A Countryside Anthology 1998

How to start, equip, operate and enjoy your place in the country

By the editors of Countryside Magazine

A Countryside Anthology—1998

ISBN 0-9729661-1-0.

Countryside Publications, Ltd.
145 Industrial Drive
Medford, Wisconsin 54451
www.countrysidemag.com

Table of contents

Country kitchen

Guest editorial

Beginning homesteading and finances

The beehive

The homestead dog

The poultry yard

Homestead health

Emergency preparation

Country neighbors

Y2K related

Shelter

After chores

Current reality as seen here

Why Oberhasli Swiss dairy goats?, pg. 257.

Guineas for tick control, pg. 251.

An attached greenhouse graces the Kalmer's solar powered homestead in Tennessee, pg. 45.

Instead of a trailer, consider building a carry-all, pg. 351.

Introduction

Going back to the land involves many arts and sciences that have been practiced for generations. Knowledge that old-timers take for granted is often regarded as novel and innovative by those who have spent their lives in cities and suburbs, and after we discover them many of us find them so exciting we feel we were born 100 years too late!

Naturally a magazine such as COUNTRYSIDE & SMALL STOCK JOURNAL, that has printed thousands of pages since 1918, is a cornucopia of old-yet-new ideas to aid and delight those new to country living.

Hefty as this book is, it contains only *some* of what appeared in COUNTRYSIDE magazine in just one year: 1998.

What a magnum opus you'd be holding if it included *everything* we printed in 1998... and the 81 years we were in business before that!

However, whether you're looking for a basic textbook on homesteading, a reference work, or just some interesting reading, 1998 is a very good year to revisit. There are several reasons.

One is Y2K.

Many people pooh-poohed the notion that computers' inability to recognize the year 2000 would lead to major disruptions in basic services such as electricity. (Electricity = lights, heat, refrigeration, water, gas pumps, communications, modern medicine, traffic lights... life as we had come to know it.)

Many others recognized the possibility. Untold millions of dollars and hours were spent by government and industry not only to avoid that potential meltdown, but to cope with it if it came. (Reporting on these efforts was a large part of COUNTRYSIDE in 1998 and 1999, but that material has not been reprinted here.)

For homesteaders, this had several implications.

One was that, for those of us who had always felt we were born a hundred years too late, Y2K sounded pretty cool! Now we could be *real* homesteaders!

In a similar vein, we had already been doing what many state and federal agencies suggested everyone should do to prepare, just in case. We could survive without weekly trips to the grocery store and most of the other things we all took for granted. After all, that's what homesteaders do.

Those of us who weren't as far along the path to self-reliance as we wanted to be started to make a greater effort. We took it more seriously, and it became more fun, too.

At the same time, a plethora of new Y2K-related products and services burst on the scene. Many of these were advertised in COUNTRYSIDE. With more ad pages, we could add more editorial pages. For the first time in 80 years, we also had enough money to increase circulation, which meant more people were participating in our reader-written discussions, which made the magazine not only fatter, but more interesting—and more helpful than ever.

Concurrently, I was planning to retire in 2000, Y2K or no Y2K. After 30 years as editor and publisher, many of them running a very small, very struggling family business, I was egotistical enough to want to go out with a bang. This included reprinting, and in many cases updating, all of the best homesteading information I had put together in the previous three decades.

The result, if I may say so myself, was a pretty good overview of modern homesteading. Maybe even a homestead survival manual. The one book I myself would want to have if I were stranded on a deserted island.

That's the book you now hold in your hands—or at least the first volume of it. Hopefully, 1999 will follow.

Y2K was a non-event... or was it? The first years of the second millennium haven't exactly been dull, and they certainly haven't made homesteading philosophy, or related skills and knowledge obsolete. Come to think of it, instead of being born a hundred years too late, maybe some of us were born a hundred years too *early*.

Or—and this is the most likely conclusion and the one I hope you reach after reading this anthology—*any* time is a good time to live beyond the sidewalks.

Jd Belanger
Lublin, Wisconsin
August, 2005

Beyond the sidewalks:

Expect the best, prepare for the worst, and then enjoy life!

J.D. Belanger
Editor

Do you have a strange feeling that something big is about to happen?

If so, you're in a slight minority, according to my mail—and so am I. (As mentioned elsewhere, our Question of the Month on catastrophes was a disaster.)

Some of us in the minority are undoubtedly psychotic; out of touch with reality. But, it's also clear from some of the letters we've received that many in the majority are either blind (or more likely in the age of tv news, uninformed or misinformed), and therefore likewise out of touch with the real world.

However, there's a third option. It's one I have always liked, and it seems even more appropriate today. Very simply, it's the observation that some tiny event almost no one notices has effects almost no one can foresee. Then, when something "big" actually happens, almost everyone is caught by surprise, and wonders where it came from.

The 212th degree

The classic example is the frog in the pot. Toss a frog into a pot of cold water on a stove and it swims more-or-less unconcerned. Turn up the heat and the frog barely notices... until the water boils.

Also, from 33° to 211°, water is liquid. It only takes one more degree to make it something entirely different.

There is a story of the tiny wisp of breeze created by the flutter of a butterfly's wings in Asia, that results in a hurricane in New York. (Sound like the Asian monetary crisis?)

And then there is one of my favorite chapters in *The Place Called Attar*—Chapter 17, The Blizzard: One snowflake fell, unseen by anyone except a daydreaming boy in third grade who was looking out the classroom window. Then another, that landed on a letter a mail carrier was delivering. They both melted, and no one paid any attention.

Eventually, of course, after a few gazillion snowflakes had landed on trees and roads and power lines—when the airports and roads and cities were shut down, and millions of people were huddled shivering in the dark—then they noticed.

This has been happening for many years. Like the straw that breaks the camel's back, the one-more-snowflake that sends a tree limb crashing onto a power line, the "final" event that will send our branch of society crashing into history hasn't descended yet. It will. And it's closer than most people realize.

As I said, most people seem to be blind, uninformed or misinformed about what's happening in the world. They simply aren't aware, or they aren't smart enough to connect the dots, or they're afraid to think the unthinkable, or they think it's both silly and useless to anticipate such matters. Some even believe that talking about such things causes them. And of course, the vast majority are convinced that "it can't happen here."

Preparation ameliorates disasters

Of greater concern to this magazine are those who see "preparation" as something sinister... an admission that something is terribly wrong, or an irrational fear of the future. At best, they claim, preparation is an exercise in futility.

It should be noted that most magazines don't even mention such things. Readers want to read happy thoughts. But are all those new stock market paper millionaires really happier than the homesteaders we read about in Countryside? Is our wonderful new world of technology and cloning and environmental degradation really a happier place than a sustainable homestead?

For three decades my mission has been to prod people into at least considering the possibilities, and to help those who accept them forge a lifestyle that will be comfortable and rewarding no matter what happens.

The Great Ice Storm of 1998

At this very moment (it's Saturday, January 10), millions of people are huddled in their homes with branches crashing around them in the great ice storm of 1998. Undoubtedly many are cold, hungry... and frightened. While a few hundred thousand are in emergency shelters—thus lending a certain credibility to the "They will take care of us" syndrome—other thousands don't have that option.

I would very much like to believe that others—instead of huddling in the dark, cold and hungry and frightened—are snug and secure on their homesteads, perhaps even giving a bit of credit to COUNTRYSIDE. If they followed our advice (or even if they're homesteaders who never heard of us) they have food, water, light and heat. While others are distraught by the lack of transportation and tv or any form of entertainment to while away the hours, homesteaders are reading or writing by lamp or candlelight, playing games, or making music, cooking, and baking up a storm. They can even "go to work!" Caring for their animals and bringing in more wood might be a real chore in the worst sense of the word under the circumstances, but how much better to be doing something than to cower in helplessness and fear!

Of course these folks mourn the distress of those less prepared. But they can no more help them now than they could have before the first frozen raindrop, when they could have urged steaders in the Northeast who are comfortable and content while the unprepared suffer and panic would have been just as comfortable and content had the storm never hit.

It's your choice... beyond the sidewalks.

Beyond the sidewalks:

Small things add up with time

J.D. BELANGER
EDITOR

At first the newspaper article was merely irritating. Then it became startling, but after I thought about it, it was just another sign of the times.

It concerned a booklet titled "Getting Rich in America: A Few Easy Rules to Follow."

Its thesis is simple: Almost anybody who wants to get rich, can. All you need is an early start, and enough luck to avoid major tragedies.

The "rules" are common sense things many of us learned when we were kids. Live modestly, don't waste money, and sock some away for a rainy day.

For example, if a 21-year-old who smokes two packs of cigarettes a day wants to get rich, the first logical step is to quit smoking and put the money into savings. At 6%, that person will have roughly $150,000 by age 71. At 15%, it would amount to more than $3 million. Add a few other frugalities, and you're talking real money.

I learned that more than 50 years ago—from my mother. So it was irritating to read that today, it takes a couple of college professors to conduct an "academic study" to discover what everybody should have learned from their mothers.

The startling reaction

The startling part concerned the reaction to the study, mostly from other "intellectuals."

Many were incredulous. The authors were stunned at how much disbelief there was in the chances of getting rich with such a simple plan. Some readers even berated them for encouraging such "nonsense."

That amazed me too, at first. But the more I thought about it, the more I realized that this simply reflects an attitude we see every day, and not only on money matters.

For example, some young homesteaders can't understand how older ones got where they are today. The youngsters want their dreams fulfilled... completely, and now. Like the incredulous readers of "Getting Rich in America," they simply can't believe the elders got there with nickels and dimes, one small project at a time.

A sign of the times?

But that same attitude is evident in countless other ways that seem to demonstrate differences between "conventional" and homestead thinking.

Most people today think it's silly to worry about saving a gallon of gas here and there. After all, there's plenty of oil still in the ground! Homesteaders realize that, like the smoker's pennies, it adds up.

Conventional thinking holds that paving productive cropland with one more mall, one more road, or one more subdivision is no big deal. Homesteaders know that fertile soil is finite. When it's gone, it's gone for good.

Why the fuss about one more extinct plant or animal? So what if the oceans are dying, rain forests are disappearing, and landfills are overflowing?

The answer is that these and hundreds of other attitudes are like smoking one cigarette. A few pennies. But one smoke becomes a pack, and then cartons... pennies become dollars, and then millions.

People who can only see the present moment have no idea where their food—or anything else—comes from. It's there when they want it, so why worry?

Homesteaders can see the details... the need for fertile soil, proper amounts of sun and rain, skill and labor... and time.

If people think they have to win a lottery to get rich and it's impossible to become wealthy little-by-little, they probably think the whole world works that way.

Homesteaders know better. They know how little things develop into big things. They see examples every day, beyond the sidewalks.

Beyond the sidewalks:

The 21st century and homesteading

Introduction:

Most people think of homesteading (if they think of it at all) as being rooted in the past. Those who know better can adapt it to the present... but not very many can see the future possibilities.

Among the reasons are several misconceptions, the main ones being a mistaken notion of what modern homesteading actually is (including its supposed anti-technology bias); the assumption that cities are a requirement for a civilized society (including technological development as well as production); and the assumption that "progress" can only mean a linear extension of recent history.

In this 10-part series we will explore these and many other myths, and show why and how what we now call "homesteading" might very well become the idyllic lifestyle humanity has sought since the Garden of Eden.

Part I: If you don't know where you're going, how are you going to get there?

Exercise: Describe your home, and life in it, 100 years from now. (Time allowed: five minutes.)

It probably wouldn't take more than a few seconds for all the standard images of the house of the future to rush through your mind. You might picture wall-size television screens or virtual reality booths, voice-activated lighting and appliances, furniture that conforms to the body sitting on it, and of course, computer-controlled everything, including your personal robot servants. If you read enough science fiction, you might want to add nutrition capsules that eliminate the hassles of cooking and dishwashing (as well as farming and grocery shopping), disposable clothing, and maybe your personal anti-gravity-powered flying saucer parked in the roof garage.

Science and technology have always been the meat and potatoes of forecasts of future lifestyles. But is all science and technology the same? More importantly, will people always be the same, in the way they think and act?

Consider this alternative scenario of life in 2100:

You wake up and trundle to the bathroom for the usual morning rituals. You use the composting toilet, and refresh yourself with water that was heated by the sun and drains into the family-size water purification system.

After dressing (hemp cloth replaced cotton as the standard many years ago), you go to the kitchen, thinking about breakfast. A peek into the earth-cooled refrigerator offers no temptations, and besides, the first raspberries might be ripe. A handful of those would be just right. However, you're still a bit groggy, so you turn on the bio-gas burner and make coffee... wondering if the debate on its health effects will ever be settled: seems like that's been going on for a hundred years!

Outside the earth-bermed house, you pause to inhale the fresh, crisp, morning country air. It's difficult to imagine, now, what the air must have been like a hundred years ago, when people still used internal combustion engines, burned coal and incinerated wastes, and the sky was crisscrossed with jet contrails.

The sun is just above the horizon but the dew is already starting to drip off the solar panels. The air is still: the windmill blades appear frozen against the clear blue sky. Old Shep emerges from his dog house, stretches, comes up to say good morning, then goes off to raise his hind leg on the windmill tower.

It's going to be a nice day.

The berries are ripe, and it takes no time at all to gather a generous supply into your now-empty cup. But you're in no hurry: rushing and stress are relics of the past. You savor the plump juicy fruits, rolling the first few in your mouth to extract and enjoy their goodness – and the delight in the first picking of the season.

While popping berries into your mouth you look over the rest of the garden, observing the progress of each crop, looking for problems, planning the work to be done and deciding on what to have for lunch and supper. That's more difficult than it sounds: there are too many choices!

The damp morning air is chilly in spite of the sun, so you move a little faster. There are eggs to gather, goats to milk, and animals to feed and water. Of course, everyone in the family has their own chores, so none of them take more than a few minutes. But on early mornings like this when you're the first one up and have them all to yourself it's nice to just wander, looking over each animal as it comes to greet you and doling out pats and rubs to those special pets.

The tranquillity doesn't last, of course. One-by-one the others come out of the house and go about their duties.

The day on a 21st century homestead has begun.

As this series continues we'll follow this family, and their little community and others like it, through the rest of the day and through the seasons: we'll see how they work (you might be surprised at how little time is spent on food production), learn, play, and interact with each other and their environment. For the skeptics who wonder where all this technology comes from, is produced and maintained, we'll have answers. We'll even address the concerns of the incredulous who can't conceive of everybody wanting to homestead (or being able to), as well as the state of cities and the larger society.

But first we should ask some even more obvious questions:

Which of these two scenarios—the high-tech totally urban one, or the more natural, country one—is more desirable, for individuals and for civilization? What are the paths leading to each one, and what obstructions might block those paths? And finally, which vision is more realistic?

For today's homesteaders, the choice between a future where people live in domed, sterile, climate-controlled cities and one where they live on small places in the countryside isn't even worth considering. If we prefer country living even now, despite all the hurdles we must overcome, how much more would we enjoy it without those obstacles! At the same time, how many more people would choose the homestead lifestyle if there were no obstacles?

COUNTRYSIDE readers are aware of the reasons many people who say they'd like to be homesteaders have for not making "the move."

One of the most common and most important is money. The grubstake needed to buy land, animals, tools and equipment. The job, most often in a city or town, required to accumulate that grubstake. The time required not only for the job itself, but commuting. The money for clothes, transportation, meals, child care... and taxes.

Then there is the money spent on "time-saving" conveniences that are needed only because there isn't time to do things because the time is being spent earning money!

How our economy works
We plant more corn to feed more pigs
We feed more pigs to buy more land
We buy more land to plant more corn
We plant more corn to ...
(Carl Sandburg, 1928)

Call it the rat race, or call it a treadmill, by any name it's a senseless way to waste a life. And our society is wasting millions of them.

There is a way out — several ways — but to get at the root of the problem we must first determine why it exists in the first place. And that brings up the second obstacle many people face when dreaming of homesteading: peer pressure.

This takes many forms, the most visible being the incredulity of friends and neighbors who think only crazy people leave the comfort and security of cities and good jobs to hack an existence out of the wilderness... or even just to muck around in the dirt and animal excrement only to put food on the table. After all, that food can easily and effortlessly be purchased at any burger stand, supermarket, or gas station.

This attitude might change if, instead of the specter of outhouses and kerosene lamps and rundown shacks — the image of living in primitive squalor and hardship — homesteading could be seen as closer to the 21st century vision briefly described above. (It certainly doesn't help that many homesteaders themselves accept this view, and worse, that COUNTRYSIDE sometimes perpetuates it. The reasons for this include the difficulties of getting from here to there, which we're now discussing, but also the lack of a clear vision of the ultimate goals and possibilities, which we hope this series will help form.)

Other peer pressures, however, are much more subtle, and in most cases much more powerful. These range from what we eat and drink, to what we buy, to how we spend our time, but they all have one common denominator: no one wants to—or knows how to—be different from others. In some cases this can be as transparent as not

Link the nine dots with no more than three straight lines that will pass through all nine dots, without lifting your pencil.
(Answer on next page.)

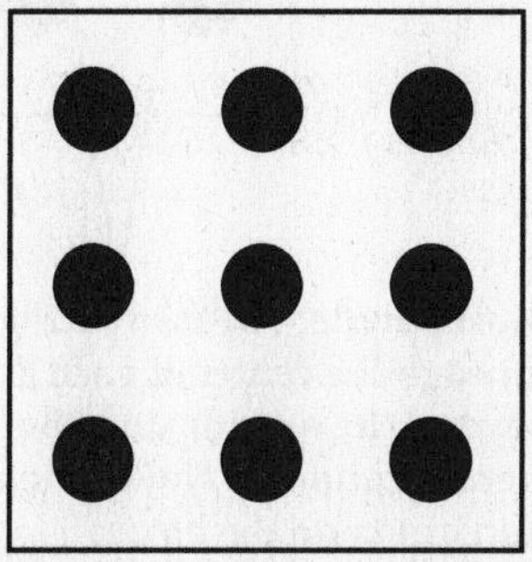

wanting to do without television or a microwave simply because we would feel deprived without them. In others, it's simply a matter of failing to think outside the box. Several excellent examples of thinking outside the box in pursuit of the homestead lifestyle can be found in Rob Roy's latest book, *The Mortgage-free Home.* (See review, 82/3) The very idea of acquiring a home without a mortgage is itself a revolutionary concept: Most people will say that's impossible... because they don't know anyone who has done it! And yet, many people have, and Rob Roy explains how almost anyone can. (He's a master at creative, independent thinking, and this book is highly recommended.)

Yes, many would-be homesteaders face obstacles to changing their lives. These are not insurmountable, as demonstrated by the tens of thousands who have already overcome them.

But of more pertinence to this discussion, what would happen if those obstacles were eliminated, on a broad scale? How many more people would be interested in, and would actually pursue a homestead lifestyle?

At this point we must digress for a moment.

In the past I, and others, have glibly explained why and how the masses might change their ways and embrace a more homestead-like lifestyle. Most often we assume it will arise from necessity, such as the Y2K computer problem or some other event that will cause civilization to falter. But this is an easy out. It's literary laziness. Worse yet, it perpetuates the image of homesteading as being a falling-back instead of a moving forward: It will become a necessity only because there won't be anything better!

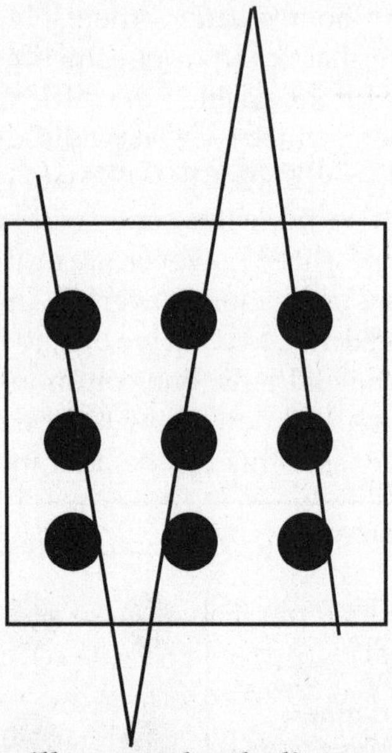

Most people will assume that the lines must pass through the center of each dot, and must not extend beyond the outside dots. But neither of these restrictions were mentioned. Never assume a thing, and strive to think outside the box!

It is, of course, a very real possibility, and one most people can more easily relate to than, say, a sudden and inexplicable change in human nature that will suddenly convince the masses to flee the cities to take up agrarian homesteading. What's more, a premonition of apocalypse apparently plays a large role in motivating many homesteaders.

Nevertheless, there are some entirely reasonable, valid, and even persuasive reasons to believe that society as a whole could shift toward homesteading without a major doomsday event... if you don't consider certain current trends and conditions indications of doom already being experienced.

Assume, if you can, that the world as it spins today is about as good as it gets. Yes, there is poverty and sickness, crime and war, but most people are relatively well-off. Progress is being made, even if in small increments, toward eliminating air and water pollution, conserving natural resources, and increasing the average standard of living. And with a continually rising stock market and constantly improving technology, life can only get better, these blithe spirits proclaim.

And yet, even in that rosy picture, there is room for our view of 21st century homesteading.

For starters, consider the massive numbers of people who will be retiring in the years ahead but have no desire to spend the rest of their lives playing shuffleboard or golf; all those who are burned out by the rat race and are already finding ways to simplify their lives; and of course all those who are already homesteading, or at least living in the country, either goaded by fear of the future or because they think that's the best way to live.

Add the societal shifts already underway: the acceptance of conservation and recycling, the increase in organically grown foods (with a concurrent distrust of agribusiness products)... and not only the dispersal of business and industry away from population centers spurred by computers, but the marked increase in home businesses and home education. We might also mention the astonishing growth of "nutri-pharmaceuticals" (driven largely by echinacea, St. John's wort and ginko biloba) and other "alternatives" as indicating a trend toward what, only a few years ago, was the purview of "kooks" of the homestead bent.

And finally, mix in the age-old desire of humankind to be close to nature, putter in the garden, have a little piece of land...

What we come up with is a tremendous base of potential homesteaders... a base which, if it proved successful in building better lives (which is entirely probable), would entice others, and they others, until all the perceived "obstacles" fell by the wayside and homesteading became a mass movement. (You'll know that time has arrived when homesteaders appear as normal people on tv sitcoms and soap operas!)

I don't see this as extraordinary at all, if we correct the image of homesteading as living in a tar paper shack without running water or any of the comforts most people consider necessities. On the positive side, we can portray homesteading not only as a very comfortable, secure, pleasant and extremely fulfilling way to live, but as an even better lifestyle than current society offers.

Even COUNTRYSIDE, even with the Small Stock Journal in its title, has conceded that animal husbandry isn't an essential part of homesteading. As most readers are by now aware, most practicing homesteaders claim that homesteading is an attitude. And the facts show that as more people become disenchanted with what the conventional or Industrial Age world has to offer, that attitude is becoming more and more prevalent.

After reaching a critical mass, or even before, the trickle could become a flood.

As the numbers of homesteaders become a "market," it's entirely reasonable to see new and innovative products developed to meet their needs. Nothing frivolous, mind you, but how about the composting toilet, small water purification plants, solar powered devices, bio-gas generators and wind electric converters mentioned in just the few paragraphs in which we described a 21st century homestead… and all that before breakfast!

These would not emanate from the giant companies and universities that are already losing their clout and prominence. Many, in fact, would be conceived and developed on homesteads, with people who have inquisitive minds, talents and skills, and education or access to information (or both). They would work to meet needs and solve problems as they encounter them on their own homesteads—the way many innovative homesteaders are working already (and as distinct from many corporate R&D efforts aimed only at putting more gizmos of dubious usefulness on the market). Many people will have ample time for such projects, as well as the shops and equipment required.

These ideas will be shared on the Internet, and in many cases almost any handy person will be able to adapt them (as they do projects in COUNTRYSIDE today). In others, products for sale might be fabricated in the homestead shops or even small factories.

Reality check: Every one of those "21st century" innovations we mentioned is already in use! But how many people have even heard about them? (You will know a great deal about these, and similar developments, by the end of this series.)

But this gets us into another arena with a multitude of ramifications, including marketing. Since we're trying to get as broad an overview as quickly as possible, we'll add this to the list of topics to return to in a future issue.

To summarize this, however, it's easy to see how homesteading could be, and in some senses already is becoming mainstream. After reaching critical mass, peer pressure would become not an obstacle but a means of encouragement.

Not everyone will agree that this path is the better one, or even possible. They will hold out for the conventional view of the future: the "smart" homes, automated industries, high-tech medicine and synthetic everything, including food. (Those who claim a homestead society is impossible because not everyone wants to live in the country should note that just the previous sentence is enough to give some of us the screaming meemies: we could just as readily say an urban society is impossible because not everyone wants to live in a city, or even in a high-tech world that ignores or even destroys nature.)

The common and somewhat reasonable argument is that science and technology will save us. No matter that they, or more specifically man's misuse of them, are largely responsible for the world we have today, which many of us find lacking. But let's ignore that for the moment and suppose that the current collaboration of science, industry and government does indeed find ways to provide food and fiber, shelter and energy, education and entertainment, without running out of raw materials or destroying the planet in the process.

Certainly, "clean" nuclear energy or hydrogen fusion would have a major impact on civilization. Cloning plants and animals, as well as other biogenetic processes, could have a profound effect on food production. The development of synthetic foods and fibers (which might be essential if natural production is made impossible by soil, water, insect, disease and other problems) could very well sustain a much larger population than we now have, with only benign effects on the environment.

The more accommodating and imaginative proponents of the technological path might try to soothe homestead types by painting glowing pictures of huge parks and gardens in or adjacent to cities, domed and climate-controlled, so any ardent gardener or nature lover could enjoy almost any growing zone, in any season.

If, as the technology sector suggests, the New Age continues on the trajectory of the Industrial Age but with new methods and materials and a renewed regard for the Earth (out of economic necessity, if not respect), the physical aspects of their forecasts are quite possible. But so is the homestead path!

Ignoring other alternatives for purposes of argument and illustration, which of the two do we want, and why? Which one is more likely to evolve, naturally? If either is deemed superior to the other (as they assuredly are by opposing camps), how could either one be promoted…or even forced?

While speculating on the answers to these questions might prove interesting and educational, they are academic.

The reason is simple: The 21st century will witness a blending of what, with great reservations, might be called city and country, or even worse, technology and homesteading. Moreover, the type or degree of technology is of no importance or significance. What will most affect the future is not technology itself, but how that technology is managed, used, and viewed. In other words, our attitudes towards it, along with our attitudes towards ourselves, our communities, our planet and our universe.

How the homestead attitude will transform the world

The revelation that homesteaders are not anti-technology will astonish many readers who, despite our repeated explanations and protests, insist on thinking of homesteading as a life of hardship and deprivation. This often applies to those who, while attracted to the philosophy and attitudes, are reluctant or unable to give up their comforts and conveniences.

This misconception—which actually consists of two—is one of the greatest obstacles keeping homesteading from becoming a more common lifestyle.

It's obvious from past issues of COUNTRYSIDE that many people do live under somewhat harsh conditions, sometimes voluntarily for personal reasons. Such a monastic lifestyle can have value, but it's not what we refer to as modern homesteading.

More commonly, primitive living is only a temporary measure in order to achieve higher goals.

(If harsh living is caused by true poverty, the involuntary kind, and the individual doesn't come to grips with it through the homestead philosophy and attitude, that person isn't a homesteader.)

In any case, hardship is not the norm, and it's not a requisite or a defining state of homesteading.

The confusion is understandable because today, we're still trapped in a black or white situation. Generally speaking, the alternatives are living a conventional late 20th century lifestyle with all the trappings, or an early 20th century lifestyle with few amenities.

But these aren't the only choices. Many of our readers provide excellent examples of how it's possible to select the best of both worlds to build a life that's better than is possible in either one. These people are role models for the 21st century homesteaders described in this series.

The problem is not in owning or using a certain device or technology (although this can be complicated by many factors, such as a product that damages the Earth by its manufacture, operation, or disposal, or involves slave labor). The real problem is what we give up in exchange for that product: how it affects our lives. What is the real cost, not just in dollars, but in what we must do (and give up) to acquire those dollars, in what we relinquish by not using some other method, or by not performing the task or function at all?

This is too complicated for conventional economics, and much of it is irrelevant to that science at its current level anyway. So we'll delve into metaeconomics... the new economic system... before this series ends.

But by then we also hope to convince even the most skeptical that modern homesteading does not involve primitive living... or antitechnology.

What about the "nostalgia" factor? Are readers who long for the good old days of simple rural living being left out in a discussion of homestead technology in the 21st century?

Not necessarily. Remember, modern homesteading involves a blending of old and new, choosing only the best of both worlds. (Strictly "modern" living has thrown out virtually everything old, and suffers for it.)

Realistically, few people are nostalgic about washboards (although we're aware of some exceptions), Saturday night baths in a galvanized tub near the stove (with the cleanest members of the family getting to use the water first), outhouses in winter, and eating brined vegetables or salt pork for months on end. These "old things" we toss out.

What we keep—and what most people are nostalgic about—are such things as warm fresh-baked bread... the sounds of animals and the aroma of well-cured hay in a barn on a winter evening... wonderful family meals...

Include a slower and saner way of life, a closer connection to nature, a greater sense of worth and purpose and increased security, and nostalgia becomes a potent tool for change.

This has been a hasty and perhaps somewhat jumbled overview of what might be involved in making homesteading the dominant lifestyle of the 21st century. In future installments we'll slow down and take a closer look at the details.

For example, what will "work" consist of, and how will it be accomplished? (We maintain that well over half of what passes as "work" today is wasted: we could easily provide equivalent goods and services in less than half the time. What's more, we'll show why a large proportion of those goods and services are unnecessary in the first place... especially in a homestead world. "Work" is a joke — or a curse — foisted on us by the Industrial Age, and that Age is dying.)

But if it takes 80 hours a week now just to make a living, what happens when we work only a few hours a day, or a few days a week or a few weeks a month? (We'll show how a ridiculous amount of money is spent because we think we have to work so much.)

With all that spare time, won't we get bored? (In the post-industrial age, leisure will be redefined. And only a small part of it will be devoted to what we now consider homestead tasks.)

How can all the people in the world, or even the U.S., possibly exist without cities? (We didn't say there will be no cities. But they'll be vastly different... and we'll present some models.)

Isn't it ridiculous to think science and technology can progress without massive government and business backing? (Name the 100 most important scientific breakthroughs and see how many were developed without such support... and we don't only mean fire and the wheel. In the coming environment we envision, that proportion could rise substantially.)

And much more of the same...next time.

Country conversation & feedback

Thanks for the "starting without a grubstake" stories

COUNTRYSIDE: A great big thank you to all those who shared their stories in the Nov/Dec. '97 issue. It provided a much-needed shot in the arm! It gave me hope, strengthened my commitment, and helped me to muster some more mettle to go through our present situation. We can do it! It is worth it! And, this too shall pass!

As I read the wonderful articles, I was reminded of some points that were passed on to us by a friend who heard a particularly motivational talk. The points pretty well summarized what all the writers were saying, in their own unique way.

There are basically four keys to success, whether it be homesteading or a business venture or whatever. They are:

1. Keep it simple. It's not going to happen overnight. Start from wherever you are, build on what you have, keeping things simple so you're not burying yourself.

2. Have a plan. Set goals, including time "limits." Plan your work, then work your plan. Put it writing; an unwritten goal is nothing more than a dream. Find someone to whom you can report your progress.

3. Stay with it! Be persistent; don't give up. Accept responsibility, and move forward. There is a degree of risk in nearly everything you do; don't let that stop you.

4. Pedal like crazy! Someone said marriage is like riding a bicycle: if you're not pedaling, you're going downhill. That has a number of different applications, including homesteading. It takes work, a lot of hard, get down and dirty work, but oh, the sweet rewards! Even if the path is mostly uphill, it's worth it!

Good luck to all of us who are striving to live our dreams beyond the sidewalks, and thanks again! – *Cheryl A. Clawson, Utah*

"No grubstake" articles are appreciated

COUNTRYSIDE: I just received my Nov/Dec, 1997 issue and all I want to say is thank you! I hope you will continue to have the "no grubstake" stories. I couldn't put the magazine down. I have always thought your magazine was the best homesteading magazine on the market and with this issue I know it. You have topped yourself.

I haven't made the big move yet, and this issue gave me a lot of new ideas. I've always been a homesteader at heart.

Thanks again and keep up the good work. – *Teresa Brown, Maryland*

We have been deluged with letters praising our November/December (87/6) issue. Many readers ordered extra copies for children, siblings, or others who they feel could use some help in learning to manage their finances. (Copies are still available for $4 each.)

As expected, a few readers took umbrage at some of the stories from people who don't quite match their image of what a homesteader should be.

A sincere thanks to everyone who took the time to write.

A culture clash in the countryside?

COUNTRYSIDE: I was very intrigued by the letter from the 13-year-old girl, but more than a little saddened by the attitudes expressed. (81/5:98)

It is good to hear from someone who is so aware of the necessity to connect with the rest of the natural realm. Too often, we imagine ourselves self-sufficient spiritually, and neglect that need to open our hearts to our four-footed (and rooted) brothers and sisters. But we are also more than just a part of the natural family – we are a part of the human family as well.

Being well-educated regarding animals means knowing the joy a horse feels while running as well as knowing the characteristics of different breeds, how many bones are in the leg, etc. Jennifer understands this.

Being well-educated regarding being human means exposing yourself to the many different types of ideas and self-expression your fellows have come up with over the centuries – how they dance and sing, as well as what they write in books; why they want to build bridges as well as how to build them.

Someone who says, "Who needs a theater when I can watch baby chicks hatch?" is as poorly educated as someone who says, "Who needs to watch baby chicks hatch when I can see a play?" Our lives are only as full as we allow them to be. The good life is not one lived in the country or in the city, but one lived with an open heart and a thoughtful and humble mind, regardless of the outer circumstances.

Jennifer, you owe it to yourself to see a play, a ballet, an opera, a story telling festival, a fine art exhibit, a symphony, and a rock concert. You can't connect with the deeper, finer aspects of your fellow pilgrims here by watching "culture" on tv any more than your city-loving relative can appreciate nature by watching PBS.

Keep yourself rooted in the natural world you love so well, but don't let self-satisfaction keep you from growing from that foundation. – *Janice Joyner, Iowa*

Article revives more memories of the Depression era

COUNTRYSIDE: The article by Wilma Carothers of Atlanta, Illinois seemed almost my own life story in many respects. Her reference to the "box in the window for a refrigerator" is familiar.

We refer to window boxes now as a place to grow flowers, but during the depression days, we had a "window box" built by my father to fit up close to the north window of our kitchen and it had a metal roof so no bugs or dirt could get into it. We kept easily spoiled items in it between mealtimes, such as milk, butter, puddings, etc. Most foods did not last more than one day but the window box served as a cooler for the times between meals.

During the hot summer months, we had another type of cooler—a shelf-like device that could be lowered into the dug well that furnished our drinking water. The cooler shelf was lowered on a chain with a handle and pulley type crank. Dug wells and such devices would be outlawed by the health department now, but then it was a common solution to the problem of preserving foods from one meal to the next.

Another thing which I have never seen mentioned or even acknowledged by various rural persons of the depression era was the way my mother fed her free-range chickens.

In the winter, she would have us all shell corn that she put in a big flat pan in the coal-wood range oven. When it was warm it would be taken outdoors to feed the chickens.

We did not have a chicken house that was heated in any manner and the chickens would run outside most all day and hunt a roost at dusk. But most of them gathered to eat when it came time to spread the food for them.

We lived on a small farm, less than 50 acres. We were seven people living in one household, from an original family of 11 children. Some of them had married by the time I could recall. But we mingled back and forth and when one household had a bumper crop of some item, we all gathered in one spot and cared for the produce. It was picked, cleaned, peeled, cut up, cooked and canned or preserved in the proper way of that time. We had no pressure canner, and no freezer. We used kerosene for the fuel in the cooking stove, and in the cold months had the use of a wood-coal range. We were "beyond the power lines" until rural electrification was started.

We were elated when we were treated to an ice cream reunion of all the family. We would freeze the ice cream in the hand-turned freezer. Crushed ice mixed with coarse salt, along with the turning of the handle to rotate the inner can with the ice cream mixture, made the ice cream mixture freeze. Everyone took turns turning the handle.

Sometimes there would be enough ice cream left over to store overnight by packing it in an ice and salt solution, wrapped in burlap and blankets. Then we'd put a dollop on our cereal the next morning.

I was born in 1921 and have become too worn out and physically unable to do much more than read and remember. However, I do have good memories of the depression years and the ways we amused ourselves and enjoyed all the times of recreation which were not nearly as many as the teen groups now have. Most of today's youth think I am ridiculous when I suggest some way to be thrifty and accumulate enough for a home of their own. Nobody wants to reuse string or paper or various other items that we would normally recycle when recycling was necessary, not just a fad.

It seemed we used every square inch of our farm for some profitable or life enhancing result. I was once given a runt pig to care for with the understanding that I could have the sale price when it was sold. Finally, when it was sold, I acquired a sum that would pay for dental work—fillings in my teeth and one cap on a front tooth.

We had no bicycle or a croquet set, which were items badly desired in that time. We did have bean bags, but they were not the chairs of today. They were little items that my mother made for us to use in place of balls when we wanted something to play pitch and catch in the yard.

My husband and I have been married 55 years and started life with nothing but each other. He had been rejected by his draft board at the time of WWII. We decided to get married while he was employed in an airplane factory so we were able to save some money until we did get ready to purchase a little rural place. It had no conveniences, so many of the tales of beginning homesteaders are right in our trend.

We have had three children, one of whom died in infancy, but two still survive and now we have grandchildren. Unfortunately they all live in another area of the U.S., which seemed to happen with the group who were born in the '40s. We write back and forth and use the telephone frequently but the old togetherness of my original family is no more. Even the farm where I grew up has been sold and subdivided into houses and lots. Recently, I talked with someone who told me that there were several houses on it but the tree that we had near our garage was still there in one of the front yards of the new home owners.

If this interests anybody, I have been glad to report it. – *Mrs. George*

Potbellied pigs are edible but not very cost-effective

COUNTRYSIDE: I want to respond to Nina Voris' question regarding pot-bellied pigs. We acquired one last fall, quite by accident. A well-meaning friend couldn't imagine letting a $3.50 pig go at a livestock auction we were at, so he bid on it and we were stuck with it.

We raised "Arnold" on corn and table scraps and this spring we had a pot-bellied pig roast. It tasted wonderful but did have a lot of fat and the carcass wasn't very big. My husband built a charcoal roaster from an old fuel oil tank and we roasted him whole.

I don't know that I would consider him cost effective. We have real pigs now that are getting much bigger much faster on the same feed.

Can anyone tell me what to do with homemade lye soap to get a laundry soap that doesn't leave soap scum on the clothes and dish soap that cuts grease? I've tried everything and have lots of "Arnold" soap to use. – *Teresa Cheatham, Wisconsin*

A response to a response to a response to a horse article

COUNTRYSIDE: One of the wonderful things about COUNTRYSIDE, in addition to the information and articles, is that it allows for a dialogue between its readers, which, in turn, allows information to be examined and sorted out, allowing, in the end, good, solid thoughts about whatever the topic at hand may be. Such is the case with the discussions about draft horses and ownership of these great creatures which began a few months ago.

In response to Mike and Maria Shanley's response to my article in Vol. 81, No. 2, which in itself was a response to a previous writer's comments, I would like to put forth a few words.

All of the information that Mike and Maria gave in their article about factors to consider when starting out was absolutely sound and accurate. However, a few other things need addressing.

My article was not a tirade against draft horse ownership or usage. It was, however, a caution against irresponsible ownership of these animals, caused either by ignorance or outright neglect.

Obviously, the amount of food will vary, horse to horse, climate to climate, pasture to pasture. Floating of teeth will also vary, horse to horse, feed to feed, age to age. Thrush can be controlled, but this also varies with climate and the surrounding available terrain. And, yes, the meat market is obviously not where the animals will bring as good a price as in an outright sale (although, contrary to what the Stanley's write, meat prices are not less than half the regular value, because there are so many horses here.) This was not the point of my comments. My point was identical to what the Stanleys wrote: "We all need to be responsible for the well-being of any life in our care." The point was that people should not be misled into thinking that animal care, especially of such a large creature, is simple, and that many people don't feed well, they don't float teeth, they don't control thrush, they don't practice discriminatory breeding, and they don't refrain from sending a horse to the butcher.

There is a glut of draft horses in my area. They show up by the dozens every Friday at the meat sale in Sugarcreek, Ohio, and that is only one sale in our area. There are several others within a two hour drive, all with weekly auctions, all with most of the horses going to slaughter. Many of them are sound, well trained horses, disposed of at auction because it is faster than waiting for a buyer to come along. Others are in a deplorable condition of health or injury, starved, bloated with worms, lame with deep thrush or curled up hooves, with broken legs with gangrene, blinded, severely maloccluded teeth, with rain rot, etc., etc., etc., many of which should have been put down long ago, but the owners just had to squeeze out the pennies per pound that their suffering horse could bring.

Because every humane society handles dogs and cats, but very few have facilities for, or expertise with, horses, my wife and I work very closely with several humane societies on horse cases. We take in dozens of horses, rehabilitating and fostering out those which can be saved, and humanely euthanizing those that can't. What we see on a week-to-week basis is disgusting and heartbreaking. Visit the slaughter auctions a few times rather than just read about them: you will begin to understand.

I am not opposed to draft horse ownership. I have had them and worked with them. I love them dearly. It is because of this that I don't want to see a first-time owner's, or anyone else's, draft horse end up being loaded into my trailer to try to be saved or worse yet, on its way to France or Japan to be put on someone's plate. – *Donald L. Miller, Ohio*

To clear a stuffy nose

To clear a stuffy nose, try this old remedy: Put several trays of ice cubes in a pan of water. Stick your toes—and toes only—in the water until they're numb. And don't laugh until you've tried it.

In Alaska, even the city can feel wild

COUNTRYSIDE: I don't ordinarily send notes with subscriptions. But after picking up a variety of "homesteading" magazines at newsstands over the years, and on occasion subscribing to one or the other, we've found more of what we're looking for in your magazine about small-time farming.

Although we live in the largest city in Alaska, it can feel quite wild. We battle moose for our garden and apple trees. We have a small dog team we use to get to our cabin (8 miles from the end of the road) and occasional camping trips.

We gather blueberries, cranberries and raspberries each fall for tasty treats in winter. We catch a freezer full of salmon with a fishwheel and my husband gets one caribou a year.

Our beehive keeps us supplied

with more than enough honey, so Christmas presents are all ready. Beekeeping is one of our most community oriented activities, with people sharing equipment and knowledge.

What I really enjoy about your magazine (it's hard to narrow it down, but...) are the articles by other readers on a variety of topics. The information is far more practical than an article by a reporter.

So keep up the fantastic work! You're needed. —*Jenny Zimmerman, Alaska*

Born a homesteader, and he's going back

COUNTRYSIDE: I have been reading your rag for some time now and find it not only educational but also very humorous.

I was born and raised in the first back-to-the-land era of post World War II. I remember when I was around five or six years old we got on the "grid." We all sat down for supper with kerosene lamps when Mom got up and pulled a chain on one bare bulb in the center of the kitchen. The family was in awe. It is something I'll never forget.

I also remember going to the john in January, sleeping in the upstairs bedrooms under a tin roof in August, and picking blackberries with the bumble bees and chiggers in July. When I was older, it was cutting wood in winter or hauling hay in summer.

I have lived in the city for over 30 years and have about a year and a half until I go back to the country. Besides clipping coupons and buying what is on sale and storing it rather than making a grocery list each week, I try to make all my business stops enroute to or from work. I'm buying building materials from shopper ads. I am buying 2 x 12 x 16 floor joists for 1/3 price of new. I just have to pull a few nails—called sweat equity—and cut some 18' down to 16'.

There is so much waste in the construction industry that unless you already live a long way from any city or growing area you can capitalize on their overstocks, overbids or on owners of huge houses that change their minds about the size or location of doors and windows.

I have lived on both sides of the fence and really prefer the country life but realize that we need health insurance (which you seem to ignore) and also some means of paying our bills when we get too old to live off the land. – *Al Wiley, Missouri*

These Yukon Gold potatoes were waist high in mid-August. The rope at the top of the fence keeps moose out of the garden.

Pigeon manure is good fertilizer in Alaskan garden

COUNTRYSIDE: In an earlier article I wrote about raising Squabbing Homer pigeons. I mentioned that pigeon manure was a very good fertilizer and won't burn plants like chicken manure will.

As an example I have enclosed pictures of my potato plants with my 15-year-old daughter (5 feet 10 inches tall) standing in one of the rows. This particular row is Yukon Gold white potatoes which are waist high. The Sangre red potatoes were slightly shorter. The potatoes were planted about June 8th and the picture was taken about the middle of August. The size and total weight per hill were more than twice what I ever had from commercial fertilizer.

Now, in mid-September, hills are producing 4-1/2 to 5-1/4 pounds per hill. Many of the red potatoes are 3/4 to one pound each and white potatoes are even larger. Red potatoes are normally small here. The Sangre are very firm, even when boiled.

Normally we have a killing frost by early September at the latest, but not yet this year. I would like to leave them in the ground to grow, but the voles (similar to a mouse) are really eating them and the beets too. They raised havoc with the peas earlier. The carrot plants are over two feet tall and they will be attacked next.

The rhubarb plants still have stalks 28 inches long and up to 1-3/8 inches in diameter.

I raked pigeon manure into each row when planted, then side-dressed the rows later. I also use a small amount of 0-45-0 super phosphate with everything.

Voles, chickweed and root maggots are the worst problems here. A clove of garlic planted with each cole plant helps keep root maggot numbers down, but they are really rough on radishes and turnips. They don't bother the celery or kohlrabi. I do not like to use standard poison for root maggots.

Using birch bark or other lightweight material to make cutouts of small hawks and hanging these from a string over the currant bushes keeps small birds out. Use a string bridle to hang the hawk so it will fly with any light breeze. Use an old fishing pole or similar to hang it from. We wouldn't get any currants without this.

The currants, raspberries and strawberries really produce using the phosphate, pigeon manure and old sawdust as mulch. I use sawdust on the floor of my loft.

Manure has many things in it which are beneficial to plants, besides the organic matter it adds. I cleaned out my pigeon loft this spring and it was only piled up outside for a couple of weeks before it went on the garden. It also has old straw which was the nesting material. It all composted after going on the garden.

The yellow rope around the top of the fence keeps the moose out! – *S. M. Mills, Alaska*

An easy way to sift compost and soil

COUNTRYSIDE: Do you need to sift a lot of compost but do not have an adequate screen? Give this low/no cost system a try.

Obtain a plastic bread/pastry tray that route delivery people use for carrying their wares to supermarkets. These are typically molded plastic, several feet square, with holes in the bottom. Those with uniformly-sized holes work best for this project.

Note: We do not condone "borrowing" one of these from behind a grocery store. We found two (one slightly cracked) along the shoulder of the Interstate.

Place the tray on a sturdy wheelbarrow and scoop a shovelful of compost onto it. Wearing thick leather gloves, move the compost around so it passes through the holes in the tray and falls into the wheelbarrow. Deposit the matter left over onto a separate compost pile for further decomposition. Take the wheelbarrow loaded with compost to the garden for use.

If you do not have a wheelbarrow, you can use a plastic trash can or similar container to catch the compost. Do not use a container that was used for toxic or hazardous materials.

If you want finer compost, use "rabbit wire" mesh attached to the inner surface of the tray.

The tray can be cleaned with a stiff brush and garden hose, or even left in the rain for a while. During the off season, the tray can be used to dry onions or store potatoes or winter squash. Finally, you can hang it on a nail in your garage or shed until it is needed. – *Robert Sulek, North Carolina*

Save the hornets; and recycle more

COUNTRYSIDE: I really enjoy reading COUNTRYSIDE. Sometimes I say, "That's a good idea," sometimes I have to laugh at what people come up with. Once in a while I'm somewhat appalled.

This was the case in "DYI pest control" (81/5:41). Why would anyone want to drown dishpans full of yellow jackets? The experts advise us not to kill hornets (a.k.a. yellow jackets) unless it is absolutely necessary, for example, if the nest is above your door or in your mailbox. They don't normally bother anyone or sting unless the nest is disturbed. Also, they eat flies, so they're very beneficial.

That said, now to my other reason for writing. This concerns the article on reusing paper and plastic. Very good ideas there, and thrifty too. But there's more!

Take your grocery bags back and reuse them the next time you shop. A bag can be used many times and you won't have so many to get rid of.

Or maybe even better, invest in some cloth or mesh bags that can be used even longer.

Grocery stores appreciate it if you bring your own bags or boxes. We haven't gotten to that point yet with other stores, but will have to try it soon.

The inner bag from cereal boxes can be used to store leftover food in the refrigerator, especially things such as pieces of meat, pancakes or waffles. Since the bag is usually plenty long, I just fold the extra underneath and it keeps just as well as in a Ziplock bag. Once used you can throw it out without feeling guilty.

Recycle everything you can. It's extra trouble to find somewhere to take it, but worth it in knowing it's good for the environment and hasn't been wasted. Remember, glass and aluminum are both 100% recyclable. – *Carolyn Vacek, Minnesota*

New tax law helps homeowners who sell at a profit

COUNTRYSIDE: Since I wrote the article on the effect of taxes on your take-home income (81/6:66) Congress has drastically changed the way home sales are taxed. In what is a great move for the average taxpayer, the law now states that homeowners can exclude up to $500,000 in gain from the sale of their principal residence. The limit is $250,000 if you're single. That's right: no tax on this gain!

Of course a few rules apply. You must have lived in the residence for the past two years and it must have been your principal residence. If you used any part of it for business and took office-in-home deductions on your tax return, that portion of the home gets treated differently (i.e., taxed!) You can use this exclusion every two years. Other minor rules apply so check them out before you sell your house.

What is particularly nice about this law is that you can buy a less expensive place. In the past, to sell your city place and buy just land frequently created a hefty tax burden. Under the old rules, you had to have a new place built and you had to be living in it within 24 months of the home sale. No more! You can take your time building.

Another advantage is that older homesteaders can sell their places and move to a smaller parcel without tax. Maybe this will free up some land for the younger folks.

Several folks can sell their individual homes and invest together on a single homestead that collectively is less expensive than several individual homes. Or you can use this rule to create your grubstake, buying fixer-uppers and selling them every couple of years after you've improved them.

As always, check out the details with a trusted advisor before you make any major financial decisions. – *Bev Carney, Wisconsin*

Tired of letters on e-mail and web sites

COUNTRYSIDE: Regarding Thomas Pitre's letter on incorrect information on web sites. I, for one, often wish all the people such as Mr. Pitre would seek out other publications and just go away. I am sure they won't as I know I am outnumbered, but I get rather tired of the letters about e-mail, web sites, etc.

I subscribe to this publication for the interesting information available and mainly because of the philosophy of the magazine. Gee, I wish we could get back to a time before all these people had computers and this was a just a super country magazine that shared ideas on the state of the world, the economy, and good wholesome ideas on surviving it all.

The letter from Jennifer L Meyer (After chores) was beautiful. I thank you for printing it. I sent a copy to our daughter and her family who will in a few short months be moving beyond the sidewalks. – *Darlene Perry, Oregon*

It's obvious that some people get the same benefits from the Internet that you get from a printed magazine, and sometimes more. If homesteaders find it to be a useful tool, we support their use of it.

Cauterizing rooster's toenails protects hens

COUNTRYSIDE: Yesterday Paul tried using a small (goat) disbudding iron on our two seven-month-old roosters' toenails. It didn't seem to hurt the birds, and it took off the sharp points so, hopefully, the hens won't get scarred backs like they have in the past.

We tried toenail clippers (the way the books suggest) but despite short cuts, they bled and made the filing job messy.

The book also describes twisting the spurs off after softening them with oil. We'll try that later. – *Paul & Joni Jackson, Wisconsin*

Many correspondents have reported good results with thrusting spurs into a hot baked potato, then twisting them off.

Down with treated wood!

COUNTRYSIDE: I saw something in the 81/6 issue that really bothers me. On page 45, there is a picture of "Home sweet home – with landscape timber addition."

To the best of my knowledge, landscape timbers are those greenish, chemically treated 4" x 8' or so pieces of "lumber" that are sold to make borders around decorative landscaping. Treated with goodies like arsenic.

I would not build a dog house with that garbage, let alone a house for my family! I really hope that the family used untreated landscaping lumber like cedar or locust (it costs more, and probably doesn't go on sale at the end of the season.)

I am sure that anywhere that sells treated lumber will tell a customer that it's "perfectly safe." It is not safe. Bugs won't eat it because it kills them. Would you use lead-based paint in a toddler's room just because you had an old can of it sitting around and wanted to save some money?

Nowhere on my farm do animals come in contact with the modern miracle of pressure treated wood, and I will tell you why. I had a wonderful dog, Czar. He chewed on treated lumber scraps one day. Some months later, he developed a tiny growth between his teeth. It didn't stay tiny for long.

He was my protector. I held him as the vet put him to sleep.

My husband is a writer and a glorified carpenter, and from time to time, he has to work with treated lumber. If he gets a splinter from treated wood, the wound always gets nasty.

I realize that my stories are anecdotal – no scientific proof of anything. But please! If you have to build a house or addition with treated landscape timbers, please spend a few bucks for something to seal it with so that you are not coming in contact with it! Please do not burn the scraps and do not make toys out of them for your kids or animals! Better yet, get rid of it and start clean.

But the manufacturers say it's safe!! Yeah, and the emperor has that beautiful new outfit, too. I worked in television and advertising for six years. I worked on a lot of commercials and I know that some people will do and say whatever it takes to sell a product. (For years the tobacco industry told everyone there was no proof that cigarettes caused cancer – when their own research told them the opposite!) When I could no longer stand participating in the great lies of television, I quit and became a nurse. As a nurse, I am obligated to help people make healthy life choices. Building a dwelling space with treated lumber is not a good idea. We move to the country to live more naturally and healthfully, not to surround ourselves with dangerous chemicals.

A useful packet of information on treated wood is available from *Organic Gardening* magazine. Contact *Organic Gardening,* 33 E. Minor St., Emmaus, PA 18098. Ask for the "treated wood package." You've heard the manufacturer's claims about how safe treated wood is. You need to hear the other side of the story to be able to make an informed decision! – *Kris Sayers, RN, BSN, MS, Ohio*

Up with recycled grease!

COUNTRYSIDE: Grease is always a recycling challenge. Here's a solution.

Set up a platform feeder on a pole. Stock with grapefruit rinds filled with grease. Birds, in particular woodpeckers, love it. – *Lewis Jett, Virginia*

Down with used motor oil!

COUNTRYSIDE: I totally agree that spreading used oil on the ground is a no-no. A quart of oil can foul thousands of gallons of drinking water.

But some of us live a long way from any recycling center that will accept used motor oil, and it piles up around the place.

For this reason I suggest burning it for heating.

If you collect the used motor oil and separate any water or sludge by letting it settle out in a drum and siphon or dip it off the top, it will mix with fuel oil and burn in a gun or pot type burner.

Filter the oil thoroughly and mix with your fuel oil in a 10 percent ration – for example, 10 gallons of used oil to 100 gallons fuel oil.

Not only will this get rid of the used oil – it will reduce your heating cost at the same time. Just be certain to remove all sludge and any water present, and to filter the used oil.

Caution: Do not use this mix in any non-vented heater or oil lamp, as toxic fumes may be present. Any normal oil stove or furnance with an outside vent will be fine. – *Swamp Fox*

This came up some years back, and we were informed by someone in the environmental bureaucracy that, at least in Wisconsin, it's illegal to burn used oil because of those toxic fumes you mention.

Dowsing works for her

COUNTRYSIDE: In response to the dowsing story (81/6:105):

My father could always find water, and the talent is said to run in families. Dad always took me along because I could also find water. I'm sure many people have the talent and don't know it.

As for determing sex, I tried it on two women when I was about 20. I was right, but people thought I was crazy. Never tried it again until I read your article.

I had a milk cow due on Nov. 19th. I laughed at myself as Muffin and I stood in the barn. It had been 14 years since I'd tried it. I used my wedding ring on a string. The string sort of quivered and then moved – the longer I held it the wider the movement.

It circled. A heifer calf.

Her due day came and went. My husband, who believes I can find water but doubted this, kept taunting, "Bull calf, bull calf."

She went overdue nine days... and had a beautiful heifer.

I did a neighbor's milk cow and 12 brood mares so far, and I want to do our beef cows to find the percentage of error.

It can be very beneficial for livestock breeders to know the sex of unborn animals. Many use ultrasound.

This is so interesting. I'm so glad a friend encouraged me to get this magazine. – *Judy Hoff, North Dakota*

Hurrah for computers

COUNTRYSIDE: In response to the lady who'd tired of letters on e-mail, web sites, etc:

When the printing press was first invented, many people were afraid of it. They thought life had been just dandy without it. They could not foresee a potential for this invention. If the printing press had not been invented, you wouldn't be able to read COUNTRYSIDE (eek!) in order to exchange all the wonderful information contained in these pages. You'd have to meet me at the post office or the country store (which could be fun, but that's another letter).

Darlene says she wants "interesting information... shared ideas on the state of the world, the economy, and good wholesome ideas on surviving it all." All of that can be found on the Internet as well as in printed material.

Computers and the Internet are not for everyone, but to some they are the greatest thing since sliced (homemade) bread. – *Heather Metheny, via fax*

My impression is that people who couldn't see any use for the printing press simply ignored it. Those who were afraid were afraid because they could see its potential – namely, to promote learning and equality, thereby eroding their power base. (This equates with certain politicians and other leaders who want to try to control the Internet today.)

Resents the name, enjoys the game

COUNTRYSIDE: This is in reply to Ruth Haskett's letter about being referred to by locals as "hobby farmers." Stings, doesn't it?

When we moved to our homestead 15 years ago, we were called "selfish" because we wouldn't be contributing to society. One person cracked that our homestead was a perfect set up for a workaholic. Another called it a "bucolic paradise." One person always asked us, "How are things down on the farm?"

Fifteen years later, none of these folks are doing well at all for various reasons. We, on the other hand, have learned gardening, canning, how to manage calves, goats and chickens, etc. We are at this point almost self-reliant and very healthy from all the work involved.

Don't let them get you down. Mostly it's just ignorance that causes people to downgrade others. – *Shirley Smith, Colorado.*

Considering what some of us are called, "hobby farmer" would be a great improvement!

Asian Shepherds are still being developed

COUNTRYSIDE: The letters and phone calls we received in response to our article on the Asian Shepherd have been heartwarming. (81/5:24.) We were fascinated to hear about the lives of people we think of as the new American pioneers.

It should be pointed out that we too are going "back to the future" with the Asian Shepherd. This is a breed in development. It takes time, as some person or group selects the best dogs for the desired traits and continues to choose breeding stock based on their ideal. We are just beginning, but hope someday to have developed an all-around farm dog, personified by the Old Sheps of earlier days, who is not a specialist.

There are plenty of specialist breeds who mostly do one thing or another—herd, hunt, protect, make good companions or whatever. There will be a need for those specialists, but we also need an all-around dog who has the genes to do a lot of different jobs. It will take detailed data sent to us from Asian Shepherd owners about health, behavior, function, intelligence, temperament, instincts and all aspects of the dog over a period of time. – *Don and Pril Zahorsky, Oklahoma*

In other words, the dog described exists only in the mind of the breeder: you can't buy one yet.

Starting from scratch at 76

COUNTRYSIDE : I want to inform you you are keeping me from my work. I am a 76-year-old homesteader starting from scratch, something I have always wanted to do. I have been at it for two years now, I have five or six things that I should be doing all at the same time, but when I get your magazine I don't put it down 'til I've finished reading it. You should come to Tennessee and help me catch up with my work.

Anyway, here is my subscription for another two years. Keep up the good work. I enjoy it very much. Thanks – *Paul Woods, Tennessee*

We'd be glad to come down and help, except for those "five or six things" you should be doing at the same time. Sounds too much like home.

Finding cheap, fertile land

COUNTRYSIDE: There are still parts of the country were you can find cheap, fertile land. Look into farming communities. You can often find abandoned farms or smaller chunks of older farms for sale.

One place to find such properties is upstate New York. No, not around Albany: that is southern New York to us. If you like the four seasons and especially winter, then look north of Plattsburg to the Canadian border. It's not unusual to find small parcels for $5,000 and up.

We bought 140 acres with a house and barn for about $35,000. Of course, it needed lots of work. But if you do it yourself you can save lots of money.

I know of a 10-acre parcel with a mobile home with a well, septic and power available and owner financing with $1,000 - $2,000 down for $17,000. Granted, good jobs are hard to find, but at that price you could pump gas and make the payments.

The people here are friendly and helpful. Yes, you will be the talk of the town for a while. And yes, every time you work on fixing up the place they will drive by slowly, but they will also give you a chance. The only problem we've had is with people from our home state.

Look in places where it might take 30-40 minutes to find the nearest Kmart. Drive the back roads. Many properties will have signs on them. Stop at the corner grocery or gas station for a cup of coffee and ask about properties for sale. Maybe even post a wanted sign on some bulletin boards or run an ad in the local paper. – *Patty Gamble, Connecticut*

Boil bones to make them safe

COUNTRYSIDE: I think it might be useful to add a caveat to the article written by a woman explaining how she stretches a chicken into several dinners. In the article she mentions that she saves the bones from the chicken after her family has nibbled the meat off of them. She then sets them aside to make a stock a couple days later.

It's a great idea. I do it myself. I just want folks to be aware that it's a good idea to immediately boil the chicken bones right after that first meal. Otherwise all those bacteria that have been introduced to the bones have a wonderful growth medium. The resulting waste products produced by the thriving bacteria include toxins that can result in food poisoning. If you don't kill the bacteria right away by boiling the meat, the toxins develop. Unfortunately, some of them are heat resistant—meaning that once the bacteria produce them they won't be destroyed if they are boiled later on. The bacteria die, but heat resistant toxins remain. – *A doctor's wife in Colorado*

"Environmentalism" is no longer a simple, clear-cut view of the world

COUNTRYSIDE: This is in support of disposable diapers. I haven't actually done the math on whether they are more or less expensive than cloth, but I know they are convenient, which can count for a lot on a homestead.

Diapers cost us about $10 a week, which seems like a lot of money. But they save time, which enables me to bake bread, clean the house, etc., etc.

You see, I use a wringer washing machine, and a clothesline or rack. It would take me hours to do diapers, since they would have to be done every day, and then I would not be able to use that time to do other things that save money. If I can bake a loaf of bread for 26¢ rather than buying a loaf for $3, I think I have saved money by using storebought diapers. If I can spin a beautiful skein of yarn for a few cents—one that would cost me at least $16 in a yarn shop—then I have saved money.

As homesteaders we have cut down on a lot of useless waste. We compost our vegetable matter, we reuse jars, we find ways to save on everything. I guess what I am saying is, don't be ashamed or feel guilty if you use disposable diapers. I would be willing to bet that the pioneer women would have really appreciated them! If you stop and consider it, I think you'll find a lot of ways that disposable diapers have helped you in your efforts to homestead.

To those who disagree, that's fine, but don't try to bully everyone into doing things your way. It may be fine for you, but impossible for others. —*Mrs. A. Peare, Maine*

I hope this won't be the next battle in the Great Dishwasher War, but rather an opportunity to open a stimulating new discussion.

"Doing the math" on this could be quite interesting, but there are several ways of going about it. In addition to the direct trade-offs for one person or family, we might also look at the cost/benefits to society. (Besides the use of resources, diapers are said to last for decades in landfills.)

This can be related to so many, perhaps even most, other "environmental problems." Are we going to weigh and measure the size of the problem—and the value of the cure—in terms of time or money saved, or in terms of environmental impact, or in some form of what we call "new accounting" that considers all of these and more? And from whose standpoint? It doesn't matter whether we're talking about spotted owls, global warming, or disposable diapers. There are some serious, and honest, differences of opinion. As yet, there are no universal tools for weighing such matters.

Around the time of Rachel Carson's *Silent Spring*, it was easy for homesteaders to be environmentalists. Today everything is much more complex.

Note: We have just received—too late for this issue—two very interesting letters with a similar viewpoint. These are a backlash to the Luddite and money-bashing attitudes others have been expressing here, and frankly, are much more in concert with the "official" COUNTRYSIDE view of modern homesteading. Watch for them in the next issue.

Bad luck tests homestead resolve

COUNTRYSIDE: I would like to write on a topic that doesn't get discussed too much. It falls in the middle of wannabe homesteading and those who are already forging on.

My family is in the stage I call "try-to-bes." We purchased a six-acre parcel complete with old farm house (a fixer-upper) about four years ago.

At the time we both longed to be back in the country where we were both raised. After 10 years "in town" for my husband and five for me (I moved straight out of "home" in the country to town with him when we married in '88.) we took the first thing we could find and afford. It was (is) a great deal.

We got the house, property, deep well, and pond for peanuts and dreamed of all we'd do with it. We re-wired, re-roofed (the first two years were spent moving furniture with every storm because it rained as hard inside as outside), re-plumbed, and built a small, open-faced barn and barnyard and tried dairy goats... twice. The first time money got tight and we sold. The second time with just a pair—they contracted pneumonia—no money for the vet and we didn't have success with home remedies so we lost them. But I'm not defeated yet—third time is a charm.

Then disaster really hit. In December of '95 my stepdaughter, who had been living with us for three years, hit puberty and ended up moving to Grandma's; my dad calls to say he's leaving his wife and is on his way to come live with us; and our well pump (which probably hadn't been serviced in 15 years or more) went out to the tune of $3,500. Then in September of '96 we lost our first baby girl (third child—two boys before) during delivery.

With all the tragedy and resulting debt we found ourselves going from no debt except a small mortgage and a small credit payment, to more debt than we'd ever had.

There went my raised bed gardens I'd planned on the last 2-1/2 years. (We have hard, concrete-like clay that pretends to be dirt.) There went acquiring my canning jar supply to start my first-ever supply of home-grown veggies. There went any more work on the house for a long time, or any more livestock or outbuildings until some of the debt could be diminished.

So here we are in the country with a barn, but no garden, no animals, only now (very moderately) trying to do some little things that require little or no money to the house ourselves—like leveling with cinder blocks that were given to us; building a carport with some scrap wood, tin and trees from our property; and hopefully saving enough to replace the field wire around the old goat yard with hog panels because our oldest (6-1/2) wants to raise hogs for 4-H and Dad says he'd like to supplement the grocery needs.

Sometime around January after

the Suburban has sold (although we really need it, but need worse to pay off the bank note that it's tied up in) and everything else that we think we can make money on and do without sells, we plan on renting out our house and property for an indefinite period—maybe even permanently while my husband's job takes us to a better salary down around San Antonio. After everything else is paid off (the house will pay for itself with rent) we are thinking mountains—beyond the sidewalks, wood heat, solar/wind-powered water system, fertile soil, etc. I've even designed a small, efficient floor plan for a cabin to fit everyone—even our newest three-week-old blessing... Elisha James McClung and any others that come along.

So you see there aren't just those who are wannabes and those who are already there. Some of us are actively try-to-bes, but we're still going to the grocery store and Wal-Mart until our dreams come true.

By the way, if any of COUNTRYSIDE's readers would be interested in renting a six-acre parcel in central Texas with well, pond, three bedroom farmhouse, and lots of privacy (only one neighbor about 100 yards down the road) please drop us a line. – *Sissy McClung, Texas*

Because of the leads and lags in the publishing world, no one will read this until well past January, and we hope your place has been rented by then.

We'd class the folks you call "try-to-bes" with wannabes: most wannabes are trying, too.

The lesson of this story might be that even the best of plans can go awry due to circumstances beyond our control. This seems to happen to many COUNTRYSIDERS... and you'll read many accounts here of how they simply pick up the pieces and carry on. Don't give up—you have lots of friends here, rooting for you!

Why did the chicken *not* fly over the garden fence?

COUNTRYSIDE:I had to laugh at Bev Carney's statement in "Chickens and fences" (82/1:45). She says two-foot chicken wire keeps chickens out of her garden? Ha!

My chickens fly over a six-foot fence. I had to put woven wire (four-inch) from the chicken house roof to the fence on all sides of the house before I could keep them in.

I only have six hens, and they only have to stay in the pen for a half-hour or so in the morning; then I let them out.

They were little last year when I was starting my garden, but this year is a whole new story. I'm thinking of making an eight-foot fence around my garden! Well, maybe seven, anyway.

Anybody else have thoughts on this subject? – *Dorothy Jones, Wyoming*

Generally speaking, the lighter (and smaller) breeds of chickens, including Leghorns, can and will fly. The heavier breeds are more likely to remain on the ground. (We note one correspondent in this issue says her Rock-Cornish crosses barely bother to walk, much less jump or fly.)

There are no doubt other differences, including what's in the garden and whether the chickens know it; what else might interest a chicken on the way to the garden, and even the distance from the chicken coop

If actual flying is a problem, clipping the feathers on one wing usually solves it. With one wing clipped, the bird can't get off the ground... or steer..

A look at attitudes, and mangel beets

COUNTRYSIDE: In reference to Chad Karnitz's column (82/1:81)—many homesteaders will not be surprised by his words. In fact, I find his attitude to be a reflection of most of society's. Thankfully, I no longer deal with it.

I attribute some of it to a lack of tolerance. Those who choose to live with other than "the norm" are always met with intolerance.

"Normal" is acquiring material wealth, buying all the latest gadgets and toys, and being a society-programmed robot.

The rest of his attitude I attribute to jealousy. Jealous, because we see the future as it is, and are doing something about it. People like him also feel an uneasiness about the future. They just don't have the courage and determination to act, so they ridicule those who do. It is easier to pretend it doesn't exist and rely on the system to take care of them in the future.

Now a question: Do any COUNTRYSIDERS have experience with growing and using mangels for livestock feed? I am considering growing some winter supplement for the goats and horses, and have found information to be limited. – *Marcella Shaffer, Montana*

Mangel beets are an old-time feed that largely faded away after the introduction of silos. Since most homesteaders don't have silos, and many can easily grow beets like a garden crop without a lot of land and equipment, it might seem that these huge roots would be an ideal homestead feed crop.

Could be. But our own experience with them was less than satisfactory on anything less than a very small scale.

Mangels are fun to grow: no doubt about that! They reach a tremendous size, and most of the root sticks out of the ground so you don't even have to dig them.

The old-time method was to wash the soil off them, remove the tops as for carrots, and store them in pits covered with straw to keep them from freezing.

When feeding, they should be chopped. (A box made for the purpose used to be a common farm tool.)

We fed them to goats, rabbits, sheep, pigs, chickens, and the family cow. None of these seemed to relish them very much, we didn't relish the work, and eventually the whole stash froze and turned to mush.

Mangels do have possibilities, no doubt, but they do require labor and management.

Save the birds with window screening

COUNTRYSIDE: I have found only one issue of your magazine in our town—ever. This magazine has much in it that parallels my lifestyle. I live on 5-1/2 acres on a small lake.

Here's a help for those folks who have large picture windows and a regular bird kill because of them. I bought nylon screening by the roll and stapled the screen on the outside of my big windows. This stops summer heat from the morning sun, and stops the reflection. Birds do not fly into the glass anymore.

I started out hanging it as a drape but stapled it to the final windows, covering them fast. I saw this used in a clothing store window to keep the sun's rays from fading clothes.

The screen is not noticeable from the inside looking out. The sun faded my furniture—but not anymore with the screening deflecting the sun's rays.

Last autumn I lost nine robins when they were flocking to go south. I haven't lost any birds all four seasons since I put the screen outside.

I have been having fun catching sky water (rain) this year. My well water is hard and this rain water is so-o-o soft. I have a PVC frame with a blanket of 6 mil plastic stretched on it, a hole in the center and a jumbo barrel below. It's been a wet year, so I have more water than I can use!

I store water in food-safe plastic containers and keep them in the dark so "things" don't begin to grow in there. I get cardboard boxes from the appliance store. It serves me well to keep the rain water in darkness. The 6 mil plastic was also free from the furniture store—wraps from Chesterfields that come enclosed in it. Wine supply stores carry the big food-safe containers. – *M. Leggett, British Columbia.*

Since you brought it up, this is a good place to mention that another one of our newsstand distributors has gone bankrupt, meaning that a few thousand more readers won't find us in the usual places. If you buy single copies and ever have trouble finding the latest issue, dig out a back issue and mail us your subscription!

And on a similar topic, in response to those who have been asking why COUNTRYSIDE is listed as "out of business" in some publication directories...

This is a continuation of our troubles with the "Countryside" magazine the Hearst Corp started a few years back. Many people confused their slick new rag with our comparatively shabby old one back then, and theirs continues to haunt us even after its death. It's amazing what an impact a few million dollars can have.

Alum, grape leaves, and pickle-making

COUNTRYSIDE: Last year I went to the store to buy alum to make sweet pickles. They were out of alum, but the lady at the store said it was possible to use grape leaves as a substitute. Not wanting to risk a batch of pickles on such uncertain information, I found alum at another store.

Still, the idea intrigues me. Can anyone confirm this practice,and maybe tell me how large a grape leaf to use? – *Leona B. Matz, Pennsylvania*

Grape leaves have been used to make pickles, probably since pickles were invented. Most recipes say to use 2-3 leaves per quart. Brined pickles call for a layer of washed grape leaves on the bottom of the crock, and another layer on top. (According to some Southern sources, scuppernong leaves are best.)

It should be noted that some modern canning experts scoff at the idea that grape leaves make pickles crispier, but they don't do any harm.

You don't have to be a scientist, or connected with a university or large corporation, to come up with ideas that change the way people do things. Here are some good examples.

Fight damaging battery corrosion

COUNTRYSIDE: Here's one that works. I discovered, by accident, that Type "F" transmission fluid stops corrosion immediately on battery terminals and exposed wiring. Just clean and brush on liberally. Lasts for years! Saves batteries and money. Any generic brand of type "F" or "FA" works. – *Ken Bynum, Florida*

A neat way to save on lamp oil

COUNTRYSIDE: I am 15 years old and am writing to you with a pretty neat way to save on lamp oil.

First fill your oil lamp tank half way with water, then put in the lamp oil. Since oil and water do not mix the oil will always be on top of the water.

This is convenient because the wick is always in the oil.

You can also make it colorful by adding food coloring to the water. – *Dan Hultquist, Iowa*

Get woodchucks to move elsewhere

COUNTRYSIDE: I have an easy way to rid yourself of nuisance woodchucks. I discovered it when I had a chicken die on me.

I got a shovel to bury it, went behind the barn, and saw a ready-made hole—a woodchuck hole. I put the chicken in and pushed some dirt over it and forgot about it.

The woodchuck left.

I have tried this quite a few times since then and no longer have any woodchucks around the barn or any place else I don't want them. A scooped up road kill rabbit, opossum or whatever would work just as well as a dead chicken I suppose.

Recently I purchased a book *How to Make It on the Land.* (copyright 1972). In it was shown an ear of corn described as pod corn. I was wondering if any COUNTRYSIDER would have some seed I could buy or know where I could purchase some. – *Valerie Reed, Michigan*

Skunk deodorizer works on cats, too

COUNTRYSIDE: I have a comment about your piece on skunks and the odor removal remedy (81/5:66). I found this same remedy in a hunting magazine several years ago. I didn't have a skunk problem, I had a cat problem.

I have found that most of the products on the market for removing cat urine odor don't work. The skunk odor remedy does. Just mix it up and sponge it on the area to be deodorized (the corner of your living room carpet, automobile floor boards, etc.) Soak the spot. Allow it to dry, then shampoo it out. (I just soak with clear water and blot with towels rather than renting a shampooer.)

Use caution and wear gloves when using this mixture. The first time I used it I had bare hands and got a slight chemical burn (as you would if you let your hands soak in bleach or hydrogen peroxide.) Because of the burning effect I won't use it on my dogs for skunk odors, although it might still work if it was diluted a bit with water. – *Abigail Madden, California*

Skunk odor remedy

Mix one quart of 3% hydrogen peroxide (from a pharmacy) with ¼ cup baking soda and 1 teaspoon liquid soap. Wash the dog (or whatever) with this, keeping it out of an animal's eyes, nose and mouth. Follow with a thorough tap water rinse. – *Paul Krebaum, Illinois*

Mice are chocoholics!

COUNTRYSIDE: By happy accident my family and I discovered that mice are chocoholics. They will turn down even plump, readily available sunflower seeds for chocolate in almost any form.

We discovered this when the mice who had invaded our pantry one autumn consistently ignored our carefully prepared peanut butter or cheese laden traps to raid (and ruin!) the bags of Snickers and Milky Way candy bars. After several days of empty traps but more ruined candy, we used bits of candy bar for trap bait. In less than four hours we caught three mice in two traps. By the next evening we'd caught the rest of the invaders.

That was about 25 years ago, before I left home. Since that time I have used chocolate as mouse trap bait in my own home with 100% success. I have used canned chocolate fudge frosting, chocolate chips, candy bars, Rollos, Hershey's Kisses and even M&Ms (broken open and "glued" to the trap with honey or syrup). Old chocolate works, but fresh chocolate enjoys a greater, more timely success rate.

Chocolate bait is environmentally safe for pets, children, and soil (wherever the deceased is laid to rest) or scavengers (who eat the deceased). It is possible to encourage ants or cockroaches with this bait, but frequent monitoring of traps and removal of bait as soon as possible will help avoid that problem. It is almost always on hand in our home (my husband and three children are chocoholics too!) whereas D-Con is not.

Hope this helps someone; it's sure been a help to us! – *Mrs. Danny (Kathy) Robinson, Arkansas*

A cheap and easy way to pick up nails

COUNTRYSIDE: I treasure every issue and use many of the hints. I just finished wrapping my cheese in vinegar-dampened paper towel to prevent fur growth and am about to shuck a pillowcase full of dried beans in the clothes dryer. Both hints were in past issues.

I am so grateful to you folks for being there that I have decided to share a hint with all.

When we re-roofed an outbuilding a couple of years ago, we had to tear off the old shingles and I was worried that our free-range poultry would eat the nails. So after picking up the shingles, I went over the area several times with a powerful magnet on a cord swung slowly back and forth at ground level.

This powerful magnet was free and just about everybody has one. They may not know it though, because it looks like an old radio, or a junked tv, or anything else that has a speaker.

Take out the speaker and remove all electric wires, but leave the paper that forms a shallow cone. At the bottom of the cone is a magnet – the bigger the speaker, the more powerful the magnet.

Most speakers already have holes around the edge for mounting. Loop cord through a couple of these holes to form a long handle. Put the speaker on the ground – magnet down – stand next to it and measure from your hand to the speaker. Make the handle a little shorter than this measurement so the magnet will be just above ground level when you walk. Then walk slowly over the area to be de-nailed while gently swaying the speaker/magnet.

Very soon you will hear ping-ping-ping as nails (and other metal stuff you didn't know was there) hit the magnet. Now and then, pull the debris off the magnet and put it in the shallow paper cone that was the speaker to store until you've finished.

I cleaned up the roofing mess with this device and also used it on the ashes after we had burned a big pile of junk. Our workshop is in the garage, so I also use it there and on the driveway to keep nails out of our tires.

My winter project is to build a straw bale insulated ice house. I'd sure like to correspond with anyone who has done this or anyone who just likes to talk homesteading. – *Sandy Stone, Minnesota*

Determining sex without ultrasound

COUNTRYSIDE: In response to the article on how to determine the sex of the unborn (81/6:105):

Many years ago we did this for fun at baby showers. We used a two-inch-long heavy duty sewing needle and a piece of thread about 24 inches long. The thread was doubled through the needle, knotted at the top, and held between the forefinger and thumb with the needle about 1-2 inches above the inside of the wrist.

After using the needle on several guests, a young lady said, "Do Mother." I did, but the needle didn't move. I looked at the young lady and said I didn't understand. She smiled and said "Mother couldn't have children. I'm adopted." – *Elizabeth Scott, Florida*

Pluck chickens with your electric drill

COUNTRYSIDE: In your superb Nov./Dec. '97 issue there was a comment regarding a chicken/waterfowl plucker that is run off an electric drill. I can't vouch for how well they work, but such units are available from Herters, 111 E. Burnett, Beaver Dam WI 53916, ph. 920-887-1765. They do have a catalog. If anyone buys one, I'd hope they'd write and let the rest of us know how well they work. – *Chuck Megan, Wisconsin*

Some new pioneers are considered lazy

COUNTRYSIDE: Today many people who are homesteading at a fairly young age like us (32 and 26) with almost nothing to start out on have it hard and it takes all of our inner strength not to give in.

We have only one vehicle and it's impractical for both of us to have jobs. Marcy works full-time as a baker and I take care of the home and land. Since we can't afford a bulldozer to clear land, I dig each and every garden plot by hand, which means removing stumps, roots and rocks.

Since we don't have electricity or a road to our cabin, I cut wood and haul it by wheelbarrow or in 10-12 foot lengths.

I built our humble six-sided 20-foot-wide log cabin by hand, myself.

I hunt, and gather herbs and plants for food and medicine.

It's funny, but I get flak for being "lazy," mostly because I don't actively participate in the American nightmare of a 9-5 job.

We are happy with our lifestyle, but sometimes the pressure of the outside world gets to us. We find solace in each other, the knowledge that there are others out there like us, and the satisfaction that we are doing what we want to do without going into debt.

Like John Trudell said in *Stickman* by Paula Iglori, "Slavery is slavery, whether you are an indentured servant, in chains, or in debt."

What we are doing was known as pioneering in the past. Now it's being lazy. Go figure. – *Ivan Cales, Jr., West Virginia*

Consider this quote from the newsletter Strategic Investment:

"Throughout history, there were few or no jobs in the modern sense, just temporary tasks. The 'job' as a permanent or semi-permanent position in an organization arose with the modern corporation... Our prediction: 'Good jobs' will soon be a thing of the past... now is the time to prepare yourself for this coming eventuality." You're ahead of the crowd!

There's lots of info for intelligent decision-making

COUNTRYSIDE: I thank Ms. Sayers for providing COUNTRYSIDERS with another option for information on treated wood (82/2).

There is so much information available, both pro and con, and in such a variety of places. COUNTRYSIDERS, in my opinion, are always questioning, always seeking new information. I would guess that most of what they do is preceded by hours of research.

So much of what we do is based on facts and whatever biases we have. Should we eat eggs? Bacon? Or anything that could raise our cholesterol? Should we raise animals for meat? Grow our own tobacco? Should we pasteurize our milk? Should we drink water with chlorine or fluoride in it? Should we turn our eggs in the incubator? Should we immunize our children? Should we compost human manure? Should we build our homes with log kits, straw bales, tires, or go traditional? Should we put in carpets, use plywood or particle board and worry about formaldehyde? Should we heat our homes with wood, coal, oil, gas, or electricity – perhaps provided by nuclear power? What about cars?

You can find information pro and con on any of these subjects, and you need to make your own informed decision on what you feel comfortable with.

Which is what we did when we built our addition with landscape timbers (81/6 – the item which instigated the letter on treated wood). Please keep in mind, our article in no way encouraged anyone to build with landscape timbers. It did not tout the virtues of using them, nor was it a how-to article.

We have enjoyed our addition for the last five years. We do not lick, bite or chew the wood, nor do we burn it, make toys for dogs or humans with it, or use it where animals might chew it. And each year the ladybugs hibernate by the thousands in the nooks and crannies and every spring emerge to work in our garden.

Homesteaders make informed choices. We made ours, and with Ms. Sayers' help, others will be able to make theirs. – *Marcy, West Virginia*

Is the fence to keep chickens in, or out?

COUNTRYSIDE: Dorothy Jones is right when she says the two-foot chicken wire won't keep chickens confined! My neighbor tried to pen hers in and ended up with six-foot fencing with extensions added to the top.

But surprisingly, a two-foot fence does keep them out. Although they can jump over the fence, they don't do it. Occasionally the rooster will jump in to see me for his daily cuddle, but that's all the problem we've had. We even put a strip of "poultry netting" up at the garage door—keeps them away from the exposed polystyrene insulation which they love with a passion. (They also know it's there—the minute the fence is down, they're pecking away at it.) I don't know if it's fear of confinement that keeps them out (although the garden sections are quite large—50' x 20' in some cases), or whether there are just enough grass and bugs elsewhere. They do root around at the base of the fence and watch me hoe and weed. I even feed them lettuce over the fence occasionally, although this is not a wise habit to develop with critters.

Half of our chickens are a White Leghorn/Rhode Island mix and we also have Asian Blacks. When they were younger, they were a lot flightier. They were not a problem in the garden until they were a year old and that's when we started fencing. Two-foot fence is easy to work with and easy to step over. I'd suggest trying it before using other drastic measures. *–Bev Carney, Wisconsin*

Know your tractor when buying parts

COUNTRYSIDE: I am writing about the picture of the tractor on in the article "Whatever works for you" in the March/April (81/3) issue.

Under the picture and in Mrs. Liska's story she calls the tractor an IH Farmall Cub. I don't know where the picture came from but it's very plain that the tractor is an M, not a Cub. My tractor-knowledgeable men say it's a Super M to boot.

There are a lot of differences between a Farmall Cub and a Farmall Super M. One is that the Cub has a wide front axle, which means the wheels stand about a yard apart, not close together as in the picture. The Cub's rear wheels are only 24 inches high and the M's are 38 inches high. The M is bigger and more powerful than the Cub.

We run a farm tractor and machinery salvage yard here in Missouri. We were mentioned in a story about fixing tractors that ran a few issues ago. If Mrs. Liska came to our yard needing a used part for her tractor, say a rear wheel, we would sell her a Cub wheel, which is what she seems to think she has. Then very soon she would be back, mad because we had sold her a part that didn't fit her tractor. But we had sold her a part for what she told us she owned.

This happens to us every so often. Sometimes someone has sold a tractor for something it was not, then when the buyer needs parts, they end up with parts that don't fit. There are those who will paint a tractor a color it is not supposed to be, and even put on decals from another brand, so they can sell it at a higher price to someone who knows nothing about tractors.

It does help very much to take along the old parts that you need to replace when you go after either new or used parts. If you have a picture of your tractor, take it along too. We call these people "city farmers" and do make an effort to find out what brand and series of tractor they do have and send them home with the right part. *–Mrs. Arnold Austin, Missouri*

We have made a few mistakes in our first 29 years on this job, but I don't recall any quite like this. That great big M on the side should have been a giveaway, but although we spend a lot of time proofreading words, we never before found it necessary to proofread pictures! And to top it off, we once owned an IH Model M ourselves. As we homesteaders say, every day is a new learning experience.

Katahdins sell well in North Carolina

COUNTRYSIDE: In contrast to Ken Scharabok's experience with hair sheep in Tennessee (82/2), Katahdins are a much in demand breed in North Carolina, and are often crossed with Dorpers. I sold two Katahdin ewes without papers, but bred to my Dorper ram, for $150—each. And that was cheap. There are people here who will pay $60-$70 and more for any Katahdin ewe they can find.

I paid $150 each for my registered just-weaned Katahdin ewes. A fellow who visited me last week had sold some of his more mature unregistered ewes for $125 each.

Yesterday I sent two Katahdin yearling wethers to the Lexington, North Carolina auction. They brought $61 each, and I netted $56.50 each. One of the wethers was sorry looking as I had made the mistake of neutering him after weaning in the middle of summer and he almost died. He never did gain weight much after that. I was shocked that someone paid $61—I wouldn't have given you 2¢ for him.

The Barbados Blackbelly is a hair sheep but are wild as can be. I won't get another, although mine is half Barbados and half Dorper. I have not been able to tame him to save my life, whereas the wild Katahdin I bought are almost pestfully tame.

If you have any more Katahdin, please let me know: there are buyers waiting! *–Pearl Ray, North Carolina*

Experience with mangel beets as livestock feed

COUNTRYSIDE: I want to respond to Marcella Shaffer concerning mangels for livestock feed.

I only raise open-pollinated heirloom seeds because we want to be as self-sufficient as possible. We ordered some yellow mangel seeds from Abundant Life Seeds (P.O. Box 772, Port Townsend, WA 98368). I grew them for the first time in the summer of 1996 with hopes of using them for fodder for our young Guernsey milk cow.

We planted two rows of them, in new ground. We used a 10-20-20 commercial fertilizer when we first planted them, and we kept them watered. We could not believe the growth on these beets!

The cow, however, was not impressed—at first. We cut them up and put them in her grain box to munch on after she finished her grain. She would eat a little, then turn up her nose.

We then tried feeding them to her over the fence, because she thinks anything coming over the fence is a real treat! She decided she liked them. Soon after she decided she loved them. Then she would come running (literally) when she saw us heading out to where the beets were planted.

We kept them in the ground and fed them a few at a time until November.

Last year we planted more mangels, the yellow and a red, and had enough until December. This last year, in addition to fertilizing, we mulched with grass. We have mild winters, so keeping them in the ground over winter will work, if you can keep the voles away from them!

I saved five or so over winter, for seed. They are now getting new growth on top, so it looks like this will work.

We will double the amount of mangels this growing season, and will plant even more next year when we have our own seed.

Anything you can add to supplement the feeding of a milk cow is money in your pocket (or money you can spend on something other than feed). We raise our own second cutting grass and clover hay, which also keeps the cost down. Daisy is fed six pounds of grain daily, all the grass hay she wants, and mangels until December. She came fresh in October and has averaged five gallons of milk a day.

As I shared in my previous letter, our two boys live with their families on our hundred-acre farm. All three families share in the milking and the milk. We still have too much milk! We fed a lot to her calf and the rest to two pigs soon to be butchered. We make a lot of butter and some very tasty soft cheese. Our favorite is when we add chopped red peppers to make a soft pepper cheese. *–Darlene Lund, Washington*

Rutabagas make good feed, too

COUNTRYSIDE: I have been extremely busy since August, when I bought a one-room schoolhouse on one acre. The yard was a major mess but I am beginning to see ground in most places now. I'm even thinking about moving there. One acre looks like a just-right size for a single 60-year-old woman.

Several comments came to mind when I read through the last issue.

Regarding mangel beets: I have no experience with these, but when I was a child my people raised acres of rutabagas. It sounds like they are quite similar.

In the fall, we children went through the field and pulled the plants. Mom came after us and cut off the tops. The tops were put in one pile and the roots in another pile, throwing distance, throughout the field. (As I recall this took several days.)

We hauled the tops in our little red wagon and fed them to the cows, without drying them or anything. I think we started out slowly so the cows could adjust to this change in diet.

The roots were thrown into a horse-drawn field wagon and hauled to the house. We had a chute made of three long boards, a bottom and two sides. This trough was put through an opened window into our 12' x 12' root cellar under our one-room house. We threw the roots into the trough and they slid into the cellar. Occasionally a parent would go into the cellar and move the trough for more level distribution.

There was an actual root cutter with a handle that turned a drum with blades that cut the roots into slices. My mom emphasized that no round roots could be fed—a cow might choke. We kids used the cutter, but when Mom prepared the feed she preferred a butcher knife.

As I recall, rutabagas were fed most of the winter. They were used as a substitute for grain. We lived in Michigan where we had very short summers. Outdoor pits didn't work there. The deer always found them and opened them.

Regarding "chocoholic mice": A friend had a country store—and mice. Once she complained about the number of candy bars she was losing to mice. An old-timer told her to leave the candy bar the mice were eating on. She said it was amazing, but the mice would finish one candy bar before starting on another! *–Marion Neely, Missouri*

Mangels and other "alternative" feeds

COUNTRYSIDE: Mangel beets do make good stock and people food. I grow the colossal long red mangel, which is relished by livestock and has the nutritive value of grain.

The greens are pretty good. They taste like Swiss chard. All the animals like the tops.

The young roots taste like mild beets, which of course they are.

Everything proceeds well through summer, but summer is when you have plenty of feed anyway.

The hard part is January, February and March. Here in the Willamette Valley of Oregon we can let root crops stay in the ground, and harvest as the need arises. Somehow, the mangels and turnips get sort of forgotten until January or February. I pull a few, take a machete to them, and present them to the livestock.

By midwinter a chicken will eat anything. Rabbits will eat them just for something to do, but the goats just look at you with those weird eyeballs.

Anyway, a little at a time, everyone gets used to the taste and texture, and they do fine.

This is also the time of the year the winter squash decides to go bad, so some of that goes to the barn too.

I think this type of feeding simply takes time to learn, and for livestock to develop a taste for it. I've seen cows tear down stalls to get to chopped-up pumpkins, but that was after they learned to eat them.

I realize my "storage system" is much simpler than it can be for those of you who have to store inside, but I hope you'll experiment with this type of feeding. We may see the day when there'll be no choice.

Since I'm on the subject of stock feed, I'm seeking info on hedge materials that might be suitable for small stock. I already feed goats and rabbits all fruit tree prunings and some materials from shrubs, but I'm interested in what feeds could develop from hedge plants. I have little room to devote to growing feed crops, and the only direction I can go is up.

I've planted honey locust for the seed pods (they're not producing yet) and mulberries for the chickens, etc., but I wonder what other ideas are out there. – *Joe D. Leonard, Oregon*

Diaper decision is a messy issue

COUNTRYSIDE: The issue of disposable diapers is a thorny one. My twin sister and I were raised without them, and our diapers are still being used as dishrags. You can't do that with the diapers of today, so you're better off, I'm told, by getting flannel from the piece goods shop.

I'm not getting down on anyone who uses them. I personally have made the choice not to buy disposables when I am a mother. My husband agrees, having been raised without them, too. There are young couples out there who are trying to be environmentally responsible and are using the logic of, "Well, my parents raised me this way, it doesn't add to the landfill, and no cranky kids wracked up with diaper rash."

Diaper rash

Boy, there's an ugly topic. Diaper rash. I knew a mother who made a loud verbal point of not raising her children unnaturally, then slapping the plastic on after a few changes. When the baby was finally put in a bath of acidophilus, it was so astonished at not being in pain, it spent several days touching its bottom to make sure it was still there.

And on a subject that would appear unrelated, I read an article in the local paper about a year ago about a woman who trains bloodhounds for police work. She personally was not fond of disposable diapers because her bloodhounds couldn't tell the difference between their odor and that of a rotting human corpse.

But when it comes down to it, sure, disposables are easy to use. So are a lot of things out there and it is easy to give in to the disposable culture, because it seems to contribute to the faster-faster-faster mode. But disposables are rather hard to biodegrade and the toxins do not go anywhere—they are not taken care of. Plastic does nothing but sit there. Cloth diapers eventually wear out, but in the meantime, they can be rinsed out and the contents added to the compost pile, just like the "wastes" of Mommy and Daddy. I hate the idea of waste, period, seeing as how where we live the soil is very sandy and even a septic tank would upset the delicate balance of nature we try to maintain. Some sugar and baking yeast does wonders for causing aerobic breakdown in the outhouse.

I suppose in my own confused way I'm saying that just because something is easy is not the best reason to do it. We have been living full-time at our home for 11 months now, and we have yet to collect enough trash to justify a trip to the landfill. Things that are safe to burn are burned, and glass, plastic, metals, even rubber can be turned in for recycling. We have exactly four small trash bags to turn in at this point and we're waiting until we actually have enough to account for the trip. We got this way when we realized just how much the county was taking us to town for garbage fees. I don't want to throw any kind of paper away, especially paper with dead presidents on it.

Lately we have been paying as much attention to the packaging of the goods as we are to the goods themselves. I will pay $7 for a tin of McCann's Irish Oatmeal rather than $3.50 for a cardboard box because first, I've got all the cardboard I need for starting fires and second, I like the tin. It's something I can use over and over again. The same goes for the tin boxes of tea at the Chinese market —whether I have a taste for Litchee Congu, Jasmine Green, or Chrysanthemum Flower, I can get them in durable, hard to ruin metal canisters. The cost is not as extravagant as I had thought at first. Especially when I saw what my family was spending on just gift boxes at Christmas.

I suppose I would change my mind if someone could come up with a good use for both dirty diapers and shredded plastic produce bags.

There's no simple solution

There's no easy or simple solution to the matter. People need to think of their land as an aspect of the entire planet. Just what exactly are you going to do with the fast food cartons, paint cans and petroleum by-product?

At least my father-in-law makes planters out of old tires and some bizarrely interesting yard ornaments out of scrap iron (the likes of which, I'm afraid, can't compete with some of his neighbors). One woman made a really spiffy grape arbor by burning a box spring mattress and then putting the wire skeleton on poles. Another neighbor has unabashedly made a two-pot planter for his front yard with an old toilet.

Just "throwing it away" doesn't solve the problem. Face it — picking up those free packets of ketchup and mustard aren't worth the hassle or the plastic. And yet who carries around a bottle of ketchup in the car for when the fast-food craze hits them? And Styrofoam! I don't know about the rest of the world, but as a teenager it was grand fun to melt that stuff using moonshine or nail polish remover (some would say there is no difference). But that was about all you could do with it!

I think it is rather disturbing that people with a lot of land can find it so easy to make private landfills out of sinkholes or other such "useless" areas. There are two farmers in this county who have inherited such land from their fathers. Their children have major birth defects. – *Marcy Wilson-Cales, West Virginia*

Other considerations in the diaper debate

COUNTRYSIDE: This letter is in response to the letter by Mrs. Peare and the time and money she saves using disposable diapers. I can understand what she says about saving time spent on washing cloth diapers and how this in turn saves her valuable time for other cost-saving projects. However, there are several things to consider in the debate between cloth and disposables.

The first I would point out is the possible detrimental effects of the disposable diapers on your child. I was severely allergic to the disposable diapers and my mother was forced, for my comfort and health, to use cloth. I would assume that even babies that show no ill-effects from having their skin in contact with plastic and synthetic gel all day are not benefiting from all the moisture held against them by plastics and gel in the disposable diaper.

The second concern I, and others, have is the environmental impact. As the editor noted, disposable diapers last and last in a landfill, or a junk ditch, if you are so unlucky as to be blessed with that hand-me-down. There is nothing quite like peeling plastic and that odd gel out of the sides of what would have been a lovely creek. The plastic part of those diapers will not biodegrade. Plastic breaks in smaller pieces but the actual compound will be here until the Kingdom comes.

That said, I will admit that cloth is time-consuming and nearly impossible to deal with while traveling. But let me pass on some tips from my mother and grandmother who became adept at working with the cloth diapers.

The trick my mother used was to take the dirty diaper and swish it in the toilet, then flush while still holding the diaper in the commode. (This assumes you have indoor plumbing.) Keep hold of the diaper as you do this! Now take the sort of rinsed cloth and hang it on a rack or line in the shower or any out-of-the way place where dripping water is not a problem. Hang up diapers until you have enough accumulated (or finally have time) to wash them properly. I realize this may not be possible at times, but if it can save a little impact on the environment, it is worth it. Especially when you consider the cost that your children and grandchildren will be paying to clean up the environment so the world will continue to be livable. Surely, that little extra drain on your time and money now is worth the health and safety of your child later. Save those disposables for emergency situations where you really cannot spare the time or are visiting and haven't room. I think once you get used to the cloth, they won't take as much time as you might think. – *Alethea Kenney, Iowa*

Stories describe their youthful years

COUNTRYSIDE: How we wish you could publish every month! I am 91 years old, and my husband is 95. We love all the stories, as they describe our youthful years in Eastern Washington. We share our copies with grandchildren and even a few great-grandchildren. It is really an eye-opener and inspiration to all of us. – *Gertrude Johnson, Washington*

When she gets ideas he gets "that look"

COUNTRYSIDE: Why does my husband get a strange look on his face when I relate an idea from COUNTRYSIDE? I've seen that look before and I hear a faint sigh escape from him. It is hard to understand, though.

There was that time, just three years ago in fact, when I mentioned building a storage room in the basement. I wanted to tackle canning and needed a place to store all the jars of produce.

His eyes rolled and I heard that sigh. "Why do we need a storage room?"

I explained the purpose and need.

"But, you have never canned anything!" he exclaimed.

"Right," I said, "because I don't have a proper place to store things." The room was built. A much too large room, according to hubby. Two shelves were put along one side for the canned goods. We also store potatoes and root vegetables in there.

Now that I had my storeroom, I could start canning. We started out with our favorite vegetable – green beans. We did a few jams and that was it the first year. The green beans were wonderful and I was anxious to can other veggies, but it was obvious we didn't have enough shelves.

They were added and each year we have canned a larger variety of vegetables and each year we have added the needed shelves. We probably will can 200 jars this year.

I still can't understand why my husband got that familiar look the other day when I mentioned the possibility, mind you I said possibility, of getting a few chickens. And that sigh was quite loud this time.

"Why chickens?"

"Why not?" I answered. And after all, I wouldn't need many, just a couple — like the couple of shelves I needed for my mini canning adventure.

I'm afraid my hubby knows me all too well. We haven't reached an agreement yet on the chickens, but then, it took me awhile to convince him about the storage area in the cellar. But he sure likes those canned green beans all year and he sure likes eggs and he sure likes chicken, so who knows what the future might hold? – *Irene F. Burt, Maine*

Suggests we change "Our Philosophy"

COUNTRYSIDE: A number of readers have directly or indirectly expressed their views on money. Here are some of the titles that caught my eye: "Are COUNTRYSIDERS 'money bashers'?" (81/4). "Homesteaders aren't money-bashers" (81/6). "She's a money-basher" (82/1). According to one reader, the wealthy are more generous than the unwealthy. To another, the opposite is so.

As I observe human behavior (including my own), I notice a tendency to highlight those events that support our beliefs and ignore the ones that don't. We can easily develop a bias without even realizing it.

I have found that rich or poor, people are people. Some of them give and some of them don't.

Those who protest a bit too loudly or defend themselves just a little too vigorously may be trying to convince themselves more than anyone else. Money is an "issue" for many of us. Who among us has a really healthy relationship with this thing called money? We muck it up with a wide range of emotions and judgments, attaching strings of all kinds to it.

Money, when you get right down to it, is merely a means of exchange for goods and services. Those who hate money or have "a certain hostility toward luxury" unwittingly short-change themselves. They constrict the flow of this means of exchange that society deems necessary in our lives. "No man needs money so much as he who despises it." — Richter (81/6:94). *Your Money or Your Life* by Joe Dominguez and Vicki Robin, is an excellent book for anyone confronting the money issue.

***

COUNTRYSIDE is a unique magazine! I appreciate the time and effort that go into preparing each issue and I'm glad so many people are eager to share their experiences. If life seems like a relentless downpour at times, COUNTRYSIDE is an inviting umbrella, opened up wide to cover a multitude of homesteader "types" as Jeff Jacob has described them (82/1:79). The diversity of the readership is COUNTRYSIDE'S strength. A generous sprinkling of editor's notes and thoughtful quotes atop each left page give COUNTRYSIDE a unique flavor. My only suggestion would be to change or eliminate this phrase in Our Philosophy: "a certain hostility toward luxury." I personally do not worship money or the luxuries it can buy but I am abashed by money-bashing. – *Ann Kuhn, Michigan*

A certain hostility to the phrase "a certain hostility toward luxury" is nothing new in these pages, but perhaps it's time to state our case again.

Even before we started printing "Our Philosophy" (and it's been in every issue since January, 1990), our view of "luxury" had little or nothing to do with money.

Try thinking along the lines of function.

Transportation can be provided by a BMW... or a rusty pickup truck. You can tell time with a Rolex... or a Timex. You can dine well on lobster and truffles... or on crawdads and puffballs.

The "luxury" we have in mind deals more with excess than with money or possessions per se.

Moreover, the "certain hostility" suggests caution and some selectivity.

But even with these caveats, even like-minded people have disagreed with the phrase, suggesting things they consider luxuries. Some of my favorites include a cold drink of water after a hot day of haying, a warm homemade quilt on a blustery winter night, and a full woodshed when the first winter storm strikes.

Or how about a new set of guitar strings, or new underwear?

Some homesteaders have said they never even think about BMWs, but a rusty pickup that runs would be a luxury for them... and one they'd feel no hostility toward!

In other words, there's also a certain amount of relativity here—and that might be the real importance of the phrase. If we have come so far that one person's luxuries have become another's necessities, maybe it's time to step back and consider what's really important. Then, if you still want a BMW or Rolex, at least it won't be mindless materialism, which is really what we're trying to get at here.

Considering all this, I think we'll keep the phrase, at least until somebody can suggest an improvement.

Big Brother is watching

COUNTRYSIDE: Although 14 years late, 1984 has finally arrived.

My telephone rang about 8:00 this morning. It was a woman from the office of my cellular telephone carrier. She asked me if I had been having trouble with my cellphone because they noticed I hadn't been using it as much as I once did.

I told her that my husband had tried to reach me several days ago and was unable to get through to me. So she suggested that I take my phone to my local dealer to have it checked. I thanked her for her concern and hung up the telephone.

Then it hit me: Someone was monitoring my telephone usage! I understand it is necessary to do so to help prevent fraud. This happened to my husband's cellphone once (running up thousands of dollars of airtime presumably by drug dealers). We were not responsible for the unusually high bill. The fraud had been detected by the cellphone carrier.

I never thought of Big Brother at that time because I was happy to know we didn't have to pay the bill. But this time it was a little scary because I had made a conscious choice to not use my cellphone unless it was necessary. I was trying to follow the advice of so many people from so many articles in the best COUNTRYSIDE I have ever read (Nov/Dec '97). Thanks to everyone for that issue. – *Nora Phelan, Illinois*

This is another topic that has several sides but no clear answers (at least to me).

If your phone actually is defective and you didn't know it, and you needed it in an emergency, you'd most likely be grateful for that call. But phone companies and other businesses are also interested in increasing sales, and "watching" is one small cog in the marketing machine.

As a businessman, I find it difficult to sympathize with those who are concerned about Big Brotherism when a company asks seemingly "personal" questions in order to target their marketing. For one thing, if a company sells widgets, and it compiles a list of widget users, that means they won't waste their money on, or bother, people who are not widget users. Besides, nobody really cares whether or not you, personally, are a widget user. You're just another name on a database.

Personally, I kind of like it when one seed company tells the others, and the garden magazines, that I'm a gardening nut, and I get on more mailing lists.

Government might be a different matter. We have heard stories about police monitoring electric bills, ostensibly because a sharp increase in power usage might suggest a marijuana farm in the attic. What's unsettling is that this kind of probing has also resulted in people getting into hot water for starting tomato and pepper plants under lights. (There's no need to mention the IRS, and others.)

When you consider all the invasions of privacy and erosions of freedom we've seen in the past few decades, there certainly is plenty of cause for concern. But if you and I pay our taxes, don't we want the IRS to nab those who don't? If we want to eliminate drugs and fraud, must we give up some of our freedoms and privacy to help?

Deciding when and where to draw the line is something Americans in general have yet to grapple with.

Questioning our thoughts and fine-tuning our approach

COUNTRYSIDE: I think everyone from time to time questions his own thoughts about the self-reliant living/homestead philosophy. This is healthy, if for no other reason than letting you and your family step back and re-examine your position and reasons. I have done this from time to time and find myself fine-tuning my approach.

Did anyone on the Titanic even consider the possibility of it sinking? They all thought they'd have bragging rights for being on the maiden voyage! They put their lives in someone else's hands, believing that if there was a problem, someone else would take care of it.

No one wants to admit that the world around us is so fragile. We all like the security of believing that tomorrow will be the same as today. We'll only have to figure out which brand of toothpaste to use.

Security, as defined within the past 30-40 years, is a myth that has been built up because of our so-called conveniences. Prior to WW II, the idea of security was totally different.

Having a positive attitude about the world around us is very important. But a positive attitude will not feed you when you are hungry, or protect you when someone is breaking into your house. A positive attitude will not stave off illness or injury. A positive attitude will only give you the reinforcement you need to know that you can overcome adversity, no matter how bad things might get. It doesn't mean it will be easy, but it means that with the determination that comes with homesteading, you will have learned and overcome.

A positive attitude is not granted, nor will it mystically appear. It is the result of studying the events and learning ways around obstructions. It is the result of confidence in oneself and one's abilities and knowing one's limits.

I believe that homesteaders must take a lead role. Not necessarily to tell everyone what we do (although that will help), but to be there to tell them "how" to do it when the time comes. Whether it is a major disaster or not doesn't matter. Their awareness can be elevated by you knowing what to do and leading them out of the problem, not by doing it for them but by showing them how.

What day, month or year the fertilizer hits the ventilator is irrelevant because no matter how well prepared we may be, there is always "one more thing" we could have, learn or do. The important point is to constantly and persistently prepare at the speed best suited to the individual and budget.

You might be amazed at how fast you can build your own self-sufficient homestead to survive and live on. And the key word here is live! – *Peggy Adkins, Michigan*

He thought his wife was nuts, but now...

COUNTRYSIDE: We made it to the other side.

We dreamed of having a home on a little land. When I suggested a few alternatives to be able to have that dream, my husband thought I was nuts. When my sister introduced me to COUNTRYSIDE, my husband thought a lot of people were nuts.

When our move from Florida to Arkansas (to be closer to family) resulted in a major cut in income, we had to start tapping our savings just to put food on the table. My husband knew we had to do something, and started thinking about some of those "nutty ideas." He wasn't willing to live in a pop-up tent, but he was willing to do without.

We now have a small home on 6.5 acres, with electric only. He's chopping wood for heat and carrying water. Next year the well goes in. We live within his income and have extra to build with.

I fully believe that knowing others live a little "different" helped my husband's willingness to do the same—for a while, that is—and allowed our dream to come true.

Thank you to all the people who have shared experiences and to the family of COUNTRYSIDE for putting it all together. – *Jackie Parish, Arkansas*

Does this mean that sex is magnetic?

COUNTRYSIDE: A few years ago when I was at a plant nursery the man ahead of me was buying a holly tree. He asked the nurseryman how to tell if it was a male or female holly.

The nurseryman took a magnet, tied to a string, from his pocket. He touched one holly, then held the magnet about four inches above it, by the string. It started to circle, and he said the tree was female. He did the same with another holly, and the magnet went back and forth: male.

I came home and tried it on our own holly. It worked. It worked on our two sassafras trees. It worked on our bladder nut bush—male and female stems. This started a type of hobby.

This works (for me) on all birds and animals, including chicks that just hatched, and even eggs.

Take an egg from a flock of chickens that has a rooster. Touch it with the magnet, then suspend the magnet about four inches above the egg. If it's male, the magnet will go back and forth. If it's female, it will circle.

Then try an egg from the supermarket. The magnet does not move: the egg isn't fertile.

Pick up a feather from the ground. It works. Old bones, it works. A roast of meat, it works.

My daughter in Florida had bird of paradise plants. One end of the bed had blossoms, the other end had none. The magnet showed male and female.

Test the clothing worn by a man or a woman—it works. Wash the clothing, and it doesn't.

I am now 82 years old and hoping to encourage someone younger to try this gift or art. I think the big secret is believing. Have fun. – *Delbert Keir, Pennsylvania*

A little planning cuts the electric bill

COUNTRYSIDE: Our electric bill for January was 21 percent less than for January a year ago. Gosh, it was nice to see it go down.

My husband has charted our electrical costs for several years, and it was disheartening to have the bill come in as high for the two of us as when we had children at home. True, prices have risen, but it bothered us to not see a reduction in cash spent.

We decided to try to reduce our usage this winter. Our plan was this:

1. Quit using the dishwasher;
2. Reduce the use of our furnace by keeping the woodstove stoked;
3. Quit using the clothes dryer.

Apparently the plan worked! A reduction of 21% is significant in my book.

We've always tried to conserve electricity by only running the dishwasher when it was full, only doing laundry when we had a full load, and turning the thermostat down at night—you know, all the tips they give you in magazine articles. About 10 years ago my husband put our electric water heater on a timer so it only heated water in the morning and evening, times of heavier use. That caused a reduction in our bill back then.

I think being fairly conservative users of electricity, the 21% reduction is even more significant than if we had been "normal" users.

I do want to point out that our experiment with non-usage of furnace, dryer and dishwasher was not absolute. We would turn the furnace on in the morning to take the chill off the downstairs rooms. (We have never heated the up stairs bedrooms—don't even have ducting up there.) Once the woodstove was fired up, we would turn the thermostat back to 60°. Also, in bitterly cold weather, the furnace would come on at night to keep the downstairs at 60°F.

I used the dryer for my elderly mother-in-law's laundry, because she like the softness a dryer produces. For ours though, I used a wooden dry rack by the woodstove. It's a great, old hardwood rack that holds a full load of wash, even towels and bluejeans. (It's also a great place to hang Christmas stockings for Santa Claus to fill.)

During Christmas, when lots of family members were home, we used the dishwasher every day, and sometimes twice a day, for two weeks.

Some plusses that came with the plan:

1. We didn't have to hear the dryer or dishwasher run and run.
2. We have plenty of fuel oil left to get us through the winter without an expensive refill.
3. Washing dishes together in the evening gives us a nice time to chat. – *Jane Keon, Michigan*

40 years a reader

COUNTRYSIDE: Please renew our subscription. We've been with you nearly 40 years (since the magazine was called *Small Stock Magazine)* and sure don't want to stop now. – *Harry & Judy Steuber, Tennessee*

Are other Romanov breeders having this problem?

COUNTRYSIDE: Are any other Romanov sheep breeders having problems with lambs surviving?

I have had only three ewes for the past four years, but no matter how many lambs are born, I never seem to be able to save more than one or two. My vet and I have brainstormed all the usual management problems and have come up with nothing.

I am especially upset as I write this, because my best ewe lost five lambs last week. Two were dead when I got to the barn, one was very weak, and two were seemingly healthy: I saw them nurse.

I got out my lamb-saver kit and went to work, but lost the weak one overnight. The two best ones started to get weaker and hunched up in the pen. Despite warming them and bottle feeding they both died within two days.

The temperature was 40°-50°F, so should not have played a role here. – *John Davidson, Illinois*

Some ideas for crafters

COUNTRYSIDE: I would like to share a couple of craft ideas that would make great gifts and would sell well at craft shows. The ideas are not my own, but come from gifts I received.

The first is a luffa sponge filled with soap. It is a piece of luffa about 5 inches long, the hollow center filled with an almond-smelling soap. It's real neat, and great for scrubbing.

The second idea is an herb bag. It is a tea bag filled with different herbs to help a person relax when taking a bath. It's a great way to use herbs you have grown.

The last idea comes from an art teacher I know. A thick white candle is decorated with dried flowers and colored tissue paper. Small flowers can be dried easily in phone books. Then they are attached around the base of the candle with melted wax, applied with a small paint brush. Colored tissue paper can be added. The flowers and tissue paper are covered with wax and a very pretty candle is created. I have seen candles like this sell for quite a bit in stores, but they are easy to make.

My family and I are going to be moving soon to 10 acres outside of Sacramento. We will be using a septic system. Can anyone tell me which household soaps (laundry soaps, shampoos, dish soaps, etc.) are non-polluting? I am also interested in any books that would tell me how to make these products, along with cream rinses and lotions. – *Claudia Judge, California*

It's amusing to consider some of the little things we all take for granted. Drying flowers in a telephone book, for example, probably seems perfectly natural to people in large cities. But if your local phone directory has 12 pages, you have to stop and think about that for awhile!

Apply that to somewhat more significant differences in experiences and ways of thinking, and it's easy to see how there can be so many different views on almost everything.

For homemade beauty products you might check a copy of *The World's Best Kept Beauty Secrets* by Diane Irons.

Food no longer provides nutrition

COUNTRYSIDE: I was watching the evening news last night while eating supper. I know that's bad for the digestion, but there was a story coming on that I wanted to hear.

The anchorman said that our government was now recommending that the whole nation start taking vitamins to supplement our daily intake of nutrients. The reason is, "We can no longer get the required daily amounts of nutrients through the food that we eat."

The spin doctors have been working overtime on this one, folks. What should have been said is, "We finally did it. We have overmedicated and crossbred our food supply to death. That super strain of broccoli we have produced can withstand temperatures from 32 degrees below zero to 100 above, and it's as green as a new mown lawn. Too bad it has none of the folic acids that the original version had."

I asked my family if they could see through that story, and what was wrong with it. My wife figured some drug company that had helped finance someone's political campaign was finally seeing a return on their dollars, and there probably is a bit of truth to that. But it was our 12-year-old son who said, "The food they're producing doesn't have what it takes anymore."

I'll admit, I took pride in the fact that the vegetables (not veggies) we were eating were all organically grown by us, and that my son who I thought at times was not listening to a thing that was being said, knew what he was talking about.

It sounds to me like the government is trying to relocate the blame, or as we used to say, "Trying to shut the barn door after the horses have got out." Keep up the good work COUNTRYSIDE. – *Grant Eversoll, Indiana*

These hornets don't like strangers

COUNTRYSIDE: I read with great interest Barbara Peters' letter ("Save the hornets? No way!" 82/3). Every year hornets (wasps?) nest on our raised garage door. I, my roommate and our three dogs are in and out all day. My head is about a foot from the nest. As far as the wasps are concerned, we don't exist.

But let a stranger go into the garage and they go on the alert. If the stranger goes in and out several times, they sting!

They must know us by sight or scent.

I have 1/2 acre and about 30 semi-feral chickens and 18 feral cats. In the spring when the tomcats fight the chickens go nuts. When the toms start to sing to each other in the daytime the chickens come running and flying from all over. They crowd into a tight circle two or three deep and elbow each other to get the best place to see! Their mouths are open and the hens seem to forget their chicks. They seem blind to everything!

Sometimes the fighting cats will roll into the crowd of chickens and even knock some down. The chickens jump up, fluff themselves, and run after the cats again.

I've heard of fox and mink playing the fool and luring birds close before catching them and now I believe it.

In a fight between a cat and a chicken, during the day anyway, the chicken wins, hands down! – *M. Cowan, California*

We have often noticed chickens reacting like this to commotion of any kind.

Dream farm turns into a nightmare

COUNTRYSIDE: When I bought my dream farm I was full of hopes and very trusting. That was a mistake. Two mistakes.

The farm had been in my mother's family for almost 100 years. Since various family members had had animals on the 36 acres, I never checked zoning ordinances.

My mother and I bought the property in 1991, with an agreement that at the end of five years it would be paid for, and divided between us. I lived in a trailer, and my mother lived in the farmhouse, both at the end of a mile-long country road.

I worked very hard and added new things each year. Besides working full-time as an RN at a hospital, I planted a medium-size garden, made spaghetti sauce, and canned and froze a few other things.

The second year I got into the rabbit business. I raised dwarves, mini-lops and angoras, and had a fair Easter trade.

The third year I bought some registered goats from an ad in COUNTRYSIDE, which I had just discovered. I found a new joy in caring for and milking the goats, and when kidding time rolled around I knew I had found something I would never tire of – I was hooked!

The fourth year I bought 25 chicks, and when they started laying eggs, it was wonderful. I was selling enough eggs at work to pay for my feed and had my own fresh eggs. They were delicious.

Then disaster struck.

A neighbor I had always been close to got angry at my mother and complained about my goats to the township supervisor. I was ordered to get my livestock off the property, because it was zoned residential. No one knew of this zoning. My neighbor (a doctor) had multiple livestock himself, but didn't have to get rid of any because no one complained.

I fought this at every township meeting, to no avail. On Dec. 21, 1995, I was told to remove my animals or pay a fine.

My nine registered goats, four to six weeks from due date, were taken away on Dec. 29. I cried for weeks. Almost five years of planning and working and bloodlines were lost. But the worst was yet to come.

After putting all of my money into the farm – more than $30,000 – my mother informed me that I was only a renter, and the property I had paid for was going to be logged. That would make the property worthless, because the trees muffled all sounds from the highway across the hill.

I was devastated. I had planned on quitting my job in three months when everything was paid off, and working on the farm. Now I had nothing, and had lost five years of my life.

We had no agreement in writing, so I had no choice. Most of my equipment, as well as my major appliances and things I had stored in my trailer, were taken and sold by my mother.

My message: Be very cautious when time and money are involved, and be sure you have a contract. Never take anyone's word about zoning – check it out yourself, and get it in writing.

I learned a valuable lesson about trust and family as well as about myself. I doubt if I will ever get over it.

I now live in another state and hope to start over, but sometimes I get very upset at all I lost and wonder if I have the energy to begin again. I hope this letter helps someone else avoid the mistakes I made. – *Vicki*

The above letter was dated January 23, 1997. In the same envelope was another, dated April 11, 1998:

COUNTRYSIDE: Since I wrote the previous letter some things have changed. I still live in the same state, but I am now married to a man who was born here.

We purchased two registered Alpine dairy goats which I was told weren't due "for weeks." Four days later my husband woke me with "There's something hanging out of your goat!" She had a beautiful doe. Five days later, the other had a buck.

We are now swimming in milk and my husband has been trying many recipes. (Does anyone have a recipe for goat milk mozzarella that melts?)

I tried to purchase my previous goats, which had been resold, with no success, so I have started a new herd. They are of excellent lineage, four and six years old, and really show themselves well in the milk pail. I enjoy the day-to-day routine of care and milking.

My husband was apprehensive and didn't want me to get goats. Now he has fallen in love with them. He gives them little treats and checks on them and talks to them when he is out on the farm working. I can't say starting over is not hard, but now I have a good husband and with his support I can do just about anything.

I now only work three days a week and spend the rest of my time on the farm. We grow most of our own food, raise our own beef, and of course now have our own milk. We try to be as self-sufficient as possible and keep trying to find ways to cut costs. – *Vicki*

"Get it in writing" might seem like unwarranted advice when dealing with a family member, but family feuds stemming from financial deals aren't at all uncommon. Better to be safe than sorry.

In response to the nonmelting cheese problem, a correspondent suggested the following (75/1:17):

If your cheese doesn't melt, try heating it longer and hotter at the end of the cooking period, until the curds get "melty" looking and will stretch.

Also, too much rennet will make the

cheese a bit too hard to work properly. You really only need a few drops to a gallon of milk to get a nice, softly set curd.

Kneading the curds seems to work them together best. Just draining won't work.

Goat milk mozzarella

Stir 1-1/2 teaspoons citric acid into 1/4 cup water. (Look for citric acid in the health food section of the grocery store, or with canning supplies.)

Add this to 1-1/4 gallons of goat milk. Warm to 88°F.

Dilute 1/8 to 1/4 teaspoon liquid rennet in 1/8 cup of water. Stir into milk gently for 15 seconds. Cover and let set 15 minutes or until it coagulates.

Cut the curd into 2" cubes, taking five minutes or more to do so. Let curds rest for five minutes.

Raise temperature to 98°F over a 15 minute period. Continue to stir gently. Keep at 98°F for 16 minutes and stir. Try to keep the curds from mating. They should be firm.

Then, either (without a microwave):

Heat curds in whey until it is very, very hot to the finger. Curds will stare to look very melty. Drain off whey and knead the curds as for taffy. Work in salt and drain well.

Or, with a microwave:

Drain curds for 20 minutes. Put one cup of curds with ½ teaspoon salt in microwave on high for 50 seconds.

Knead curds like taffy. Return to microwave for 10-25 seconds, and knead again.

This correspondent said she had heard that you can't make mozzarella from goat milk—you have to add cow milk—but this recipe worked fine. However, real, original mozzarella is made from *water buffalo* milk.

That Cub tractor just won't go away! Let's see if we can get it right this time...

In the top photo Pete Liska and friend John are restoring the Farmall Cub.

The other shows the finished restoration.

The Farmall Super M we showed in 82/2 was restored by, belongs to, and pictured John, not Pete.

Another spider bite experience

COUNTRYSIDE: I would like to add some information on Brown Recluse spiders (82/3).

My granddaughter was bitten by one, twice, on the same leg, while sleeping. The spots were dark purple and one, up under her buttock, was as large as a saucer. The other was about two inches across.

We covered both areas with Black Ointment and covered them with a large bandage. It was changed and more ointment added each day. In a few days large yellow points came up all over the dark area. We continued the treatment until all the yellow was gone and the purple faded. She also took echinacea and golden seal.

She never missed a day of work.

Black Ointment is a blend of several herbs. – *Marjorie Russell, Idaho*

Please note that when we pass along any information on health matters of any kind, it's a matter of informing readers only about what other readers think and do. The RN on our staff is leery of many home remedies, but the journalist is against censoring ideas and methods some people believe in. We obviously don't want to endanger anyone, but we are aware that many home remedies do have merit. We provide the information: you make your own decisions.

Community cannery has a helpful guide

COUNTRYSIDE: Please send a gift subscription to Mrs. Flossie Raines, who manages our community cannery. She is most helpful and generous in advising the novice and assisting the experienced canners. She tries to keep informed as to when and where produce is available locally.

We have a complete Ball kitchen, equipped to do anything a canner would want. I wish all counties offered something like we are so fortunate to have.

Mrs. Raines also teaches sewing and quilting. As you can imagine, we think of her as one of our local treasures. – *Pam Harell, Florida*

When we investigated community canneries back in 1977 there were about 120 of them, and we heard they used to be quite common and popular. The Hernando County (Florida) Cannery seems to be typical.

It's a fully-equipped community canning and preserving kitchen, with everything from a blancher-sterilizer, stainless steel steam jacketed kettle, several 16-qt. pressure cookers and a stainless steel preparation table, right down to the paring knives. You bring your own jars, lids, and spices. The fee is $10 per year per family. No family could afford or justify the expense of a setup like this... and the best part of all is, you get the experienced guidance of Mrs. Raines.

The Ball Co. no longer provides such facilities, but for information on someone who does contact Joel M. Jackson, 110 S. Claypool, Muncie, IN 47303. Note that these units cost $25,000 to $100,000 or more. They're definitely a community project... and the community will have to make good use of them to justify the expense.

Magazine is hard to find, but it's focused

COUNTRYSIDE: You do a fantastic job. Keep it up, please.

For the last two years I've been picking up issues at the grocery store, but lately, either they've stopped carrying it or others are beating me to the punch. So... here is my subscription.

May I add that for awhile I was buying several magazines of this type and became disappointed. They seem to lose their focus and have very little helpful info anymore. So my choice is COUNTRYSIDE. It focuses on helpful ideas, suggestions for inexperienced homesteaders, and is a wholesome, family magazine. – *Judy McDowell, Missouri*

Thank you very kindly, although not everyone agrees with you. Actually, I myself thought we had lost our focus... which we're (hopefully) regaining with a bang... which some people won't like. Maybe that's why there are now more than 5,000 magazines published in the U.S.

That number of titles for limited newsstand space, along with the continuing problems of magazine distributors, means we (and most other small magazines) continue to lose newsstand sales. Getting your own subscription was a smart move.

Money and interest

COUNTRYSIDE: I enjoyed the well-written and interesting articles in the May/June issue by Art Horn and The Intentional Peasant concerning prudence, economics and money. I agree with most of their thoughts, but they both omitted one critical fact concerning money creation and inflation. (Ed. note: I'm sure they missed many "critical facts" in their brief articles: Even entire books can't cram in everything there is to know.)

As The Intentional Peasant says, banks create our money by making loans. They also charge interest on those loans. The problem is, the money to pay the interest is not created. Therefore, at any given time it is impossible to pay back all loans plus interest outstanding. It is only when additional loans are made that enough money exists to pay the interest on previous loans. This is the true cause of inflation. We frequently hear from a variety of sources that wage and price increases cause inflation. For the most part they are the result, not the cause. When the Federal Reserve raises interest rates to slow the economy they are guaranteeing more inflation since more money must be

created to make higher interest payments.

The idea that our government should have to borrow money that is created out of thin air by the Fed and then pay interest to boot is totally absurd and benefits only those few at the top of the heap that control the financial world. Our constitution clearly states that Congress has the power to create and value money. Unfortunately, a majority of our congressmen who didn't understand the function of money created the Federal Reserve System in 1913, thinking that financial stability would result. In fact, the result has been the Great Depression in the '30s, numerous recessions, and constant inflation. I'd say this is failure.

We have all become so accustomed to living with this financial situation that most folks think it's inevitable. I don't. There was a time when it was accepted knowledge that the Earth was flat and the center of the universe. Over time and with much castigation, a few courageous people showed otherwise. I believe the same is true of the financial and economic world.

Many books are available concerning these subjects, but I would recommend one in particular, as it is written in layman's language and explains in more detail what I have written here. It's *The Truth in Money*, by Theodore R. Thoren and Richard F. Warner. If it's not available in your local library you can order it from Liberty Library, 300 Independence Ave. SE, Washington, DC 20003. – *Charles R. Bobb, Pennsylvania*

As the old saw goes, if all the economists in the world were laid end-to-end, they still wouldn't reach a conclusion. So far be it from those of us with bigger fish to fry to become too embroiled in their debates except as a matter of curiosity... and in order to form personal opinions we can use to guide our own lives.

For me, this means that the important point is that our "economic system" is a human artifice that has been formed by the fears and concerns of the day, based on unproven theories and without consensus, even among those who spend all their time studying and pondering such things.

Diaper dilemma

COUNTRYSIDE: THE cost of disposable diapers, both financial and environmental, can be argued back and forth endlessly. My opinion is that disposables are harder on the wallet ($30/month/child in our household) and the planet. But the use of nonrenewable resources to make them and the landfill space they take up far outweigh the energy needed to launder cloth diapers, especially since many of us use solar or wood heat for drying.

But we still use disposables in this house. This is a small source of guilt for me. My husband and I consider ourselves good environmentalists (almost environmental extremists). We practice sustainable farming, organic gardening, we reuse and recycle, avoid consumerism, and built a passive solar house. But we still use disposable diapers. Why? Because they are so much less trouble.

When I had my first child in cloth diapers I was changing his diaper on an average of 30 minutes throughout the day. I washed a huge load of diapers every three days. We had no dryer so I used solar or wood heat for drying. Boy, I was a good little environmentalist.

Then spring came, with finishing the house, gardening, and all the other homestead chores. I started treating myself to disposable diapers so I could have more time to get things done.

My second child never experienced a cloth diaper.

If our finances got tight, the luxury of disposable diapers would be gone in a flash. Because that is what they are: a luxury. Just like electricity, a flush toilet and hot running water. You pay more for these luxuries both with your wallet and in the health of the planet. We could live without them, but boy, they sure make life easier. – *Kathy Dice, Iowa*

P.S. Since writing this I have started using cloth diapers to help my daughter with toilet training, and I am still finding them a big pain. The photo speaks for itself.

A city spoiled brat?

COUNTRYSIDE: The lady who wrote (an article we won't mention) sounds like a city spoiled brat. If she had been raised as a pioneer she would have been thankful for such a country home and a good husband. He's okay, and headed in the right direction. She better love him while she's got him.

I miss my dear husband. He was nearly 92. We were both western hillbillies. I was born in Long Beach and got to the country when I was nine. I soon learned to milk a cow and to ride a plowhorse, bareback.

The three of us and our cousins herded the turkeys and killed rattlesnakes. We each carried a walking stick for protection.

Talking about pioneering, we moved out on a salt grass prairie where we milked 19 cows. They ran on company land for one dollar a head (calves free). We would get on the horses after school, round up the cows, and bring them into the corral to be milked.

Each of us girls owned a cow of our own, and we had a goat for a pet. We had rabbits, chickens, ducks, geese and turkeys. My job was to monitor the eggs and see that they got to a setting hen or goose or turkey.

We didn't know any better than to enjoy our country life. If I had it to do over again, I would still choose the country. I'd love to still be out and at it, but can't quite swing it any more.

Keep plugging along, out there. – *Madonna J. Wilson, Oregon*

We were recently informed (by someone who hates references to "wannabe homesteaders") that the word "wannabe" originated with girls who want to be like Madonna, the singer. We think they should wannabe like our Madonna, the 80-something homesteader, whom we always enjoy hearing from.

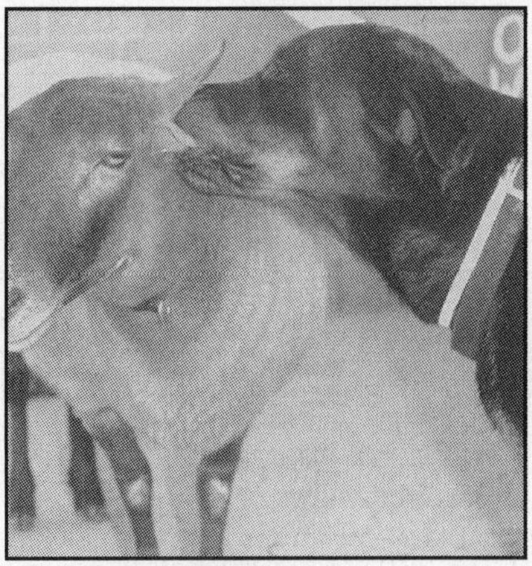

Sheep thinks she's a Rottweiller dog

COUNTRYSIDE: Here is a picture of our Rottweiller, Bijou, with our sheep, Hazelnut. Our Rott was grown when we got our lamb and it took careful training (with a muzzle!) and much supervision, but today they are best buddies. (The sheep is two years old.)

She has taken on a few of the dog's traits and behaviors, though. She's gotten rather pushy when it comes to treats from the house, and "paws" at the gate to get up near to the house, where she loves peeking in the windows. She also eats Pedigree dog biscuits on occasion!

We've also had chickens that we enjoyed very much.

Not bad for ex-city folks, turned ex-military, turned California desert homesteaders, having a good time and building memories and funny stories for our girls. It helps ease the difficulties of living in today's "society." – *Gary & Melinda Dorsey, California*

It's just for a while

COUNTRYSIDE: In your stories about getting started, no one mentions that after picking up aluminum cans, driving ancient trucks, working 2nd jobs, etc., there is a plus side.

After you are debt-free you can splurge on new coveralls or something nice you have waited years for. It doesn't have to be blood, sweat and tears forever. It's just temporary.– *John & Sweetie Viniolas, Indiana*

Anybody have a bone grinder they aren't using?

COUNTRYSIDE: The National Poultry Museum in Bonners Springs, Kansas, is looking for a bone grinder.

Back in the late 1800s and early 1900s such grinders were in common use. Poultry raisers then didn't have "factory-made" feeds. Ground-up bones were a good source of protein, which was then included in a mixture of ground grains such as corn, wheat and barley.

In those days there was little knowledge of need for vitamins such as those found in cod liver oil. So you can say a bone grinder was essential to those who had to make up their own chicken feed mixtures. (A few years back I had a German poultry supply catalog that still offered bone grinders.)

We'd like to find one for the poultry museum so the story can be told of early nutrition for chickens.

My dad started in the poultry business on a farm in Iowa back in 1921. Even at that time there were no manufactured poultry feeds in Iowa. With the help of the Iowa State College at Ames, he got his first information on poultry nutrition. The protein was tankage, the very crudest form. (Tankage is the animal residues that remain after rendering fat in a slaughterhouse.) He had his own small mill to grind the grains, with cod liver oil added. He had no mixer, so his formula was hand-mixed with a shovel.

We moved from the farm to a larger chick hatchery in Fort Dodge. Along with our growing hatchery business, Dad started his own feed mill. I remember my mother gave Dad a most expensive book on poultry nutrition. I wonder what our modern feed nutritionists would think of the information in that book from about 1925?

Dad also developed friendships with owners of two other small feed mills, and they exchanged information, experiences, and feed formulas.

Some ingredients they used especially in the chick starter rations were kelp, powdered milk, and oat meal. They soon learned that oat meal (oats without the hulls) was not good, as some of the chickens developed rickets. From then on, whole oats were used.

Dad did considerable testing to offer some excellent feeds, but producing the best elevated the price, so changes had to be made to achieve a favorable merchandising cost. *– Loyl Stromberg, Minnesota*

For many years Morrison's Feeds & Feeding served as our bible on animal nutrition, because it contained the "old-time" information most homesteaders demand and couldn't find elsewhere in a world of store-bought feeds. This book was so popular, and revised so often, I assumed that everyone involved in animal husbandry had a copy right next to The Merck Manual.

So I was somewhat surprised when I phoned a university veterinarian with a question and mentioned Feeds & Feeding, and she had never heard of it. (She also wasn't the least bit interested in what some "outdated" book said.)

At the same time, it's amusing even for us to reread some of our early issues (from the 1920s) reporting on the new discoveries of "vita mins" (suggesting "minerals" essential for life, although no one knew exactly what they were or what they did).

Wise words of warning on wonderful Wyoming

COUNTRYSIDE: During the last decade or so I have noticed a steadily increasing migration to Wyoming by people with big dreams and small pocketbooks. They seem to call themselves the "new wave" of homesteaders. They're looking for cheap land and a place to call their own.

Well, folks, I've lived in Wyoming for 40 years and the article in 82/1 prompted me to write this letter.

Wyoming is a beautiful, free, wild state with plenty of wide open spaces, low taxes, and few people. There is a reason for that. Wyoming does not adapt herself easily to human populations in general and especially not to starry-eyed back-to-the-land dreamers with a shovel, a few garden seeds, and no money.

The first wave of homesteaders came in the early 1900s and were mostly gone by the late '30s. They starved out and left, froze out and left, or droughted out and left. I can show you the graves of those who never left at all.

I'm not telling you we don't want you here or that you can't make it in Wyoming. I'm just trying to caution folks so they don't leave their hopes, dreams, finances, and maybe their bones on the windswept high deserts of Wyoming.

The article referred to a site north of Rawlins, an area with which I am familiar. It's not the best area in Wyoming, nor is it the worst. But to say the area is marginal for homesteading would be to pay it a compliment.

There are good areas for homesteading in Wyoming, however the bulk of it is marginal or worse. The economy of Wyoming is based mostly on energy production, mining, and large-scale livestock production, because that is what adapts best to the land.

Our climate is extreme, with snow and frost possible any month of the year. In many parts wind will be your constant companion. The most adequate description I can give of Wyoming weather is that it is prone to violent temper tantrums.

Cheap land will probably be alkali/greasewood flats where the only thing you can grow in your garden will be beets (they're remarkably salt tolerant). That is, if you can get water to grow beets.

To make this as short as possible let me just give you some pointers and then if you want to discuss Wyoming further, write to me.

1. Be aware of the water situation. The lack of it is probably the main reason Wyoming still has a low population and wide open spaces.

2. Be aware that in more marginal areas it could take your entire 40-acre homestead to support one milk cow.

3. Realize that we in the higher areas never put our winter clothes into storage.

4. Look at the elevation of where you would like to locate. If it is above 5,500 feet, it could be challenging to raise anything other than native vegetation. Remember that each 1,000-foot increase in elevation is equal to moving 300 miles north.

5. Look at the map. If the place is a long way from anywhere else, there is a reason.

6. Be aware that the per capita income is not real high, but living expenses are right up there.

Be aware that Wyoming is a "fence-out" state. You must fence your property to keep other people's livestock off your land. They do not have to help with labor, money or materials.

8. Buy the very best land you can possibly afford and know what makes the land good or bad. Do not buy land sight-unseen.

9. Don't try to come broke and start on a shoestring. It can be done, but you probably won't like it. Picture yourself in the winter, out of money, out of propane, and there's not a decent stick of firewood within a 20-mile radius of your purchased sight-unseen Wyoming homestead. You're in trouble.

Don't get me wrong: I love Wyoming and I'll be here until I die. My wife and I have our own 40-acre homestead and we consider ourselves rather successful considering the altitude (6,400 feet). We raise a good garden and livestock in a zone 3 area. With our experience and a good start, self-sufficiency is possible but unrealistic. We have good soil and water in a great area, but until it's paid for we both work full-time jobs and homestead the other 16 hours a day.

Wyoming is a beautiful and magnificent lady, but she will not take to her bosom the sick, lame, feeble, stupid or unprepared. – *John F. Gallenbeck, Wyoming*

This is good advice that, with minor changes, can be applied almost anywhere. There will always be surprises and disappointments: The object is to keep them to a minimum, and manageable.

Farm tours provide extra income

COUNTRYSIDE: Welcome to Hirschey's Canna Lily Farm tour site! That is the seed to start the newest crop on our farm.

Small farms (and some larger ones too) are enchanted with the possibility of adding some income from farm tours. Even the University of Minnesota and the extension services are getting involved. In fact, that is how local farms have created an agritourism organization called Country Heritage Adventures. Twenty-two farms are involved in this organization, and ours is one of them.

We raise sheep, Angora goats, Angora rabbits and other farm animals. We try to have every animal pay its way, although the occasional pet does find a home here. An example is Penny, the French Alpine dairy goat who gets bred only every couple of years and doesn't produce enough milk to pay for her feed. But she was our son Shane's best buddy and constant companion when he was four years old.

A visitor to Hirschey's Canna Lily Farm enjoys the sheep.

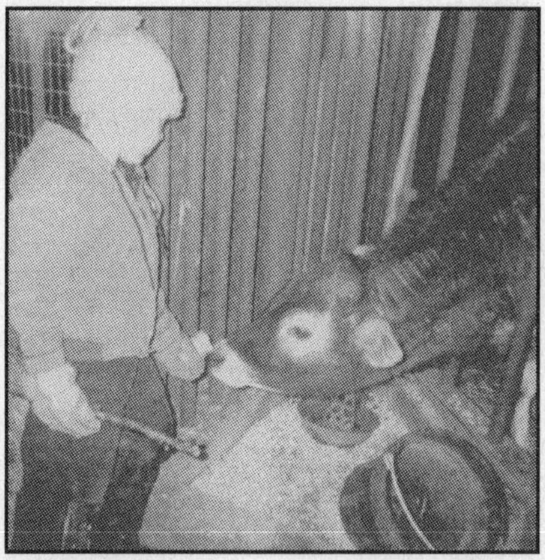

Travis Hirschey and a friendly steer.

The chickens keep a watchful eye on visitors.

Then there is QT, who lived in the basement where we have a portable pen for bottle lambs. The boys insisted that QT come to the living room to visit. I wasn't totally sold on that idea, but Grandma stepped in and suggested using a diaper while she visited. What a great idea! Not only did it allow QT to visit the boys in the living room and get very well socialized, but it gave her access to nursing homes and schools where I gave wool spinning demonstrations as she laid quietly by the spinning wheel or wandered around, visiting lots of welcoming hands. Even though her wool and size are not the quality we are aiming for, she will be on the farm forever.

Since we began giving tours, many of the animals have learned to wait for the cups of corn visitors are carrying and come greedily for their portion.

We charge a fee to show people how we raise the sheep and give short demonstrations on carding and spinning wool, weaving and felting.

Interested visitors can ask questions about the 1850s barn and other turn-of-the-century outbuildings we use. We give an educational as well as entertaining tour and add another income source to our small farm. It's not a great source of income, but along with sales of handspun wool and handmade products in our haymow gift shop, it feeds the animals, keeps the hens laying, and puts food on the table. We also have off-farm jobs, but feel the tours and wool products will be helpful when the day comes to retire and spend more time enjoying our homestead.

To visit or get information on our farm contact Lynn Hirschey, 19475 Jacobs Ave., Faribault, MN 55021. For information on agri-tourism in general contact your local extension office or Wabasha County Extension, 611 Broadway Ave. Ste 40, Wabasha, MN 55981-1613. – *Lynn Hirschey*

About that diapered lamb...I hate to bring this up, but were they cloth, or disposable? Oh, never mind: we've heard enough on that.

Some old-time tips on chickens and uses for pork rinds

COUNTRYSIDE: Here are some old-time tips:

Limber neck in chickens: In the spring when chickens run around looking for worms they sometimes run across an old dead animal or something the dogs drug in which is full of maggots, which they eat. Then the chickens lay around with limberneck, barely able to cluck.

Mix turpentine in meal dough, and spice it with red pepper mixed in a bowl. Force small amounts of this down the chickens' throats and you can save them. (Ed. Note: The real culprit here is botulism, which is caused not only by fly maggots but also by spoiled food, such as improperly home-canned vegetables, that might be given to chickens. Laxatives such as Epsom salts are also said to be helpful, and there is a *Cl. botulinum* antitoxin.)

Uses for pork rinds: Grease bread pans. Grease rifle barrels, rubbing with a soft cloth afterwards. Puts a sheen on the metal and prevents rust. Grease boots so water and snow won't penetrate the leather. Use for animal and fish bait. Grease saw blades. If you use a crosscut saw on pine, use a meat rind or coal oil (kerosene) to cut resin off the blade. Throw a slab in a pot with green beans and cook. – *Lester Queener, Tennessee*

If you use the same pork rind for all of this, it should sure give those green beans an interesting flavor!

Expert says "Don't can milk"

COUNTRYSIDE: Published in a recent edition (82/4) were two procedures for home canned goat milk. As a low acid food, milk should never be canned at home.

Clostridium botulinum, the bacteria responsible for the illness botulism, forms very heat resistant spores that cannot be destroyed using waterbath canning methods, even if the process time is one *hour* or more. This bacterium can be expected to be occasionally found in milk as it is widespread in soils and dust. Although the organism often causes food to spoil prior to producing its potentially deadly toxin, this is not always the case. Normal looking foods have caused botulism. Both animals and humans are susceptible to botulism so this method is not appropriate even if limited to animal foods.

Clostridium botulinum spores can be destroyed using a pressure canner but the specific temperature/pressure combination necessary to achieve this destruction must be determined for each food product. Safe methods have not been determined for milk. Commercially, evaporated milk is canned but the processing times for this product are not applicable to single strength goat milk canned in glass jars. Therefore, I consider the pressure canning method provided in your publication to be potentially unsafe.

The best method for preserving excess goat milk is to freeze it, even if it is less convenient that room temperature storage in jars. – *Linda Harris, Ph.D., University of California*

We submit this for the record—and anyone who wants to do everything according to the book. (But then, some "book people" warn that home canning of any kind is risky...an attitude that would put homesteaders out of business.)

For another angle see "Culture clash confuse canners: Who are you going to believe, Grandma or the USDA?", also in issue 82/4 (page 161 in this anthology.)

Hard-earned freedoms are valued

COUNTRYSIDE: I am a new subscriber and enjoy your magazine very much, but I must comment on a statement that was made at the end of the letter titled "Big brother is watching." The editor stated, "If we want to eliminate drugs and fraud must we give up some of our freedoms and privacy to help?" I sincerely hope not!

The freedoms we enjoy in this country have been hard earned, and to give any of them up could put in jeopardy all of the others.

I would like to tell you something that happened in Chicago a few years ago. The people living in the inner city housing projects were tired of the rampant drug problems they were having. A proposal was made by the police department to give the police the authority to do random searches in order to send a message to the drug dealers. The people of the projects thought at the time that if it would help clean up the neighborhood, giving up a little freedom would be worth it. They figured the extra police presence on the street would help scare away the bad influence.

Before too long the good citizens living under those circumstances were being subject to early morning raids of their homes, police pat downs in the halls of their apartments and humiliating scare tactics. They could not believe they were living in the same country. Did it help curb the drug trafficking problem? No, not at all! Did the people think it was worth if even if it had? No!

Fortunately, the people of the projects still lived in a country where that kind of behavior by our law enforcement is illegal. They retained legal counsel and the police raids stopped.

We live in a wonderful country where we can think and live how we want as long as we don't infringe on other people's rights. To lose that because we thought giving up a "little" freedom was okay would be a terrible tragedy. "Is life so dear or peace so sweet as to be purchased at the price of chains and slavery" (Patrick Henry). Personally, I think not. – *Jim Boles, Utah*

The "statement" you quote was a question. It was followed by this statement: "Deciding when and where to draw the line is something Americans in general have yet to grapple with."

We mentioned police monitoring electric bills and seeing a surge in power use, busting into a private home. When that happened in a nearby town, I didn't hear one word of protest.

If, instead of finding an attic marijuana farm, the police discover a gardener getting an early start on this season's tomato seedlings, a few people get upset. But most don't squawk, as long as it isn't their home that's raided.

We also mentioned certain IRS tactics, which achieved notoriety during the recent congressional hearings. Very few people have the money, or the guts to fight the IRS.

However, even rah-rah Americans can and do become upset by many, many news reports about widespread and widely varied loss of freedoms. A common one concerns people carrying large sums of cash which authorities "assume" came from drug deals.

One we repeated here concerned a man who paid cash for a plane ticket. This raised the suspicions of the ticket agent, who notified the drug police, who found that the man was carrying several thousand dollars. Actually, he owned a landscaping business and was on his way to purchase plants. Nevertheless, it took years and more thousands in legal fees to get his money back. (Some people never recover their confiscated possessions.) Anyone who reads and makes note of such items could cite hundreds of similar cases.

Not all of these involve corrupt, or even overzealous authorities. For example, if you make a bank transfer of $10,000 or more, you (or your bank) are required to fill out and submit a CTR (Currency Transaction Report-Form 4789) to the IRS. Moreover, the sum is accumulative: Many transactions of a few thousand dollars are reported.

Not filing the report is a felony. You could be clean as a whistle, perhaps wiring money to an adult child who is buying a house or a car, or sending a money order to a brother with unexpected medical expenses. Simply failing to file the report could mean a five-year prison sentence and a $250,000 fine.

Not all abrogations of freedom concern drugs. Many readers have also urged us to report on the many horror stories of so-called "Swampbuster" laws. Farmers have been wiped out, financially and emotionally, for plowing a low spot in a field, even when it has been cultivated for years, not for any rational ecological reason, but because of bureaucratic ineptitude.

These cases are legion, and proliferating, but for the most part they're beyond the scope of this publication. Some of our readers are paranoid about them, while others appear to be totally unaware...or wearing heavily tinted rose-colored glasses.

However, this leads us to some very interesting speculation that is making the rounds in certain circles, involving the infamous Executive Orders. These are regulations, already set in place, that would give the president almost dictatorial powers "in case of national emergency."

Considering the widespread apathy mentioned above on matters of lesser concern, how many people would protest if, say, Y2K suddenly became a "national emergency"? Like the Chicagoans mentioned, most people who expect the government to take care of everything would probably clamor for such a move. The others, who are the ones we hear from, are especially concerned about prohibitions on "hoarding" and other matters of concerns to homesteaders, but how many freedoms would be lost... with almost unanimous approval of the U.S. electorate?

Eternal vigilance is the price of liberty. Something to think about.

Quick comments

Here's a sampling of what readers have been saying about 82/4:

• I just got the July/August issue and I really love the changes. I was getting tired of hearing how people found their dream homestead. – *Lynda, Pennsylvania*

• It is refreshing when someone of your influence has the courage to stop and evaluate the realities and priorities of his life.

I'm in total agreement: It isn't a matter of "if," it's a matter of "when." Than you for being there. – *G. Ingram*

• Thanks for the eye-opening, galvanizing July/August issue. You have gotten me off my lazy behind and working hard every weekend to prepare my homestead and myself for self-sufficiency as soon as possible. – *Robert, Missouri*

• Thank you for the July/August issue. We are seriously planning for the difficulties that might arise, and found your articles a confirmation that we're doing the right thing. Keep up the good work. – *Sharon, Georgia*

• Wow! What a magazine! (Just got the latest issue.) Thank you and bless you for your courage and determination. – *Bonnie, Illinois*

An interesting observation: More and more correspondents are asking us not to print their names and addresses.

Some thoughts and observations after 20 years in the military and 30 of homesteading

I last wrote to COUNTRYSIDE nearly 30 years ago, shortly after we had started our journey down the narrow, twisting trail we dreamed would lead to self-sufficiency.

Little did we realize then just how difficult, sometimes seemingly impossible, realization of our dream would be. We quickly discovered that the trail we had chosen was booby-trapped with snags, pitfalls and stone walls sufficient to stop all but the most determined. But we persisted, from the Arizona desert to the northern Arizona mountains to the western slope of the Rockies. But that's another volume.

I wanted to respond to the latest issue, first by stating that it's reassuring to realize we're not the only "nutty doomsday soothsayers" in the world.

As a member of Uncle Sam's military I spent most of my 20-plus-year career in foreign countries. I made it a point to travel as far away from the military reservations as I could, to visit the local people, most of whom could be classified, if it's possible to classify people, as "primitive homesteaders." The majority were uneducated, family oriented, down-to-earth, open, trusting and all the other adjectives you can use to describe good people.

Everywhere I traveled I was always made welcome. I've eaten kimche that had been buried behind a Korean hooch long enough to ferment to the point it brought tears to my eyes. I've eaten sheep intestines roasted on a spit by a Turk family that earned their living laboring in the poppy fields. I've sipped Italian booze, the name which escapes me, but I do remember that every bottle contained a grub of some sort. I don't recall very many details about my three, or maybe it was four, days of the Munich Oktoberfest, but I must have enjoyed the experience.

I could go on and on, but the main point I want to make is that everywhere I was fortunate enough to have visited I was made welcome by hard-working, honest, down-to-earth people. The strange thing about the whole experience was that I couldn't speak the languages, nor could most of the people I met speak English, but we still managed to "talk."

I returned to the U.S. in late 1968 and retired in 1969, a stranger in my own country. The country had changed. The people had changed. The country I remembered no longer existed.

Honesty and integrity seemed to have all but disappeared. Personal responsibility was becoming a rare commodity. Immediate gratification had become the primary driving force of everyday life. A true, honest smile had become so rare it did little more than arouse suspicion. Traditional family structure and values had started to disintegrate. Freedom, as I had experienced growing up and for which I had served more than 20 years to preserve, was becoming "antisocial,", "extremism," "anti-American" and "undemocratic."

I was also concerned about the then-developing credit monetary system. I doubted that it could survive over the long haul. History has proven that every major civilization experienced similar cycles, from poverty to prosperity and indulgence, currency deprecation and eventually decay and collapse. I don't remember where I read it, but, "A great civilization is never destroyed from without until it is first destroyed from within" seems to describe my perception of what the future had in store.

I wondered...if the people I found in other parts of the world could maintain the values I respected, values I had grown up with, and live long happy lives, why not in my own country?

I remembered families, dirt-poor by modern standard, lacking all the modern "plastic gadgets" so essential to the modern American, were happy and healthy. Their children were raised by the family, at home, not by day care centers, baby sitters and the public school system. The had no health insurance, no government guaranteed pension, no government guaranteed anything, and Grandma wasn't exiled to the old folks' home. They were independent and happy families living in close-knit communities.

I was convinced that real people with basic values must still exist somewhere in my country. I found them in the remote rural areas.

Now that I've got that out of way, on to the Y2K problem...

I wonder, is the predicted Y2K catastrophe perhaps a bit simplistic? Please don't misunderstand. Meltdown could very well be caused by the operating system's two-digit limitation. I am concerned, but collapse of the world's computer systems is but one of the many possible triggers which I suspect might very well lead to inevitable economic disintegration. The problem is extremely complex. If programmers somehow manage to solve the problem in time to prevent meldown, then eventually another crisis, a catastrophe beyond anyone's control, may well blow the American straw house into oblivion.

Perhaps the simple solution would be to change the date to "1984" which would allow us to experience the Brave New World before we discover Atlas Shrugged.

I'm convinced that we will experience serious economic trauma with the inevitable collapse of our credit-based monetary system. I can't change it. I can't prevent it. I learned years ago that to worry about thing or events I can't change or control is an exercise in futility. The only option I have is to attempt to put my family in the best possible position to survive it.

Could the predicted Y2K disaster, if it in fact occurs, be an engineered collapse? Would not the collapse of the world's computers prove a benefit to many of the world's bankrupt governments and corporations? Wouldn't it be handy to be able to point the finger of blame for an inevitable economic meltdown at a machine?

I worked for a few years as a computer engineer for Honeywell Information Systems, and I find it difficult to believe that the problem is as complete as some may want us to believe. At the risk of sounding simplistic, I can very quickly write a short routing for my PC that would solve the problem.

Another aspect of the problem that might be worthy of consideration is with both parents holding down full-time jobs the real income and standard of living of the average American family has fallen steadily over the past few years. I wonder, wouldn't the response be less violent, making "control" much easier if the inevitable collapse of our economy could be engineered to take place gradually over a long period of time as opposed to a sudden depression? Remember, the 1929 Depression didn't find the average American suddenly waking up in abject poverty. It was a gradual process that took several years after the stock market crash.

In any case, my responsibility begins and ends with my family, and I've worked hard to put my family in a position to survive. I'm concerned about the national computer crash leading to power blackouts, food shortages, riots in the cities, and all other catastrophic events imaginable. They might happen, then again, they might not. In either case it would be irresponsible and unforgivable not to be prepared.

Whatever the cause, when and if the "bust" comes, whether it's gradual or sudden, it will be human nature to search for and punish scapegoats. Most will never accept responsibility for their mistakes or their refusal to see reality. After all, any catastrophe must be the result of someone's violation of "human decency." It's much easier to point a finger than it is to look in the mirror. "Jeffy did it" doesn't change reality but it certainly makes the unprepared feel better.

It reminds me of a midwinter storm we experienced a few years ago. Power lines were down for almost a week. Most of my neighbors suddenly found themselves without heat, without enough food to last more than a day or two, and absolutely no way to survive short of moving in with relatives or going to a community shelter. We were one of the rare families that stayed home, warm, dry and well-fed, simply because we were prepared and not dependent on anyone.

I'm truly concerned about my neighbors, most of whom don't know how to raise a callous, much less a garden. What do I do if I suddenly find a family standing on my front porch asking to be fed? If I feed them once who will feed them tomorrow? What happens if I refuse because I only have enough to feed my own family? What do I do if my winter's supply of potatoes stored in the root cellar suddenly makes me guilty of hoarding?

I've seen starving people in several parts of the world, and in every case all normal standards of behavior are abandoned in the search for enough food to survive. If they didn't have it, they took it by any means necessary from those who did. Starving people have no conscience. – *R.L. Twining*

At 70, she's ready for anything

COUNTRYSIDE: Thank you for publishing my favorite magazine for a good many years now. More power to you for the coming changes, of which I have preached for years and no one listened.

As a widow looking age 70 in the eyeball I can say I've been there, done that. Buying a farm in my "past" middle age took hard work and every penny I could scrape up, but I am debt-free and can face anything that could occur in 2000. Have done without everything before and could do it again. – *Betty Preston, Missouri*

Two highly recommended novels

COUNTRYSIDE: Just received your Countdown to Year 2000 issue and the title alone really gave me a nudge to get on with things. Also to highly recommend two novels.

Earth Abides, by George Stewart, is a real classic. The second is *The Missing Persons League* by Frank Bonham. It is termed "juvenile fiction" so it is suitable for younger readers or those adults who don't mind reading books aimed at a different age group.

They both deal with the collapse of modern civilization. In the first book it occurs suddenly and completely. The second describes a slow but inexorable slide downwards. Both have characters that will be easy for homesteaders to relate to, as they are "down to earth" (no over-muscled types with machine guns here) and shown in their day-to-day existence.

The natural environment is a prominent player as well.

I've reread these books several times, as I find them so inspiring. *Earth Abides* has been reprinted several times, and can be found in libraries and used book stores (under science fiction, but don't let that scare you away). – *Eric Duncan, California*

Long-lost friends find us again

COUNTRYSIDE: It has been a long time since we've read and enjoyed COUNTRYSIDE. Although it had been a part of our daily living for a lifetime, we often wondered what happened to it.

When we were on vacation we stopped at a general store in a small town in the Rocky Mountains in Colorado to use the facilities. The store had a soda fountain and we decided to get ice cream. My husband Jerry was looking at the magazine racks.

Lo and behold, he says "Look at this" and held up a copy of your magazine with "Countdown to Year 2000" on the cover.

It brought back floods of memories and comments like, "Well how about that, look at that title, do you think it's the same magazine?"

Jerry has read it cover-to-cover and we have had much discussion about it.

It almost seems like our lives have rounded a bend in a long road and caught a glimpse of the past and the future at once.

We are very interested in what you have to say. Please start subscriptions for us and for our children. – *Janet Sweet, Colorado*

Even the best places aren't perfect

COUNTRYSIDE: I read with interest in the July/August issue the letter from the gentleman from Baggs, Wyoming. I too am a transplant, having lived here for 20 years. We live in the Northeastern part of Wyoming that is just about equal distance between the Black Hills and the Big Horn Mountains. Sounds great, right?

Wrong. Our area is classified a high semi-arid plateau. This year our last snow was June 3rd and today (June 17th) our temperature is 44°F.

Don't get me wrong, I love the area I live in, but it does take some getting used to.

Our county (Campbell), is called the energy capital of the U.S. Lots of oil wells, natural gas, and 15 operating, above-ground coal mines. But don't think of coming here for a job. We have a higher rate of unemployment than the national average. And if you remove the coal miners, our average wage is only $5.85. Include them and it goes up to about $7.25.

But that doesn't stop the economy from being based on their pay. Land here is about $1,000/acre, and that is bare prairie.

We also have lots of scoria (clay that is baked when coal burns underground). It is difficult to build on because of the shifting. Imagine building a house on a pile of broken clay pots, and don't even think about a basement.

It has taken us six years to get our garden to a semi-fertile state. We rent 2.5 acres and have had horses, goats, sheep and steers, at one time or another. The manure was great and it continues to improve our soil. But it will take years and I don't know if we will be here that long.

For the last three years we have fought the grasshoppers for every bit of produce we got. This year the man who heads our county's weed and pest control office stated in the paper he would not plant a garden because the hoppers are going to be the worst yet.

We are anywhere from 100 to 175 miles from the next largest town. We have a hospital, but many are sent to Billings, Montana (approximately 200 miles away) or Casper (125 miles) or even Rapid City, South Dakota (175 miles).

Our children are bussed to as far away as Jackson Hole for athletic games. We have only one four-year college and that is in Laramie (four hours away), but we do have a small two-year college district here.

One of the things I love most about Wyoming is the lack of people. Some come expecting it to be one long vacation or hunting trip. We have had blizzards in April and during the winter it is not unusual to have a week or more of -50°F wind chill. For those of us who thrive on the cold it is great. Others never leave their homes.

There is also the lack of sunlight to contend with and many have special lights they sit in front of to compensate.

Do I love Wyoming? You bet I do! But my husband says working 12 hours a day when it is -50°F is not what he wants to do with the rest of his life. He is looking for an island where the temperature does not go above or below 70°F. – *Linda Bartles, Wyoming*

A geological note: Technically, scoria is defined as porous, cinderlike volcanic lava. It has nothing to do with clay or burning coal.

A personal note: We continue to be both amused and chagrined by readers asking us where they should live, as well as by those who complain about their present locations.

A preferred location is dependent on so many seemingly insignificant factors it is highly unlikely that anyone could investigate all of them without actually living in a place for a while, probably several years. And some of them can change overnight with the arrival or departure of a neighbor, business, local official or what-have-you. Even the weather changes.

Obviously, no two people give all these factors the same weight. Therefore, no one else can give you advice on where to live, any more than they could tell you who to marry.

The grass is always greener on the other side of the fence, no matter which side you jump to. Maybe the happiest people are those who spend more time looking within themselves than at their surroundings.

Food storage and other questions

COUNTRYSIDE: I can and dry food but because of medical problems this year a garden was out of the question. I have been looking for something to tell me what the shelf life is of purchased products. I think it would be of interest to a lot of readers. Things like deodorant and shampoo. I have had travel sizes that have developed off odors. Flour, cornmeal, coffee, etc. I always keep extras but I have gotten some kind of bug in cornmeal, etc. What things can people realistically expect to be able to keep and for how long?

We have a lot of the tools, wood-burning stoves, a few chickens and the room to grow as much as we can eat but if your health or other reasons prevent you from growing a garden right now it would be helpful to know what you can store and for how long. We have enough of the essentials to get by for a while and a few of the luxuries like soap and shampoo would be nice.

My husband and I both love the magazine and it is nice to know that we are not the only ones with an uneasy feeling—not just because of the Y2K problem, but because things just haven't felt right in a while. It's been way too long between cycles and the economy is just too "good."

A comment about water storage: Here in Alabama a few years back we had the big blizzard and I had bought gallon containers of water knowing that the power would be out for a while. To my surprise some of the containers sprung leaks. I guess I had not realized until then how thin the plastic is that they are made of. Other than buying high priced igloo coolers, do you have any suggestions? Keep up the good work and when the time comes, enjoy your retirement. – *Ivy Blackburn, Alabama*

The shelf life of most items is quite arbitrary depending on brand (ingredients), packaging, and storage conditions. A key factor is that you can't depend on any figure, as anyone who has encountered an unusable product direct from the store shelf can attest. Store as recommended (and using common sense) and hope for the best, but be prepared to substitute or do without.

"Bug" infestations of milled grain products such as flour and cornmeal are quite common. If they can't be stored in a freezer or vacuum-packed (with a Food Saver or similar device) the best solution is to store the whole grains, and to grind them as needed. (The grain can also present storage problems, of course. We'll look at some solutions in a future issue on growing, handling and using grains.)

Water storage: The five-gallon water jugs used in office-type water coolers are made of much tougher plastic than gallon jugs, although these can spring leaks too. Rubbermaid makes a six-gallon "Water Can-tainer" that is heavy duty and sells for $10-$15. For serious water storage, Freund Can Company offers a wide variety of containers. For a catalog write to 11535 S. Central Avenue, Alsip, IL 60803; 800.363.9822; www.freundcan.com.

Bees, and other varmints

COUNTRYSIDE: Our four-year-old child got stung several times by an insect that seems like a cross between a bumble bee and a hornet. It is big like a bumble bee, but it is black and white and appears to attack other insects, and it doesn't leave a stinger. These are ground-living and very nasty tempered.

This is the second attack in our family this month, and our little one didn't fare as well as his daddy. JT is allergic to insect stings, and we want to avoid any more trips to the ER. We have too many uninhabited acres around here to wipe out every nest and what are these nasty little beasts anyway? What can reliably stop the reaction time of his allergic reaction to get us to the hospital in time? (We live 25 miles from a hospital or town and 911 is worthless out here when it comes to response time.) Any suggestions?

Also, Jimmy has created the ultimate small varmit gun. He took a Ruger 10/22, added a Bushnell .22 varmit scope, and then added two AA maglites. (The clip for pockets fits right onto the forearm locking ring that locks barrel and stock together.)

Now when there's a possum, fox, coon, bobcat or even wild domestic cat in the henhouse or any of the other outbuildings, he has a clear target. It won't work on bears or panthers, but those are not abundant here. – *Jimmy & Suzie Hyde, South Carolina*

Your bees could belong to the family *Anthophoridae*. But there are more than 900 different species in that family of bees, so identification is difficult.

What goes 'round comes 'round

COUNTRYSIDE: If you haven't already seen it, check out the article by Donella Meadows in the most recent issue of *Whole Earth* (#93, Summer 1998, p. 100). It gives an introduction to several different economic/political cycles, how they interact with each other, and their economic origins. It is very well written and lucid.

Her analysis of where we are in the current cycle appears to be similar to yours, because in her concluding section, she says: "Most of them (economic cycles) would say now that we're right at the bottom of the trough, though perhaps riding high on a short-term business cycle... Card-houses are tumbling down. There could yet be a spectacular implosion, if overvalued financial assets come back down to earth quickly."

This is the best introduction to long-term cycles I have seen.

Donella Meadows was one of the coauthors of *Limits to Growth and Beyond the Limits*. She had another article in *Whole Earth* #91, in which she discussed systems analysis, with an emphasis on how to intervene in systems to change where they are headed. – *Mike Benz*

It seems to me it would be pretty difficult for a homesteader to ignore natural cycles, and observing them is one of the rewarding aspects of the lifestyle.

Many students of cycles are interested in long-term social cycles, which are difficult to measure. So they turn to economics, where data is plentiful and easy to quantify...and easy to relate to social conditions.

Except for the indications of the coming crash, it might be difficult to connect this with homesteading. But I can see a day, perhaps in a distant future, when cycles become a science that both draws on and contributes to the total homestead experience.

Eat your tomatoes and plant them, too

COUNTRYSIDE: I planted seeds for tomatoes, peppers, etc., and grew them under fluorescent tubes for the container gardening we do.

Last year, we had a bumper crop of tomatoes and peppers and invested in a food dehydrator. We dried loads of tomatoes and peppers, put them up in clear glass and clear plastic pint jars saved from peanut butter and such, and stored them in a zero Fahrenheit freezer all winter.

We also are experimenting with saving seeds from open pollinated varieties, but have not tried it with tomatoes, such as Principe Borghese, simply because we couldn't figure out how to clean tomato seeds. (See 82/4 for information on this.)

On May 20th this year, as we were cutting up some dried tomatoes into a salad, on a whim, I took a few of the crisp, dried tomato slices from the jar... and laid them on top of some soil in a four-inch pot, sprinkled a little peat moss to cover them, soaked the pot real well and set it under the fluorescent lights. Didn't think I'd get anything out of the experiment so wasn't expecting anything.

Lo and behold, on June 4th I noticed two of the healthiest tomato cotyledons I've ever seen, sticking up about an inch out of the soil of that four-inch pot!

Now I'm wondering if drying tomatoes would be a way to save seed. Have you heard of this method? – *Yolanda*

Although this is what we might call somewhat unconventional, the physical treatment of the seeds themselves doesn't differ markedly from the method we discussed in the July/August issue (82/4). In both cases they are dried without damaging heat, and kept dry.

The one caution would be freezing, which kills some seeds. You'd think tomatoes would fall into this category, yet we routinely grow cherry tomatoes from volunteer plants even with our -40°F winters. Nevertheless, I'd prefer to store them at above-freezing temperatures. And that's how we store our dried tomatoes anyway, since eliminating the freezer is one of the main reasons for drying.

Of course, you didn't have to "plant" the entire tomato slice in order to get a plant—just the seeds. In this case you could "have your cake and eat it too."

There's a lot going on in Texas

COUNTRYSIDE: We've been thinking about "chicken tractors", but your movable coop is great! A knockoff will be located in central Texas shortly.

I'm very impressed with your approach to newcomers and how well you are integrating it into the ongoing guidelines for experienced home owners.

A Dallas support group has been formed to share and motivate like-minded people in Y2K readiness. While that's all well and good (the more prepared people, the better off we all are), lifestyle redirection makes a lot more long-lasting sense. – *Clint & Jo Wilhelm, Texas*

Another example:

COUNTRYSIDE: Thank you so much for sending copies of *The Have More Plan*. We are part of two Y2K/homesteading groups, and those books went fast!

Could you please send us 25 more? So many people are joining our group that we are having a hard time keeping resources for them. We are not reselling these books—just providing them at cost to the group. – *Cathie Lund, Texas*

Which would you rather drink?

COUNTRYSIDE: Isn't it ironic that so-called dairies and others who feed their cows processed chicken manure and ground-up newspapers made palatable with molasses, and inject them with antibiotics and growth hormones, then have milk collected in tank trucks where it is treated with formaldyhyde, then sterilized, pasteurized, and homogenized, beating out all the nutrients only to add chemical vitamins, are allowed to sell their milk with no questions asked while someone who feeds their stock good grain and hay and is sanitary in handling their wholesome all-natural milk isn't allowed to sell it at all?

I realize that the public does need some means of protection, but if pasteurizing kills the "bad" bacteria, doesn't it kill the "good" too?

Somebody has their priorities mixed up. – *Alice Wagner, Florida*

They don't make 'em like they used to

COUNTRYSIDE: I really enjoy reading your magazine, especially Jd's articles. I enjoy most of the articles by good old everyday folks, and I have been around long enough (72 years) to know that lots of their ideas are sound.

I would like to add my two cents' worth about canning in mayonnaise jars. I used plenty of them for canning about 30 or 40 years ago when they were made of stronger glass. Jars rarely broke. The jars we get mayonnaise in today are not as strong, and my experience with them has not been as good. They break under pressure when canning.

Another thought: When making a pickle recipe that calls for apple cider vinegar, be sure the vinegar is made from apples and not apple cider-flavored grain vinegar. It makes a difference in the taste of the pickles. – *E.L. Powell, Alabama*

One step forward, three steps back; But then...

COUNTRYSIDE: We finally got the courage to move to a bigger place. For the last nine years, my five children and I have tried to make a go on the 1-1/4 acres my husband left us when he died.

After thousands of dollars of improvements and even more invested in sweat equity, I finally couldn't take it any more. Every step forward was followed by three steps back. A bad roof and bad septic finally forced me to look at what I was trying to do.

Another straw that broke the camel's back came when I received a notice from the county agent that there was a complaint about too many hoofed animals. Not to worry, I only had a few extra goats that a friend would take. I called the agent to get an extension so I had time to build some pens.

Did I get a surprise! The report he read to me said I had 40 – count them, 40 – wild horses, burros and goats on a half acre, along with a five-year-old running around unsupervised with a loaded handgun! I laughed and asked him to read that again. (I would like to frame that one).

Imagine his surprise when I told him that I had one burro, 10 goats and five children but no handgun on our 1-1/4 acres. Needless to say, he gave us a three-month extension and bent over backwards trying to help. I felt like someone had let the air out of me. I found out the person who turned me in had been a friend and neighbor who had been running all her neighbors away little by little since her illness. I was number four.

I took stock of our lives and our home and decided I needed more peace of mind than our place afforded us. We started checking out areas in Montana and Idaho, but were unable financially to make the move. I was ready to give up when I saw an ad in our paper.

Five acres, all fenced, two mobile homes, well, fruit trees, grapes, animal pens, take over payments. Curiosity got the better of me, and I checked it out. We signed the papers two weeks after looking. I think it is one of my better decisions.

The new place is only 15 miles from a town of 970 population. Family, friends and my older childrens' schools and jobs are still close by, but we have the peace and quiet I crave. The older children live in the second mobile home.

There is a lot of work to do, but as a family co-op (those who work, eat), this gives us freedom and togetherness. The $61,000 price tag almost made me hesitate, but pulling together made it a lot easier to take on.

It's worth the price just for the peace of mind. I feel better prepared to provide for us as Y2K draws closer. Thank you for the support your magazine has provided over the years. The issues have been read to death. *– Elizabeth Froehner, California*

Retiree devotes time assisting others in self sufficiency

I am a retired Air Force officer who returned to my hometown 27 years ago where we bought 3.5 acres of wheat land just outside the city limits of Plainville, Kansas (population 2,000) and have developed total self-sufficiency capabilities with two water wells and one acre of garden.

I am now devoting much of my time in assisting others in becoming self-sufficient in preparation for the coming bad times, which I believe includes a stock market crash, banking system failure, economic depression and terrorism in U.S. cities.

Within a 30 mile radius of Plainville there are several families that have relocated here to have security, simplify their lifestyle and become as self-reliant as possible.

Terry and Sherri Rowe and their two sons have established a model homestead on 42 acres of land and welcome the opportunity to assist newcomers in finding land and developing self-sufficiency capabilities.

As High Plains Water Company Inc., I am in the process of planning and building a bottled water plant in Hill City, Kansas for which we will offer distributorships with protected territory to market three- and five-gallon bottled water, water coolers/dispensers and a full range of household and commercial water treatment and purification equipment.

Our bottled water plant will also include a self-sufficiency center that offers a full line of pressure cookers/canners, can sealers, food processors, non-electric steam water distiller, Hard Red winter wheat in five-gallon buckets and other items that are needed for independent living. For our full product line, see www.conquestinc.com.

I look forward to receiving your magazine and the invaluable articles therein for new homesteaders and others who want to get into the self-sufficiency mode.

Keep up the good work! *– Ned Colburn, Conquest International/High Plains Water Company Inc., 1109 SW 8th St., Plainville, KS 67663; www.conquestinc.com*

Another example of why you should never phone in a classified ad

COUNTRYSIDE: Here's another entry for your citified classified ad dept. "For sale: 3.2 bottom plow."

(Hint for non-farmers: 3-point, 2-bottom plow.) *– Bill Mackenroth, Pennsylvania*

Glad to be back again

COUNTRYSIDE: How great to find you again. A friend sent me an issue and whoops, off I go again in search of land and barns. Thanks for the zest, the encouragement, the ideas, the dreams, and some back issues! *– Cathy (and 50 goats), California*

Stockpiling isn't the same as hoarding; Community canneries can be useful

COUNTRYSIDE: I would like to comment on two paragraphs in your Sept/Oct 1998 issue. In the article A planning guide for the future: What to do now, the author states the following: "Walton Feed sells food reserves, mostly to Mormons. Although they are encouraged to stockpile food, not all do it. If they did, Walton Feed couldn't meet the demand. Enter non-Mormons. Walton Feed is sold out."

Granted that to stockpile means "to accumulate and maintain a supply for future use," it is not exactly what Mormons are encouraged to do. To me, stockpiling has a connotation similar to hoarding. Mormons are encouraged to store a year's supply of food for their families. And they are encouraged not just to store it, but to use it so it will have continual rotation. In my estimation this is neither hoarding nor stockpiling. It is what every homesteader aims to do and what every pioneer had to do to survive winter, drought, famine, and whatever else. Anyone who expects to show up at a Mormon's doorstep to be fed in a famine because they have "stockpiles and stockpiles" of food is mistaken.

There are many advantages to having a usable and continually rotated storage of food that COUNTRYSIDE has always made clear and which I won't go into.

Although Mormons are counseled to store a year's supply of food for their families, the way that year's supply is stored is up to each individual family. Some prefer to use cans of dehydrated foods, others prefer to can and put produce into a root cellar either from their own gardens or that which they have bought. Others prefer to take their pick of goods from the local supermarket; others have a year's supply "on the hoof," or any combination of these.

Walton Feeds is not the only company which sells emergency and dehydrated foods. There are many all over the country. And Mormons and non-Mormons alike can take advantage of the Mormon church-owned canneries in their own area.

Church-owned canneries supply the canning equipment and sell cans, lids and food stuffs. Some have wet pack and dry pack, but most nowadays are changing to only dry pack. You can buy the food stuffs and cans to take and can at home with your own equipment or you are welcome to can at the cannery itself. There is no charge for using the equipment at the cannery, but an appointment must be made.

Also, many local Mormon church congregations plan canning events in members' homes. Non-Mormons are always welcome. Just call a local Mormon church (found in the phone book under "Church of Jesus Christ of Latter-day Saints") and ask for the phone number of the president of the Relief Society (the women's organization in the church). She is usually the one who knows this information or can find it out.

I have found that buying some foodstuffs at the Mormon canneries is less expensive than other places, sometimes not. And not all canneries carry the same things. You will need to call the cannery in your area and ask for a price list and information.

I hope that this is of help to others and clears up the idea of Mormons having hoards of food around.
– Thor

I would have expected that the differences between hoarding and stocking up would have been apparent to COUNTRYSIDE readers, after all we have said about this... including nearly a full page in that issue (82/5).

For more on community canneries (Mormon or not) see our July/August issue.

Alternative energy:

The earth-sheltered passive solar Kalmer home is topped by a solar water heater on the roof. The house is constructed of cedar cordwood covered with hand-split oak shakes.

Solar power: It's nothing new, and it's here to stay

Douglas A. Kalmer
Tennessee

About 20 years ago I bought a 2,000 square foot uninsulated house in upstate New York which got me interested in solar space heating. After the usual insulating and weather-stripping, I added an attached greenhouse and built a window box solar space heater. These worked well enough to make me want to explore further solar possibilities.

After reading everything I could on the subject, I decided to build a passive solar earth sheltered home in Tennessee. I researched the subject by reading magazines and books and visiting every solar building I could. The book that gave me the best perspective on the history of solar design and its uses was *A Golden Thread: 2,500 Years of Solar Architecture and Technology.*

I'd like to give you a summary of what I've learned.

The evolution of solar technology

Solar powered home and water heating technologies have been evolving for thousands of years. The effectiveness of many of even the oldest solar technologies, especially the simpler ones like passive solar architecture, have been adequate for centuries.

The steady evolution of solar architecture and technology has been periodically interrupted by the discovery of apparently plentiful and cheap fuels, such as new forests or deposits of coal, oil, natural gas and uranium. Successive civilizations have short-sightedly treated this energy capital as income. This attitude persists today.

We speak of "producing" oil, as if it were made in a factory, but we don't produce oil; all we do is mine it and burn it up. Neglecting the interests of future generations who are not here to bid on this oil, we have been squandering, in the last few decades, an inheritance of hundreds of millions of years. Only recently have we begun to come full circle to the same realization that similar boom and bust cultures have reached before us: that we must turn back to the sun, and seek elegant ways to live within the renewable energy income that it bestows on us.

It is very important to appreciate the lessons of earlier cultures, lest we repeat their mistakes.

From the wood-short Greeks and Romans onward, people became aware of the limits of their dwindling fuel resources. They then rediscovered much of the earlier knowledge of permanent, practical solar energy.

At several points in history—the latest being today—observers of the energy scene have bemoaned the absurdity of having to rediscover and reinvent what should have been practiced continuously. Today we stand precisely where several earlier

This attached greenhouse was built for about $250. Barrels filled with water provide thermal mass.

cultures have stood. We have suddenly learned the transitory nature, the vulnerability, and the high social, ecological, and even economic costs of depending on nonrenewable hydrocarbons to hold our society together. But we still play elaborate games of self-deception by giving these precious fuels (and the electricity made from them) tax and price subsidies which in the U.S. alone total roughly $100 billion a year. Although some available solar technologies are more expensive than oil and gas, almost all cost several times less than what we would have to pay to replace them with nuclear power or synthetic fuels.

Perhaps this is the last time the inevitable solar age will be temporarily forestalled by a false sense of abundance. For unless some new form of energy now wholly unknown is discovered soon, there are no long-term energy alternatives other than nuclear reactions kindled artificially or the natural energy flows driven by nuclear fusion sited at the appropriate distance of 93 million miles.

The Greeks ravaged forests for fuel and building materials 2,500 years ago. By the fifth century BC many parts of Greece were totally stripped of trees. This led to the earliest examples of solar architecture based on the changing seasonal position of the sun.

The Greeks knew that in winter, the sun travels in a low arc across the southern sky; in summer it passes high overhead. They built their homes so the winter sunlight could easily enter the house through a south facing portico, similar to a covered porch. Overhanging roofs and eaves shaded the house from the high summer sun.

Socrates said, "In houses that look toward the south, the sun penetrates the portico in winter, while in summer the path of the sun is right over our heads, and above the roof, so that there is shade."

The Greeks planned cities so that each house had good southern exposure. In the first century AD Romans had solar rights laws.

About 500 BC the great Greek playwright Aeschylus noted that a south facing orientation was a normal characteristic of Greek homes. It was a sign of a modern or civilized dwelling, he declared, as opposed to houses built by primitives and barbarians, who, "though they had eyes to see, they saw to no avail, they had ears, but they understood not. But like shapes and dreams, throughout their time, without purpose they wrought all things in confusion. They lacked knowledge of houses turned to face the sun, dwelling instead like ants in sunless caves."

Sophisticated solar communities were built by the Pueblo Indian tribes of the American southwest. The Anasazi built sky city Acoma with full sun exposure.

The use of solar heat in horticulture also has a long history dating

This solar water heating panel was purchased used, for $100, and works fine. The small panel at top left is a 10 watt photovoltaic panel which powers the pump.

back to early Rome, where the earliest glazing materials were thinly split stone, such as mica or selenite.

During the 1600s, the French and English developed a technique of constructing fruit walls, vertical or sloping masonry walls facing south or southeast, to which they attached the branches of fruit trees or grape vines. The walls absorbed solar heat, and would greatly lengthen the growing season, even allowing tender blossoms to survive a hard freeze.

Solar water heating has a shorter history, starting with bare metal tanks painted black and tilted to face the sun. An 1891 patent combined that technique with the solar hot box, increasing the tank's ability to collect and store heat. This was our nation's first commercial solar water heater, called The Climax.

Visible light makes up only 46 percent of the total energy emitted from the sun, while 49 percent is in the infrared band, which we experience as heat. The remaining portion is in the ultraviolet band. Earth intercepts only a tiny two billionths of the sun's total radiant output, but this is the equivalent of 35 thousand times the total energy used by all people.

Anatomy of a direct gain passive solar home

For the past 15 years, I've been living in a solar collector—otherwise known as a direct gain passive solar home. It is naturally well lit, thanks to many large, evenly spaced windows on the south wall. These appropriately shaded windows allow direct sunlight to reach the back of the building in winter, but allow no direct sunlight inside in summer. The light which does enter strikes the textured, brown concrete floor, slip formed stone walls, and large stone fireplace, gently warming these surfaces which absorb and store heat, moderating temperature fluctuations. Having insulation on the exterior of the building allows these thermal masses to remain at or near room temperature, absorbing heat during sunny days and radiating warmth at night. This makes interior temperatures very stable, naturally staying warm in the winter and cool in the summer. Because the floor and walls are doing double duty as thermal flywheels, temperatures also remain very even throughout the house.

The attached greenhouse viewed from the outside.

This simple system is effective enough to require backup heat only after cloudy days in December, January, and February. My only backup heat is a large stone fireplace, modeled after the high thermal mass Russian and European designs. Mine also provides domestic hot water. My space and water heating bills are near zero.

Passive solar systems are simple in concept and use, have few or no moving parts, require little or no maintenance, and require no external energy input. Passive systems collect and transport heat by non-mechanical means.

Active systems employ hardware

All of the post and beam framing and poplar paneling were cut from the property. Doug Kalmer made the cherry cabinets from local lumber.

The homemade window frames use patio door replacement insulated glass units. The open design allows circulation of air and better light distribution.

and mechanical systems to collect and store heat, often using some outside energy source such as electricity for fans and pumps.

The greenhouse effect is most commonly demonstrated by leaving a parked car in the sun with the windows rolled up. We all know how hot that can get because it lacks storage. In a passive solar building, your windows are your collectors, your walls and floor are your absorbers and storage. Water and phase change materials can also provide storage. Typically one-half to two-thirds of total surface area is masonry. An open design aids heat and light distribution.

A direct gain building is the simplest live-in solar collector—heat storage and distribution all in one. They work well on sunny days and in cloudy climates by collecting and using every bit of energy that passes through the glazing, direct or diffuse. Masonry thermal storage materials include concrete, concrete block, brick, stone and adobe.

Indirect gain is when sunlight first strikes a thermal mass, located between the sun and the living space, commonly called a Trome wall.

An attached greenhouse is a combination of direct and indirect gain.

Isolated gain is when collector and storage are isolated from the living space.

Temperature fluctuation can be controlled by operable windows or vents, shading devices, and a backup heating system.

Windows can still receive 90% of possible gain when oriented within 25 degrees east or west of true south.

Incorporating solar design into a new structure is fairly simple and low cost. My passive solar, earth sheltered, post and beam framed house cost about $8 per square foot to build, not including labor. There are no special materials required—just a rearranging from typical design. Looking at ordinary homes, I usually see picture windows facing the road, when it would have been a simple change initially to orient to the south, providing a lasting energy gain in winter, instead of a loss. South facing windows provide a net energy gain; all other directions are an energy loss.

Also, many homes are built with brick or stone on the outside of the insulated shell, when a reversal of positions, with insulation exterior to the thermal mass, would greatly improve the homes' thermal stability and comfort at little or no added cost. Having heat absorbing masonry materials as part of the home's interior structure, such as floors and walls, can reduce overall building costs, especially when, if things are designed correctly, the need for a furnace or boiler can be eliminated, or at least downsized.

Sometimes there are minor problems with having sunlight entering your home. At times I find a certain chair too brightly lit for comfort, but I just move to another. This is the advantage of spreading the windows out along the southern wall. You have some solid wall in between windows, to minimize glare and provide some shaded areas. I suppose the sunlight also helps fabrics fade, although I haven't noticed this occurring. People in more populated areas may have some privacy concerns with a lot of large windows facing their neighbors, but this can be designed around, possibly going to a Trome wall, or indirect gain system.

Solar design in existing structures

Even though it's simpler to incorporate into a new structure, a lot can be done with existing structures. Energy conservation must be the first step, since there is little use collecting solar heat if you can't hold onto it. Weather-strip and insulate, possibly adding exterior insulation. Consider moveable insulation for doors and windows at night. A small addition of a double door or airlock entry way can increase energy efficiency, and give you a place for all those shoes and coats.

An attached solar greenhouse, or sunspace, can provide heat, food, beauty, and additional room. Plants thrive in them. My 8' x 18' attached solar greenhouse cost $250 to build, and my wife enjoyed it and what it can do for plants so much that we now have a 22' x 48' freestanding greenhouse for her plant business.

Properly placed vegetation is also important, even for houses with no solar aspect. Deciduous trees, shrubs or vines on the east, west, or south sides will lose their leaves in winter to allow sunlight in, while providing cooling shade in the summer. Evergreen foliage on the north side will buffer winter winds.

Solar hot water

Solar hot water can be added to existing structures, as I did to my house nine years ago. I am now past the point where the money I invested in the solar water heater equals the money I would have spent on electricity to heat water. Consider the fact that in the next five to eight years you are going to pay the cost of a solar water heater, whether you buy one or not. It's your choice—you can invest in solar now, demonstrating your support for sustainable energy, and getting free hot water after your payback period, or continue to pay ever-increasing energy bills, which indicates your support for maintaining the status quo.

Cooling

Passive solar design is not just about heating. Many solar design considerations also help with summer cooling. Thermal mass resists overheating, direct earth contact through slab-on-grade, and earth sheltering all contribute to cooling in hot weather. The most efficient shape of building for maximum winter solar gain is elongated along the east-west axis, giving a large south facing wall and smaller east and west facing walls. This design also minimizes unwanted summer heat gain on the hot east and west sides.

Radiant barrier placed in the attic or roof system can reflect 97% of radiant heat, keeping the excess solar gain in summer from the living spaces. Light colored roofing also helps. During the hottest months, I place soaker hoses along the ridge of my roof, to trickle water slowly enough so it evaporates before reaching the edge, for a solar evaporative cooling effect. Vegetation is usually the best shade, because it is later arriving in the spring, when we need more solar gain, and usually provides shade into fall, as well as providing its own evaporative cooling effect.

There are several low-cost, low-tech devices that anyone can use, such as an integral passive solar water heater which is basically a tank in a box. Window box collectors, window greenhouses, and attached greenhouses can help heat the house. Solar food dryers, cookers and ovens can also reduce utility bills. Many of these can be homemade, inexpensively.

Due to the window design, December sunlight penetrates to the back of the home, while the hot June sun doesn't come in at all.

Thanks to the thermal mass, the stone stays warm for days from one evening's fire. This unit also heats water.

Some typical questions that I get about my solar home are: Doesn't it get hot inside in the summer? No, proper orientation and shading prevent sunlight from entering the building during the summer months, keeping it cooler than the average home.

Doesn't it cost more to build? No, properly done it can cost less.

Does it have to face south? Yes, in this hemisphere it does—within 25 degrees east or west of south.

As sure as the sun will rise tomorrow, our energy costs will also continue to rise. Getting heat from sunlight is economical, ecological, dependable, readily available, time tested, powerful and empowering. This free and equally distributed energy source arrives at our homes almost daily. Let's all try to make better use of it, for our own well-being as well as the planet's.

Come with us to visit the 1998 Midwest Renewable Energy Fair...
and the homestead of the future

Forecast for alternative energy:

Sunny, and exciting!

For three days every summer for the past eight years a small town in central Wisconsin becomes the alternative energy capital of the world.

In June, about 10,000 people from 49 states and 30 countries descended on the Portage County Fairgrounds near Amherst (population 700) to examine solar, wind, and other renewable sources of energy, along with alternative construction methods, vehicles, and communications, and a variety of social issues. They attended workshops and took notes like eager college students, gazed skyward at whirling windmills (one with a blade span of 27 feet), and admired solar panels the way some people admire new cars in dealer showrooms. Some scurried from exhibit to exhibit as if afraid of missing anything, while others engaged in long technical discussions with vendors and other experts. Children cavorted in the streets formed by colorful carnival tents—when they weren't attending their own activities which ranged from "Durwood the Dinosaur and His Conservation Tips" to the energizing sing-along with Tom Pease. There was good food, lively music, and rousing speeches by Ralph Nader and Annie Young.

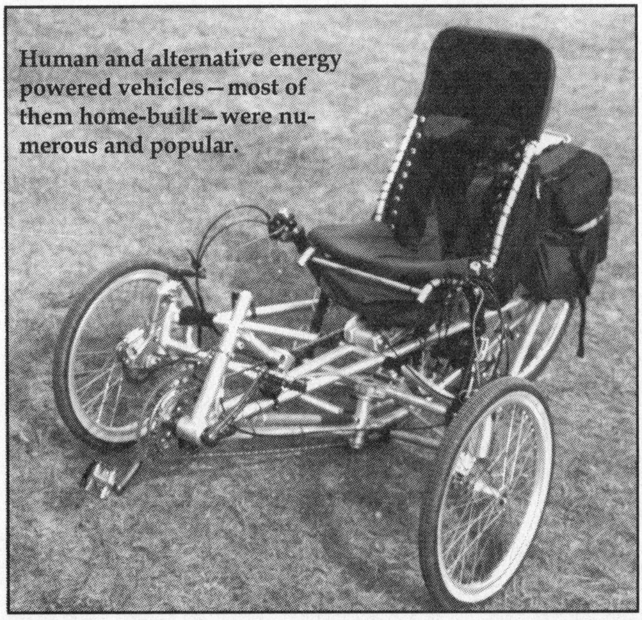

Human and alternative energy powered vehicles—most of them home-built—were numerous and popular.

This extravaganza is known as the Midwest Renewable Energy Fair.

Forecast for the future: Sunny—and exciting

The 129 workshops, most held in 12 large, colorful tents, made homesteaders wish the event lasted three weeks, not three days. Even though some sessions were repeated, it was impossible to attend every one that pertained to making the homestead both energy-independent and more pleasant.

They covered Photovoltics; Electrical Storage and Controls; Wind and Water; Housing; Transportation and

There were solar ovens of all kinds.

Fuels; Perspectives; Sustainable Living Skills; Renewing the City; and Children's Workshops.

Within these categories were sessions on PV systems for the beginners and "New Developments in Photo-voltics: Amorphous Silicon"; the history of wind machines and PV/Wind hybrid systems; straw bale construction and cordwood building and earth sheltered construction; gardening in the north; saving seeds; cooking with the sun; community living; and a panel discussion on the spirituality of sustainable systems. You could learn about methane, ethanol and fuel cells, ground-coupled heat pumps and Stirling engines, sustainable agriculture and the ABCs of socially responsible investing.

Just as instructive and exciting were more than 80 booths and exhibits featuring huge wind electric converters and small ones—large arrays of solar panels and tiny ones for powering radios—solar cookers, steam power, batteries, wood and pellet and masonry stoves and energy-efficient home appliances as well as hemp, ham radio, and recumbent bicycles.

There was a display of alternative energy powered vehicles, and a model solar home, in an "eco-village."

And if you were overcome by all that, you could have visited the massage tent.

It was, in brief, a preview and celebration of the homestead technology and culture of the future...and it was all available right there in Amherst.

On the following pages you'll find some highlights of just a few of the sessions of particular interest to homesteaders.

The future of solar is at hand

Dr. Richard Komp of Sun Watt Corporation said new solar cell materials that are now in production slash the manufacturing cost from $5 a watt to $1 a watt. This makes solar electricity competitive with fossil fuels.

The cost reduction hasn't reached retail levels yet for several reasons, including manufacturing capacity, the developers' desire to recoup their research and development investments, and supply and demand. Expect this to change in the next year or two. And when prices come down, demand will soar, production and competition will increase, and electricity from the sun will follow the pattern of calculators and computers: They will be everywhere.

When this happens, Dr. Komp expects solar electric output to increase at a rate of 1,000 megawatts a year—equivalent to one new nuclear power plant each year.

He touched on quantum physics and "momentum space," the bottom line being that modules have gone from 20 microns to 0.35 microns thick, with a resulting increase in efficiency. (Ten percent power efficiency is the "magic number" for solar cells.)

Today, abut 75% of the solar cells manufactured go to underdeveloped countries where most people live far from fossil fuel power plants.

Although the useful life of a solar cell depends on how it's made, he once tested a German-made photographic light meter, which works on the same principle. It was still accurate—and it was nearly 80 years old. (Pocket calculators use modules that decay.)

Also of interest: Photovoltic (PV) cells are made from silicon—sand—which contributes to solar power's being a "clean" source of energy. Some are being made from reject computer chips—and at least one large manufacturer subcontracts work to Silicon Valley computer chip makers.

And note this in connection with Countryside's Homestead 2100 series: entire solar electric systems, including the batteries, are being manufactured in what amounts to cottage industries in under-developed countries such as Nicaragua.

Dr. Richard Komp

Water-powered pumping

Water rams are a time-honored device to raise water to higher levels using the power of a flowing stream or river. Michael Welch explained how a Folk Ram uses a 26-foot drop to lift 175 gallons of water a day 150 feet to a storage tank at his Arvata, California home. There are other manufacturers, and you can make your own, mostly from standard plumbing parts...and shoe leather.

Rams can be used with heads as low as three feet. (Flowing water is a requirement with these devices: they will not pump water from a lake or pond.) With a greater fall, water can be lifted as high as 300-500 feet, he said. There is no set ratio of supply to delivery because of variables, although a formula does provide some generalizations.

For example, with a drop of three feet, and raising water 18 feet above the ram, a chart provides a number of .09. Multiply this times the gallons per minute entering the ram times 1440 to get the estimated gallons per day the ram will pump.At a height of six feet the number is .24; at 12 feet, .12.

Example: With a drop of three feet, and a flow of two gallons a minute entering the ram, you can expect to pump 259 gallons a day to a height of 18 feet...using only the power of the falling water itself.

How it works: Water flowing into the ram strikes an impulse valve, opening it to allow water into the main chamber, which also includes air. When the pressure in the chamber reaches a point where no more water can enter, the impulse (or impetus or waste) valve closes.

A flapper valve (compared to the valve in a toilet) opens and the air in the chamber forces some of the water into the delivery pipe.

As this process is repeated over and over again, water is forced up the delivery pipe and into the holding tank.

Welch told of some friends who were hiking in a remote area of California's gold country hearing a rhythmic clicking. Curious, they searched for the source of the sound. Beneath the forest floor they discovered a water ram, still pumping away after who-know-how-many-years. These machines are durable and virtually maintenance-free.

Solar ovens were very much in evidence, including this "Villager," which can bake 50 loaves of bread at once.

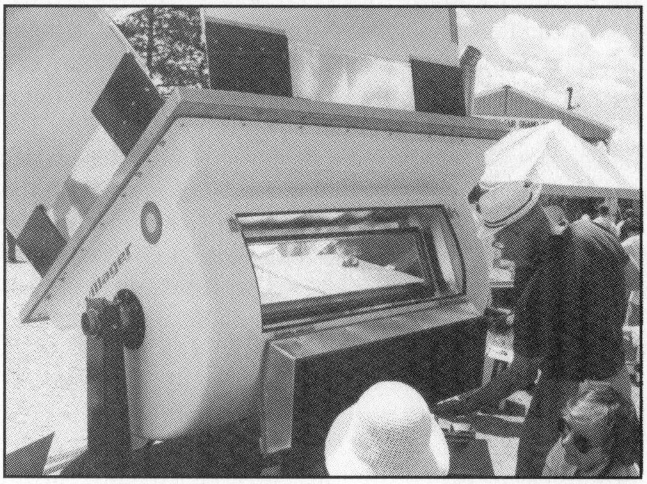

There was lively music and fun for kids of all ages.

Some models, however, use brass valves that can be worn by sand in water. Those using hard rubber last longer under such conditions, Welch said.

Also, in climates such as Wisconsin's, there is potential for freezing. The water must be kept moving and it's a good idea to house the ram in an insulated box.

Welch displayed a **High Lifter**, a somewhat more sophisticated version of the ram, using pistons. This can operate on a flow of as little as one quart per minute. Used for household, livestock or irrigation water, it can pump 750-1500 gallons per day. It was suggested that the high lifter could be hooked up to a hand pump to increase the lift.

Another form of "energy-free" water pumping is the **sling pump**. This is used in flowing stream or river.

It consists of a cone that is tethered in the stream. The cone is lined with tubing, wound in a spiral. The tube is progressively smaller as it passes from the large to the small end of the cone.

On the small end of the cone are vanes or propellers which make the entire unit revolve in the current like a cement truck. Because of the vanes, these generally require a stream at least 18 inches deep and one free of floating branches or other debris that might damage the unit. It should be removed from the water when flooding causes such conditions.

How it works: As the sling pump slowly turns in the stream, the open tube alternately grabs a drink of water and then air. As these pass through the ever constricting tube, the air compresses, but water doesn't. When the two get to the end of the cone the compressed air forces water through a swiveling coupler into the delivery tube.

Sources and more information: For an excellent source of more information, pumps, and many other items, contact Alternative Energy Engineering, PO Box 339, Redway CA 95560, 1-888-840-7191; www.alt-energy.com; energy@alt- energy.com.

Folk hydraulic rams are priced from $795 to $1,095; High Lifter pumps are $775.

Sling pumps (and others) are available from Real Goods/Jade Mountain, 360 Interlocken Blvd., Broomfield, CO 80021; 1-800-442-1972; www.realgoods.com and Lehman Hardware and Appliances, PO Box 41, Kidron, OH 44636; 1-330-857-5757. Prices range from $869 to $1,300.

Masonry stoves

In climates like that of central Wisconsin, home heating isn't an option when the sun is low in the sky during short and frequently cloudy days. The common alternative, renewable source of heat is wood, but that has its shortcomings.

Builder Mark Klein (Gimme Shelter Construction, Amherst, WI) looking for an environmentally appropriate and aesthetically satisfying method of home heating with wood, believes the answer is the masonry stove.

Masonry stoves burn wood, but at very high temperatures (1500°F-2000°F) for short periods (about two hours). The heat is stored in the mass of the stove (they weigh two tons or more) and then is slowly released to the house.

What this means is that the stove is tended only once or twice a day even in frigid weather; it uses 20-30 pounds of wood per burn—a small fraction of what a conventional stove or furnace would consume under similar conditions; and the high temperature combustion results in low emissions. It's possible to have creosote problems with a masonry stove, Klein said, "but you have to work at it."

Along with the lack of creosote, low surface temperatures after the burn and the elimination of overnight fires are also considered safety features.

Traditionally, small pieces of wood have been used in these stoves. But when they were developed in Europe in the 18th century that was all that was available. In what might be considered a preview of the oil crisis, the fuel-efficient stove was developed to conserve a dwindling resource. Larger pieces can be used, but wood that is three inches in diameter is recommended to get that fast, hot burn needed to make these stoves work as intended. At least 20 pounds of fuel is needed for a good burn.

How they work: The very hot fire superheats the wood gases which are then routed through a long flue. (Flues are configured in various ways within the stoves.) The gases transfer their heat to the thermal mass and are relatively cool when they reach the chimney. When the fire has died down, a damper is closed and the stored heat radiates into the house.

While simple in principle, making owner-construction possible, Klein recommends the kits available from several manufacturers, mentioning Envirotech and Heat-Kit. Relationships, between the size of the combustion chamber, length of flue, chimney size and radiant surface area is quite precise. With the factory components, the guesswork has been eliminated.

Much of the workshop session was devoted to questions and answers about bake ovens and cooking ranges, which can be incorporated into the stoves. However, the Gimme Shelter Construction booth at the MREA Fair provided other information about the stoves themselves.

Asking why masonry stoves are often referred to as "Swedish" stoves, we learned that there are four basic types. Along with the Swedish are Russian, Finnish and German styles. Ovens, ranges, corner units, see-through fireboxes, heated benches and domestic hot water are options offered by various manufacturers.

For more information: The Masonry Heater Association of North America (11490 Commerce Park Dr., Reston, VA 22091; 703-620-3171) is a trade organization and can furnish names and addresses of member builders, dealers and manufacturers.

With a straw bale wall nearing completion, cordwood guru Rob Roy (left) looked over the wall started by fair-goers under his direction.

Ed Eaton

Al Ruton

Envirotech, PO Box 323, Vashon Island, WA 98070 (800-325-3629) manufactures components at prices starting around $4,000.

Straw bale construction

Ed Eaton is with Solar Energy International, Carbondale, Colorado, an organization that conducts workshops on earth-friendly construction and other topics. He spoke on the history and recent renaissance of building long-lasting, low-cost, fire resistant, energy efficient homes with bales of straw. In addition to the high insulating properties (R 40-55), straw bale construction is known as a do-it-yourself project. One house shown in the slide presentation was built by a group of Girl Scouts.

Rice straw is the most commonly used material, with wheat in second place. Thousands of acres of rice straw are burned every year in California. (A 1996 initiative banning straw burning has been recinded.)

However, any kind of straw (not hay) can be used. Use what's available.

How the straw is baled is more important than its type. You want good, tight, "square" (but rectangle) bales, preferably three-string.

There are straw bale housing in Nebraska that are 200 years old and still standing. Some people living in straw bale houses didn't even know it. Eaton said.

Straw bale construction can be load-bearing or in-fill.

The in-fill technique is often used with timber framing, although steel studs are becoming popular, and are cheaper than wood in some cases. Bale quality is more important with load-bearing walls.

If load-bearing, the straw should be allowed to settle before finishing the walls. Two weeks is standard. Most building codes don't allow load-bearing straw walls, especially where snow loads are a problem. (As of now, only Pima County in Arizona allows them for houses.)

The first row of bales must be above grade, or the straw would act like a wick. In the southwest, a rubble base, with no foundation, is common. Soil-filled bags are used for the first course, and the straw bales are added on top of that. If building on a cement slab, a rise or foundation ridge of at least two inches is required. Tar or tar paper goes over this.

Where termites are a problem, a termite barrier is required. Termites don't eat straw, but they live in the straw and eat the wood.

The first row of bales is impaled on rebar imbedded in the concrete.

The bales of load-bearing walls must be pinned, tying three layers together with bamboo or rebar. Pinning isn't necessary for fill-in construction.

Run plumbing in the floor, not the walls, because of potential water problems. Other forms of ductwork can be in the walls. A weed whacker works well for cutting ducts.

Bales that must be cut to fit around windows, doors and corners, can be cut with a chainsaw, hay knife, or weed whacker. Remake the bale by making a "needle" to pull the bale twine through the straw.

There are two schools of thought on finishing the walls. One covers the straw with chicken wire before plastering. The other uses a "slip-coat," a thin layer that can be sprayed on the wall. The plaster goes over that.

Straw bale houses aren't always as inexpensive as some people expect. One reason is that walls represent only 20% of the cost and structure and the studs, headers, etc. are very important. Some straw bale houses have cost $125-$160 a square foot. Others, however, have come in as low as $60 a square foot, which is competitive with conventional building methods.

Methane

Al Rutan, Liberty Center, Iowa, has been conducting workshops on methane since the first Fair. While sessions covering other technologies have expanded, he remains the lone voice promoting methane.

That, he jokes, is because methane is the only alternative energy technology with a "100% failure rate."

Actually, that isn't quite true. There are more than 200 methane plants operating in his home state of Iowa (where he uses hog manure to produce the gas). There are even more municipal methane plants, working with human waste.

But none of them are cost-effective. The problem is that in the winter it requires more heat to make the process work than the process delivers.

An example he cited was St. Cloud, Minnesota. The city spent $17 million to build a methane plant that costs $250,000 a year to heat the slurry so the bacterial process will convert human waste to methane gas.

Some farmers produce methane...and simply torch it off to get rid of it.

"It works as a process for getting rid of manure, but it's a total failure as energy production."

St. Paul, Minnesota, has a greenhouse that for years featured a grapefruit tree. The structure was heated with municipal methane. "We can grow grapefruit in Minnesota—if it's paid for by taxes."

Farmers do have one advantage over municipalities:

they can use warm manure. But this isn't enough.

The slurry used in methane production doesn't heat up, like compost. And it needs to be at 95°-100°F, usually for a holding period of 40 days. In addition, stirring is essential. (This is not "beating" or "whipping." In his system, the stirrer makes three slow turns per hour.)

The latest experiment is being conducted on a poultry farm with 80,000 layers, a $600 a month power bill, and two tons of manure a day. It utilizes a 9,200-gallon digester (a junked tanker truck) with a waterbath underneath and heavy insulation. While he has doubts about some aspects of the system, he says "Never tell a visionary it won't work."

Contact: e-mail: arutan@commonlink.net; web site: www.commonlink.com/~methane. A video is available.

Model home

It's not actually a "home"—no bathroom or kitchen, for starters—but it's crammed with goodies to delight alternative energy nerds and homesteaders alike.

Previously, the model home was erected before the fair and dismantled afterward. Now a 10-year contract with the Portage County Fair has enabled MREA to build a permanent structure showcasing solar space and domestic water heating, both wind and solar production of electricity, as well as straw bale and cordwood construction.

For space heating, solar heated fluid (a food grade polypropolene glycol) is pumped (with a 10 watt 12 volt solar-operated pump) through tubing in the floor. The tubing is about two feet beneath the floor and buried in sever feet of sand, which serves as thermal mass. This mass warms up in the summer when the most insolation is available and releases heat during the winter.

A separate loop, for the back-up heater, is located close to the floor surface for quicker heating.

Domestic hot water is heated by two solar panels on the roof.

There are three different electrical systems, demonstrating two grid-intertie inverters and one stand-alone (battery based) system. The Omnion grid-intertied system uses 1500+ watts of Solarex solar modules wired in a high voltage array to efficiently put clean solar power on the local utility grid. The Trace grid-intertied system uses 1200 watts of Siemens modules on a Wattsun tracker (a rack that move to follow the sun throughout the day) and a 1500 watt Whisper Wind turbine to put wind and solar on the grid. The Trace system also provides battery back-up of the system during utility power outages. The third system has a Solpan power center connecting a small Wattsun tracker (with 250 watts of modules on it) through its charge controller to a 24 volt battery. The Solpan also connects the battery to the systems inverters (an Exceltec and a Heart) to provide the model home with grid-free 120 vac (volts AC) power.

Two alternative construction methods are employed in the house, straw bale and cordwood. The straw bale wall is post and beam in-fill.

The model house features super-efficient insulation and south-facing windows that are shaded by eaves in the heat of summer but allow the sun to shine in the winter.

Jd Belanger, Steve Kalmon, and Chris LaForge contributed to this article.

The Midwest Renewable Energy Association model home is now a permanent fixture at the Portgage County (Wisconsin) Fairgrounds. It demonstrates wind and solar power, straw bale and cordwood construction, and energy-efficient construction methods. The solar panels on the roof provide heat, while those on trackers (left center and top right) produce electricity.

Below: **The control panels and other devices related to the power and heating systems.**

Old technology:

A short history of wind power

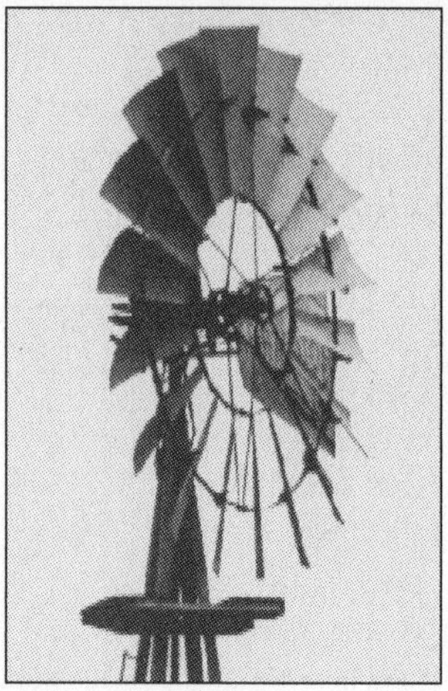

We don't know when someone first experimented with harnessing the power of the wind to do useful work other than to propel a boat. A primitive horizontal windmill was used in Persia as early as the 10th century, but it could have been used three centuries earlier.

The "Dutch-type" windmill was widely used throughout northern Europe by the end of the 12th century, in the south by the 14th, and then in America. These machines, which caught the wind with huge sails, were most often used to grind grain, but by the end of the 19th century many also powered the tools used to manufacture farm implements.

In 1854 Daniel Halladay devised a mill with many vanes or sails which made a smaller diameter wheel possible, most being about eight feet. He also worked out the principle of self-governing, maintaining a steady speed.

This "American-type" windmill was first used extensively by the transcontinental railroads pushing across the prairie. Many were manufactured by the Eclipse Wind Engine Company, under a patent issued in 1867. These mills, with their 22-1/2-ft. diameter wheels, pumped the large quantities of water needed by the steam locomotives.

Water was as vital to the settlers as it was to the railroads, but in the early days the average settler couldn't afford to buy a windmill. Consequently, most of their wind machines were homemade and cheap, constructed chiefly of wood, and often of whatever scraps were available.

While this might lead us to note with some amusement that certain aspects of homesteading haven't changed much in 100 years, there's a lesson here about the resourcefulness of those homes-steaders which can be duplicated today, and in the future.

In 1899 Erwin Barbour of the United States Agricultural Experiment Station of Nebraska traveled through the Dakotas, Nebraska, Kansas and Oklahoma, collecting data which he presented in a bulletin on homemade windmills. Because individual homesteaders designed their own and had different ideas, skills, materials and circumstances, there were literally hundreds of different designs. Some undoubtedly worked better than others, but the significant thing is that nearly every one of those homesteaders was an inventor as well as a builder.

Barbour was able to classify those hundreds of designs into seven types: jumbo, merry-go round, battle-ax, Holland mill, mock turbine, reconstructed turbine and shop-made turbine.

- With the distribution of this extension bulletin, the designs (and their names) spread quickly.
- This encouraged a certain uniformity.
- Almost as certainly it discouraged individual innovation and experimentation.
- Water-pumping windmills increasingly became factory-made rather than home-made. At one point there were about 150 manufacturers.

Innovations continued, of course. There were fanless mills, multi-wheeled mills, and by the 1930s and 40s, windchargers that generated electricity.

After WW II however, windmill sales fell drastically, and only two of the 150 companies remained in business. Small gas engines could be used even when the wind wasn't blowing, and rural electrification offered even more convenience.

What might have happened to wind power if gas and electricity hadn't been available, or cheap? What might wind power be today if it had been the beneficiary of all the research and money that went into electrification of home and farm appliances? What inventions involving wind power might have been made, on homesteads, if the incentive hadn't been removed?

And then...what might happen in the future...in the realm of wind power as well as other technologies... if circumstances and fate intervene again?

Pumping water by hand

COUNTRYSIDE: We are looking for an appropriate way to pump water from a 12" drilled well. An electric pump works very well, but obviously only when the electricity is on! We're looking for an emergency backup muscle-powered system. I understand there is a danger of contamination with the old-style hand pumps, in addition to the fact that they are generally inadequate for a 70-foot well.

Any suggestions as to the proper equipment and a place to locate same would be deeply appreciated. – *C. K., Pennsylvania*

According to Water Supply for Rural Areas and Small Communities (World Health Organization, 1959), a hand pump can be used in a well of any depth. However, when the water level is more than 16 feet the cylinder is attached to a drop-pipe and placed in the well.

In addition, the deeper the well, the less water can be delivered by one person using a hand pump. The example given: one man can pump nine gallons per minute from a 20-foot well; but only 1-1/2 gallons a minute from a well 100 feet deep.

Some hints about avoiding electrical hazards

You might find it strange that we talk about "the lights going out" and electrical safety in the same magazine. How can electricity be dangerous if there isn't any!

It's logical to assume that during blackouts or brownouts more people will be exposed to electrical dangers. That's because then more people will be messing around with generators and other equipment that they pay little attention to when everything is functioning normally.

Bruce Burdge
Virginia

Electrical hazards are all around us. The use of electricity for power, light, and processing operations is so universal that we accept it with only an occasional thought of its ability to harm or destroy. Electricity is something everyone uses frequently with just the flip of a switch or the push of a button, but it is also something that should be treated with respect.

A hidden aspect of energized electrical equipment is that it "looks normal;" that is, there are no obvious signs that tend to discourage one from touching.

Getting a shock is akin to being bitten by a snake. It happens fast and is usually a surprise. Keep in mind, however, that conditions must be exactly right for you to get an electrical shock. Just touching a wire won't necessarily do it.

Remember that current must flow in a continuous closed path from its source through some device or load and then back to the source. If for some reason you happen to become the link in an electrically live circuit, you will receive the shock. You must make the connection. You must be touching the live wire and at the same time come in contact with a grounded object or another live wire. Your body must form the link or make the connection to complete the circuit.

All of this means that electricity does not need to flow in wires to make the return trip to its source. Electricity can return to the source through any conductor, including the human body, that comes in contact with the Earth directly or comes in contact with another conductor that in turn touches the Earth.

Water has the characteristic of making some poor conductors good ones. This means that if you are taking a bath, swimming in a pool, touching any metal water pipes or faucets, or standing on the ground or on a damp concrete floor, you become a conductor to ground. Now all you have to do is touch a hot wire or come in contact with a live circuit, and a shock will most likely occur. It is self-evident that a dangerous current can flow when the skin is wet, and it is significant to observe that in the majority of electrocutions from low voltage, there is an indication that the skin was moist or wet. Summer, when the body is damp with sweat, constitutes the period of maximum peril.

The obvious and important lesson to be learned is that extra precautions must be taken when it is likely that the skin will be moist or wet.

To avoid dangerous situations it is only necessary to observe one of the most important rules. Never work on any electrically live circuit, fixture, motor, etc. Before reaching for a screwdriver or wire strippers, simply disconnect or kill the circuit you are working on. Do this at the source—at the fuses or circuit breakers in the panel box. Lock and tag it out with a padlock. De-energizing equipment, including locking and tagging out, is the best worker protection there is.

Simply removing a fuse or turning off a breaker is not enough. Someone can easily reset a breaker or replace a fuse and cause a tragedy.

Keep in mind that water is a good conductor. Never do any electrical work while you are wet or standing in a damp location. If the ground or floor is wet, put down some boards as a temporary work platform, or better yet, wait until it is dry.

Always be on guard against sloppy wiring practices. The person who was there before you might not have observed proper wiring techniques. Labels in panels might be misleading.

Each year more than 1,000 persons in this country die from electrical shock. Many of these fatalities are due to accidental contact with low voltage (120 volt) circuits.

The term "low voltage" may be deceiving because to some people, low voltage implies low hazard. While the voltage may be low, voltage is only one factor in determining the danger of electricity. Other factors are of equal importance. Electrocutions have even occurred from contact with voltages as low as 30 volts, hence, any circuit of this or higher voltage should be treated with respect.

There are no absolute limits or known values which show exact injury from any given amperage. The difference between a current which can just be perceived and one which can be immediately fatal may only be a difference of 100 milliamperes. Further, in low-voltage shock, there is a much greater danger of having current in the range which will cause ventricular fibrillation (convulsive movement) of the heart, a condition for which there is no field treatment or cure. On the other hand, high-voltage shock frequently causes paralysis of breathing and many victims of this are saved by CPR.

The number of amperes (measurement of flow) flowing in a circuit with a given voltage will be inversely proportional to the resistance. Therefore, great variations are possible even with the same voltage.

Assuming a 120-volt circuit under ideal dry conditions and 100,000 ohms resistance, the amperage passing through the skin could be calculated as 120/100,000=0.001 amperes (1 milliampere). If, however, the resistance of the skin were reduced due to perspiration and the person was standing on a wet or damp area making the resistance 1,000 ohms, the amperage might be 120/1,000=0.1 ampere (100 milliamperes)—more than enough to kill.

What all this boils down to is that de-energizing equipment and all energy sources provides the best protection available. Other ways to protect yourself may include: don't use metal ladders; use appropriate tools, gloves, etc.; be alerted by "electrical hazard" signs; be aware of overhead power sources and their distances; use the correct protective covering if called for; don't bypass electrical safety devices; inspect extension cords for insulation breaks, use only grounded or insulated power tools; use portable "ground fault interrupters" when needed; only do the electrical work that you are qualified for; use common sense; look around before starting any work—take a good look: it could save your life.

Lightning

Another electrical force that we have to contend with is lightning. If you are in the open around metal and water, you are subject to the dangers of lightning. A person directly hit by lightning will likely be killed; however, a near miss can produce a serious shock.

Effects of lightning include severe burns and cardiac arrest, and should be treated as any other severe electrical shock. CPR will often revive a lightning victim, even one who may have been "dead" for a while.

Lightning is the leading weather-related killer in the country. Between 100-150 people are killed each year. Some safety advice is to stay away from water and open fields. Don't stand near a tall isolated object. Don't use the telephone, except in an emergency. Safe shelters include inside an all-metal vehicle or well engineered buildings.

Use common sense and stay alive.

Some tips on electrical wiring

TIMOTHY S. BAKE
MICHIGAN

When putting a new plug on a wire, push the wire through the back of the plug before stripping off the insulation. This will prevent fraying of the fine wires of most electrical cords.

When you remove the insulation from the wire, do it by slitting the insulation around the circumference of the wire and twist the insulation as you pull it from the wire; this will twist the wires neatly together and help prevent loose strands of wire which could cause a short circuit between the terminals.

Never remove the ground plug from a 3-pronged plug. If the device ever shorts out internally (or if you plug a modified plug in backwards in some cases) the outer shell of the device will become electrified and the electricity will seek the most convenient path back through ground, most likely your very conductive body. It takes less than 1/10 of an amp of current through your heart to stop it.

When wiring a house, put in lots of plugs to avoid the need for extension cords. Most household wiring is fused for 15 amps. Extension cords are usually rated for about 10 amps. That means your extension cord could be turning into a torch at 14 amps while your circuit breaker is unaffected.

Do not coil up an extension cord. An extension cord can heat up and needs to dissipate that heat to the air. When coiled it cannot get rid of the heat and is heated by the adjacent loops of the cord which causes it to heat quicker and become a fire hazard well below its rated amperage.

You may wish to install outlets higher than normal where you plan to place tables in a permanent location. An outlet just above the table top would be convenient for toasters, computers, etc. and eliminate the need to crawl under the table every time you wish to use something.

It would be a good idea to consider a ground fault circuit breaker in areas that might be susceptible to wet conditions. These are able to detect improper current paths and turn off the electricity if your body becomes the most favorable path for electricity. Circuit breakers weaken a bit every time they trip. A 15 amp breaker that has tripped a few times will trip at a lower amperage and will continue to deteriorate with use. If you have a circuit that keeps tripping, split the current load by putting another wire run with its own circuit breaker and replace the circuit breaker that has been tripping with an appropriately rated breaker.

Make sure that you follow the local building and electrical codes for your area. The rules may seem arbitrary and excessive, but they usually have been made with local conditions taken into consideration.

Reprinted from COUNTRYSIDE September/October, 1992.

Around the homestead:

The cistern: A solution for declining water quality

Bill & Judy Mackenroth
Pennsylvania

A few years back, the orphanage up the road decided (despite Newt Gingrich) that there wasn't any future in orphans. They figured that old folks who didn't want to maintain their own homes any more offered greater potential. So they built some condominiums which they can re-sell when the residents die.

That worked even better than they had hoped. They built another complex right next door to the first one. Then the cornfield across the street from our house sprouted another condominium.

The real problem with all these new people (who seem to be nice enough neighbors) is that most of them came from the city and don't think twice about where their water comes from.

When people began moving into the newest complex, water could only be pumped once a day. That lasted about a month; then our well went dry, since the complex's wells are deeper than ours. I had to make some choices.

I could drill a deeper well, but where was all of their sewage going? To top that off, our next door neighbor's well went from having a high iron content to having a high sulfur content (rotten egg water!) as well. The complex must have fractured the seams in the water table while drilling their wells.

There were two problems to solve: I needed water for the animals; and I needed water for us. My wife's mulching system takes care of the garden. I needed a good temporary system that would provide water quickly without spending a lot of money that would be needed later for a permanent system. Since I have a good slate roof, I opted for building a cistern instead of drilling a new well.

Animals get rainwater

For the animals, I catch rainwater off the barn and outbuilding roofs in five-gallon buckets. It is stored in 55-gallon plastic barrels with removable lids. This keeps us in animal water until the dry season in mid-August. When the rainwater runs out, we pump water from the creek located about 1/4 mile from the house.

I have a self-priming pump that runs off the 12-volt DC truck battery. To save money, I use regular extension cords and three-prong outlets. Since this is a DC system, a pump wired to a regular three-prong plug could get burned up real quick if someone plugged it into a 110-volt AC house outlet by mistake. I changed the way the plug is wired onto the extension cord to keep this from happening.

When you look at an outlet, there is a large slot with a silver-colored screw which is neutral (close to ground potential), a smaller slot with a hot 115-volt AC copper-colored screw and a small green-colored screw which is ground. I wired the positive side of the battery to the large slot and the negative side to the ground wire. The hot wire doesn't connect to anything if anyone plugs the pump into the house outlet by mistake.

We also use rain and creek water to flush the toilet. To flush a standard toilet, take a bucket (two gallons is usually sufficient), pour it into the bowl (not the tank) from waist level. The water pressure will flush the bowl. Continue adding water to refill the bowl to the appropriate level for your toilet.

I have a friend with a good well who lets me have drinking and household water when needed. A hose fills 55-gallon drums strapped to the back of a pickup truck. I have barrels waiting in the basement so I can just siphon the water from the truck into the house. To do this, I have two specially cleaned hoses used exclusively for this purpose. After all, it's drinking water.

To get water into the house's plumbing, I disconnect the old rod and tube pump from the house's water supply and attach a shallow well pump to use the original pressure tank. A suction hose goes from the cistern to the basement, where it empties into a white barrel (I used white so I could check the water level from the stairs).

A check valve is attached to the hose just above the white barrel. When the water gets low, I just transfer water from one of the other barrels to the white one.

Tips for saving water

Here are a few water-saving tips.

1. I shut off the hot water to the bathroom sink. It takes about a gallon to get water from the hot water tank to the tap, and that adds up quickly. I keep a kettle of water on the bathroom space heater. This can be mixed with cold water for washing.

2. For shampooing, I pour straight hot water from the bathtub faucet into a bucket reserved for this use. Hot and cold water are mixed for the right temperature. Use a plastic cup to dip out of the bucket to wash and rinse.

A few watery notes from Judy:

People often ask us why we don't "force" the nursing home/apartment complex to drill us a new well. Usually, my answer is "Why would I want that?" As I write, they are putting up a new hospital complex. I'm not sure whether this means more nursing home-type rooms or emergency care. Maybe they'll just go for more condominiums.

The sign says there will be 100 new suites available this fall. Where is all that medication they wash down the sink or urinate down the toilet going to go? Into our water table! Why would I want to raise my food organically and drink that?

You quickly learn how wasteful you are with water once you lose it. Do you know it takes an entire 55-gallon drum of water to wash one load of laundry in an automatic washer? No wonder we used to use the old wringer washer.

I have two dishpans in my kitchen sink. The dirty dishes have been put into the cool rinse water pan from the last washing to soak. I then put straight hot water into the dishwashing pan. As I wash the pre-soaked dishes, the water is accumulating in the washing pan.

By the time the pre-soaked dishes are washed, the pan is about half full of water. I add the next batch and let them soak while the first batch air dries.

The old rinse water is emptied into a five-gallon bucket. The second batch of dishes goes into the empty rinse pan. When I have a pan full, I begin to rinse the dishes, allowing the rinse water to accumulate in the pan. If the water gets too dirty or greasy, I just add it to the five-gallon bucket of waste water, add soap to the rinse water, making it the new wash water and start off with fresh rinse water. At the end, the waste water can be used on plants or for cleaning the porch.

Never run water when washing or bathing. Use enough to do the job, but don't let it run indiscriminately. It's amazing how much clean water goes down the drain.

The hose is another major water waster. I really miss it for washing the driveway and rabbit cages, but I cringe when I think of how many hundreds of gallons of water it took.

I have also discovered a wonderful way to shower. I bought a new Hudson three-gallon spray tank like they use to spray chemicals on plants. That's why I bought a new one. Even a used one that was scrubbed thoroughly would have residual contamination.

One teakettle of hot water to two gallons of cold water provides enough water for two showers. The tank stays outside the tub/shower. Just pump up the pressure according to the directions. Since the spray is a gentle mist, it uses a low volume of water. The flexible hose has the advantage of being able to spray exactly where you need it, making rinsing very efficient. The sprayer can also be used to mist seedlings.

We recently purchased one of those sun shower units, which is a vinyl solar-heated bag that holds one to five gallons of water. I hope to try it with rainwater and see how it works.

We use less water in a week than the average single person does in a day.

There are some concessions. The constant washing of cloth diapers isn't practical, so I use disposable diapers even though I'm not thrilled with their impact on the environment. I also take my laundry out to wash. Hauling all those buckets of water into the basement to wash clothes was not my idea of a good time!

Apart from that, the ingenious system my husband has devised has enabled us to use the regular water system. Guests don't even realize we're using an alternate water source, and I appreciate the convenience of hot and cold running water.

Around the homestead:

12 volts pressurizes shower water

Marcella Shaffer
Montana

One thing everyone agrees on: nothing feels as good or is as welcome as a warm shower after a long hard day. For the homesteader or survivalist with only the barest basic bathing facilities, a warm, pressurized shower can be utopia.

A recent discovery changed our simple but functional bathing methods into an enjoyable and even luxurious experience. The 12-volt Low Power Shower (patent pending) is a pressurized shower unit powered by 12 volt DC power. It is simple to install and operate and is exceptionally versatile, making it suitable for use almost anywhere.

The Low Power Shower was created by Jesse McGee of Bonners Ferry, Idaho for use in his own DC-powered backwoods home. He experimented with several different pumps and shower set-ups to find and design a system which delivered sufficient pressure, conserved water and was reasonably priced. Two adults can shower with just five gallons of water and an average of 1.5 amps of power. Jesse began selling his shower units locally by word of mouth and at energy fairs and swap meets. He refined the device after talking with customers.

For the energy-independent home, the shower can be permanently wired and affixed in the shower stall. When traveling or in times of water or power outages, it can easily be clipped to any 12-volt battery (clips supplied), hung up and used. If you want to shower outdoors while camping, simply clip to a battery and enjoy. If climate and privacy permits, a permanent outside shower could be created by using a small solar module and/or a battery. The Low Power Shower consists of a small pump, tubing, wiring, in-line switch and fuse and shower head.

The pump is placed in a container of warm water such as a five-gallon bucket. Water is pumped from the container to the shower head which can be hung up or permanently affixed. The in-line switch controls the pump, while the in-line fuse protects against excessive current.

For most efficient power and water usage, turn the pump on to get wet. Turn the pump off, lather up, then turn the pump back on to rinse.

Make your own decorative stones

Jim Hunter
Arkansas

After pricing decorative edging stones for my wife's herb garden, I decided to experiment and make my own. Here's what I did. Experiment and find out what works best for you.

For molds, I used disposable aluminum pans in the largest size I could find. An entire paper bag of pans was purchased for a quarter at a yard sale. Then I assembled my supplies—pans, readymix concrete, small smooth gravel from our creek bed, a trowel and water.

After mixing the concrete according to instructions, it was at a consistency where it plopped off my trowel. Then I put the gravel on top, tapping the stones down with the trowel. Then I let the cement dry for eight hours. After being popped out of the molds, they were ready for placement in the herb garden.

The same pans can be used over and over again as needed. We've made over 500 decorative stones for walkways around our homestead for just $20.

If you use larger pans, be sure to embed a layer of chicken wire or hardware cloth in the concrete mixture so the stones have enough strength to keep from breaking while they are supporting weight.

The concrete left over after pouring the base for Countryside's solar panels was used to make a "stone-like" path to the front door. But unlike Jim Hunter, we used a store-bought flagstone-shaped mold. We recommend it for projects like this. Neighbor "Uncle Dick" gave Jd and Tammy a hand.

COUNTRYSIDE'S **solar array provides more than 1,300 watts at peak power. Part of the garden is in the foreground.**

Power from the sun

Even people who have a genuine interest in solar often lack understanding of just how different it is from the almost universal power grid system of electricity. It involves much more than just saying good-bye to the grid and installing solar panels and an inverter. If it were that simple, there would be far more solar-powered homes and businesses today.

More than anything else, the decision to go solar becomes something of a lifestyle. One must be a true energy miser when depending on a solar system. While solar is a viable energy alternative, it definitely has its limitations, and they must be considered before the choice is made.

It's also possible to become a frugal energy consumer without going to solar. You would save substantial sums on your electric bill and avoid the considerable expense of a solar conversion.

Despite the high monetary cost, there are some very legitimate reasons to go solar. There is the undeniable benefit of being independent from the electric oligopoly. Some people have philosophical objections to using nuclear-powered electricity and fossil fuels, and they are willing to do whatever it takes to live according to their beliefs. Then there's the potential disruption of utility services.

While it is expensive when compared to conventional electricity, solar power is actually more economical than the grid in some applications. The cost of bringing power lines to rural and isolated homesteads is often in the tens of thousands of dollars. As many COUNTRYSIDERS have discovered, going with solar was the right choice for their remote households.

Solar has proven useful in a wide range of niche situations. It is often the only practical power option in rural African villages. Solar technology for lighting and electricity for construction zone signs and other portable devices is routinely found in America. Solar calculators commonly sell for less than $10. A growing number of motor homes use solar panels to meet their electrical needs.

As the cost of solar power continues to decrease, the use of solar panels should expand. Since the market for solar power is still relatively small, the benefits of economies of scale on prices have not taken hold yet. Perhaps in the not-too-distant future, contractors will be able to install solar on new homes at prices that are comparable to wiring into the grid today.

The photovoltaic cell

These silicon wafers are the heart of a solar panel. Semiconducting cells convert sunlight into electrical energy through the photovoltaic process, hence the name. Like computer chips, the silicon in solar cells is made from highly refined sand. The wafers are layered with boron and phosphorus atoms before a metal coating is applied.

The top side of the cell is painted with an anti-reflective coating. This vastly increases the cell's ability to absorb sunlight. The cells are wired together in panels or modules for increased efficiency and energy output.

Photons, which are bundles of energy from the light, strike the cell and provide enough power to dislodge the positively charged boron atoms and the negatively charged phosphorus atoms. When the cell is exposed to sunlight, these imbalanced electrons flow in an effort to equalize the balance. This activity creates an electrical current, which can be transferred to a power storage unit such as a battery.

Why choose solar cells over a generator? Solar is virtually maintenance free, which is a real benefit for those who aren't mechanically inclined. Just keep the panels clean and cleared of snow and debris, and those cells will keep trickling electricity with little fuss or bother. Solar also eliminates the need to store large quantities of gas, diesel or LP, and frees the sun-powered homestead from price fluctuations for petroleum products. Some solar users do keep a generator around as a backup source for winter and emergencies, but their fuel consumption is modest compared to full-time generator users, and they don't have the constant noise that comes with frequent generator use.

Picking the right system

Most people give little thought to electricity. Move into a home, and the wiring and connections are already in place and functioning. On rare occasions, the fuse box or other obsolete components may need to be replaced.

The first step was embedding a 6" diameter 20' long well pipe in almost five yards of concrete.

Chris LaForge and Carl Hansen work on the wiring while Amy Wilson starts assembling the tracker frame.

When working with solar, every energy-using device needs to be considered. Even the masters of energy frugality will find that they can inadvertently overload their systems. You don't have to trash your appliances and gadgets—just don't try to operate them all at once while the lights are on!

Since the marine (deep cycle) batteries used for energy storage are 12 volts, the most common standards for solar systems are 12 or 24 volts. Photovoltaic supplier and consultant Windy Dankoff (P.O. Box 548, Santa Cruz, NM 87567) recommends a 24-volt system for homes, since it offers lower per-watt cost and higher efficiency. A 12-volt system may be sufficient for cabins or a small household.

One reason Dankoff prefers the 24-volt system is for capability to power electric motors above 1/4 horsepower. He offered other reasons for going with the larger system.

"Long wire runs from PV (photovoltaics, or solar cells), to a DC well pump, or to other generators, can be very costly at low voltage/high current," he said. "The longer the distance, the larger the wire must be to reduce losses. Cutting the current in half by using twice the voltage can cut your wire cost by nearly 75 percent."

Unless you have an inverter to convert direct current (DC) into the alternating current (AC) that comes from the grid, you'll have to stick with electrical devices designed especially to operate on DC. Inverters are designed to handle widely varying amounts of wattage and are priced accordingly.

Some inverters also have a stand-by charger feature, which juices the battery when a generator is running and also has an automatic transfer switch to send generator power to the house circuits. According to one solar specialist, inverters produce a modified square wave AC, which is popularly known as modified sine wave. This is slightly different than what comes from the grid, but it works well with most electrical appliances.

Reportedly, some Apple computers, sewing machine speed controls, copy machines, laser printers and some Makita and DeWalt tool rechargers burn out on the modified sine wave AC. If just one or two de

The frame went on the top of the 10-foot pole (the other 10 feet are buried) with the help of a makeshift platform.

The 12 panels are wired together.

vices might have problems, a small true sine wave inverter will handle the load. Also check the surge rating of an inverter to see how well it will handle short stretches of heavy power use such as when tools or appliances are started.

Getting on track

While a stationary panel array will consistently produce power, a tracker powered by a small electric motor moves solar cell panels with the sun's rays and gathers sunlight more efficiently.

This is a close-up of the tracking mechanism. The lever with the holes in it allows the solar array to be tilted toward the sun for maximum exposure in both summer and winter.

"Depending on the atmospheric conditions, a tracker will add 30 to 40 percent in sunlight gathering efficiency," according to solar power installer and instructor Chris LaForge. "The tracker points the panels directly into the sun, which is when they produce the most energy. Tracker motors use very little electricity. The payback time on a tracking system is pretty good."

If money is tight, the tracker can always be added later. However, this device does pay for itself by providing extra energy. To have the kind of wattage that a tracker system can provide, the only other alternative would be buying additional solar panels for a stationary unit. Unlike the current system of heavy-handed government intervention and subsidies for special interests, the solar shopper bears the full cost of the purchase. To quote a popular Libertarian credo, there ain't no free lunch when your electricity comes from the sun.

Will I have enough power?

How do you calculate the amount of power that a solar system will produce? Take the number of sunlight hours for your area and multiply that by the kilowatts the system is rated to produce. Keep in mind that the figures listed are averages and will vary with the seasons, especially in colder climates.

Obviously, the prospective solar buyer will need to do a thorough energy audit. Your electric bill should show average energy usage over various time periods. That will give you an idea of how many adjustments and changes might be needed to go from a grid life to solar.

On the lower end of the price scale, LaForge's $1,500 "billboard" system features two solar panels that produce enough power to supplement usage in an apartment or small home. He said, "It's designed to show people that solar power works. This is a fairly portable system."

If you're willing to go one step up the ladder, a larger stand-alone system can be put together for $3,000 to $4,000.

"I'd get this if you're concerned about electricity being cut off or don't have much money," LaForge said. "This system will run a few lights, some power tools or other appliances and a computer." While this may seem like a high price for a modest supply of electricity, keep in mind that your monthly light bills will be eliminated or greatly curtailed. If Y2K does play havoc with the grid, it could actually turn out to be a very wise investment.

The Countryside solar/wind system

While we're not completely energy independent yet, Countryside has taken a major step in that direction with the installation of an 18-panel, 1.35 kilowatt solar array and tracker supplemented by a 900-watt wind generator. The 24-volt inverted system is metered, and power can be sold to the local utility. Local power companies react with everything from genuine confusion to thinly veiled hostility when dealing with a customer who is going the solar route.

"The utilities all react differently," LaForge said. "The right thing to do is to pay the retail price instead of wholesale, because it's clean energy. In some parts of Europe, the utility companies are paying twice the retail price for clean energy until the cost of the system is paid off. Then the utility companies pay one to one for alternate power."

The solar panels were up and operating for several months before the wind generator was added in early September. Even a light breeze is sufficient to get the blades turning to create renewable, pollution-free energy.

"It takes about a 7 MPH breeze to start making power," LaForge said. "There are quite a few people who want just the wind system if they live in windier areas."

Is solar or wind the better option? LaForge urged alternate energy enthusiasts to consider the best of both worlds.

"I'm sold on hybrids," he said. "I like the idea of having two power sources. We can put a system up pretty quickly. It costs a little more to put up a system that is completely off the grid."

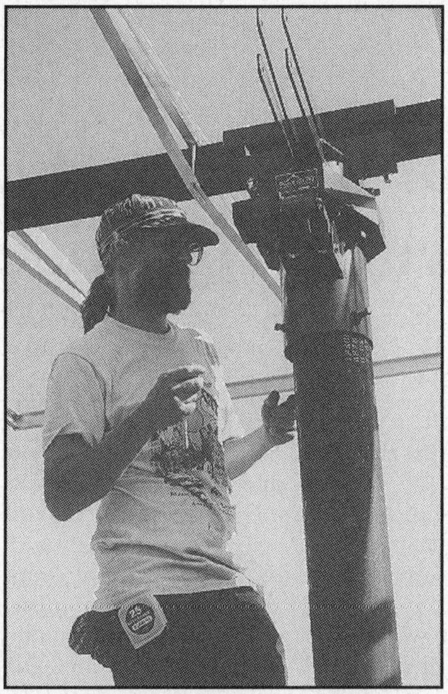

Chris LaForge, of Great Northern Solar in Port Wing, Wisconsin, checks out the tracking mechanism which keeps the solar panels facing the sun for peak efficiency.

The future of solar energy

Once considered the province of hippies and eccentrics, solar and wind power has attracted a broader base of interest in recent years. Y2K has only created more demand for freedom from centralized electricity.

"Business has skyrocketed this year," LaForge remarked. "I have several people who are ready to install systems right now. Our bread and butter customers are people who are more than a quarter mile off the grid, but that profile is changing. Environmentalism has changed a lot. People are aching for good information. If you're not thinking outside the box today, you'll be in trouble when the box disappears. More people are concerned about what I call our environmental catastrophe."

Chris and Carl at the control panels in the battery room.

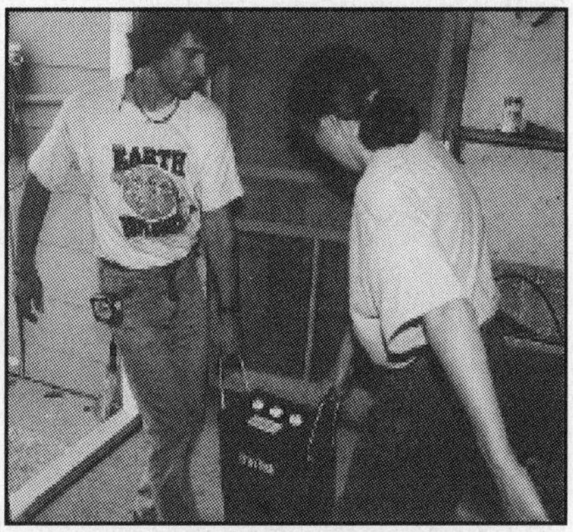

Carl Hansen and Amy Wilson bring in one of the Trojan (L-16W) batteries. They weigh 126 lbs. each.

Even city dwellers can tap into renewable energy.

"Wind power isn't the best choice in cities because of liability concerns, but there's solar," LaForge said. "I did a workshop in St. Paul, Minnesota. After the workshop, a couple who are environmental activists went to their bank to get a loan for a solar system. There's a 1.35 kilowatt clean energy system operating in the middle of St. Paul."

LaForge has made renewable energy his career for the past decade, and there are employment opportunities in the field.

"I instruct everyone from the beginning local user to the person who wants to open their own solar business," he said. "The Midwest Renewable Energy Institute is developing a curriculum that will certify people to do national quality electrical installations."

While it isn't "cost effective" according to traditional economic measurements yet, things could change very quickly for alternate energy. Remember the gas lines of the mid-70s and the heyday of the OPEC cartel? Mix in the uncertainty of Y2K with unpleasant events to come, and the mainstream media may suddenly "discover" solar and wind decades after Countryside and other "fringe" sources were on the scene.

– Al Doyle, Countryside staff

The most important aspect of home power is learning to conserve it

You can get a taste of what it's like to live with solar (or wind) power even before you set up your system.

The first three rules for alternative energy systems are conservation, conservation and conservation. You can practice that (and benefit from it) even if you never go solar.

Many people dream of buying a wind or solar electric system and kissing the power company good-bye, with little or no change in their lifestyle. But unless they are already very frugal power users, it doesn't work that way.

The typical off-grid home uses only about 10% - 20% as much electricity as the average American home. Think about that. To match the typical solar powered home, you'd have to cut your use of electricity—not in half, but by 80-90 percent!

This can be done anywhere, any time. All it takes is a little knowledge, determination, and the right attitude.

Electric power is cheap. Too cheap, and artificially cheap. (The same applies to food, gas, and much else.) We do end up paying some of the costs in other, hidden ways. In the case of electricity, this includes air pollution, nuclear waste, depletion of nonrenewable resources and others that don't show up on conventional balance sheets.

When something is cheap and readily available with little or no effort on our part, we tend not to give it much thought. With electricity, this means we flip switches and leave lights on and add appliances, seldom considering the consequences... unless the bill even for cheap electricity gets higher than we expect.

Solar power is not cheap. Unless you're fortunate enough to come across used components (and have enough knowledge to know what to do with them) even a minimal system will cost several thousand dollars. That's more than most people pay their utility in years.

And what do you get for that? You can have a few lights, maybe a radio or tape player, and possibly an appliance or two, all used judiciously.

But even a larger system costing $20,000-$30,000 isn't going to provide all the electricity you're probably accustomed to using now. It will still require conservation.

For starters, forget about electric heat of any kind. No electric water heater. No electric kitchen range. No clothes dryer, and definitely no air conditioning. Most refrigerators and freezers use more power than the typical solar installation will produce.

This doesn't mean owners of solar homes live as harshly as those without any electricity at all. It does mean that they apply homestead principles and thinking to things most people simply take for granted.

Those energy hogs just mentioned have alternatives. Wood and active or passive solar heat are viable options. Wood-fired, LP and solar water heaters are available, as are wood and LP kitchen stoves. Super-efficient refrigerators and freezers with very efficient compressors and much more insulation use about one-fourth as much power as ordinary models. (They also cost much more, although not as much as the additional solar panels needed to run standard models would cost.)

Most solar homes convert sun power to 120 volt AC, which means they can use all the "normal" household appliances: tv, vacuum cleaner, sewing machine, kitchen and power tools, water pumps, you name it. Even high-wattage tools can be used, briefly and prudently: toasters, hair dryers, microwaves, and even washing machines.

The operative word is prudently. Conservation. If you only have one or two kilowatt hours a day to "spend" on your electrical needs, you're going to learn to budget... or do without... just as you budget money. And the results can be just as satisfying.

You don't have to disconnect your home from the power grid to conserve electricity.

Is it worth it?

If a solar array costs so much, produces so little, and requires more expensive lights and appliances, why bother?

In some cases, solar is actually cost-efficient. Many homesteaders have told us of power companies wanting $20,000 and more to run lines to their homesites... which aren't always or necessarily in remote areas. When grid power is going to be that expensive, or impossible to buy, alternative energy is the only alternative.

Some readers are undoubtedly thinking of Y2K preparedness: If the grid goes down (which many, including a congressional panel looking into Y2K and electricity, think is likely), it might be nice to make your own. However, electricity isn't a top priority for survival, so unless you have everything else in place, have some extra money, and have been considering going solar anyway, Y2K shouldn't enter into your decision. On the other hand, if you do have everything else in place and have been wanting solar power (as most homesteaders do), Y2K might provide a great excuse for doing it now.

The main reason most homesteaders with access to cheap grid power install solar is very close to the reasons they homestead, period. They want to step aside from the Industrial Age and its consumerism mindset. They want to be more independent. They want to help promote sustainability, conserve natural resources, lessen the demand for nuclear power, live closer to first causes... and a host of other hard-to-describe desires.

In this regard, being off the grid might even be seen as a symbol of homesteading. It's fun, and it feels good... and it's pioneering a trail into the better life we envision in the 21st century.

—Jd Belanger

Many homesteaders use smaller, less expensive systems with success

Not all alternative energy installations are as large or as complicated as COUNTRYSIDE'S. Here's an example of what a frugal homesteader can do, as reported in COUNTRYSIDE in 1991.

ROBERT BUSHEY
ARIZONA

Having grown up in a Midwest farming area, I never paid a great deal of attention to newfangled devices or inventions. As I reached middle age I heard of the new solar energy systems which at first I thought was just another wild, somewhat hare-brained idea to make money.

But after I sent for a catalog of solar products, and later bought an isolated, 41-acre East Arizona site, I found out how truly useful, economical to use, and efficient these solar power systems can be.

My new country land was a full 15 miles from any town, on a 7,000-ft. mountain plateau in a semi-desert wilderness area. There were no utilities available: no phone, tv, gas, or water line hookups or connections—and no electric. To bring in a single utility line this far might cost thousands of dollars. Perplexed as to how I would survive in my 23' travel trailer, I talked with a local solar systems dealer.

I was amazed to learn I could have almost full power installed at a surprisingly small cost of a little over $1,000. By buying a trio of used solar collector grid-type panels for only a little over $500, I saved almost 60% of the cost of three new solar panels. A few 12-volt storage batteries cost a little over $100 each, a small inverter unit, only about $70, and the rest of the system's cost went for wiring, accessories, etc.

I soon found my new power system could supply enough power to run my trailer's full interior lighting, plus household appliances and color tv. My solar grid collector panels, on a pole-type adjustable mount to move with the daily path of the sun, could supply a full 110 watts of power. These panels simply collected normal daily sunlight, converted it into electricity, then transferred this by wiring to my few storage batteries kept in my tool shed just outside my trailer. Then, from the inverter, the power was transferred to my trailer's electrical system.

Electricity from the sun is useful, efficient, clean, and quiet—much unlike the noisy generators I've heard some of my neighbors use.

I've found that one real advantage of my solar energy system is that it is fully self-contained. It requires no connection to any outside power source. Thus, using only normal sunlight which is plentiful in my area, it means I never, for the rest of its useful life, ever again have to worry about paying monthly utility bills. It will pay its own cost fairly soon.

The sun's energy can be stored for up to several days in case of stormy weather or overcast skies. My new power system effortlessly and quietly provides me with steady, reliable power, and gives me a sense of security as I know sunlight will never fail me.

I'm told that if I had more collector panels, costing about $300-$400 each, new; or a larger inverter unit, about $400; I could run my optional gas-electric stove and refrigerator off the solar electricity. (At present I run them on bottled propane.)

Besides providing steady, reliable power from nature, and being economical, easy-to-install and almost maintenance-free, these new systems are also ideal for isolated, hard-to-reach areas. Farmers or those in out-of-the-way places can save hundreds or possibly even thousands of dollars yearly. Some new types of solar units can power electric fences, fence gates, power tools, sluice or irrigation gates, and pump water.

"Early adapters" put up with bugs

COUNTRYSIDE'S current system is not our first foray into alternative energy. This time, fortunately, it's working much better.

We wrote about wind and solar power, and made some half-hearted attempts at constructing home-built windmills and solar heaters, in the early 1970s. But it wasn't until 1977 that we installed a 12-volt Wincharger and a working solar heater. The windmill charged a marine battery which ran a fan that blew warm air into our building.

It was a very small, demo setup. And after the wooden windmill blades broke—twice—it was abandoned.

Shortly afterward, we ordered a much larger three-blade wec (wind electric converter). The four-legged tower was erected. But before we could install the windmill itself, the company issued a recall: seems they were having trouble with the blades tearing off in high winds.

Then they recalled the generator, because it was wound backwards.

Finally (and not surprisingly), they went out of business.

Solar electric panels were simply too much for our budget, but we did get a solar water heating unit. That too, was unsuccessful.

So alternative energy sat on the back burner at COUNTRYSIDE for 20 years. During that time the quality and reliability increased, while prices decreased. We're back in the game.

The Intentional Peasant ponders progress

THE INTENTIONAL PEASANT
MARYLAND

Almost all of us are in favor of progress: a better way to shell corn, get the garden cleaned up for fall, heat the house, bring in a few extra dollars, whatever. To most of us, progress means better, easier, cheaper or faster ways to perform a task. Sometimes it means a more responsible way to perform one, like contour plowing or terracing—making sure our runoff doesn't destroy the creek. So progress, then, means better; better for us, and better for our neighbors—at least to the point of our not doing harm to anybody, upstream or down.

When this peasant was manager of a customer-contact department, he coveted the company's automatic typewriters. Now there was progress, with upgrades almost daily. First, there was the old dual-magnetic contraption. Then countless no-name improvements, followed by the Xerox that needed a pilot's license to operate, and finally the $3,000 Exxon.

So it was when this antique IBM PC-XT turned up in the Pennysaver for pocket change that a decades-long hunger was stilled. This beat-up, recycled old thing represented real progress for the peasant without apparent harm to anybody. No harm, that is, except to the folks who make the paper paste the peasant had been using to glue up revisions to his 300-plus page manuscripts.

The handy little pocket or desk calculators we have today are surely a big improvement over a #2 pencil and a ruled pad. They're cheap and can be had in wild configurations, like scientific, calculus and building trades models. But here is where we're getting into a trade-off situation.

Along with the improvement, we find a devil in the rumble seat. Kids are pretty well finished with arithmetic today after the third grade. They can take tests with calculators by their sides. The "educators" want the pupils to understand the math principle; they needn't actually be able to do calculations, like with a pencil. Heaven protect our young from dead batteries!

"The computer is down"

A similar situation developed in the office mentioned above. In the pre-computer days, actual human beings could do actual transactions—as in figuring the intricate cash values of life insurance policies. The people who could do that are gone. The computer does it all, thank you. Very efficiently, too, but when "the computer is down," all work stops. Nobody knows how to do the transaction manually, not even the systems analyst who installed it. The documentation is, um, no longer available. When one reads in Spengler that civilizations collapse when they become overextended and have gotten too complicated, one thinks of those things and wonders: A horseshoe nail?

One would be hard put to find anybody who would prefer a mule to a tractor or to a big tiller for really serious tillage. Yet when we lived in a place called Randallstown, the black man next door would plow perhaps five acres with an enormous mule that he obviously loved dearly.

Now Tiller the Hon was a nice piece of machinery, but I don't recall anybody ever loving him or pulling morsels for him from the hedge rows. Anyway, he didn't live as long as the mule.

The clothes dryer is another gadget that has changed the way most Americans live. You can even buy stuff to make the duds "smell clothesline fresh." This one almost defies comment, but a deal of rope wouldn't make a patch on the dryer's considerable appetite for Reddy Kilowatt.

On the other hand, the home freezer seems close to being on the plus side of the homestead ledger. In 1940, Grandma had to tool the Model A six miles into Crozet, Virginia to visit her hindquarter of beef in the freezer locker. The hogs were taken care of at home, mostly sold off the place. Two or three socking great hams always dangled in the smokehouse—a real low-tech way to go and of minor impact on civilization as we know it.

It's hard to keep up this peasant's reputation as a misotech, or hater of technology, when so much of it is so darned useful. But sometimes he has to agree with Albert Einstein (who no doubt wasn't talking about dryers and freezers) when he said "Technological progress is like an ax in the hands of a pathological criminal."

Still, if one owns a restaurant, why would one do without a Cuisinart or perhaps even a pressure oven? Is there much equipment more useful around the family kitchen than a Vita-Mix or a big pressure canner?

The city as technology

If you don't object to the stretch, the modern North American city is probably our most awesome piece of technology. Ivan Illitch thinks they've become too complicated and costly, as "city dwellers must... rely for every one of their needs on complex institutional services. It is extremely expensive to keep (the city) even minimally livable." He described apartment buildings as a place to store consumers between trips to the supermarkets. R. H. Tawney nodded, "Systems prepare for their own overthrow by a preliminary process of petrification." Where we live it's really petrified.

Generations of our forebears left the land to come to these places for a less grueling, more predictable way of life in the cities. In exchange for pure air and water, hard work, and better food than money can buy, they received soot, carbon monoxide, undigested hydrocarbons, chlorinated water, a flush toilet, hard work, corn flakes, Bisquick and today, Eggbeaters, margarine and Mylanta.

This was a complete reversal of the colonial situation described by Charles and Mary Beard: "It was the man fired by the passion for owning a plot of ground who led the vanguard of settlers all along the frontier from New Hampshire to Georgia; to him, cheap land meant freedom, to his family a rude but sufficient comfort."

A case could be made that technology made the rude sort of comfort insufficient. In the city there were sidewalks, indoor plumbing, trolley cars, movie houses, restaurants, libraries, museums, wages, sewer rats, and influenza epidemics. But things seemed better, especially when there was no money back home to buy one's own ground and too many brothers to carve up Mom and Pop's place to provide for everyone.

In the city, one died more slowly. There were the physician's shots and potions and in extreme cases, his carving knife. If one worked hard, saved and was patient, there might even be enough put by to cover the price of one of Mr. Ford's Tin Lizzies.

Now as to Mr. Gore's favorite hate, it is sure that Henry Ford thought he was making real progress and doing a fine thing by his perfection of the assembly line method of building automobiles. But by the 1980s, Bob Easton was praying in Shelter, "With luck, we'll run out of oil before terminal Los Angelesization grips the Earth." Ivan Illitch pointed out that the speed of transportation was counterproductive. That is, the faster we went, the longer we spent going.

Today in southern California or the northeastern U.S., it isn't unusual at all to sit in one's car for an hour each way, coming and going. Ancient Rome redux. As if this wasn't punishment enough, half of these prisoners inflict "music" on themselves. One can see their cars pulsate to the beat of The Heet or one of their clones.

The surviving automakers and their foreign competition are doing their part. Television commercials show their raciest, lushest models whispering along just below the speed of light, the handsome hunk's blond mop blowing in the backdraft, a supermodel at his side, tresses whipping in the wind. These ads frequently end with the admonition Always Drive Safely. Nobody in Tokyo, Detroit or Munich cares to remember Mahatma Gandhi's observation "There's more to life than increasing its speed." Or the accident insurance rate.

The car hasn't been much of an improvement over the bygone farrier's two-block walk to the livery stable or the grocer's apartment "over the store." Today, the couple too old to drive is in a pretty pickle if they don't live on, say, the 33rd floor of the John Hancock Building or in Peaceful Acres retirement home.

As it is used today, the car is the single greatest pollution source in the country. Yet neither Dan Rather nor his clones have done a really intense segment on the problem. And cars kill a lot more of us than guns without safety locks, drugs in unlocked medicine cabinets or crazed teenagers with Lizzie Borden complexes. Let's see now, what industry is it that does 3.5 prime-time tv ads out of every 10?

Our destructive ways

Maybe it's not so much that the family car, pickup or van is a problem in and of itself, but we tend to use our technology in destructive ways. For instance, any homesteader who tries to do without a pickup or a big trailer is either flat broke or a fool, or some combination of the two. The problem is born when 200,000 cars with single drivers pile downtown in major metropolitan streets five days and 50 weeks of every year. Meanwhile, alternate transportation goes begging, then finally rots. Who wants to take the bus or the metro when it's so neat to cruise on downtown in one's Catera, the Caddy that zigs?

There is hope that a big part of the car pollution problem will eventually go away. It comes from a strange quarter: from technology itself. The personal computer is already making it possible for a considerable number of people to work at home and leave the driving to nobody. Already, people in India and Bangladesh, where an elite is better educated than most North Americans are, is doing systems analysis for firms in the States who can't find talent here.

Is this education?

But we face another dilemma in the U.S.: What is the future for the millions of the products of our public schools who can't read, write or cipher? How can there be genuine education without these basics? Further, our students are burdened with the credentials problem. One must get the diploma, just as the Straw Man did, whether they know anything or not.

In a society that values useless junk "knowledge", any kid who opts not to play the game but who knows many useful and important things is written off as a hopeless ignoramus.

But the diploma that is a lie will not impress the employer's mainframe, even if the holder's "self esteem" is off the top of the dial. This is the other face of our technological progress "problem." The youngsters who can make their computers jump through hoops, with or without credentials, will be the valued resource of the upcoming century.

At first blush, the problems we face as a culture seem to be rooted in our technology, but are they really? Does our national predicament really arise elsewhere? Our national attitude toward our little water planet seems very much like the attitude of the wolf toward the sheep.

Lewis Mumford put it, "...we formed the habit of using the land, not as a home, but as a means to something else—principally as a means to the temporary advantage of profitable speculation and exploitation." Is this attitude, and our tradition of law-made real property, at the root of our love for nuclear-powered clothes dryers and throwaway packaging, along with our penchant for covering thousands of square miles of our countryside with concrete runways for a rapacious single-passenger steel capsule?

Is our posture of speculation and our attitude toward our land—as a resource to be used and in reality thrown away—at the bottom of every major problem we face today? Have the slash-and-burn habits of our European ancestors who first migrated here really changed much?

This peasant's warm regard for the homesteader rests on the freeholder's respect for the land, the attitude of the husbandman. This is the polar opposite of the consumer's credo "I am what I buy," and the sick world of rising expectations, a world which Ivan Illich described as "not simply evil—it can only be spoken of as hell."

Karl Hess said of the ethic of consumerism, of our national penchant for buy-and-throw-away, that its essence "is that those caught in its grasp behave as though the ability to purchase is in fact an ability, a manifestation of merit, of expertise, and further, they behave as though what they purchase actually confers on them real characteristics, actually defines them as human beings."

Really, why should little Leroy learn to read when he can make more than his father earns, just by dealing heroin on the school playground? The solution, our leaders tell us, is to give little Leroy some self-esteem—unearned, undeserved self-esteem for a kid who will never learn anything more sophisticated than techniques for avoiding ending up under a city bridge in a pool of his own blood. Leroy will never even make a decent wage laborer, the grist of the mill of our institutions which have until recently required more and more of this human fodder to go tottering on. We have created a very strange nation with severe social problems and a compulsive missionary complex to reshape the world in our image—a sobering thought, indeed.

Further, our institutions built on wage labor give rise to the quintessential company man, the specialist. From the assembly line worker whose job description is limited to slapping a windshield into Cavaliers, to the attorney who does only limited partnerships, we live in the world of the specialist despite George Bernard Shaw's warning that "no man can be a pure specialist without being in the strictest sense an idiot." We keep proving Shaw's point until we will be faced at last with the medical practitioner who is a specialist in the left great toe. Sorry, but one must take their sore little toe elsewhere.

If one suggests we return to our roots and retrace our steps to determine where we took a false turn, that person is described as a reactionary, a gloom and doomer, unrealistic, and is generally dismissed as an eccentric of no great consequence. If a person suggests that the Agriculture Department's "get big or get out" edict was one such false turn and that the proper advice would have been to get out of commercial one-crop industrial agribusiness, one is admonished that the problems besetting the farmer are complex and will never yield to such simplistic measures.

We peasants just don't understand the problems, you see. Right. It's like taking out your own appendix, like daring to observe the transparency of the emperor's new clothes. We should leave these things to experts—to specialists.

For homesteaders, the way ahead is clear enough. A good example, Amish style, is far better than long sermons like this one if Joe and Jane Sixpack are going to have any 21st century at all. The future could belong to the freeholder, if he isn't buried under an avalanche of escapees from the dying city.

We have what Spengler calls a society entering its cultural winter, when the best possible place to be will be on the land, even if it's half an acre or less. Here's R.H. Tawney again, "...the past has shown no more excellent social order than that in which the mass of the people were masters of the holdings which they plowed and of the tools with which they worked."

In the end, even Henry Ford was moved to observe, "No unemployment insurance can be compared to an alliance between a man and a piece of land."

Not all technological breakthroughs come from giant companies

The latest example of garage tinkerers and basement inventors to come to our attention: Paul Brown, of Kendall, England. "They said it couldn't be done," but he found a way to send phone and data signals along the wires carrying ordinary electric current. Because these wires snake into virtually every home and business, power companies could offer cheap phone and data services. By one estimate, this would lower Internet access costs by 33% to 50%.

And yes, the discovery was made in his garage... after many hours of work, but with a budget of $3,300 for two student assistants.

Pondering technology & money bashers

Greg Holmes
Washington

Many homesteaders, in their letters, express distaste for technology and money, while showing care for "the Earth" and the simple life. While I believe I understand their hearts, I'm afraid their words sound like regurgitated ideological nonsense.

Consider technology bashing. The word "technology" has been pasted with overtones of ominous meaning. No one derides the wheel, but isn't it a technology? Soon the wheel becomes a cart, and eventually you're stuck in a traffic jam, cussing about the modern world.

Are these technology bashers drawing lines: more complex technology is bad, but simpler technology is good? Isn't a car just wheels, levers, and simple chemical reaction? Is a complex series of inventions and ideas really different than just one or two simple innovations? There's no logical sense in that per se—perhaps polluting technologies are bad, or maybe just technologies not within the capabilities of the lone, independent homesteader, but let's keep our criticisms and words accurate.

I hope the day comes when every homesteader can have superconducting, superefficient appliances, solar cells and batteries for dirt cheap, or perhaps buy a simple, non-polluting, cold fusion generator that will make current, inefficient, polluting energy sources extinct. It won't happen if everyone becomes a homesteader. There have to be techno-geeks and greedy capitalists, or in 100 years we really will have problems.

I can understand a yearning for simpler times, but through rose colored glasses, we forget they also had their problems. Today's maligned technologies were the cure for many of those problems, and future technologies can solve today's problems, too. To say that lives will not be improved in a future day is arrogant and lacks vision. We cannot go back, but we will go forward or just stagnate where we are; let's make a decision based on something other than sentimental yearning.

The money bashers also seem to show lack of depth in their rhetoric. Money is simply a tool for exchange (albeit a government manipulated tool). All homesteaders praise "barter". Money standardizes and facilitates this to the nth degree, allowing an exchange network. People in drought plagued areas can eat, everyone can have a diverse diet, and Christmas trees come to Kansas wheat fields. At what point does this become evil—when I trade firewood for a goat, or when I trade shares on Wall Street, or somewhere in between?

To criticize money itself, or the exchanges of free people seems insane. I suspect the money-bashers would rather criticize the interdependence of others, and the necessity of so many exchanges to obtain needs and desires, but why this recurring theme of bashing others to prove the superiority of the homesteading lifestyle? Naturally, those with homesteading hearts have felt the crush of the busy, interdependent world, but don't you imagine the overwhelming majority of folks live happily filling their niche? To the extent that they may be brainwashed consumers "stuck" in such a lifestyle brings up questions of social and economic freedom, not the evil nature of money, and successful homesteaders stand as anomalies in such theories.

"Caring for the Earth" is a term that is wielded as having some sort of almost religious meaning. There are implications that everyone understands, but no one talks about. Being frugal, recycling, and not being consumerist sound like good, self-centered, economic sense, and refraining from chemical farming in favor of organic methods seems less expensive, more healthy, and keeps the farm in natural balance—it's easier to work with nature than against it. Are we being good to the Earth, or just good to ourselves? Each of us must manipulate nature to sustain our lives—we impact the Earth by our very presence. Even caterpillars will kill a tree, and a beaver will dam a stream.

Are any of us wise enough to draw a line, and decide when the Earth is being abused? Is it when we make a clearing for a new chicken coop, or plow up a field, or when a big company makes a strip mine, or perhaps when we use a cast iron pan created from that mine? Can anyone tell me what's better for the Earth, an outhouse or a $2,000 composting toilet; just how do you decide? If property rights are less important than an arbitrary line defining earth abuse, do property rights mean anything?

I think some homesteaders are not content to homestead for themselves, but think everyone should follow their lead. They use terms forged in the fire of ideological debate to describe their homestead values. They criticize and advise, and there's nothing more fun than bringing such rhetoric to the light of reality. Are Countrysiders deciding the way the world should be run, or celebrating and sharing the homesteading lifestyle? Personally, I'm game for either or both, let's just be honest when we're preaching and bring on the next issue.

I've had a little time to ponder some

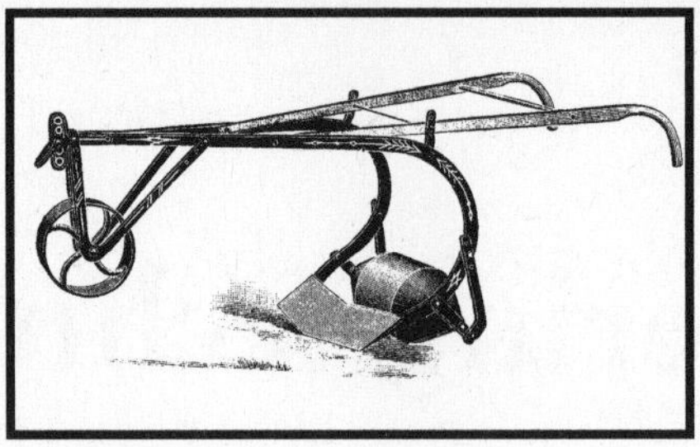

of these thoughts, because they've been with us ever since I became the editor, 30 years ago.

"Where do you draw the line on technology?" some said, even back then. "Hammers and nails are technology. Fire is technology! You can't just pick some arbitrary cutoff point between a caveman's club and a computer and say one side is good and the other side is bad."

Which is true—but irrelevant for those of us who have come to grips with the situation.

It's not technology we're concerned about. It's the use of technology. And it's the cost—not just in dollars, but in the total expense to society, including the environment and individual and community welfare.

Using fire to keep from freezing to death is an acceptable use of that technology. Using fire to burn down your neighbor's house is not.

That's simple enough. But as technology becomes more complex, so do the distinctions. And our philosophy says we have anxieties about technological complexities.

I do take exception to the statement that there will be no scientific and technological progress "if everyone becomes a homesteader." We might not have the same view of technological progress... but I rather suspect that the real problem is that we don't have the same view of homesteading.

I'm intrigued by the number of comets that are discovered by "amateur" astronomers using relatively simple equipment in their backyards. By guys like Jobs and Wozniak, who developed the Apple computer in a garage. By all the people toiling in home shops who come up with creative solutions that make life better or easier.

Advice on buying a greenhouse

"For the first time, our home-started flowers were as big as those in the garden centers."

BEV CARNEY
WISCONSIN

Last spring, we decided to purchase a greenhouse in which to grow our garden seedlings. Neither of us are particularly good at construction and we couldn't put up a lean-to, so we turned to the catalogs.

Boy, were there a lot of decisions to make! We spent hours poring over catalogs and brochures advertising various makes and models ranging from small and cheap to big and extremely expensive. Our favorite was a rigid fiberglass model with screen-type doors and an automatic venting system. It was expensive—a 10' x 12' model would have cost about $2,000 and that was far more than we were prepared to spend. Plus you needed to dig footings and put it in a permanent location—we weren't prepared for that either. Reluctantly, we put that brochure aside.

Although we've been using cold frames for years, neither of us had any greenhouse gardening experience. We weren't exactly sure what we wanted, but we made a list of what we thought was important.

A list of demands

Of major importance was cost. We didn't want to bankrupt ourselves on this purchase. Second, we didn't want to have to replace the plastic every three years or so. We hate using plastic and wanted one to last as long as possible. Third, we wanted one that wasn't on a rigid foundation. If this was a "permanent" structure, it would be added to our property taxes and we would pay for it forever. Plus, being new at this greenhouse stuff, what if we put it in a poor site? Fourth, we wanted the most interior space for the size we would choose. Fifth, we wanted one that we could easily put up by ourselves in an afternoon.

A lengthy list, but we found several different models that met most of these criteria.

Three made the first cut

Working backwards, there were three companies offering "up in an afternoon" models within our price range ($300-$800). The desire for greater interior space ruled out any greenhouse with a "hoop" shape. We wanted straight sided walls, as that wouldn't limit what we could grow close up to those walls.

There were still three models to choose from. All of these were "relatively" portable—that is, you couldn't really pick them up and move them, but you could disassemble and reassemble without digging new foundations. The longevity of the plastic did eliminate one company—their standard greenhouse plastic lasts three to five years and we figure three is probably more the norm.

So we were down to two models: one made of corrugated plastic providing two layers to keep in the heat, and the other made of "rip-stop" fabric supposed to last 10 years. A tough decision. We called for samples of both "fabrics" and bent and stabbed at them to test durability.

But one major trait affecting our choice was light transmission. The corrugated plastic allowed 75% of the light to pass through while the rip-stop fabric allowed 85%. We weren't sure if 10% difference was critical or not, but it seemed that the more light the better, so we chose the "rip-stop" model. And after one growing season with this greenhouse, we're real happy with it.

Our greenhouse ended up as a 11' x 12' structure and cost $529 including shipping. This price included the "optional" double zipper doors for each end and the anchoring kit as well. This model had the added attraction of being less expensive than most. We felt we got a good amount of greenhouse for our money. We have learned some things that might help you if you decide to go greenhouse shopping.

Ventilation is important

Probably the most important is the issue of a self-venting system for your greenhouse. It gets mighty hot in there. And when it gets that hot, your plants dry out quicker than you can imagine. Even with both doors open, the interior temperature usually hovers around 90. Fortunately, I'm home from April 16 to January 1 so I was available to make sure the plants were watered often enough. (Even with all the attention I gave them, they still dried out on me a couple of times.) If you can't be home all day, automatic venting would probably keep the temperature low enough to prevent such rapid drying. Or you could check into some sort of automatic watering device (perhaps on a timer) that would water the plants during the day. Or perhaps a wicking system might work. The venting and watering system would probably both require electricity, although I think there are some solar-powered, temperature-controlled vents available. Perhaps a box fan set in the doorway would provide enough air movement to force out some of that hot air.

Second, your greenhouse will be cold at night, especially in early to mid-Spring. Here in Wisconsin, we had a very cool spring and we spent hours moving the plants from the greenhouse to a warmer building before we finally broke down and bought a heater. A 11' x 12' structure is not really big enough to store enough heat retaining material to guard against nighttime freezes. So plan on either moving your plants a lot early in the season, or using a good heater. We had to spend $60 to get one strong enough to heat the space. And of course, we soon found that we had to spend another $40 to get proper extension cords to run the 150' out to the greenhouse. So your greenhouse will cost you money to own! Perhaps you can get a "lean-to" greenhouse and use the stored heat from a building or a wall, thus saving the need to heat.

Buy more greenhouse than you think you'll want. Ours was jammed to the gills after the first season. Fortunately, we can add on to ours if we want to, but I think for now, we'll just be more selective in what we grow.

We can probably be more creative in the use of space too. We had sawhorses set up with ladders as shelves. We could set out about 44 standard size flats without using the hanging space or double layers of shelves. Already, though, I have sold four flats of flowers and two tomato seedlings and I wasn't trying to sell anything. So the potential for some extra income can be added incentive. That might make expansion worthwhile.

Be prepared to "babysit" your house for a while. We put our greenhouse up on a Saturday and on the very next day we were hit with 30-50 mile per hour sustained winds for two days and nights. Our neighbors just assumed we had lost the structure, but we hadn't. Unfortunately, we hadn't quite finished erecting it so it popped off one anchor. We were home though, so we could fix the problem shortly after it happened.

But just like a cold frame, you can't just put your plants in the greenhouse and check them once a day. Even regular strong winds whipped the doors from their fasteners, flailing them all about. (We've since learned better ways of holding up the doors.) Like I've said, the plants dry out incredibly fast.

When situating your greenhouse, try to put it where you'll have access to water. During the height of "seedling season" we were hauling 10-12 gallons of water daily to the plants. This year, we plan on asking for hoses for Christmas!

All in all, we've been very pleased with greenhouse gardening. Our tomato plants were stocky with very thick stems and produced rapidly and well in the garden. Our flowers also took right off and for the first time, our home-started flowers were as big as those in the garden centers.

We did find, however, that summer growing doesn't work too well. We planted three tomatoes directly into the ground in mid-June. They didn't do well at all. First off, we needed to remember to water them and we frequently forgot. Most importantly though, it got hot in there, frequently 110° and higher. That's just too hot for the plants to thrive and set fruit. We had hoped to get the plants going well and keep them after frost, but it didn't work out (at least this year). In the future, we'd also like to grow greens out there until at least Christmas.

Can this greenhouse be made to pay for itself? I don't know. I do know I can easily sell more seedlings. While vegetables are popular, there is increasing interest in the flowers that gardening centers just don't carry. In addition to the flats I sold, I gave away at least six more and probably could have charged for them.

While seedling sales for us will never pay the whole price, we are very pleased with the quality of the seedlings we raised.

Keeping deer out of the garden

Faye Buice
Georgia

I would like to share a trick we used this year to keep deer out of our garden. When I say "garden" I mean pea patch. The deer ate a lot of our garden before we tried this.

When the peas came up and had three leaves we began to see deer tracks all through the patch. We knew we had to do something if we were going to harvest any peas. I remembered reading that deer don't like strong odors and the only thing I had on hand was a few boxes of moth balls.

Our pea patch is surrounded on three sides by hardwoods, so we broadcast handfuls of moth balls through the tree line all around the patch, then hung old pantyhose by one leg tied to a tree limb and a handful of moth balls in the toe of the other leg that hung about three feet from the ground. The odor was very strong.

We did not lose even one pea vine and harvested about 15 bushels of field peas.

This spring I am going to tie bundles of moth balls in my fruit trees just to see if it will keep worms out of my fruit (after the blooms fall, of course; I don't want to keep the bees off the blooms). I am also going to tie small bundles of moth balls to part of our corn stalks just to see if it has any effect on corn worms.

Deter crows, too

We have another trick to keep crows from pulling up our young corn. We cut black garbage bags into strips, leaving about four inches at the uncut end. This makes a rattling sound at the smallest breeze and is almost constantly in motion when hung from long sticks pushed into the soft, plowed ground at an angle. By the time the young corn is big enough for the first cultivating (a couple of weeks) you can remove the sticks and garbage bags and store them away for the next season. We have used them several times before having to make more. These can also be hung from any tree limbs that happen to hang out over the edge of the field. We haven't lost any corn to crows since we started using this trick, about 10 years ago.

Some readers are alarmed when anyone mentions using moth balls in or around the garden. "Look at the label," they say. "Do you really want those toxins in the soil that grows your food?"

An alternative is to sprinkle the plants with a solution of eggs mixed in water.

Spinach: a great cool-weather crop

Elizabeth & Crow Miller
New York

When we grow spinach, we're dealing with a strictly cool-weather crop. As soon as long days and heat come, spinach refuses to produce. We've tried heavy mulches, drip irrigation and shady locations to extend its growing season into summer. Something in spinach's genetic make-up triggers the plant to send up a seed stalk as soon as those long, hot days arrive.

Oddly, spinach will germinate with ground temperatures as low as 35ºF, but will refuse with soil heat above 80ºF. This is quite the opposite of most vegetables. We've found it better to grow Malabar spinach, beet greens and Swiss chard for summer use.

We plant our spinach from early February (in our solar greenhouse) to early May, and pick up again with plantings in late fall. This planting system frees us from bolting spinach and poor germination.

Spinach loves nitrogen

We've also found that spinach is both shallow rooted and a lover of nitrogen. Plants like spinach, which need to make rapid growth for best flavor and tenderness, do better in a light soil than a heavy one. By working some compost into the top couple of inches of soil, we put the nitrogenous plant food right where it will do the most good for those shallow roots.

The only other ingredients needed are a micro-nutrient foliar spray (fish 20%, seaweed 80%=3 ounces into a gallon of water) and water, but not too much. It is best to plant spinach in a well-drained, sunny location (spinach prefers full sunlight along with cool weather).

We sow the seed in ground that has been thoroughly watered a day or two previously, so that by the time the seeds are in the ground all excess water will have percolated or evaporated, yet there will be plenty of water held in the germination zone by soil particles.

As long as the soil doesn't dry out, don't water again until after the seedlings emerge. This greatly cuts down on the possibility of dampness-related diseases.

After the plants are established, we water whenever the top 1/2 inch of soil dries out. We also cultivate shallowly around the seedlings to remove weeds and promote fast growth.

From an initial sowing of one seed to the inch in rows a foot apart, we thin to a plant every four inches. I cultivate after thinning, and again at mid-growth if time permits. Handled like this, spinach becomes an easy vegetable to grow.

We begin harvesting when I can pick enough leaves to make a meal. By successive sowings every 10 days, we have a supply all spring. I sow in rows by themselves, or between rows marked out for large cole crops like cabbage.

During the fall and winter months, we pick the outer leaves as long as the plants generate rapid new growth, extending the season. I've found that, protected in a cold frame from freezing temperatures, spinach will produce all winter.

This crop grows best between October and May, just at the time of the year when nutritious homegrown vegetables are in shortest supply.

A simple garden seeder can save your back

Grant Eversoll
Indiana

Being a physically challenged homesteader, I sometimes have to find easier ways to do things. Like most people I have good days and bad days, but my bad days can put me out of commission for a week or more at a time. And when it's time to put out the garden you sometimes have to work around the weather. I cannot be unable to work when it's time to put seeds in the ground.

Running the big red rear-tine tiller is one thing I can do that doesn't hurt my back. Using it is just like a slow stroll in the park.

But putting seeds in the ground… that's a different story. Ten minutes of that and I'm done.

I looked into getting a garden seeder but the price range did not fit my budget. So I made one myself in about 15 minutes. It could have been made more substantial but I needed it now and I was not sure if my patent was going to work so I slapped it together with that good old handyman's friend, duct tape.

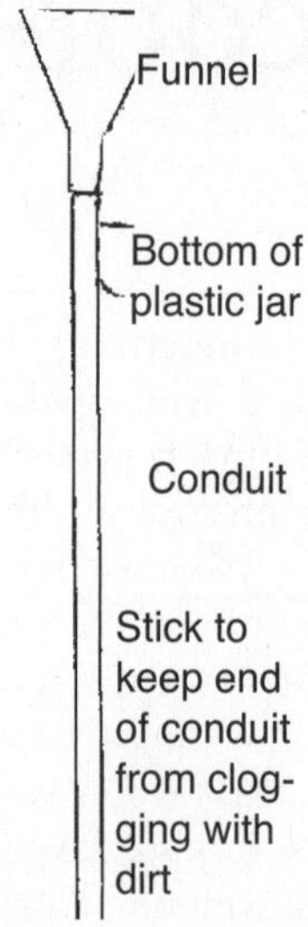

My seeder consists of one four-foot piece of conduit, one funnel, the plastic bottom of a peanut butter jar, and duct tape. These were all items I had laying around the shop.

The funnel and the conduit are pretty self-explanatory, but the peanut butter jar is the key to making this thing work.

Tape the jar to the side of the conduit right below the funnel, open side up, and fill it with seeds. You can reach into the seed cup and drop the seeds into the funnel without losing any seeds or fumbling with seed sacks.

With this method I can space my seeds better so there is less waste. I save time. And most of all, I save my back.

The only drawback I have found could be remedied easily. You cannot rest the bottom of the conduit on the ground or it will get clogged with dirt. This could be fixed by taping a stick to the bottom of the conduit that will protrude past the end of the pipe, keeping the opening out of the soil.

I planted all my seeds with this and the garden looked better, with fewer bare spots and more uniform plantings.

As we homesteaders know, you can do anything if you try.

Shower simple

Dorothy Schmelzer
Texas

Here's how to enjoy a shower without piped in running water.

For several months I have been using a camping "solar" shower bag. I save gallons of water using only one big soda bottle per shower.

"I don't mind doing chores. I can rest while you're doing my homework."

The camping shower bag is on a heavy clothes hanger so it can be hung on the shower curtain rod.

To fill the bag, I use a large soda bottle filled with warm/hot water from the tap. The bottle's mouth fits into the bag for filling water. Of course, the solar bag, or the soda bottles, could also be heated in the sun. The bag has a long hose that can be easily directed to any part of the body for the water spray.

I use a recycled "409" spray bottle (it has an expanded spray) filled with diluted bubble bath ($1 a bottle here) to spray my whole body, except my face, which is done separately. I then rinse off using the solar bag spray hose.

If I didn't have a bathtub, I would use a wash tub or a plastic storage bin to stand in and a plastic shower curtain made of recycled plastic from a furniture store dumpster.

The greywater can be used to water trees, shrubs and flowers.

To avoid fiddling with the hose open and shut valve, I use a clothes pin to pin the hose on the side at the top of the bag so the unused water will not leak out.

I use the solar bag hose to rinse my head when I wash my hair, too.

Camping solar shower bags can be purchased at sport and camping stores or from Real Goods, 555 Leslie St., Ukiah, CA 95482-5576; www.realgoods.com.

This retaining wall at a home in Ogden, Utah, made from used tires, is both attractive and safe. (Note the rocking horse swing, also made of used tires.)

Tire crafting and gardening: A toxin and pollution report

PAUL FARBER
UTAH

Because of recent letters of concern, I have collected much in formation on the toxicity of the products I use in tirecrafting. These sources include OSHA, EPA, USDA, *Toxics A to Z*, Material Safety Data Sheets, and others.

I can only find one toxic substance in the rubber tire: zinc. Zinc and cadmium are in sheet metal galvanize. Toxins are added to some silicone caulk/sealants to resist mildew. I could find no record of toxins in acrylic latex paint nor in the bonding agent "Emulsa Bond."

Toxics A to Z says "Zinc is a naturally occurring trace element required for human health, although there are more reports of adverse effects from zinc deficiency than from zinc overload. Compounds of zinc will cause stomach distress if too much is ingested... Because the body rids itself efficiently of zinc, there is little risk of buildup."

Ground or chopped tires in growing medium

USDA researcher and compost expert Rufus L. Chaney, Ph. D., reports, "Tires normally have 0.5% Zn (zinc). In many situations, when rubber was used in plant growth media, or burned tires residues were on soils, Zn killed plants. There is an interaction between soil or medium pH and Zn toxicity. At a reasonable rate of application, rubber would be a high grade Zn fertilizer over time because the Zn in rubber is purified, with very low Cd (cadmium) concentrations."

Gardening in tire retainers and containers

I was told of a study where submerged tires with exposed metal belts leached trace amounts of heavy metals into the water, and might do the same in your garden. I have not found the source of this report, but for obvious hazardous reasons, tires with exposed wires should be avoided.

Dr. Chaney said that whole tires start to decay within a few decades (20 years or more), and removing the sidewalls or turning them inside out would probably not accelerate this process.

To avoid zinc contamination, I recommend that at least once every ten years, either replace or clean and coat all your garden retainers and containers, inside and out, with a toxic-free sealant. I use exterior acrylic latex mixed with "Emulsa Bond." I also rotate the soil in my vegetable retainers every year and retire it to my flower gardens after five years.

Water gardens and fish ponds

In my latest *Tire Recycling Is Fun* book, I recommend using galvanized steel for the bottom of the water containers. I was assured that this product is harmless. I am no longer sure.

From Toxics A to Z we learn that galvanized steel is steel with a thin protective layer of zinc or zinc alloy

"Tire crafting" is a far cry from simply filling an old tire with dirt and planting something in it, as this attractive fountain demonstrates.

which includes cadmium. Unlike zinc, cadmium has no known health value, and can accumulate in the human body to cause many chronic diseases. Cadmium is widely used in a myriad of products and industrial processes, and is a trace element in commercial fertilizers. From these sources cadmium is taken up by plants and animals and enters the food supply.

I am currently experimenting with covering the sheet of metal with fiberglass cloth between several layers of latex/E.B. paint. Try plastic instead of sheet metal. I am also testing scratched plastic windows discarded from a local glazing service. Concrete works, but is too heavy and permanent for me.

Coat the inside of your water containers with a toxic-free sealant before you use them.

Used tire pollution

Used tires provide an ideal haven and nursery for a variety of vermin, including mice, rats, spiders, wasps, and mosquitoes. I was told of a wall of tires stacked around a race track in southwest Arizona. When seen at night through headlights, it sparkled and shimmered, the entire surface being covered by cockroaches.

Fire is always a danger. Tires are not easy to ignite, but once started, they burn extremely hot and are difficult to extinguish. Tires are more likely to catch fire while being stored than are the finished projects.

Respect fire codes in every aspect of tire crafting.

Keep on hand only as many tires as you can craft within a month. If you must store them, re-stack them and dump any accumulated water at least twice a month.

Visual pollution

Few things look more trashy than used tires scattered or heaped around a place. This also reflects on the character of the people who live there.

All tire projects can be made functional while still looking like junk. The more common examples are seen in landscaping and gardening. These projects are either poorly thought out, or aesthetics were thought too difficult, or never considered. These prevalent examples are why tirecrafting has such a bad reputation.

Well planned useful tire projects, skillfully and attractively crafted, displayed in pleasing surroundings, will inspire all who see them, and will convert the skeptics as well.

Benefits of container gardening

The physical and psychological health benefits, as well as family and community bonding associated with home and communal gardening, are all well documented, but gardening is available to only a fraction of those who desire to participate.

Modified tire retainers filled with homemade compost/growing medium provide the only method of gardening that can offer affordable, available, quality gardening to everyone, no matter how limited their funds or poor their existing soil, or how limited or irregular the available space. They can be used where the essentials of gardening never existed before, such as on a rocky hillside, ocean beach, alkali flat, porch, mobile home space, house boat, roof top, and on and on.

Many who were previously excluded can experience the joys of gardening. Tire containers are safe, sturdy and flexible. They can be held onto, leaned against or bumped into, without injury to you or the container. They can be modified to accommodate anyone, including those with poor balance; who have limited ability to bend over, stoop or reach; are wheelchair confined, or blind. Children as well as the mentally challenged can enjoy their very own garden. The therapeutic value of making and painting their own containers is also priceless.

Health, safety and social benefits from tire projects far outweigh any easily preventable risk factors.

Get minimal water use and maximum crop yields with no hoses—no electricity—no moving parts:

Grow your own food with totally automatic watering

Horace McCracken
Arizona

This garden, in the high desert of Arizona, was not watered at the surface all summer. Water is supplied automatically below the growing soil, and "soaks" upward by wicking, or capillary action, as well as being drawn up by the roots. Production was abundant and the vegetables were of top quality. No pesticides were used. This 3' x 16' bed and another small one, not visible here, produced approximately 250 pounds of vegetables, of 20 different kinds, in 1997.

Note that only the area within the enclosure contained the growing soil and was watered. The various squash vines traveled out beyond the edges—almost blanketing two juniper trees—and the tomatoes grew upward in the 8' tall cage. Thus the system multiplies the benefits of the watered area and works perfectly in barren, infertile places, such as rocky terrain, paved areas, concrete floors, and rooftops.

How it works

Water is maintained underneath the growing bed in a series of perforated plastic "distribution tubes," which are made from irrigation pipe. The outer annular orifice is partially filled with fine sand, which comes up out of the orifice and spreads out under the growing bed. Water is held about 3" deep in the distribution tubes by a float valve.

Garden sizes may range from a few square feet on up to thousands for commercial use.

The distribution tube

This design has been developed to fulfill four functions:

1) Contain the liquid water beneath the growing bed so it does not leak.

2) Provide a sure and controlled method of distributing water into the sand layer.

3) Permit visual inspection of the water level.

4) Make it easy to remove those roots which can live under water and can continue growing until they plug up the water inlet. (Most vegetables will not do so.)

It has been determined that water will soak outward at least 2-1/2 feet from the center point. This contributes to the recommendation that the maximum bed width be about 4', and suggests a spacing between tubes of approximately 40", as seen here.

The float valve

The float valve itself is an ordinary stock watering tank float valve which has been modified for this purpose. The present material of choice is redwood, coated with silicone sealant. The transparent cover facilitates inspection. This is all ready to hook up from a supply hose, and thence to the garden.

Note that the supply may be at any pressure, from that of a shallow tank just above the valve, on up to city water pressure.

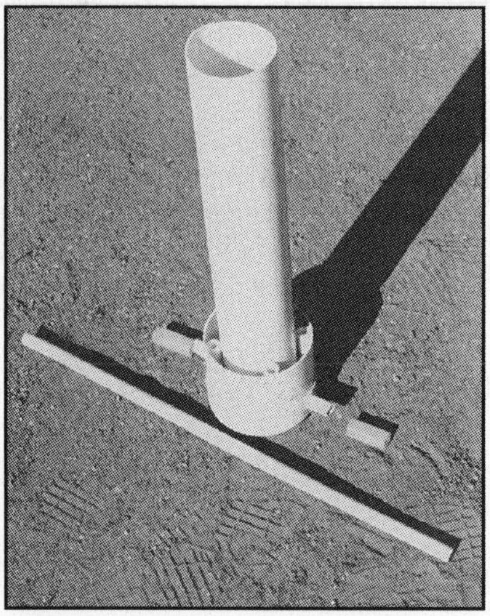

Distribution tube and connecting tubing

Distribution tube, cross section

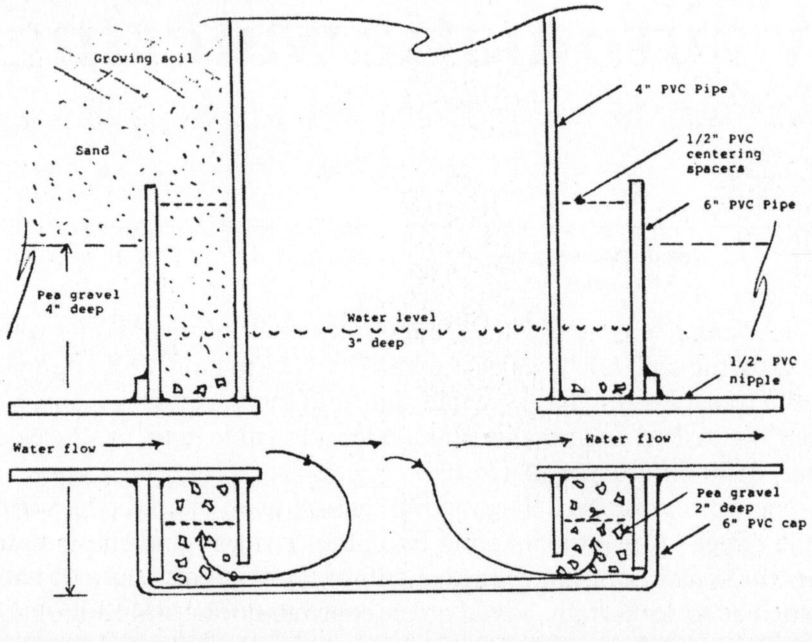

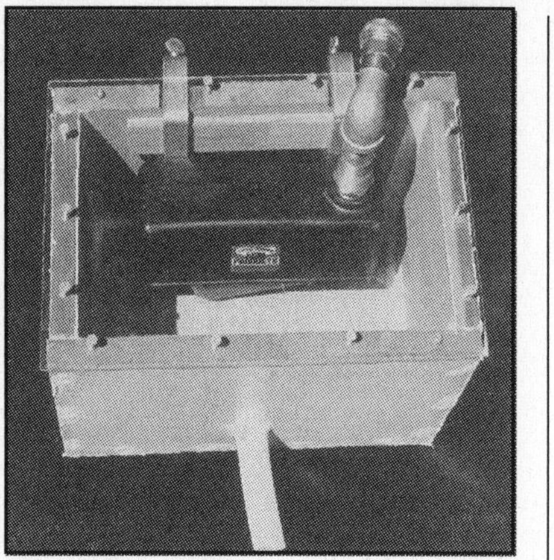

Float valve

Construction

Used railroad ties would be another way to build the walls but, as checked out here, these would cost more and require more labor. The bed could also be set into the ground, but in most cases I believe it will be preferable to construct it as a raised bed.

Pressure-treated lumber would be another option, but it is difficult to avoid concerns that those toxic chemicals might leach into the soil. Ordinary lumber, of course, would last only a few years.

Ferro-cement deserves consideration. You could also think about building the garden inside an actual stock watering tank, but these are unnecessarily expensive for this purpose.

It appears undesirable to have a bed more than 4' wide, as it would become unduly difficult to attend to the plants.

Note that there is no limitation as to the actual shape of the enclosure. It may be round, or follow a contour around a hill, be configured to fit a decorative garden, etc.

Waterproofing the bed

The entire floor and enclosure may be of concrete, but making the floor this way seems unnecessarily expensive. The preferred choice is to line the bottom and 8" up the walls with an impervious membrane. Ordinary 6 mil polyethylene seems too light for this service. A few of these gardens have been built using a vinyl impregnated fiberglass cloth, which is expensive.

Level the area and outline the enclosure.

The best present choice is an industrial "pond liner" plastic film, made of laminated high-and-low-density polyethylene. I buy it from the manufacturer, cut to my width of 5'7", and I cut it to the length required by the customer.

To obtain the length needed for a given bed, add 1'8" to the inside length of the bed. For example, for this 12' bed, the membrane length was 13'8".

The people who build industrial ponds could not be satisfied with a membrane which could be penetrated by rodents. The manufacturer reports no problem in this area. Based also on my 40 years of experience with water systems, I am confident that this material will be free of rodent damage.

The second course of blocks holds down the edges of the membrane. Note that the final distribution tube has been moved aside to show the opening for the storm water overflow.

Assembly of the membrane and water system.

That final tube is, of course, sealed at its outlet.

Remember that the function of this membrane is not to contain liquid water, but rather to prevent water in the moist growing bed from soaking down below and being lost.

I see no effective limit as to the length of such a system, up to perhaps a hundred meters. At some point, the size of the interconnecting tubing would become a limitation. Presumably one would not make individual beds that long, as such length could become a handicap in attending the garden.

Note also that a single float valve can supply a number of beds in parallel, just so long as they are all at the same level.

With regard to storm water overflow, note that in ordinary gardening, when a big storm comes along the excess water just drains on down through and out to waste, carrying nutrients away with it. With this system, a container can be provided at the outlet to catch such valuable water, and it can be returned to the garden through the distribution system (or sprinkled on the surface.)

Turn the water on, let the level get stabilized, and adjust for 3" depth desired in the distribution tubes by raising or lowering the entire float box assembly.

I think it's important to insure aeration under the growing bed, here using pea gravel. Such gravel may be less expensive than soil in some locations.

The gravel depth shown here is 4".

Ordinary concrete construction sand is too coarse to soak water adequately. In my region there are occasional strong winds with blowing dust. This dust settles in low places and behind obstructions, and has proven to be an excellent choice for soaking up the water. I sift it through 1/4" screen to remove large objects. I don't want the sand to go all the way to the bottom of the annular orifice, so about 2" of pea gravel is put in at the bottom. Then the sand goes into the orifice to below the level at which the

A layer of gravel is installed.

water is held, so that it always "has its toes in water."

Spreading out on top of the pea gravel then, this 2" layer of sand continues all the way to cover the bed of gravel.

Here it can be seen that the water is beginning to soak outward after a few hours.

In other locations, river mud may be a suitable material for the "sand" layer. For larger projects, the choice of these materials may need to be done on a case-by-case basis.

The growing medium is being installed.

The growing medium

These bed walls were built up to a total of 24" using three concrete blocks and the cap block. It appears that an optimum depth of growing soil is about 14". Some vegetables can do well with less, and a few prefer more, but this is a good single number.

So we start with 4" of pea gravel, plus 2" of sand, plus 14" of soil, for a total of 20". If the walls were made with half block on top (4" high instead of 8"), this would have worked. In that case, the growing soil would have been piled up a little higher than the top edges, because it will settle with the passage of time. Doing it with the 24" walls, it will settle down below the top edge, which can be an advantage. If trying to start plants as early as possible in the spring, it is necessary to cover the bed when freezing is expected, and the raised edges make this easy. (I had to do that, I believe, five times last year.)

A layer of fine sand is applied.

A close-up view of the distribution tube, the gravel and the sand layer.

In this case, the growing soil was made up of about 40% well-aged horse manure which I ran through a shredder, 40% wind blown silt, and a few other materials, including a little aged chicken manure, aged compost, perlite and shredded newspaper. A few pounds of ground blue crab shells were mixed in to contribute trace elements. I would have used more seaweed if I had had it.

Earthworms thrived in this year's garden, and I will put some in as soon as the soil is moist.

A great deal remains to be learned about the soil mixture(s) and customers' experience is solicited. All such information will be assembled and made available in subsequent years.

Caps on tubes

It is desirable to keep the distribution tubes covered to prevent entry of debris and small animals.

pH, soil testing

For most household vegetables, a pH around 6.4 is a good average, while a few prefer it slightly on the alkaline side, around 7.5. For best results, it will be worthwhile to use litmus paper and a simple home soil test kit to make these determinations at the start-up and a few times a year. These materials are commonly available in hardware and garden stores.

For serious/commercial gardening, it will be desirable to have two or more growing beds, maintained at optimum pH for the plant selection. Soil test kits I have seen list the pH preferences of many common plants.

Watering

Seeds/transplants are watered at the surface for two or three weeks, long enough to get their roots down into the permanently moist zone. After that, the plants get all the water they want, never too much nor too little. Yield is maximized, commonly being multiples of those of ordinary surface-watered gardening.

Adding fertilizers at the surface, as is commonly recommended, will not accomplish much, as the surface stays dry. If the needed nutrients are available in soluble form, it is very easy to fertilize the whole garden immediately and uniformly by putting them into the feed water supply. Such nutrients become available to the plants beginning the first day. "Teas," made by soaking manure, compost, etc., are a valid option.

The surface of the soil stays dry to the touch. It amounts to a permanent mulch two or three inches deep, greatly restraining the loss of water by evaporation from the surface. Of course, when the rain does come, the plants use that water and don't draw as much from below. This adjustment is entirely automatic.

Water conservation

Based on my long experience gardening here and there most of my life, I believe that the water economy will be substantial. My guess is that this system will save 25% compared to conventional gardening, producing the same amount of food.

Salt accumulation

When watering at the surface, by any method, some portion of the water always evaporates from the soil, resulting in a buildup of salts. This is a widespread and serious problem with irrigation.

With the watering system described here, such buildup has to be reduced, probably greatly, because evaporation from the surface is greatly reduced. In this high desert climate, the 12" of annual rainfall we get may be sufficient to rinse away such accumulation as does occur.

Plant selection

So far, I and others using this system have grown dozens of varieties of vegetables, herbs, and flowers. More than 90% of the species tried have grown successfully. I did not have pH testing in the early stages, and imbalances there surely accounted for some of the 10%. Plant selection will vary widely around the world, and I will assemble and pass along such information as it becomes available.

What I can say with confidence at this point is that this method of watering is beneficial to virtually all ordinary residential and commercial plants.

Flowers can be grown this way, of course. Suppose that you have an apartment complex, with requirements for keeping the vegetation in good order. Automatic watering would translate into measurable dollar savings of water and labor rather quickly.

Greenhouse use

This system works excellently in a greenhouse. For example, last winter Barbara Kerr, the solar cooking specialist, got hundreds of tomatoes from one plant, and had to keep cutting it back to prevent it from overrunning the room.

Organic gardening

With this method, you can be just as free of synthetic fertilizers and pesticides as you want. One fact stands out: strong, healthy plants resist insect attacks better than weak/diseased ones. No pesticides were used on this garden all last summer. Some squash bugs did begin to appear toward the end of the season. They have the potential to wipe out a whole garden of squash, but they weren't numerous enough to prevent me from getting a bumper crop. I didn't have any problems with aphids, and I picked off a dozen tomato worms. Diligence will always be needed in this matter. There are many sources of information on such controls as soap solutions, diatomaceous earth, biological predators, etc.

How much will it cost?

By way of illustration, for a system of the size shown, the costs (not counting gravel, sand or growing medium) were about:

Blocks (78 @ 87¢, 26 @ 64¢)	$85
Membrane ($1.31 per lineal foot, 13.74 ft.)	$18
Float valve assembly	$50
Distribution tubes (4 @ $25)	$100
Tubing, inlet/outlet	$10
TOTAL	$263

Compared to hydroponics

I built and operated a small hydroponics system once, have read about them, and have visited a few residential and commercial installations, but don't yet have a good direct comparison. The indications I have at present are that this method does the same job and costs far less than hydroponics, and does not require electricity nor all the attention to soluble fertilizers.

Using solar distilled feed water

This gardening work amounts to a branch-off from my decade of pioneering solar distillation. In many places around the world where people need/prefer to live but where food and drinking water are being imported from great distances, it can be economically rational to use solar stills to purify saline water for the garden.

For instance, while installing such a dual system last year on the island of Saint Martin, in the Caribbean, I bought one tomato, at $2.50 per pound, that had been imported from France! In my opinion, the residents of that island would be ahead financially and would be more secure if they had several thousand of these gardens.

I can supply solar stills, and am willing, as a consultant, to teach others how to build them.

Security

Those of you with long memories will recall the tens of millions of "victory gardens" during World War II. By now, most of the people in the industrialized world have made themselves dependent on importation of food and energy from far-away places. That transportation system is vulnerable to disruption. It is a deeply satisfying sense of security to be growing somewhere around half of one's own food, and doing solar cooking, solar food drying, canning, and root cellar storage.

Other benefits

This method makes gardening possible for some people whose health or busy schedule would otherwise prevent it.

A major benefit is that it makes gardening a lot more fun. One can enjoy it free of the drudgery of dragging hoses around every day.

You may have heard of some activity being "about as exciting as watching grass grow." Well, we may be a little oversold on the benefits of "excitement" in this society, but I can assure you that drinking lemonade in the shade and watching your garden grow can be very satisfying indeed.

A name for the system

I would dearly love to come up with a name for this system in a class with Kodak™ or Frigidaire™, but so far no luck. If one of you can come up with a winner in this department, I will give you a nice reward.

"My favorite tool"

DR® Field and Brush Mower gets high marks

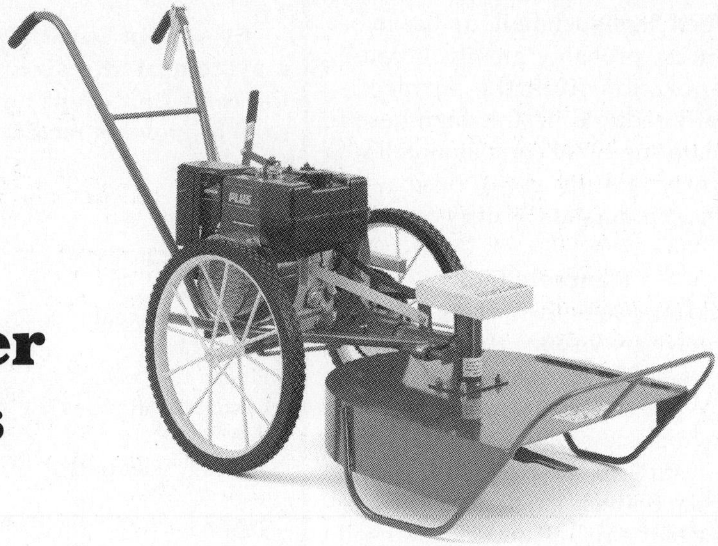

Bruce Pankratz
Minnesota

After a few summers of watching an army of black raspberries march across my land I knew I had to fight back. Armed successively with scythe, garden shears and gas-powered trimmer, I fruitlessly retaliated before finally surrendering. The scythe was hurting my back, the shears took too long, and even the gas-powered trimmer was no match for the brush. I knew the only way I was going to keep the black raspberries and brush from taking over my land was to get a brush or sicklebar mower.

After sending for information from the ads in the country magazines I finally settled on the DR® Field and Brush Mower. The first time I used it I was so excited I decided I wanted to do a testimonial and get my picture in the newsletter *Country Home Products* sends to people who buy their products.

My chance came the next Spring when I was on my land in northern Wisconsin. I was mowing around a tree when I heard the distinct clang you hear as a mower hits a rock—then the silence of a dead engine. I had accidentally nicked rocks before, but this one sounded like a direct hit. I pulled the mower back, thinking I had broken something, but found the blade had actually cut the top off of a big rock.

The chunk of rock was about 12" long, 5" wide and 3" high. It must have had some cracks started already, so when the mower came along it actually chopped off the top.

This was my big chance. I called for my dad, who was visiting for the day, to come over and take my picture holding the chunk of rock for my testimonial. That done, I examined the mower for damage and could find nothing wrong except some minor dents in the blade.

We had used a disposable camera. It must have been defective, because the picture never turned out. That was probably good though. Mowing rocks is dumb.

But the story does show several things about the DR®. First, the mower is rugged. Second, it really cuts. Third, its safe use requires country common sense. Fourth, it is easy to use. And fifth, it's fairly easy to maintain.

What the story does not illustrate is that you have to pay for what you get.

Rugged

This mower is like a larger, supercharged version of a regular lawn mower. It has one blade for lighter work which mulches, and a second heavy duty (five pound) blade. (By the way, I cut the rock with the lighter one.) The mower looks somewhat crude with its simple design using belts and pulleys. The belts slip rather than anything shearing off when you hit immovable objects.

Cutting

With an 8 horsepower engine, the mower goes easily through the black raspberries on my property in northern Wisconsin. The blade chops up what it cuts so often it seems like the raspberries have vanished after the magic machine passes over an area. Heavier cutting, like bushes with several dozen 1/2" trunks, is slower but possible. I have cut down small trees up to 1" in diameter but a small saw is a better tool in these cases. The mower does not mulch trees.

Common sense

The DR® is not a city toy. Its power can turn little rocks into bullets that ricochet off tree trunks back towards your face. Eye protection is mandatory. Its value in going up hills and over small logs means you mow in places you would never dream of mowing in the city. With that comes the need for extra caution. I wear shoes with steel toes when mowing, but fortunately have not found out if they do much good against the blade. It also is tempting to work around the mower while the blade is spinning when common sense says it's time to shut it down until you are ready to mow again.

Easy to use

The mower takes a few tries to start when I have let it sit for a month, but once started it starts up right away when you shut it down temporarily. Once you start the mower you pull back on a long lever to engage the blade and squeeze a handle to make the mower move forward. That's it for controls, other than the choke on the engine.

Easy to maintain

The manual is clear, with good illustrations. For someone with minimal skills with fixing machinery the manual serves the purpose. The manual has checklists for daily use and seasonal storage. The company's newsletter also has reminders about getting ready for storing the machine for winter and getting it ready again in the spring. There is a separate manual for the engine, but it only addresses simple items and does not cover fixing the engine, which is something many people would not attempt anyway.

Cost

The biggest drawback is cost. I bought the mower for $1,250, plus an amount I cannot remember for shipping, in 1995. You can answer an ad in a magazine for any of the mowers and the companies will send you their current prices periodically for the next several years. Country Home Products has prices that change throughout the year. They are the lowest in the off-season so we bought in January. The company will ship to a local trucking warehouse so you can pick up the box and save a little more money that way.

Country Home Products also sells other items. Based on my experience with three seasons of using this mower I definitely am thinking about saving my money for their Power Wagon to haul firewood up the hill to our future retirement house. Maybe then I can find a way to get my picture in their newsletter.

Wild foods:

Please don't eat the daisies... (but daylilies are okay)

René Fahey
New York

More than 40 different wild foods are found on our New York homestead, and over half of them grow within an acre of our log cabin.

Wild foods are both practical and delicious. Our table is adorned with them, deliciously prepared, almost every day of the year.

These food plants are used all over the world. The same plants that you may have looked at as "just weeds" in your backyard are eaten as delicacies in many countries.

Foraged plants are an important part of every homestead. They have been our mainstay in hard times and in times of plenty. They are a delicious source of variety and enjoyment. In fact, many of the wild foods that grow on our homestead are so good that we cultivate them in our garden for fresh vegetables in summer as well as through the winter.

In this article I will cover one of the most productive wild foods—daylilies.

Not a good first impression

We were trying out a new food. I excitedly dug up a large quantity of daylily tubers.

I had read that cooked daylily tubers have a delicious flavor and a texture similar to sweet corn.

After they were cooked they had a delightful golden color that made them look delicious. After seasoning this new food with oil and salt, they were ready to eat.

The first few spoonfuls tasted quite good—tender and somewhat crunchy with a mild sweet flavor all its own, but nothing like sweet corn.

I could not enjoy it for long! After the first bite or two I began to notice an unpleasant aftertaste that was quite mild but enough to make eating daylily tubers at a meal undesirable. No one else at the meal enjoyed them either.

We all knew that some foods are excellent for keeping you alive when you would otherwise starve. Daylilies fit into this survival food category perfectly.

I almost decided never to serve daylily tubers at a meal again. But I discovered that sometimes even the worst tasting foods can be made into delicious delicacies that can be served at the finest meals for the pickiest eaters. After experimenting, I came up with a recipe that makes daylily tubers into the gourmet food you would expect from the wild.

I have served this daylily dish to my students at the survival course and they all declared it delicious.

To my family, daylilies have become not just a survival food, but a treat looked forward to by everyone. Daylilies are one of the most abundant year-round wild foods. When other foods are low you can count on daylilies being there when you need them.

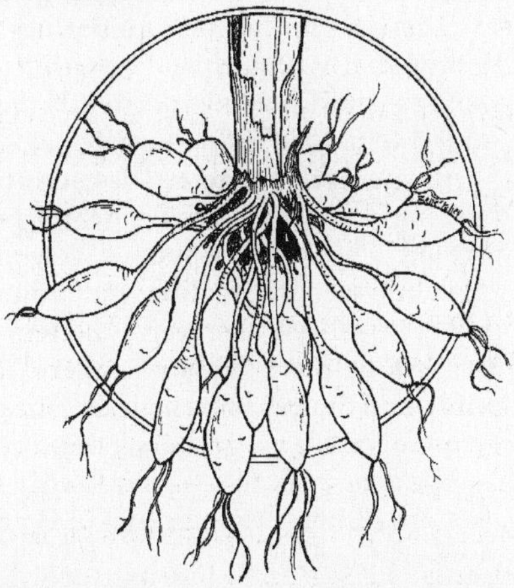

Daylily tubers (Art by René Fahey)

This one plant produces four different foods which can be gathered at different times of the year. I will cover each of these separately and show you ways to cook them.

Food from the tubers

Daylilies grow in spreading clumps in large patches. The long grass-like leaves of the plant mark a buried treasure of golden tubers that are just waiting to be discovered. Like all wild foods, daylilies are a security you can depend on when you need it most. Each separate plant produces about 15 little tubers that are about half an inch thick and an inch long. When digging daylily tubers you needn't worry about wiping them out. A clump taken here and there will only give them a much needed thinning and cultivation.

Preparation and cooking

The small tubers can be tedious to prepare when not done properly. First, dig the clumps of tubers and give them a rough wash in a large container of water. Then cut the tubers from the plant and remove the little feeder roots. Give the tubers a final wash and rinse by rubbing them between the hands until the water comes out clean.

Boil tubers in salted water for 15 to 20 minutes. This is the way most books recommend eating the tubers. You may try eating them at this point. If you find that aftertaste is delightful to your palate then you won't have to go any further to enjoy your daylilies.

Following is a recipe which makes the aftertaste disappear and brings out a delicious flavor that everyone likes.

Fried daylily tubers

1 cup daylily tubers (cooked and mashed)
1 large egg
1/2 teaspoon baking soda
Whole wheat flour
Oil

Let the mashed tubers cool. Mix in egg, baking soda and just enough flour to thicken to the consistency of thick pancake batter. Mix together and fry like pancakes.

The flowers and buds of the daylily are an important vegetable eaten regularly in China and Japan.

Gather the unopened buds when they are nearly full sized and boil them for a few minutes with only a little water. Season with butter and salt and serve like green beans. They are very delicious and are similar to green beans, only smoother and very tender.

To make delicious daylily fritters, gather the nearly opened buds and fully bloomed flowers and dip them into a rich egg batter and quickly fry in hot oil until golden brown. This wonderful food is fit to serve at the finest meals.

To give soup a delightful flavor, add daylily buds and flowers during the last few minutes of cooking. They give the soup a desirable gelatinous quality which acts as a thickener.

The Chinese and Japanese appreciate the daylily flowers and buds so much that they not only use them fresh, but they dry them to use year-round as well.

These dried lily buds are sold in Chinese markets and in some health food stores. Before you add them to soups, soak them until soft and then use them as you would the fresh flowers and buds.

Early in the Spring when the young shoots are a few inches high they can be added to early Spring tossed salads. When the young daylily shoots are less than 6" high they are ready to eat like asparagus. Boil the greens for a few minutes and season with oil and salt. They are very tender with a mild sweet flavor.

Warning

The Chinese have reported that daylily tubers and leaf shoots might contain a toxin which can affect the eyes or even cause blindness in some cases. Chinese reports indicate that the toxin builds up in the body over the years from eating large amounts of tubers and leaf shoots of the daylily.

This food has been eaten for thousands of years and continues to be eaten in China and Japan. Chances are you would have no ill effects even if you ate daylilies every month of the year in small quantities.

With this caution in mind, you can enjoy a few delicious dishes of daylilies every year without having to worry about your health.

Daylilies were originally introduced as a garden flower and have gone wild. Look for daylilies on old, abandoned farms and in ditches along roads and railroads.

Once you find a patch you will be able to go back year after year, and harvest as many as you need.

René Fahey lives with his family on a 90 acre self-sufficient homestead where he teaches simple living and survival skills. René specializes in wild foods.

How to share an idea with more than 50,000 homestead friends... with just one stamp!

New readers frequently ask how they can participate in our network. It's as easy as writing a letter or sending an e-mail!

There are no "writer's guidelines" (and no compensation except the satisfaction of sharing an idea or experience and seeing your letter in print). Simply write to your COUNTRYSIDE friends the way you'd write to any other friends, and send it to us. We'll do the rest!

We get letters and articles scribbled in pencil on the backs of recycled ad flyers and school papers... neatly penned on printed stationery... computer-printed... by e-mail—and we welcome them all!

While we love to hear what you're thinking and doing, we obviously can't print everything we receive. Letters with innovative ways of doing things, or that will help other homesteaders in some way, have a better chance of being published than those that, interesting though they might be, have less practical value for our large and diversified community.

We also want to see your family album photos and drawings!

Our address: COUNTRYSIDE, 145 Industrial Dr., Medford, WI 54451. E-mail: csymag@tds.net.

Folklore:

Planting by the moon

Not by its light... but according to its phases

John McAndrews
Pennsylvania

I had a short article in Countryside about moon sign planting and how the Almanacs differ in times of the moon's changing from one sign to another. I have had an unexpected amount of SASEs, many just a plain self addressed stamped envelope in an envelope addressed to me, or a bit of a note asking for more information—but not specific questions that I could be of help with. I have not written any books on the subject. I was just trying to share my experience with fellow countrysiders.

I have found that it is as beneficial to use the signs of the moon for greater success when planting seeds indoors for transplanting, as when planting outdoors, directly.

Some people scoff at planting by the signs as being anti-Bible or against God's will. The Bible goes against fortune tellers and false prophets, but advocates the use of the signs and moon's benefit. To everything there is a season. And a time to every purpose under Heaven: a time to be born, and a time to die: a time to plant, and a time to pluck up that which is planted... (Ecclesiastics 3:12). "The precious things put forth by the moon" (Deuteronomy 33:14). Many Amish people plant by the moon, and we know how successful they are.

Here I'm going to try to explain moon sign planting and the symbols found in an ephemeris.

An ephemeris has a row of columns showing Sidereal Time, Sun, and Moon, which is the column you need to look at. Each day will show the moon's position and what day and time it will change. The symbols are the signs of the zodiac (Aries, Taurus, Gemini, Cancer, Leo, Virgo, Libra, Scorpio, Sagittarius, Capricorn, Aquarius, and Pisces). All books use the same symbols.

There are four groups of three signs each divided into the elements: fire, earth, air and water. The fire signs are Aries, Leo and Sagittarius. The earth signs are Taurus, Virgo and Capricorn. The air signs are Gemini, Libra and Aquarius. Water signs consist of Cancer, Scorpio and Pisces. Many books show only planting by the water signs. This is a quick generalization, which I don't follow.

Basically, planting by the signs is divided into two types of crops—above ground and below ground (root crops.) The phases of the moon can also be used—first, second, third and fourth quarters (often referred to as new moon, first quarter, full moon and last quarter). It's helpful to combine these with the proper moon sign for better results.

Putting it together

With that, here is some general advice on planting by the signs.

♈ *Moon in Aries*—dry, barren, fiery. Destroy weeds, pests, etc. Good for tilling, plowing and cultivating. Good also for harvesting. Being a dry and barren sign, it helps keep weeds from sprouting and roots of weeds from resprouting when you weed the garden.

♉ *Moon in Taurus*—moist, productive, earthy. Good for root crops, especially potatoes. Promotes hardiness. Good also for lettuce, cabbage, kale and other leafy vegetables. Promotes short leafy plants. Promotes quick growth to root crops. Also a good sign for transplanting. Taurus moon in second quarter promotes very good root growth.

♊ *Moon in Gemini*—dry, barren, airy. Destroys weeds, unwanted growth, pests. Good for harvesting. Do not transplant or plant in Gemini. Mow your lawn in Gemini and it will help slow the growth of the grass.

♋ *Moon in Cancer*—watery, moist, very fruitful. Used for watering gardens and irrigation. Very productive. Extensively used for planting. Good for grafting and budding. Plant below ground crops. Also good for cover crops like wheat, rye, oats. Under Cancer, seeds germinate quickly. Favorable growth, abundant yields. At full of the moon plant beans. New moon, lentils. Sow peas following the new moon, not following second quarter; this gives little yield. Moon in Cancer is also a good time to prune grapes.

♌ *Moon in Leo*—dry, barren, airy. Most barren sign. Only use for destroying weeds and unwanted roots and trees, cultivation. Harvest fruit and root crops. Cut grass to retard growth. To permanently destroy bushes, briars, weeds, unwanted trees, cut off in 8th month in moon's fourth quarter in Leo.

♍ *Moon in Virgo*—moist, barren, earthy. Cultivate, destroy unwanted pests and weeds. Do not plant or transplant vegetables. Good vine growth and flowering—little fruit. Plant flowering vines for good results.

♎ *Moon in Libra*—moist, semi-fruitful, airy. Gives good pulp growth (tomatoes, peppers, etc.) and roots. Excellent for flowers and vines. Good for seeding hay, corn fodder and livestock feeds. Good for above ground crops and vegetables and those of which the flower part is eaten (cauliflower, broccoli.) Libra is ruled by the planet Venus—the mythological goddess of beauty. If you want the prettiest flowers around, plant them in Libra!

♏ *Moon in Scorpio*—watery,

fruitful, moist. Scorpio is the next most fruitful, second to Cancer. It is used for the same purposes as Cancer. Very good for sturdiness and vine growth. Also helps corn plants survive drought. Excellent for planting corn. Do not harvest potatoes or other root crops when moon is in Scorpio as they may rot. Plant for abundance of flowers. Good for vegetables, cereals, berries. Sets plenty of fruit. Helps offer hardiness against frost. Good for transplanting. I planted my corn in Scorpio in 1995 and had excellent results even though we had a drought-like summer here. Many other gardens lost corn. So, it is a good sign to plant under for drought protection. Pumpkins and squash grow best when planted under Scorpio. It is good for transplanting tomatoes as it gives better resistance to cold and drought, which they are quite sensitive to.

♐***Moon in Sagittarius***—dry, barren, fiery. A poor time to transplant or plant. Good for cultivating and weeding. Also for harvesting. Fruits like apples, pears, etc. keep better when harvested under Sagittarius.

♑***Moon in Capricorn***—moist, semi-fruitful, earthy. Favors root crops like turnips, beets, potatoes. Provides rapid growth of pulp stalks (celery, rhubarb, etc.) or roots. Not good for grains or seeds. Also good for onions, peanuts. Good for applying organic fertilizer. Good for pruning or grafting as it promotes quick healing of the wood. Very good for planting ornamental shrubs and trees.

♒***Moon in Aquarius***—dry, barren, airy. Destroy weeds and pests; cultivate. Good for harvesting root crops and fruits. Seed planted in Aquarius is likely to rot. Plant pine trees and onion sets.

♓***Moon in Pisces***—moist, fruitful, watery. Pisces is third most fruitful. Very good for planting and transplanting. Especially good for root growth. Also assists drought resistance. Good for planting in dry soil where you want good, deep root penetration. It supposedly produces the shortest top growth of all the signs. Good for promoting sturdy root systems on fruit trees, providing abundant fruit crops. Encourages growth of root systems—may cause misshapen tubers etc., as the plant's energy wants to go past tubers into the root system.

Summary

Planting: Use Cancer first, Scorpio second and Pisces third whenever you can, unless the nature of planting points elsewhere. Try to combine the moon's phases if possible for better results. Fertilize when the moon is in Cancer, Scorpio, or Pisces. Use Taurus or Capricorn if needed. Fertilize in third or fourth quarter.

Harvesting: food root crops in Aries, Leo, Sagittarius in third or fourth quarter. Gemini or Aquarius root crops for seed best harvested at full moon. Grain to be stored or used for seeding just after full moon in dry signs as above under harvesting. Fruit in decrease of the moon in dry signs. Water or irrigate when moon is in Cancer, Scorpio or Pisces, second best in Libra.

Mowing grass: Mow in the third or fourth quarter to decrease growth, first or second quarter to increase growth.

Pruning is best in the decrease of the moon. Scorpio and third quarter help retard branch growth and produce better fruit growth. Ornamental trees during the moon's decrease in a fruitful sign. Spraying to destroy weeds and pests is best in fourth quarter and barren signs.

The moon's phase is indeed important but on a tight time schedule the sign takes precedence.

For further reading on planting by moon signs:

Planetary Planting and Astrological Gardening by Louise Riotte. Storey Publishing, Pownal, Vermont. For a catalog call 1-800-441-5700.

Llewellyns Annual Moon Sign Book and Lunar Planning Guide and *Llewellyns Annual Organic Gardening Almanac.* Llewellyn Publications, PO Box 64383, Saint Paul, MN 55164-0383.

A quick reference for planting by the signs

Asparagus—Cancer, Scorpio and Pisces.

Beans—Cancer, Scorpio, Pisces, Libra, Taurus, second quarter.

Broccoli—Cancer, Scorpio, Pisces, Libra first quarter.

Brussels sprouts—same as broccoli.

Cabbage family—same as broccoli; also Taurus.

Cauliflower—Cancer, Scorpio, Pisces, Libra first quarter.

Corn—Cancer, Scorpio, Pisces first quarter.

Eggplant—Cancer, Scorpio, Pisces, Libra.

Kale—Cancer, Scorpio, Pisces first or second quarter.

Lettuce—Cancer, Scorpio, Pisces, Libra, Taurus first quarter.

Mustard—Scorpio first quarter.

Spinach—Cancer, Scorpio, Pisces first quarter.

Okra—Cancer, Scorpio, Pisces, Libra second or third quarter.

Onion seeds—Scorpio, Sagittarius second quarter.

Onion sets—Taurus, Libra, Pisces third or fourth quarter.

Peas—Cancer, Scorpio, Pisces, Libra second quarter.

Peppers—Scorpio, Sagittarius second quarter.

Potatoes—Cancer, Scorpio third quarter.

Red beets—Cancer, Scorpio, Pisces, Capricorn third quarter.

Tomatoes—Cancer, Scorpio, Pisces second quarter.

Squash—Cancer, Scorpio, Pisces, Libra second quarter.

Note: when you move your seedlings from the house to the greenhouse, also use the proper sign as if planting. It is a new growing environment and the right moon sign will help them to adjust and grow better.

The importance of flowers

Bev Carney
Wisconsin

When planning our garden, our focus used to be almost exclusively on vegetables. We'd comb the seed catalogs and get several varieties of each veggie and start them from seed ourselves.

But when it came to flowers, well, that was another story. Who had time and space for a variety of flowers? As lovely as they were to look at, you couldn't eat them. It was enough for us to buy some marigold plants and pop a few in here and there. After all, we had peonies all over the side yard. Who needed more than that?

Fortunately, we moved to a much bigger property and were inspired to try planting a wildflower bed. We planted cosmos, larkspur, cleome, yarrow, daisies, dame's rocket, poppies, coreopsis and blanket flowers.

While we greatly enjoyed the flowers, we noticed a marked increase in the number of little flying insects buzzing about. Most of them were unknown to us, but the garden certainly didn't suffer. Perhaps we were attracting some of the beneficial insects we'd read about.

The following year, we added another flower bed and got more good insects and a lot of little wasps. We were onto something!

One season found the hairy vetch cover crop in full flower and the patch was attracting more bees than we'd ever seen. The vetch was right in the

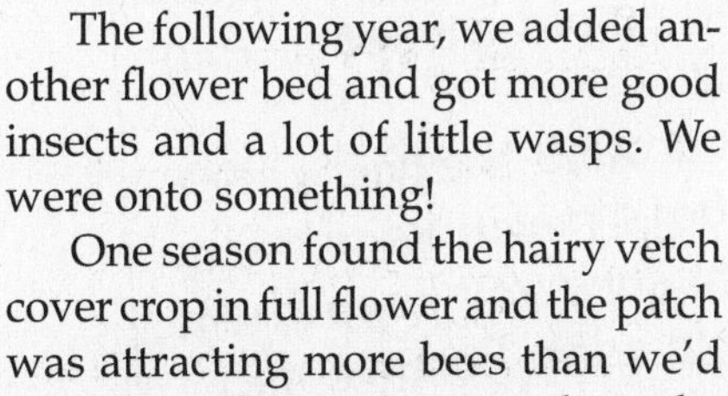

middle of the garden and that got us to thinking of interspersing the flowers right in with the vegetables. Now we make sure that flowers throughout the garden get the same priority as the vegetables themselves.

Flowers have become even more important in the garden since the decline of the honeybee. Studies have shown that about 95% of the wild honeybee population has been killed off by mites. A great many of the domestic bees have also died. There are so many fewer bees that it just makes sense to do whatever you can to attract what bees there are.

Although studies have examined which beneficial insects like which flower, we don't pay too much attention to these. Rather, we plant a wide variety of flowers and try to make sure that we have things in bloom for as long as possible. One of the earliest is dame's rocket, a wonderful flower that closely resembles wild phlox. And of course, remember the dandelion provides some much needed food for the bees. We have a ground cover called gill of the green, which while horribly invasive, also feeds the early insects. Daisies also bloom early. Cleome and cosmos are particularly nice to intersperse because they're so tall and they're also annuals. Dill and carrots also attract some interesting bugs (including larvae of the swallowtail butterfly).

Even if your plot is small, make sure you get some flowers throughout. You'll be rewarded by great color as well as increased production.

If you can't afford to build a pond to put a boat in... put the pond in the boat!

Gail Moore
Texas

My husband has always wanted two things: a pond, and a new boat. He has an old (1953) fiberglass 14' boat that needs a new transom.

Well, he finally got his new boat and was trying to decide what to do with the old one. We didn't figure anyone would want it, so we discussed burying it when we dug the pond.

I was thinking up silly ideas and told him, "Since it costs so much to hire a dozer ($65/hour and do-it-yourself) why didn't we just get the tiller and some shovels, dig a hole large enough to fit the boat in and bury it up to the seam around the top? Fill in the top few inches above the transom area (to match the side height) with a board and fiberglass from a boat repair kit. Take the red/green (port and starboard) lights from the bow and reposition them inside under the top in the same location they came from. Install in-ground pipes for a recirculating pump, and you'd have a fish pond in the shape of a boat.

"Add water, water plants, fish, wiring for lights, a nice rock edging and some plants around the outside. With some ground cover plants, fancy grasses, banana trees, and maybe a trellis over the boat, you'd have your own paradise! You could even put in a little waterfall or fountain on it."

By that time he was looking at me very oddly. He said, "That's a great idea!" I thought he was joking—but he wasn't!

The more I think about it, the better it sounds. I guess I'll learn to keep my mouth shut!

Fishing worms

Another idea: When I lived in Missouri for a few years, any time I wanted to go fishing it was just a matter of taking a stick and turning over dried cow patties or digging through leaf mulch in the woods and coming up with all the nightcrawlers I could use. Here in Texas (this part anyway), the extreme temperatures make it impossible for nightcrawlers to survive. I've tried raising them in a shaded raised bed with no luck. Since the little buggers are so expensive ($2.75 a dozen!) when I do buy some I hate to turn loose the unused ones and I sure don't like to keep them in that little, tiny 1/2 pint container.

So I got a five-quart, plastic ice cream bucket with a lid and put used coffee grounds, used tea leaves, veggie scraps, shredded cardboard, paper and a light mist of water in there with my crawlers. Punched holes in the lid with an ice pick and covered the bucket of worms and put them in the refrigerator! They seemed to like their new house and they live a very long time.

I've never had any reproduction in the bucket, but I usually always have fishing bait. (I don't get to use them up very fast as I don't catch many fish!)

I used to have an old chest freezer (latch removed, of course) that I used to raise red wiggler worms. I filled it with old, rotten, shredded cloth material, shredded cardboard boxes, paper grocery bags, leaf mulch, potting soil, kitchen scraps, clippings from haircuts—you name it—everything went into it (No bones, grease or meat scraps.) Boy, did we have worms!

Getting irises to bloom

Mrs. Collier
New Mexico

This letter is exactly why I love Countryside; can you believe the nice people that read this publication! What a joy to know they're out there near Ol' Mother Earth somewhere! This came to me simply addressed, "La Luz, N.M." That's one reason I like small towns!

Dear Mrs. Collier,

I was reading your column in the Countryside Nov./Dec. issue and saw your question about your irises not blooming. The answer the magazine gave did not include an answer I would have given, so here it is....

If, by chance, when you transplanted them you covered the whole corm, tuber or root, whichever the roots are called, they will not bloom. The sun must bake the iris root to make it bloom. If the roots are covered with soil, just uncover the top of the roots so the sun can get to 1/2 to 2/3 of the top of each one. If this was the problem they should bloom for you after this is corrected. If that was not the problem I am sorry, that is the only answer I know. I made that same mistake when I started planting irises and an old gardener told me what to do and it worked.

If the weeds get so thick around the roots that the sun can not bake the roots it will keep them from blooming also. But I am sure you keep them weeded, I mentioned it just in case. Forgive me.

I enjoy Countryside magazine to the fullest and have taken it for years. My wife Alice and I read it together.

A subscriber friend,
John and Alice Peterson
OH

Understanding the balance of soil, plants and insects

ELIZABETH & CROW MILLER
NEW YORK

Why do weeds, insects and disease become a problem? Why don't they bother every plant in a row? Organic farmers and gardeners have learned to recognize edible weeds and are tolerant of weeds in general. But I wasn't satisfied with eating weeds instead of sweet corn. I wanted to know why each weed was growing this year in this exact spot.

Weeds function as part of nature's soil-balancing process. They sprout at a given time, often after years of dormancy, because of an ideal combination of soil chemistry, moisture, temperature and various other conditions. The right combinations allow them to thrive while their roots secrete hormones that inhibit other seeds from sprouting. It's a case of survival of the fittest. Each type of weed accumulates certain chemicals over the course of its life. When it dies it is consumed by soil microbes and its nutrients return to the soil.

To control weeds, the organic gardener can pull and compost them before they set seed, till annuals under as a green manure crop, or test the soil and provide soil conditions that don't favor weed growth. Weeds can indicate soil problems: mustard suggests lack of sulfur, sorrel indicates acid soils, plantain and dandelions thrive on compacted soils. In each case, correcting the soil problems should reduce the weed problem.

Solving most gardening problems is a lot more interesting than spraying everything with pesticides. Develop an understanding of soil, then use your knowledge of soil, plants and insects to figure out how to have the healthiest garden possible.

The garden:

Just taking a handful of soil and sifting through it tells a lot about its texture, color, and water content, and will give you some idea of its resident population of roots and insect life.

Soils high in sand are easily identified by their gritty texture and their tendency to both absorb and lose water quickly. They react quickly to change of temperature and are easy to till. Because there are large spaces between particles, there is generally plenty of air available for roots.

Soils high in silt absorb water much more slowly and therefore tend to erode easily during heavy rains. Because the spaces between particles are smaller, they also dry out more slowly during dry spells, but they pay for this feature by having poorer air exchange abilities than sandy soils.

Soils high in clay absorb water very slowly, but clay soils can store nutrients efficiently, releasing them slowly as needed.

The fourth mineral-containing component of soil is organic matter. The term "organic matter" covers a wide range of substances, most of them chemically complex, including partly-decomposed plant and animal remains as well as humus, the end product of the decay process.

Humus is nature's storehouse of carbon, nitrogen (N) and other minerals necessary to plant and microbial growth. It is often listed separately as a component of total organic matter because of its importance in the tilth and food and water holding ability of soil.

One way to check your soil type is to put some in a quart jar with water, shake it up, then let it stand for 24 hours. By then it will have settled, with sand on the bottom, silt layer next, clay on top, so you have a pretty good idea what your garden soil mix is.

Or, to get a close look at the make-up of your soil, dig a deep hole and observe the layers of the soil profile. From the top down, you will see first the organic matter of the rooting zone, then down through successive layers to the soil's rock layer.

Soil compaction: You may deal with compaction by adding a soil conditioner. Humic acid, for example, clumps soil particles somewhat, creating air spaces between them, thus improving the structure. Farmers and gardeners with problem soils, either extremely heavy clay or pure sand, need to add quantities of organic matter.

Working the soil deeply and deep cultivation can help overcome compaction. Or, plant a deep rooting cover crop like birdsfoot trefoil, crownvetch or sweet clover. As the roots of these crops begin to work downwards through the soil they create channels through which water and nutrients move more freely.

The roots of a farm or garden's well-being are found in the living Earth. With a better understanding of how the soil ecosystem cooperates with plants and insects, we can learn how to manage our food production better, and help assure the health of our soil, crops and ourselves.

A "family/market" garden

KEITH E. NARMI
ARKANSAS

We have what I call a family/market garden. We deliberately plant more than we need in our 1/2 acre garden, and we sell the surplus.

Last year sales amounted to $800. (People will pay more for fresh, chemical-free produce, and since our garden is completely organic, we get a premium price.) We kept $200 for seed money and canning supplies, and the remaining $600 was donated to charity.

Our success with sweet corn was particularly noteworthy. Three dollars' worth of seed planted four rows, each 100 ft. long. We planted in late April and harvested 90 days later, in late July. We put up 65 pints of corn off the ear for us at a conservative value of $33. We froze 12 bags of ear corn for us at a value of $12. We sold 10 bags of ear corn (8/$1), for another $10.

The husks were fed to our cattle, with a feed value of $10. Our chickens pecked at the cobs, worth about $2. We pulled some whole stalks and chopped the roots off to feed the pigs – feed value $3. Others we dried and bundled for sale to a local company…35 bundles at $1 each or, $35 in sales. The cobs were put into low spots in the road after the chickens cleaned them.

Here is the summary: A $3 investment in seed supplied us with corn for the year, fed stock, and generated outside sales with a total value of $105. None of the corn or byproducts were wasted. I think that's a return of 3,500 percent in 90 days. I don't think there is a Wall Street fella around that can match that! Every once in a while you need to sit down and figure out what your sweat is worth.

Pigs play an important role

I would recommend pigs as part of any garden plan. We just bought six (50 pounds each) pigs for $21 apiece. They are in an 8' x 16' pen in the garden. (It's January, but the ground isn't frozen solid here in Arkansas.) The pen is moveable by pulling four metal T posts, moving the pen, and putting in the posts and attaching the corners of the pen to them with baling twine.

We feed the pigs chopped corn at a cost of $15 per week. Every day the pigs are given one wheelbarrow full of manure to go through. The pigs consider this a treat and as they go through the manure, they work it into the garden. The pen is moved daily.

By the end of March they should have worked all our manure into the garden before we plow. Once plowing begins, the pigs are placed in their pen adjacent to the garden and supplemental feeding continues.

By the end of April the garden is in and weeding begins. The pigs get all the weeds and household waste and supplemental feeding is cut back. By June produce is being harvested, weeding continues and pigs get all the waste. By the end of September the garden is done.

The pigs have not been moved but the area they've been in is now a bed of organic matter weighing several tons. Now we go back to moving the pigs through the garden (two moves per day). They clean the garden of plant residue of any type. By early November they go to be processed and will dress out at about 160-180 pounds each. We sell the pigs before they are processed for $1.50 per pound, dressed weight. We keep one for our freezer and sell five. Again, people will pay a premium price for an organic product.

Here's how the numbers add up for our pig enterprise:

$126 for feeder pigs + $700 for feed = $826. If all the pigs dress out at 160 pounds and we sell five at $1.50 per pound, our gross is $1200. Our pig is free. We pay $100 for processing. Total profit is $274 cash and 160 pounds of excellent meat.

The end result is, we have animals that worked manure into the garden over the winter, made organic compost out of waste and cleaned the garden for us, provided meat and made us some money.

Rachael Ramiccie enjoys visiting the homestead of her aunt and uncle, Kathleen and Gary Roberts, in Florida.

Living with Nature:

Save the hornets? No way!

Barbara Peters
Montana

A comment about the letter by Carol Vacek titled "Save the Hornets; and Recycle More":

I certainly disagree with her about yellow jackets. They may have a good side—that I don't know about and won't argue with—but the downside is what I don't like. They are the worst pests of summer to me! One cannot have a picnic or plan an outdoor get together without the yellow jackets coming to the feast and outnumbering the people.

They aren't gentle guests, either. They are aggressive. I don't for one moment believe the conventional wisdom saying they only sting in self defense. I've been stung by them more times than I can remember and I never saw a nest of them or was doing anything aggressive towards them. They want sweets, they want meat, and maybe something in-between. They linger in the garden, crawling over the plants and under them; they linger around the doors hoping to get into the house; they hover like minute helicopters between the car and the house and wait for me to carry in a bundle of groceries and then wham, bam, thank you ma'am! There is no way I can appreciate those beasts.

However, the thing that really set me against the yellow jackets was when they invaded one of our bee hives one summer and eventually over took the hive and killed it. They were after the honey, of course. The bees didn't stand a chance because they can only sting once and then it's curtains for the bee. No such restriction on the yellow jacket; he can sting as often as he wants and he doesn't die for it. That's not very fair odds.

After they killed one hive and wiped out the honey they went after a second hive, but by then the men in the family got geared up to defend the hive, successfully. However, it was fortunate that the end of summer was upon us and the first hard frost put a crimp in the yellow jacket population and so they forgot about the bees. Nowadays I'm not that forgiving to the yellow jackets.

They eat flies. Well, maybe they eat flies... but that I've never seen, and I have seen turkeys, ducks and chickens, and even my cat eat flies!

There are wasps around; they are reputed to eat insects and be beneficial. They haven't reached pest proportions and they have never stung me either, nor have they gone after the bees. Consequently I don't mind them.

I had to laugh at the article on "Chickens and Fences" by Bev Carney. I've never found poultry and gardens to be compatible. I know others will disagree, and talk about the weeding benefits and the eradication of bugs, etc. I've seen chickens roaming gently in others' gardens and admired the scene, but in my garden with my poultry it's a different matter. I lock up my poultry during the growing season in sheer self-defense. I tried it the other way and it doesn't work for me. They get all the garden wastes and the garbage from the house anyway and eventually I get it all back as manure and compost; the little dears don't roam freely except from Fall to Spring.

I was interested in the photo taken in Alaska of the child and the potato vines. I was impressed by the comment that the yellow ribbon fence kept out the moose. We use a "yellow" ribbon fence, but it is electric (solar). I circle the planting area to keep our own creatures out but it doesn't work for deer, who sail over the fence with ease and grace and feast on the garden. Maybe moose don't jump as high as deer. I'm curious if the fence is electric. I didn't want us to go to the time or expense of putting up a seven- to eight-foot deer proof fence so I solved that by putting one dog in the garden and another in the orchard at night. That keeps the deer away. Needless to say one has to provide food, water and shelter in the area they are leaving the dogs. The dogs go off duty in the morning, and from late fall until spring planting time. Doesn't take the deer long to know when the dogs are gone and then back they come to clean things up.

And Great Pyrenees dogs...

For those who were interested in my article about the Great Pyrenees a couple of years back:

We have been at our present location for seven years and we still have the dogs. In that length of time we have never lost a sheep, goat, or any other livestock to predators, and now the dogs are doing double duty in the garden as I mentioned. However, one of the dogs doing night duty is a Chow... (giving credit where credit is due).

I'm curious about hearing from others in regard to growing worms under rabbits. I have heard that the common red wiggler, sold by so many, is good at eating manure and making compost and apparently okay as fish bait, but it won't live in your garden. Is that correct? I would like to try worms under the rabbits, but this is in an unheated building and I want to apply the worms to the garden in the compost created, and I want them to live there. Can I use ordinary earth worms found outside? It seems if those kind work well on manure under rabbits they should then live outside in the garden when they get put back there. I would like to hear what experiences others have had in this department.

Appreciates nature, but has the sense to recognize a dangerous situation

LYNN SLOAN
TENNESSEE

I would like to add something regarding the letter "Save the hornets." (82/1).

Hornets and yellow jackets are in the same family *(Vespula)*, but they are not the same species. The bald-faced hornet, which is common here in Northeast Tennessee, is classified as *Vespula maculata,* while the yellow jacket is divided into two subspecies, the western yellow jacket *(Vespula pennsylvanica)* and the eastern yellow jacket *(Vespula maculifrons)*. (This information comes from the *Audubon Society Field Guide to North American Insects and Spiders.)*

According to this book (and personal experience), both yellow jackets and most hornet species become easily agitated when their nests are disturbed, and the female workers sting repeatedly to protect the larvae.

Yellow jackets feed primarily on nectar, as do most hornets, although I have observed them on more than one occasion feeding on carrion. Both species' larvae require insects pre-chewed by the adults. According to the book, the adults too consume a certain amount of insects for their protein needs.

To respond to the writer's comment/question, "Why would anyone want to drown dishpans full...?" Well, let me tell you. I appreciate nature and I endeavor to provide a balance on my little piece of Earth, yet I also have the common sense to recognize a dangerous situation.

One summer a few years ago our property seemed to become infested with yellow jackets. Even our bird houses were overrun. Parent birds were ousted by the stinging hordes and many baby birds were killed.

The numerous crawdad holes became subterranean fortresses. Mowing the yard required protective garb and sometimes had to be abandoned 'til late in the evening.

We were no longer able to sit on our deck in the mornings or evenings without being stung.

When it was no longer safe to let the children go outside to play or the livestock to graze our little field, I knew something had to be done.

Since I dislike chemical interventions, we began to systematically identify occupied nests and after sunset began burning each one. The *Field Guide* recommended using a transparent bowl set firmly into the ground over subterranean nest entrances. The adults are confused by the inability to escape and seek food, and since they will not dig around the apparent obstacle they soon starve to death. This method does work fairly well, however, I doused two very large nests with lighter fluid and burned them immediately.

During my nursing career, I saw several unfortunate people who had one way or another disturbed a nest of yellow jackets and became severely ill from the injected toxins. I remember quite well two particular individuals who did not recover.

I feel that I must responsibly protect my children and the livestock which sustains our family from an imbalance of potentially lethal insects the same way I would feel compelled to protect them from marauding animals. Yes, I do love, respect and enjoy nature, and I try to balance the wonders of nature and the needs of my family. Quite honestly, it sometimes seems hard to do. Yet, I will keep trying, keeping in mind the COUNTRYSIDE Philosophy.

Adult Bald-faced hornet: 5/8"-1" long; wings smoky brown

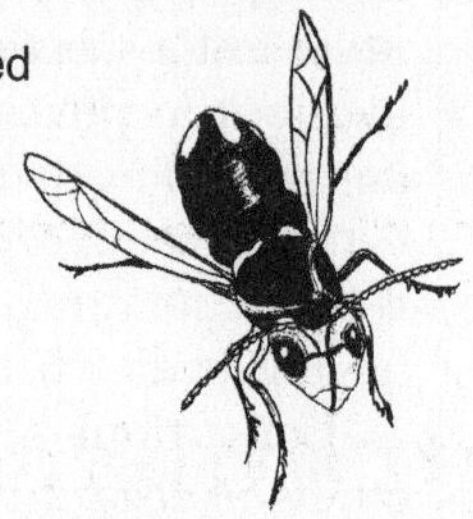

Nest of the Bald-faced Hornet

Adults are black with white to pale yellow patterns on face, thorax and abdomen. All die in winter except young mated females which overwinter in soil or among leaf litter. The nest is chewed wood pulp which turns gray when dried. Nests vary from the size of an apple to the size of a football. They're usually constructed in bushes and trees at the edges of meadows.

Nest of the Yellow Jacket

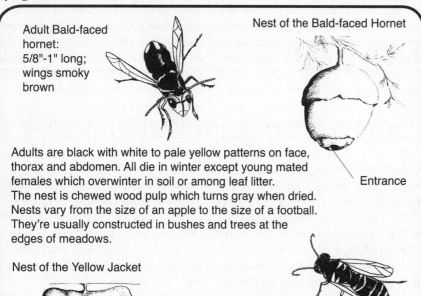

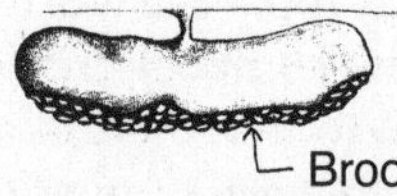

Adult Yellow Jacket: 1/2" - 5/8" long

Adult Yellow Jackets are smaller. Head, abdomen and thorax are striped with yellow or white on a black base. Again, all die in winter except mated females. Nests are constructed in the ground, in stumps, fallen logs, or anywhere near ground level where they are sheltered from the elements.

Artist: Lynn Sloan

Nature:

The much-to-be-feared Brown Recluse spider

GWEN LEMONDS
VIRGINIA

The brown recluse spider produces a bite that gives little or no pain at first—but is extremely toxic. This creature is more to be feared than the black widow spider—which is more easily identified.

Within 24 hours a purplish-red blister develops at the site of the bite, and extensive "tissue death" occurs beneath the bite, producing a very deep and angry ulceration extending down to the bone, often lasting for many weeks or months, if it's not fatal. It takes months to heal and leaves a deep puckered scar—at best.

Since there is no antidote and no anti-venom, the only treatment generally recognized medically is that of wide surgical excision, or cutting away any flesh containing venom—or amputation, in hopes of physically removing all of the venom.

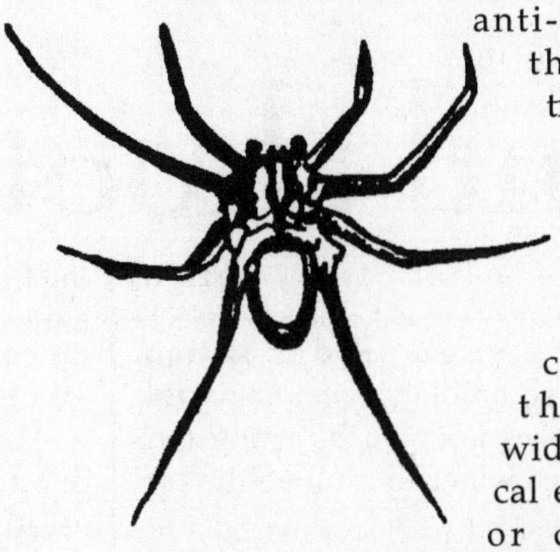

It has been found that the treatment of choice for brown recluse spider bite is a compress of powdered charcoal applied as soon after the bite as possible, preferably during the first 24 hours, with frequent changes (about every 30 minutes for the first eight hours). The next day, the time interval for changing the poultices or compresses (mixed with water, cornstarch and charcoal) can be lengthened to two and then four hours.

An anesthetist, on hearing the report of how charcoal poultices are a near-specific for the extremely toxic bite of the brown recluse spider, related that just the previous day he had anesthetized a lady for the second time, to do a more extensive amputation of her foot from the bite of a brown recluse spider that had bitten her over two months before. The first amputation had not removed all the damaged tissue, and it had failed to heal.

Charcoal compresses are also quite effective for persons extremely allergic to bee stings. Also apply charcoal poultices to snake bites, one after another, every 10 minutes until the victim can get to the emergency room. If the snake is venomous, swelling appears in about 10 minutes.

Charcoal should also be taken by mouth. Put one tablespoon in about 4 ounces (1/4 cup) of water or juice. Pour into a small jar—cap carefully— then shake vigorously and drink through a straw. Charcoal absorbs toxins of all kinds, incredibly so!

In cases of gangrene of extremities—toes, feet and legs—charcoal poultices have been known to save these parts of the anatomy from being amputated.

The webs of ecology:

Forecast Lyme disease by watching acorns

If you want to know how harsh the winter will be, look at the stripes on a woolly bear caterpillar in the Fall. And if you want to know how prevalent Lyme disease will be two years from now, look at acorns.

Scientists scoff at the wooly bears' predictions, but they applaud the acorn connection. After all, they discovered it.

Lyme disease is caused by a bacterium. The bacterium is carried by ticks. Ticks live on deer and mice. Deer and mice eat acorns. When there are more acorns, two years later there will be more mice and deer... and ticks and Lyme disease in humans.

Researchers at the Institute of Ecosystem Studies in Millbrook, NY, the University of Connecticut, and Oregon State University found that in years following a big acorn crop, there are eight times as many tick larvae as in years following a poor acorn crop, and about 40 percent more ticks on each mouse.

There was a large acorn crop in 1994. Two years later, 1996 set a record with more than 15,000 cases of Lyme disease reported to the Centers for Disease Control and Prevention. In 1997, the total dropped to about half that.

There was a big crop of acorns in the Northeast in 1997. That means 1999 should be a year of high risk for Lyme disease.

With the old way of thinking, some people would probably want to eliminate Lyme disease by cutting down all the oak trees. But even if that were possible or acceptable, it would disrupt other natural cycles in the forest, with unknown outcomes.

Today, you don't have to be an observant and thoughtful homesteader to know that everything is connected to everything else—and that science has only begun to trace the wondrous webs of ecology.

Foraging:

Stalking greens, potherbs and shoots

Julie Hunter
Arkansas

Warmer weather brings a time of rejuvenation, a time to revitalize our systems, which have become sluggish from the cooler weather and diet.

It's time to begin to seek out those growing things that are full of vibrant elements to aid our bodies.

But just what is a green? Greens are plants which can be used raw or cooked like any cultivated green vegetable like lettuce or spinach. A potherb is any plant that must be cooked in some manner in order to be eaten. Shoots are the new growths of many plants.

Many greens and potherbs are available from early spring to late summer. Shoots and stems may be edible only in the early spring.

Below are a few plants to be on the lookout for. Some may not taste like their cultivated cousins, but are worth trying. Some greens are more appetizing if mixed with other greens. Stir frying greens will enhance the flavors of others. Adding onions or other herbs can add flavor to some of the greens.

Greens or potherbs having bitter taste improve with at least one change of water. Cook most greens only a short time. Greens and potherbs can also be dried to use during the winter in cooking.

Dandelions
(Taraxacum offici-nale)

Use the tender young shoots and leaves before flowering, adding the leaves to a tossed salad or putting them in scrambled eggs. Cook the older leaves later on by using two changes of water to remove the bitter taste.

Make dandelion pancakes or waffles by adding the yellow flowers to pancake or waffle batter. Be sure to gather the flower heads in the morning and remove the green calyx, because it is bitter.

The roots are good in the spring, if boiled in salted water, changing it once. For a coffee substitute bake the scrubbed roots in a 275 degree oven for four hours or until the roots snap and are dark brown inside. Grind the roots in your blender or food processor.

Lamb's-quarters
(Chenopodium album)

The entire young plant and tender new leaves of older plants are used as salad greens or potherbs. It is available all summer and contains more vitamins than spinach.

Plantain (Plantago rugelii and Plantago lanceolata)

Of the two most common varieties, one has a narrow long leaf and a white flower cluster, while the common plantain has rounder, wider leaves and sends up green flower spikes.

Use the young leaves in salads with an oil vinegar dressing. To cook plantain, just boil it quickly in very little water until tender, but still crunchy.

For a tea high in vitamins A and C, steep several leaves in a cup of boiling water for 30 minutes. In our area the cooled tea is applied as a poultice for insect bites.

Parch or grind the seeds for something that tastes like wheat germ and use in your recipes where wheat germ is called for.

Purslane
(Portulaca oleracea)

Gather this creeping plant for use raw or boiled. Put the end tips of purslane in a tossed salad.

Add chopped purslane to a rice casserole. In a greased casserole add 1/2 cup uncooked rice, 1 cup meat stock, 1 cup water, 1 tablespoon grated onion, 1/2 cup butter, 1/2 cup grated cheese, 1 cup purslane, plus salt and pepper to taste. Stir slightly and bake 350 degrees for 45 minutes.

Roll the stems and leaves of purslane in flour, dip into an egg batter, reroll in cracker crumbs and fry for a yummy snack.

Use the fleshy stems in your favorite dill pickle recipe, in place of cucumbers.

Stinging nettle
(Urtica gracilis)

Use gloves to gather the young plants in the spring when they are not more than 8 inches tall. Cook in at least one change of water. Once stinging nettles are washed and cooked or steamed they lose their stinging quality.

Red clover
(Trifolium repens)

Eat the young leaves and flowers raw, but don't eat large quantities of clover raw, as they can cause bloat.

Try making biscuits substituting dried clover blossoms for part of the flour.

Pick the flower heads in full bloom, but before they start to turn brown. Dry them slowly, and use them for a light yellow tea that is quite delicious: add 1 teaspoon dried, crushed flowerheads to 1 cup of boiling water and let steep for 3-5 minutes.

Watercress

(Nasturtium officinale)

Eat the leaves and tender shoots that grow above the water raw. You can also cook it like spinach. Make certain that you get your watercress from running water. If there is a question that the water in which it grows might be contaminated, soak it in water with a water purifying tablet before using.

Shepherd's purse

(Capsella Bursa-pastoris)

The young leaves, flowers, and seeds may be used in a tossed salad. It may also be boiled as a potherb, using only one change of water. Indians gathered and ground the seeds of this plant into a meal for breads.

Dock

(Rumex... various species)

All of the young leaves are edible as a spinach substitute, so dock can be utilized either in a fresh salad or cooked. It is often used here with poke, lamb's-quarters, wild lettuce, and dandelion leaves to make a "mess of greens", being cooked in two hot water baths and seasoned with salt, pepper, butter and vinegar.

Chickweed

(Stellaria spp.)

Chickweed remains above ground all winter, so is a wild edible food source all year. Use the young tips of stems in salads. It tastes very good steamed or cooked briefly.

Scrambled eggs with chickweed are also delicious. For chickweed soup add 1 cup of chickweed to 4 cups of milk, 4 tablespoons chopped onion, 3 tablespoons cornstarch, 2 tablespoons butter, plus salt and pepper to taste.

Thistle

(Circium vulgare)

Clippers, scissors, and gloves are necessary for thistle picking. Cut the stalk when young, strip off all the leaves and thorny stickers.

The peeled stems can then be eaten raw or cooked in salted water. They have a bit of a celery flavor.

As emergency food the stems can be gathered late in the summer. Even though they are fibrous and tough, they are still tasty. Pull the stems through the teeth and discard the stringy part.

Cattail

(Typha latifolia)

The cattail is a source of food the entire year. In early spring the new shoots from the roots make good pickle substitutes.

In early spring dig up some of the roots. Peel the outside layer and the spongy layers away leaving the central core. Cut this core into 4-inch pieces, dry them for a day, then rub out the flour to use for biscuits, pancakes, or whatever, giving a nutty taste to baked goods.

After the flour has been taken out, one can then make jelly by boiling the remains of the roots for 10 minutes in enough water to cover them. For every cup of liquid, add an equal amount of sugar. Add a package of pectin for every four cups of juice. This jelly is delicious and looks a bit like honey in both color and taste.

After the cattail shoots are above the ground, but under two feet tall, the central white core is wonderful eaten raw with a hint of cucumber taste. Boil it for a few minutes in salted water, and it is an asparagus substitute. These shoots can also be blanched and frozen for winter use.

The green bloom spikes can be gathered and prepared as one would corn on the cob. Put the spikes in boiling water for 5 minutes, drain, eat with butter and salt to taste.

Next the green bloom spikes turn bright yellow as they become covered with pollen. Put a plastic bag over the entire head and shake. Use this pollen in pancakes, muffins, and cookies, substituting pollen for part of the wheat flour in any recipe.

Field sorrel

(Rumex acetosella)

Use field sorrel in tossed salads. However, it contains potassium oxalate, which can be poisonous if eaten raw in large quantities, so only use a small amount at a time. Boiling it causes it to lose its poison potential.

Cat brier

(Similax tamnoids)

Snap off the flat, fleshy stems of this bristly climbing plant. Use this asparagus-like vegetable served raw, boiled, or in a casserole. The greenbrier shoots can also be placed in a dill crock. Layer shoots with dill seed or fresh dill weed, onion slices, hot peppers, and wild grape leaves in a brine of one part salt, 1/2 part vinegar, and 10 parts water. Let ferment for two-to-three weeks, pack into sterilized jars and seal.

The root can be dug in the fall and throughout the winter. Clean and dry the roots, cut them up, and pound on them to make flour to be used in baking.

The orchard:

Apples...

A wealth of varieties not found in stores are available to the home orchardist

An agricultural tome of the 1950s listed over 1,000 varieties of apples, all of which had been introduced by European settlers. (The native American variety is a small, hard crab apple.)

And although there has been a trend in this century to "standardize" the apple, the lovely pome hasn't gone the way of the square tomato. There are still hundreds of varieties to choose from for eating, drinking and preserving.

Here are a few of them and their outstanding characteristics.

Jonathan: brilliant red with crisp, tender, often red-tinged flesh; both sweet and tart, aromatic; winter apple; good for eating and cooking.

Idared: related to Jonathan, but better keeper.

Northern Spy: yellow skin with bright red stripes; fragrant, juicy, somewhat tart, old-time favorite, good keeper.

Russett: several varieties, share fine, sweet taste and keeping abilities; often gnarled in appearance.

Rome Beauty: large red, fat and squatty, best for baking, but also good eating; yellowish flesh, mild and juicy.

Beacon: attractive red fruit with yellow flesh, medium tough, juicy, subacid; not good keeper, best for baking, but early tart all-purpose apple.

Puritan, Paulared, Viking: similar qualities to Beacon.

Greenings: several kinds, golden or green skin, flesh firm and yellowish; good keepers, thought of as the "pie" apple but in last century esteemed as a fresh dessert fruit.

Wealthy: medium-sized, greenish yellow skin, blushed and striped with red; flesh tender, white and crisp; good fresh and for sauce, poor keeper.

Manet: medium-sized, early, creamy yellow skin striped with crimson; aromatic, juicy, fine-grained and tender; best fresh and for sauce, poor keeper.

McIntosh: subject to apple scab, important commercially; large red apple with tender, aromatic, juicy flesh that's whiter than the Jonanthan; good keeper.

Macoun: turn-of-the-century improvement on the McIntosh, similar in appearance, but has more character in taste and aroma, and a finer texture. Does not keep well; excellent for eating.

Cortland: similar to McIntosh with lighter red skin color and firmer flesh that's good for salads because it discolors slowly; all-purpose; good keeper.

Winesap: medium-sized, somewhat oblong, crisp tart, tangy, deep red skin, firm, yellowish flesh, excellent for eating and cooking.

Stayman Winesap: very hard, juicy red apple with white freckles, all-purpose.

Spartan: red-green skin, white-to-green flesh, good for eating, baking, sauce.

Snows: dark red, tart, white flesh, excellent keepers, old-time favorites, make best taffy apples.

Red Delicious: long-stemmed, oblong, red with sweet flesh; good keeper, best for salads, turns mushy when cooked.

Golden Delicious: long and tapered with rosy, bright yellow skin and white flesh, delicate taste; good for cooking, baking, canning, jelly and apple butter; favored for baby food, very sweet.

Secor: late fruit, red striped with red blush, juicy with bright flavor; excellent keeper.

York Imperial: greenish yellow with a strong red blush; mildly sweet, aromatic, spicy; good for pies because it keeps its shape in cooking.

Whitney Crab: large crab apple, lemon yellow skin tinged with red, flesh yellow, crisp; used for pickling and fresh; gets mealy in maturity, most popular of larger crabs.

Note to readers who ask to see articles from older, out-of-print COUNTRYSIDES: This one is reprinted from our September, 1977 issue.

Apple sources

"For flavor, go to the old varieties." —The director of the British National Fruit Trials, which maintains a living museum of more than 3,000 varieties.

Here are two sources with awesome selections of apples you won't find in the supermarket... or at most local nurseries:

Southmeadow Fruit Gardens, 10603 Cleveland Ave., Baroda, MI 49101, lists more than 280 varieties of apples, along with other fruits and berries.

Schlabach's Nursery, 3901 County Road 135, Millersburg, OH 44654 offers more than three dozen different apples, as well as other fruits and berries.

The woodlot:

What can a tree be used for?

Once they get past the obvious uses like furniture, tooth picks, houses and paper, most people are hard-pressed to think of other products made from trees. The fact of the matter is, there are thousands of products – many of which we use every day – that we aren't aware are made from timber.

When man first discovered fire, he realized the value of trees as firewood. Later, when we began building shelters, we used trees for lumber. In the process of making lumber, however, there was a tremendous amount of waste: sawdust, bark and wood scraps all had to be hauled away and that created more problems.

Then scientists began to analyze the structure of trees and they found a veritable cornucopia of useful material.

The bark of the tree is used in the production of chemicals, resins, waxes, vitamins, plywood adhesives, plastic fillers, lacquers and oil-spill control agents. It is also used as a fuel in forest industry mills, for mulches and soil conditioners.

Wood flours and melamine resins using cellulose filler are principal components of dinnerware, toys, handles for cooking utensils, telephone housings and camera cases.

From ethyl cellulose and other chemical-based cellulose we make tool handles, photographic films, sausage casings and football helmets. Acetate filament yarns make textile products such as clothing, drapes and rugs. Nitro-cellulose is used in making solid rocket propellants and explosives.

Torula yeast is a high-protein product made from wood sugars as a by-product of the pulping process in papermaking. Different types of torula are used in baby food and cereals, in feed supplements for cattle, fish and chickens and in pet foods. Torula has been found to make bees and lobsters grow faster.

Turpentine and tall oil reclaimed from the paper-pulping process are important ingredients in paint, varnish, adhesives, asphalt, printing inks, rubber products, soaps and polishes. Synthesized essential oils are used in chewing gum, toothpaste, menthol cigarettes, detergents and shampoos.

Bark, ground wood and spent pulping liquors provide a source of energy for the pulp and paper industry. Nationally, more than half of the industry's total energy is self-generated from these residues.

Forests and water

Still another forest product that is vital to our existence – without which we wouldn't survive, in fact – but which few would ever think of is water. Our forests collect, clean, regulate and recycle much of the water we use and drink every day.

Forests are natural water regulators. Forest soil can absorb up to 18 inches of water from rain, then slowly release it back into natural channels and watercourses. And forest soil cleanses the water too, removing the impurities. That's why so many municipal reservoirs are located as close as possible to forests.

Trees absorb carbon dioxide and release oxygen, they help keep our water supply fresh and protect our wetlands. And trees are renewable. There are no "dry holes," no "exhausted veins," no "bottom of the barrel" in a forest.

But if we are to continue to enjoy this precious natural resource, we must practice good forest management.

Who's the smartest? A cat or a pig?

When it comes to animal intelligence, people give highest marks to their pets, and put chickens and turkeys at the bottom of the IQ poll.

A survey of Oregon State University faculty and students ranks the dog and cat as most intelligent with the pig and horse close behind.

Next came the cow and sheep. Last, in a dead heat, were the chicken and turkey.

The survey of people's perception of animal intelligence was conducted by OSU animal scientists Steve Davis and Peter Cheeke. They said perception of intelligence influences how animals are treated. "The smarter we think animals are," Davis said, "the more humanely we care for them."

Those surveyed included faculty and graduate students in animal science, zoology, veterinary medicine, English, and philosophy, plus members of the Oregon branch of the American Association of Laboratory Animal Sciences, who are in charge of university research animals.

"There are really no differences between the groups of respondents and their perceptions of relative intelligence," Davis said. "Regardless of profession or educational background, rankings of intelligence came out remarkably alike."

Respondents were asked to assign a number to the different species with 1 being the highest intelligence and 5 being the lowest. Overall, dogs earned a 2.1 ranking and cats 2.3. The pig and horse were tied at 2.6.

The animal science faculty and students and veterinary medicine faculty rated the cat and pig even. Philosophy faculty rated the pig smarter than the cat. "Maybe they have pot-bellied pigs as pets, or maybe they've seen the movie, 'Babe,'" Davis theorized.

Ranked at the bottom in perceived intelligence were the cow (3.2), the sheep (3.5) and the chicken and turkey (both at 4.0).

Proposed rules on organic farming raise hackles, and questions

Late Bulletin: At press time the news arrived that the government has backtracked on its proposal after receiving more than 200,000 letters of protest. Irradiation, genetic engineering and sewage sludge will not be allowed on products labelled organic.

Should foods altered by genetic engineering, undefined toxic ingredients, sewage sludge, irradiation and antibiotics be considered "organic"?

Martha Brown, Editor
The Cultivar
The Center for Agroecology and Sustainable Food Systems
University of California

The U.S. Department of Agriculture's proposed rule which would govern the National Organic Program has been met with a storm of protest by groups and individuals from the organic farming, marketing, and certification communities, as well as from consumer and environmental organizations.

The proposal grew out of the 1990 federal Organic Foods Production Act, intended to establish a national definition of "organic" for farmers and food processors. Currently, many states and a number of private certification organizations have their own rules governing inputs and practices that can be called "organic." The organic industry hoped that setting a national standard would create a level playing field for farmers and food processors, help build consumer confidence in the organic label, and increase opportunities for both interstate and international commerce.

As proposed, the USDA's rule would do just the opposite. After a seven-year effort by members of the National Organic Standards Board (a decision-making body established as part of the National Organic Program) to come up with a set of practices acceptable to the organic community, the USDA has chosen to ignore many of the Board's recommendations in proposing national organic standards.

The proposed rule opens the door to use of genetically engineered organisms, food irradiation, undefined toxic "inert" ingredients, sewage sludge, and other materials currently prohibited by organic certifiers in California and elsewhere. Conditions under which livestock could be called "organically raised" are also questionable, allowing for confinement with no access to the outdoors, up to 20% non-organic feed, and antibiotic treatments.

These possibilities alone are enough to dilute the existing definition of organic and damage consumer confidence in the industry. In a recent press release, Sierra Club Executive Director Carl Pope said, "If USDA's proposed rules are adopted as written, consumers will lose all faith in the 'organic' label, and a $3.5 billion industry in organic products will be threatened."

The International Federation of Organic Agriculture Movements has also responded, noting that the possibility of genetically engineered organisms and the proposed prohibition of private certification based on standards higher than or in addition to federal requirements will "drive a wedge through the heart of the U.S. organic movement and effectively destroy the hard-won consumer confidence in organics – presumably the reason for a law in the first place."

As written, the proposed standards would not be acceptable to many foreign governments and private certification groups, negating efforts to expand overseas markets for U.S. products.

In addition, the proposed rule ignores the authority granted to the National Organic Standards Board (NOSB) by Congress, shifting decision-making over materials which could be used in organic production to the USDA. This means that even if a list of inputs acceptable to the organic community were established, the USDA would be in a position to alter the materials standards without NOSB intervention.

Missing the bigger picture

Also disturbing is the USDA's reductionist approach toward organic production. Nowhere in the rule is the bigger picture of agroecosystem health and biodiversity addressed. These issues have been central to the efforts of the Center for Agroecology & Sustainable Food Systems (the Center) and a priority for existing certification groups.

For example, California Certified Organic Farmers (the state's oldest organic certification group) defines organic agriculture as "an ecological production management system that promotes and enhances biodiversity, biological cycles and soil biological activity. It is based on minimal use of off-farm inputs and management practices that restore, maintain, and enhance ecological harmony."

The proposed rule's failure to include language that speaks to agroecosystem health is one of the red flags noted by Center entomologist Sean Swezey. "The USDA can't get away from the idea that organic products are just commodities," says Swezey, who also acts as a technical representative and member of the California Organic Foods Advisory Board.

"The Center's research has continually emphasized that organic farming is a process that needs to be verified in the marketplace. It's not merely a final product with a list of approved inputs; the performance of organic farming is as identifiable as a trademark, and should be. The USDA needs to be informed that organic farming has always wanted performance and process to be revealed in the label."

Swezey explains that private certifiers such as CCOF look not only at what goes into an organic product in terms of inputs, but also at how farmers manage their land. For example, CCOF requires a grower's farming plans to include cover cropping, crop rotation, composting and other practices which protect and enhance

Organic market growers are proud of their produce; they don't want to see the "organic" label watered down.

natural resources. Says Swezey, "The proposed rule seems to negate the idea of materials and performance standards being rigorously reviewed in the certification process. They seem to want to evade high standards with very vague language."

Center member Thomas Wittman, a long-time organic farmer, believes that rather than tax farmers for the right to call their product organic—as the proposed rule would do—the government should be supporting organic growers for their efforts to protect the environment. "We're already doing what the government is trying to get conventional growers to do, especially in terms of limiting soil erosion and using cover crops," he says.

Adds Swezey, "The consumer has a certain picture in mind when they buy an organic commodity that includes the way the farmer is farming. The rule in many ways will obscure that picture and make it difficult to hold organic farming to accepted and well-known performance standards."

Swezey believes the California law that now governs organic certification in the state should be the model for any national program. "A number of the Center's staff and farming clients have been involved in crafting a very effective law, one that holds growers to higher standards than the proposed rule. Adopting the federal rule as written would mean diminishing or losing 15 to 20 years of effort in California," he says.

Rule prompts action

Wittman notes one positive result of the USDA's efforts. "The proposed rule has galvanized the organic industry into one very strong lobby, which has never happened before. We're looking at a big environmental movement in the making."

Public interest in the rule is already evident. In the first 10 weeks of the comment period, the USDA received more than 12,000 letters to its web site <www.ams.usda.gov/nop> and extended the comment period an extra 30 days (to April 30).

Swezey also sees a silver lining to the controversy over the proposed rule, viewing it as an opportunity to influence existing attitudes toward organic production. "The rule represents a very interesting emergence of the disharmony between national agricultural policy and the organic industry," he says. "We need to strive to educate the USDA and political decision-makers as to the uniqueness of both the process and the product in organic commodities."

Nutrient content of some fertilizer materials (%)

Material	Approx. NPK	Mg	Ca	S
Activated Sludge	(6-2-0)	1.8	0.9	0.4
Basic slag	(0-5-0)	3.4	32.0	0.2
Blood meal	(13-0-0)	0.4	trace	trace
Bonemeal, steamed	(2-11-0)	0.3	24.1	0.2
Gypsum	(0-0-0)	trace	22.4	18.6
Limestone, dolomitic	(0-0-0)	12.0	21.0	—
Limestone, pure	(0-0-0)	trace	40.0	trace
Manure†, beef	(0.7-0.5-0.6)	0.1	0.1	0.1
Manure†, dairy	(0.5-0.3-0.5)	0.1	0.2	0.1
Manure†, pig	(0.5-0.3-0.5)	0.1	0.6	0.1
Manure†, poultry	(1.3-1.3-0.6)	0.3	1.8	0.2
Manure†, sheep & goat	(1.4-0.5-1.2)	0.2	0.6	0.1
Monoammonium phosphate	(12-50-0)	0.3	1.4	2.6
Peat	(3-0-0)	0.3	0.7	1.0
Phosphate rock	(0-6-0)	0.1	33.1	trace
Potassium sulphate	(0-0-50)	trace	trace	18.0
Sulphate of potash magnesia	(0-0-22)	11.0	trace	22.0
Tankage	(7-10-0)	0.3	10.9	0.4
Wood ash	(0-2-5)	0.2	14.0	trace

† fresh manure, as it comes from the animal: urine, feces, but no bedding.

Starting wildflowers from seed

Your patience will be rewarded

JULIE HUNTER
ARKANSAS

Starting wildflowers from seed can take patience. However, the patience is rewarded by being able to have a wide variety of wildflowers growing in your own yard.

Below is a list of tools and materials that can be helpful for establishing healthy wildflowers:

√ Plastic seed flats with clear plastic domes
√ Plastic or foam pots and cups
√ Some kind of trays to catch drainage from the plant pots
√ Homemade or commercial potting soil
√ Perlite or commercial seed starter mix
√ Purchased plastic or wooden labels or some kind of materials for making your own labels
√ Marking pen with waterproof ink
√ Hand mister
√ Long snouted indoor watering can
√ Measuring spoons and cups
√ Scissors
√ Tweezers
√ Table knife
√ Something to make holes in soil
√ Pressers (boards of different sizes for firming soil in pots and flats)
√ Paper towels
√ Whiskbroom and dustpan
√ Soil and wall thermometers
√ Notebook and reference materials
√ Four foot shop lights
√ Tables or benches for propagation
√ Egg cartons for elevating trays of young plants or seeds

If using 6.4 ounce foam coffee cups as plant pots (we often recycle foam cups gathered from various events we attend; we wash them out and they're ready for use), cut a 1/2 inch hole in the bottom of the cup for drainage and remove one inch from the top. This way 32 cups will fit into a plastic flat, and the plastic dome will fit over the flat.

If you do not have plastic domes, cover the flats with plastic wrap or clear plastic after planting and watering the seeds. You can also use a clear plastic bag, closing it with a twist-tie.

Fill the cups 3/4 full of potting soil and press firmly. Then fill the pot to within 1/2 inch of the rim and put 2-4 seeds in each cup. Cover the seed with perlite or a sterilized seed starter mix.

Push large seeds 1/2 inch into the pot and firm the soil over them. When using very fine seed, take a pinch of the seed and sprinkle it on the surface of the soil, but do not cover the seeds. However, do press down to make certain all the seeds make a good contact with the soil.

Label each container as to the kind of plant that it contains. After the seeds are planted put the cups in a container of water until moisture dampens the surface layer of the planting mix. Remove them from the water. Do not let the mix become soggy. Put the pots in the flat and cover.

Put the flats under the shop lights and lower the lights to within six inches of the flat. Use lengths of light chain fastened to the light fixtures with open hooks to make for easy height adjustment, as the seedlings grow.

Daily test the soil. Keep it moist, but not soggy. Apply a fine mist of water over the top when necessary.

When the seeds have germinated remove the cover. At this stage when the seedlings need moisture, mist with chamomile tea until the seedlings have developed their second set of leaves. (1 chamomile tea bag in 4 cups of boiling water; allow it to sit for 24 hours to ensure a strong brew at room temperature.)

After the seeds have germinated, the first leaves will appear. You might want to feed them with manure tea once a week as a starter feed.

Be sure to thin the seedlings to two to three plants per container. Fill extra containers with potting soil to receive the extra plants. Grasp the leaves between the thumb and finger while lifting the plant from the soil with a fork (a cocktail fork from a garage sale works well for us). Place the seedling in the new container, putting the root ball and part of the stem in the hole that you made beforehand. Press the soil around the plant and put the container in a pan of water until the top soil is moistened. When the remaining plants grow large enough to handle, plant the extra seedlings in individual containers also or take your scissors and cut the stem off close to the top of the soil.

Water less, withhold fertilizer, and lower the temperature a few degrees during the last week your seedlings are indoors.

Move the flats to a sheltered place outdoors, where they are protected from the wind and direct sunlight. Watch the plants carefully to add water, cover them, or move them indoors overnight until temperatures stabilize.

Transplanting seedlings is best done on a damp, cloudy, windless day. Disturb the roots as little as possible. Water each plant as it is placed in the soil, and firm the soil around it for good contact with the roots.

Protect your new planting from sun, wind, and cold weather in the beginning using whatever system has worked well for you in the past: floating row cover, brush or leafy branches stuck in the ground, bottomless plastic jugs, etc.

Growing celery substitutes

JULIE HUNTER
ARKANSAS

To get that great taste of celery one doesn't have to tackle growing demanding celery, but can grow instead three dependable and easy to grow cousins—cutting celery, celeriac, and lovage. Each contains some sodium and will add a slightly salty taste to any food without use of the salt shaker along with that unique distinctive celery flavor, some of the crunch, and wonderful aromatic celery-like seeds.

Plant cutting celery that looks like parsley in the spring. Start the seeds indoors two to three months before your last frost date. Because the seeds are tiny, just dust them with a bit of covering. Keep the growing medium moist, but not wet. Set out the plants 12 inches apart. Cutting celery will grow into a bush that sends up thin new stalks around its edges as it grows.

Varieties to look for are Zwolsche Krul, an old Dutch cultivar with dark green leaves, Par-cel, an old European heirloom variety with curly leaves, French Dinant with branches that grow outward, and HeungKunn, a Chinese cutting celery with a spreading growth habit.

Start celeriac plants 10-12 weeks before your last spring frost. Set seedlings 8-12 inches apart in loose soil. It is known as celery root or knob celery, because it develops a thick and round underground root that looks like a hairy baseball. Peel off the cover, and the white inside is smooth and tastes like celery. It is wonderful diced or grated, cooked or raw.

Harvest celeriac by pulling it out of the ground after mild frosts in the fall when the nighttime temperatures are in the 20's. Just shake off the dirt, cut off the tops, and store the roots in sawdust or straw in your root cellar, or in a loosely closed plastic bag in your refrigerator's crisper drawer until you are ready to use them.

Lovage is a large perennial that tastes like celery with all parts being edible from the roots to the flowers. After it is established it is one of the first plants to send up green shoots in the spring.

Start lovage seeds indoors about eight weeks before the last spring frost in your area. Plant them two times the diameter of the seed deep. Transplant seedlings when they are two or more inches high. Because a mature plant can reach six feet in height and two to three feet across, space seedlings four feet apart.

Lovage has a more intense flavor than celery, so use less of it than celery. Lovage will go to seed in the early summer. Cut the whole plant to the ground and new leaves will emerge and continue to grow most of the summer. Otherwise its texture and taste will be too strong for eating.

Be sure to try drying the leaves of cutting celery or lovage to use during your off growing season. Just trim the leaves from their stalks and dry them slowly. When the leaves are crispy store in a glass jar or other airtight container. Use as needed to add that celery flavor to soups, stews, salads and vegetable dishes.

A few sources:
Abundant Life Seed Foundation
PO Box 772
Port Townsend, WA 98368
Web: www.abundantlifeseed.org

The Cooks' Garden
PO Box 535
Londonderry, VT 05148
Web: www.cooksgarden.com

Nichol's Garden Nursery
1190 Old Salem Road NE
Albany, Oregon 97321-4580
Web: www.nicholsgardennursery.com

Pinetree Garden Seeds
PO Box 300
Gloucester, ME 04260
Web: www.superseeds.com
Also, check your favorite catalogs.

Saving tomato seeds

Tomato seeds are best saved by fermentation.

This is done by squeezing the seeds and pulp into a container. (Plastic deli containers work fine, and even homesteaders who don't buy things like that can easily find them. If you can't, use a bowl of similar size.) Don't fill the container more than about half full.

Leave it, uncovered and out of the sun, in a place where you won't mind the fruit flies. Don't stir or mix it.

Depending on the temperature, in three to five days a white mold will form on the top, with seeds at the bottom. Skim off the fungus and either strain the rest through a coarse sieve or add a little water and clean the seeds with a swirling motion, like panning gold.

Spread the seeds on an absorbent surface such as a paper plate or several thickness' of newspaper, out of the sun, until they're dry.

Store them in a small airight container in a cool place. The refrigerator is fine. Be sure to label them as to variety and date, and any other information you feel is pertinent.

Properly stored, they should be good for five years or more.

You might note that other sources list different lifespans for the same seeds. Among the reasons are variations in storage conditions and many other factors. It's best to use the freshest seeds possible, but even then, proper storage is mandatory.

Growing lima beans

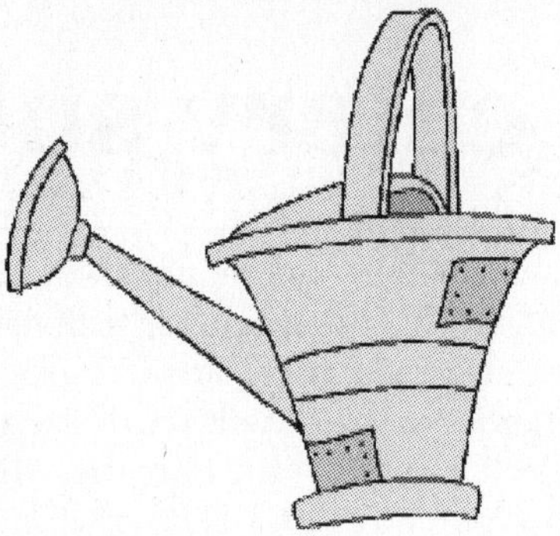

ELIZABETH & CROW MILLER
NEW YORK

Lima beans provide both carbohydrate and vegetable protein, thus making an important contribution to your family's diet. Limas are easier to shell than crowder peas, stand more heat and drought than green peas, and sustain less insect damage than green beans.

We use green manure and sheet composting procedures to improve the soil for bean plantings. During fall cleanup we spread leaves, grass clippings, and vegetable stubble over the future bean site. We also add some dolomitic limestone to the sheet compost.

We sow winter ryegrass to serve as a green manure crop, but natural grasses and weeds will serve the same purpose. Green manure is a crop to produce organic matter that is tilled into the soil. We till this growth into the soil just a week before we plant our limas. Succulent green tops and roots of these indigenous plants provide excellent fertilizer for our young plants.

All rows are spaced three feet apart to accommodate the tiller for cultivation. Limas bush out quite a lot anyway; even in lighter soil, we plant at least 2-1/2 feet apart.

Tilling keeps out weeds and helps the soil form a "dust mulch." As weather becomes hot and dry, this dust mulch atop the soil breaks the capillary action, preventing evaporation of soil moisture. At this point, we no longer till the limas, as the dry weather discourages most weeds, and the limas are too large to allow the tiller to pass between them without damaging some of the blooms and pods.

Limas will grow even in very dry soil. After they bloom, if weather is dry, we soak the soil thoroughly between the rows. This encourages the pods to fill out well, and the plants will bloom again for second and third crops.

We exercise care in watering: too much causes the beans to rot. It seems to encourage bean leaf beetles, too. For the most part though, insects show a minimum interest in lima beans. We interplant marigolds in the bean rows and have no problems with bugs.

When your lima beans plump up, with pods all the way to the tips, pick the mature ones, leaving the flat pods for a later picking.

When limas seem to finish bearing, we water again, and perhaps loosen the soil around them with a hoe. In a few days, the limas wave a new crop of blooms, and we're on our way again with more limas.

Whether you like them large or small, fat or flat, bushy or climbing, you can find a lima to add satisfaction to your gardening and to your diet.

Raised beds raise eyebrows

JUDY SMITH
MISSISSIPPI

How come every gardener I know has a beautifully planned, perfectly lush vegetable garden and I don't? I know I try as hard as they do. I put every inch of corn and peppers on graph paper. I plan how not to crowd the broccoli and how many square inches of carrots to put in.

I dig for hours on my wide beds. I hand-pulverize every clod, always with a plan at hand. Never mind how hard I work; the garden will soon become a national eyesore.

My double-dug, intensively manured and strawed, carefully not-walked-on beds always end up sinking during the first hard rain. I spend entire days stealing dirt from every corner of the yard to build them back up.

The "experts" can talk all they want to about those beds being easier to weed, but that ain't necessarily so. I've decided that these experts are Yankees and Yankees must not have the weeds we have here. Up through 24 inches of mulch come healthy Johnsongrass and crawley-grass. The books say eight inches will stop them—but not for me.

Those folks also say that the walkways become compacted from all the walking and never a weed will grow. But for me they certainly do. I spend more time hoeing the paths than I do picking vegetables.

But my worst worry has been the comments of my neighbors. In various towns since my conversion to raised beds six years ago, my neighbors have said,"Who you gonna bury in that?" The neighbors are right. The danged things always look like graves. I never answer their questions, I just smile wisely and let them figure out who.

This year being above par for my gardening, I've done myself one better. Husband Carl found an old arched rose trellis at the dump and brought it to me. I stuck it in the ground on the end of the longest grave. Wouldn't you know it? My grave now has a headstone! I intend for the butterbeans to eventually cover the trellis, but until they do, I'll have to live with The Look.

Living with neighborly ridicule, slovenly beds and under-enthusiastic produce isn't easy. In fact, it's depressing. The one thing I've asked all my friends is, "Please, don't give me any more pretty gardening books!"

Reprinted from Volume 70/4.

Restoring old apple trees

Those ancient, gnarled gems can be made productive again

Lea Landmann
Countryside Staff
(Reprinted from 61/9:12, 1977)

One of the legacies of our predecessors in the countryside are myriads of picturesque but unproductive old apple trees dotting the face of the land, particularly east of the Mississippi. These ancient gnarled gems can be used for more than their shade, according to former orchardist Chiatanya York, Union, Maine, executive director of the Maine Organic Farmers and Gardeners Association.

At a workshop in Bar Harbor he outlined a program for restoring these relics of Johnny Appleseed.

While his talk was eminently practical, he opened it on an almost mystical plane. "A good grower will meditate upon the tree, studying it for at least one-half hour to get the feel of it before he begins any restoration. When you walk into an orchard that has been mishandled or neglected, you can almost feel the anger in the groves. Remember to be considerate of the tree and foster its health in its geographic setting." Chiatanya said. He also recommends spending time studying and walking through older orchards which have been pruned to "open center." This should be done prior to any pruning to your own apple trees. It's also a good idea, he said, to invite yourself to spend a day assisting a commercial orchardist in his pruning tasks.

Chiatanya stressed that "sanitation should be put into double capitol letters. Remove all of the old fruit, twigs and leaves from under the tree. Keep the grasses trimmed and compost all of the debris into a hot pile, using the freshest possible horse manure to get the action going."

His step-by-step restoration method is as follows:

Pruning: Remember that there's a definite relationship between the crown of the tree and its root system. They almost exactly correspond, so you don't want to do too much alteration at any one time. Those roots need a chance to adapt. Except for removing suckers, the restoration should be spread over a two to three-year period. Be considerate of the tree; you don't want to get it out of synch with its root system. It will take five to six years before the trees regain equilibrium.

Start with the deadwood—any that is lichen-covered and/or gray, that is obviously brittle with no green layer. Prune when the tree is asleep or dormant. (In Maine that's from mid-October to the beginning of March.) Be careful not to prune too near the tree's "wake-up time" in early spring. The worst time to prune a tree is in mid-summer, August in Maine. However, you can selectively prune off the suckers and waterspouts in summer to leave that much more available nutrition for the fruit.

Chiatanya's orchardist friend, Steve Page, says that two weeks after petal fall is the best time to remove excess fruit — fruit that touches another. A little selective pruning can be done at this time also, according to Page.

After studying the tree and eliminating the deadwood, consider the sun. The idea is to open up the tree to the air and sun so that a robin can fly through it. An old tree is apt to have many interlacing branches. You'll keep one of any pair of them. The open center form, always stressed in the past, limited yields. If a modified central leader plan is followed, you wind up with kind of a Christmas tree shape. Go with what branches you have and open them up, leaving most "risers," unless they're overshadowing the lower branches that go straight down to achieve a feathering effect. The tree will be your guide. Page says to bear in mind while pruning, that the ideal angle for a bearing branch is 45 degrees.

Sometimes while pruning, you will accidentally break and tear off a branch. Then do a bark tracing down from the tear using a heavy-duty case knife. Check it again next season to make sure it's healing properly. If not, redo it entirely. (See illustration.)

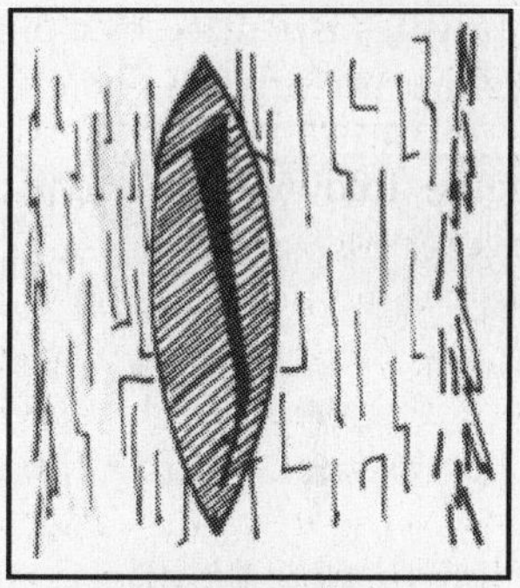

Bark tracing

Tools: You'll need pruners, both a small pair and some loppers, a hatchet, long-handled hooks, and a pole saw-hook combination. A good, rugged, thick tree saw is a must. Remember to push and pull both when operating that saw. You have to be a bit of a monkey when you work with trees, but the long-handled saws and the proper equipment help quite a bit. Those saws should be kept sharp, not only for ease, but because you're using an entirely different set of muscles when pruning a tree. You'll tend to tire very easily because of this, so it makes sense to keep those tools in top condition. Dull tools are also rough on a tree.

Painting: Immediately after pruning, paint any wound larger than a dime in size with an asphalt base paint. Oil or water base paints aren't *satisfactory*.

(Note: The University of New Hampshire has done considerable research on painting tree wounds and the results indicate that in most cases it is best to leave wounds, particularly the smaller ones, unpainted, because painting appears to inhibit callus growth over the wound. Chiatanya still likes to paint, however, feeling that it seals the wood from insects, disease and rot.)

You can make your own tree painting rig. Just buy an inexpensive oil can with a screw top. Unscrew the cap and shave down the handle of a plastic-handled paintbrush so it will fit in the oil can spout. Tape on a handle of rope or clothesline; fill the can with paint; and tie it on your belt or preferably, the hammer holster in your coveralls and you're in business. You can also use a long-handled paint brush, suspended by a piece of clothesline run through a hole drilled in the handle. Be sure to wear old clothes; it can be a messy job.

Family album:

Susan Lamb, Ohio, has what she calls a "postage stamp homestead." On 1/2 acre she has rabbits, chickens, and this 30' x 40' garden. "I raise 90% of everything we eat," she said.

Do a bark tracing around old injuries. Cover the area with orange shellac if it's quite large; otherwise use the black tree paint. If the tree is injured, and if there's one-half to two-thirds of the cambium left, try to heal it.

Scraping: If you look carefully at the tree bark, you'll see many little holes, most of them caused by birds that are after insects living in the bark. Scraping every couple of years when the tree is dormant is a necessary sanitation to remove those insects and their eggs and lichens. Spread a sheet under the tree, and taking an old, fairly blunt hoe, scrape the bark off carefully all around the tree. If you see any green, you're scraping too hard. Carefully gather up all of the scrapings from the sheet and burn them.

Whacking: Old orchardists practice this for fun. After pruning, painting and other repair work in the early spring, take a shovel handle and gently thump all around the tree trunk. It wakes up the tree, and it does seem to respond. You can even chant "I want apples" as you're doing it. The whacking loosens extraneous bark and gets the juices flowing, they say.

Fertilization: The best all around fertilizer for fruit trees is well-balanced compost from a hot compost pile. Work into the pile some rock powders like green-sand, granite dust or feldspar, some rock phosphates for potash (maybe wood ashes, although they leach away very quickly), potassium and trace elements. Add one of the meals, blood, cottonseed, or fish, for nitrogen.

The compost should be applied two feet from the trunk of the tree to one foot beyond the drip line. First, take a grub hoe and loosen all of the soil in the area. Then work the compost to 1 to 1-1/2 inches deep. Do this in fall or early spring, making one heavy application followed by lesser amounts every three or four years. With a crowbar, dig holes as deep as possible about every two feet and work in about 1/2 cup of rock powder and additional compost.

You can judiciously and sparingly add some chicken manure along with the compost, but the wisest use of manure in an orchard is to compost it first. Fertilize before June 1 in Maine so the new wood will have sufficient time to harden before winter.

Mulching: If you only do one thing to a fruit tree, mulch it. The mulch can be pulled back at least two feet from the trunk to discourage rodents. Some people are against mulching because they feel it will harbor insects and create an environment for scale. If in doubt, try one tree each way.

Clover or alfalfa can be planted in the orchard, mown, and then thrown back under the trees as mulch. However in some cold climates legumes can be counterproductive. According to Dr. Warren Stiles, Maine's state "apple man," warm rains in August release nitrogen resulting in slow fruit ripening and late growth that might not harden off thereby incurring winter kill.

You can mulch with hay, straw or seaweed or other organic material commonly available in your area. It's a good idea to create as varied mulch as possible.

Insect Control: Before the buds begin to swell (from March to early April in Maine) use a dormant oil spray made out of biodegradable liquid soap and 10W motor oil. When the flower buds are beginning to open, you can use a finer spray made from inexpensive miscible oil.

Cover the whole tree with the spray to give it a protective shield and to smother insects so they can't break dormancy. A small pump pressure rig can also be used for spraying; it would also be useful around the farmstead for applying seaweed foliar spray and compost inoculant.

Another control for insects can be made out of equal parts of cow manure, kaolin, sand, and diatomaceous earth and brushed on the tree. This will seal out bugs and feed the tree at the same time.

Liquid seaweed used as a foliar spray not only fertilizes, but it seems to be quite successful as a fungicide and seems to act as an insecticide, although it's not known why. Spray it on the trees when they're in the green tip stage, the pink tip, in mid-season, and then a couple of times later in the summer.

Pyrethrin and ryania compounds have been used effectively against insects. For fungus and bacteria, the best control is sanitation; also keep water out of any holes or "wells" in the tree as it will cause rot.

Mechanical insect controls include "yucky stuff" like bear grease, axle grease and tanglefoot. Apply a three-inch band of one of them all around the trunk about one foot above the ground. That way you can see the insects you are dealing with because they'll get stuck in the stuff.

Some research with plastic balls covered with tanglefoot done by Dr. Eugene Carpovich, Mt. Vernon, Maine, indicates that reddish-orange is the best color for attraction. There are also traps baited with a sex attractant and tanglefoot so the insect will get stuck in it.

For codling moths, cut bands of corrugated cardboard, secure them with elastic and the moths will use them to shelter in. When you see the pupae inside, remove the bands and burn them.

Chiatanya explained that apple trees naturally run in cycles of fat and thin years. While trees drop some fruit every year, in a heavy year, if they are overburdened, they will drop more excess fruit in June. Commercial chemical orchardists try to even out those cycles by spraying preservatives on the trees so they won't drop apples until fall when the pickers can get to them. The spraying means more fruit will drop in spring with the larger ones remaining on the tree "held" until fall.

The commercial people also subject the tree to any number of biocides, and the apple itself undergoes everything from being gassed to being coated with those biocides and preservatives.

For sure, those apples won't keep the doctor away, but a beautiful organic apple just radiates good health and nutrition.

Taming
the wild apple tree

Woods and scrub land often contain wild apple trees which have been seeded by animals. Some of these trees can be brought into production for the homestead, given the proper set of conditions and enough time.

One of the considerations is how much the wild tree is overshadowed by other trees. Can you cut the other trees back to the apple tree's drip line and then add another 10 feet?

If so, cut the other trees and take drastic action on the wild tree itself. Cut out most of the tree, leaving some new, thrifty, spaced suckers for sapling wood and using the old root stock. Just before the trees start to leaf out, you can put in scions or grafts. Scions should be stored in polyethylene bags in the refrigerator until used.

John Deppe, who has revived many old apple trees, advises ignoring the new varieties of apples and sticking to the old tried and trues like Russett, Black Oxford, Wolf River, Yellow Transparent, the Snows, Delights or Greenings as well as some of the newer scab-resistant varieties like Prima and Priscilla.

He doesn't recommend the practice of digging up wild root stock and transplanting it before grafting, feeling that the chances for success are much higher if the wild tree is left in its original location.

The rejuvenation process of grafting should spread out over three or four years. And during the restoration, remember that the object is to draw up the tree, encouraging the branches to grow high up in it.

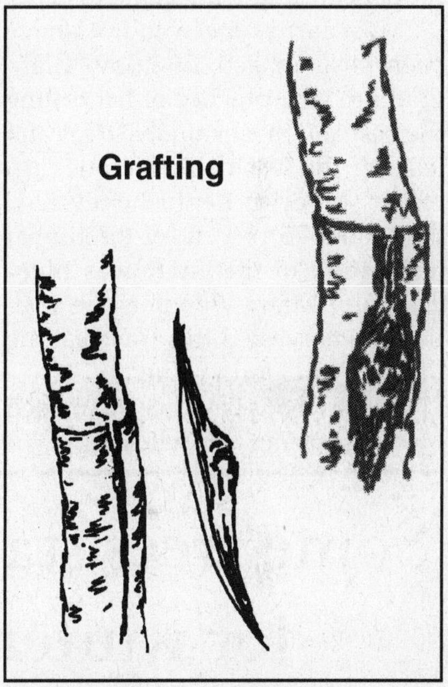

Grafting: The best way to learn this skill is by watching an old-timer do it. The second best is to consult a basic text on fruit science at your local library, and then practice.

The general outlines for grafting are to take the scion, split it open a bit, leaving attached a thin sliver with a wide back and a thick front. Line up the green or cambium layers on the branch with that of the scion. Then seal it with heated beeswax or grafting compound to keep out the air and its moisture. Check it in a couple of weeks to see if it is taking. If not, do it again below the unsuccessful graft.

The woodlot:

Multipurpose woodlots require management

Woodlots have many uses, and on most homesteads they serve more than one purpose. Woodlands can provide building materials, firewood, shade for livestock, hunting, cash from timber products, recreation, wildlife habitat... or simply the satisfaction of protecting an "unspoiled bit of wilderness."

All of these can be enhanced by proper care and management.

Most farm-type woodlots have been mismanaged, often by "high-grading," the practice of harvesting the best and most valuable trees and leaving the less desirable ones. (A recent survey in Kentucky revealed that about 75 percent of the timber harvesting in that state was high-grading.) Many woodlots are continually harvested this way, leading to lower long-term value.

Other woods have been damaged by over-grazing and wildfires.

Many new owners of wooded rural property have a strong Earth ethic and are determined to "protect" their trees. But if these woods have been mismanaged in the past, simply leaving them to nature might not be the wisest course. In addition, managing for multiple use makes the most sense for most homesteaders.

As with most aspects of homesteading, the first step is to take inventory, to see what you have now. Second, set a goal or objective, and third, develop a plan to reach that objective, both short and long term.

What species of trees are in your stand right now? What is their age, size and general condition?

If the stand was recently high-graded, it might be prudent to remove some of the remaining trees. If they were passed over because of disease or injury, because they are misshapen or stunted or of an undesirable species, cutting them for firewood or some other low-end use might be compared to removing weeds from a garden: it will make more room and free up more sun, water and nutrients for more valuable specimens.

But "value" is a subjective term, depending on your objectives. A large hollow tree might be useless from a timber standpoint, but important from a wildlife management one. If a magnificent tree that would make a high grade sawlog is the only one of its kind in the area, it could have long-term value as a "mother tree." Hence the importance of relating the inventory to the ultimate goal.

If a woodlot was recently extensively cut over, thinning might be called for. This is another garden analogy, but in this case, since all the plants (trees) have equal or similar value, removing some will provide more space, light and nutrients for those remaining, resulting in faster and better growth and a more valuable stand. In other cases, fast-growing low-value trees might be removed to make room for more desirable species.

Overgrazing might have resulted in an unbalanced stand, with older trees, but no replacements coming along because the seedlings were eaten or trampled by livestock. This calls for yet another management strategy.

Timber that is of harvestable size will begin to deteriorate, eventually becoming worthless, while retarding the growth of nearby trees. Whether or not to cut such a tree depends on your inventory, and objectives.

A truly "natural" woodland can require ages to develop, and in most woodlots, human activity has upset and disrupted the balance that would have occurred naturally. But with knowledge, thought, and proper care, we can give nature a much-needed boost... and provide forest products for our homesteads at the same time.

Some trees start getting ready for winter in August

Homesteaders aren't the only ones who plan ahead and prepare. Even trees do it.

In temperate zones, trees start to "shut down" for winter as early as August. They gradually reduce active growth and prepare to go dormant.

Many begin to lose leaves and show color that is a forerunner to vibrant fall foliage. In some areas, the yellow poplar is one of the first trees to leaf out in the spring, and one of the first to begin losing them in the fall.

Trees in the shut-down mode are often more susceptible to disease and insect attacks. Leaves of black locust trees, for example, frequently turn brown in early August. This browning is caused by the locust leafminer whose larvae eat the leaves of locust trees as well as birch, apple, beech, cherry, elm and oak, according to Doug McLaren, extension forest management specialist for the University of Kentucky. "Insects don't eat the entire leaf. Instead, they 'mine' the inner part of leaves, removing the green-colored chlorophyll and leaving a brown-colored skeleton. This is why so much brown is visible."

These insect attacks usually don't kill the trees unless they have already been stressed by other factors, such as extremely dry conditions earlier in the growing season.

But dry conditions in late summer can also cause trees to drop their leaves in order to reduce evaporation.

The garden:

For high yields, garden intensively!

Elizabeth & Crow Miller
New York

When asked to name the single most important factor in achieving higher yields, our answer is always—soil! Building up the soil was the only thing we did at our Spring Meadow farm, where yields increased seven-fold just five years after this former piece of farmland was converted to organic, raised beds. Last year we harvested more than 800 pounds of tomatoes from a single 100 square foot bed!

As an organic grower, you're already well aware of the importance of adding organic matter to your soil to keep it healthy and productive. A deep, organically rich soil that isn't compacted encourages the growth of healthy, extensive roots that are able to reach more nutrients and water.

The fastest way to get a deep layer of fertile soil is to make raised beds. And the best way to make raised beds is by double-digging, creating a fluffy bed of deep, friable soil that extends 24 inches below the soil line and a foot above it.

Yes, double-digging does take some work initially, but the rewards are worth it. You'll get at least five times the yield of regular row planting out of a double-dug method that emphasizes using loose, fertile soil to get the highest possible yields from the least space.

Designing your vegetable garden as a series of beds is space efficient. With raised beds, more space is devoted to plants and less to paths than in a garden planted in rows. You can produce half a ton of vegetables in 450 square feet with raised beds. A conventional row garden of the same size would produce only half that amount.

One year we kept track of the time it took to plant and maintain a 30 by 30 foot garden, planted in raised beds. It only took a total of 27 hours of work from mid-May to mid-October to produce 2,100 pounds of fresh vegetables. That's a year's supply of food for a family of four for little more than three days of work.

How do raised beds save so much time, you ask? Plants in beds grow close enough together that they shade out competing weeds, so you spend less time weeding. And the close spacing in beds also makes watering and harvesting more efficient.

How you shape your beds can make a difference. Raised beds that are gently rounded to form an arc are more space-efficient than raised beds that are flat on top. A rounded bed that is five feet wide across its base, for example, will give you a six-foot wide arc above it, creating a planting surface that's a foot wider than that of a flat bed. That foot might not seem like much, but multiply it by the length of your bed and you'll see that it makes a big difference in total square foot planting area.

In our 20-foot long sample bed at Spring Meadow, for instance, rounding the top took our total planting area from 100 to 120 square feet. That's a major league gain of 20% more planting area in a bed that takes up not an inch more ground space.

To get the maximum yields from each bed, pay attention to how you arrange your plants. Don't plant in square pattern or rows. Stagger the plants instead, by planting in triangles. By doing so, you can fit 10% to 14% more plants into each bed.

Plants don't reach their full size when crowded, and you'll end up with less yield per square foot. When we increased the spacing between romaine lettuces from 8 to 10 inches, we doubled the weight per plant. Remember that your weight yield per square foot is more important than the number of plants per square foot. Overly tight spacing can also stress plants, making them more susceptible to diseases and insect attack.

No matter how small your garden, you can grow more by going vertical. Grow space-hungry vining crops—tomatoes, pole beans, peas, squash, melons, cucumbers, etc.—straight up, supported by trellises, fences or stakes.

Growing vegetables vertically saves time, too. Harvest and maintenance go faster because you can see exactly where the fruits are. And upward bound plants are also less likely to be hit by fungal diseases thanks to the improved air circulation around foliage.

Interplanting compatible crops saves space. Consider that classic combination of Native Americans, the three sisters: corn, beans and squash.

Sturdy cornstalks serve as a support for pole beans, which twine around the stalks as they grow, while the squash grows freely on the ground below, shading out competing weeds.

Succession planting allow you to grow more than one crop in a given space. Many organic gardeners, in fact, can grow as many as three or four successive crops in a single area. Let's start with lettuce, for example. Pull the lettuce out when the weather turns it bitter. Follow with a fast-maturing corn, (Ashley 60 days), then pull up those stalks after harvest and finish with more greens or even some over-wintering garlic. The basic idea is to always have something growing in any given space.

As soon as a crop is finished we pull it out, work more compost into the soil, add some 4-6-4 organic fertilizer, dunk the transplant in a mixture of fish/seaweed, and plunk in a new plant.

A transplant needs less time to reach maturity than a direct-seeded plant, so start as many of your crops as possible indoors or in a greenhouse. For even faster turnover in the garden, choose early maturing varieties.

The garden:

How to build a raised bed

ELIZABETH & CROW MILLER
NEW YORK

At Spring Meadow, for seven years now, our raised beds have provided us with early onions, lettuce and cabbage. Our raised beds show proudly over the landscape, soaking up the extra warmth while the excess moisture drains down, leaving the rich topsoil ready to be worked by understanding hands.

There are two ways to build a raised bed. The impatient gardener will buy a truckload or two of good topsoil from a reliable person and deposit it in some suitable spot in the garden exposed to the full sun. Then they will industriously raise the soil level to a height of at least 10 inches. If they have a compost pile, they will top off the raised bed with its rich soil and plant their seeds.

But you can get much better results first by setting aside a load or two of soil with the help of your trusty Garden Way cart. Next, spread a narrow band, not more than two feet wide, of old hay, leaves, manure, straw or other crop residues across one end of the raised bed. Then, scooping up some soil next to the strip, cover it lightly to a depth of about two inches.

Make a second band where the soil was removed, also about two feet wide, and cover it with soil. Continue making crop residue strips until the entire bed has been treated. Cover the final band with the cart full of soil you saved at the start.

Rake the bed smooth and allow to stand for several days. The weight of the soil will compress the buried vegetation, after which the bed may be planted safely. On our beds we plant onions, lettuce and cabbage during the last days of March. It is a wonderful sight to see the first rows of green become more pronounced with the passing days.

If desired, sheathing boards, 10 to 12 inches wide, may be used to enclose the raised bed, making it a box garden.

A slower but gratifying method

While the second way of building a raised bed is much slower, the rewards are indeed gratifying. Best of all, the job may be done over a long period or several seasons at times most suited to the gardener. Start by marking off the desired size of the bed. If it is to be fair-sized, it should be started half that size so the built-up half will be producing vegetables while the remaining half is being completed.

Strew old hay, leaves, anything organic, thickly on the ground. Cover with soil. Let the weight of the soil compress the vegetation. This is the foundation of the bed.

Now toss weeds (these are high in minerals) on this bed as they are pulled in the garden. Add lawn clippings. In fact, add the small amount of organic wastes encountered daily about the home and grounds. These small additions will grow surprisingly over the days. Cover with soil again.

Continue to add more organic materials on top. In the fall, add cornstalks and the wealth of dead garden vegetation. Again cover with soil.

In the spring, this bed may be planted even if it is only a few inches higher than the surrounding area. The idea is to keep adding organic substances and soil until the desired height is reached.

Once this is done, start building up the remaining portion of the bed. This can take one or more seasons and can be done at any time of the year.

Experience has shown us that rows may be planted quite closely together on the raised beds. The soil is so rich from the abundance of decomposed organic materials that there is an abundance of plant nutrients in it. Growth is rapid and steady because the bed drains well and is warmer than soil on lower leaves. Planted early in a raised bed, peas are tender and fast-growing. Lettuce plants may be thinned from it to be transplanted in the main gardens. Onion greens and small bulbs are ready for the table about the time most people are preparing to plant them.

How can you beat a system that cures gardener's itch and produces early vegetables at the same time?

Once the raised bed is established it takes little maintenance over a gardener's lifetime. Should the raised bed at any time be in the way for some reason, it offers no disposal problem. Simply haul the rich soil into the garden and spread it.

I feel that a raised bed is a valuable part of any garden, and if you make one, I'm sure you'll agree.

(Reprinted from COUNTRYSIDE, 1989)

A living soil is basic to organic gardening

ELIZABETH & CROW MILLER
NEW YORK

The basic premise of organic/sustainable technology is that a healthy soil produces healthy plants, which in turn will provide nutritious food for people. A healthy soil is one that is teeming with varied life forms. This biological activity in soils is dependent upon the physical structure and the mineral balance. A healthy soil is characterized by a complex of inter-dependent microflora, microfauna, and mineral cycles.

In just one gram of soil there are 20-million bacteria, one million fungi, millions of actinomycetes and 800,000 algae. These invisible agents are the major forms of microflora. As fertility increases, so does the number and variety of soil lifeforms.

While we can't see or even realize the complexity of these cycles, the organic gardener must build a suitable habitat for soil life so that they, in turn, can create a fertile soil. There is no one way of doing this. Differences in climate, geography, soil type, financial resources, access to material, amount of leisure time, physical ability, equipment and especially the mental attitude of the organic grower, dictate how each garden or farm will develop.

There are as many methods of as there are gardeners. The organic/sustainable approach stresses the importance of incorporating large amounts of organic matter in order to create a healthy soil. Many organic farmers simply back the manure spreader filled with compost up to the family garden and "let 'er fly." Some gardeners feel that the purchase of a blended artificial fertilizer each spring will feed their plants adequately. Other gardeners, knowing the ignorance of using artificial

COMPANION PLANTING GUIDE

Vegetable	Likes	Dislikes
Asparagus	Parsley, tomatoes, basil	
Beans	Beets, cabbage family, cucumbers, potatoes, carrots	Onions, garlic, gladiolus
Bush beans	Strawberries, cucumbers, corn, celery, potatoes	Onions
Pole beans	Corn	Onions, beets, kohlrabi, sunflowers
Beets	Lettuce, cabbage family, onions	Pole beans
Cabbage family (cabbage, cauliflower, kale, kohlrabi, broccoli, Brussels sprouts)	Early potatoes, nasturtiums, tomatoes, celery, aromatic herbs	Strawberries, pole beans
Carrots	Peas, leaf lettuce, chives, red radishes, leeks, rosemary, wormwood, sage, tomatoes	Dill
Celeriac	Leeks	
Celery	Leeks, tomatoes, bush beans, cabage, cauliflower	
Chives	Carrots	Peas, beans
Corn	Potatoes, beans, peas, melons, squash, pumpkins, cucumbers, broad beans in large plantings	
Cucumbers	Beans, corn, radishes, sunflowers, cabbage, marigolds,peas	Potatoes, aromatic herbs
Eggplant	Green beans	
Kohlrabi	Beets, onions	
Leeks	Onion, celery, carrots	
Lettuce	Strawberries, carrots,beets, radishes, cabbage, cucumbers	
Onions	Beets, strawberries, tomatoes, lettuce, summer savory, chamomile (one plant every four yards)	Peas, beans
Peas	Radishes, carrots, cucumbers, sweet corn, beans, turnips	Onions, garlic, potatoes, gladiolus
Potatoes	Beans, sweet corn, peas, cabbage, broad beans, nasturtiums, eggplant (to lure Colorado beetle), marigolds	Pumpkins, cucumbers, squash, sunflowers, tomatoes
Pumpkins	Corn	Potatoes
Radishes	Peas, lettuce, chervil, pole beans	
Soybeans	Helps everything	
Spinach	Strawberries	
Squash	Corn, nasturtiums	Potatoes
Tomatoes	Asparagus, parsley, cabbage, onions, chives, carrots, marigolds, nasturtiums	Kohlrabi, potatoes, fennel
Turnips-rutabagas	Peas	

Plantings of aromatic herbs throughout the garden or as a border have a good influence on all vegetables. The most aromatic are lavender, hyssop, sage, parsley, chervil, tarragon, chives, thyme, marjoram, chamomile and lovage. On the other hand, keep wormwood and fennel well away from vegetable plants (except carrots) as they have an inhibitory effect.

fertilizer, spread bags of crushed rock powder, natural phosphates and other soil amendments, relying on the natural minerals, while many older gardeners just add mulch each year and state that any tillage of their garden is unnecessary.

Many of these different approaches can lead to a healthy soil, something more often due to the energy of the gardener rather than the efficiency of the method. The structures of any one gardening method, however, can lead to the over-emphasis of a single factor and risk the danger of imbalance. Good gardening is a matter of balance or as the adage goes, "moderation in all things."

Gardeners often do too much. The adage "more is better" has caused untold harm. Adding too much old hay, cultivating too often, pouring limestone on the garden out of a bag and rototilling four times to get a fluffy seedbed, are just some of the sins many gardeners have committed. Truly unpardonable are the deadly overuse of artificial nitrogen, insecticides, fungicides and lamentable practice of soil fumigation.

Instead of forcing the garden to conform to our theories, some of this time would be better spent in observation. we need to change our approach from one of manipulation to one of nurture. Only then can we create a harmonious balance.

Remember, without our small soil creatures and microorganisms, our plants would not be fed.

Ruminations in the mulch

Ruth Stout had the right idea

THE INTENTIONAL PEASANT
MARYLAND

The Ruth Stout system of permanent deep mulch has one serious drawback: slugs. Besides this, it can harbor wet, rotting conditions, unfriendly fungi, and destructive animal life. Still, here in the Middle Atlantic region, when supplemental water is not available, it is an essential method for getting any crop at all during a dry year.

Ms. Stout simply drew back the mulch along the proposed row and planted in the soft, moist soil underneath. Then she pulled a further layer back over the row and the seedlings eventually peeped through. She mulched with whatever was free: straw, spoiled hay, or leaves and litter. Here in Big Town, what are free are immense quantities of bagged leaves. These bloom like big, black flowers every fall along the sidewalks and only require transport to the garden, nothing else. Also, they come complete—as often as not—with their own supply of slugs. This old peasant uses little else other than a sagacious sprinkle of Ra-Pid-Gro, unless darling daughter arrives with a load of interesting profit from the floor of a stable.

Making do with what is at hand and cheap—or preferably free—is what sets the homesteader apart (not so?) from "the bewildered herd." This, together with a strong preference for things natural and unbuggered-with. But don't we detect a strong preference within ourselves for a reasonable austerity? Not necessarily of the hair shirt variety—although that has certain rewards, too—but living lightly on the land? Krishnamurti thought that "where there is prosperity without austerity there is violence, there is every form of unethical luxury (and a) society which is utterly corrupt and immoral." Isn't it this kind of society that we attempt to distance ourselves from as we go among our chemical-free tomatoes and free-ranging chickens?

Too, many of us are card-carrying misotechs—haters of technology—even as we mess with our computers and solar panels. But we appear to select our technology, with much soul searching, from the yearly swarm of the latest thing buzzing around our heads.

One of the nicest things about the work of fetching the bagged leaves is the opportunity to sprawl supine in the mulch and contemplate the sky, clouds, and eternity. Sprawling just so becomes more attractive with each passing year, as the bags grow heavier for a creaking, old back. On those rare occasions when one turns and finds oneself eyeball to eyeball with eight feet of mature black snake, one can rest assured that Mr./Ms. Snake will be more upset than the gardener is. Besides, snakes generally do not eat elderly, bearded peasants. Gardeners meeting other specifications are on their own. Last year this same serpent, or a close relative, got into a nest of bunnies, to a horrifying squeal from one of the victims. One moves away with a sad sigh; life goes on, dog-eat-dog and snake-eat-bunny.

In one such sprawl in the mulch this peasant was thinking that no healthier food exists on the planet than good food raised on good soil with little added to it. This food, which includes honey "raised" by the bees, is surely its own reward. Eating so might well put the degenerative diseases—heart and artery trouble, cancer, and the rest—right back into the 1940 range: close to zilch. Well, yes, but the sneaky little modifier good, alongside soil, is the problem.

In her Pennsylvania garden, Ruth Stout at least started with genuine dirt, regulation soil, admittedly not in superlative shape at the outset, but horticulturally promising. She did not start with the raw stuff of which jugs, pots, and dinner plates might eventually spring. Here in the mulch garden on borrowed land up the hill from Peasant Hovel, it might be smarter to grow bricks rather than plants, but plants are more useful on a daily basis. As its fourth summer approaches, the earthworms have been doing journeyman service in the "topsoil" below the leaves. Perhaps in eighteen or so more years...In the meantime, praise be for Ra-Pid-Gro.

To the average consumer, the word picture which appears at the mention of soil is likely to be either amber waves of grain or the filthy stuff ground into the knees of Junior's jeans. There are more kinds of soil than there are hamburger chains and more kinds of word pictures than grains of sand at Coney Island. But we all live by this mental shorthand, concepts, not so? If we use the word crops, the readers of COUNTRYSIDE think immediately of the garden. The agribusiness CEO thinks of what's planted in the thousand acres north of the creek. The hydroponics practitioner's mind flicks to the greenhouse growing matrix. To the disinterested office clerk on the 34th floor, the word gardening may conjure up a picture of some hick in bib overalls and a cap that says John Deere dropping seeds into the Earth, then going inside to start the water boiling. Of course, none of the pictures is correct at any two points and at any two times, but without concepts, word pictures, our minds would have to work terribly hard.

This mental shorthand does have its drawbacks, the most telling of which is that it can encourage mental laziness. Perhaps that's why the television and radio sound bite has been so successful in shaping our opinions. (We who don't want our opinions shaped simply neither watch nor listen.) Walter Cronkite was "the most trusted man in journalism." He told us what we should think. And this sort of thing encourages us to accept what is as what must be. We must have air conditioning, drive a Belchfire Eight, jet 3,000 miles to attend Earth Day, add that extra wing to our eleven existing rooms, and take up line dancing. Daddy works two jobs and Mom works as a full-time chauffeur for the kids—all to keep the myth alive.

The mental giant Marilyn Voss Savant recently answered a reader in *Parade* who wanted to know why everything we did ended with ourselves worse off than before. She replied that every time we change the present in some significant way, we alter the future environment of our fragile little water planet. Driving gas hogs, flying home for Thanksgiving, cooling the office, all seem very nice things to do, but each is a debit on the future, a charge for future payment by our grandchildren. Marilyn pointed out that we have adapted over the centuries to this exact environment. The incremental charges against the environmental account must eventually fall due. At that time, Katie, bar the door!

People who are trying to be gentle with the planet often have a mental picture of themselves as wearing the white hats. (An observation from personal experience.) The guy in the Belchfire Eight with the solid-gold Omega on his wrist is wearing an eighty dollar Stetson, but it is definitely black. But, like Will Rogers, most of us only know what we read in the papers or, lately, see on the tube. And the advertisers that pay for both are selling Belchfire Eights and solid-gold Omegas.

Well, we say, that's business; that's competition—which flashes up a new word picture. The word competition, depending largely on how one earns one's living, can mean the cutthroat, dog-eat-dog world of business or else the force that pushes enterprise in the general direction of efficiency. Likewise, downsizing can mean the heartless expulsion of loyal workers or the natural and necessary force operating in definition two above. At any rate, word pictures serve the purposes of business quite well, even if the system seems not designed to work to the well-being of Mother Earth.

Well, there's all that, but ruminating in the warm mulch on a pleasant spring day with old Henrietta safely pulled off the road, one feels at last beyond the sidewalks, if only by 200 feet or so.

Here's how to make compost

1. 2-6 inches of rotted hay
2. 6 inches of leaves, weeds, grass clippings, kitchen garbage
3. 2 inches manure
4. 1 inch of wood ashes and/or rock powders
5. 2 inches of topsoil
6. Enough water to dampen the whole pile, but not to soak
7. Cover of plastic, boards, tarp, etc. to trap heat

Repeat numbers 1-6 until the pile is several feet high. Mix this pile every two weeks. Turn the outside material to the inside of the pile. This pile will heat to 160°F or so.—*Jim & Julie Hunter*

Extend lime with compost

Mixing lime with compost might make the lime go farther. Literally, farther down in the soil. Scientists studying various fertilizers found that only on plots with composted sewage sludge was the lime able to favorably change soil pH deeper than the six-inch rototilled layer. On plots with commercial fertilizer, the lime was effective only in the first six inches. Scientists theorize that the sludge compost chemically assists the movement of calcium from the lime. They are now designing follow-up studies to this surprise finding, which could be very helpful to farmers and gardeners dealing with acidic soils. – *Soil Microbial Systems Lab, Beltsville, Maryland*

Quick and easy compost method

I have been reading many articles on composting and most of them complain about the back-breaking work of turning the compost. I have come up with an easy way.

Using my front tine tiller to loosen the dirt, I dig a trench about three feet wide, three or four feet long, and a foot-and-a-half or two feet deep.

I shred and store dry leaves in the fall. Each time my husband mows the lawn during the summer he dumps the grass clippings in the trench. I add the desired amount of leaves, mix them with the tiller, and use the garden hose to give them the right moisture. About every three days I run the tiller through them and add moisture if needed. This method will produce usable compost in two weeks.

If space is not a problem, you can run the tiller all the way through the trench, turn around and run it back through. Where we are living now, space is at a premium, so I just run the tiller the length of the trench, shove it into reverse and back out. It sure beats turning by hand or waiting a year to get compost without turning. – *N.A., Colorado*

Seed corn size differs

My seed dealer has small, round seed corn, and large, flat seed corn. He says there's no difference—except in price. (The small seed is anywhere from $5 to $15 a bag cheaper.) Since I only buy one bag a year the savings don't amount to much, but would I get a better crop using bigger seeds? – *W. L., Wisconsin*

Tests have shown that small, round seeds perform just as well as large, flat seeds. The only problem might be your planter dropping doubles...two seeds in the same hole. (This isn't a problem with plateless planters.)

There are differences in germination between large and small seeds, but these are not consistent, according to researchers at the University of Wisconsin. Sometimes hybrids with small seeds outperform those with large seeds, and sometimes it's the other way around.

Corn seed varies in size and shape according to its position on the ear, weather conditions, and hybrid type.

Fall garden tip

Here is a quick tip for separating tomato plants from support cages.

Pull up plant and cage all together. Stack in a pile in an out-of-the-way open spot. After the plants are good and dry set them on fire, cages and all. The fire is done in about five minutes. The cages aren't damaged and I believe the heat kills some harmful critters and possibly some viruses.

Here is an old method of getting more out of your wheat: I hadn't heard of this even though some of you may have. Let your cow or other grazing livestock feed on the wheat until spring (April in Texas). Then take them off of it and let it head out.

Crops & soils:

Some weeds and their uses

A weed, as Ralph Waldo Emerson observed, is simply a plant growing in the wrong place.

He also might have said it's a plant growing at the wrong time. There are many examples of plants we now consider weeds that were once treated as valuable plants.

Crabgrass, for example, was once recommended as a forage crop in the south by the USDA. Crabgrasses were the first cultivated grains and were grown for food for thousands of years. The seeds are nutritious, and it's still an important cereal crop in some parts of the world. (Survivalists, take note!)

It's a strange world: while science and agriculture work to make crop plants grow better, crabgrass is considered a nuisance...because it grows too well.

Lamb's-quarters—a British native and a spinach relative—was once considered one of nature's most delicious vegetables. Young plants were gathered and boiled, used in salads or made into soup. Lamb's-quarters has more iron, protein, vitamin B12 and vitamin C than raw cabbage or spinach. It also has more calcium and vitamin B1 than raw cabbage.

The seeds of lamb's quarters taste something like buckwheat. Dried, they can be ground into flour. Pioneers added them to breads, pancakes, muffins and cookies.

Lamb's-quarters leaves are a source of ascaridole, an oil used to treat for round worms and hook worms. The plant was once valued in Europe as an important animal fodder.

When spinach was introduced from Asia in the 16th century, lamb's-quarters became a "weed."

Broadleaf plantain is a European native that was once considered a valuable medicinal herb and a tasty vegetable. The leaves contain a fluid that was used to treat cuts, scorpion stings and snake bites.

Some people still use young leaves of broadleaf plantain like spinach and brewed to make a tea, and the seeds are popular with birds.

Quack grass has been used for medicinal purposes for thousands of years. The underground stems, or rhizomes, are the useful part. About 11 percent of the rhizome is a sticky, gel-like substance which possibly accounts for its use in medicine and other products such as glue.

Thistles native to the Mediterranean were used for medicinal purposes for more than 2,000 years, and the roots of some species were used as food.

Chicory is another European native with several uses. The roasted and ground roots have historically been used as a coffee substitute, and the young leaves are still picked as salad greens.

Purslane was brought to the U.S. by immigrants for its value as a salad green. The succulent leaves have a lemony flavor.

Dandelion's use as food is still common: young leaves of this European native are used in salads, the flower heads are used to make wine, and the dried and roasted root is brewed as a coffee substitute.

And surprise: at least one company has been selling dandelion seed to people who presumably don't have enough wild ones!

Jerusalem artichoke is an American native. Its potato-like tubers are eaten raw or cooked, and can also be made into a flour.

Milkweed is also a native of the Western Hemisphere. Young shoots are used like asparagus, and there has been a lot of experimenting with using its pod plumes as a substitute for goose down.

Others, including the notorious **kudzu** and **multiflora rose,** once touted by extension agents, are now cursed by most landowners afflicted with them. The **white and yellow sweet clovers,** while still valued by some farmers and many homesteaders as soil improvement crops, are considered weeds by many others.

There's a mirror image to this. The best-known example is the **toma**to which, when introduced in Europe from the New World, was considered a decorative plant—but poisonous. Today the tomato is the most popular vegetable garden crop in the U.S.

Who knows what plants might be considered weeds—or valuable plants—tomorrow!

Canada thistle

Canada thistle is one of the toughest, most persistent, most difficult to eradicate weeds there is.

This perennial has roots that may reach 10-15 feet deep. They contain buds that produce more new shoots. One plant may spread over a 20-foot circular patch in one year... and that's from root spread alone.

The stored root reserves keep the thistle coming back. Those reserves are sufficient to keep the plant alive for two years even if no topgrowth is permitted.

Food reserves peak as the plant matures. Those reserves keep the plant alive in winter and enable it to produce new growth in the spring.

Tillage and herbicides are most effective before the summer and fall buildup of nutrient reserves, but controlling this field and garden pest is a tough, long-term job.

Phosphorus, potash and trace elements

The best time to build up your soil's mineral reserves is in the late fall, when the harvest is in.

This past season, you probably worked large amounts of organic soil conditioners (organic fertilizers, soil amendments and compost) into your garden beds, but you may have short-changed it on such key minerals as phosphorus, potash and trace elements.

Late fall and early winter are the times to apply those nutrients, before you get the message the hard way next year. And you have a large variety of materials to use, ranging from surface rocks to undersea deposits.

Rock phosphate, for example, includes phosphatized limestones, sand stones, shales and igneous rocks. The rock ranges from 28% to 38% phosphoric acid.

Colloidal phosphate is a finely divided type of rock phosphate, obtained from the settling ponds used in hydraulic mining of phosphate rock. It usually contains from 18% to 24% total phosphoric acid, and recommended application rate is about 50% more than rock phosphate.

Ordinary **superphosphate** *is* made by mixing phosphate rock with sulfuric acid. **Triple superphosphate** *is* made by mixing rock phosphate with phosphoric acid. Organic farmers and gardeners have never used these superphosphates because of the residues from the process and the excessive availability and leaching of the phosphate.

A great many farmers and gardeners have found that the effect of rock minerals on plants is almost doubled when organic materials, like manure and compost, are applied at the same time. The natural acids produced by decaying humus increase the availability of the mineral nutrients to plants.

Natural mineral sources of **potassium** are mainly available as **granite dust** and **greensand**. The potash content of granite dust varies between 3% and 5%, sometimes more.

Not all granites are similar in the release of potassium to plant roots in the soil. Favorable types include: (a) granite which contains abundant small flakes of dark mica, and (b) granite which apparently originated by the conversion of ancient sedimentary rocks of complex composition (sometimes called granitized rocks, migmatites, and some of the hybrid granites).

Greensand, originally an undersea deposit, contains from 6% to 7% potash, plus many trace elements. Besides supplying potash, greensand is valuable for improving the soil's physical structure.

When estimating how much to apply to the garden, don't be afraid to lay it on thickly in late fall and winter. Use about 10 to 15 pounds per 100 square feet every three or four years, spreading in fall directly on the soil surface, then tilling it in with a tiller (gardeners) or disk (farmer). In spring and summer you can dust a mixture of phosphate and potash (equal amounts) in the row. Some gardeners spread handfuls around growing plants or add them to the backyard compost pile.

The way these elements become available is through **chelation**, a process by which nutrients are literally pulled out of soil minerals and rocks by certain compounds. Humus is one such compound converting insoluble minerals to available forms.

Many soil fungi normally produce a variety of compounds that behave as chelators. This may well be a major function of the mycorrhiza fungi which act in the role of root hairs for certain trees and other plants. Without their fungus partners, these plants either grow poorly or are unable to develop at all.

While chelators are not new, during recent years some of the chemical companies have been aggressively marketing synthetic chelates. These posed the danger of being so strong as to dissolve too much of the stored

Fertilizer values of some manures

Can rabbit manure be used in a garden? I know other small animals' manure can be used, but I live in the city and my area is not zoned for certain animals. I am trying to be self-sufficient—as much as I can, in the city. *– Ann M., Michigan*

Yes indeed, rabbit manure can be used. In fact, it has more nitrogen—usually the most important and most valuable fertilizer ingredient—than any other commonly used manure. Composting is recommended when using any barnyard manure.

Here are some statistics on various barnyard byproducts.

Animal	Tons excreted per year per 1,000 lbs. live-weight	% nitrogen	% phosphoric acid	% potash
Rabbit	4.2	2.4	1.4	0.6
Sheep & goat	6.0	1.44	0.5	1.21
Swine	16.0	0.49	0.34	0.47
Chicken	4.5	1.0	0.8	0.39
Dairy cow	12.0	0.57	0.23	0.62
Beef steer	8.5	0.73	0.48	0.55
Horse	8	0.70	0.25	0.77

How to plan your root cellar

It's possible to live without a root cellar...but then it's possible to live without chickens, a garden, or wood heat. But would you want to? Not if you're a homesteader! There is nothing so pleasant, so reassuring, as going into the root cellar on a cold and snowy evening and gathering up the makings of a hearty meal—all from produce you grew yourself last summer. Seeing shelves of mason jars and the bin of potatoes and bags of onions and all the rest fills you with a sense of security that even money in the bank can't provide.

When most people think of preserving food today, they probably think of freezing or canning. But root cellaring—for those fruits and vegetables adapted to this form of preservation and which includes more than just roots—is much easier, less time-consuming and less expensive. Since you never have to worry about the availability of canning jar lids or power failures, it also provides more security.

About root cellars: "Cellars" are not, and never were, always directly under the house. The word cellar comes from the French cella, meaning a storeroom or pantry. When root cellars were a part of almost every home they were often to one side of the house, and frequently they were separate structures altogether.

Today, when most modern homes have heated, carpeted, paneled basements (few people even call them cellars any more), a separate root cellar might be the best and most economical way to store food. Even if your home has a damp, cool, unheated basement, you have many options as to where and how you build your cella or storeroom.

The first thing to consider is **temperature**. The main idea behind root cellaring is to provide "natural refrigeration" for food products but to avoid freezing.

Different fruits and vegetables have different storage requirements, but most of them fall within a range of 35°-40°. The easiest way to maintain this temperature naturally is by using the insulation properties of earth: hence, the popularity of dug root cellars. If dug below the frost line, the cellar remains cool during the hot months and above freezing even during the most frigid time of the year.

The second major requirement is **humidity**: for most crops, 90-95 percent. Again, earth is a natural and logical source of this moist air.

The third requirement is **ventilation**. One reason is that you can manipulate the ventilation to maintain some control over temperature. For example, in the fall, when you fill your cellar, it might not be cool enough. But by admitting cool night air and blocking out the warmer air of Indian Summer days you can decrease the temperature of the cellar appreciably.

Ventilation can also be used to waft off excess humidity, and also the odors and ethylene gas given off by some stored products.

A root cellar should be dark, since sunlight will increase the temperature but more importantly, foods keep better in the dark.

Still another consideration and a very important one (but for you rather than the produce) is **accessibility**. A root cellar is useless if you don't use it, and if it's too far from the house or the entrance is blocked by three feet of snow you're more likely to say the heck with it, forget about the potatoes and onions and carrots, and make macaroni and cheese.

Planning the root cellar: With these basics in mind you can begin to plan your cellar.

The actual design is of little consequence. There are many designs for root cellars as there are for houses or barns. Like houses and barns, cellars can be small cubicles or palace-like structures; plain or fancy; cheap or expensive. It's your choice.

As a first step I would suggest determining how much room you'll need. In other words, what are you going to store, and how much of it?

The basics would probably be canning jars and potatoes. What quantities of each will your family need for a year? The jars will be on shelves along one or more walls, and potatoes are commonly (and best) kept in a slatted or otherwise ventilated bin.

For illustration purposes let's assume there are two people in your household and you'll need enough for, let's say 300 main meals a year that you can't take directly from the garden. Including jams and jellies, juices, canned fruits and canned vegetables, as well as a supply of frozen and perhaps dried produce, let's say you decide that about 300 quarts of canned foods would tide you over for a year.

Since one square foot of shelf space will hold nine canning jars,

Phosphorus, potash...

(continued from previous page)

up nutrients in a short time, leaving little for future crops to draw on.

You have many materials available to increase your garden's mineral reserve. Make sure you don't forget to build it up in plenty of time for your next year's garden.

One more thing: the best way to really know what your soil needs is to have it tested. This takes the guesswork out of feeding the soil.
– *Crow Miller*

you'll need about 34 square feet. If you use 12" boards for shelves, that's also 34 linear feet. If you want to use standard six-foot lengths, six of them will hold your year's supply of canned goods...and if you stack them up the actual space required is a mere one by six feet.

The average American eats about 50 pounds of potatoes a year. Since it's impossible to grow and harvest exactly 100 pounds of anything—and you'll need extra for company anyway and any leftovers next spring can be used for seed or fed to the chickens or rabbits—let's just say that in this case a potato bin 18 x 36 inches and perhaps 24 inches deep would do quite nicely.

How far you go beyond this depends on how serious you are about self-sufficiency, as well as on what you like to grow and eat. (If even this is more than you care to bother with but you still want to avoid the supermarket a little, see the box on small-scale storage.)

Onions are best stored in bags hung from the ceiling, so while you don't have to make special plans to increase the area of the storage room for those, keep ceiling height in mind.

Carrots, celery, beets and similar crops are stored in or even under the floor, and will require additional floor space.

Squash and pumpkins should be on shelves. If you grow and store those, sketch that shelf space into your plans.

Do the same for apples and other fruits.

You can make a template, much like designing a house or the layout of a room, and move things around to see how they fit. As in most similar cases, it will be better to have too much storage capacity than not enough, and increasing the size of your storage room a bit at this point probably won't take much extra cash or labor anyway.

How big should your cellar be? Many plans (which you might get from your county agent) suggest a space 10 feet square, but you can pack an awful lot of produce into that. Eight by 10 should be plenty for most people, and with good organization even a floor area of 5x8 will hold the equivalent of many shopping carts full of good meals. But deciding what you're going to store, and how much, and playing with that on paper will give you a good idea of your own requirements.

Construction: Now that you know where you're going to build your cellar and how large it's going to be, it's time to make some decisions on the actual design and construction techniques.

There are no rules, beyond the requirements of temperature, humidity, ventilation and darkness. Here the primary considerations are the location, how the cellar will blend in with the rest of your homestead, and of course how much money you want to spend.

If you have a fairly damp (but obviously not flooded) cool basement, that might be the most logical and efficient location. In most older homes (and even many newer ones) it's possible to partition off a corner of the basement to make a first-class root cellar, with very little labor or expense.

Or you might consider extending the basement, by digging a cellar next to an existing wall. Such a cellar could have access from outside, or from the basement, or both. In the latter case you could take produce directly from the garden to the storage room without lugging baskets and crates (and mud) through the house, and yet get to that produce even in deep snow without even putting on a sweater. Proximity of the outdoor entrance to the garden is desirable, but so is a location on the north side of the house. Your individual situation will dictate your choice.

If neither of these are feasible and you opt for a new excavation away from the house, the ideal would be to cut into the north side of a hill. If you don't have a hill, or one with a north slope, a cellar on level ground will work, but will require a little more effort.

If you need ideas or help on the actual construction, get some advice from someone with experience. But if you have built a goat shed or anything else you can probably build a root cellar. Root cellar walls are usually made of concrete, block, or stone, but the new forms of treated wood have also been used and many people will find that easier to work with. (Ours is wood...the outside was tarred and then covered with plastic before backfilling, and it's lasted about 15 years so far with no visible problems.)

The aspect that leaves most people scratching their heads is the roof, particularly if you intend to pile three feet of soil on top of it.

In some climates and under certain conditions, the sod covering we usually associate with an outdoor root cellar might not be necessary. If the cellar is deep enough to make use of the Earth's heat during the winter, and soil is massed up to the height of the walls, a normal wooden roof with a very well-insulated ceiling might suffice. This pretty well describes our own root cellar. Although there is an unheated room over it, the ceiling is not particularly well-insulated. It has never dropped below 32°F even during extended periods of -20°F outdoors.

But you can easily pour a concrete roof that will support an insulating soil cover.

Begin by constructing a wood roof. Depending on the size of your cellar you would probably want to use 2x6 beams with 2x4 or 2x6 joists running perpendicular to them. Cover this with 3/4 treated or exterior plywood. Cover the plywood with 6-mil plastic so the plywood doesn't suck moisture from the wet concrete, forcing it to dry too quickly and lose strength. Don't forget to install your ventilation pipes at this point! Build a form of 2x6 lumber around the roof to hold in the concrete until it's cured.

A concrete roof must be reinforced with crossed bars or rods: you've probably seen highway construction crews use this material when building concrete bridges.

Before pouring the concrete brace the beams and joists with 4x4s: wet concrete is heavy, and of course has no strength to support anything until it dries.

Pour six inches of concrete over the plastic.

Then you're ready to start backfilling, but don't simply fill the trench around your new cellar. There's a trick that will help prevent the walls from caving in.

Start backfilling, tamping the soil firmly as you do. But when you get about three feet from the top, fill with a few inches of gravel, and install a four-inch perforated drainpipe on top of that. The pipe (usually a slinky-like corrugated tubing) should slope (about an inch every eight feet) from the back of the cellar to the front. This isn't for drainage, but to keep water and ice from expanding the soil and putting undue pressure on the wall.

When backfilling is completed and the concrete has cured, attach rigid two-inch sheets of Styrofoam to the top of the roof with construction cement. Cover this with a sheet of six-mil polyethylene.

Now you're ready to cover the roof with two to four feet of soil.

Finishing the interior: Coarse sand or gravel makes a good root cellar floor.

Shelves should be sturdy: filled mason jars are heavy! Either use two-inch lumber, or provide plenty of supports.

The choice of shelving lumber is important too, since dampness will take its toll. Pine or spruce won't be your first choice, and you probably won't care to use treated lumber for this application, either.

It's a good idea to leave an air space behind the shelves, particularly with concrete walls.

Install your ventilation pipes, a solid door (insulated, or a double door, if it opens directly outside), and you're all set to dig potatoes.

Home storage of vegetables

Harvesting your garden bounty or extending your garden growing season for more vegetables does little good if one month after you pick your produce, it's spoiled. This fall and winter, when supermarket produce is most expensive and most of us can't run out to the garden and pick a fresh bunch of celery or panful of beans, it's gratifying to know that you can visit the fruit cellar or make a trip to the pantry or freezer, and not be disappointed. Below is a list of recommended storage conditions, storage duration times and highest freezing point for several vegetables.

Commodity	Temp. (°F)	Relative Humidity (%)	Avg. Storage Life	Freezing Point (°F)
Beets	32	95	1-3 months	30.3
Brussels sprouts	32	90-95	3-5 weeks	30.5
Cabbage	32	90-95	3-4 months	30.4
Carrots	32	90-95	4-6 months	29.5
Cauliflower	32	90-95	2-4 weeks	30.6
Celeriac	32	90-95	3-4 months	30.3
Celery	32	90-95	2-3 months	31.1
Chinese cabbage	32	90-95	1-2 months	—
Dry Beans	32-50	65-70	1 year	unaffected
Endive	32	90-95	2-3 weeks	31.9
Garlic	32	65-70	6-7 months	30.5
Horseradish	30-32	90-95	10-12 months	28.7
Jerusalem Artichoke	31-32	90-95	2-5 months	—
Kale	32	90-95	10-14 days	31.1
Kohlrabi	32	90-95	2-4 weeks	30.2
Leeks	32	90-95	1-3 months	30.7
Onions	32	65-70	5-8 months	30.6
Parsnips	32	90-95	2-6 months	30.4
Peppers, Dry	32-50	60-70	6 months	—
Peppers, Sweet	45-50	90-95	8-10 days	30.7
Potatoes	38-40	90	5-8 months	30.9
Pumpkins	50-55	70-75	2-3 months	30.5
Rutabaga	32	90-95	2-4 months	30.1
Salsify	32	90-95	2-4 months	30.0
Sweet Potato	55-60	85-90	4-6 months	29.7
Tomatoes, mature green	55-60	85-90	2-6 weeks	31.0
Turnips	32	90-95	4-5 months	30.1
Winter Radishes	32	90-95	2-4 months	30.7
Winter Squash	50-55	70-75	3-6 months	30.5

Northeast Regional Agricultural Engineering Service

The problem of weeds

From our files: This article is reprinted from our June, 1979 issue, but it was old even then. It was written in 1914 by A. L. Stone of the University of Wisconsin Agricultural Experiment Station.

It's worth repeating for several reasons, not the least of which is the portrayal of common farming methods before chemical agriculture came on the scene. But the descriptions of certain weeds and their control will also be of practical importance to modern homestead gardeners and farmers alike.

Life periods of plants

With respect to duration of life there are three classes of plants, viz,

Annuals,
Biennials,
Perennials.

An annual comes up from a seed, bears flowers and seeds and later dies; all within one year.

A biennial grows from a seed but produces only leaves the first year. The root and sometimes the leaves live through the winter. The second year a flower stalk comes up, seeds are produced, and the plant dies.

A perennial is one the roots of which live on year after year unless killed in some way. Depending upon conditions, the plant may or may not produce seed every year.

Methods of reproducing and spreading

Plants reproduce themselves in various ways: first, by seeds alone; second, by roots alone; third, by seeds and roots both; and fourth by runners, suckers, etc.

Practically all annual plants reproduce themselves by seed only. Biennials, also, except for the one winter through which the roots live, reproduce themselves by seeds. Perennials may propagate by means of the roots only as does the horseradish which in many places is a bad weed. This plant was introduced into Wisconsin from a warmer country and while its roots live on for many years it produces no seed. Canada thistles in many cases spread only by the roots and bear no seeds, while in other instances, where the conditions are favorable, a large amount of seed is produced.

The wild morning glory when growing in cultivated ground often produces no seeds but spreads rapidly by its roots. There are other noxious weeds which reproduce and spread both by seed and root like the ox-eye daisy, the snapdragon or butter and eggs, the bouncing Bet, perennial sow thistle, quackgrass, and several more.

The importance of knowing the habits of any weed lies in applying this knowledge to the eradication of the plant. For instance, it would by useless to summer-fallow a field in order to kill an annual weed like the wild mustard which can be kept from spreading by any method that will prevent it from bearing seed. Whether the root is removed from the ground or not is of little consequence if no seeds are allowed to form.

On the other hand it would be equally unwise to attempt to destroy quackgrass by preventing it from bearing seed when, in many cases, it really spreads more rapidly by root stocks than by seed. Hence to intelligently eradicate any weed one must know its life period and its habit of growth.

Methods for eradication annual and biennial weeds

For purposes of eradication the annual and biennial weed may be treated alike. Both may be kept from spreading or reproducing themselves by preventing them from bearing seed.

Means of control

Annuals and biennials:

1. Cutting or pulling
2. Thorough tillage of cultivated crops
3. Rotation of crops
4. Spraying with chemicals

Perennials

1. Summer fallowing
2. Partial summer fallowing and smother cropping
3. Thorough cultivations with crop
4. Smothering with tar paper, etc.
5. Application of salt brine, gasoline, etc. (Update note: Today we know enough not to put gas or petroleum products on the soil.)

The important thing is to decide which is the best way to prevent the plants from bearing seed, and the way chosen will depend upon whether the plants are scattered or whether they are growing closely together in large patches or fields.

Where annual or biennial plants are scattered there are two ways of killing them, either by pulling them up by the roots or by cutting them. When the plants are pulled up they may safely be dropped where pulled in the field. However, if the seed-pods are once formed, plants usually possess sufficient vitality to ripen the seeds even when they have been pulled up and thrown on the ground. In such case the plants should be carried to some place where they may be burned.

If annuals are to be cut, this

should be done if possible beneath the surface of the earth. Any other method is apt to leave one or two small branches on each plant and the entire food-supply furnished by the well-developed root is sent to these branches. They thus grow very rapidly and are practically certain to ripen their seeds unless cut a second time and even then the seedpods will probably have formed and necessitate burning of the plants.

A good tool for cutting scattered plants is the "spud."

Methods for large patches of fields

Where annuals or biennials are growing in large patches or thickly infest whole fields, other methods than pulling and cutting must be used.

Cultivation: Careful and thorough preparation of the seedbed for every crop is a great factor in control of annual weeds. Fields which have been fall-plowed usually have a hard crust over them in the spring. The weed plantlets growing in the soil are not noticeable until cultivation breaks the crust and the white or pink stems of the young weed-plants are thrown up, sometimes by the thousand. Exposed to the sun and wind, they are practically all killed.

This same cultivation turns a new lot of seeds up to the surface to sprout, and within two or three days a new crop of weeds is growing. Another cultivation kills this crop; it would not require many such operations to practically free the crop-producing portion of the soil from weeds.

The disk-harrow is an especially valuable tool for fitting fall-plowed land for a crop and killing the young weeds. Even after the crop is planted, the field should be harrowed whenever possible to kill whatever young weeds may have appeared.

The value of such cultivation was shown in one instance where seven acres of a certain field were not harrowed. The weather later prevented further cultivation. On portions of the field which had been harrowed a two-hundred-bushel crop of potatoes was produced. On the unharrowed portion, the weeds took complete possession. They were so thick that the potatoes were choked out and no attempt was made to harvest the crop.

Many farmers hesitate to drag corn, potatoes, or sugar beets early in the growing season, for fear of tearing out or covering up some of the young plants. If the dragging is done during the middle of the day or when the plants of corn or other crops are somewhat withered, little damage will be done. More weeds will be killed by one dragging while they are young and tender than by several cultivations when the plants have become larger and harder to kill.

Besides killing the weeds, cultivation ventilates and warms the soil, supplying much better conditions for germination of the seed and giving the crop a strong, vigorous start. It also encourages chemical action and provides the nutrifying and other bacteria with better conditions in which to work, and to render available a larger amount of plant food. Every good farmer has discovered this secret and no matter what the conditions are, insists on a careful preparation of his land for crops and plenty of the right kind of cultivation afterward. In fact, many farmers even insist that quackgrass and Canada thistles are blessings in disguise because their presence necessitates more intensive preparation of the seed bed, and better and more frequent cultivations of the crop than is often otherwise given.

The importance of careful cultivation both for weed eradication and its effect upon the soil and the crop cannot be over-emphasized. This fact in a measure off-sets the expense incurred in the process of eradication. Where crops like corn and sugar beets are drilled-in, killing the weeds in the row, while they are small, is especially important. If allowed to grow to any height it is necessary to cover the weeds with dirt in an endeavor to kill them. This requires deep cultivation, and may cut off many of the roots of the corn, retarding its growth and lessening the yield. To offset this damage, it would be well to plant a little additional seed in the beginning.

Rotation of crops: Perhaps one of the best means of successfully combating weeds is by rotating the crops grown upon the infested fields.

A good rotation, especially for the dairy farmer, is one requiring four years and may include the following crops:

- First year: corn with clean cultivation;
- Second year: grain crop with clover (10 pounds), timothy (eight pounds);
- Third year: two crops of clover hay;
- Fourth year: timothy meadow, or pasture.

For the second year of the rotation barley, oats, or spring wheat may be grown, as best suits the farmer's convenience. In the fourth year a crop of timothy hay may be cut or the field pastured, whichever plan best meets the needs on each particular farm. The sod should be manured and plowed in the fall and the field made ready for corn the succeeding spring. The degree of success obtained with this or any other rotation is largely dependent upon persistent cultivation of the corn or other cultivated crops.

Shorter rotations are not apt to be very satisfactory for weed-control, although in some cases and on some soils they serve the purpose admirably. Longer rotations, particularly those including alfalfa, would be even more satisfactory for the eradication of weeds. The establishment of a good crop rotation of a field is usually a guarantee that annual or biennial weeds will be largely destroyed and that even the perennial weeds will be partially controlled.

A few weeds can produce an enormous quantity of seed. At this Station actual counts have shown that a well developed plant of pigeon grass will produce 142,000, red-root or rough pigweed 330,000, barnyard grass 1,290,000, and tumbleweed 5,000,000 seeds. These are among the common weeds infesting cornfields and none of them should be allowed to go to seed, because one crop of weed-seeds will cause untold trouble.

In this rotation if the corn is kept

clean and cut close to the ground the field can be left unplowed and the ground for the oats and grass seed be prepared by disking and harrowing thoroughly the next spring. The thorough and careful cultivation of the corn should have killed all the seeds and weeds in the crop-bearing surface of the soil so that the grain-crop following should be practically free from weeds. If the ground were tplowed a new crop of weed-seeds would be turned up, to grow in the grain unless killed by thorough cultivation before the grain is sown. If properly carried out, this rotation will prevent the production of weed-seeds on the field for four years, as practically no weeds grow in the hay if a good stand is secured.

"Are four years of persistent work enough to kill all weeds?" They would be, were it not for the great length of time during which weed-seeds may lie dormant in the soil only to grow and reproduce their kind when turned to the surface. Instances are known of weed seeds growing after having been buried for 10 and even more than 40 years! Hence the need of continued rotation.

Chemical spray checks: Another effective method with some weeds, notably the wild mustard, is to apply some sort of chemical spray. Various chemicals have been used with varying success. Iron sulfate and common salt have given good results and are comparatively cheap. The former can be bought for one dollar per hundred pounds; salt at half that price. A 20 percent solution of the iron sulfate or a 35 percent solution of the salt is effective and easily made by placing 100 pounds of the former or 125 pounds of the latter in a vinegar or kerosene barrel, filling with water and stirring until completely dissolved. It should be applied on a fair day after the dew is off, at the rate of one barrel to an acre. If rain falls within 24 hours, a second application may be needed. A sprayer throwing a fine mist that will settle gently upon the plant should be used. Success depends upon reaching all portions of the plant with the spray. The one ordinarily used for potatoes throws too course a spray. The proper implement should develop a pressure of 100 pounds to the square inch. By using a sprayer with a 20 foot boom, a man with a good team can spray 20 acres a day, provided he has a helper to make the solution for him.

This method is advisable only where mustard is very thick. It will kill only the plants which are in the grain at the time of spraying and will have no effect what-so-ever on the millions of seeds buried in the soil. Its effect therefore extends only to the year's crop. The spraying would need to be continued for several years or until the mustard plants would not be thick enough to make spraying profitable, when the remainder of the work would have to be done by hand.

Probably a much greater destruction of wild mustard would result from plowing and cultivation. Successive crops of seeds would be turned to the surface, sprout, and as rapidly as the young plants appear, they would be killed by cultivation. By continued repetition of this process, the crop-bearing surface of the soil could probably be freed from mustard in a single season.

Methods of eradicating perennial weeds

While there are many perennial weeds which are proving troublesome on Wisconsin farms, two are pre-eminently noxious, because of their peculiar nature and habits, viz., quackgrass and Canada thistles. Description of these weeds and the methods whereby they may be destroyed follow.

Quackgrass

Quackgrass grows to a height of from one to five feet, depending upon the fertility of the soil and the character of the season.

Its roots are fine and fibrous, like those of other grasses. It also has underground stems or root stocks, which give this plant its noxious character. They must be killed to eradicate it. This is difficult to do, for they possess great vitality. They resemble roots and are sometimes mistaken for them. They look like other stems, except that the color is nearly white and the joints are much closer together, usually not more than 1-1/2 inches apart and often less than that. At each joint new roots are thrown out and at many of them new stems start. In this way the grass spreads rapidly and a piece of the rootstock with one of these joints on it will produce a new plant, although it may be not over 1/2 inch long.

The leaves vary from three to 12 inches in length and from 1/4 to 1/2 inch in width. They are rough to the touch on the upper side and smooth on the lower. The parts which clasp the stem (sheaths) are shorter than the distances between the joints (internodes).

The head is from three to eight inches long and from 1/4 to 1/2 inch wide. It is slender and at first glance much resembles English Rye Grass. The divisions of the head (spikelets) in Quack Grass are turned with the flat side to the stem (rachis), while in Rye Grass the edge of the spikelet faces the stem. When the heads first appear, they are narrow but grow wider as the plant approaches maturity.

The seed of quackgrass is about 1/2 inch long and 1/16 of an inch wide, light brown or yellowish when ripe, and resembles the oat, except that it does not close up so much on the furrow side. At the larger end of the seed and in the furrow there is a club-shaped appendage (rachilla) about 1/16 of an inch long.

The leaves and roots of bromegrass are often mistaken for quackgrass and while the plants are young it is extremely difficult to distinguish them. The roots of Kentucky bluegrass and red top are also mistaken for those of quackgrass, except that they are much smaller. It is not possible to confuse these last named grasses with the quackgrass after they are headed out, for all of them in general outline resemble oats, instead of rye or wheat, as is the case with quack. The heads of different plants vary greatly in appearance. In some the flower covering (glume) bears only a sharp point at the end. In others the glume bears a distinct beard (awn) 1/2 inch long. Some plants are light and some are dark green in color but in general characteristics all are alike.

How it is spread: The whole plant grows rapidly and ripens its seed usually in July. Where growing in meadows, it may be gathered in the hay, whence it gets into the manure and so scattered broadcast of the farm.

If growing in grain it may be harvested and threshed with the grain, and if the grain is not graded with extreme care some of the quackgrass seed will be sown on the fields the next year. If the hay or grain is sold on the market the seeds may be carried for long distances to establish patches of the grass on farms far removed from the place where the hay or grain was produced. The seed, and, in some cases rootstocks also may be carried from farm to farm by the spring floods or the seed may be blown from place to place by the wind.

While quackgrass may have some feeding value, it is not relished by stock so much as cultivated grasses are and its presence prevents the production of crops of much greater economic value and importance.

Canada thistle

Like quackgrass the Canada thistle is a perennial plant. In height it ranges from one to three feet, depending on conditions. It is said to have received its name from the fact that it was found in the French settlements in Canada, although it was later introduced by the Dutch into New York and by the English into Vermont and New Hampshire. In England it is called "corn thistle," "green thistle" or "creeping thistle."

The Canada thistle does not have rootstocks like the quackgrass, but has true roots, the parts of which are capable of producing plants. There are tuffs of rootlets at intervals on the horizontal root. These roots are about 1/4 inch in diameter, almost white in color and it is from these that new plants are thrown up at intervals as they extend their length through the soil.

When undisturbed by cultivation the roots are apt to lie near the surface, but go deeper in cultivated soil and where it is particularly loose and porous may be found at a depth of three feet. The roots are very hardy and by means of the sharp growing points will sometimes send shoots up through two or three feet of hard packed clay soil. When the plant begins its growth in the spring, a rosette of leaves is formed close to the ground from the center of which a flower stalk is set up.

The stem is rather slender, somewhat irregular in shape, seldom more than 3/4 of an inch in diameter and bears few spines. It separates into several branches near the top, each branch bearing a flower.

The leaves are bright green in color, smooth on the upper face and rough or hairy beneath. The lower leaves are from three to eight inches long and from one to one-and-one-half inches wide and the edges are curled or wavy. The edges are cut or divided and bear a large number of sharp stiff spines, which on the mature plant are yellow or almost white in color. The leaves are easily distinguished from those of the common or bull thistle, the leaves of which are very rough on both surfaces and bear a large number of spines of varying lengths.

The heads are purple, about an inch long, 3/4 of an inch in diameter and bear no spines but simply stiff scales or bracts. They differ from the heads of the bull thistle which are often two inches or more long and an inch in diameter and covered with sharp, stiff spines.

The seeds are smooth, brown, about 1/8 inch long and larger at one end than the other. The larger end bears a shallow depression or cup, from which projects a sharp point. Once seen and known the seed will not be forgotten. Every seed bears a tuft of downy hairs, called a "pappus," by the aid of which it may be carried a mile or more during the high winds preceding some of our summer storms.

The seeds may be carried from place to place by water in the shape of spring floods, creeks, rivers, irrigation and drainage canals. They may also be shipped in hay or grain, but the most prolific source of introduction is through grass and clover seeds. For this reason all grass and clover seed should be carefully examined before sowing to make sure that it contains no Canada thistle seed.

Habits: Canada thistles seldom bear seed in cultivated fields but in clover or grass fields, in pastures, groves or fence rows where they may develop undisturbed for a time,

About checkrows:

Most schoolchildren know (or once did, at least) that Indians taught the European settlers in America how to plant corn: in hills, with a fish in each hill for fertilizer.

When corn-growing became more mechanized, it was planted in checkrows; that is, there were rows going both north-south and east-west, with enough room between all the rows to drive a horse and cultivator.

With the introduction of herbicides and even more mechanized farming, such cultivation was considered unnecessary. Then corn could be planted in rows going in one direction only, which allowed the spaces in the rows going the other direction to be filled in with corn plants. This, of course, increased the yield per acre.

As the push for greater yields continued, along with the development of herbicides as well as pesticides, chemical fertilizers, new corn varieties and new machinery that allowed planting with less space between rows, the "population" or number of corn plants per acre continued to increase.

If corn is planted in checkrows—rows that are, say, four feet apart in both directions—there will be about 2,722 plants on each acre.

But if the rows are only 18 inches apart, and the plants are one foot apart in the rows, that same acre will contain almost 10 times as many plants.

The combination of all these factors accounts for the tremendous increases in corn yields in the 20th century.

seed is often produced abundantly. Whenever seed is produced on plants growing in cultivated fields only a few of the heads on each plant bear seed, the rest being sterile.

While Canada thistles produce more or less seed, yet the increase of these pests is due largely to the roots which spread out rapidly in all directions and are transplanted in widely different portions of the farm by the plow, drag, and cultivator.

Methods of eradication

Many methods have been devised and advocated for the eradication of quackgrass and Canada thistles. The success of any method depends very largely upon soil and weather conditions and a method which has proven entirely successful under one set of conditions has frequently failed when used under somewhat different circumstances. Quackgrass is more persistent and more difficult to eradicate than the Canada thistle, hence any method which will eradicate quackgrass will surely destroy Canada thistles or any other perennial weed.

Some methods may be used effectively and economically on small patches, but will prove too costly for large areas. The method should be wisely selected and suited to the circumstances.

Methods for large areas

This method is successful except on sandy soils which leach badly, soils that are continuously wet, or are so porous that the horizontal roots are too deep to be reached with the plow. No crop can be grown while this treatment is being given. Then the field should be plowed as soon as possible after the crop has been removed, but should not be plowed while so dry that the soil turns up in large lumps, making it difficult to work. The depth of the plowing is very important as the success of the method practically depends upon it.

First ascertain the depth at which the horizontal roots or rootstocks are growing, and regulate the depth of the plowing so as to turn them to the surface. In meadows, or pastures, or any other place where the plants are not cultivated or otherwise distributed, the rootstocks of quackgrass will be found usually within two or three inches of the surface. In cultivated ground they grow deeper, in some cases below the usual plow line.

After plowing, the field should be cultivated often enough to prevent all leaf growth, for every time the leaves get above the surface they supply the root with food, thus prolonging its life.

Hence the cultivation must be done before the leaves appear above the ground. The plant breathes through its leaves and if its breathing apparatus is destroyed, it dies for lack of air. The succeeding spring the ground should be plowed again just deep enough to turn to the surface any roots which the cultivator may have failed to reach the preceding autumn.

The object of the cultivation is to drag all the roots to the surface where the wind and sunshine will dry them out and kill them. In a damp season the roots should be removed from the field by use of a horse rake and a big fork. A spring-tooth harrow or some other good digging tool is preferable to a disk-harrow. The latter cuts up the roots into small pieces; it require more work to get them all to the surface where they will be killed, and a single portion of a quackgrass rootstock bearing a joint will start a new plant even though it is only one-half inch long. It has been shown that an inch long will often produce a new plant, so it is unwise to cut them up with a disk harrow. The field should be plowed at varying depths at least three times more during the season, to make sure that all the roots are brought to the surface and killed. The cultivator should be kept going during the time between plowings to prevent all leaf growth.

In case there is any doubt about the complete eradication of the weed, corn planted in checkrows (see box on previous page) to allow for cultivation both ways should follow the summer-fallow. Close watch should be kept of the field and if any weeds appear they can be removed by hoeing. It is not probable that any weeds will survive the preceding treatment but it is well to be certain.

This fallowing method is more certain to result in complete eradication than any other which has been tried. It gets rid of the weeds with one year's work. The thorough cultivation of the soil puts it into splendid condition, a much larger crop will be obtained the following year than possible had the weeds remained, and the field will continue to bear good crops after the weeds have been eliminated. The dead rootstocks of the quackgrass will be converted into humus and so increase the water-holding capacity of the soil. For these reasons it is as economical a method as one which allows the production of crops but extends the treatment through several years.

Variations of the fallow method

Cultivating with a crop: Where the quackgrass or thistles are to be removed while a crop is being raised plowing should begin the preceding summer or autumn, the earlier the better. This should be followed by careful cultivation until the ground freezes up. The next spring, plowing should begin as soon as soil conditions permit and be repeated at intervals of four weeks until the first of July.

Between plowings thorough cultivation should be practiced. On the date mentioned the seedbed should be carefully prepared and the land sown to millet or buckwheat at the rate of three pecks per acre in either case. The previous treatment will have so weakened the weeds that the millet or buckwheat will be well established before the weeds recover sufficiently to begin growth.

Hemp as a smother crop

Hemp is another crop which has lately been introduced into Wisconsin, and which has already shown its value as a smother crop for weeds. It requires a very fertile soil for best results, but will do well on all but our more sandy soils. The preparatory treatment of an infested field should include the application of 20 loads of barnyard manure per acre followed by the partial fallow as outlined for use with the millet and buckwheat. Hemp must be sown by May 10th in Wisconsin, hence not much spring cultivation other than a careful preparation of the seed bed can be given. Sow the hemp with a broadcast seeder or grain drill at the rate of one bushel of seed per acre. Experiments conducted by C. P. Norgord of this station show that success is practically sure on fertile soils but cannot be expected on poor soils or on badly infested fields where insufficient preparatory work has been done. All of these crops grow rapidly and provide a dense shade which smothers the weeds.

This means almost sure death to Canada thistles, but often fails with quackgrass and must be adopted advisedly. If followed by plowing again in the fall after the crop succeeding spring, all weeds will probably be killed. This method allows the production of a crop during the process of weed eradication, but it is not so certain of success.

Methods for small areas

Covering with paper: Quackgrass and Canada thistles in patches not over two rods square can sometimes be economically killed by cutting the weeds close to the ground just when in bloom and covering with tar or some other heavy building paper. The strips of paper must overlap sufficiently to prevent the plants from coming up between the strips and should also extend far enough beyond the edges of the patch so that no plants can reach the air and sunlight.

The paper should be weighted down with earth or stone to hold it in place. If the surface is nearly level it would be better to use planks or fence rails to hold the paper in place because the earth is apt to retain moisture and cause the paper to rot. (Update note: Today, this method frequently employs plastic sheets or rolls.)

This method can only be used successfully on fairly level ground where the paper can be held close to the surface. In a dry season 60 days is usually sufficient to destroy the weeds, but it is best to leave the paper on until time to plow in the fall. Should any plants survive this treatment they will be so weakened as to be easily killed the succeeding season.

Close cultivation: Where it is not possible to use the foregoing method either because of unevenness of ground or for any other reason, close cultivation may be practiced. The patch should receive the same thorough cultivation as recommended for large areas, except that much of the work may be done with a hoe.

Methods for Canada thistles but not for quackgrass

Growing alfalfa: Canada thistles have been completely eradicated where good stands of alfalfa were secured and maintained for three years or more. To secure this result the ground should be heavily manured and plowed as early in the summer or fall as possible and cultivated as already described, continuing the cultivation until early June, when the seedbed should be carefully prepared and alfalfa sown at the rate of 25 pounds per acre.

The preceding treatment will have weakened the weeds. The manure will give the alfalfa a good start and provide a rapid growth sufficient to prevent the thistles from growing. This method was tried by several members of the Wisconsin Experiment Association who claim that it is a complete success.

The sod method: The same results as above noted can sometimes be secured by manuring heavily and seeding down thickly to perennial grasses, such as Kentucky bluegrass, red top, English rye grass, etc., but the stand must be almost perfect and the land allowed to remain in grass for a series of years.

Salting the plant: Cut off the Canada thistle while in bloom just beneath the surface of the earth and apply a large handful of salt, or better yet, a half pint of stiff salt brine where the thistle is cut off.

Occasionally this treatment needs to be repeated, but usually one application is sufficient. This method is especially effective when stock is pastured on the field, for in their efforts to get the salt they help to destroy the thistles.

Gasoline for thistles: Gasoline may be substituted for salt and applied the same way. Carbolic acid may also be used, but must be handled with care. Neither of these is practicable, except for scattered plants or with very small patches, as the material is too costly. (Update note: Again, this is included for historical information only. Do not put gasoline on the ground.)

Farmers should act at once

Farmers cannot afford to ignore the danger from the encroachment of these various weed; yet there is a lamentable lack of concerted action to get rid of these enemies of crop production. Land in this state is too high-priced to be destroyed by weeds. It is time that those interested in agriculture realized the situation. The legislature has named a certain number of weeds which must be kept from seeding. They are quackgrass, Canada thistle, burdock, white or oxeye daisy, snapdragon or butter and eggs, cocklebur, perennial sow thistle, sour dock, yellow dock, wild mustard, wild parsnip, and Russian thistle.

There are laws on our statute books to compel the cutting of these weeds before seed is produced, but to prevent seeding is not sufficient. Steps must be taken to rid the soil of the roots as well as of the seed, if complete freedom is to be obtained. Cooperation between farms in the same locality and between farmers, the Experiment Station, and the Legislature, is necessary before satisfactory results will be secured. The fact that the most noxious weeds can be eradicated should be emphasized and active efforts put forth to prevent these pests from taking possession of Wisconsin farms. Only by continuing the fight to the end with method and thoroughness can ultimate freedom from noxious weeds be attained.

Self-sufficient gardening:

Feeding a family of four from the garden

With good soil, good weather, and some experience, a space about the size of a two-car garage will feed a family for a year

COUNTRYSIDE: In the latest issue someone said you need two acres of garden to grow all your food for a year.

Are there any guidelines for this? What to plant, how much seed, how many rows of each, for a family of four? – *Elliott Reynolds, New York*

I don't recall any reference to two acres of garden... and I'd dispute it if I did. Unless, possibly, your rows are so far apart you're cultivating between each one with a horse or tractor! But few homesteaders today use such old-fashioned methods.

With any type of intensive planting and well-built-up soil fertility, a half-acre or less should suffice for most families of four. Under ideal conditions, and with experience, much less. John Jeavons, in *How to Grow More Vegetables* (than you ever thought possible on less land than you can imagine) (Ten Speed Press, Berkeley, CA, first edition, 1974 and still in print) claims you can feed a family of four with a garden of 1,302 square feet—including paths! (An acre is 43,560 square feet, or almost 35 times as much.) This, of course, requires some very intensive gardening, and enough experience to make it work.

We might also point out, once again, that small gardens frequently produce more than large ones. The reason is simple: Smaller gardens are likely to get better care, while large ones, especially those planted by beginners, often become overwhelming and by July are lost in weeds and neglect.

But these variables suggest already —even before getting into the more difficult part of your question—why we have always disliked presenting such information even as "guidelines." How fertile is your soil? What are you going to plant (or what do you like to eat)? What varieties? What is your climate like? How much do you know about intensive planting?

And when we get into things like weather that varies from year-to-year, pests and diseases that also vary, timing of plantings (another big variable in our gardens, depending on weather and other projects and priorities)... that's why we always say asking a question like this is like asking "How long is a piece of string?"

Really. The only substitute for experience is beginner's luck. And experience alone is no guarantee. When we moved 250 miles north it took three years to learn how to garden all over again.

With these disclaimers (and many others we could add), here are some of the "guidelines" so many people are asking for.

What, when, and how much to plant for a family of four with a six-month growing season

Not all seeds germinate, and you'll thin out weaker plants

Weights of seeds

It might seem silly to count seeds, but for our purposes here, it makes more sense than weighing them. The reason is simple.

There are about 72,000 celery seeds in one ounce. 23,000 carrots. Onion, 9,500. Cabbage, broccoli and Brussels sprouts, 9,000. Beets, 1,600; beans, 100-125, sweet corn, 120-180.

So although it might seem silly to talk about planting 32 cabbage seeds, it's actually more helpful than talking about 0.007 ounces or 1/48th of a teaspoon.

Six weeks before the last frost, plant:

Vegetable	#Seeds
Cabbage	32
Broccoli	16
Brussels sprouts	8
Cauliflower	8
Head lettuce	96
Leaf lettuce	56
Celery	96
Parsley	16

About four weeks later these will be thinned by half and transplanted. At that time plant directly in the garden:

Spinach	234
Bush peas	1,370
Carrots	1,414
Beets	100
Onions	380 sets
Radishes	60
Garlic	32 cloves
Chard	12

At the same time start in flats:

Tomatoes	56
Bell pepperes	48
Eggplant	8
Dill	8

On the last frost date plants potatoes (68.25 lbs should be 546 starts) and start in flats:

Cantaloupe	40
Honeydew	40
Watermelon	160
Cucumbers	48
Sweet basil	8

Two-to-four weeks later transplant what's in the flats and plant early corn, 168 seeds; pumpkins, 8; and sunflowers for seeds, 8.

As the peas and carrots are harvested, plant the melons in their place. Replace the early brassicas and lettuce with bush green beans, 752 seeds, and bush lima beans, 224.

As the first corn comes out replace with 31 lbs. of sprouted potatoes, or 248 pieces with one or two eyes each.

About 14 weeks after the last frost dig the first potatoes and replace with corn, 168 seeds. Start another 16 broccoli seeds, 32 cabbage, and more lettuce.

A good and experienced gardener using intensive methods in good soil can far outproduce the average backyarder…or commercial farmer. But some of their "tricks" can be used by anyone with time, patience, desire and ambition.

For example, a seed packet might suggest planting seeds four inches apart, in rows 36 inches apart. If a plant only needs four inches, why not make the rows four inches apart too? Plant four rows together and then leave the wider space for walking, and you'll get much more from the same area.

Succession planting – harvesting one crop and immediately using the space for another – increases the yield per square foot, as does growing viney crops on trellises rather than sprawling over way more real estate than their root systems require.

And something as simple as a mounded raised bed (as opposed to a flat topped one) can add growing space.

The payoff: Less time, less effort, and more food.

Vegetable	Seed per 100 sq. ft. oz.	Yield (US av) lbs.
Artichoke, Jerusalem	10.5#	50
Asparagus	159*	5
Beans, Lima, bush	45	8
Beans, Lima, pole	22	8
Beans, snap, bush	8	10
Beans, snap, pole	8	10
Beets	1.5	35
Beets plus greens	1.5	55+
Broccoli	.01	25
Brussels sprouts	.01	36
Cabbage	.01	60
Carrots	.2	65
Cauliflower	.01	29
Chard	.4	150
Collards	.025	80
Corn	16	19
Cucumbers	.2	40
Eggplant	.015	55
Garlic	14 lbs.	40
Kale	.01	16
Kohlrabi	.22	34
Leeks	.1	120
Lettuce, head	.008	73
Lettuce, leaf	.016	51
Muskmelon	.09	100
Mustard	.055	30
Okra	.64	100
Onions	.2	85
Parsley	.08	25
Parsnips	1.9	100
Peas	2-4 lbs	7
Peppers, green	.064	46
Potato, Irish	25 lbs	69
Potato, sweet	12 lbs.	33
Radish	3.9	50
Rutabega	.07	70
Salsify	4.4	70
Spinach	.37	25
Squash, yellow bush	.37	65
Squash, winter	.37	50
Squash, zucchini	.24	100
Tomato	.006	60
Turnip (w. tops)	.13	50

* roots

What we eat

Food	Average per capita consumption per year (lbs)
Potatoes	49.3
Lettuce	24.9
Apples	16
Tomatoes	11.4
Onions, dry	10.2
Cabbage	8.4
Celery	7.3
Cantaloupe	6.6
Sweet corn	6.6
Carrots	6.1
Cucumbers	4.0
Bell peppers	3.3
Pears	2.4
Bananas	20.8

Gardeners and farmers know that seeds planted in ground that's too cold will not germinate. Also, the steadier the heat, the fewer number of days will elapse between germination and ripening.

Germination temperatures of some common crop seeds (Farhrenheit)

Crop	Lowest temp	Highest temp	Optimum temp
Wheat	41	104	84
Barley	41	104	84
Pea	44	102	84
Corn	48	115	93
Bean	49	111	84
Squash	54	115	93

Can you make yeast and baking powder?

Where do yeast and baking powder come from? I would like to grow or make my own, if possible.—T. F., Hawaii

Yeast is a plant, a tiny fungus, that's found everywhere. So it does grow… but you have to "plant the right kind of seed" if you want to grow the kind of yeast that will make your bread edible.

Back in 1985 a countrysider described the "everlasting yeast" which had been in her family for generations. This is the "seed" you need, but finding it will be a problem we can't help with.

The main active ingredients in baking powder are a carbonate and an acid substance, mixed with starch or flour. We can't help you stay away from the store to buy the sodium acid pyrophosphate and sodium bicarbonate and rice or corn starch one recipe we found calls for (42 g., 30 g. and 28 g., respectively) but you might try this:

Six ounces cream of tartar; 2-2/3 ounces bicarbonate of soda; and 4-1/2 ounces of flour. (Even if you don't care to be that self-reliant, you might want to remember this the next time you run out of baking powder.)

These obstacles contributed to the early popularity of sourdough, which uses a starter… which can be made in the kitchen.

The garden:

Yes, you can grow rice in zone 6

ELIZABETH & CROW MILLER
NEW YORK

Although rice is a tropical crop, early maturing varieties can be grown as far north as Long Island. And you can harvest enough rice from your garden to feed your family for a year. (A 100' x 15' bed will produce about 170 pounds of rice. A 15' x 15' bed will produce about 50 pounds.)

Rice grows best when it has 40 days with temperatures above 70°F and when night temperatures do not drop below 55°F. If you live in such an area, an always muddy, low lying site with hard-packed soil (where everything else you ever tried to grow was swamped) is the best place for your patch. Ideally, you want a level area that retains water well to keep the rice evenly irrigated.

Presoaking seeds will enhance germination. Put the seeds in a cloth or burlap bag and tie it closed. Then place the bag in warm water for 24 hours. Drain it and allow the seeds to dry for another 24 hours before planting.

Till the planting site to one foot deep and enrich the soil with well-made compost. If you plan to flood (and the best yields are harvested from paddies), dig a trench 1-1/2 feet deep and seven inches wide around the site.

In warmer climates you can direct seed, but if you live in a shorter season area you should plant a small bed, then transplant. For direct seeding, we suggest flooding your site shallowly, then sprinkling the seed into the water. The seeds will root right through the water.

If you opt for the transplanting method, select a warm, sunny spot in your garden. Water the soil thoroughly, or use a mucky planting medium if starting indoors in flats. About one month before your last frost date, sow the seed and cover with a small film of water.

About three or four weeks after sowing (when three to four leaves appear) transplant your rice seedlings. We start seeds in our greenhouse around April 15th, then transplant three to eight stalks on nine-inch centers about May 15th. After sprouting, thin to two plants per foot, because rice patches require diligent weeding.

For the next 90 days watering and weeding are your priorities. Watering in the morning is best because that will allow the afternoon sun to warm the water sitting in the garden. Keep about one inch of water on the patch during the day for best growth.

Weeds? Standing water in a paddy will destroy many of them. We suggest a different approach: Allow the water to drain completely from your patch once or twice during the season and then pull all the weeds before watering it again.

A member of the grass family, rice plants grow tall and thin during the long, hot days of summer. About 60 to 85 days after you plant a semi-dwarf variety, the plant will flower. Most rice is self-pollinating, but excessive wind, rain, and especially cold, can inhibit pollination.

About 30 to 40 days after flowering, heavy, golden-brown heads should develop from the flowers. Allow the soil in the rice patch to dry just before harvest, which will let the plant dry and speed the final ripening process. When about 85% of the heads have turned golden, you're ready to cut.

A scythe or sickle is a good tool for harvesting small stands of grain. Bundle the sheaves and hang them in a well ventilated spot to dry. Next, thresh rice as you would other grains.

Sure, rice may require more work than your average garden crop, but the challenge is rewarding.

Use the tiller wisely to protect your soil

The University of Kentucky College of Agriculture reports that soil compaction is the biggest problem for many gardeners. Compacted soil is an unfriendly growing environment for plants, and it can be prevented with a little thought and planning.

According to UK horticulturist John Strang, "Compaction transforms plant-friendly soil into a difficult environment for plant growth by making it harder for plant roots, water and air to penetrate the soil. Major causes are excessive rototiller use, foot traffic in the garden and working in the garden when the soil is too wet... Compaction limits availability of air and water to the roots."

Excessive rototilling destroys soil

structure and creates a "plowpan", or compacted layer, just below the tilling depth. Instead of using the rototiller to control weeds, a two to three-inch layer of mulch can perform the same job. Mulching also helps retain soil moisture and keeps tomatoes and other edible plant parts off the ground.

Stang advised home gardeners to avoid working or walking in the garden if the soil is too wet. A simple test of wetness is squeezing a handful of soil. If it forms a muddy ball rather than crumbling apart when you open your hand, it would be wise to stay out of the garden.

Walking between plants and rows will also reduce compaction in primary growth areas.

Make a good mouse trap better

GRANT EVERSOLL
INDIANA

After constant nightly rebaiting of the mousetrap, I succumbed to the evils of using poison. I would rather have rid myself of the rodents another way, but I was at my wit's end and figured it was either us or them.

I'm not sure which is worse—sharing our food supply with the small, four-footed feline beast, or smelling their decaying bodies within my wall studs. Things worked out well this time when none died inside the house, but what about next time?

While talking to my brother, he mentioned the method that he used to trap mice. It's not really a better mousetrap: It's just a mousetrap that works. This could be called the politician's mousetrap, because you earn their trust, then hit 'em when they're not looking.

All you need is a paper bag or small box. Open the box or bag at both ends and place the trap inside in the middle. The varmint runs inside into the dark where it feels safe and lets its guard down, then...the rest is history.

If you're squeamish about mice, you can dispose of the pre-bagged mouse, trap and all. Otherwise, remove the mouse from the trap, wash and re-use it. If the trap doesn't have the smell of death washed away after the kill, it will not catch another mouse.

Ed. note: Although that last statement is commonly heard, some of us have had experiences that lead us to question it.

Reduce pains with a homemade rice bag

LEONA SULLINGER
PENNSYLVANIA

There is one thing that homesteaders aren't afraid of—hard work. But it catches up to all of us eventually. I would like to share a pattern for a pain reliever called a rice sack. It's sort of like a heat pad, only it conforms to your body and is not plugged in. They are quite simple to make.

Take a piece of flannel, fleece or something woven or tightly knit. Cut it to 14"x 18" and sew the length together. Right side together first, then turn it inside out.

Make two handles out of webbing, wide shoestrings, or melt macramé cord together. Take one end of the sack and zig zag it shut, then fold one of the handles and sew it down. Fill with about two pounds of dry rice.

Sew end shut, then fold over the second handle and sew down. I double seam everything to prevent leaks.

Heat two to three minutes in the microwave, and use the handles to position the bag. The first usage may require a longer heating time.

If you are off the grid, I suppose you could use heat-resistant sleepwear flannel and heat it on an iron skillet on the wood stove. You'll have to experiment. If you can't sew, use a wool sock that has no holes.

My favorite place for the rice sack is around my neck or across the forehead and temples for sinus headaches. It's good for arthritis, and I wrapped it around an injured arm. It's nice for warming up toes after winter chores. These sell commercially for about $10, but you can make one for less than $1 and sell them for $4. Remember to write directions on fabric with a permanent marker before sewing or attach a heating instruction tag.

I give away a lot of rice sacks as gifts. I use scraps of material in making them, and I love to sew and weave carpets and piece quilts. My husband says I hoard things. I say I'm saving them for future reference, but I may have to live to be 100 to use them all.

Keep working hard, then heat your rice sack and relax those tired, achy bones and muscles.

New life for dead aerosol spray cans

COUNTRYSIDE: A tip I've been meaning to pass along for quite some time now is even more appropriate for cooler weather.

When an aerosol can has plenty of liquid left but no propellant, place it in a pan of hot water for a few seconds and it will recharge enough to get you through a job. I have one can of WD-40 that I've used that way several times. It's still about 1/3 full. A similarly dead can of ether started an old Farmall on several cold mornings. Of course one should never place the can over flame or in the microwave.

I brought in 20 turkey poults day before yesterday, and started digging through back issues and indexes. It took awhile, but I found what I was looking for. – *Paul Whitfill, Texas*

Seed-saving has many benefits

Diane M. Heeney
South Dakota

Saving seed will not only reduce gardening expenses, but it can enable you to have control over size, disease resistance, maturity dates, flavor and overall quality of your produce.

Your seed should come from healthy fruit or plants with a better-than-average yield. If you're going for size, progressively choose larger fruit sources. It is not desirable to save seed from hybrid parents, as they come from inbred stock. Some of their saved seed will be sterile. Be sure to mark your seed plants as soon as you decide you will be harvesting from them.

Correct seed storage is necessary to insure viability. Seeds should remain in their natural pod or husk until dry and hard or brittle. Small seeds that have a tendency to shatter or blow away can be encased in a fine mesh or paper bag. Don't use plastic, as it encourages mildew. Onions, carrots and cabbage do well with bag harvesting.

After collection, dry seeds for a week before storage. Spread them on newspapers or fine screen to increase ventilation. Berry seeds can be retrieved by pushing the fruit through a sieve, washing off the seeds, then air drying.

Heat and humidity can hurt germination, so store in a cool, dry place. Mold can form if jars are used, since seeds can re-absorb atmospheric moisture. Simple paper envelopes (sealed and labeled) are an easy solution. Picking seeds on a warm, dry day can go a long way in preventing mold.

Lettuces are a self-pollinating annual. They don't need to be isolated. Harvest from the last plant to go to seed after the yellow flowers turn to whitish wisps. One plant can amply supply your family.

Peppers are also self-pollinating, but some crossing can occur from insect activity if two or more varieties are planted less than 50 feet apart. Don't harvest from green fruits, as the seeds are immature. Wait until the pepper is red.

Tomatoes are self-pollinating, so varieties don't cross. Save your very best fruit on the vine until quite ripe, but not rotten. Put the whole tomato in a glass jar and let it ferment for several days. The pulp and worthless seeds will rise to the top, where they can be skimmed off. The good seeds will sink to the bottom, where they can be strained, rinsed and dried. This process eliminates seed-borne diseases such as bacterial canker.

Beans should be left on the vine until they rattle or can't be dented by your teeth. If you have a very special variety, a 100-foot isolation barrier should be used. Average garden varieties don't need that much space, as they are considered self-pollinating.

Pumpkin/cucumber/cantaloupe cross-breeding tales can be intimidating. The species *C. pepo* has many cousins such as zucchini, baby jack o' lanterns, pattypan squash and acorn squash. Most oddities occur within the family tree. Crosses occur only within a species, so pumpkins can't cross with cantaloupes. Isolate plantings by 100 feet when in doubt. Fruit rinds should be hard to the fingernail, and the seeds washed and dried.

Biennial vegetables don't set their seed until the second season. These include parsnips, kale, carrots, beets and cabbage. They must be kept from freezing if left over winter in your garden. This can be accomplished with mulch, or you can dig and store in a cool place over the winter. Replant the best of the stored specimens in the spring.

An added bonus to saving radish seeds are the zesty pods that go so well in salads and stir fries. Purchased packets seem to be getting more expensive and have fewer seeds.

To summarize, pick the healthiest fruit, let it stay on the vine until fully ripe, rinse pulp off if necessary, and dry thoroughly. Keep the seeds from molding in storage. Isolate your plantings if cross-pollenization might be a problem.

I took a Master Gardener's course through our Extension Service last year. I highly recommend it. Even accomplished gardeners can learn something. The fee was nominal.

Easy, economical seed drying

Fall is seed drying time. The harvest season brings to many small farmers the problem of gathering, processing and storing seed. Whether preparing it for planting next spring yourself, or preparing it for sale, the job is vital.

Many seeds require some drying as a part of their preparation process. Melon, squash and pumpkin, to name a few, require some drying time. Even corn and bean seeds frequently need drying before storage. Since artificial drying with heat is sometimes bad for the seed, the following is a cheap natural method.

Secure a number of used window screens. These can be purchased at farm or town auctions at prices ranging from 50¢ each to as little as 50¢ per half-dozen. They are usually 4-4-1/2 feet long and about 30 inches wide. This gives about 1,600 square inches of drying space per screen.

The screens need to be set up in an open or ventilated room or loft and may be either suspended from above by wires, or they may be set up on a saw horse arrangements or chairs, or use your own creativity. Seeds are then spread out in a thin layer on the screens and left until dry. Since air passes up through the screen and flows through the layer of seed, thorough and efficient drying is possible. This is one of the cheapest and most efficient ways to dry seeds.—*Bill, Missouri*

The machine shed:

Farm tools: Part IV

Tools for secondary tillage

JEFF RAST, FARMER/DIRECTOR
THE CENTER FOR
SMALL ACREAGE FARMING
IDAHO

For as long as I can remember, I've enjoyed the sight, feel and smell of a mellow, healthy soil. Producing such a soil condition is the goal of secondary tillage. More specifically, secondary tillage takes the coarseness of a soil subjected to deep, primary tillage and makes a smooth, weed-free seedbed with soil particles fine enough to establish good contact with the soon-to-be-planted seed.

In this article, I will present some of the tools used in secondary tillage with a view to seed-bed preparation. There are plenty more tillage tools designed for cultivation (weed control) after the crop has been planted. Those will be presented in the next article in this series.

Disk harrows

Disk harrows are one of the most versatile field tools of any kind on a farm. (A much larger version of this tool is the disk plow intended for primary tillage, but its use has declined considerably.) Disk harrows fall into two classifications: tandem and offset. The disks in both types are concave shaped plates which cut into the soil, lifting, turning and mixing the soil as it is pulled through the field.

In a tandem disk, two groups or gangs of disks are arranged in somewhat of a v-shape followed by two more gangs arranged in an opposite v-shape. The disk blades are normally 16 to 18 inches in diameter and are set about seven inches apart. Most tandem disks are constructed with a rigid frame work which works well in loamy soils. Some tandem disks, especially older models, have a "floating" framework which is better suited to stony fields.

An offset disk resembles a tandem disk cut in half from front to back. The forward gang of disks is set at an angle which is a mirror image of the trailing gang of disks. Usually, offset disk harrows have larger disks, up to 20 to 24 inches in diameter, set on a spacing of nine inches. Obviously, this one is designed for heavier duty work.

The angles in both types of disk harrows can be adjusted to regulate the cutting depth and mixing action. The sharper the angle between front and trailing gangs, the deeper the disk will cut. If front and trailing gangs are parallel to each other (perpendicular to the line of travel), the cutting and turning action is very light.

Spike-tooth harrows

The spike-tooth harrow is one or more gangs of steel spikes fastened in a series of rows. New spikes are usually about eight inches in length and have a diamond-shaped rather than round cross-section. A single gang is about five feet wide. Depending on your tractor's pulling capacity and tillage needs, you may pull from one to as many as 10 gangs at a time. Obviously, a 50-foot-wide harrow finds itself at home on a large-scale grain operation rather than a small-scale farm.

The spike-tooth harrow is designed to break down large soil clods and to level the ground to a limited degree. The depth of penetration can be altered by the angle of the teeth to the ground. The more vertical the teeth, the deeper they harrow.

Another use of the spike-tooth harrow is to set the teeth at a shallow angle and lightly harrow in seed that was broadcast on the surface. This is especially applicable for cover crops, green manures and pastures.

Spring-tooth harrows

These harrows are a series of flexible C-shaped iron teeth arranged in patterns similar to the spike tooth harrows. Because the teeth are so broad and flexible, they do not perform as aggressively as the other harrows, which can be an advantage in stony ground. For the purposes of secondary tillage though, the spring-tooth harrow has been eclipsed by the more effective disk and spike-tooth harrows.

Though much less versatile than the previous harrows, the spring-tooth still has two helpful applications. It can be used to dig out roots of quackgrass and other weeds. Also, the flexible teeth make it a good candidate for cultivating alfalfa, as it can dig up weeds without damaging the alfalfa crowns as badly as any other kind of harrow would.

Due to their limited usefulness,

you should be able to find one of these in a scrap pile on some farms. But don't bother bringing it to your place even if it is free) unless you know you'll use it.

S-tine Cultivators

A more modern, vigorous and versatile version of the spring-tooth harrow is the S-tine cultivator. This cultivator can be mounted to the three-point hitch or used in a hydraulically operated trailing version. The teeth of the S-tine are narrower and sturdier than the teeth of a spring-tooth harrow. It can work at depths similar to a disk harrow but does not turn, pulverize or mix the soil to as great a degree.

Corrugated rollers and cultipackers

Many fine-seeded crops such as alfalfa and many of the vegetables need a firm seedbed to ensure a good contact between the seed and the soil. In this case, you need to use a roller. Two common varieties are the corrugated roller and the cultipacker. The corrugated roller comes in varying widths and is basically a heavy rolling tube with ridges every five or six inches. The ridges break up clods as the roller packs the soil.

The cultipacker is similar except that in place of one continuous roller, there is a series of compacting sprockets or packing wheels each with a solid or toothed ridge. The cultipacker tends to leave a more even surface than the sharply ridged corrugated roller.

Rototillers, vertical tine tillers and spading machines

Rototillers are understandably popular on everything from small gardens of several hundred square feet on up to small farms with several acres in production. Every model from the front-tine shoulder beaters to the large rear-tine varieties find useful applications in soil preparation. With just one pass, you can dig and pulverize soil and mix in compost and plant residue.

But a caveat is in order. Rototillers are hard on most soils, especially if used every year. In addition to chopping up much of your indispensable earthworm population, rototillers hasten the breakdown of organic matter by exposing so much soil to oxygen and light. Oxidation (chemical breakdown of materials in the presence of oxygen) occurs so rapidly in response to rototilling that it is simply not sustainable on an annual basis unless you are incorporating vast quantities of organic matter. Furthermore, fine soils with high silt or clay content will compact under the beating action of rototiller tines. While the tines are supposed to cut through the soil, the cutting action soon turns to a beating action as the tines dull with wear. So what's a person to do?

Two similar, and gentler options are available. The first is a vertical tine tiller which is a series of rotating pairs of vertical tines which mix the soil somewhat like a kitchen mixer combines ingredients. This tiller avoids the compaction problems of the rototiller and minimizes oxidation losses because it does not expose new soil to the surface. *The 1938 USDA Yearbook of Agriculture* speaks of such a machine being in use at that time. Now, however, we have to import these machines from Europe. The Lely Corporation in Wilson, North Carolina sells these tillers in the United States.

Biological pest control?

Hay fever is running rampant in Budapest, Hungary, and ragweed has flourished there recently—some say because of Chernobyl. To reduce the pollen, the mayor has hired sheep to graze the fields of ragweed on the city's outskirts.

Another option is the articulating spader. This is truly an amazing machine which can attach to a BCS walking tractor or, in larger sizes, attach to the three-point hitch of most tractors. At first glance, it resembles a rototiller. But instead of rotary tines, a series of spades cuts into the soil with a double-digging action. Clods are broken down as the spades throw the soil against the frame. This prepares the soil well without the compaction of a rototiller. While soil oxidation losses are higher than when a vertical tine tiller is used, the losses are lower than those caused by a rototiller.

Hand rakes and spading forks

For biointensive mini-farming with raised bed production, secondary tillage is accomplished by means of hand rakes and spading forks. Granted, such farming is extremely labor-intensive, but it boasts two advantages which no other production system can claim. First, it is easier on the soil than any of the more mechanized methods, escaping entirely the compaction caused by machinery travel. Second, it also holds the title for being the least expensive method in terms of capital outlay. For very small farms (mini-farms) with adequate labor available, this method is not only economically viable, but often superior to the alternatives.

As with all tillage tools from large plows for primary tillage on down to the hand rakes and spading forks, best results are achieved by working the soil at the proper moisture content. Even with these hand tools, you can damage the soil if you work it when it's too wet. The soil should have good moisture content, yet crumble easily. In using the spading fork, the soil should be of a consistency that you can lift a spadeful of soil, yet have it crumble easily when you bounce that spadeful on the fork a couple of times with a rapid jerking motion. The rake will often break the soil even finer as you use it to smooth and level the planting surface on your raised beds.

Jeff directs The Center for Small Acreage Farming.

Country kitchen:

A baker's holiday in Germany

Denise Fidler
The Country Baker
Indiana

The strong and pleasing aroma of fresh brewed coffee lingers in the air as I lay in bed wondering if I am dreaming or am I really here in Germany? The gentle clatter of china and silverware downstairs and the softly spoken "Deutsche" assures me that I am really here in the land of hearty, dark bread! I can hardly get downstairs fast enough to savor the intense robust flavor of the coffee that the Germans brew so strong.

"Guten morgen" from my husband and I and "Good morning" from my friend Anke and her husband Michel. The coffee is as rich and satisfying as I remember it being 12 years ago and the traditional German breakfast of fresh bread (little hard rolls), assorted cheeses, mustard, thinly sliced meats, jams and pickles is no less satisfying.

I was very intrigued by the assortment and texture of the colorful breads. Some were very dark, pumpernickel perhaps. Some were very seedy and rough, including several with toasted pumpkin seeds on top—these were my favorite.

Anke explained to me that most Germans go down to the corner bakery (backerei) for fresh bread every day. When Jim and I walked to the backerei one morning, it was clearly the busiest place in town at 6:30 A.M. This very small and simple bakery had such an impressive assortment of loaves of bread, rolls, pastries, cakes and fancy desserts that it would make some large scale American bakeries ashamed of their lack of colors and textures of their breads and rolls.

One of my goals while visiting Germany was to explore as many bakeries as I could and to try, with what little German I know, to discover some of the tricks of their trade.

I soon discovered that some of the darker breads were baked very slow for long periods of time using a sourdough starter—perhaps even a rye starter. This produces a thick and chewy loaf of bread that stays fresher longer.

Some of the shapes and types of bread are indigenous to certain locales. For instance, while visiting the beautiful city of Munster, we noticed very large circular mounds of dark bread in almost every bakery. I was also able to find this same bread in Frankfurt at a beautiful bakery in old Sachsenhausen. Also in this bakery were baguettes which I thought to be unusual for a German bakery to have.

My excitement with exploring these wonderful bakeries came to a peak when we entered the Black Forest and I found some Schwarzwalder Bauerbrot or dark farm bread which is also indigenous to the Black Forest region. This same backerei had some kamut bread which was satisfying as well.

Of course the pastries and cakes were to die for, and being that we were in the middle of the strawberry season there were strawberry cakes and pastries in every bakery! It was hard to decide what to eat whenever we were in a cafe, but whatever we chose was always satisfying and never too sweet. Black Forest cherry torte tempted our taste buds through the scrupulously cleaned glass display cases of every backerei we entered. (I found no dust in Germany, and believe me, I looked in every restaurant and store that I could!) Of course we gave in and were not disappointed!

Early one morning, Jim and I enjoyed (well, at least I did, I'm sure he would have rather been golfing) observing a German baker and his staff busily preparing the day's breads and pastries in the charming village of Drensteinfurt. The bakers pulled crusty-brown, oval loaves out of the ovens by means of a long wooden paddle and then sprayed the loaves with water to produce a shiny crust. There were little cut out bears made of bread dough with raisin eyes that were prepared special for some children! Machines mixed and rolled the dough into various lengths and then some were cut into stars and filled with ruby colored jam or vanilla pudding. Customers were coming and going. Some had hurried looks on their faces, but most were taking their time, catching up on the local news or weather. It really amazed us that such a small town had so much activity bustling around a bakery, of all things!

This probably comes as no surprise to any German readers, as I came to realize that most villages and towns have bakeries. In our fast-paced world of strip malls and convenience food marts, the baker has been replaced by commercially prepared quick frozen, chemical laden donuts, pies, cookies and breads. The county I live in has a population of over 60,000 and we have no bakeries that bake healthy and hearty whole grain breads.

One of my favorite brotchens was the roggenbrot or rye brotchen. These were made into little squares and looked very dense and tan colored. The taste was slightly sweeter than most of the breads I had tasted and biscuit like in texture. It was wunderbar (wonderful)! Most of the rye bread that we get here in the U. S. is white bread with caramel coloring added and if you are lucky a little rye flour!

In only a few bakeries did I notice sandwich type breads that were baked in loaf pans. Most of the breads of Europe are baked free form, thus allowing the bread to stay fresher longer while promoting a thick and chewy crust.

Our friends wanted to know what baked goods were popular in America. We told them that cookies, lots of cookies in all shapes, colors, sizes and flavors—especially chocolate chip, peanut butter and oatmeal raisin—were available in almost any American bakery. We did not see any cookies in the bakeries except for fat, frosted bagel-without-the-hole type things that didn't even look like cookies. I was told that these were "American" cookies. I don't think so!

We also told them that muffins were very popular in all sorts of flavors—blueberry, raspberry and banana being some of our favorites. Our friends were not familiar with muffins but we managed to find some in a quaint little bakery in Munster. These muffins had an American flag stuck in the top of the crust for the Fourth of July and were made with fresh red currants. I made these when I got back home to Indiana and they were a hit with my children and very pretty as well.

We also told them that bagels, (or, for lack of a better definition, chewy boiled and baked brotchens with a hole in the center) were quite popular in many bakeries here and although my German friends have never tasted a bagel before (and probably never care to after that definition) I told them that they were not alone as I also know an American that never has either!

The thick and hearty muesli that we were served at the Cafe Journal in Heidelberg was very satisfying and fresh tasting; the combination of flaked rye, oats and chopped raisins and sunflower seeds and other grains kept us satisfied right up until lunchtime. The only drawback to me was having it served with warm milk!

This young German baker carries on his father's trade.

Jim and I have come to learn a new appreciation for such a simple meal: cheese and bread. Of course, this isn't any cheese (like Velveeta) or any bread (like Wonder) but some very thinly sliced emmantaler, gouda, or the very popular and slightly woodsy smelling brie, along with some hearty whole grain breads. It makes for a very satisfying meal.

We have this quite often at home now and sometimes add fresh fruit and muffins. It's surprisingly quick if all of the cheese and meat are pre-sliced the night before. You don't need much. Just a slice of emmantaler, and a thin slice of salami or Black Forest ham or the meat of your choice and a little mustard and some strong black coffee and you are on your way to enjoying a deliciously simple European breakfast. Good quality soft brie cheese is wonderful alone on bread or spread with jam on top.

And of course I wouldn't do this article justice without mentioning the wonderful smooth and chocolatey nutella! Spread generously on bread or tucked inside a warm crepe, this hazelnut flavored chocolate spread is simply sublime. If only they would team it up with peanut butter… what a marriage that would be!

Here is a recipe I came up with that is reminiscent of the hearty farm breads and brotchen of Germany. This bread keeps very well, four to five days, without much crumbling.

Hearty farm bread with mixed grains and seeds (Bauerbrot)

5 pounds hard red wheat flour
5 cups rye flour
1 cup toasted sunflower seeds
1 cup toasted pumpkin seeds

In bowl of electric mixer with dough hook attachment, or large bowl if kneading by hand, place:

6 cups hot water (135°F to 140°F if using SAF yeast or 115°F if using regular yeast)

2/3 cup raw honey
1/4 cup lecithin granules or oil

In order given add:
3 cups red wheat flour
3 cups rye flour
1-1/2 cups flax meal (may grind this in a coffee mill or blender)
1/3 cup whole flax seed
3 tablespoons SAF yeast or 5 packages of regular yeast*
3 tablespoons dough enhancer or 1 crushed vitamin C tablet (optional: this helps to make a higher rising and lighter dough)**
2 tablespoons sea salt

Slightly mix the above and let it sit until double in size (approximately 20-30 minutes) then add enough of the remaining flour to make a smooth and elastic dough by kneading 15-20 minutes by hand or 8-10 minutes in the mixer. After the dough is properly kneaded, it should stretch easily and show little "windows" or thinner parts of the dough that you can see through. This is the gluten or "glue" that holds the bread together. If your bread just pulls apart then it is either under-kneaded or over-kneaded. However, it is very hard to over-knead bread dough by hand.

Let the dough rise until double (30-60 minutes) and then punch it down. This step is not necessary when using the electric kneader unless you like a real tender bread; however, I prefer to punch this particular recipe down.

Preheat your oven to 375°F and place a baking stone inside. This produces a crispier crust. A greased or floured cookie sheet will do, but don't preheat it: just let your dough rise directly on it.

After the dough has doubled in size, punch it down and shape it into round mounds or individual little brotchen or rolls. Roll the tops in the remaining 2 cups of rye flour and slightly press down into the roasted sunflower and pumpkin seeds. Slash the tops with a sharp knife and place on a well floured wooden pizza paddle or kitchen counter and cover with a light tea towel. Let rise until double in size (15-45 minutes) and gently transfer to preheated baking stone that has been generously dusted with flour.

For rolls (brotchen), just shape dough into golf ball sized balls and place on greased cookie sheets or flour-dusted pizza paddle or counter.

For a crispier crust, throw a cup of cold water in the oven and quickly but gently close the oven door. Bake for 20-30 minutes. (Rolls take less time, approximately 18-20 minutes, depending on the size.) Be sure to throw a cup of cold water into the oven every 5-10 minutes or until bread is well browned and hollow sounding when tapped. Cool on wire rack and enjoy!

This bread freezes well. I use extra-heavy-duty freezer bags (or you may double bag). To reheat, just wrap frozen or thawed bread in foil or parchment paper and place in a preheated 350°F oven for 20-25 minutes for frozen or 10 minutes for thawed. You will have a surprisingly fresh and crispy loaf of bread to serve!

Pretzels (brezeln) abound everywhere in Germany and make a wonderful midmorning or afternoon snack. Although this next recipe is not exactly like the large and chewy pretzels found in many German bakeries, it can hold its own due to the wonderful flavor imparted from using whole wheat flour and by brushing melted butter on top. These are a favorite at our house and I don't know if they freeze well, as they have never been around long enough for us to find out!

Buttery soft pretzels (Brezeln)
6 cups fresh milled Prairie Gold hard whole wheat flour***
1 teaspoon salt
2 teaspoons dough enhancer (option)
2 tablespoons honey
1-1/2 tablespoons SAF yeast
2 tablespoons powdered milk
2 cups hot water 135°-140° F

In bowl place water, honey, and 3 cups of the flour. Add yeast, salt and dough enhancer on top and mix. Add enough remaining flour until dough starts to clean sides of the bowl. Knead for 8-10 minutes in the mixer or 15-20 minutes by hand. Cover dough and let rest for 30 minutes.

Divide into 16 pieces, shape and dip into the pretzel wash and place on greased parchment lined cookie sheets. Sprinkle with coarse salt (lightly, a little bit goes a long way!).

Cover and let rise until double and bake at 500°F for about 10 minutes. Do not overbake. This is the secret!

Place on wire racks to cool and brush with plenty of melted butter. These are good sprinkled with cinnamon sugar over the melted butter. Omit coarse salt if you plan to do cinnamon pretzels. These keep about two days. Serve with plenty of sweet mustard.

Pretzel wash
1 cup warm water
1/4 cup baking soda
Mix thoroughly in shallow bowl.

Notes:
*SAF yeast is a professional bakers' yeast and is now available to the general baking public in some specialty or grocery stores in 1 pound packages. It does not need to be proofed. It has more live cells than regular yeast, therefore you use about 1/3 less. I use 2-3 tablespoons for 10 pounds of bread dough. If you use 2 tablespoons it will take longer for the bread to rise but I feel what you lose in time you gain in flavor so if you are not in a hurry then opt for the longer rise: the flavor is worth it!

SAF yeast must not be added directly to the water or it will die. Be sure to place it on top of the flour when adding it.

If using regular yeast, be sure that your water is between 110°F - 115°F. Add the yeast directly to the water and about 1 teaspoon of honey or sugar and let it sit or proof for about 15 minutes. The mixture should be bubbly. If it is not, throw it out and buy some new yeast.

**Dough enhancer is a natural dough conditioner consisting of whey powder, vitamin C and tofu powder. It helps to lighten up the loaf and ensures a higher rising. It also helps to extend the shelf life of

Buns and animal breads can be found in many different shapes.

the bread if it is around long enough to last! This is an optional ingredient. A crushed vitamin C tablet produces similar results although will not help to preserve the loaf.

***Prairie Gold flour is a high gluten hard Spring wheat grown in the mountains and valleys of Montana. It is ideal for baking bread.

If you don't have access to high gluten hard whole wheat flour, then mix your whole wheat with half white flour or add 1/4 - 1/3 cup vital gluten to lighten up the loaf. It is always better to use a high gluten flour for bread baking as the gluten acts as glue to hold the bread together. It stretches like bubble gum and forms little bubbles when carbon dioxide gas is released inside the bread from the yeast interacting with the proteins in the wheat.

If you use a nonglutenous flour such as barley, rye, corn, rice or millet, then no matter how much yeast you use, you will not get a bread that rises unless you add gluten or wheat flour. Gluten may be purchased at health food stores or food co-ops.

If you have trouble getting your bread to rise, it could be your flour or grain. There are over 30,000 different varieties of wheat but there are two categories that are worth knowing about: hard and soft. Hard is the high-gluten wheat used for baking with yeast. Soft pastry wheat is best suited for non-yeasted baked goods such as muffins, pancakes, cookies etc. If you are used to eating whole wheat baked goods then you may find that you prefer to use a hard wheat in all of your baked goods, as we do. But pastry wheat may not be used to bake bread, as it will turn out real heavy and crumbly due to the lack of gluten.

For more information on baking with whole grains contact Denise Fidler, The Country Baker, at 8751N 850E, Syracuse IN 46567. Phone: 574-834-2134, Web: www.countrybaker.com; or e-mail: country baker@countrybaker.com

This bread is easy, fast, versatile and delicious

Teresa Turner
Texas

I make this bread on a regular basis and not only is it good—it is simple and very versatile. You can give bread a different taste for each meal just by adding a few additional ingredients.

I sometimes roll out the dough and sprinkle with cinnamon and sugar, then roll it up and proceed to make a very easy cinnamon bread. Or after removing from the oven, I brush with melted butter (oil works) and sprinkle with various herbs (basil, sage, garlic, caraway or oregano are good ones to try.) I make an Italian seasoning blend with herbs from the herb garden and this mixture is sprinkled on top to make a mild flavored Italian bread to go with spaghetti, etc. My husband's favorite way is brushed with butter then lightly sprinkled with sugar.

Since it is a "three cup of flour" recipe, it is best to use a standard loaf pan (8-1/2 x 4-1/2 inches) to produce a high-domed loaf. I also have used my stainless steel mixing bowls (7 inches in diameter) to bake round loaves. I can start this two hours before meal time and serve it warm from the oven. Everyone loves it.

Quick Rise Gratification Bread
1 cup whole wheat flour
2 cups white flour
1/4 teaspoon salt
1-1/4 cups water (warm—110°-120°F)
2-1/4 teaspoons yeast (calls for Rapid Rise, but I've used all kinds)
1 tablespoon brown sugar (honey works well also)

Mix the flours and salt together in a large bowl. In a separate bowl (I use a 2-cup measuring cup) put 1-1/4 cups of warm water, sprinkle yeast over water and add brown sugar. Then stir until all is dissolved. Pour the liquid into the flour mixture and stir until dough starts pulling away from the sides of the bowl.

With floured hands knead dough (right in the bowl) for five minutes. Cover with a damp towel and let rise in warm spot for 45 minutes or until doubled in size.

Punch the dough down and turn onto a floured surface and knead 10-12 times. Then shape into loaf and place in a greased loaf pan and let rise again for 35-40 minutes.

Use a sharp knife to gently make three slits diagonally to allow steam to escape. Bake in a 400° oven for 35 minutes or until crust is golden. Remove onto wire rack, brush with oil or melted butter and let cool.

At my house it is usually half gone by the time it cools. My husband and son love it hot from the oven. Leftover slices make excellent toast.

Country kitchen:

Here's a tasty, healthful, inexpensive snack

Becky Tahara
Nebraska

A while back, a mother wrote in requesting snack foods. But, due to a recent move from the sunny island of Guam, I haven't had much time to dabble with a response. It's a little late, but nevertheless, here's my idea for a very inexpensive and healthy snack that tastes pretty darned good. I pack it in my husband's lunch every day and it seems to be the one thing he always eats but never tires of.

Black Bean Dip

2 cups cooked drained black beans
1 teaspoon ground toasted cumin seeds
1/2 teaspoon coriander
1 clove garlic
2/3 cup chopped fresh parsley (or cilantro)
1 teaspoon olive oil
1/2 lemon or lime
Something hot—jalapeno, serano chilies, Thai peppers, whatever. I like to use the dried pacific peppers that we grew when we lived on Guam.
1/3 cup chopped toasted walnuts (optional)
2 tablespoons minced Spanish olive (optional)

Puree the ingredients together in a blender or food processor. My cookbook says you can mash the beans by hand but I haven't tried that. I'm sure it would turn out chunkier that way, and maybe some people would prefer that.

Once this is made, we use it as a dip with the following recipe for an Armenian flat bread. It is sort of a replacement for tortilla chips. It very easy to make and is also a great source of fiber.

Lavash Crisp Bread

2 cups bread or all-purpose flour
2 cups whole wheat flour
1 pkg. dry yeast (this is more for flavoring and texture than for rising)
1 tablespoon salt
1-1/2 cups hot water
1/2 cup milk
1/4 cup toasted sesame seeds and/or poppy seeds

In a mixing bowl place 1 cup each of the 2 flours and add the yeast and salt. Stir well to blend. Pour in the hot water and beat with a wooden spoon to thoroughly mix for 3 minutes. Add the remaining cup whole wheat flour and stir vigorously to blend. Add the remaining white flour, 1/4 cup at a time. Don't overload the dough with flour. It should be soft and elastic but not sticky.

Knead dough and let rise until doubled in size. Punch down dough and let rise for another 30 minutes.

Prepare a lightly floured work area. Divide the dough into 12 balls. Roll out each ball until it is very thin but still fits on half of a cookie sheet. Place two crisps per baking sheet. Brush with milk and sprinkle with sesame seeds.

While the first batch is in the oven, roll out the second batch, and so on. Bake at 400°F for 10 minutes or until light brown. Be careful that you don't overcook, there seems to be a fine line between raw and very brown.

Put the baked lavash on racks to cool. Store those not eaten immediately in a dry place. Stored in a sealed carton or bag, the pieces of cracker-like bread will keep indefinitely.

This cheesy soup is fun to make

Kathy Fite
Ohio

Cheesy Homestead Soup

1/2 cup butter or margarine
1 cup flour
3 cups milk
2 pints home-canned chicken broth
1 teaspoonWorcestershire sauce
2-3/4 cups cheddar cheese, grated
2 pints frozen or canned corn

Melt margarine in large sauce pan over low heat. Add flour and stir until it's mixed well. Turn burner up to medium high and add milk, stirring constantly until mixture comes to a boil. Keep stirring and let it boil for just a minute or so to let it thicken. Then turn heat down to low and add Worcestershire, broth, cheese and the corn last.

This soup is very tasty and filling and also fun to make. After I made it a few times I quit measuring out each ingredient and just started dumping whatever felt right. You can substitute another vegetable for the corn or add more than one vegetable. Brown rice is good to add if you want to stretch it a little further.

"It's a hoof trimmer. Made it myself."

Order zucchini seeds now (and file these recipes!)

Late last summer you probably swore you'd never plant another zucchini. But by now, the memories of bushels of squash you couldn't even give away are starting to fade, and you find yourself drawn, even if reluctantly, to the zucchini descriptions in the seed catalogs. After all, it doesn't make any sense to not plant something just because it grows too well!

Go ahead, order those seeds. Just be sure to file these recipes where you'll be able to find them next summer.

KIMBERLY THIMMING
WISCONSIN

I have spent quite a few years growing quite a few varieties of zucchini. My favorites are Sunburst (also called Butter Scallop) and Black Beauty.

Some people say they can't sell or even give away their extra zucchini. Here's an idea that worked well for me. Make copies of a few recipes and set them out next to your basket of zucchini or include it with each bag you give away. You might be surprised to find return customers.

My best idea is to use them small, substituting them for cucumbers in dill pickles recipes. Use your same dill recipe—delicious! And, you use up a lot of them.

I have 29 zucchini recipes, but these are my favorites:

Chocolate Zucchini Cake

1/2 cup butter or margarine
1/2 cup corn oil
1-3/4 cups sugar
2-1/2 cups flour
1/4 cup cocoa
1 teaspoon baking soda
2 eggs
1 teaspoon vanilla
1/2 cup sour milk (add 1 tablespoon vinegar to 1/2 cup milk)
1/2 teaspoon salt
1/2 teaspoon cinnamon
1/2 teaspoon ginger
2 cups grated zucchini (I leave the peel on but remove the seeds from the large ones)
1/4 cup chopped walnuts (if desired)
1/4 cup chocolate chips

Cream oil, butter and sugar, add eggs, vanilla and milk. Add dry ingredients. Stir in zucchini. Nuts and chocolate chips can be mixed in or sprinkled on top. Bake at 325° for 45 minutes.

Zucchini Patties

2-1/2 cups grated zucchini
2 tablespoons onion, chopped
1/4 cup grated parmesan cheese
1/4 cup flour or instant mashed potato flakes
1 egg
2 tablespoons mayonnaise
Salt, pepper, oregano and parsley

Mix together, form patties and fry until brown on both sides. I enlarge this recipe for my family by grating potatoes with this. Or, peel the zucchini and use some potatoes with it, and you might be able to fool the "non-veggie" eaters in your family.

Zucchini Casserole I

6 cups diced zucchini
1/2 cup onion, chopped
1 pound ground beef
1/2 pound cheese of your choice
1 can cream of mushroom or celery soup
Topping of buttered crumbs or French fried onion rings optional

Parboil zucchini until almost tender. Brown ground beef with onion. Layer meat, zucchini and cheese into casserole dish. Top with soup and crumbs. Bake at 350° for 45 minutes.

Zucchini Casserole II

2-3 zucchini, sliced and sautéed in butter until tender
3 medium carrots, shredded
1 onion, chopped
1 can cream of chicken soup
1 cup sour cream
2 cups seasoned croutons

Mix vegetables with soup and sour cream. Put half of croutons on bottom of 9 x 13 pan. Pour vegetable mixture over. Top with rest of croutons. Bake 350° for 25 minutes.

Mock Apple Cake

4 cups flour
2 cups sugar
1/2 teaspoon salt
1-1/2 cups margarine
1 teaspoon cinnamon

Mix until crumbly. Measure out and reserve 1/2 cup for filling. Press half of remaining crumb mixture into a jelly roll pan pushing up the sides. Bake at 375° for 10 minutes.

Filling:
8 cups zucchini, peeled and thinly sliced
2/3 cup lemon juice
1 cup sugar
1 teaspoon cinnamon
1/2 teaspoon nutmeg

Place in pot and simmer, covered, about 20 minutes. Add the 1/2 cup reserved crumbs. Stir well and cool.

Put cooled filling onto prepared crust. Top with remaining crumb mixture. Bake at 375° for 30-35 minutes.

"Tastes like apple" zucchini pie

MRS. CATHY HARRELL
TEXAS

2 or 3 medium zucchini (6 cups)
2 cups water
2 tablespoons fresh lemon juice
1/8 teaspoon salt or to taste
1-3/4 cups sugar
2 teaspoons ground cinnamon
1/4 teaspoon allspice
1/4 teaspoon ground nutmeg
2 teaspoons cream of tartar
2 tablespoons all-purpose flour
2 tablespoons cornstarch
1/4 cup chilled butter, cut into small pieces
1 unbaked 9-inch pie shell
1 unbaked 9-inch top crust

Preheat oven to 400°F. Peel zucchini and cut in half lengthwise. Cut each half in half lengthwise again, then remove the seeds and cut crosswise into slices about 1/4 inch thick. Cut enough zucchini to total 6 cups sliced.

In medium saucepan bring the water to a boil over high heat. Add the zucchini, reduce the heat to medium-high, and cook until tender but still crisp (about 3-4 minutes). Drain in a colander.

In a medium bowl toss together the drained zucchini, lemon juice and salt. Set aside.

In a small bowl combine the sugar, cinnamon, allspice, nutmeg, cream of tartar, flour and cornstarch and mix well. Add to the zucchini and mix well. The mixture will be rather runny and loose.

Spoon the mixture into the unbaked pie shell and dot with half the butter pieces. Add the top crust, pinch together the edges to seal and dot the crust with the remaining butter pieces. Bake 40 to 45 minutes or until golden brown. *–from Dori Sanders'* Country Cooking Cookbook

They'll love the name of this cookie

Mildred Stout
Missouri

Bacon Grease Molasses Cookies

1-1/2 cups bacon grease
2 cups white sugar
2 eggs
4 tablespoons sorghum molasses–not blackstrap
4 cups flour
2 teaspoons baking soda
2 teaspoons ginger
2 teaspoons cinnamon
1 teaspoon ground cloves
1/2 teaspoon salt

Mix together and form into small balls. Place on cookie sheet. Mash with glass bottom that is dipped in sugar. Bake at 350°F for 10-12 minutes.

A few variations on lemon cheese

Chris Gallo
Texas

A few variations on Marcy Wilson-Coles "lemon cheese" in issue 81/4:77, also in the book *Your Goats... A Kid's Guide to Raising and Showing* by Gail Damerow (Gardenway Publishing) page 112.

First, I should tell you we don't use fresh milk. We use the one gallon glass jars to keep milk extra cold in the fridge. When the milk level gets below the spigot (mostly cream) we dump it in a 5-quart plastic bucket that we keep, covered, in the freezer, until it's full. Then we thaw out the milk, sometimes in the fridge, sometimes on the counter, just until we can get it into a cooking pot.

We follow the recipe–well, pretty much. Heat the milk between 165° and 200°F.

If you don't have lemons, the concentrate works fine. Add a little at a time, until you get the consistency you want. We use about one cup concentrate to one gallon of whole, raw goat milk.

If you don't have or like lemon, or lemon concentrate, apple cider vinegar works nicely too. Use the same quantity as concentrate. Vinegar will give you a little different texture and flavor, but not much different.

I let the curd set in the whey 15 to 60 minutes. The whey pours off more easily if you can give it a longer setting time.

If you don't have real cheese cloth (or an old ham bag) you can use a laundered nylon stocking, runners and all. Strain the curds and whey in the stocking (we retain the whey for the chickens) then hang for an hour or so. It doesn't hurt to leave it for 3-4 hours, although the longer you drain it the drier the curds will be.

Turn the stocking inside-out to release the curds, crumble the chunk of curd with your fingers and add salt (again we use about 1 teaspoon pickling salt per pound of cheese) and spice if you'd like. Mrs. Dash's Herb and Garlic or Extra Spicy are nice blends to try, if you don't grow your own (1 teaspoon is great plenty).

Or you can halve the salt and add crushed fruit and sweetener for a nice summer treat on crackers or unleavened bread. Last week we tried this with 1/3 pound curd, 5 large crushed strawberries and 1/2 cup sugar.

If you'd prefer a slicing cheese, drain the curds from the whey, no longer than two hours, crumble, add salt (herbs optional) pack back into the stocking and press, increasing pressure every hour until you don't see whey come out when you add more pressure.

We started pressing cheese with two pieces of countertop covered boards and bricks for weight. As you can imagine, these were some odd-looking cheese wheels. I finally popped for a real cheese press from Caprine Supply (PO Box Y, Desoto, KS 66018) last year. It sure is a lot easier to sleep when you're not listening for the crashing sound of bricks. And if I'm not too heavy handed with the crank on top the cheese actually looks wheel-shaped.

"I told her it was a mild case of indigestion, but she insisted on a second opinion."

What everyone should know about *Camellia sinensis*

Debi Blazei
Wisconsin

Next to water, tea is the most widely consumed drink in the world. On any given day about half the population is drinking it. Nowadays tea sipping cannot only delight the senses, but it just might be good for your health as well. New research shows that regular consumption of tea has been linked to lower risk of both heart disease and cancer. You can drink it hot or iced and with sugar or lemon. It's flexible enough to suit every taste, plus it's cheap and easy to make.

When we talk about tea, we mean one of three kinds: green, oolong or black. All three come from the leaves of one plant—the tea bush *Camellia sinensis.* All three teas boast rich amounts of naturally occurring compounds called flavonoids. Scientists believe it may be these compounds that could account for the lower risk of cancer and heart disease among tea drinkers.

Tea is made by harvesting and drying the leaves of the tea bush. Depending on how quickly you dry the leaves after picking them, you end up with green, oolong or black tea. Green tea is not heated, but steamed, rolled and crushed. The leaves are steamed and packaged immediately after being harvested. Black tea comes from leaves that are air-dried and crushed to release their juices. The juices and leaves are then oxidized (allowed to react with oxygen). Firing stops the oxidation and seals in the delicious flavor. Oolong tea falls between green and black, being only partially oxidized.

Don't waste time worrying over which tea varieties might have the greatest health benefits. The tea that's best is the tea that you drink. So find a flavor that suits you. Whether you enjoy it first thing in the morning, at the end of your exercise routine or before going to bed, tea-time may soon come to mean anytime.

How to read a tea box label? If it's tea you want, read a list of ingredients and make sure you see the words "tea," "black tea" or *Camellia sinensis.* There should be no mention of herb or herbal on the box. Herbal teas come from leaves, flowers, roots, bark, seeds or stems of herb or spice plants. Common herbal ingredients include fruit pieces or flavorings, spices, mint leaves, rose hips, hibiscus flowers, carob, ginseng—but no tea.

Yogurt making is a simple process

Mackie Allgood
Texas

Why should making yogurt be so difficult? Desert nomads for centuries managed with fewer conveniences than most of us. It is an easy method of preserving milk where refrigeration is limited.

The science is simple: grow "good" bacteria in fresh milk before the "bad" bacteria get a chance while making the environment wrong for others to grow. Yogurt making bacteria, lactobacilli, grow at 105° to 112°F. Their preferred food is milk. They multiply rapidly in milk while producing acid that slows down even its own growth.

1. Use freshly scalded containers and whisk. Milk from a healthy goat or cow has only the bacteria you introduce.

2. Strain fresh (new) milk into a clean container.

3. Mix in 1/4-1/2 cup active yogurt.

4. Keep it in a warm place (105°-112°F) for about 5 hours. I use an insulated box heated with a 15 watt bulb.

5. Set some aside as starter for the next batch.

Powdered milk can be mixed in warm water and substituted. Follow instructions above from step 3.

The lactobacillus that makes buttermilk grows at a different temperature: 70°-75°F. Use fresh buttermilk starter and proceed the same except for temperatures and time—overnight. *(Mackie Allgood is a retired bacteriologist.-Ed.)*

Can this homemade tomato soup

Teresa Turner
Texas

I canned about 10 dozen quarts of tomatoes this year, everything from spaghetti sauce to hot sauce and so on. (We love grilled cheese and tomato soup for a winter lunch.) I found this recipe in *Tastes From The Country* cookbook.

Easy tomato soup—to can
1/2 bushel tomatoes
2 bunches celery
6 onions
4 bell peppers
1 cup flour
1 cup butter
1/2 cup salt
1-1/2 cup sugar

Wash vegetables carefully. Place in large soup pot and cook until soft. Force through small hole colander or use food processor. (I use a Victorio Strainer and it works great.) Return to pot. Make a paste of flour, butter, salt and sugar. Add to puree and boil for 20 minutes, stirring constantly.

Fill hot, sterilized jars leaving one-half inch head space. Seal. Process in boiling water bath for 15 minutes. Yields 10 pints.

Stalking the wild acorn

There are many good reasons to learn about foraging "wild" foods. It is, of course, a survival skill, and a part of simple living and living with nature. But foraging also preserves old and now largely neglected knowledge. Here's a good example.

MARIE BURKE
CALIFORNIA

There are about 50 species of oak trees. We have several of them in California: black, live and blue oak, to name a few. But the most important to the Indians was the white oak. They used the bark for medicinals and the acorns for medicinals and food.

The Wintu Indians are just one tribe that has a ceremonial dance and gathering during the time acorns become abundant. The "grandfather trees," usually the oldest and largest, were honored and belonged to a family group, being passed down from one generation to the next according to tradition.

Acorns are still gathered by the women and dried in two-foot round, shallow, loosely woven baskets. Only the largest, with no blemishes, are picked off the ground and either dried to be stored and used later or ground for mush or flour.

The acorn's meat is bitter because it contains tannic acid. This must be leached from the nuts before they can be used. This can be done several ways. The easiest for my purpose is to soak the chopped or ground nut meats in water in a sieve until they taste sweet. Usually this takes about 24 hours of setting in clean water, soaking, rinsing and letting them set again, repeating the process. Then I dry the meats on a screen or spread them on a cookie sheet and roast them 7 minutes at 275°F for nutty flavor. I

like the roasted taste this gives, but it makes the nut meats harder to grind for flour.

I use the acorn flour in any simple bread recipe. You can add regular flour half-and-half for raising.

The Indians added red clay to the flour before baking on a bed of hot rocks covered with leaves above and below, overnight. They also mixed the dough with water cooked to make a soup. The ground meal was "put-by" and left to mold on top. The mold was then scraped off and used like penicillin.

The humble acorn we city folk used to rake off our lawns as a nuisance is gathered widely on our place today. The Wintu have gatherers who choose the largest nuts for the elders as "gifts" and for feeding the infirm among them by making a strengthening mush to nurse them back to health.

Oak acorns contain calcium, magnesium, phosphorus, potassium, sulfur, fat, protein and carbohydrates. This I learned first hand from my Cherokee neighbor who bought the acreage across the way. He has been instrumental in opening our eyes to how well the Indians here survived with the salmon, nuts, bulbs, plants, herbs and roots. All it takes is hard work and know-how.

One way to shell green acorns; cut around the circumference and peel off halves. But any way is okay. The tannin dries your hands.

So gather a few! They add up fast. One plastic shopping bag full will make about 3-1/2 cups of flour. You can also grind them medium-fine and use like walnuts in cookies, on top of crumb cakes or sprinkled on ice cream.

We didn't start out to be homesteaders (big mistake!). We thought we needed the conveniences, but we are learning more and more to live with less and less. Keeping it simple really gives you time to enjoy this wonderful world we were given to take care of.

Recommended reading: Earth Medicine Earth Food *by Michael Weiner. "The classic guide to the herbal remedies and wild plants of the North American Indians."*

Bacon "jerky" is lower in fat

Strips of bacon can be cooked like jerky to remove much of the fat.

Cut bacon strips in half. Pull out and set oven racks at highest and lowest positions. Put a fat catching container on the bottom rack. Hang the bacon with toothpicks from the top rack over the catching container. Push in both racks and set oven at 200ºF. Leave the door slightly ajar. Check periodically until cooked as desired.

Several pounds can be cooked in a short period of time.

To preserve cooked strips, separate them into meal servings and freeze them in quart zip-lock-type bags. To serve, simply heat.

This pre-cooked bacon is great for camping trips. *– Ken Scharabok*

Favorite winter homestead meals

BOBBIE SPRAGUE
TENNESSEE

We have two meals for those days when the temperature outside is the same as inside your freezer. The first is my Pantry Soup. The more you put in, the better, even if you add store-bought canned vegetables to what you put up yourself. Measurements are not something I use, so I'll just list the ingredients. Add as much or as little as you want.

All you do is put everything in the pot and cook it all day.

Pantry Soup

Chicken stock and meat (turkey works too)
Small potatoes, quartered
Green beans
Lima beans
Corn
Tomatoes, diced
Green peppers, chopped
Onions, chopped
Celery, chopped
Mushrooms, chopped
Small amount vinegar (to taste)
Garlic
Salt
Pepper
Any other seasonings to taste

A form of Brunswick stew

When a storm is forecast I get out my big pot and fill it and put it on the back of the stove (or on the kerosene heater) so we can eat anytime. Since I do not measure, the cook is in control of the taste.

Ground beef or venison
Cubed pork
Cut-up chicken
Onions, chopped

Brown all above ingredients in light oil. Add:

Peppers, chopped
Mushrooms, sliced
Lima beans
Corn
Stewed tomatoes
Small potatoes, quartered
Barbecue sauce (homemade is best) or salsa will work
Seasonings to taste

The more you experiment, the better.

JANE KEON
MICHIGAN

I usually start this on weekend winter mornings when I know we'll be working outside all day. The promising smells help keep us warm, even if our toes are icy cold in our boots.

Pork Hocks

3-6 pounds smoked pork hocks (depending on how much meat you want)
1 quart water
2 teaspoons salt
Black pepper
1 quart sauerkraut
2 large onions, chopped
6 or more potatoes, chunked

Simmer the hocks in water with salt and pepper until the meat falls off the bones. Separate the meat and dig out the marrow and put in the pot with the sauerkraut, onions and potatoes. Simmer until supper time. Excellent heated up with more potatoes added for the next day.

This is not your crunchy vegetable Chinese restaurant dish, but a hearty stew with plenty of red meat.

Chop Suey

2 tablespoons cooking fat
1 pound pork, cut up
1 pound beef, cut up
6 stalks celery
5 onions
6 ounces soy sauce
3 cups bean sprouts
2 cups mushrooms
1 quartwater
1/4 cup molasses
Black pepper
No salt

If using canned mushrooms and sprouts, drain them. Brown the cut-up meat in the fat. Add onions and celery. Add remaining ingredients and simmer all afternoon. Serve over rice with chow mein noodles on top.

CINDERELLA FAY
MINNESOTA

Chicken or Rabbit & Dumplings

2 chickens or rabbits
3 quarts water

Simmer in a big kettle until tender. The time will vary depending on how old the animal is when you butcher it. I normally do this a day ahead and store in the refrigerator overnight. If you don't have a refrigerator—any cold spot will do, but don't let it freeze! At my house, on cold winter nights anything that is not in the refrigerator freezes!

Carrots
Onions
Peas
Potatoes
Garlic
Celery seed
Bay leaf
Salt & pepper
Corn starch
Cream (or milk, water)
Chicken bouillon

These are the vegetables and spices I usually use, but they are all optional as you can omit or substitute any depending on what you have on hand.

Take the meat off the bones and set aside. Remove most of the fat that has hardened on top of the broth. Simmer broth, vegetables and spices for about 10 minutes. Thicken slightly with cornstarch mixed with cream. Not too thick because the dumplings will soak up a lot of liquid.

Dumplings

3 cups flour
6 teaspoons baking powder
1-1/2 teaspoons salt
3 tablespoons shortening
Milk

Sift together dry ingredients. Cut in shortening. Add enough milk to make a thick drop batter.

Add the meat to broth and return to a boil. Spoon dumpling batter on top of bubbling stew. Cover and let simmer for 12 minutes—don't peek! After 12 minutes remove from heat and serve.

Guaranteed to warm and fill 8-10 hungry souls and burn their lips and tongues too if they're not careful.

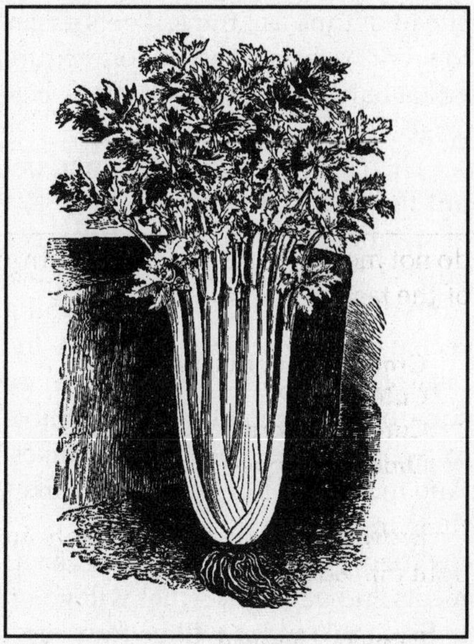

BARBARA FISCHER
MISSOURI

Here are a couple of casserole recipes that we like in the winter. Both are very flexible as to amounts of ingredients.

Casserole I

Brown 1-2 pounds of ground beef with some onion. Add drained green beans, one can or pint per pound of meat. Add one can tomato soup per pound of meat. Pour into a greased casserole dish, cover with mashed potatoes and grated cheese. Bake in medium oven until hot and bubbly.

Casserole II

Brown 1-2 pounds ground beef with onion. Add corn—canned or frozen (drained) to suit taste of your family. Add ketchup or barbecue sauce to suit taste. Pour into greased casserole dish, cover with mashed potatoes and grated cheese and bake in medium oven until hot and cheese is melted.

These are both good with coleslaw and cornbread. I usually make one of these when I have leftover mashed potatoes.

CYNDY AHO
MINNESOTA

Thanks for the harvest-time recipes in Vol. 81 No. 5. As the cook of the family, I'm always looking for something different to fix whether it's to can or cook. I have always enjoyed canning and freezing since I was a young girl. I'm looking forward to reading about what other cooks are making from their winter larders.

Here is a daily menu of some of our family favorites:

For breakfast, plain yogurt with homemade jam stirred in, with or without granola. Canned grape juice. Homemade oatmeal bread, toasted, with butter and jam. And with plenty of fresh skimmed milk, as are all of our meals.

Blue-barb Preserves

(I got this recipe from COUNTRYSIDE in a "Menu of the Month" back in the '80s.)

3 cups rhubarb, finely chopped, simmer until tender
3 cups blueberries, crushed, add to rhubarb and stir in
7 cups sugar

Bring to a rolling boil over high heat, boil 1 minute, stirring constantly. Remove from heat and stir in one 6-ounce bottle of Certo. Stir and skim after 5 minutes. Ladle into hot jars. Process as directed for jams. Makes 7-8 cups.

Apricot Syrup

(Yes, good on pancakes and waffles and French toast, but we like it stirred into our yogurt too.)

5 cups ground apricots
1 cup water
3 tablespoons Sure-Jell
1/4 cup lemon juice
1/2 teaspoon butter
4 cups sugar

Combine all but the sugar in large pan and bring to a rolling boil. Add 4 cups sugar all at one time. Bring to a boil, stirring constantly and boil 1 minute. Ladle into hot jars and process. Makes about 4 pints.

To top off a noon meal of homemade vegetable soup using beef bones from the freezer and vegetables that I've canned, we might have:

Sourdough Applesauce Cake

This is from Carla Emery's book. I revised it to fit my family. I use home canned applesauce.

Mix together 1 cup starter, 1 cup applesauce, 1-1/2 cups flour and 1/4 cup milk. In another bowl, cream 1/4 cup butter with 1/2 cup white sugar and 1/2 cup brown sugar. Add 1 beaten egg, 1/2 teaspoon cinnamon, 1/4 teaspoon nutmeg, 2 teaspoons soda and a pinch of salt. Add the starter/applesauce mixture. Fold in 1/2 cup dates, raisins or nuts or a combo of each. Pour into a greased 8 x 12 pan. Bake at 325 degrees for about an hour.

Oatmeal Bread

Combine 4 cups each oatmeal and boiling water. Add 1/4 cup butter, 1/2 cup dark brown sugar and 4 teaspoons salt. Stir until butter and sugar melt.

Dissolve 1 package yeast in 1-1/2 cups warm water and stir into oatmeal mixture. Gradually add 3-1/2 to 4 cups flour to make a soft dough. Add more flour as needed. Knead and let rise, punch down and shape into 3 loaves. Place in large greased loaf pans. Let rise again and bake at 375 degrees 35-40 minutes.

For our supper I like to make pizza, as it can be made ahead of time, or if I'm running late, I can make it quickly. Here is my crust recipe.

Pizza Crust

Combine 3/4 cup very warm water with 1/2 teaspoon sugar, 1/2 package yeast and 2 teaspoons oil. Let sit until yeast dissolves. In another bowl mix 1 cup wheat flour, 1 cup white flour and 1/2 teaspoon salt. Add yeast mixture and stir well. Let dough rest at least 10 minutes. I like to make my dough at least an hour ahead of time as I think it gets easier to work with and has a good texture when baked. I think the taste is better too.

Then I grease a 9 x 13 pan and pat out the dough in it. Then add pizza or spaghetti sauce to taste. My sauces are Ball canning mixes with tomatoes from our garden. (I haven't found a recipe for either sauce that I like the taste of, and I would have to purchase some of the vegetables and the spices to put in so I use the canning mixes. And most important, my family likes them too.)

Then I can get creative as far as meats and vegetables that will go on it. Since this pizza will be four servings, each family member can have what they like on their quarter. Top with cheese. Bake at 350 degrees for 15 minutes or if you are pressed for time at 400 for 10 minutes or until cheese starts browning.

With our pizza we will have quick coleslaw.

Quick Coleslaw

Chop up about 1/2 cabbage. Dress it with mayonnaise and yogurt. Also get out the bread and butter pickles and use some of that juice for flavoring. It has that vinegar, sugar and onion-pepper to give an extra zip to your slaw. You can also chop up some of those pickles with the cabbage. If so, you probably won't need the juice.

We don't need dessert, but if someone drops in it would be nice to have something to serve them. So I'll bring up some peaches and bake peach crisp.

Peach Crisp

Grease 9 x 13 pan. Put in 2 quarts drained sliced peaches, 1/2 cup reserved peach juice and a few drops almond extract.

Topping

Combine 1-1/3 cups brown sugar, 1 cup flour, 1 cup oatmeal, 1/2 teaspoon nutmeg, 4 tablespoons butter. Mix until crumbly and press over peaches. Bake at 350° 45-50 minutes. Serve with fresh cream or ice cream.

VICTORIA BROWN
CALIFORNIA

Goulash

Fry some hamburger. Add canned tomatoes, any type of vegetables, rice, chopped potatoes, onions, garlic, some water and your favorite spices. Cook until rice and potatoes are done. Thicken with cornstarch and enjoy. This is a basic recipe. You can add anything your family likes.

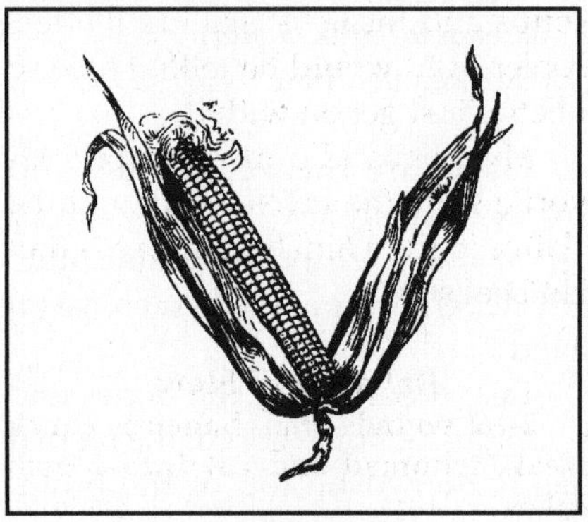

DONNA MCCRITE
OREGON

One of our favorite meals is one we call Irish pizza. It can be adjusted to fit any size family and to suit any taste.

Irish Pizza

Peel and shred 3-4 medium potatoes. Heat a large skillet and put in 2-3 tablespoons of butter or oil. Spread shredded potatoes evenly over the bottom, then top with your toppings. Our favorites are ham or smoked sausage, cooked green beans, corn, chopped tomatoes, onions, or whatever else you have on hand.

Beat 3-4 eggs along with about 1 teaspoon of salt and 1/4 teaspoon of pepper, then pour over your "pizza." The eggs help to hold it together. This is then topped with shredded cheese of your choice. We prefer colby or cheddar.

Then just put on the lid and let it cook until brown on bottom and potatoes are soft—approximately 25-30 minutes.

TERESA TURNER
TEXAS

It is a very hot and humid day (97°F) here in east Texas (August 19th) and I am digging out my family's favorite winter recipes. I wish I could say thinking about these cold weather soups and meals is making me feel cooler but I would be telling a lie so I better just get on with it.

My husband's number one favorite stew (he loves it although he claims it gives him heartburn) is Italian beef stew.

Italian Beef Stew

2-1/2 pounds lean, boneless chuck steak, trimmed and cut into 1 inch cubes
1/2 cup flour
Vegetable oil
3 medium onions, chopped
3 large carrots, scraped and cut into 2 inch pieces
3 medium potatoes, peeled and cubed
1-1/2 cups water
2 stalks celery
1 pint whole kernel corn, drained
1 quart whole tomatoes, undrained
1 clove garlic
1-1/2 teaspoons salt
1 teaspoon pepper
1/4 teaspoon oregano
1 teaspoon Italian seasoning

Dredge meat with flour and brown in small amount of vegetable oil in an 8 quart Dutch oven. Add remaining ingredients. Cover and simmer 2-1/2 hours or until vegetables are tender. Serves eight. This goes great with homemade bread.

Another favorite around here is chicken fried steak & gravy.

Chicken Fried Steak & Gravy

Tenderized round steak
Salt & pepper
All purpose flour
Baking powder (add a little to flour to make it fluffy)
Melted shortening (use melted instead of oil—it makes a better gravy)

Rinse steak with water; sprinkle with salt and pepper. Let stand a few minutes to bring out the juice. Dredge both sides with flour. Cook in hot melted shortening over medium-high heat until brown. Turn and brown on other side. Drain. Don't cook it very long—the meat is usually done by the time both sides are browned. The quicker the meat cooks the juicier it stays (in this case.)

Gravy:

Put 2-3 tablespoons of drippings in skillet and all the crumbs. Stir in a heaping tablespoon of flour. Stir well to moisten. Cook a few minutes to brown the flour. Add 2 cups milk, stirring constantly until thick as desired.

Serve this with mashed potatoes, green bean casserole or corn and homemade biscuits.

The following recipe does not include anything from the garden; however, I do use fresh goat milk and fresh eggs for this great pancake recipe.

Sweet Milk Pancakes or griddle cakes

1-1/2 cups sifted flour (can use white, wheat or half-and-half)

2 teaspoons baking powder
1/2 teaspoon salt
1 cup milk
1 egg
2 teaspoons melted butter

Sift dry ingredients into bowl. Add thoroughly beaten egg. Then add milk and melted butter and mix well with large spoon. For a thinner batter add more milk. Bake on a hot griddle (large cast iron skillet works), slightly greased. Drop the batter by spoonfuls onto the hot griddle and when bubbles appear turn and cook the other side. Serve hot with butter and maple syrup (or honey). You can also sprinkle confectioner's sugar and squeeze lemon juice onto them.

For sour milk pancakes use same recipe but add 1/2 teaspoon baking soda. If you don't have sour milk on hand, add one tablespoon vinegar to one cup milk.

We are off the grid and interested in a greenhouse. I would love to hear from someone who heats a greenhouse with something other than electric (wood, propane, etc.) Also, I have been enjoying the letters from the families who are homeschooling. Each issue is filled with informative, useful, encouraging information and I look forward to each one.

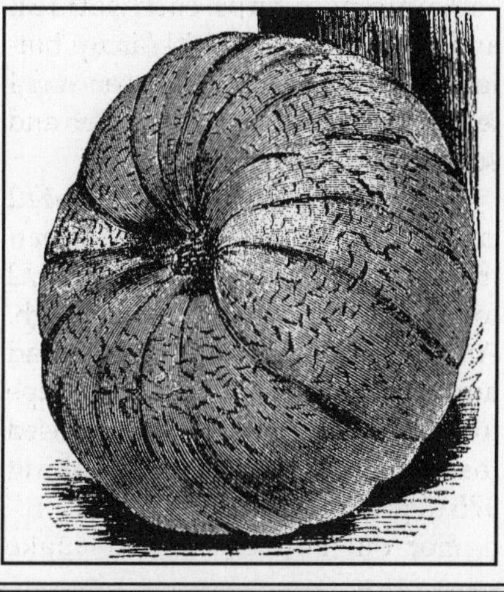

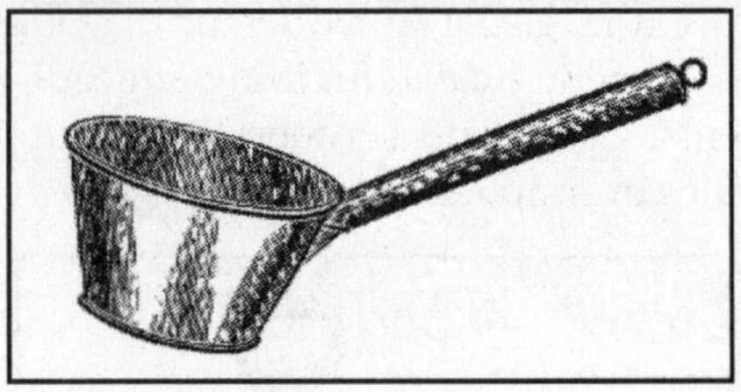

Gail Grundl
Wisconsin

I made up this recipe for spaghetti sauce. We like it so much I don't use store-bought anymore. It's very quick and easy.

Spaghetti Sauce

Brown 2 pounds ground beef or ground venison. Add 1 quart of stewed tomatoes, 1-1/2 teaspoons each basil, oregano, Italian seasoning and 1 clove crushed garlic. Simmer 30 minutes to 1 hour. Add salt and pepper to your taste. It will be thick and not runny.

Jan Hoadley
California

It seems funny to be answering a cold weather question while currently in an area that doesn't get cold...but having grown up in the Midwest and living briefly in Montana and Colorado I think I remember well enough! A few good cold weather ideas to warm up those cold days:

Brown some cubed meat — beef, lamb, venison are all good. Put in a crockpot . Add cubed potatoes, bits of carrots, onions or whatever vegetables you have available. Cover with water and set to cook on "slow" (or put on top of the woodstove for the day, covered). Come evening you'll have a tender, easy, "no effort" dinner.

Or brown ground meat; add diced onion, cubed potatoes and water to cover; season; and cook over medium heat until potatoes are soft. Uncover, if desired stir in a little flour for "gravy". Top with cheese if desired.

Combine tomato soup with water. Add Italian seasonings. If desired add browned ground meat, pepperoni or other meat. Serve with croutons or crackers and top with cheese.

The *best* meat loaf

This dish has gotten rave reviews from American and Australian visitors who swear I've spent all day in the kitchen, even though the Australian friends saw me make it in about 10 minutes!

Combine 1/2 pound beef with 1/4 pound lamb or venison and 1/4 pound sausage (turkey or pork works well). Mix this well. Add diced onions, a little seasoning, oatmeal or crackers (until it's almost "dry") and then add half a can of sloppy joe sauce (homemade or store bought). Set the other half-can aside. When meat mixture is thoroughly mixed, press into loaf pan. Cook at 350°F. for about 40 minutes, then pour the other 1/2 can of sauce over the top and cook for about 15 minutes more. You may top with cheese if desired or serve as is with potato, corn and/or bread.

Wash, peel and cube potatoes. Boil until done. While they're cooking prepare a white sauce (most cookbooks have a recipe using milk, butter, flour). When potatoes are done, drain and stir in white sauce to coat. Top with bacon bits, cheese or as desired.

Baked pheasant & rice

2 pheasants, cut into serving pieces
1-1/2 ounce envelope dehydrated onion soup mix
14 ounce fresh mushrooms
3/4 cups long grain rice, uncooked
3/4 cup milk
1 10-ounce can condensed cream of mushroom soup

Blend mushroom soup and milk; combine with rice, mushrooms and juice and onion soup mix. Arrange pheasant on top. Brush with melted butter, sprinkle with paprika and bake uncovered in preheated oven at 325 F. for 1-1/2 hours. (This can also be used for guineas or chickens if you don't have pheasants or don't hunt.)

Dutch Oven Duck

2-3 pounds duck, cut into small pieces and browned in skillet. Remove and place in Dutch oven or baking dish. To the drippings in skillet add 1 cup diced onion, 1 cup diced celery, 2 tablespoons grated orange rind, 1/2 cup maple syrup, 1-1/2 cups sauterne wine. Mix well, pour over duck and bake at 300° approximately two hours or until tender. Serve with rice.

Irish Goose

Clean and dry an 8-pound goose. Rub inside and out with salt and pepper mixed at the ratio of 1 teaspoon salt to 1/4 teaspoon pepper.

Boil 10 medium potatoes, diced; reserve water for basting. Put 1 tablespoon fat in skillet and partially cook 1 cup chopped onions and 1/2 cup celery but don't brown.

Combine potatoes, onions and celery with: 1/4 teaspoon pepper, 1/2 pound ground salt pork, 1 teaspoon poultry seasoning, 4 slices of bread (crumbled), 2 eggs (beaten) and 1 teaspoon salt. Stuff goose and roast in a moderate oven 3-4 hours basting occasionally with potato water.

Creamed Venison Over Biscuits

(This could also be used with lean beef or lamb)

1 pound ground venison and 1 small onion, chopped. Sauté in 1 tablespoon oil in skillet until brown. Drain off excess oil. Add 3 tablespoons all purpose flour, 2 beef bouillon cubes and 1 teaspoon Worcestershire sauce and simmer for 20 minutes. Serve over biscuits (or toast).

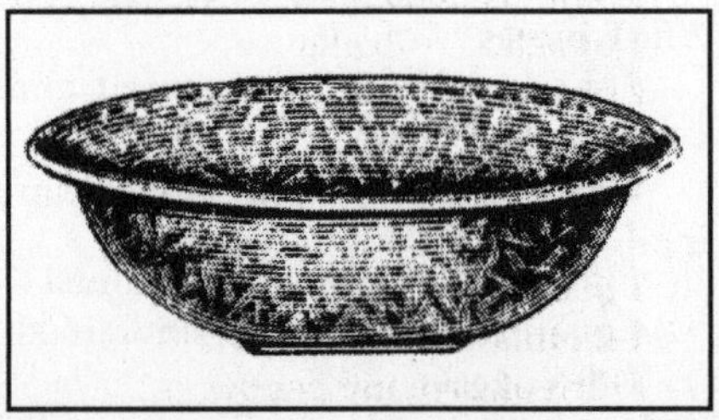

CONNIE B. SNYDER
FLORIDA

Here are two of our favorite winter soups.

Portuguese Chicken

1 chicken, cut up
7 potatoes, diced
1 teaspoon cinnamon
1 onion, chopped
3 ribs of celery, chopped
Salt and pepper to taste

Cover chicken with water and cook until tender. You can take the chicken off the bone, or leave the pieces whole. Add the rest of the ingredients and cook until potatoes are tender.

Potato Soup

8 potatoes
1 onion, chopped
1 clove garlic, chopped
4 or 5 slices of bacon, cut up
A handful of mushrooms, sliced

Put everything in a pot, cover with water. Add salt and pepper to taste. Cook until potatoes are tender.

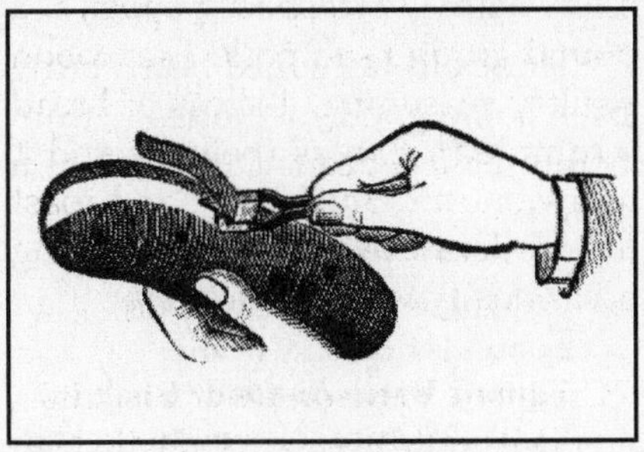

CHRISTINA VAN NORMAN
MARYLAND

This is by far my very favorite wintertime meal. It is best eaten with some hot, fresh bread.

Potato Leek Soup

3 pounds potatoes
1 bunch leeks
2 cups corn
4-5 stalks celery
1 teaspoon Old Bay seasoning (heaping)
1 quart milk
1-2 pints sour cream
Pinch of cayenne pepper

Peel, boil, and cut potatoes into cubes. Wash and slice leeks thinly, then sauté in butter until softened. Be sure not to brown them. Cut up the celery into small pieces. Add the Old Bay and cayenne pepper. Sauté until soft. Put everything together and let simmer at a low heat uncovered. Don't boil, as you don't want the milk to curdle. Keep stirring. Let sit for 30-40 minutes so that flavors blend. Add salt to taste and enjoy.

DONNA WEITLISBACH
INDIANA

Venison Stew

2 pounds ground venison
1 pound ground sausage
2 cups lima beans
2 cups corn
1 envelope sloppy joe mix
1 quart tomato juice
1/3 bottle hickory smoked flavor Worcestershire sauce
Salt & pepper to taste

Fry meat until done. Cook vegetables (if frozen) or use canned. Combine all ingredients and heat through.

Venison-Veggie Skillet

1 pound ground venison
1 cup onion, chopped
3/4 cup green peppers, chopped
1 clove garlic, minced
1-1/2 teaspoons salt
1/4 teaspoon pepper
1 teaspoon chili powder
5 cups zucchini, sliced
2 large tomatoes, peeled & chopped
1-1/2 cups corn
2 tablespoons pimentos, chopped
1/4 cup parsley, chopped

Sauté venison, onion, green pepper and garlic in skillet until well browned. Add remaining ingredients. Cover and simmer 10-15 minutes or until tender.

CONNIE DUBOIS
TEXAS

Russian Stew

1 pound beef or pork cut into bite size pieces or even hamburger
1 large onion, diced
2 stalks celery, diced
salt
pepper shakins*
1 bay leaf
1 quart canned tomatoes
1/2 cup elbow macaroni
2 large potatoes, diced—no need to peel

Brown meat in small amount of oil, add onion and celery. Brown lightly and add enough water to just cover the meat. Season to taste with salt, pepper shakins, bay leaf. Add tomatoes. Simmer until meat is tender. Add 1/2 cup of elbow macaroni and 2 large potatoes which are diced into bite size pieces. Simmer until potatoes and pasta are tender. If you need to thin add some water while cooking. This recipe is for two people; adjust amounts for a larger family. Great to cook on a wood stove.

*Note: pepper shakins are my own blend of sweet bell peppers and hot peppers which have been dried and put through a blender, then packed into recycled spice containers. A great way to use an excess of peppers from your harvest. Each batch has a different heat factor so use carefully in soup, stews, eggs, baked potatoes—anything your little heart desires.

Country kitchen:

More winter favorites... that are good anytime!

DEBRA REYBERN
TEXAS

During the cold days of winter (we will have about 10 of them here in south Texas) we enjoy lots of stews, soups and casseroles. One that has become a year-around favorite of our family is noodle, egg and onion. It is great in both summer and winter. We have shared it with several families with rave reviews. Some serve it as a side dish while we eat it as the main dish. We usually do not serve anything else with it, but it goes well with any fresh vegetable.

We call it noodle, egg and onion for short, although it also has fresh tomatoes. With fresh picked tomatoes, onions and farm fresh eggs all you need to have on hand is macaroni to make a wonderful and nutritious dish. When my husband first made this dish years ago, he explained that it was something he picked up during his many years in Germany. I thought I would pass, but I took a bite just to say I tried it. Now it appears on our menu regularly. We have been known to have it twice a week when the tomatoes are at their peak.

Noodle, Egg and Onion

2 large, fresh tomatoes, diced very small
1 small onion, diced very small
1/4 teaspoon salt (optional)
1/2 teaspoon pepper
1/4 to 1/3 cup canola or olive oil (olive oil tends to be a bit strong unless you are used to its taste)
Flavored herb vinegar to taste, about 1 tablespoon. We use balsamic or tarragon vinegar.

Combine the above ingredients in a bowl and let sit at room temperature while preparing the remaining ingredients. You want the mixture to be a bit soupy and slightly tart. For the very best flavor, make a couple of hours ahead of time and allow the onions and tomatoes to marinate in the oil and vinegar.

Boil and drain 2 cups elbow macaroni.

Scramble 1 farm fresh egg per person in a bowl. (Egg substitutes like Egg Beaters or Second Nature also work well if you choose.)

In a large skillet melt 1 tablespoon of butter. A cooking spray will also work. Add cooked macaroni and stir to coat in the butter. Add the scrambled eggs. Stir the macaroni and eggs until the eggs have fully cooked like scrambled eggs. Be careful not to burn the macaroni or eggs. Put into serving bowl.

Spoon the macaroni and egg mixture onto the plate. Then spoon generously the onion and tomato mixture on top.

Dig in, it is delicious.

Keep leftovers in separate bowls for reheating the macaroni and egg.

MAGGIE OAKLEY
ARIZONA

If you're concerned about the mystery-meat in bologna try this.

Cold cuts?? Lunch meat??

2 pounds hamburger
1/2 teaspoon ground pepper
1 teaspoon garlic powder
1/2 teaspoon (or more) mustard seed
1/2 teaspoon seasoned salt
3 tablespoons Morton Tender Quick
1/2 teaspoon liquid smoke
1 tablespoon red pepper flakes

Mix everything together with your hands until thoroughly blended. Shape into two equal-sized rolls. Seal as airtight and watertight as possible in foil. Refrigerate for 24 hours.

Leave in foil and put in a large kettle of boiling water. Boil for one hour. Remove from water and let cool until you can handle it. Remove from foil and rewrap in plastic and return to refrigerator.

You may add minced garlic for some added zip.

These old-fashioned beans bring back some good memories... from before baked beans came out of a can.

Molasses Baked Beans

2 pounds dry navy beans
5 quarts water, divided in halves
1 can (28 ounces) tomatoes, undrained and cut up
1-1/2 cups ketchup
1 cup butter, melted
2 large onions, quartered
1/2 cup packed brown sugar
1/2 cup molasses
1 tablespoon salt
1 tablespoon liquid smoke or BBQ sauce

Place beans and 2-1/2 quarts water in a 6-quart Dutch oven; bring to a boil for 2 minutes. Remove from heat and soak for one hour. Drain and rinse beans, return to pan with remaining water. Bring to a boil. Reduce heat; cover and simmer for one hour or until beans are tender.

Drain, reserving cooking liquid. Return beans to pan; add remaining ingredients and mix well. Cover and bake at 350°F for 2 to 2-1/2 hours or until beans reach desired consistency, stirring occasionally. Add some of the reserved cooking liquid if too thick.

This is super tasty and the slow roasting time really warms up the house.

Spicy pot roast

1-1/3 cups chicken broth
1/4 cup soy sauce
2 tablespoons molasses
2 tablespoons corn syrup
2 tablespoons sugar
2 teaspoons chili paste or hot sauce
1 teaspoon five-spice powder
1 bottom round roast (2 pounds)
1-1/2 pounds carrots cut into 2" chunks
1 pound parsnips or turnips cut into 2" chunks
1 pound onions, quartered
2 large potatoes cut into 2" chunks
1 tablespoon dry sherry

Heat oven to 325°F. Combine broth, soy sauce, molasses, corn syrup, sugar, chili paste or hot sauce and five-spice powder in large Dutch oven. Add beef, spooning mixture over top of roast. Cover and roast one hour and forty-five minutes.

Add carrots, parsnips, onions and potatoes. Cover and roast 45-60 minutes more until beef and veggies are tender. Remove veggies with a slotted spoon; spoon onto serving plates. Slice beef thin; arrange on plates.

Stir sherry into sauce and spoon some sauce over beef and veggies. I thicken the sauce a bit with corn starch. You may serve over rice or noodles.

Another good-tasting house warmer.

No Peek Chicken and Rice

1 cup rice
2 cups boiling water
1 can cream of mushroom soup
1 can cream of celery or cream of chicken soup
1 cup chopped celery
1 cup chopped onion
1 chicken, cut up
pepper
paprika
1 package dry Lipton onion soup

Mix rice, water, soups, celery and onion in a 9 x 13 pan. Lay chicken pieces on top. Sprinkle with pepper, paprika, and dry soup. Cover with foil and bake 2-1/2 hours at 350°F.

To make your own onion soup mix:

4 teaspoons beef bouillon
8 teaspoons dry minced onion
1 teaspoon onion powder
1/4 teaspoon seasoned salt

Here's a good one pot dish for a busy day.

Pork Chops Creole

4-6 rib or loin pork chops about 1/2" thick
1 cup diced celery
1 medium onion, chopped
2 teaspoons chili powder
1 can (1 pound) red kidney beans
1 can (12-16 ounce) whole kernel corn
1 cup uncooked rice
1 can condensed tomato soup
1 soup can of water
1-1/2 teaspoons salt
1 teaspoon oregano
1/4 teaspoon pepper
1/2 cup whole black olives

Brown pork chops in a large Dutch oven; remove and set aside. Saute´ celery and onion until softened in the same pan; stir in chili powder and cook one minute. Stir in kidney beans and liquid, corn and liquid, rice, tomato soup, water, salt, oregano and pepper; mix well. Heat to boiling. Arrange chops on top and cover with lid or foil. Bake at 350° one hour or until meat is tender. Garnish with black olives.

MARY & GEORGE TILLEY
WISCONSIN

Tomato Juice with Garlic and Dill

To can:
8 quarts ripe tomatoes, cut up
1 bunch fresh dill weed
1/3 cup sugar (optional)
5 large cloves fresh garlic, slivered
1 teaspoon dill seed

Equipment needed: Two 8 quart stainless steel saucepans; small stainless steel skillet; large boiling water 12 new flat canning lids. canner; jar lifter; wooden spoon; ladle; canning funnel; Foley mill or Squeezo strainer or sieve; 11 pint and 1 half-pint canning jars with screw bands;

Directions: Wash tomatoes, core and discard any doubtful parts. Cut into eighths. Boil along with dill weed until tomatoes are soft, stirring often, about one-half hour. Run through Foley mill, Squeezo strainer or sieve to remove skins, seeds and dill weed. Reheat juice and boil gently for about another half hour.

Meanwhile, wash and sterilize jars. Boil flat lids in skillet with a little vinegar added to the water. Keep lids in hot water until ready to use.

Just before canning, add slivered garlic and dill seed to the boiling juice. By adding it this late in the process, you won't overcook the garlic. If your tomatoes are end-of-season tart, add a little sugar to taste. Salt is unnecessary. Boil the mixture for 5 more minutes, then maintain a low boil while you fill each sterilized jar, wipe its rim and seal with a new lid (from the skillet with hot water.) Put on screw bands fingertip tight—do not overtighten. Process sealed jars in a boiling hot water bath for 20 minutes. Remove jars and place on towels on counter to cool.

Yields 9 to 11 pints. Each pint makes two nice glassfuls, just about right for two people on a cold winter morning. Savor those bits of garlic.

MARY GIBSON
MONTANA

Vinegar Candy

2 tablespoons butter
2 cups sugar
1/2 cup vinegar

Melt butter, add sugar and vinegar, stir and boil to hard crack stage. Pour into buttered pan. When cool enough to pick up, pull it into strands as you would taffy. Cut bite-size pieces and put on buttered plate to cool further. The candy should be translucent and have no vinegar taste.

Country kitchen:

Stashing the basics: Avoid a trip to town

DEBI BLAZEI
WISCONSIN

What are some of the basic generic items to keep on hand? We all have those favorite food or snack items we keep stashed away, but what about the basics to see you through until the next trip to the grocery store? I think we all have flour, sugar, salt and those type of items on hand, but what about spices?

I have a large family and we live in the country, so extra trips into town are not a good option for us. With about 15 years of cooking experience, I have compiled a list of basic spices to keep on hand. I always try to plan my meals for a few days in advance, but usually I decide in the morning what to have for supper. By always having the same basic spices in my pantry, I know I can prepare any of our favorite and quick meals.

I always have soup bases and gravy mixes on hand. Leftover meat can be cut up and served with gravy over mashed potatoes or rice in a pinch. If I get up in the morning and it's cold or rainy, I can make a quick pot of soup with whatever vegetables or meat I have, by using one of my soup bases.

I always have some chamomile tea bags in case someone is having trouble sleeping or has a stomach ache. A box of crackers can always be found toward the back: you never know when the flu will strike one of my kids.

I keep minced garlic, chopped onions, green and red peppers, all dehydrated, to add to soups, stews or casseroles. Chili powder and seasoning salt can be added to any hamburger dish or casserole to perk it up. Ground cinnamon, cloves and nutmeg are three good items to have. You can always find a cookie recipe that uses those ingredients.

Parsley and cilantro are a necessity for my pantry. I use these a lot. In addition to the great taste they add to foods, you can't beat the color. Even fried potatoes or scrambled eggs look like a gourmet meal.

Vegetable Soup

GRACE CARTER
CALIFORNIA

Large pot—I use one bigger than the one that comes with sets of pots and pans, probably 6-8 quarts

1 quart stewed tomatoes, or 1 can plus a can of tomato sauce, if you want reddish soup

1 or 2 chopped onions

1/3 of a bunch of celery, chopped—just slice the old ends off a whole bunch and start slicing the entire bunch at once—much faster

3 or 4 large carrots, sliced as thick as you like

1 or 2 chopped, peeled turnips, if you like

Chopped garlic, if you like

1 tablespoon dried basil

Handful of dried or fresh parsley, chopped

1 teaspoon dried marjoram or oregano

1/2 teaspoon dried thyme, if you like

1 can or frozen package string beans

1 can or frozen package of corn or hominy or use both

Black or red pepper to taste, crushed or ground

Chopped greens—spinach, 1 package frozen chopped or beet greens or 1/2 to 1 head iceberg lettuce chopped. Chopped cabbage or Brussels sprouts work fine too.

1-2 cups white, pink, red or pinto beans or small limas. These can be cooked or raw. If raw (dry) be sure to stay with small types.

Starches—(these add body, thickening and flavor, but can be left out):

1/2 cup barley
1/2 cup bulgar wheat
1/2 cup rice, white or brown
1/2 cup wheat berries
1/4 cup corn meal or masa harina

Use singly in amounts given, or in combinations totaling no more than 3/4 cup, or you will end up with a very thick mixture like a casserole or Mexican sopa seca (dry soup). That's fine too, if you like. Using any of the starches will also make leftover soup that is thicker than the first.

Any other vegetable laying around that needs to be used up, such as cucumber peeled, seeded and chopped, or a zucchini sliced or what-have-you.

Enough water to look like soup—remembering that any dry ingredient is going to take up water. Just use somewhat more than looks right. You can add more as it cooks.

Bring to a boil, reduce to a simmer and cook covered 2-3 hours or more. I like longer and slower to develop the flavors, but if that's not convenient, just turn off after the time and let cool down with the lid on and reheat to boiling to serve. A crock pot works but is too small and the flavor is never as good for some reason.

If you didn't use much starch in the soup, or none, you can make dumplings on the soup. This makes you look like you really know what you're doing and is easy. If there's a lot of starch and the soup is thick, skip it—the 20 minute simmer with no stirring can burn a thick soup to the bottom of the pan.

Anyhow, the dumplings:

1 cup flour
1/3 cup dry milk powder
1 teaspoon or more baking powder

Stir together with enough water to make a dough-like biscuit dough—but sticky. Drop by tablespoons onto slow boiling soup, put lid on and cook for 20 minutes without lifting the lid. These are so good, and no fat.

If you don't want red soup, just leave out tomatoes and use soy sauce, Kitchen Bouquet or soup base mixture with plenty of herbs.

Basically, you are cleaning out the refrigerator into the soup pot. The only vegetables that don't go well in this, or not in any amount, would be beets, sauerkraut, cauliflower or broccoli, and you can get away with a little bit of them.

Singing Cake

JACQUE SCHWENKE
OKLAHOMA

3 eggs, separated
1 cup butter
2 cups brown sugar
2 squares bitter chocolate, melted
1 cup raisins
2 teaspoons cinnamon
1 teaspoon cloves
4 cups sifted cake flour
1 cup strawberry jam
1 cup chopped nuts
2 teaspoons baking powder mixed into 1 cup buttermilk.

Beat the egg whites until stiff, set aside. Cream the butter and sugar. Add egg yolks and stir. Add melted chocolate and stir. Add raisins. Add cinnamon, cloves, and flour, stir. Stir in nuts and jam. Now add the baking powder to the buttermilk and quickly stir into the cake mixture. Fold in the stiffly beaten egg whites.

Quickly pour into greased and floured angel food cake pan. Bake at 350°F until cake stops singing, about 45 minutes.

Make sure you time this so your guests are present during the baking. Once the cake is baked, the effect is over.

(Note: This is the corrected version from 84/6:29. The original recipe was not printed correctly.)

Zucchini Jam

LINDA YOUNGREN
MAINE

This recipe makes great jam, without much work.

6 cups peeled, grated zucchini
6 cups sugar
2 tablespoons lemon juice
Fruit—fresh, frozen or canned—1-2 cups (drained)
6 ounces Jello

Add a dab of water to zucchini. Bring to a boil and cook 6 minutes.

Add sugar and lemon juice and cook 6 more minutes.

Add fruit and Jello. Cook 6 more minutes.

Turn into sterilized jars and seal.

I have tried (Jello flavor/fruit) strawberry banana/rhubarb; berry/blueberry; raspberry/mixed berries; orange/pineapple; and strawberry/rhubarb.

Connie's Wild Plum Jelly

CONNIE J. REA
FLORIDA

Use approximately 5 pounds of wild plums or enough to fill a medium roast pan or Dutch oven 3/4 full. Do not remove stones.

Add water to cover and bring to a boil. Reduce heat and simmer until plums are soft. Remove from heat and mash into a pulp, skin and all. Drain through a sieve with small holes, or cheesecloth if you prefer. Let drain for an hour or longer.

You will need 5 cups of juice. If you do not get 5 cups, add water to make 5 cups. Sometimes I get more than 5 cups. I then measure and add water to make two batches or save the extra until I cook more plums.

You will then proceed by the directions on the pectin package of your choice, Sure Jell, Ball's etc.

Place in hot, clean jars. Seal, then turn upside down for 15 minutes or so. This makes 10 to 11 half pint jars.

Paw Paw Pie

1 cup sugar
1/2 teaspoon salt
1 cup milk
1-1/2 cups cut up paw paws, peeled & seeded
1 egg

Place all ingredients into pan and stir together. Cook over medium heat until thickened. Pour into unbaked pie shell and bake until the crust is done. Top with whipped cream if desired.

Strawberry Rhubarb Jelly

This is from a great new book, *The Big Book of Preserving the Harvest,* by Carol W. Costenbader ($18.95, available from the Countryside Bookstore).

1-1/2 pounds red rhubarb stalks, washed and cut into 1-inch pieces
1-1/2 quarts strawberries, washed, hulled and crushed
6 cups sugar
6 ounces liquid fruit pectin

Puree rhubarb by pulverizing in a blender or food processor.

Prepare your jelly bag by pouring boiling water through it. Squeeze out excess moisture. Line bag with a double layer of cheesecloth. Place both fruits in bag, let drain, and squeeze gently to remove excess juice.

Measure 3-1/2 cups strained juice in a 3-quart saucepan. Add sugar, mix thoroughly, and boil to dissolve sugar. Remove from heat and stir in pectin.

Return to heat and bring to a full boil. Boil exactly one minute. Remove from heat and skim off any foam with a metal spoon.

Ladle into sterile 1/2 pint jars, leaving 1/4 inch headspace. Seal and process 5 minutes in a boiling water-bath canner.

Yield: 7-1/2 pints.

Yogurt Cream Cheese

Make yogurt following your favorite recipe. Then, instead of refrigerating it, pour it into a collander lined with three layers of cheesecloth. Let it drip for a minute, then lift the four corners of the cheesecloth and tie them together. Hang the bag and let it drip for 6-8 hours. Store in refrigerator.

Using the humble soybean

Grown on big commercial farms for animal feed and industrial purposes, this little bean also deserves a place on the homestead

The humble little soybean, one of the most nutritious, most versatile vegetables in the world, is one of the least known food crops in this country. For families and groups who want to grow their own, it is probably the single most valuable vegetable crop possible in a homestead plan.

Most of the soybean crop grown in this country is used for oil for industry and for animal feed, but the oriental peoples have practically lived off this vegetable for centuries. Rice supplies most of their carbohydrates, but the soybean supplies them with most of their oils, fats, and proteins. "The yield of protein from soybean, weight for weight, is approximately twice that of meat; four times that of eggs, wheat, and other cereals; five to six times that of bread; twice that of lima and navy beans, walnuts, filberts, and most other nuts; and12 times that of milk." [(1)] Considering that the actual yield of soybeans per acre (approximately 25 Bu) compared to the acreage needed to raise beef, the difference in protein yield is fantastic. And just as important, the kind of protein available in soybeans closely matches the human diet requirements.

Soybeans are used for food in a great variety of ways. They can be cooked and eaten the way we eat navy beans, sprouted for green vegetables, made into soy sauce, fermented, brewed, cultured, ground into grits, or milled into flour.

This article is about flour. Soy flour can be used in bread, cookies, gravies, and sauces. It can be mixed with water and sugar to make a very nutritious soy milk. The milk can be curdled into soy cheese, or Tofu. Tofu can be flavored and seasoned, steamed, fried or broiled for an endless number of dishes.

Soy flour comes in three varieties: defatted, refatted and full fat flour. Defatted flour has had its natural oils removed during processing. If some of this oil is returned to restore nutritional value, it is called refatted flour. Flour made from the whole bean is called full fat flour. These flours are available commercially in health food stores at ridiculous prices. But you can make the most nutritious of these, the full fat flour, in your own kitchen.

The Agricultural Research Service, USDA, at Peoria, Ill., has developed a simple process for making full fat flour for village technologies.[(2)] It can easily be adapted to homestead scale production. The process is outlined below:

1. **Soaking**
2. **Immersion cooking**
3. **Air drying**
4. **Cracking**
5. **Winnowing**
6. **Milling**

The equipment you will need is: a large canning kettle; cloth bags; cloth, paper or flat metal trays; a food grinder; an electric fan; and a flour mill.

Fill the cloth bags 1/2 to 1/3 full of cleaned raw beans and place in the kettle with clean water at 75 degrees or less. Preferably start soaking in the early morning to allow plenty of sunlight hours for drying. For a better flavor to the flour, add one part baking soda to 100 parts water to the kettle. After 4-6 hours, remove the bean bag and briefly drain.

Place the bags in boiling water for ten minutes. At higher altitudes, 15 min. is required. The cooking does not destroy the protein, but makes the beans safe to eat.

After cooling, spread the beans out on the cloth, paper, or metal trays. Quick drying is important to prevent the beans from spoiling. Insure good air circulation and expose the beans to as much sunlight as possible. Protect the drying beans from dust, dirt, rain, and dew. If they are still not dry in 30 to 36 hours, finish drying in a low oven. A light toasting of the bean will greatly reduce the beany flavor, so you may want to roast the beans in an oven to finish drying anyway. Be careful not to over roast them, as they will burn rather easily. To test the beans for proper drying, place a few on a hard, flat surface and strike sharply with a mallet or flat stone. They should break apart easily with the hull separating cleanly from the meat of the bean.

The dried beans are then cracked in a food grinder set for coarse grind. This breaks up the beans for milling and loosens the hulls for easy separation in the next step.

The hulls are removed by winnowing. This can be simply done by slowly pouring the cracked beans into a paper tray in front of a fan. Several passes may be needed to remove all of the hulls.

The bean meat is then milled into flour with a hand mill or a small electric flour mill. Four pounds of raw beans will make a little over three pounds of flour.

Store the flour in clean airtight containers, away from moisture, rodents and insects. Be sure to thoroughly clean all of your equipment to prevent spoiling the next batch.

Full fat flour can be used in many ways to fortify your diet with high quality protein. This flour contains 41-42% protein. To get the most use out of this flour, I suggest that you get the two cookbooks listed in the references. [3],[4] To give you a start and an idea of what you can do, here are just a few recipes and ideas.

Soy flour cannot be used alone for breads, as it doesn't have the gluten necessary for proper baking. But it can be used to extend and fortify other flours. Soy flour is also sensitive to heat, so when baking, start with a moderate oven and increase the temperature as you become more familiar with its character.

Soy Biscuits

1-1/2 cups wheat flour
1/4 cup soy flour
2 teaspoons baking powder
3/4 teaspoon salt
1/4 cup cooking fat
1 cup less 2 teaspoons water

Sift together the flours, baking powder, and salt. Cut fat into mixture with a fork. Stir in water. Drop by spoonsful on greased baking sheet and bake in moderate oven till golden brown.

Soy Corn Bread

1 cup cornmeal
3/4 cup wheat flour
3/4 cup soy flour
1/4 cup sugar
5 teaspoons baking powder
3/4 teaspoon salt
2 tablespoons melted fat or oil
1 egg, beaten
1-1/2 cups water

Combine all ingredients in a bowl and stir. Pour into a greased baking pan and bake in a moderate oven 30 min. or till golden brown.

Yeast Soy Bread

2 cups soy milk, scalded (see below)
3 tablespoons oil
1/2 cup honey or brown sugar
1-1/2 teaspoons salt
1 cake yeast in 1/2 cup warm water
5-1/4 cups wheat flour
1-3/4 cups soy flour

Add oil, sugar, and salt to milk. Cool. Add yeast, water and mix well. Mix in flour until a medium stiff dough. Knead and let rise. Knead again and form into loaves. When loaves have doubled in size, bake in moderate oven till golden brown.

Soy milk is a nutritious beverage that can be used in place of cow milk in any recipe; in making yogurt, gravies, soups, etc. Many prepared baby milk formulas are made from it. Soy milk will also curdle and sour like regular milk and can be used to make soy cheese, or Tofu. A simple recipe for making soy milk from soy flour is:

Soy Milk

4 cups water
1 cup soy flour
1/2 teaspoon salt
2 tablespoons sugar or honey

Mix soy flour into water gradually to prevent lumping. Bring to a rapid boil for 10 minutes and cool. Add salt and sugar. If you use honey, do not allow to set long before drinking, or it will spoil quickly.

One of the most interesting things you can do with soy milk is to make tofu. Allow the milk to set in a warm place to sour and thicken. Use sugared milk, not the honey variety. Then, when the milk has thickened to a jelly consistency, cut into pieces with a knife and place in a sauce pan with water to cover and bring to a boil. Pour through cheese cloth bag and wring as dry as possible. Shape into blocks and allow it to firm up in refrigerator.

Tofu has a rather bland taste by itself and can be easily flavored to taste like meats or sugared and spiced for sweet meats. It can be deep fried with a batter, pan fried in cakes, scrambled like eggs, or added to soups and casseroles.

For easy meat-flavored tofu steak, pre-cook tofu over boiling water for 15-20 minutes. Cool and slice into 1" slices. Fry in a greased pan, handling the pieces gently so they don't break up. Add salt, soy sauce, and a meat flavored sauce, such as bouillon and soy flour, and simmer. Top with pads of butter or margarine (many margarines are made from soy oil, by the way) and enjoy your low cholesterol, high protein steak.

The soybean is the single most versatile agricultural crop I know of. Industry uses its oils for paints, inks, varnishes, plastics, lubricants, cooking oils, and on ad infinitum. Its protein is commercially extracted, spun, woven, twisted, and tied into imitation meats of every description. It's used to feed cats and dogs, cows and hogs. And now it's time that we, America's over-fed, under-nourished citizenry, get this marvelous little bean into our kitchens like good Mother Earth intended.

The versatile soybean

Soybeans have been a staple in China for thousands of years, but in America, they have been treated like an industrial product. They're used to make paint, varnish, soap, glue, plastics, lubricants, cooking oil, and margarine. They are defatted, spun, extruded and compressed to make imitation ham, beef and chicken. And they are used for livestock feed. Few people here make use of their natural flavor, versatility in cooking, and economy.

And they're easily grown in any garden.

References

[1] Chen, Philip S., Soybeans For Health, Longevity, and Economy. The Chemical Elements, South Lancaster, Mass., 1956.

[2] Mustakas, G.C., Albrecht, W.J. et al., Full-fat Soy Flour by a Simple Process for Villages USDA publication no. ARS-71-34, Aug. 1967.

[3] Jones, Dorothea van Gundy, *The Soybean Cookbook,* ARC Books, Inc., New York, 1968.

[4] Cottonseed Flour, Peanut Flour, and Soy Flour; Formulas and Procedures for Family and Institutional Use in Developing Countries. USDA Publication no ARS 61-7, July 1969.

This article first appeared in COUNTRYSIDE *in 1971.*

Puttin' up pawpaws

Marcy Wilson-Cales
West Virginia

I have been literally swamped with mail asking about canned cakes. Well, I can't take credit for inventing it. I got the brainstorm reading a back issue of Countryside (77/1:16) right as the dreadful storm of pawpaw season was about to crash down on my head.

Perhaps you know about pawpaws. If not, you should. They can be fearsome things, pawpaws—large and mushy and possessed of no keeping abilities whatsoever. These are northern cousins of the banana, if bananas can be pale green-blue and potato shaped, and possessed of large bean-shaped, tooth cracking seeds if bitten into without caution.

As fruits go, they seem to be totally without grace, but you either love them or hate them. When we sell them for their brief season at the flea market, it isn't uncommon for them to get raved by over grateful people—or ranted at by people who wouldn't take a pawpaw if you paid them.

At any rate, once the fruits come in, you've got to do something ASAP, and as I baked a fair amount of pawpaw bread, cake and cookies to sell alongside the raw fruits, the canned cakes were a good enough idea. Every year, we manage to cut ourselves a nice little profit, which is always worth the while.

When baking cakes in a can, be assured this is no new idea. Gourmet and specialty shops sell such cakes in small but decorative jars, with a fancy label pertaining to "Granny" and her kitchen. As presents go, the effort is highly appreciated, as the fancy kind easily sell for $8 for a bitty thing.

In response to the questions I received in the mail, a canned cake is like any other canned anything—it will keep. I don't see how it can keep longer than a year when you've got that craving for something sweet, or with holidays, parties and birthdays to think about. Canned cakes with a little ribbon and a handmade label are perfect for party favors, 4-H projects, and keeping kids vaguely out of trouble.

Don't use mayonnaise or small-mouth jars—wide-mouth jars are the rule! These are cakes you'll want to pop out, not jelly you'll have to dig for! If you really want to show off your baking skills, check out the all-glass, glass-lidded canning jars Lehman's Hardware imports from Europe. While a little expensive, they are truly beautiful, and you don't have to buy lids for them every year.

Basic rules for canning cakes:

Grease the insides of your jar up to 1" from the rim, just where you would stop filling a jar under normal circumstances.

Fill the jar only halfway with the cake batter. Wipe any batter from the top sealing edge or the jar. It will expand nicely in the baking.

Canning jars are designed to endure high amounts of heat (and pressure). If a jar breaks on you for some odd reason while being baked, don't worry. A jar that breaks would have violated the seal anyway. Good riddance.

Old fashioned blue jars, despite their age, work fine, but the blue will put a weird cast on the contents.

Bake the canned cakes at the same temperature you would with a normal cake pan. Normally, the length of baking will be cut in half.

When done, pull the hot jars out and quickly screw the lids and rings on them and set aside on a towel to absorb the heat that could damage your counter top. As the jar cools, the cake will pull down in the lid, vacuum sealing the contents.

I feel heavy or moist cakes are perfect for canning. Banana breads, fruitcake, applesauce cake, pumpkin breads, spice cakes, zucchini breads, fudgy cakes, etc., all work just fine.

Pawpaws are interchangeable with any recipe calling for bananas. The flavor will be somewhat different, and much richer, but they behave the same. I simply use Betty Crocker's recipe for banana bread, using pawpaw pulp instead. If I want to make fruitcake, I simply add as much chopped pecans, dried cranberries, raisins, dates and figs as I can cram in them.

Good luck, and any good ideas will be appreciated.

Pawpaws are available from Raintree Nursery, Inc., 391 Butts Rd., Morton WA 98356; 360-496-6400; www.raintreenursery.com

Pawpaws are getting a boost from research

Vitamin-rich sweet desserts and drinks from America's largest native fruit, the pawpaw, could become commercially available within the next decade. Scientists with USDA's Agriculture Research Service (ARS) and more than a dozen universities are testing 28 existing pawpaw cultivars to find the best to develop into commercial varieties.

Ripe green pawpaws weigh up to two pounds and are about five inches long. The bright yellow flesh has a custard-like consistency suitable for baby food and ice cream. The taste has hints of banana, avocado and pineapple.

Kentucky State University is leading the effort to commercialize the fruit, in collaboration with the private PawPaw Foundation. ARS researchers are providing technology to propagate and preserve the germplasm.

The researchers are also trying to expand the cultivated range of the fruit. So far, pawpaw trees are growing as well in their new Oregon home as they do in their native range from New York to Michigan and from Nebraska to the Florida panhandle.

Cast iron in the country kitchen

Heavy, clunky, out of place in a streamlined high-tech kitchen, inexpensive, and definitely old-fashioned. What more could a homesteader ask for?

That's why although they win faint praise from most modern cooks, cast iron utensils are frequently listed among homesteaders' favorite tools. There are many other good reasons.

Cast iron heats slowly and evenly, with none of the hot or cold spots often encountered with utensils of more modern materials. But if it takes a relatively long time to heat, once it attains the desire temperature it maintains it particularly well. There is none of the too-hot or too-cool frustration so common with thinner, lighter pans. This is especially good for sauteing and stir-frying, cooking methods for which the heat needs to remain high.

Also of great importance to homesteaders, cast iron pans are nearly indestructible. (The only cooks we're aware of who ruin cast iron skillets are those who do a lot of "blackened" cooking, where extremely high heat is required, sometimes cracking the pans.) Under normal use, cast iron can literally be used for generations.

An often-overlooked attribute is that with long and continuous use, cast iron is the original non-stick material. That's because iron is porous, and can be "seasoned." When the pan is covered with a very thin layer of cooking oil which fills the pores, cast iron will easily match the most highly-touted and expensive "non-stick" cookware, and without requiring the coddling of plastic spatulas or spoons. With years of use, the protective layer builds up to a black, flat, even surface that is a sure sign of a well-loved tool. A bit of water and if necessary, a few swishes with a brush, and the pan is clean.

New cast iron can be aggravating, which might account for some people avoiding it, or trying it and giving up in disgust. The same porosity that allows seasoning can also make an unseasoned pan a real chore to clean. But the eventual "heirloom" pan is well worth the time and effort.

There is a great deal of folklore, almost a mystique, associated with seasoning cast iron, and many countrysiders have shared methods handed down by their mothers and grandmothers. But the principle and basic method is simple.

Wash a new (or any unseasoned) pan with a steel wool soap pad and hot water, and then with detergent. Dry it thoroughly. A warm stovetop or oven is ideal.

Coat the entire inside with vegetable (non-salted) shortening, such as melted Crisco. Put it in an oven at 375°F for about an hour, turn off the oven, and let the pan cool in the oven to room temperature.

A newly-seasoned pan should not be washed with soap or detergent (or horrors, in a dishwasher!) because this destroys the seasoning. However, if a cooking disaster makes it absolutely necessary to soak or scrub the pan with detergent and hot water, it's no disaster for the pan. Simply repeat the seasoning.

To clean ordinary pot mess, use plain hot water and a plastic scrubber or stiff bristle brush. For less stubborn residues or for a more thoroughly seasoned pan, it's possible and better to avoid water entirely. Scrub the pan with table salt moistened with oil to loosen cooked-on particles.

Cast iron can't be dried adequately with a towel, and besides, the towel will turn black. Put the pan on a burner over low heat (or on the wood stove) until it's dry.

Even then, rust—the worst enemy of cast iron—can sometimes form, especially during the early years. This is easily removed with a little oil and a dish cloth (although most people will prefer to use a paper towel). Many cooks also give their cast iron this treatment before each use. (The cloth or paper will turn black.)

If you do manage to do a really good job of burning something into a carbon that bonds with the iron, you haven't ruined your tool. Remember, cast iron is almost indestructible! Here's an easy way to salvage it that, as someone once said, makes cast iron "the only pan in the world that's actually fun to clean!"

Build a big, hot fire—in the fireplace, wood stove, outdoor grill, or even campfire ring. Toss the skillet into the coals, and wait for the fire to die out and the pan to cool. That's it. Season it again and it'll be as good as new… or better, because cast iron improves with use and age.

Many homestead cooks wouldn't be without their cast iron skillets of various sizes, as well as Dutch ovens. Other utensils available in cast iron include corn bread pans (some shaped like small ears of corn) and muffin pans.

There's just something about a stew in a cast iron Dutch oven, simmering on a wood stove on a brisk winter day, that can't be duplicated by any modern, high-tech cookware. It's one of those little details that makes homesteading so hard to explain… and such a pleasure.

Because cast iron can last for several lifetimes, and because so many modern cooks can't be bothered with it, skillets and other utensils can often be found at yard sales and other sources of used items, at very reasonable prices. As noted here, even the worst can be cleaned and rehabilitated. This is definitely a case of a city cook's trash becoming a homesteader's treasure.

But even if you must buy new, cast iron is a wise investment.

Cast iron, and more

Doug Taylor

I really enjoyed the tips on cast iron cookware. I have been fortunate enough to be able to pick up many pieces at yard sales. Once I even got a whole bunch of saucepans that someone had left in the weather for who-knows-how-long. Knowing that you can hardly ruin cast iron, I decided to try a shortcut.

I used spray oven cleaner on them until I got rid of all the rust, grease and oil that were in them. Then I seasoned them as usual and had myself, and both of my daughters, great, cheap, pots that will last for longer than we will use them.

I have found that when I run into someone having burned food in my pans that after soaking you can get most of the burn off with a putty knife and finish with the oven cleaner.

I have found that a real time-saver, not to mention unwanted heat, is to not make any jams or jellies during canning season. Instead, I put all of my fruit intended for either in the freezer and then do the jams at my leisure. It makes it much less of a push and then when I do make it, the heat is wanted instead of being another problem to deal with.

The problem of tomatoes having too little acid in them has been a concern for quite some time. It was one of the situations stressed when I took a master food preserver course over 15 years ago. What the instructor recommended was to add one teaspoon of vinegar per quart of tomatoes and then it was again possible to process as a fruit. I started doing this just as a matter of course and have had no problems. The amount of vinegar is so small that it really isn't tasted.

Another real time and effort saver has turned out to be my crockpot. Nothing new, you say. Well maybe, but the combination of getting my dinner out of the way first thing, and keeping the heat outside is a real bonus.

I have found that with about a cup of liquid you can "bake" chicken, ham and roast. Just season as usual and put it on low. I use my chest freezer for the table and it keeps it all out of harm's way.

My last tip is about a book that I have been very happy with. It is *The Complete Make-a-Mix Cookbook*. It was put together by three ladies who didn't have enough time to start at the beginning every time they needed to get a meal together. It's from HP-Books, a division of Price Stern Sloan of Los Angeles, CA. The authors are Karine Eliason, Nevada Harward and Madeline Westover.

I started making my own "Bisquick" many years ago and this book picks up from there. Of course, any time there is a call for shortening I use lard. Yes, there are some brands that are just that, with no hydrogenating done to them, or if you have time, lard is very easy to make. With this wonderful book and the white whole wheat that is available through Trader Joe's I have been able to produce some really great baked goods that many people have no idea are almost healthy for them.

Cast iron cookware

Paula Walker
Illinois

I have read about using the cast iron camp Dutch ovens for outdoor cooking. Since we use cast iron pans for all our indoor cooking, I decided to give it a try outside. Food just tastes so good in a properly seasoned and cared for cast iron pan.

Many of you probably already have the camp Dutch ovens, but I'm always late to the party. I thoroughly enjoy cooking and baking, but I'm not very heat tolerant. I just hate heating the house up and then trying to cool it down with more electricity to run fans or air conditioning. Enter the camp Dutch ovens.

You can use charcoal briquets under the oven and on the top recessed lid. If you have an ample supply of firewood, just burn some down to hot coals and use it. You may burn a few meals until you get the hang of it. The coals are much hotter than you might think.

Instead of becoming worried and depressed after reading about the Y2K problems that may lie ahead, I decided to make lemonade out of a lemon. I have always felt that I was a closet pioneer just waiting for an excuse to live as one. I decided cooking outdoors pioneer-style was right up my alley.

What is more therapeutic than sitting around a campfire with family and friends enjoying the smell of stew or roast cooking? I can also hear the chorus of outdoor life. Sure beats what's on television!

I called the Lodge Company of South Pittsburgh, Tennessee (423-837-7181) to find out what stores carry their Dutch ovens. I was told that some Wal-Mart, Target, Ace or TruValue hardware stores and Service Merchandise stores carry them nationally. Look in the camping rather than the housewares section. Twin-K Enterprises of Logan, Utah carries Lodge products. They have a cookies and accessories brochure. Write them at P.O. Box 4023, Logan, UT 84323. Utah is the most popular state for Dutch oven cooking.

The Lodge Company will sell Dutch ovens directly to the customer if they can't be found locally. They offer a free catalog of all their cast iron cookware.

I hope this will encourage some of you closet pioneers to get out in the great outdoors and cook some of your meals without electricity or gas. You may need some more strong shelves to hold all those Dutch ovens! Many happy meals to you.

Why eat whole foods?

Jennifer Stein Barker
Oregon

In 1990, I was running a cross-country ski lodge in the Wenatchee Mountains of Washington state. Both my guests and I thought that my cooking was pretty healthy, because I served vegetarian food with lots of fresh ingredients and some whole grains, but I was still using plenty of white flour, sugar, and fat. I even had a can of that white stuff they call "vegetable shortening" stashed in the cupboard for my piecrusts!

Then I met the man who was to become my husband. Lance didn't like to eat any processed food at all, but he was ever-so-tactful. He ate my food, even when it made him feel uncomfortable. He knew I had a potential, so with a hint here and a comment there, he convinced me to change my way of cooking. I started using 100% whole grains in my baking, even in desserts. I never need to add bran any more, or worry about whether or not we get enough fiber. There's more flavor in everything too.

I threw away the can of white stuff the next year when I moved to Lance's 40-acre homestead in the eastern Oregon pine forest. I didn't buy any more margarine, either. Artificially hardened fats (look for the word "hydrogenated") are worse for your arteries than the ones nature made, like real butter, because your body doesn't know how to react to foods not found in nature.

We don't get hung up on our food choices. We eat whatever's put in front of us when we go out, and sometimes that includes highly processed foods or meat. We just figure that if we eat right at home, which is 95% of the time, we'll be better able to stay healthy.

At home, we don't eat meat at present because Lance grows all the vegetables we could possibly eat. In our chilly, dry High Desert climate, this means we currently eat a lot of cabbage-family, root vegetables, greens, peas, and potatoes. Garlic grows great here, so I use it generously. We are learning how to grow feed crops, and only when we can give them wholesome food will we get goats and chickens for meat, milk and eggs. For now I buy milk and eggs from the small, local health-food store.

For fruit, we get strawberries, raspberries, gooseberries, and rhubarb from our garden. Our apple trees aren't big enough yet, so I buy apples by the box from a nearby orchard. Combined with the organic grains and other natural foods from the health-food store, our garden produce furnishes us with a very healthy diet and plenty of organic matter to compost and improve our native soil (which was a good starting point for soil, but very low in nitrogen and organic matter.)

As I began to cook this way, I found that there weren't very many recipes for the way I wanted to make things. I like my food ingredients simple and unprocessed, but I like a lot of herbs and seasonings so the food is flavorful and interesting. I also don't like overly fussy, involved preparation. I started writing down my original recipes and collecting them in a looseleaf notebook. As the notebook got fatter, Lance encouraged me to think of writing my own cookbook.

I queried a few publishers, but got dampening replies from them. Since I didn't have to prove anything to myself (I used the recipes in the cooking classes I taught at the local community college extension, and knew they were good), I decided to publish at home. Using a desktop publishing program that a friend had given me, I typed up camera-ready copy for a 196-page book. I did my writing on my laptop computer powered by the solar panels which provide all the electricity at our homestead.

I made a local project out of the book. I got a few bids, then ended up taking the business to the local printer because I could talk to him in person. He delivered the boxes of finished pages to the multi-purpose room at the Seneca City Hall (pop. 230). I paid friends and friends-of-friends to come and help collate. For two days, we all walked around long tables to the beat of the boom box, picking up pages.

Now I have boxes of books in my bedroom, and whenever I get an order, I punch and bind them with those plastic combs that allow a book to lay flat when open. I sell the books mail order. I kept the price as reasonable as I possibly could, because I figure people like me don't have a lot of money. We make a little on each copy, not a lot, but as you know, homesteaders live well on less. I pay the postage because I figure if I can wholesale them to stores, I can pay postage for people who are willing to search me out and buy direct. Try the recipes below, and then if you like my style, send for a cookbook!

Recipes from *The Morning Hill Cookbook* by Jennifer Stein Barker

More-Than-Tabbouleh

This traditional Middle Eastern salad can be turned into a main-dish salad with a few simple additions.

Serves 4 as a main dish:

1/4 cup dry lentils
1 1/2 cups bulgur wheat
2 medium-sized tomatoes, diced
3 tablespoons minced fresh parsley
3 green onions, thinly sliced
1 teaspoon minced fresh mint
1 small cucumber, peeled, quartered, and sliced
1 medium carrot, sliced thin
3 tablespoons lemon juice
1/2 cup olive oil
Pepper to taste
1 head red- or green-leaf lettuce

Boil the lentils in a small pan with 2 cups of water until they are tender, but still whole. Place the bulgur in a large bowl, and drain the cooking water from the lentils over it. Put the lentils in the refrigerator to cool. Add enough more boiling water to the bulgur to cover it, and let soak until all the water is absorbed. Taste the bulgur, and if it is not tender, add a little more boiling water as necessary and soak until tender. If you add too much water, the bulgur will have to be drained and squeezed in cheesecloth to remove the excess moisture.

When the bulgur is tender, add the lentils and all the other ingredients. Toss to mix thoroughly, then cover and chill for two hours or overnight. Serve on a bed of fresh leaf lettuce.

Borscht

Serve with a dollop of yogurt and a sprinkle of dill weed for a traditional touch. Good with rye bread, too. Serves 4 as a main dish:

2 tablespoons oil
1 medium onion, diced
3 cups shredded cabbage
3 or 4 carrots, coarsely grated
4 beets, peeled and grated, or 1 can shoestring beets
1 15-ounce can crushed tomatoes
4 cups stock or water
4 tablespoons tomato paste
1 tablespoon honey
3 tablespoons vinegar
2 tablespoons lemon juice

Heat oil in a 5 or 6 quart stock pot or Dutch oven. Add onion and sauté until soft. Add cabbage, carrots, and beets (if fresh), and a little water, and sauté another 10 minutes. Add more water if the vegetables start to stick. Add tomatoes, stock or water, tomato paste, honey, and vinegar (if your beets are canned, add them now, using juice for part of the stock). Bring to a boil, lower heat to simmer, and cook, covered, until vegetables are tender, about 30 minutes. Stir in lemon juice and serve.

Variation: leave the beets out. Instead, add two potatoes, quartered and sliced thin. It may not really be borscht without the beets, but it sure is good anyway.

Chili Potatoes

A new twist on old favorites. Be sure and get the best chili powder you can find. The best kind is made from ground roasted chilies and nothing else. My favorite place to buy it is El Ranchito Mexican Grocery and Restaurant in Zillah, Washington.

Serves 2 to 3 as a main dish:

2 pounds small red potatoes, diced
1 tablespoon olive oil
1 medium onion, diced
1 large clove garlic, minced
6 medium mushrooms, sliced thin
2-3 teaspoons chili powder
1/2 teaspoon cumin
1/2 teaspoon oregano, crushed
2 tablespoons tamari
Tabasco to taste (2 dashes)
1 green pepper, diced 1/4 inch

Scrub and dice the potatoes, leaving the skins on. Steam or boil the diced potatoes until they are tender (save the water for soup stock).

Meanwhile, heat the olive oil in a deep heavy skillet, preferably cast iron. Add the onion, and braise with a little water as necessary until the onions are golden all the way through and quite soft. When the onion is about half done, add the garlic and mushrooms. When the onions and mushrooms are almost perfect, add the chili powder, cumin, oregano, tamari, and Tabasco to taste (starting with two dashes), and enough water to keep it from burning. Simmer a few minutes, then add the green peppers and simmer three minutes more. There should be just enough water in the mixture to keep it from burning.

The potatoes should be done by now, but if they aren't, then put the chili mixture aside and keep warm for a few more minutes. When the potatoes are done, stir them into the chili mixture, mix well, and serve with a big salad, red wine and corn bread!

Strawberry-Almond Torte

This delightful dessert is the perfect way to take advantage of the bounties of strawberry season.

Makes one 10 inch torte:

1/2 cup crunchy almond butter
1/2 cup honey
2 egg yolks
1/2 teaspoon almond extract
3/4 cup whole wheat pastry flour
1/2 teaspoon cinnamon
1/2 teaspoon baking powder
2 egg whites, beaten

Filling and glaze:
3 pints strawberries
1 tablespoon orange juice concentrate
2-3 tablespoons honey
1-1/2 tablespoons cornstarch

Prepare a 10 inch springform pan by oiling the sides lightly and lining the bottom with bakers' paper. Preheat the oven to 350 degrees.

In a medium bowl, beat together the almond butter, honey, egg yolks, and almond extract until well-blended. Sift together the flour, cinnamon, and baking powder, and stir into the almond butter mixture. Gently fold in the beaten egg whites.

Spread the mixture in the prepared pan and bake for 25-30 minutes, until it is golden and springy to the touch. Run a knife around the inside of the pan, and then remove the sides. Remove the cake from the bottom of the pan, and cool on a rack. Prepare the glaze.

Wash and hull all your berries, and reserve the best for the filling. Mash the less perfect ones until you have 1 cup of mashed berries. Add the orange juice concentrate and 2-3 tablespoons honey (depending on the ripeness of the berries). Dissolve the cornstarch in the berry mixture. Heat gently on the stove, stirring constantly, until the mixture comes to a boil and thickens and clears.

When the cake is cool, and the glaze is still hot, assemble the torte as follows: Turn the cake upside down on a large plate. Spread a thin layer of the glaze over the cake. Arrange the good berries artistically on top. Pour the rest of the glaze over the top of the berries, working it over and between them carefully. Chill at least 1 hour before serving.

Jennifer Barker can be reached at 15013 Geary Creek Rd., Canyon City OR 97820. (541)542-2525, e-mail: jbarker@highdesertnet.com, web: www.highdesertnet.com/morninghill

Canning salsa

CINDY POPECK
GEORGIA

Salsa—to can

5 pounds ripe tomatoes
3 cups chopped onions
2-1/4 cups chopped hot pepper (see hint below)
1 cup vinegar
2 tablespoons minced garlic
1 tablespoon salt
1 tablespoon cumin
2 cans tomato paste

Parboil tomatoes to remove skins (see hint below). Core and chop tomatoes.

In very large pot, combine all ingredients. Bring to a boil, stirring occasionally. Reduce heat and simmer for 30 minutes or to desired thickness. Fill 5-6 sterilized jars, leaving 1/2" headspace. Run a wooden or plastic utensil inside the jars to remove any air bubbles. Wipe jar tops and threads and cover with hot lids and bands. Process in boiling water bath for 15 minutes.

Hints:

If you have too many tomatoes and not enough time to process them, tightly pack the whole tomatoes in freezer bags and put the bags in the freezer. When you're ready to use them, hold each tomato under warm running water and the skin will slip off. This saves a lot of time over parboiling. I made two batches of salsa this year from last year's frozen tomatoes.

When you're cutting up fresh tomatoes, place your cutting board inside a cookie sheet. The sheet will catch the tomato juice and make clean-up a lot easier.

To make really hot salsa, use at least 1/4 cup chopped habanero peppers.

When cutting up hot peppers, be sure to wear rubber gloves and do not touch your face or eyes with the gloves. It's also a good idea to wear safety glasses to keep from getting shot in the eye with pepper juice.

This recipe also makes good taco sauce. Just run the sauce through a blender or food processor before canning it.

***

Boiled, fertilized, partially-incubated duck eggs are considered a delicacy by Filipinos (who call them balut) and Vietnamese (hot vit lon). The eggs are incubated for 17 of the 28 days it takes to hatch a duckling. Ducks which have been crossbred for high egg production (up to 290 per year) are available from Metzer Farms, 26000 Old Stage Rd., Gonzales, CA 93926 (800-424-7755).

***

If you have livestock or pets, don't throw away water from canned vegetables. It contains vitamins and minerals and can be offered to pets or livestock.

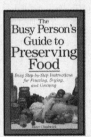

Planning for canning

Canning is a big job As with any big job, it pays to plan ahead

MARILYN B. NOYES, PHD
HOME ECONOMICS PROGRAM LEADER
JEAN ALDER, MS, HOME ECONOMIST

Many homemakers preserve food for their families. The most common method used is freezing, probably because it is quick and easy. Canning takes more time and energy, but is preferred by many for preserving the large quantities of fruits and vegetables available during the summer season. Time spent preparing and planning for canning will make canning days go more smoothly and be more enjoyable.

Get ready: Use updated canning guides

All canned food should be prepared following tested recipes. Research is done continually to provide the basis for updated recommendations. Many new guidelines, especially for tomatoes, have been released recently. Check your canning books and update them if necessary. The Extension office in your county has reliable, up-to-date low cost guides.

Assemble equipment

Review the equipment needed. A large deep pot is needed for processing fruits and a large pressure canner is essential for vegetables, meats, poultry, fish and other low acid mixtures. Review the recipes you will be using and get the ingredients, jars and supplies ready in advance. Wash the estimated number of jars needed the day before you will be canning. Set upside down on clean dishtowels or paper towels. Sterilization is usually not necessary.

A checklist of other equipment would include: Jars (not chipped), new lids, sharp knife, clean cloths, measuring cups, garbage container, cooling area, newspaper, pad, sugar, cardboard, racks or board, salt, hot pads, rings, funnel, and jar lifter.

Get organized

Plan to organize your family's activities for canning days. Keep meals simple but nutritious. Cook ahead if possible. Have laundry and other chores caught up. Check your appointment calendar and rearrange if necessary. Arrange for child care if possible, or plan activities to keep the young ones busy. Some mothers of young children like to do their canning before the kids are up or after they go to bed. Youngsters underfoot can add stress to an already busy day. Be reasonable in estimating the time required to complete canning. The time required for preparation, waiting for water to boil, processing and cool down time will probably be at least 1-1/2 hours per canner load. You may need to process part of the produce one day and part the next. The reduction in quality is probably more acceptable than an overly stressed parent or overdoing to the point of exhaustion!

Get set

Preparations on the day you can or freeze are important too. Sharpen knives if necessary. Start with a clear and clean counter space, sink and table. In apartments with limited space, you may need to put canisters, spices or decorations usually found on the counter and table in a box and store them temporarily out of the way. Dress in clean, cool, and comfortable work clothes. Some fruits stain clothing, so don't wear good clothes. Tying your hair up will keep you cooler and help prevent unwanted hair in food. Set up your work flow in an organized manner. Right handed people work more efficiently if tasks move from right to left. Left handed people work best from left to right.

Go

Now is the time to get to work. Can you get others to help? Neighbors or friends can work together, sharing costs and work effort. Husbands can accept responsibilities. Children should learn to help according to their ages and ability. Time spent working with our children is more fun, the children feel needed, and it can be a good time to talk and teach. Other work-saving hints include: Do as much of one task at a time as possible and practical (wash all jars, prepare all lids, etc.). Divide work into manageable parts (prepare one cooker load at a time). Don't start more than you can finish. Fruits peeled too far in advance turn brown; also beets will turn dark. Heated products that are to be hot-packed will not be safe unless reheated before continuing. Clean up as you go.

To keep foods from discoloring:

Peeled and cut up (halved, quartered, sliced or diced) apples, apricots, nectarines, peaches, and pears will discolor when exposed to air. While it's important to can them as quickly as possible, discoloration can be retarded by keeping these fruits in a solution of 3 grams (about one level teaspoon) of ascorbic acid to 1 gallon of cold water.

Ascorbic acid is usually found with other canning supplies in supermarkets. But if you can't find it, vitamin C tablets will do the same job. Crush and dissolve six 500 milligram tablets in a gallon of water.

Citric acid powder is sometimes sold for this purpose, but it's less effective.

Culture clash confuses canners

Who are you going to believe, Grandma, or the USDA?

Life isn't as simple as it once was. Even something as old-fashioned as home canning has been affected by technology and the modern world.

This sometimes puts a magazine like COUNTRYSIDE in an uncomfortable position. If we print your grandmother's tried-and-true recipe for canning spaghetti sauce, we alarm the home economists who are absolutely certain we're contributing to widespread agony and death. If we print the home economists' dire warnings about the absolute necessity for using a pressure canner, hordes of old-timers descend on us with disdain, and stories of their own experiences.

As for using or not using mayonnaise jars for canning... we won't even mention that anymore.

Curiously, perhaps, even some "modern high-tech" methods don't pass muster. "Canning powders," and processing in the microwave—or even the dishwasher!—wouldn't seem to have much appeal for homesteaders, but home economists don't approve of them either.

On the brighter side, we can recall when it was very difficult to get any endorsement or even acknowledgment of home canning from university and government experts: it wasn't safe, they said, it certainly wasn't economical, and what kind of nut would do all that work when they could buy a can or frozen package of the same thing for pennies? That, at least, has changed, at least in some quarters.

Nevertheless, home canning seems to be another one of those areas where you gather your own information, meld it with your own outlook and attitude, and make your own choices. Home economists are understandably cautious, and sometimes over-cautious. People who have "always done it that way" are understandably confused, or even skeptical about the new rules: "How come we didn't all die from food poisoning years ago?"

And a magazine that strives to blend the best of both worlds will continue to irk both factions from time to time... as well as those in the middle who demand explicit "facts" in black and white.

Home canning under pressure: an overview

All vegetables, as well as meat, poultry and fish, must be processed in a pressure canner. The water bath method (processing jars in boiling water not under pressure) is considered safe only for jellies and jams, brined and fermented foods, and high-acid products (namely tomatoes—although extension people point out that many modern varieties of tomatoes are no longer acidic enough to qualify for this exemption).

A good pressure canner is a major investment. However, in addition to the safety factor, they also save time.

There are two types of pressure canners, those with a dial gauge, and those with a weight gauge. It's essential to understand how to operate the pressure cooker you're using, following the manufacturer's directions.

An accurate pressure gauge is essential for getting the food to the proper temperature.Most county extension offices have the equipment to conduct this test, which should be done at least once a year.

Check jars and covers for cracks, chips, dents or rust. Wash them in hot soapy water and rinse well. Sterilization isn't necessary. Metal lids with sealing compound may need boiling.

After processing (which varies with the food you're canning), remove the cooker from the stove to where air can circulate around it. Do not place it on a cold surface, and do not run cold water on it to speed up cooling.

When the weight or gauge shows that the cooker has cooled enough to decrease the pressure safely, wait another minute or two, then remove the weight or open the petcock, depending on the type of cooker you're using. Make sure there is no pressure left before carefully removing the lid.

Directions, not recipes

There are no "recipes" as such for basic food preservation by canning, but rather directions for preparing and processing. In other words, if you're preserving corn, or beans, or beets, you don't add anything except water. (Salt is optional.) These directions come with most canners, or are available in basic cookbooks.

Six potentially deadly canning sins

CHARLOTTE P. BRENNAND, PHD
EXTENSION FOOD SAFETY SPECIALIST
UTAH STATE UNIVERSITY

1. Making up your own canning recipe. Without scientific testing, you will not know how long the product needs to be processed to be safe.

2. Adding extra starch, flour or other thickener to recipe. This will change the rate of heat penetration into the product and can result in undercooking.

3. Adding extra onions, chili, bell peppers, or other vegetables to salsas. The extra vegetables dilute the acidity and can result in botulism poisoning.

4. Using oven instead of water bath. The product will be under processed since air processing is not as good a conductor of heat as water or steam. The jars also may blow up.

5. Not making altitude adjustments. Since boiling temperatures are lower at higher altitudes, the products will be undercooked.

6. Not venting pressure cooker first. Lack of venting can result in air pockets which will not reach as high a temperature.

Country kitchen:

Favorite recipes for summer canning

Over the years, many readers have shared their favorite canning recipes with us. Here's a selection to keep you busy this summer, and well-fed next winter!

Catsup

1 gallon tomato juice (unseasoned)
2 cups sugar
3 tablespoons salt
1-1/2 cups vinegar

Tie together in a cloth for easy removal when done cooking:

1 tablespoon pickling spice
1/3 teaspoon red pepper flakes

Cook on a low flame, stir often until it is the thickness desired. Remove spice bag before canning. Makes approximately 3 pints. Very good and easy.

Tomato Juice Cocktail

5 quarts tomato juice
1/2 cup brown sugar
1 tablespoon salt
1 tablespoon celery salt
1 tablespoon onion salt

Boil five minutes, pour into jars and seal. This tastes a lot like V-8.

Spaghetti Sauce

1/2 bushel tomatoes unpeeled, cut in quarters
7 green peppers
3–4 hot peppers
12 large onions
2 heads garlic
1 cup oil

Cook these ingredients until mushy. Put them through a Victorio strainer, food mill or blender and into a large ovenproof container. Add:

8 small cans tomato paste, mix well
1 cup oil
1 cup sugar
1/2 cup salt
1 tablespoon basil
1/2 cup oregano
1 tablespoon black pepper
10 tablespoons grated cheese
Mushrooms

Bake the mixture at 350° for 6 hours or until sauce is desired thickness.

Pack hot in sterile jars and seal. Yields about 10 quarts.

Blender Corn Relish

1 medium onion, quartered
2 sweet red or green peppers, seeded and sliced
2 cups coarsely sliced cabbage
1/2 cup water
2 cups vinegar
1 tablespoon dry mustard
1/2 tablespoon mustard seeds
1/2 tablespoon celery seeds
1/2 tablespoon salt
1/2 tablespoon turmeric
3/4 cup sugar
4 cups fresh corn

Fill blender container three-quarters full with mixed onion, green pepper and cabbage pieces. Add water and half the vinegar. Cover. Blend for six seconds (puree). Empty into saucepan. Repeat with remaining vegetables and remaining vinegar. Add corn and remaining ingredients to vegetable mixture. Bring to a boil and simmer for 20 minutes. Pack immediately into hot jars and seal. Makes four pints.

Cabbage and Beet Relish

1 pint chopped boiled beets
1 pint chopped cabbage
1/4 teaspoon white pepper
Pinch red pepper
1/2 teaspoon salt
1 cup chopped celery
3/4 cup sugar
1 cup vinegar
1/2 cup water

Peel beets, mix all ingredients and let heat through. When boiling, pour into sterilized jars to within 1/2 inch of top. Put on cap, screw band firmly tight. Process in a boiling water bath 5 minutes. Yield: 2–3 pints.

Apple Pie Filling

4-1/2 cups sugar
1 cup cornstarch
2 teaspoons cinnamon
1/2 teaspoon nutmeg
1 teaspoon salt
10 cups water
3 tablespoons lemon juice
3 teaspoons yellow food coloring
6 sliced tart apples

In a large saucepan blend first four ingredients. Add salt and stir in water. Cook until thick and bubbly, then add lemon juice and food coloring. Mix well. Pack apples in hot jars and fill with the mixture. Process in water bath for 20 minutes. Makes 6 quarts.

When making pie, pour into unbaked crust and bake for 50 minutes at 400°.

Quick Grape Juice

1 cup Concord grapes, washed
1/2 cup sugar

Put grapes into sterilized quart jar, add sugar, fill to within 1/2 inch of top of jar with boiling water. Put on cap, screwing the band firmly tight. Process 10 minutes in a boiling water bath.

Grape Juice

1/2 cup sugar to each quart of juice

Remove from stems and wash sound ripe grapes. Cover them with water and heat slowly to simmering. Do not boil. Cook slowly until the fruit is very soft, then strain through a bag and add sugar as above. Pour into sterilized jars to within 1/2 inch of top of jar. Put on cap, screw band firmly tight. Process 10 minutes in boiling water bath.

If only enough water is added to start grapes to cooking and the sugar omitted from the recipe, the juice may be used to make grape jelly when jars are opened.

Concentrated Grape Juice

1 cup grapes
1/2 cup sugar

Put into a quart jar, fill with hot water, process 10 minutes in a boiling water bath, and let sit for six weeks.

However, if you double the amount of grapes and sugar in the same jar, you have concentrated your mixture so that by adding a quart of water on opening you get two quarts of grape juice instead of one, and saved yourself one jar in use and storage space.

Victoria Sauce

This has some unusual ingredients, but it tastes very good with meat.

8 cups chopped rhubarb
1/2 cup chopped onion
1-1/2 cups chopped raisins
3-1/2 cups brown sugar
1/2 cup vinegar
1 teaspoon salt
1 teaspoon ginger
1 teaspoon cinnamon
1 teaspoon allspice

Mix rhubarb, onion, raisins, sugar and vinegar. Boil slowly until thick. Add spices about five minutes before removing sauce from heat. Pour, boiling hot, into hot jars and seal at once.

Spiced Pickled Beets

Cook beets until tender. Slip skins off and slice. Combine:

1 cup beet juice
3 cups sugar
3 cups vinegar
4 teaspoons cinnamon
2 teaspoons salt
2 teaspoons ground cloves

Bring to a boil and simmer five minutes. Fill jars with beets and syrup and process 30 minutes. Makes enough syrup for eight to 12 pint jars.

Condensed Tomato Soup

6 medium onions, chopped
1 bunch celery, chopped
Water
8 quarts tomatoes, cut-up
3/4 cup sugar
1/4 cup salt
1 cup butter
1 cup flour

Add enough water to onions and celery in a large kettle to start a good boil and prevent scorching. Add tomatoes and cook until vegetables are tender. Put through a strainer and return to the kettle with sugar and salt. Cream butter with flour and add to boiling puree, stirring thoroughly. Simmer until mixture thickens slightly, like thin gravy. Put into hot jars and process 20 minutes at 10 pounds pressure. Makes 10 to 12 pints.

To serve: Combine soup and a pinch of baking soda per cup with an equal amount of milk or water and heat.

Zucchini Relish

12 cups zucchini, chopped or grated
4 cups onions, chopped or grated
1/3 cup salt
1 teaspoon ground turmeric
1 teaspoon whole celery seed
3/4 teaspoon nutmeg
1/2 teaspoon white pepper
1 tablespoon cornstarch
2-1/2 cups vinegar
4 cups sugar

Sprinkle salt over zucchini and onions in a bowl and leave in refrigerator overnight. Drain and rinse in cold water. Add remaining ingredients. Bring to a boil and simmer 20 minutes, stirring often. Ladle into hot jars and process 10 minutes in boiling water. Makes 4 to 6 pints.

Zucchini Sweet Chunks

6 or 7 large zucchini, washed and cut into chunks
4 pounds onions, sliced
5 tablespoons salt
2-1/2 cups vinegar
6-1/2 cups water
3-1/2 cups brown sugar
1 teaspoon dry mustard
1 teaspoon ground cinnamon
1 teaspoon nutmeg
1 teaspoon whole cloves
1 teaspoon turmeric
1 teaspoon ginger
1/2 teaspoon white pepper

Combine zucchini and onions in a large kettle and sprinkle salt over. Let sit while making the syrup. Mix remaining ingredients and bring to a boil, stirring thoroughly to dissolve sugar. Pour over vegetables and boil 25 to 30 minutes. Stir often. When zucchini is transparent, pour into hot jars and process 10 minutes in a boiling water bath.

Applesauce

Grind apples up in food grinder on the medium blade, skin and pulp together. Add 1 tablespoon lemon juice per quart and cook to an "applesauce texture."

The result is a sauce retaining the nutritive value of the skins plus a pink glowing color from cooking the red skin and pulp together. After cooking and processing the sauce becomes very smooth and it is difficult to even tell that the peel is there.

Cook with the sun!

Would you like to make use of the sun's energy, but think it's too expensive, or too complicated? Think again!

COUNTRYSIDE'S Steve Belanger made the ovens shown here at a cost of pennies, in 1-2 hours each.

Note that this is a project anyone can use, even on an apartment balcony!

Using the oven

We're located above 45° latitude (closer to the North Pole than to the equator), and when these ovens were tested in April the noon sun was only about 45° off the horizon. On a cloudless day (also somewhat rare here in April) with an air temperature of 50°, these ovens easily reached 200°, and with a little time and proper positioning, 250°. It took about four hours to bake four small potatoes, but the wait was worth it: in a taste test, the slow-cooked sun-baked spuds won hands-down over those baked in the kitchen.

We baked some potatoes in a covered cast iron pan, and wrapped others in foil. The cast iron took longer to heat up, but resulted in a superior product. The pan also stayed hot when the sun went behind a cloud.

Dry beans also take about 3-4 hours, but other vegetables, cut-up pieces of chicken and fish should be cooked in an hour or two.

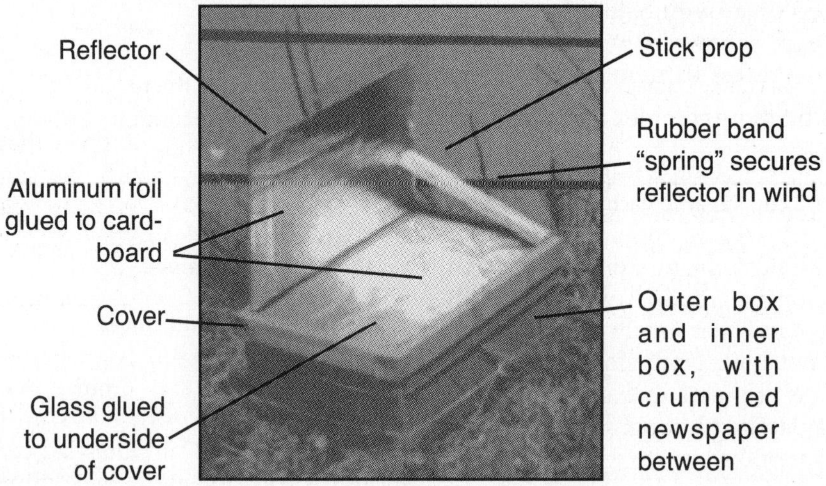

Box in a box

This simple solar oven consists of two cardboard boxes, one inside the other. The tops of the two boxes are level, but there's about an inch of space between them on the sides. This space is filled with crumpled newspaper for insulation. The inside of the smaller box is covered with aluminum kitchen foil attached with Elmer's glue.

The cover was constructed from the cardboard of a third box. It was cut, folded and taped to fit snugly over the outer box.

The reflector was made by cutting, on three sides (see illustration), an opening as large as the inner box.

On the inside of this cover we glued a sheet of glass from an old window, which we cut to fit. Again, Elmer's glue did the job.

Glue aluminum foil on the inside of the lid flap reflector, prop the reflector up with a stick... and you're ready to cook with the sun!

Materials: Three cardboard boxes (or two, if you can find one with a ready-made cover); 8 feet of aluminum foil; 1 piece of glass; a stick; rubber band; Elmer's glue. Construction time: About an hour and a half, not counting scrounging up materials. Cost: Pennies, for the foil: everything else is easily scrounged.

A solar oven can be any size you choose to make it, but it will be most efficient if it's just large enough to hold the container you'll be cooking in. Aside from that, the deciding factors might be the size of the glass or boxes you have on hand.

Note also that heavy plastic could be substituted for the glass, although with some loss of efficiency, and other insulating materials could be used instead of newspaper. Avoid foam materials that might be susceptible to outgassing, however.

This oven, known as the SunStar, is a bit more complex and takes longer to construct, but it's still simple.

The basic "oven" itself is a box in a box (in a third box, as shown in the drawing, but we only used two).

The main difference here is in the more efficient reflector.

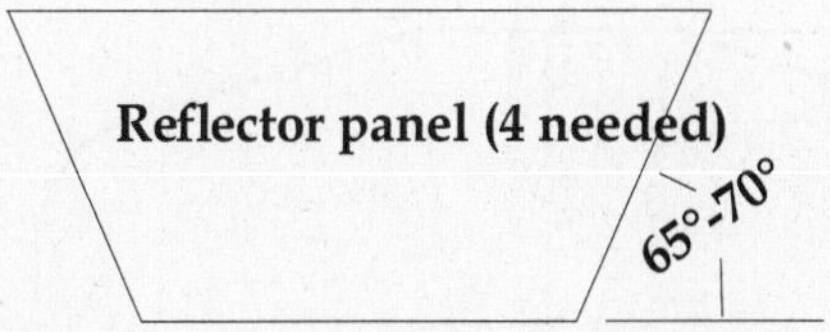
Reflector panel (4 needed)
65°-70°

3 The reflector is the tricky part. The pieces should be cut at a 65°-70° angle. You can determine this by using a protractor. If you don't have one handy, fold a piece of paper in half at one corner as shown below, and then in half again, giving you a 22.5° angle (90° ÷ 2 = 45° ÷ 2 = 22.5°). Place this on a 90° corner of a piece of cardboard and cut it on that angle. (90° - 22.5° = 67.5°.)

You'll need four of these reflector panels. If your oven is square, they'll all be the same size. If you used rectangular boxes, measure the length and the width to determine the length of the bottom of the reflector panel and cut two of each.

Assemble the pieces with tape. Glue aluminum foil to the inside.

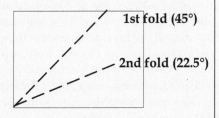

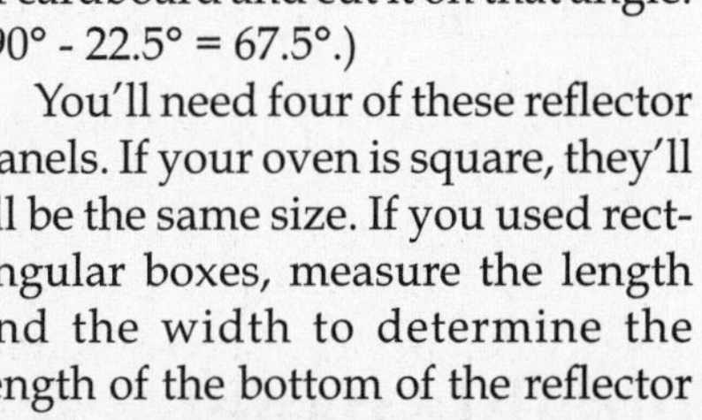
1st fold (45°)
2nd fold (22.5°)

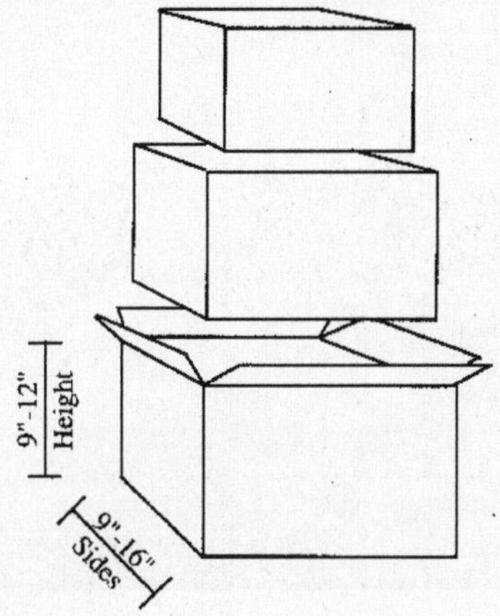
9"-12" Height
9"-16" Sides

1 Find or make three boxes that will nest together with about an inch of space between them. Fill the spaces with crumpled newspaper or other insulating material.

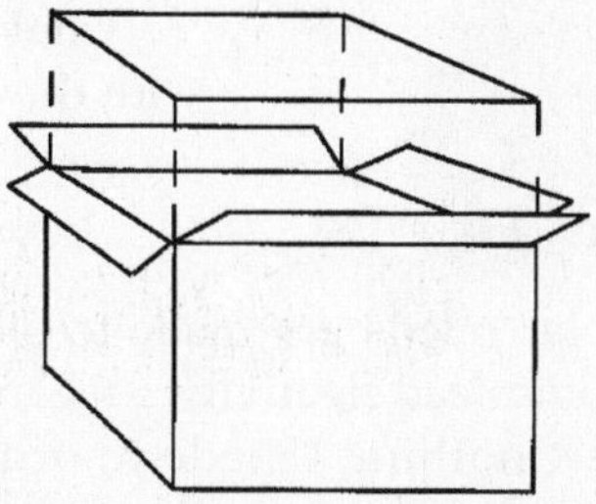

2 A glass cover goes over the inner boxes. It should fit snugly to minimize heat loss. One oven maker suggests using weather stripping to help create a seal. Since this glass is the oven door and will be handled frequently, it's a good idea to tape the edges for safety.

The inside can be painted black, or covered with black paper or other material.

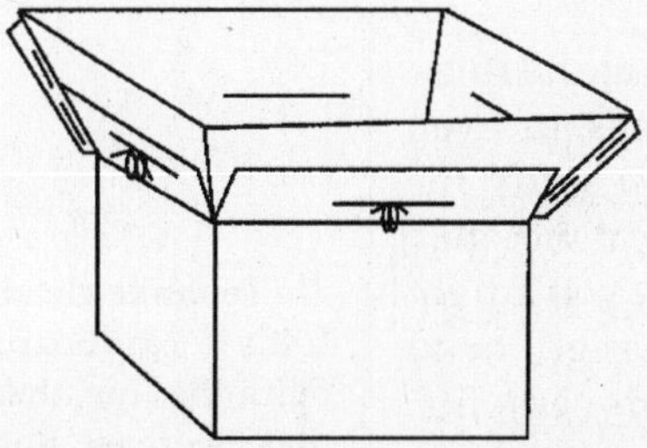

4 We found suggestions on several ways to attatch the reflector to the oven box. One involed poking holes through the outside oven box flaps and the reflector, and lacing them together, as shown here. (Note that extra flaps were left on the four reflector panels so they can be laced together too. This would be a good idea if storage or transportation is a concern, because the reflector can then be dismantled when not in use.) We simply taped it all together.

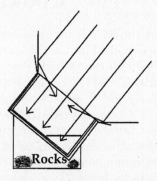

Rocks

5 The oven needs to be tilted toward the sun. This could be accomplished by propping it up on rocks or a log, by making a stand, or by setting it inside a larger box that will hold it at the correct angle.

With the box tilted as shown here, a level shelf inside is a necessity when cooking anything liquid. Taken into account when determining the size, this merely involves one more piece of cardboard.

Cooking with the sun

Solar ovens are made-to-order for homestead creativity... meaning there's nothing "made-to-order" about them! The size might be determined by the size of the boxes you can find, or on the size of the piece of glass you have, just as easily as by what you intend to cook. Some people use thermopane (insulated glass) to increase efficiency; others use two sheets of ordinary window glass, providing an airspace between the two by cutting a "gasket" sort of spacer from cardboard or other material. Some people paint the cardboard to preserve its lifespan, while others build ovens from plywood or even metal.

In other words, there are no rules, no specific measurements, or even ironclad directions. You study the concept and let your creativity go.

After building one, you might want to try another design, or to experiment with improvements. Indeed, many solar oven enthusiasts have several, often cooking and baking at the same time. (Yes, with a little experience, you can bake cookies, pizza, and even bread, in a solar oven. Putting a heat sink—a dark-colored brick or rock or chunk of metal—in the oven will help "preheat" it while the bread dough is rising and will result in more uniform baking.)

When using a solar oven you'll have to pay attention to a few things that microwave users never consider. Obviously the sun must be shining, and the brighter the better, and the higher the angle the better.

For maximum efficiency, make your oven as small and as shallow as you can for the utensils you'll be using. Then use the smallest pot possible, preferably black. Cast iron works, but a thinner pot will heat up faster.

Use as little water as practical, and cut the foods into small pieces for faster cooking.

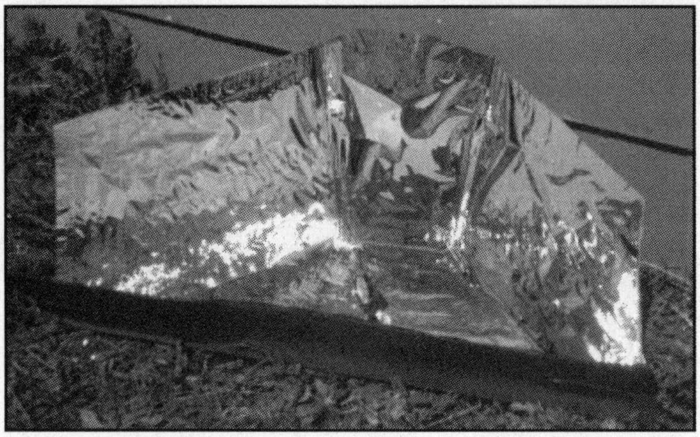

For more information on solar cooking we recommend *Heaven's Flame*, by Joseph Radabaugh, available from Home Power, Inc., PO Box 520, Ashland OR 97520.

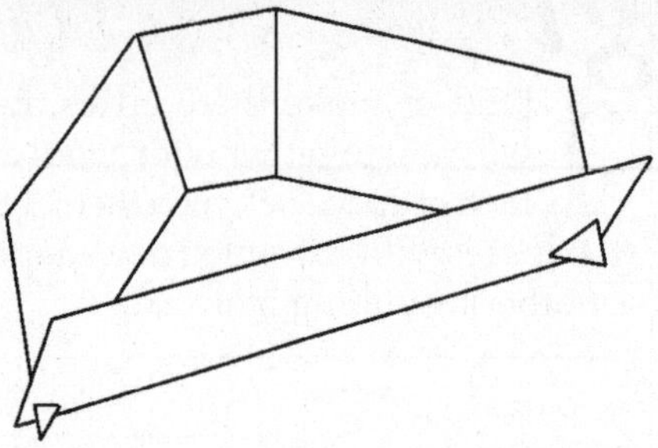

To make clean folds in cardboard, mark the line, then make a crease along it with a blunt tool such as a spoon handle. Fold the crease against a hard straight edge, like a table.

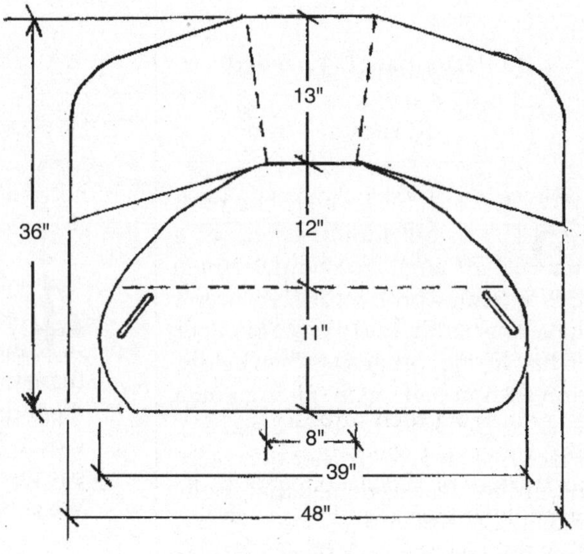

The "Cookit" foldable panel

This model has no glass cover, making it the simplest and cheapest oven we made, but was the least effective. (Many solar oven designs were developed for use in Third World countries where cooking fuel is scarce or unavailable, and where glass is probably hard to come by too. This one was reportedly widely used by refugees in Kenya, where they get more sun than we do in Wisconsin in April.) Cooking in boilable bags might work well with this unit, but we haven't tried that.

Technically, this is considered a cross between a solar oven and a curved concentrator. Ours measures 12 inches deep and 38 inches wide, with the back reflector being 13 inches high and the front one 11 inches.

The hay box:
The original slow cooker

W.R. Matthess
Real Time Systems Ltd.
N. Ireland

I was recently struck when reading *The War Time Kitchen Garden*, a BBC book, that during the Second World War the population of Britain needed detailed instructions from the Ministry of Agriculture and the Ministry of Food in order to survive the rationing then imposed. One of the things that was rationed was the amount of electricity one could use in cooking meals, and so the simple hay box cooker was recommended to the public.

Hay box cooking

During the Second World War the hay box came into its own. The Ministry of Fuel informed the British housewife that it took the burning of five pounds of coal to supply electricity to an oven for two hours. This same coal could be used to make 100 bullets!

In addition to fuel rationing, gas ovens were often difficult to cook on, as gas was cut off following air raids, or the pressure was just too low.

The hay box cooker had been used extensively during the First World War and many people turned to it again in WWII as a cheap form of cooking.

The general idea is that the box be very well insulated on all sides, top and bottom, and that the pot of food be boiling before putting it in. This is not an entirely unfamiliar idea these days as many people cook beans overnight in a vacuum flask. The hay box acts like a large vacuum flask by simply retaining the heat in the cooking pot so that the food can continue to cook slowly over a long period of time, usually about 10 hours or overnight.

Our boys love woodworking and were eager to get their hands on electric saws and the like, however having other things to do that morning I looked around in the shed for a ready-made wooden box. We found an old packing trunk with lid.

My source of information on hay box cookers then told me to line the box on all inside surfaces with four layers of newspaper, attached with a staple gun or drawing pins.

Next make a thick mattress of hay, any old material would do.

Then the pot must be placed in the middle. Any pot could be used, but it would need to be one which could be heated up to the boiling point, and with short handles to fit easily into the box.

It is essential that the pot be filled up to the top, excluding as much air space as possible. A Dutch oven would do well.

Hay could be packed in around the pot and another mattress stuffed with hay should be laid on top, at the same time making sure there are not cinders sticking to the underside of the pot that might set the hay on fire.

Not having a bag of clean hay available, I decided to line our trunk with some slabs of rigid insulation foam. We then poured in polystyrene packing chips all around the pot and on top, and lined the lid with the same rigid foam.

This worked very well, but I would caution that polystyrene chips are rather messy and must be completely removed after each pot is taken out, which is inconvenient. Our toddler was convinced that they were edible and we spent some time gathering them up from around the house.

After about 10 hours the dinner was cooked well, and the meat very tender. I brought it up to the boiling again in order to thicken the gravy (beef stew).

23 ways to save money (and increase quality)

RENEL HALL-BECK
SOUTH DAKOTA

Here are a few ideas to help you save your hard-earned dollar and probably increase quality in your life style.

Household:

1. Use homemade or simple ingredients to clean, such as bleach, ammonia, cleanser, vinegar and baking soda.
2. Use lemon to freshen the air, tone the skin, and mildly bleach surfaces or blonde hair.
3. Plant a garden.
4. Have a compost pile.
5. Recycle whenever possible.
6. Make your own soaps, shampoos, lotions, creams and facial cosmetics.
7. Buy an aloe vera plant. Use for homemade cosmetics and first aid uses.
8. Simple, good cleaning increases the value of items you sell and brings out hidden value of items purchased used.

Kitchen:

1. Buy bakeware at thrift stores or garage sales.
2. Make your own specialty items such as flavored oils, flavored vinegars or flavorings.
3. Bake your own bread or buy at a bakery thrift store. Bread is easily frozen and used when needed.
4. Buy in bulk whenever possible or join with a friend to buy large quantities together.
5. Can or freeze your garden's or summer's bounty of fruit and vegetables. Making your own jams, jellies and sauces can mean great savings.
6. Buy food as close to the source as possible. Buy directly from the farmer or a wholesaler.
7. If you don't raise your own animals for meat, purchase meat on the hoof from a farmer/rancher and have it butchered to order.
8. Make your own often-used items such as breakfast cereal, syrups, bread and spice blends.
9. Buy spices in bulk or mail order. Buy spices whole (they last longer) and grind, using a mortar and pestle, what you need.
10. Buy nuts whole and crack your own. Store them in the freezer to keep them fresh.

Gifts:

1. Plan for Christmas or gift-giving months in advance.
2. Give homemade items whenever possible.
3. Buy children's toys out of season and on sale.
4. Buy end rolls from a newspaper publisher/printer. Use this paper as wrapping paper. Decorate as necessary.
5. Use newspaper comic strips as wrapping paper for children's (or adult's) gifts.

Kitchen cosmetics

RENEL HALL-BECK
SOUTH DAKOTA

Do you know those cleansing and moisturizing lotions are really easy to make? It's as easy as following a recipe. Actually, creams and lotions are a simple mixture of oil, wax and water. The results you want, such as cleansing vs. body lotion, depend on the particular oils or their amount in the recipe.

Let's talk about the ingredients. The best wax to use is beeswax. Beeswax is a natural emulsifier (helps bind the ingredients together) that's full of nutrients for your skin. Use nut oils or a combination of oils, such as almond, grapeseed, or wheat germ. These oils have vitamins, which are good for your skin. Using herbal teas, flower waters, or essential oils can enhance nutrient properties. Please research what would be best for your skin type. Here are a couple of recipes to help you get started.

Basic Cleansing Cream

1/2 ounce beeswax
1 ounce lanolin
1 ounce distilled water
3-4 ounces almond oil
Pinch of borax

Put beeswax and lanolin in a heatproof bowl and melt slowly over warm water. Gently add oil and stir. Remove from heat. Slowly add water, stirring constantly until thickened. Stir in borax and put into sterilized jars and refrigerate. Use cream within a few weeks.

Rich Moisturizing Cream

1 tablespoon beeswax
2 tablespoons cocoa butter
3 tablespoons lanolin
1 tablespoon distilled water
5 tablespoons almond oil
5 drops essential oil
Pinch of borax

Put beeswax, cocoa butter, lanolin and oil in a heat-resistant bowl. Place bowl over simmering water and stir until the mixture melts. Remove the bowl from the pan and slowly add the water to the mixture, stirring constantly. Keep stirring while the cream begins to cool, then add the essential oil and borax. Stir until the cream has thickened and transfer it to sterilized jars. Keep refrigerated and use within a few weeks.

A last thing to remember: to make a cream firmer, add more beeswax; to make it softer, add more oil. Adding more water will make it lighter and fluffier. Always add a pinch of borax to help bind the ingredients together.

Have fun making your own lotions.

***

To extend the life of felt tip marking pens, store them with the tip down.

Country kitchen:

Liz's Garden Fresh Salsa

6-8 large, fresh tomatoes, chopped and divided
1-3 hot peppers, diced
4 large cloves of garlic, minced
2 large stalks of celery, diced
2 small cucumbers, diced
1-1/2 cups cooked beans (pinto, kidney, black, etc.)
1/2 bell pepper, finely diced
1/2 cup cilantro, chopped
1 lime or 2 tablespoons vinegar
1 teaspoon chili powder
1 tablespoon cumin
1/2 teaspoon salt
1 large onion, chopped

In a blender puree half the tomatoes with the hot peppers. Add 1/2 cup beans and puree with mixture. Pour into large container, then stir in remaining ingredients, seal and chill. Serve with chips, on tacos, omelets, home-fried potatoes...use your imagination. Very flexible recipe. Remember to adjust hot peppers according to your tolerance. Omit them if necessary. – *Elizabeth Van Cleve, California*

Spiced Watermelon Pickles

7 lbs. watermelon rind
3-1/2 lbs. sugar (7 cups)
1 pint vinegar (2 cups)
1/2 teaspoon oil of cloves
1/2 teaspoon oil of cinnamon

Peel rind and cube. Cover with hot water and boil until you can pierce with a fork. (Rind should be slightly transparent.) After rind is cooked, drain. Mix sugar, vinegar, oil of cloves and oil of cinnamon. Bring to boil to make syrup. Pour boiled syrup over well drained rind. Let stand overnight. The next morning drain syrup and reheat, pour over rind again and let stand overnight. On the third day reheat the rind and the syrup together. Pack in sterilized jars and seal. Makes about 4-5 pints depending on size of watermelon. 7 lbs. of rind is about 1 medium to large watermelon.

Zucchini Salsa

1-1/2 cup diced celery
4 cups grated zucchini
10 cups diced tomato
6-8 diced jalapeño peppers (optional)
3 small diced green peppers
2 large diced onions
1 tablespoon garlic powder
1 tablespoon sweet basil
2 teaspoons ground oregano
1/2 cup cider vinegar
1/4-1/2 cup Worcestershire sauce
2 teaspoons Morton's All Seasoning Salt (optional)
Later add: 2 cups tomato paste

Boil all ingredients except tomato paste 1/2 hour, stirring occasionally. Add 2 cups tomato paste and boil another 15 minutes. Hot pack in sterile jars. Makes 3 quarts. – *Mary Gibson, Montana*

Jerusalem Artichoke Pickles

1 gallon small artichokes
1 cup salt
1 gallon water
2-1/2 cups sugar
1 clove garlic
1 tablespoon turmeric
3 tablespoons mixed pickling spices
8 cups vinegar (5%)

Scrub, rinse and drain artichokes. Dissolve salt in water. Pour over artichokes. Let stand 18 hours. Rinse. Drain. Add sugar, garlic, turmeric and spices (in bag) to vinegar. Simmer 20 minutes. Pack artichokes into hot, sterilized jars. Heat syrup to boiling. Pour, boiling hot, over artichokes. Process 15 minutes in boiling water bath. Yield: 4 quarts.

Sourdough Bread

For those who bake bread regularly, sourdough has a special appeal. The starter is simple to make. The bread itself is less complicated, and requires less time.

Milk and flour starter: Mix a cup of milk with a cup of flour. If the milk is pasteurized, let it stand out for 24 hours beforehand. Place in a scalded crock or glass jar. Keep in a warm spot, covered with a towel.

"Leftovers" starter: Mix a cup or two of any two-day or older rice, cereal, fruit, vegetables or milk with two and one-half cups whole-wheat flour, and enough water to form a sponge. Stir daily for three or four days, until a distinctly sour smell arises.

Yeast starter: Dissolve a tablespoon of dried yeast granules or a cake of yeast in a cup of warm water. When the surface froths (about 10 minutes), gradually stir in two cups of whole grain flour and another cup of warm water. Beat thoroughly.

These starters will be ready to use in two to five days. Generally, the warmer the atmosphere is, the faster the yeast will work.

Ed Brown, author of *The Tassajara Bread Book,* offers this recipe for sourdough bread which makes four loaves. The same dough can also be the basis of sourdough English muffins, cinnamon rolls, or anything else you make with bread dough.

The night before:

Add two cups of starter to nine cups whole-wheat flour, without mixing. Then mix together while adding seven and one-half cups water a few cups at a time, until a thick pasty batter is formed. Beat well.

The next morning:

Remove two cups from sponge to replenish starter. Fold in one cup oil, two tablespoons salt, and 10-12 cups flour gradually. When dough comes easily away from bowl but is still a bit sticky, place on a floured bread board and knead for five minutes, adding more flour as necessary. Dough will be a little softer and stickier than normal yeasted bread. Cut into four sections and form into loaves. Place in oiled bread pans. Slit tops. After two hours rising in pans, brush tops with water and place in a preheated 425° F oven for 20 minutes. Brush tops with water again, turn oven down to 375° F, and continue baking for 60-90 minutes.

Spoon Bread

1 cup cornmeal (white or yellow)
1/2 teaspoon salt

2 tablespoons sugar
2 tablespoons bacon or other grease
Boiling water (about 1/2 cup)

Mix the first four ingredients in a bowl and add just enough boiling water to make the mixture workable. Mix it.

Spoon the mixture into hot grease in a skillet. Brown on both sides.

Serve hot, with butter.

This is good with soup, stew or any meat.

The 5 secrets of good homemade bread

1. Use the highest-quality ingredients you can get, especially flour.
2. Do not over-sweeten, especially with molasses. Let the taste of the grain come through.
3. Allow sufficient rising time to develop flavor and texture. Long, slow rising at fairly low temperatures is best.
4. Use at least some salt. It will improve the texture and bring out the flavor of the grain.
5. Go easy on the yeast. More yeast doesn't make a higher-rising bread, but it will make it rise too quickly. This might produce a coarse-textured bread that will go stale rapidly, and has an under-developed or perhaps an unpleasant yeasty flavor.

The 7 secrets of high-rising whole wheat bread

1. Use high quality, high gluten flour made from at least some hard wheat.
2. Use potato cooking water or whey, to feed the yeast.
3. Use a small amount of solid fat. Oil makes a heavier dough.
4. Go easy on the sweeteners: they require more yeast, and overpower the wheat flavor. You can use diastolic malt.
5. Knead vigorously.
6. Allow sufficient rising time. Use sponge method.
7. Use at least a little salt. Bread may fall and be course-textured without it.

Eggs make a lighter, airier loaf, but one which aslo stales more quickly.

Mayonnaise Biscuits

Mix:
1 cup self-rising flour
1/2 cup sweet milk
1/4 cup mayonnaise (can use salad dressing, regular, light or fat-free)

Drop into greased muffin tins. Bake 10 minutes at 400°F. Makes 8. – *Mary Williams, Illinois*

Mayonnaise Yeast Rolls

Dissolve 1 package dry yeast in 1 cup warm water

Mix with:
2 cups self-rising flour*
1 tablespoon mayonnaise
1 tablespoon sugar

Drop into greased muffin tins. Bake 25-30 minutes at 350°. Makes 1 dozen.

* Self-rising flour: 1 teaspoon baking powder to each 1 cup of flour.

Kielbasa

3 lbs. pre-frozen (or certified) pork butt, with fat, cubed
2 lbs. beef chuck, trimmed and cubed
1/2 cup ice water
1/4 cup nonfat dry milk
3 tablespoons salt
1 tablespoon sugar
1 tablespoon paprika
2 teaspoons fresh finely ground white pepper
1 tablespoon finely minced garlic
1/2 teaspoon ground marjoram
1/2 teaspoon ground thyme
1/2 teaspoon ground celery seed
1/2 teaspoon ground finely ground coriander
1/2 teaspoon nutmeg
1/4 teaspoon ascorbic acid or 1/2 teaspoon saltpeter
4 foot medium hog casings

Grind the pork through a coarse disk and the beef through a fine disk. Mix together with the other ingredients.

Stuff the casings and tie off into 8-10 inch links.

Cure in the refrigerator for 24 hours.

Smoke at 180°-190°F for two hours.

Bring a large kettle of water to 160°-170°F and simmer the sausage for half an hour.

Place the links in a kettle of cool water for half an hour, dry, and store refrigerated for up to two weeks.

Pickled Artichokes

10 lbs. small artichokes
2 large sliced onions
2 cups sugar
1/4 lb. mustard (1-1/2 cups)
4 tablespoons turmeric
4 tablespoons mixed pickling spices
1 cup salt
3 quarts vinegar

Scrub artichokes well, pack in jars with sliced onions. Mix sugar, mustard and turmeric together and add spices and salt. Dissolve well in vinegar, place in kettle and bring to boil. Pour, hot, over artichokes. Seal and process 10 minutes at simmering point in hot water bath. Yield: 4-5 quarts.

Fool-proof kraut

For foolproof kraut that cannot be distinguished from the old-timey crock kraut, and to make as many or as few quarts as wanted, here is my recipe:

Shred cabbage and pack tightly into quart jars up to 1/2" from top. Add 1 teaspoon canning salt and 1 teaspoon sugar. Pour boiling water over cabbage and up to the top of the jar. Remove air bubbles by taking a butter knife or spatula handle and gently go around inside of the jars. Screw the caps on loosely, but not tight. Place jars inside sink or pan where bubbling water won't make a mess. Ferment for 24 hours. Then remove the lids and add enough boiling water to fill the jars again to the top ½". Seal as tightly as you can with your hands. Then set in a sunny spot for three days (preferably outside).

Process quarts for 20 minutes in boiling water bath. Store for a minimum of three weeks before eating. – *Vicki Parrish, Oklahoma*

Learning to cook on a woodstove

Deborah Moore
Michigan

When my companion and I began our 18-month transition period of moving to and living in the woods, we also began a period of education. We discussed and planned much. We bought books and magazines and took classes on everything from solar collecting to gardening.

One subject evaded me: cooking on a wood-burning stove. Every time I saw a magazine that flashed headlines on wood stoves, my hands would tremble in anticipation as I reached for it. However, the wood stoves in question were for heating, not for cooking.

Since we were looking at a self-sufficient lifestyle and wood on our 160 acres was virtually free, there wasn't even a consideration to use anything but wood for heating and cooking. Our land is approximately 95 percent maple, a steady source of excellent quality hardwood. Labor intensive yes, but since we were quitting our jobs, we had the time.

Initially, we tried to find a real antique stove for our kitchen. Since the 20' by 24' kitchen/dining/living room was to be the main focus of our new house, we wanted the stove not only to be functional but attractive as well. The antique stoves we found were either attractive but of questionable functionality, or functional and downright ugly.

We bit the bullet and bought a brand-new, old-fashioned looking Enterprise King from Lehman's (if you ever have the chance to visit there, do it!). To this day, I'm glad we spent the extra money. Not that there aren't good old stoves out there, but we never found one.

Our stove has a warming oven overhead, a tip-down butter warmer, a washable porcelain clad oven with thermostat and an optional water jacket. The firebox has a side lifter lid and easily takes a 20-inch log. And it looks good.

But I still didn't know how to cook on it.

Being an experienced cook (translation: I love to cook), I figured I was tough. I was smart! I was inventive! I was lost. So I learned the hard way, by trial and error, lots of practice and even more patience. I've burned a few things, but only because I wasn't paying attention.

The functioning of the stove is really quite simple. They will last for generations with proper care, since there is so little that can go wrong with them.

One end has a firebox, and outside the firebox are vents. Mine has four "dials" which regulate how much air is fed to the fire. The more you open the vents, the hotter the fire. The ash door can also be opened for a surge of air, but this needs to be watched very carefully.

There is a sliding mechanism towards the back of the firebox. This diverts the smoke coming from the fire to go around the oven box before it escapes up the chimney. This heats the oven more consistently. The position of the slide unit is most important before lighting the stove.

Because a draft needs to be created when first firing up, the slide needs to be directed to the chimney. The positioning for my stove is to the right to light, to the left to bake. If you forget to reposition the slide, the result will be a roomful of smoke.

You can't set it at 350°F and walk away! The biggest challenge is keeping the oven heat even. Unlike a gas or electric stove, when you put something in the oven to cook and the temperature drops as the food absorbs the heat, nothing kicks in to compensate. What to do? Feed the fire wood that will burn quickly and offer more heat.

As the food begins to cook and its internal temperature rises, a longer, slower-burning piece of wood will maintain the heat. Open the oven door if it gets too hot—but not for long. Your oven may even have "hot spots" like mine. During baking, I turn bread or cookies 180 degrees halfway through the baking time. Stay in the kitchen when there is cooking to be done. In winter, it's the best place to be.

Range top cooking is similar to a gas or electric stove, but you have more room available. The entire surface is hot, not just four little burners. No, those circles are not burners, as I once thought.

The surface area can be divided into three major temperature zones. The hottest is right over the firebox, whether it is on the right or left. The next warmest would be in the center, and the coolest is the front of the side opposite the firebox. After the coffee perks over the firebox, it stays warm sitting on the far right corner.

Everything needs to be watched carefully, as the heat can drop or flare in a very short time. Don't be discouraged. Once you get used to the heat always being there (it doesn't shut off with the twist of a knob), cooking on a wood stove is easy.

Grilling takes some patience, but it can be done. You can get pretty good results by removing one of those little circles over the firebox and placing a heat-resistant grate over the flame. I use half of a hamburger basket meant for grilling. I also lay aluminum foil around the opening to keep splatters to a minimum. Since most barbecuing is done inches above hot coals, some adjustment is necessary. I let flames do the grilling rather than coals. Since the grate is so much further from the heat, I use a hotter fire.

The cleaning and care you give your woodstove is important. Most cook stoves have three types of surfaces. There is cast iron, porcelain or enamel-finished sheet metal and decorative trim. A wet rag or sponge wiped daily on the decorative trim should suffice. For baked-on spots, a bit of non-abrasive cleanser like Soft-Scrub works very well. Prevention is the best approach to cleaning. Avoid spilling or splashing, since you can't wipe it up right away.

Don't put a wet pot on the stove. Remember, the surface is cast iron and will rust, even when hot. The least of your cleaning worries will be the rust ring, but the worst will be the ring underneath the rust that is there forever. Spots that are left on too long will pit the cast iron. By first taking a razor blade to spills, you can scrape up lots of gunk and save your buffing pad and shoulder.

Scotch Brite Very Fine is a metal sanding pad that is unsurpassed for cleaning even the toughest spots on cast iron surfaces. Always buff back and forth in one direction, from front to back, or you will get a scratched look. Always let the surface cool before buffing, or you will melt the cleaning pad.

Once the entire surface has been buffed, use a soft flannel cloth and wipe a thin layer of cooking oil over the whole surface. This seasons the top and makes it easier to clean the next day.

A word of caution: The oil has to be spread thinly. I've used too much, and when I lit the stove the next morning, the kitchen smelled like cooking popcorn.

When necessary, you will need to wipe down the metal back splash and warming oven. Warm, soapy water or a non-abrasive cleanser will do the trick. Clean the soot from under the oven monthly in the summer and weekly in the winter when the stove is constantly running. There is a small opening concealed by a decorative nameplate directly under the oven. Use a long-handled scraper to remove the blackish soot and hardened chunks. It's best to do this when the stove is cool, or the draft will keep pulling the soot back in. Don't forget the sides of the ash compartment. Cinders don't always fall into the ash pan.

One of the most overlooked areas for cleaning is the top of the oven box. Remember, you keep diverting smoke around the oven. If enough ash collects there, it will have an insulating effect, and your oven won't heat properly.

A friend and neighbor (around here, a neighbor is anyone who lives less than 10 miles away) complained that her recently purchased antique stove was giving her fits when she tried to maintain a steady temperature. I didn't hear another complaint after making this suggestion.

The cooking surface is made up of two to four panels of cast iron. Remove these panels when the stove is cold and set them on newspapers, as they are sooty. This exposes the top of the oven box. The first time I did this was after a year of cooking, and I had over two inches of ash. Carefully brush this ash into the firebox, where it can fall into the ash pan. Do this too quickly and you'll raise an ash cloud.

Then take your long-handled scraper and scrape the sides of the oven box. Soot will fall to the bottom, where it can be removed through that little hidden door. The whole process should take about 15 minutes, and it will make a world of difference in your oven temperature. This cleaning should be done monthly or bimonthly in the summer and weekly in the winter.

The gasket around the top of the stove should be carefully inspected every year and replaced if it is too worn. I never concerned myself with the gasket. Two and a half years later, there was no gasket left! My stove had lost its air tightness, and I hadn't even noticed.

Most gasket packages I've seen include 84 inches of material, but my stove requires 100 inches. There is no loss of efficiency when material is pieced together. Just scrape the old stuff off, lightly sand, wipe off, glue and install the new gasket. This takes only 15 minutes and a few dollars, but what a difference it makes. It is always wise to keep a few gaskets in storage. You never know if they'll be available in a few years.

Cast iron pots and pans are nice, but certainly not necessary for wood stove cooking. Ceramic casserole dishes are great. Use common sense with pots that have plastic or wooden handles. Don't put anything into the oven that wouldn't go into a conventional oven, and don't position handles over the cooking area that you couldn't expose to a gas burner. Never put a plastic bowl on the stove, even if you think it's cold.

I purchased two pieces of cast iron cookware for $5 at an estate sale last summer. They were valued at over $80 new in a catalog. The old pieces cleaned up quickly and are among my favorites. One major advantage of cast iron is that it stays hot. That might not seem like a big deal until you serve a pot of stew or spaghetti on a cool evening.

Use the warming oven to your advantage. I keep four plates (two meals) and two soup bowls in my warmer. Having a pre-warmed plate at mealtime can make a big difference. I also have a biscuit stone (a terra cotta disk that is heated and put in the bottom of a basket of biscuits or rolls) that I rarely remember to heat up on time, so I just leave it in the bottom of the oven.

What I cook since we moved to the woods has changed, but that's because we've changed the way we eat. We eat less meat and more homegrown vegetables, more soups and bread. I now have the time to bake, and homemade, fresh-baked bread tastes like heaven. Soup is easy to simmer on the stove.

We have very little waste, because everything goes into a soup jar. This is something every cook can do. If you open a can of mushrooms, pour the juice into a jar and freeze it. After you cook vegetables, pour that liquid into the jar. I even save the liquid from soaking the roasting pan. To prevent overeating, put the last few mouthfuls of veggies, rice or potatoes in the soup jar. It makes for some very interesting, economical, healthy and work-free soup. For me, it's a conscientious thing to do, as I care about not wasting things.

Here in the Upper Peninsula, the weather is fairly cold all the time, so the stove is always running except in mid-summer. The first thing I do in the morning is light the stove. While the kindling is catching, I feed Muffin, our 15-year old cat. Then I add three or four pieces of wood, light the kerosene lamp, check the temperature outside and add larger logs to the fire. Now it's time to put the coffee pot over the fire box. Then it's back to the warmth of the bed. It takes about 20 minutes for the water to boil and another 20 minutes to perk. By the time the coffee is ready, the room is also warm.

I bake something almost every day. Since our refrigeration (an antique ice box) is limited, I bake only one loaf of bread at a time. Cookies and biscotti are favorites around here. Dinner is usually started around 4 P.M., and I let the fire go out. The coals are ready to be knocked down into the ash pan by 9:00.

Since I don't want to mess with all the details when it's cold in the morning, I lay a new fire, clear the stove top and fill the coffee pot at night. I'm ready for a new day.

Country kitchen:

Advice on safe canning

Elin Larson
Virginia

In a recent issue a reader wrote of the difficulties of keeping meat for the winter, and mentioned canning it. She said she wanted to buy the huge canner from Lehman's Hardware that covers two stove burners because it "would make the job go faster."

The huge canner from Lehman's is a water bath canner. It cannot be used for meats, starches, vegetables or any other low-acid food. It can be used safely only for high-acid fruits, pickles, relishes and high-sugar jams, jellies and preserves. All low-acid foods must go in a steam pressure canner at 240°F and at least 10 pounds of pressure (more at higher altitudes) on a gauge checked every year at the Agriculture Extension office.

There is no safe way to can meat or other low-acid foods in a water-bath canner. Never use a pressure saucepan, microwave canning, dishwater canning, or a water bath canner less than 13 inches deep. Most aluminum crab pots (20-quart size) or blue speckled enamel "canners" are too shallow.

Also avoid the widely distributed "steam canner" in which bottles are placed on a rack on top of a shallow pan full of boiling water covered with a deep domed lid whose edge is at the level of the bottoms of the jars and cooked in unpressurized steam. Some people call this method "steam canning," but it is really hot water vapor canning. It is not an adequate substitute for water bath canning or for steam pressure canning.

Don't use any of the weird methods like oven canning, putting an aspirin in each jar, or inverting freshly filled jars of hot preserves to kill the bacteria on the bottom of the lid. This last method breaks the seal you carefully made, and it isn't hot enough to kill the bacteria. However, it is hot enough to burn your hand.

Leave your jelly glasses upright and process them for the required time in a water bath canner. Pouring hot food into a waiting jar, putting the lid on and putting the jar away isn't recommended either. All home-canned foods must be prepared with a water bath or steam pressure canner as appropriate.

I don't recommend sealing jars with wax or using old-fashioned canning jars. Use two-piece metal lids with the rubber sealing ring glued onto the upper lid. Don't use zinc caps, two-piece glass lids or lightning-type glass jars. They're not safe.

Get your canning directions either from the latest edition of the *Ball Blue Book* or the USDA canning book which has been published by Dover Books. The canning advice in the homesteading classic *Stocking Up II* is getting out of date. For safety, use the Department of Agriculture's procedures. You may use other recipes, but get your canning times and methods from the USDA book.

Don't change or amend recipes unless you know what those changes will do to the processing method. For example, adding even a small amount of vegetables to canned tomatoes means you'll have to use a pressure canner. It's okay to can tomatoes in a water bath canner if you add two tablespoons of bottled lemon juice per quart. Don't use fresh lemon juice unless you know its acidity. Using more lemon juice of unknown acidity isn't good enough. If you can't use lemon juice of correct acidity, put your tomatoes in a pressure canner.

Lehman's water bath canner is excellent. It's a stainless steel rectangular box with handles, lid and rack. It costs $125, and it will hold 15 quart jars, more smaller jars, or 48 quarts of soup. It can be used on a wood stove or gas or electric range. This is an excellent utensil for canning large quantities of high-acid fruits and high-sugar preserves.

Lehman's and your local farm supply store sell good quality steam pressure canners. They are also available at some hardware and discount stores. Get the largest size available, which holds 22 quarts of soup or seven quarts of home-canned food. While half gallons of fruit juice are sometimes canned, that is too large a size for food, since the heat doesn't penetrate all the way to the middle, leaving some of the contents unsterilized. Some canning books list processing times for foods in half-gallon jars, but stick with quart or pint jars. Some dense foods such as pureed squash and pumpkin pie filling must be canned in small jars only.

Relishes and mixed vegetables without a high acid content must be canned in small jars, even in a steam pressure cooker. The old method of putting sliced cucumbers and spices in a jar, then pouring boiling vinegar, water and salt on them is no longer recommended.

You may still pack your pickles that way, but boil the pickles in a water bath canner for the required time after they are sealed.

Incidentally, a steam pressure canner can be used for water bath canning if it's deep enough. Thirteen inches is sufficient. Just don't pressurize it. The largest steam pressure canner now available will cover only one stove burner. Make sure that your canner(s) are used properly and are in good working order.

In my opinion, canners with the weight and the pressure gauge are better than the kind with the "rocker" weight that rattles to indicate the pressure and doesn't have a separate pressure gauge. I wasn't able to get a rocker weight canner to work properly, so I went back to the other kind.

Instead of buying new canners, I have been rehabbing old ones. Remember that Presto still has parts for even its 50-year-old canners, while other brands generally don't. I bought a Magic Seal canner from an old lady. This is the canner shown in the harvest kitchen drawing as well as *The Have More Plan.*

The Magic Seal is so old that it has wooden handles instead of bakelite, so I guess it was made in the 1920s or '30s. It was in excellent condition, but the gasket was old. A replacement was unavailable, but I went to an auto parts store and got a gasket making kit. It consists of a sheet of rubber material, a pattern for tracing the original gasket and instructions. Many older cars need gaskets that are no longer manufactured, so that's why I was able to find the kit in an auto parts store.

All pressure canners and cookers (except for a few modern ones with a precise metal-to-metal fit) need a gasket. A gasket can easily be replaced when it wears out. I worry that the gasketless seal on a modern aluminum canner will become scratched, bent or otherwise unusable and unrepairable.

My next steam pressure canner came from a junkyard for $10. The place had several acres of car parts and an acre of other things, including household items. It was an old Presto Model 7, made about 1940, with no weight and an aged gasket. I knew I could get parts for it. I bought a new gasket, pressure plug and weight for $22.97 at the local appliance store. After a good bath and repairs, the old machine is equal to a new $150 pressure canner. It will only take quarts and smaller jars, but half gallons aren't recommended anyway.

Feedback on baking powder

COUNTRYSIDE: In 82/5, you told T.F. from Hawaii that you couldn't help him stay out of the store for ingredients to make baking powder. Back in the '30s, many "poverty" housewives screened corn cob ashes from the cookstove and substituted it measure for measure for baking powder. I'm sure it isn't the quality of Calumet or Clabber Girl, but it does work after a fashion if nothing else is available.

Let's hope times don't get that bad again, but it doesn't hurt to have the knowledge just in case! Isn't that what COUNTRYSIDE is all about? Keep the information coming. – *Charles Turner, Iowa*

Baking powder

COUNTRYSIDE: The simple recipe for an aluminum-free baking powder calls for mixing two parts of cream of tartar with one part of baking soda and cornstarch in a medium to large bowl. Blend thoroughly before storing in an airtight container.

If you like, arrowroot may be substituted for cornstarch. – *B. Roop, North Dakota*

Everlasting yeast

COUNTRYSIDE: My code word is "a thrifty cook," because that is what I am. Here is my recipe for Everlasting Yeast:

1 quart warm potato water
1/2 yeast cake or 1/2 tablespoon dry yeast
1 teaspoon salt
2 tablespoons sugar
2 cups white or whole wheat flour

Stir all ingredients together. Place mixture in a warm place to rise until ready to mix for baking. Leave a small amount of everlasting yeast for a starter next time.

Keep covered in the refrigerator until several hours before it is to be used.

Add the same ingredients except yeast to the everlasting yeast starter for the next baking. By keeping the everlasting yeast starter around and remaking it each time, yeast can be kept on hand indefinitely. – *Judy Way, Wisconsin*

Potato yeast

COUNTRYSIDE: In reference to your yeast making in 82/5, I believe the "seed" you're referring to is hops. (Ed. note: No, the seed referred to is airborne yeast that multiplies.) My husband says his mother used hops in making her own yeast.

He didn't remember what all the ingredients were, but she did use cornmeal and flour and made it into somewhat of a cornbread. It was then dried, cut in squares and stored in an empty oatmeal box with a lid for future bread making.

The following is a recipe given to me by my husband's aunt. She has been deceased for several years, so I can't get any more information on it.

Yeast starter

4 large mealy potatoes
2 quarts cold water
1 cup loose dry hops
2 tablespoons white sugar
4 tablespoons flour
1 yeast cake dissolved in 1/4 cup warm water

Tie hops in a piece of coarse muslin. Place in kettle with potatoes and water. Cook until potatoes fall apart when pureed with a fork. Remove potatoes and simmer slowly. Mash potatoes and work in sugar. When smooth, add three tablespoons of boiling hop tea. Stir in one tablespoon of flour. Repeat four times, beating and stirring each time to remove lumps.

Stir in the rest of the tea and squeeze the bag. Strain liquid into a bowl and let cool to lukewarm. Stir in dissolved yeast, cover and set aside to "work." When it ceases to sing, hiss and bubble, the fermentation is complete. This will take four to five hours in hot weather, about seven hours in cold weather.

Pour into jars and seal. Keep in a cool place. Open only when needed and shake well each time. Will keep one month in refrigerator. Half a cup of starter will make three loaves of bread with 10 to 12 cups of flour.

We purchased some hop seed from Gurney's. This is a vine, and the hops resemble Chinese lantern flowers. We grew them, but when we decided to move the hops to a different location, we lost them.

I haven't tried the recipe yet, but Aunt Emma was a great cook, and I have no reason to doubt that it will work. Too many skills have become a lost art. I feel that we should keep as many skills as possible. – *Evelyn Eickmeyer, Illinois*

Favorite recipes from Florida

Naomi Livingston
Florida

Green tomato mincemeat

3 pounds chopped green tomatoes
3 pounds apples
2 pounds raisins
8 cups brown sugar
1 tablespoon salt
1 cup suet, chopped
1 cup vinegar
2 tablespoons cinnamon
2 tablespoons cloves
1 teaspoon nutmeg

Chop and drain tomatoes. Measure the liquid and discard it. Add an equal amount of water to pulp. Scald and drain again. Repeat this twice, adding fresh water each time. Add rest, cook until thick. Seal in jars.

Mincemeat cookies

1/2 cup shortening
1-1/2 cups sugar
3 well-beaten eggs
3 cups flour
3/4 teaspoon salt
1 teaspoon soda
1 cup canned mincemeat or one 9 ounce package with 3 tablespoons of water

Drop on greased cookie sheet, bake at 350°F for 10 to 15 minutes. Makes four dozen.

Switchel

During the Depression, my mother made switchel and haymaker's switchel:

1 gallon water
2-1/2 cups sugar
1 cup dark molasses
1/2 cup apple cider vinegar
2 teaspoons ground ginger

Haymaker's switchel

2 quarts water
1 cup brown sugar
3/4 cup vinegar
1/2 teaspoon ginger
1/2 cup molasses
Mix and refrigerate.

Corn and potato chowder

2 tablespoons butter
1 cup chopped onion
Cook until tender
Add:
2 cups diced potatoes
2 cups water
1/2 teaspoon salt
1/4 teaspoon pepper
2 cups fresh or canned corn
1 13-ounce can evaporated milk
Paprika
1/2 cup cooked ham, chopped
Mix together and stir in at end:
1/4 cup flour
1/2 cup water

Clam soup for a crowd

1/2 pound margarine
3 pounds onions
1 bunch celery
5 pounds potatoes
2 to 2-1/2 cans tomatoes
1 large can V-8 juice
1 bottle French dressing
Salt and pepper to taste
8 dozen minced clams with juice

Add enough water to margarine, onions, celery and potatoes so they will not burn. Add tomatoes, V-8, French dressing, salt and pepper; simmer. Add clams and simmer. Add clam juice and simmer.

Potato pancakes

5 tablespoons flour
1-1/2 pounds raw white potatoes, peeled and grated
1 small onion, peeled and grated
1 egg, unbeaten
1 tablespoon salt
1/8 teaspoon pepper

Mix all ingredients. Lightly grease medium skillet. Drop heaping tablespoons of mixture onto hot skillet. Drain on brown paper, serve with applesauce. Goes well with pot roast or other main dishes.

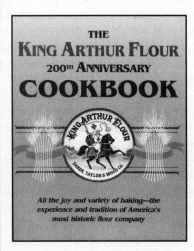

Guest editorial:

The Alpha Strategy revisited

Now that the years of irrational exuberance are behind us, some old but rational ideas might come in handy

THE INTENTIONAL PEASANT
MARYLAND

At a family get-together some years ago an in-law, the wife of a locally-well-known attorney, was amused to learn that, peasant-like, we stockpile durable things that will be needed when the world goes sour and the nation goes belly-up. That's when, not if.

Well, from her standpoint, it probably does look a bit cockamamie. Her husband being in that magical top-five-percent income stratum, she hasn't likely missed a meal except for perhaps a flat tire 10 miles from the nearest cassoulet au vin.

Another lady, a goddaughter approaching 40, was complaining good-naturedly about her mother's "cheesy" propensity for washing out plastic baggies. When she elicited stony stares from the assembled codgers and codgettes, she gasped, hand to mouth, "Oh, no, not you too?" One and all, we nodded silently.

Perhaps it's simply that we came from that "second generation" who, following the profligate first, have generated a profligate third. Or maybe those we love and respect never tire of telling us of how it was in the 'thirties—with a third of a nation out of work, out of money, and with their navels heading for their backbones. Anyway, to us waste seems irresponsible, devoid of empathy for Mother Earth, and not just a little bit tacky.

Even so, there are other compelling reasons for saving, preserving, and putting by. John Pugsley described many of them in his 1980 book, *The Alpha Strategy*.

Simply put, Pugsley advocated saving durable things rather than money, as a hedge against inflation, deflation, and civil unrest. Anyone with a pencil or a long memory knows that the "interest" on savings, after being taxed relentlessly by the IRS, has not kept pace with inflation. While we paid a tax on our phantom increase, we were ending up with less spending power. Oh, the numbers might look fancy, but the actual buying power of those dollar numbers was disheartening.

Where one had the ability, Pugsley argued, it was far better to save things one was sure to need down the road a piece, which would increase in dollar-value and not be subject to income taxes.

But the *Alpha Strategy* is also good medicine in a deflation. While the price of stuff—in real terms—may go down, the price tag's dollar numbers aren't likely to show much decrease. This is because we have been generating too much money, creating the weird situation where you have a genuine deflation, probably the mother of all depressions, and rising prices. More importantly, we may not have many dollars in our pockets to spend, after the music stops.

Now, this author was not directing the *Alpha Strategy* at peasants, at least not primarily. In the higher plateau of his plan, one saved copper sheet goods and tin ingots. But the lower rungs suited us, personally, very well in 1980, because we were, and still are, stranded by circumstances in a large city not known for peace, quiet, and brotherly love on any significant scale. Those are rural virtues. So a plan that could make us independent of public systems—long enough for the cavalry to arrive—seemed very attractive.

As Pugsley suggested, we saved any durable items we thought we'd need: paper goods, for example, stashed under the eaves. We don't discard clothes or linens promiscuously, either. In a disaster, our linen closet would bed down Cleveland.

Well, Grover at least.

In the food line, we freeze some and can a lot—especially our own tomato paste for pasta sauce. We were going to get out of this tomato growing hassle, so we laid in some commercial sauce, the expensive kind sold in its own Mason jar. Ugh! It was such a jolt, we decided we'd go back to growing our own, hassle or not.

We will sometimes pick up an extra box of sugar cubes for the larder. Granulated sugar turns to five pound bricks in captivity, but one might try storing quarter cups of it for baking—all pre-measured and ready for the recipe.

Food, paper goods, and household products need careful thinking. We buy an awful lot of canned goods on sale and with coupons. We don't eat most of this ourselves, but make it part of our tithe and put it in the poor collection at church on Sunday.

We prefer to make our own "convenience food" and freeze it. The jocular reference to cassoulet above aside, we make our own, put it into dessert cups, and freeze it. Things like that.

Rotation is critical. There's nothing quite like coming upon a cache of 1979 soup on a back shelf of your larder.

As recounted here before, we buy whole grains—wheat, barley, and whatnot—and store them in glass wine gallons as recommended by Wild Bill Kaysing in his many books. Alternatively, we could buy nitrogen-packed grains from one of the many suppliers such as Happy Hovel.

Our library holds many how-to, do-it-yourself, and formula books. We accumulated many hand tools and laid in boxes of nails, those wonderful square drive screws (the ones with the machined threads), and other fasteners of almost every description. Should the power fail, there's an electric generator to work the sump pump and keep the freezer healthy. That's just the nose of the alligator, but you get the idea.

Being here where a water well is illegal, I distill water and rotate 30 glass gallon jugs of it. Carmela drinks what comes out of the tap, having a weakness for fluoride and chlorine cocktails. Since this peasant knows what fluoride does to enzymes, he figures that his Cipro antibiotic gives him all the trouble he needs.

The only large undertaking we might consider in these late years is installation of a coal-burning Petit Godin in the basement. For us, anthracite would be easier to stash than wood.

Having lived with this gradually increasing system for almost two decades, it seems to have done pretty well for us. We have, as one might expect, fouled up on occasion, but it is gratifying to happen upon a box of Kleenex bearing a price tag of thirty-nine cents when the current gouge is ninety-eight.

Even so, the psychological aspect of saving goods does take its toll. Carmela is used to thinking of wealth as money, of which we have little to none. This is despite her father's experience of retiring "set for life" with a $10,000 annuity he started during the heyday of advertisements which went, "How I retired to Florida with an income of $40 a month."

When she totes up where we are in the great dollar race, the result is acute depression. That's because we have come so far from Webster's definition of wealth as the total contents of our physical estate, not the number of little slips of green-printed paper secreted under the liner of our undies drawer.

But thoughtful souls have only to consider the Hamburger Law to put their heads back on straight. In 1942 15 cents bought two Little Tavern (or White Castle) hamburgers and a hefty glass bottle of Coke, quite a filling lunch. Almost everything is reducible to the peasant's Hamburger Law which decrees that fiat currency is always, in the fullness of time, reduced to the level of bathroom tissue, no matter how regally printed and impressively sealed. The Alpha Strategy is our attempt to escape the ravages of the Hamburger Law—which is why this peasant is now going to raid the freezer and broil up his own homemade convenience food from the stash: a handmade hamburger.

How to get started without a fortune

It requires great desire

Richard Brock
Wyoming

I think the first thing that anyone considering a move to or creating a homestead should do is take a look at why you want to make the move. What do you expect once you get there? What are you willing to give up to get there and to stay there?

I think most of us have a desire to be self-sufficient. To have a simpler non-complicated life. A life with fewer, or even better, no bills.

I started off wanting to live like they did 100 years ago. Yeah, right. I also wanted tv, the computer, etc. Here's where my problems started.

We got real lucky. We found 108 acres 22 miles north of Rawlins, Wyoming for no down and low payments. This is not the best property in the world but with a lot of work it can be made into something. Rawlins is a town of about 9,000 people. There are jobs here but the pay is not real good. So, when we moved here from Illinois we started our own little business.

Once we got here we looked at our property. It wasn't bad. Good access, nice views, but it was still desert property. This is a very windy area, great wind power. I could find positive in all negatives. We found a little house we could rent for $150. Pretty good. We will save a lot of money so we can move out to the property sooner.

We got the business going and did pretty well the first year. We didn't save any money but we were still happy to be here.

The second year things went downhill. We ended up with a lot more bills than we started with. The only good thing that happened was that we found a small, older mobile home for $2,400 and the lady was nice enough to carry a note for us. No down and payments of only $100 a month. We even got someone to move the mobile home to our land for free. Great.

I bet you think we are out there right now, huh? This is where things don't even make sense to me.

Somehow I decided that we would just use the property as a weekend getaway until we got a few things. You know, things that you really can't do without. A windmill, a big generator, a mini dish for tv, etc.

So how do we get all of these things that I thought that I wanted to get away from so bad? Well, my wife got a job as an assistant manager at an apartment complex. We had to move to the complex for the job. The rent was reduced to $325 per month for us. Oh, that helps. We still have our own little business that I work full time, plus we both clean carpets in our free time. So, we are getting closer to moving, right? Wrong.

Something always happens to put bumps in our path. We probably let things happen, but they do happen. This is how things should have gone. As soon as we got the mobile home out on the property we should have moved there. We would have saved a lot of money and we could have had a lot of things that we wanted by now.

So why am I telling you all this? All you wanted to know was how to get the property or farm you want without being rich!

Well, the land is out there. What you have to decide is how bad you want your dream. As for me I have learned that I didn't want it as badly as I thought I did.

I always thought I knew that the whole idea behind being self-reliant was to change your whole life. I guess I thought you could pick and choose what you wanted to change. I believe that on a whole we are very spoiled people. What were once considered luxuries are now considered the basics.

If we haul water for a while, put in an outhouse, simplify our ideas a little, we could move out there right now, right this very minute. Will we? Probably not. Is it because we are low income people or because we want more things out there before we go? I am learning that it is pretty simple why we are not there yet. We don't want it bad enough.

In the back of this magazine there is a real estate section. Look at it. Call or write those people (and tell them you saw their ad in Countryside) and find out what they have. Go to the library. You can find books on building anything. Remember, people lived for a long time without electricity. I wonder how they did it.

If you have the desire, a real desire, you can do it. You can have your homestead. More than likely if you are paying rent you can buy some land somewhere. You may have to build on it or do a lot of improvements. You may not have utilities, but I'm telling you that it is there. I found it, you can too.

Knowing what to do with it after you find it is the hard part.

Note: Richard Brock called the other day to let us know that recent issues of Countryside have inspired him. They have decided to move onto their land—now.

For them, it was a 15-year journey

Jeff & Annie Kusilek
Wisconsin

As usual I really enjoyed my latest Countryside (81/4) especially the article about Coco the guard llama. I also liked Sandra Gratton's article about their search for their "right" place. I think they set an excellent example for all who are looking for their own little piece of heaven. They showed perseverance, determination, self-discipline and the willingness to re-think their priorities—all qualities any homesteader needs to have. I think they will succeed in their new venture.

I sympathize with your Ohio reader who is getting discouraged in her dream to have a homestead of her own but can't seem to save anything to get started. My husband and I went through a long period (15 years) to get where we are now. (And there are those who feel we've moved down the scale—maybe they have a different scale?)

For the first four years of our marriage we rented homes, but during this time we scrupulously paid our bills and made loan payments on time and whenever possible paid off loans early. This gave us an excellent local credit rating.

Our first home was financed by Farmers Home Administration which gave us very low mortgage payments because of our large family (five children). After three years living in this small home in town, we began looking for a hobby farm. Like the Gratton's, we ended up taking one of the first properties we looked at. It was a small former dairy farm. Originally we saw it through the listed Realtor, but the price was very high, considering the condition the property was in. We talked to the lenders that were carrying the liens against it and were given to believe that foreclosure proceedings were in the near future.

Sure enough, within six months the farm was auctioned off on the courthouse steps. (Literally. They really did hold the auction on the steps of the courthouse!) Jeff went and bought 198 acres for $60,000. He had to write a 10% down payment—which our bank was happy to cover (all those early payments, you know). Because the farm was assessed at over twice what we paid for it and had CRP payments of over $8,000, Farm Credit Services financed us for $75,000 ($60,000 for the farm plus $15,000 to begin fixing up the house.) At this time, Jeff was working full time as a welder at about $12 per hour and I was (and am) a full-time mom.

We spent three years renovating the house and goofing around with some chickens, calves and pigs and, of course a garden. Then we decided to sell the farm and milk cows. We couldn't stay and milk because it was too costly to put the milking system back in the barn and buy the cows, too.

We sold the place and invested the profits in a herd of Jersey cows. Because we owned our cows with no debt we were able to purchase a small dairy farm for $60,000 and nothing down (the cows were secured as the down payment). Here again, our past credit history stood us in good stead. We also were very fortunate to find a small locally-owned and controlled bank with a free-thinking loan officer and no approval board. At this time, our mortgage payments were $250 per month—less than the rent for a small house in our area. We had a huge 20-year-old house, a dairy barn and a large pole-type machine shed, all on 145 acres. We then sold off 40 acres to another couple who wanted to hobby farm, for $15,000 (our debt went down to $45,000) and later sold the same fellow another 40 acres for the same price (our debt now $30,000.)

Stray voltage forced us to stop dairying and later fire took the barn (the insurance money took care of some personal debts: auto loan and feed loans) but we were a little upset as we had planned to try milking again when the stray voltage problem was corrected.

Since we couldn't milk at this location anymore we began really looking to get debt-free somehow. We had taken some of the insurance money from the fire and purchased an abandoned school on a two acre lot with a view to salvaging the usable lumber from the school and re-selling the lot. Now we began thinking about building there instead. So we listed the building site and 25 acres for sale. We set our price to cover our debt plus give us a good start on our new house plus some "dickering" room. We sold in three weeks to a couple who came in with exactly what our bottom line was. (No debt now plus we still owned 40 acres in addition to the two acre lot.)

We built a log home with poplar logs cut locally and sawn out by a neighbor with a portable bandsaw. We invested in new, energy efficient windows and put in very good insulation. The house sits on cedar piers (concrete work is expensive) with a four foot crawl space formed by treated plywood walls and with a silo tarp floor (heavy black plastic) to prevent too much humidity from rising into the crawl space. There was an existing well and septic system from the school and we are on the grid for now.

Our house is two and one half stories. Main level includes an entry porch and laundry room, a great room, and a full bath. The second level is a "bunkhouse" with six bunks for our daughters, a small open area that serves as a school room and will have a loft over for our son, and a sewing room with dressing area with a sleeping loft above for Jeff and me. The lower level is log construction but the second story is stud walls with boards and battens inside and out.

We chose the framing-over-log method because we had lots of sawn lumber after trimming our logs to size and because it was getting very hard to set the logs in place after we got eight or nine feet in the air. We have lots to finish still—siding, a small utility shed, wiring, miscellaneous trim and doors, etc.... but after one year we have a home that we are very happy with.

Last week we were able to trade some labor to get a garage moved to our lot. The garage will provide shelter for our three mares and a small tack/feed room. The building itself was free—the lot it was on had been condemned and we could have it if we had it moved before the bulldozers came.

We are now mortgage-free and the only loan we have is $400 left to pay off a pickup. Last summer we sold the last 40 acre parcel we owned to allow us to purchase another large van and to get some winterizing done on our house. Our total cost in our place here has been about $45,000 now, all paid in cash. Our banker tells us that our credit is still good with them and that they would be glad to work with us at any time (even though we have run into some tough times in the last years and did make some late payments. However, we have also paid ahead and are still on schedule to pay off our one remaining loan on time.)

I know that our situation is unique, as is everyone's, and obviously these circumstances aren't going to arise very often, but these are some things that I think many people can try to do to put themselves ahead of the game.

1) Keep your credit rating good—no credit cards, pay on time, pay off early. Talk to your creditors before they get worried over your late payment. We've found ours to be very understanding as long as they are aware of the situation.

2) Invest your time and labor helping others. We have traded for building stuff, meat, milk, eggs and a computer printer among others. We haven't always got cash, but we can often make time.

3) Set your goals, dream and plan and be ready to act when the time comes.

4) Think creatively. We had struggled to live conventionally on my husband's fairly good income and we continue to struggle on much less, yet by thinking of unusual solutions we seem to be able to get those things which are most important to us. For instance, a railing system for our stairs could have cost upwards of $1,000 if purchased at a lumber yard, but we happen to like our peeled log railing just as much and it didn't cost us more than $5.00—the cost of some screws, electricity, and gas for the chain saw.

5) Remember that every penny spent—whether at a garage sale, a thrift store or at Tiffany's—is still spent—it's not coming back. Avoid the temptation to buy something simply because it's a good buy. I really do think that this is the single biggest problem most of us have. We did it just this spring: we bought a riding lawn mower for $5—great buy right? Wrong! No motor and a new one is going to cost about $200—which we do not have. So it's just $5 gone. But maybe we can sell the tires... or maybe not. Don't rationalize a purchase. If you have to justify it, you don't need it! I have to stay away from thrift sales, auctions, and discount stores because I just don't always have the will power I need not to buy.

It's a process

Debra Davis
Illinois

I absolutely must respond to the July/August Question of the Month, how to get started. This is a question we asked ourselves two years ago. The answer is, I think, very much related to the question of "what is a homesteader" and has more to do with the process than with a finished product. Let me share our story.

We never set out to become homesteaders, really. Although my husband and I both grew up in small rural communities, we met and married near Chicago and spent our first eight years in city apartments. Homesteading? Hardly...but there was the annual trek to a strawberry patch and jam made on our apartment stove. We tried starting seedlings on the radiator cover and coaxed tomatoes and beans from the urban soil behind our building. One year we rented a 10' x 4' garden plot in a neighborhood park and grew mammoth zucchini to the delight and amazement of our three children.

No, we weren't looking for a "homestead," but we did want a bit more space to garden, so our next step was to get a very small house in a very small town, for very little money (a first-time buyer's program) far enough from the city to be affordable. This meant a 45-minute drive for my husband but we felt the tradeoff was worth it, so we spent seven years there, growing a large garden, learning to can and freeze, and acquiring every kind of handyman skill that our little fixer-upper called for. And adding three more children!

Then we came across Gene Logsdon's *Contrary Farmer* and we knew that we were homesteaders at heart. Now, how to find land? The search began in earnest.

How far from his job would we have to go in order to find acreage we could afford? Too far. Another job change, this time to a small metropolitan area. We drew circles on maps and contacted every Realtor within a hundred-mile radius of the job. We spent weekends and evenings looking at countless farms.

After two years of searching, and selling our little house, we finally found it—an 1888 farmhouse on five acres, with barns, in good shape. The long commute for my husband is not ideal, but like the rest of our "homestead in progress" we hope it may change someday. For now it is the price we must pay to live on five acres, to raise chickens, pigs, calves and maybe turkeys this year—to give our children plenty of good hard work to do and the satisfaction of raising our own

She's a money basher

K. O'Brien
Wisconsin

I am an unashamed money basher. It is not money itself that I bash, but the attitude that money creates. To me it represents a false security of the ability to buy happiness, health, comfort, and a better, easier life.

My family takes the attitude that the best things in life are free. We use money to provide the necessities of living. We gave up the dangling carrot approach to living and stopped chasing those greenbacks to concentrate on being together as a family, the powers of nature, the pleasures of the garden, and the satisfaction of basic survival. Our homestead grows slowly as we do it ourselves by having long range goals to work towards. If success is measured in dollars we lose the race.

Many people own recreational vehicles valued at more than what our two meager acres cost. Many people also travel to areas like ours for their vacations, leaving the city for two weeks of rest and relaxation. We live on a year-round camping trip full of adventures, challenges, learning experiences, beauty and fun.

I have found the unwealthy person to be much more generous than the wealthy in proportion to their total value. Sure it's great to feed off the scraps of the rich because they are always tossing out used items for the new, improved, better whatever it is. And that tossed out whatever was probably hardly used anyway. It is garbage to the giver, a veiled generosity to the receiver.

When a family has three chickens and gives me one, that is the caring generosity of friendship that sustains. When I needed $250 for an unexpected circumstance a friend with thousands offered me a loan at 10% for 90 days. Another friend who didn't have very much demanded that I take the money and pay it back when I could. It was paid back within the month, with respect and many favors to follow.

I am also likely to find a non-materialistic friend to spend time with when everyone else is too busy working, commuting, or eating out to have any time left to spend leisurely with friends.

Both my partner and I do work part time to earn the essential money for supporting our two kids and home. He has to travel to the city two hours away for a week at a time about 16 times a year to earn under $10,000 a year. He is a scenic artist in the theatre and has found a way to keep doing what he loves to do without being totally immersed in the constant city squabbles of day-to-day life. He packs his own food and spends his free time shopping at second-hand stores and outlets to bring home bounties of gifts. He has managed to use the best of both worlds to his advantage, and ours. Sometimes the breaks are very welcome, sometimes they are hard, but his travels remind both of us of how lucky we are in our rural paradise.

I am a college graduate with 12 years' experience in the theatre. I started giving that up when I started having kids. Now I work for $6 an hour at a local greenhouse and on an organic farm. I am a hard worker for $6 an hour, but I am getting so much more than money in the process. I am supporting a form of agriculture I believe in; I am constantly learning and teaching my kids about gardening, eating and nature; I can grow a glorious bounty of vegetables and flowers to enjoy all year round; I am healthy and in good shape from the exercise of work and good eating habits; and I enjoy watching my labors grow.

To be in the middle of a field under a huge sky of bouncing clouds, surrounded by lush, earthy smells, watching bald eagles, cranes, herons and ducks flying overhead, to hear all the birdsongs echoing through the trees up the ridge, and to feel the creek rushing cold over my sweating skin, to work as a team to harvest beauty from the Earth—this is the life I have chosen, and I love each season on a day-to-day basis.

There is no secret to success for homesteading. It takes goal setting, planning, and will. If you want to do something bad enough you will find a way to do it. If obstacles keep cropping up maybe your desire isn't strong enough. You either work at it one step at a time or you dive off of the cliff to sink or swim. (If you sink you will probably come out of it as an experienced swimmer the next dive in.)

Just don't think that big bucks will buy you a happy homestead life. It's a drive within yourself and a desire to sustain the Earth that creates a homesteader. The move is not a question of how will I make money in the country, but how will I make a living?

We started looking at 20-acre farmettes and ended up with two acres and a trailer. It's what we could afford. Sometimes it drives me crazy to be living in a tin can, but we are doing what we want to do now. If we had waited to amass enough cash to buy a dream farm we would still be in the city chasing money. Instead we are living with chickens, rabbits, cats, dogs and wildlife and are beginning to build our own home. If we were in the city we wouldn't be together as a family and we would be watching our children grow up viewing the world from a much different angle.

But even as a money basher, if money rained down on us, I would collect it and hope I would put it to good use. I just don't want to be chasing it. I do know that without it I have more respect for money because I must be very conscious of how I spend it. I know I would not be as self-reliant if I had a lot of money. My attitude towards it would gradually change. The accumulation of money would cause a need of more money as the standards are upgraded. And the cycle begins and before we are aware of it the pursuit of money has usurped the pursuit of happiness.

There are many different kinds of poverty and wealth. We have chosen to be economically disadvantaged. We live off of what we can make, not trying to make enough money to live by marketing standards. We are very happy doing what we are doing. There is no price tag that can measure our life beyond the sidewalks.

Start small, and grow into it

Douglas A. Kalmer
Tennessee

Long before I became old enough to have a say in the direction my life would take, I knew I loved the natural world of plants and animals, hills and streams of my boyhood. Machinery also fascinated me, but after two years of tech school and several years in the repair business all I knew was what I did not want to do—spend the majority of my waking life repairing an endless stream of broken machinery.

But how to integrate the two? How to free myself from 45 years of economic servitude so I could afford an overpriced, inefficient house, supporting bankers and builders with one-third of my income for 30 years, keeping myself in food from giant agribiz, making those monthly payments for energy, electricity, gas, gasoline, taxes, etc.?

Then a friend gave me a subscription to *The Mother Earth News* (this was the early '70s.) A whole new concept began to develop in my mind: Homesteading—I could build my own home, grow my own food, provide most of my energy needs!

My whole life has been pointing in this direction. I am a generalist, interested in many things, not a specialist the modern world demands. I cherish my personal freedom, never fit comfortably in the nine-to-five grind. I felt I could take care of my needs in a more direct manner, more efficiently than corporate America could.

But, I was stuck in the city—in debt, nine-to-five, no yard and constant noise of traffic and neighbors. I read everything I could about homesteading, gardening, building, solar energy and began to do whatever I could—grow a few tomato plants, build shelves, a table, a greenhouse. Learn, read and do.

Instead of paying rent I bought a run-down house on a city lot and spent years fixing it up, learning carpentry and plumbing, wiring and sheet rocking. I still worked nine-to-five and did extra repair work after hours, working late nights on the house.

This was a sort of "forced savings" plan where I just bought materials as I could afford them and added my sweat equity over the years.

Selling the city property and buying 34 acres and a trailer in a rural location in the southeast gave me no mortgage, no rent, a long growing season and mild winters—all homestead friendly. We built a solar home, started several businesses, got chickens, ducks, goats, cows, tractors and trucks—not all at once of course.

I used the library to learn whatever I needed to know, at least as far as a book can teach. Then you need to go out and just do it!

I should mention that *Mother Earth News* introduced me to the writings of Helen and Scott Nearing, best known for their book *Living The Good Life.* I used many ideas from the Nearings. One I consider important is their '"childfree" choice. This frees much time and energy and money to put toward achieving your homestead dream, not to mention helping an overcrowded world.

The key would be—start small and grow into it!

Good luck and have fun. We are!

Mrs. Mildred Culver's mother, father and oldest sister, on their homestead in White Butte, South Dakota in 1911.

Mildred Culver sent this photo and some information about her family. Her father (Carl Pickler, Sr.) was born in Austria. He met her mother in America and they lived in Wisconsin before moving on to homestead land in South Dakota with one child. After a series of setbacks and five more children, they moved to Washington.

Among her memories of the old homestead... the singing of the meadowlarks, the swimming hole where she learned to swim by watching the frogs... and their half-coyote dog, "Fanny."

Mrs. Culver lives in California.

Analyzing your BUDGET

What to do when there's too much month left at the end of your money

As we have seen in many recent articles, some people, regardless of income, have a great deal of trouble managing their money, while others seem to do it with ease.

The problem boils down to one simple and logical fact: You can't spend more than you take in. (Going into debt doesn't increase your net worth.)

Limiting spending to less than income requires a budget. A budget is nothing but a systematic plan for the expenditure of a usually fixed resource, such as money or time, during a given period.

Some people (usually frugal ones) can allocate their money intuitively, or at least unconsciously, or out of long habit. Others need to track their expenditures more carefully. And still others need to examine their current spending patterns in detail, analyze them, and use the results to develop better standards or habits.

We asked several readers in the latter category to share their personal financial figures with us. These are people who say they want to own their own homesteads, free and clear, but can't seem to get off the treadmill of earning and spending.

The information they provided was analyzed by experienced financial counsellors, who suggested possible courses of action.

Everyone concerned hopes that these examples will help others in similar situations by demonstrating how budgeting and budget analysis works and how it can be used to improve your life.

This is a report prepared for someone we'll call "Tami," who provided the figures on the next page. The counselor also spoke with her to gain additional information and insights. Both prefer to remain anonymous.

Your basic problem is you are spending more than your in-come. Easy to say, but not so easy to remedy.

I will try to go through my recommendations item by item and explain my reasons. Of course, only you and your husband can decide if it will work for you.

Housing. You are very top-heavy in the housing category. The $603.44 (38%) is based on $1,588.07 overtime income. It would make your housing budget even worse if you went without overtime income (38% of $1,178.45 is $447.81).

In other words, you currently are over budget in housing based on net income without overtime $448.74, or $293.11 based on the net with overtime.

In order to maintain your current housing it will be necessary to reduce all other areas as much as possible. Reduce your phone bill to no more than $40 per month and preferably $30 or the minimum amount for service in your area plus one or two short long distance calls. (Write letters!)

Is there any way to reduce your electricity and gas or water bills?

After giving the matter careful consideration, you might want to consider moving to a lower-priced home, or even renting. That is a big decision which only you two can make after investigating alternatives.

Food: Reduce to $150 to $200 per month.

Use the cash/envelope system instead of the checkbook. This will force you to plan carefully. Since you have the *Tightwad Gazette* I won't go into many ideas for saving, as most are covered there. Basically it's a matter of cooking from scratch. I would suggest that you have the kids and your husband carry lunches from home most of the time. Let the kids buy school lunch when they have pizza or some other special item on the menu.

Also, plan a cooked breakfast of oatmeal, homemade pancakes with homemade syrup, or eggs, rather than buying $3 per box of cereal. Undoubtedly you are up on ways to save in this area.

If you want to buy half a beef, you would need to accumulate the money in the envelope by spending less than the $200 until you have the cash to do so.

	Current amounts (Tami provided)	Recommended % and amounts		Budget suggested by counselor
Housing*	$896.55	(38%)	$603.44	$856.55
Food	300.00	(12%)	190.56	200.00
Auto	182.00	(15%)	238.20	232.00
Insurance	42.00	(5%)	79.40	42.00
Clothing	104.30	(5%)	79.40	50.00
Entertainment	61.75	(5%)	79.40	0.00
Medical	24.00	(5%)	79.40	24.00
Tithe	10.00	(10%)	159.00	10.00
Misc.	104.30	(5%)	79.40	50.00
Loans	103.50	(5%)	79.40	103.50
Savings	0.00	Whatever is possible.		20.00
TOTAL	$1,828.40			$1,588.05

*(Mortgage/taxes/ins. $502.55 & utilities $394.00)

Income with overtime $1,588.07

Income without overtime $1,178.45 (approximately)

(All percentage amounts are based on monthly income with overtime. You should actually be basing your budget and percentages on net income without overtime. The percentage recommendations come from Larry Burkett's Family Financial Planning Workbook.)

A Countryside reader provided these actual income and spending figures, which were analyzed by a professional consultant.

Auto: This is an area where you spend less than budget percentage for gas and oil. However, if you factor in repairs, you would actually be over budget.

I suggest putting $50 per month into a separate savings account for auto repairs/replacement so you'll have the money available the next time you need repairs. Otherwise, you'll have to take a loan again, which you really cannot afford to do.

Insurance: You are well within budget here.

Clothing: I took one-half of the Wal-Mart amount or $104 for clothing. You need to reduce this to no more than $50 per month.

You said most of the kids' clothing is given to you and since you stay home your needs should be minimal. I'm not sure what your husband's needs are. However, for the next year you need to try to stick to the $50.

I would suggest using the envelope system here too. If the money isn't in the envelope, don't buy clothes. This will require planning ahead for school clothes, winter coats and boots, etc.

Entertainment: I put eating out ($40) and cable ($22) into this category. Frankly, right now you cannot afford either. Until you get the loans repaid you need to eliminate spending here.

When you have to be away at meal time, plan ahead and fix a picnic to take along. I had to do this for several years and still do on occasion because we don't care much for fast food. It actually can be an adventure with kids if handled right.

Medical: You are under budget here. This is an area that concerns me as it seems unrealistic. I suspect the $24 per month is what is needed for diabetic supplies. You need to increase your budget in this area to cover insurance deductible, dental and eye exams and costs of eyeglasses. A simple office call is at least $35 and prescriptions are out-of-sight these days, so unless your insurance pays 100% you need to budget in your share of medical costs.

For now, you will have to leave things as they are, but this is an area that needs to be increased to reflect actual spending as soon as possible. Obviously, when you need medical attention you're seeking it, but don't have it budgeted. Not good!

Tithe: You're under budget percentage here.

Miscellaneous: The other half of Wal-Mart went here. I suggest you use the envelope system here too. If you don't have anything in the envelope, you can't spend. Leave your checkbook at home when you go to Wal-Mart and take only the appropriate envelopes.

Loans: You will pay these off entirely when you receive your income tax refund. Until such time the payments will continue at $103.50 per month.

Warning—if you get behind with Avco they will get a judgment and will garnish wages. If you find yourself being threatened by them, consider going to them and offering them a security interest in your 1997 income tax refunds. If you do so, be sure a specific amount is stated on the security agreement so you will be sure to receive the remainder of the refund.

Also, if it is necessary to do this,

ask if you can suspend payments and let the tax refund take care of everything. That will allow you the $103.50 per month now to start building your emergency fund.

If they garnish wages, you'll be in the soup because you won't be able to pay anything. It is vital you build an emergency fund so you do not have to take a loan again. On your current budget you simply cannot afford loans.

Savings: For now, $20 per month. You've got to start somewhere! Add the $103.50 to this when the loans are repaid. You must get a safety cushion built up. Otherwise, you will not be able to survive with your current level of income and expenses.

An acceptable emergency amount should be equal to six months' net income. The ideal is that this amount is not touched except in a true emergency.

Amounts added to that are for "planned expenses" such as medical emergencies, digging up your sewer or other stuff that happens just when you don't need it. All of this will take time.

You mentioned buying a computer to start a home typing business. At this time I don't see that as feasible for a couple of reasons.

First, you don't have the capital you need without borrowing. Second, you need additional income now. A home business would require a year or longer to build a sufficient client basis to provide income, and it could possibly fail. In the meantime, you would not only not have the income you need—you would have payments to make on the computer. Just not practical for now.

Last year we were asked to take four foster children aged 8, 6, and twins 5. I spent hours and dozens of calls trying to find before and after school daycare. Someone who would get the girls to school and pick them up daily. Someone I could depend upon to be there if school was canceled for snow or other reason.

Since you have a van and are going to school with your kids anyway this might be a possible source of income for you. A couple hours before and after school and the security of knowing someone will pick them up if a blizzard cancels school would mean a lot to parents, especially those who work out-of-town. It wouldn't provide a huge amount of income, but on the other hand, it would not require any capital investment. It would still leave you free during school hours to do your housework, baking, etc.

If you do baby-sit, be sure to keep good income records and report the income to the IRS. You will also be required to pay self-employment tax on your income, so be sure to factor it in.

Going back to work doesn't seem to be a good option for you unless you could find a job locally during school hours.

If you do start earning income, I suggest you put it into savings and not include it in any budget area. It may very well need to be added to medical which undoubtedly will need to be adjusted. Since it will be seasonal and undependable, don't get to depending on it.

Just to give you an idea of "planned" expenses—this past year we've had to dig up our sewer, replace a car, replace our roof, $1,200 of dental, replace the lawn mower plus a few other items I can't recall at the moment. Of course, this wiped out our savings so we must start at ground zero and rebuild as quickly as we can.

However, if we hadn't had savings we would have had to borrow and be $10,000 in debt with interest to pay. We would have had a big pit to climb out of before we could begin rebuilding. (Lord willing, we'll be able to rebuild before the next disaster strikes!)

Anyway, you see my point. With savings, you finance yourself rather than paying interest to someone else. That is the only way to achieve any sort of financial peace of mind.

I don't say financial security, because I don't believe it really exists. All we can do is our best and hope that is good enough.

You are fortunate to not have massive consumer debts. You aren't starting at ground zero, but you're not far off. You've already gotten rid of the credit cards, which puts you a large step ahead of the average family.

Your main problem area is taking your checkbook with you to Wal-Mart! Stay-at-home moms tend to go shopping as "cheap" entertainment. It is only cheap if you don't buy anything!

Seriously though, it would be a good idea for you to use the cash/envelope system and leave your checkbook at home. Use the checking account to pay mortgage, utilities, etc. and cash for food, gas, miscellaneous, and clothing.

As I said before, the only area where you are seriously out of balance is housing. I'm not sure that is something that can be helped with today's housing costs.

If you're willing, give the budget a try for the next couple of months and see how it works. There will be areas where it's not going to work so we'll adjust until we find something that works.

There's no room for debt on a homestead

The vast majority of correspondents who have complained about money problems face a common obstacle: they're in debt.

In most cases, these are people of modest means. Some of them would have a hard time making ends meet even if their entire income went to current expenses. But when some of that income has to be diverted to pay for items that in some cases might already be used up, plus the interest on that debt, it's like throwing money down a rat hole.

Most successful homesteaders avoid debt like the plague, and if they can't avoid it entirely, they work their way out of it as quickly as possible. It's impossible to be self-reliant when you owe money.

"Budget? Ha! After I pay the bills there's nothing left to budget!"

While preparing our recent articles on personal financial management, numerous readers told us it was impossible for them to budget, because it took all their money just to pay essential bills. Many others had no idea where their money goes, and even more had no handle on their net worth. (Many didn't even know what that meant.)

We asked about a dozen of those readers to fill out the forms shown here. One of those is analyzed in this issue and we plan on looking at others in the future.

But you might want to plug in your own figures. Several of our volunteers said that just sitting down to gather the data opened their eyes. Now they can see where their problems lie, and where to start to correct them!

These aren't complicated, although it might take some work and effort, or even discipline, to track and record expenses. If you want to control your finances, this is basic and essential information.

Note: For homesteaders, "other" assets include such items as tools and livestock, which are often considerable and which, ideally, pay handsome dividends. Non-material assets such as security and peace of mind, despite their importance, don't show up on this type of balance sheet.

Monthly Expenses

Housing:
- Rent/mortgage ____
- Gas/electric ____
- Telephone ____
- Water ____
- Insurance ____
- Taxes ____
- Repairs/replacement ____
- Other ____

Subtotal: ____

Food ____

Auto:
- Gas/oil ____
- Repairs/replacement ____
- Insurance ____
- Licenses ____
- Payments ____

Subtotal: ____

Insurance:
- Life ____
- Health ____
- Other ____

Subtotal: ____

Clothing ____

Entertainment ____

Medical ____

Tithe/giving ____

Child care ____

Child support/alimony ____

Misc.:
- Personal care ____
- Laundry ____
- Meals out ____
- Other ____

Subtotal: ____

Savings ____

Credit cards ____

Personal loans ____

Other ____

Total expenses ____

Assets & Liabilities—Net Worth

Assets
- Savings ____
- Investments ____
- Insurance cash values ____
- Other ____

Total assets ____

Liabilities
- Mortgage ____
- Car loans (list each) ____
- Credit cards (list each) ____
- Personal loans (list each) ____
- Other: (List)

Total liabilities ____

Net worth
(Total assets - total liabilities) ____

Monthly income

(List husband & wife separately)
- Gross income ____
- Overtime ____

Subtotal: ____

Minus payroll deductions:
- Taxes and Social Security ____
- Insurance ____
- Union dues ____
- Other ____

Subtotal: ____

Other income:
- Business/farm ____
- Interest/dividends ____
- Alimony/child support ____
- Social security ____
- Gov't assistance ____
- Pension ____
- Other ____

Subtotal: ____

Total combined income ____

Small farming:

Self-sufficiency and farmers

Farmers joke about "selling at wholesale and buying at retail." Should they become more like homesteaders?

Jeff Rast, Farmer/Director
The Center for
Small Acreage Farming
Idaho

As an advocate of sustainability in agriculture, I've long felt that the farmer should enjoy a high degree of self-sufficiency. The more sustainable the farm, the more self-sufficient is the farmer and his or her family and vice versa. Even if the nation's economy should crumble, farm families should enjoy a resilience unavailable to their urban counterparts.

To avoid misunderstanding, let me make an important clarification before proceeding any further. While "self-sufficiency" implies independence, I do not equate it with an independence from one's neighbors or even one's local community. Human souls are socially interdependent. Always have been and always will be. We derive a strength and richness of character through such interdependence.

The self-sufficiency I have in mind is one which gives a person or a family independence from the prevailing economy. It's an independence in which the farmer produces much, if not most of the food for the family. It's an independence in which a local community of farmers produces all of the food they need. "Need" is the key word. We farmers in the north may want to dine on a banana or grapefruit now and then, which is just fine. However, if self-sufficient or community-sufficient (a more realistic, stable and edifying goal), we can produce all the food locally to supply our nutritional needs.

Please be careful this haying season, or you might wind up like this! This photo came from John Favinger, Kentucky.

This whole issue grabs me every time I think about how dependent farm families are on grocery stores to supply their own food "needs." Our increasing specialization in agriculture has created a generation of farmers who produce a smaller portion of their own food needs than has any other generation of farmers in history! What an insult! These farmers, as a result of their specialization and mechanization, are also more dependent on the national economy than any preceding generation of farmers. In my naive way of thinking, this is absolutely inexcusable!

We must pursue a more self-sufficient, community-sufficient farming system. And it should serve as a model for the nation. We should be working to pursue what Abraham Lincoln considered the greatest of all arts – "the art of deriving a comfortable subsistence from the smallest area of land." But now, farms are far larger than Lincoln could have possibly imagined. And those farmers buy much, if not most, of their family food supplies from the grocery store.

Lincoln didn't use the word "subsistence" as we so often think of it —eking by with barely enough food in some run-down shelter. I wager that he meant something more along the lines of self-sufficiency. That's more consistent with the other term he used: "comfortable." But the term comfortable is so subjective. Our society has skillfully and progressively redefined so many luxuries as needs. This strikes at the very heart of any pursuit of sufficiency.

This critical factor—the viability of our consumption or life-style goals—determines how successful we will be in our pursuit of self- or community-sufficiency. In other words, must I raise my family in a large home with oak trim, a whirlpool spa, elaborate drapes and a 3 car garage, or would a simple 1,500 square foot home with no frills suffice? Must we drive late-model vehicles with all the bells and whistles? Do we need three televisions... or do we need any at all?

Our answers to questions like these define our consumption goals. And our consumption goals can make enormous demands on our income potential and the production potential of our farms. This is one reason why consumer debt in our nation has reached dizzying heights. We want, want, want, want. The idea of learning to be content with a simple lifestyle is almost abhorrent. Darn near un-American! Our consumption goals have been exacting unsustainable demands on our productivity and resource potential.

Every now and again, an economic recession or depression comes along to slap our consumptive mentality with a reality check. Such reality checks hurt. Some people don't survive them. However, those who had previously learned to be content with simplicity weather the economic storms well.

I recently read the results of a survey which focused on two major questions: How much is your gross family income, and how much more would you need to make in order to be content?

The gist of it was that the more people earned, the more money they felt they needed in order to be satisfied. Clearly, then, the bells and whistles of life do not provide contentment. In fact, those on the lower end of the income scale seemed to have the highest level of contentment. There seemed to be a connection between contentment and simplicity.

I'm frequently asked if a family can actually derive a livable, full-time income from a small acreage. My general answer is yes, but I usually qualify that answer based on who asked the question. It all depends on how they define "livable."

I am not saying we need to return to subsistence farming wherein our children read by candlelight; Mom washes clothes on a washboard by the creek; and Dad does all his field work with a planting stick and a hand scythe. Not at all. But a definite emphasis on simplicity is in order. And compared to our current consumptive habits, a simple lifestyle would still be quite comfortable, if we'd just make the effort to adapt.

Learning to honor manual labor again as a healthy activity would be one step in the right direction. Besides, manual labor is often financially superior to many of the costly mechanized alternatives, especially for profitable, small-scale farming.

Working with your children out in the fields, or fixing fence or feeding the animals, will develop their creativity and character and physical strength better than some electronic joy stick in front of a video screen. Working with your spouse on the farm provides excellent opportunity to build a solid relationship. Granted, it creates more opportunities for conflicts to arise. But if those conflicts happen in an environment of a mutual commitment to each other and to simplicity, then it's more likely that those conflicts will be resolved for the sake of unity.

Conversely, in a fast-paced, complicated world, those conflicts can be glossed over and ignored with the result that people drift apart.

Pursuing such family-sufficiency and community-sufficiency provides social and economic benefits which endure despite difficult times. I can't think of one valid excuse for anything less.

Jeff Rast directs The Center for Small Acreage Farming and edits the newsletter, Small Acreage Farming, a monthly publication promoting sustainable, small-scale farming for the land, the people and rural communities. For a sample copy, send $2.00 to The Center for Small Acreage Farming, PO Box 219, Fairfield ID 83327. A free brochure listing other publications and services is available.

Book review:

A homestead encylopedia in one volume

A homestead encylopedia in one volume Husbandry, *by Nathan Griffith; 295 pages; illus.; indexed; paper; $18 + $2.50 shipping (available from the Countryside Bookstore, 800-551-5691).*

If you're looking for a book that covers just about anything having to do with homesteading you can think of, your search is over.

In fact, if you had to choose one book to get you started and keep you going in a self-sufficient lifestyle, this one should certainly be a top contender.

Nathan Griffith has managed to explain the basics of almost every homestead project without getting bogged down in endless details. You won't find dozens of recipes for cheese, soap, or vinegar, but you'll find the basics, and by golly, you'll be able to make them!

Need information on smithing? Developing a spring? Training a horse? Hedges? Concrete? You name it, and you'll find it here.

Husbandry is illustrated with woodcuts from old books, and it mirrors the overall feel of those delightful old treasures. But its updated focus on "husbandmen" (the author avoids "homesteader") makes it much more valuable. Don't miss this one. — Jd

Why farmers go to farmers markets

Jeff Ishee
Virginia

Most conventional farmers in this country do not attend local farmers markets... and there are many reasons why.

In the latter half of this century, emphasis in agriculture has focused not only on feeding our own towns and communities, but on feeding the world. And if I were the CEO of a corporate farm, I really couldn't find fault in this logic. After all, look at the size of the market! I wouldn't be concerned about how many bushels of green beans were going to be picked this week. I would be more concerned about the number of ships that I was going to fill with grain and send to China!

But more and more often, farmers are taking a second look at the local needs of agriculture, where there are fewer middlemen to siphon off all the profits in farming. And that's only one reason farmers are going back to the market.

Farmers typically record gross sales of $200 to $600 per day at an established market in season. Some of the bigger growers can realize more than $1,000 per day.

Farmers markets usually offer a prime location that costs much less than a private retail outlet. Rather than taking the full burden of insurance, advertising, physical facilities, and other marketing costs, a farmer can share these expenses with others.

Customer feedback is often immediate, offering the farmer first-

hand knowledge of what the shopper really wants. If a farmer wants to experiment with different varieties, he can try them out at the market before committing to a larger scale of production.

There are minimal start-up costs and immediate access for new farmers. All you really need is a table, some baskets, and a truck to get you to the market.

Farmer-to-farmer relationships are usually very positive at the market. Growers share information and successful methods they use in their own operations. And, if you need to go to the rest room or get another cup of coffee, a neighboring farmer will usually watch your stand while you are away for a few moments.

It's just plain fun to sell at the farmers market. You can joke around and have a good time.

I've seen many farmers with pick-your-own operations or roadside stands who just got tired of the arduous hours. They would comment, "I always have to be here at the stand, six days a week, from 7:00 A.M. until dark. I just can't get anything done on the farm." But because most farmers markets are either one or two days a week, the farmer is free not only to market his crops, but to produce them with an emphasis on quality. Most farmers look forward to "market day" because it offers them a chance to stop and talk with people, tell a story or two, and make some new friends who appreciate what they do.

Because most farmers don't utilize farmers markets as their sole outlet, they use the market as publicity to gain new customers who will buy their products in other ways (community supported agriculture, on-farm sales, restaurants, etc.).

While our nation becomes more and more conscious of the vital link between farm and markets, the growth of local farmers markets will continue. All of the trends and indicators reveal an ever-increasing demand for fresh and healthful food. More and more, consumers want food that was harvested yesterday by a local farmer, not three weeks ago and 1,500 miles away.

This is an excerpt from Jeff Ishee's book, Dynamic Farmers' Marketing: A Guide to Successfully Selling Your Farmers' Market Products; *farmsteadatcfw.com. Used with permission.*

Home business:

Beware of work-at-home scams

KEN SCHARABOK
TENNESSEE

Almost every classified advertising section of newspapers, magazines and other periodicals, plus tv and radio, carry advertisements for work-at-home ventures. The advertisements sure sound interesting. People in need of extra income and time on their hands see cash floating before them as promised in the advertisement and it doesn't cost much to get started.

How can you tell if the offer is a scam?

Even with improved consumer fraud legislation, people who have been taken in often do not complain since the amount they lost is small and they are embarrassed to admit they have been fleeced. In addition, local police authorities are reluctant to spend the time to pursue small claims and the companies themselves are adept at completely disappearing before enough complaints pile up. People who fell for the scam may also place similar advertisements to try to recoup their losses, further perpetuating it.

I am reminded of the classic story about the advertisement along the lines of "Become a millionaire within a year!". All you had to do was send in $5 for information. Reportedly all the buyer received was a short letter telling them to place similar advertisements to get 200,000 people to send them $5 each for the same advice. What's the old saying about, "If it sounds too good to be true…"?

A common scam is envelope stuffing, where you supposedly receive envelopes, labels, the envelope contents and so much per envelope mailed. However, any company which direct mails can buy equipment to do 10,000 mailings per hour, which are then bulk mailed at a substantial discount to first class. Why would they need to subcontract it to people working out of their homes?

Other popular scams are managing vending machines or pay phones; independent travel agents or book or movie reviewers; overseeing display racks for greeting cards or computer software; performing data entry, billing and marketing services; mail order with merchandise supplied; area code 900 pay-per-call telephone numbers; producing promotional or event buttons; selling trading cards and grocery coupons.

Somewhat related scams have included providing information on well-paying state or federal jobs, how to obtain confiscated vehicles for a fraction of their value, participating in chain letters and using your home personal computer to provide income.

Some companies which furnish kits to assemble have now started to have their material delivered by commercial overnight services to avoid coming under mail fraud legislation. Often their advertisements stipulate your work must be of acceptable quality, and unless they really have a market for it, it seldom is, or you wind up working for less than minimum wages.

An example cited by the Dayton, Ohio Better Business Bureau involved a person with an interest in woodworking sending $50 in response to an advertisement which said $350 per week (which works out to $18,200 per year) could be earned assembling and decorating wooden picture frames. It took the purchaser an average of an hour and a half to produce each frame, for which he was paid $3.25. At this rate, he would have to work some 162 hours a week to make the projected $350 (and there are only 168 hours in a week!).

At that time, the Dayton Better Business Bureau offered the general warning to beware of any work-at-home opportunity which:

• Does not have a telephone listing in the city which is given as their business address (call information). Often scam artists use a mail drop box via which their mail is forwarded to them to make them more difficult to locate.

• Was advertised in classified sections of national magazines or tabloid newspapers (or local paper with an out-of-state address or phone number).

• Requires an up-front payment to get started or to pay for the materials.

• Makes extraordinary claims about potential earnings, within a very short time and with little effort or investment on your part.

• Does not conduct personal interviews.

• Does not supply all materials.

• Requires employees to pay for employment.

The bureau said they were not aware of any work-at-home opportunity which provided even a minuscule return on time and investment.

Based on my research, I'll add some more recommendations:

• Beware of any company which will not readily provide the name, address and telephone number of all their clients so you can call some at random for verification of their information. This includes correspondence courses which are supposed to lead to well paying jobs. (Actually, this is a very good test of their credibility since a company which has been highly successful in sponsoring work-at-home or career opportunities will want to promote it through success demonstrations.)

• Don't take testimonials from past clients at their face value. Scam operators are not above writing their own testimonials or they may be actual testimonials, but from only a handful of clients who actually thought they did well.

• Insist everything be in writing and then file it. If you later have to file a consumer complaint this will help provide supporting documentation.

If you do get taken, there are some recourses:

• Contact your local or regional Better Business Bureau to file a formal complaint, even if the money involved is minor. If enough complaints are filed, action by the appropriate office might be taken to prevent others from being victimized.

• The National Consumer Fraud Information Center, 1701 K Street NW, Washington DC 20006, sponsored by the National Consumers League, operates a hot line which assists in filing complaints. Counselors are available at 800-876-7060. They will pass the complaint on to the appropriate authorities for investigation. If fraud has caused a financial hardship, they can also refer you to the appropriate agency for assistance.

• For fraud committed over the Internet, there is a complaint site at www.fraud.org. It was created by the National Consumers League, MasterCard, law enforcement agencies and state attorneys general as the Internet Fraud Watch Program to gather information for possible further action.

• The Federal Trade Commission will take consumer complaints at FTC, Correspondence Department, Washington, DC 20580. Call 202-326-2222 for what information to provide. While it does not intervene in individual disputes, information provided by consumers may indicate a pattern of violations requiring its action.

• Within each state the attorney general office or consumer protection division is empowered to investigate consumer complaints and possible violations of state laws. Look under State Government in the yellow pages of your state's capital phone book (check local library for copy). If you cannot locate what seems to be the right department there is normally a number to call for directory assistance for the state's departments and agencies.

Before investing any money in a work-at-home opportunity contact the following:

• The Federal Trade Commission at FTC, Public Reference Department, Washington, DC 20580; 202-326-2222. They have available a number of publications on consumer fraud, included Work-At-Home Schemes. Their publications can also be accessed via the Internet at http://www.ftc.gov.

• The American Home Business Association, 4505 S. Wasatch Blvd., Salt Lake City, UT 84124; www.homebusiness.com; 800-664-2422. Ask if the company you are interested in is a member and, if so have any unresolved complaints been filed against them.

• The National Association of Home Based Businesses, 10451 Mill Run Cir, Ste 400, Owings Mills, MD 21117; www.usahomebusiness.com; 410-363-3698 serves as a clearinghouse for legitimate home-based business opportunities. To receive their certification work-at-home companies must submit the full details of their operation for review. They will advise if a particular company's operation has been cleared with them.

When contacting a company for further information ask if they are a member of either or both of the above associations. If not, let the buyer beware!

On the assumption they cannot all be bad apples, a book store can order a copy of *The Work-At-Home Sourcebook: Over 1,000 Job Opportunities with Names, Addresses and Complete Information* by Lynie Arden for you.

In addition to what may be in stock at a larger bookstore, Books in Print lists a number of references on the successful operation of home-based business; however, only the version on CD disk on a personal computer is of any real use for researching titles.

If you do get victimized chances are very good your name will go on a "sucker" list to be sold or traded to other similar companies. All you can do is to throw away their mail or hang up on the calls. "I am not interested, goodbye!" works.

Work-at-home opportunities should not be confused with cottage industries, where work is subcontracted out by legitimate companies to home workers or where home workers market through a national mail order catalogue company. Examples are craft items and hand-produced clothing. However, even here the same warnings apply. The national group for this endeavor is the National Association for the Cottage Industry, PO Box 14850, Chicago, IL 60614.

My recommendation: thoroughly investigate before sending any money and, if taken, sic as many people on them as possible.

Family finance:

Find barters in unexpected places

GRANT EVERSOLL
INDIANA

I am not going to waste your time telling you about the homestead budget. Being a homesteader on a very tight budget, it is usually a struggle trying to keep both ends in sight let alone trying to get them to meet. Then one day the water system goes down and the end that was almost in sight moves clean out of view.

We live one-half mile from a large park (camping, swimming, golf, etc.). For the past 10 years it has been the site of the annual "Official Indiana State Pickin' and Fiddlin' Contest."

We planned to take the whole family down and spend the day listening to some of the best bluegrass pickers from all over, but two things happened to put a crimp in our plans.

One, they raised the price of admission. For us that meant $20. (Two would get in free.) We could swing that ($3.33 each for 12 hours of entertainment is not bad.) But when the water pump went out, $220 that we did not have shot a big hole in a day filled with bluegrass.

To help supplement our income I do some freelance writing and had planned on getting a story from the event. Not only had our family day out been disturbed for lack of funds, but we lost possible future earnings as well.

But then, the night before the event, our 12-year-old daughter received a call from the president of her Junior Optimist Club asking her if she could help park cars at the contest. We asked if they could use some adult help, and bingo, we were in.

The deal was that we would work from 8 A.M. until noon parking cars and we kept our "official" badge.

This worked out better than if I had planned it. While parking cars I had a chance to talk with everyone who came (I worked the "put your car here" end of the line) and a ton of different angles for stories were handed to me on a plate.

Noon came, the biggest part of the crowd had arrived, and our time in the box was done. We went home, grabbed lunch and picked up our other three children and headed back to the park. We planned on paying for one of the oldest two, but when we returned they smiled and waved all of us in.

Three of us worked (if you can call it that) for four hours for $15 worth of tickets ($1.25 an hour). As my wife says, "We work cheap." But being homesteaders, at times our time counts for nothing, for time is all we have.

We have already decided to volunteer to help park cars next year.

It's your credit: check it!

ANONYMOUS
TENNESSEE

Changes to the federal Fair Credit Reporting Act implemented in October 1997 offer more protection to your credit record, easier access to it, and more formal procedures for correction of error.

Previously just about anyone could order a credit report through a credit reporting agency. Now, a document must be provided on which you authorized access to your credit report. This also applies to medical records.

You can obtain your own credit report for a nominal amount, such as $8. However, if you are requesting it because you were denied credit based on it, the report is generally free. (The three major credit reporting agencies are Equifax (800-685-1111), Experian (formerly TRW) (888-397-3742) and Trans Union (800-916-8800).

You can dispute anything in your credit report which you think is inaccurate. You have to tell a credit reporting agency, in writing, and the agency has to investigate it within 30 days by going to the company which provided that information. The credit reporting agency then reports back to you. If you still don't agree, you have the right to say so in a statement, not to exceed 100 words, which must be attached to your credit report.

Previously, if the source of the information did not answer an inquiry by a credit reporting agency, the information stayed on your credit report. Now the reverse is true. If the source doesn't respond to the inquiry the information can be removed if the credit reporting agency believes you have provided sufficient evidence.

You must be informed if a credit report is being used against you, such as denial of a job application, and you must be given the name, address and phone number of the credit reporting agency which provided the report.

You can tell a credit reporting agency to remove your name from lists for unsolicited credit and insurance offers. You can request a form to complete and return for this purpose.

You have the right to sue credit reporting agencies, report users or sources of information for it for violations of this act.

Financial experts recommend you review your credit report at least every two years.

A pamphlet, Fair Credit Reporting, is available from the Federal Trade Commission, Consumer Response Center, Sixth & Pennsylvania Ave NE, Washington DC 20580 (202-326-2222 or www.ftc.gov).

A summary of the recent changes to the Fair Credit Reporting Act can be obtained from the National Center for Financial Education, PO Box 34070, San Diego, CA 92163-4040 (or www.ncfe.org).

A good credit report is an extremely valuable asset. Take steps now to insure all of the information is accurate so you won't have to spend several months trying to remove inaccurate information after you have been denied credit, leases or unemployment based on it.

Family finance:

Another way to save money: Start a buying club

Bev Carney
Wisconsin

Several Countryside correspondents have talked about buying clubs and how they can save you money. They're right—buying clubs save both money and time, and have the additional benefit of helping you organize your needed shopping.

We started our buying club three years ago through the North Farm Cooperative, which serves all of Wisconsin, Michigan, Illinois, Minnesota, Indiana, and parts of Missouri, Iowa, Ohio, Wyoming, South Dakota, North Dakota, and Montana.

Starting a buying club is relatively easy. All you need are some interested people! Our "club" started out as an individual family and has since expanded to three families with various others ordering from time to time. The major determinant for size is the minimum order your club is required to place. Since we're close enough to North Farm to pick up our orders, our minimum is only $100. If you'll need to rely on North Farm's delivery truck, your minimum order will vary—the usual minimum for delivery is $500. However, if you live on an established truck route and will accept a road drop, your order can be as little as $100.

Of course, these rules apply only to North Farm. A buying cooperative in your area will probably have different rules and minimums. But the $500 is not too difficult to come up with if you order infrequently. We have twice reached this minimum without really trying. If you require delivery however, your club will probably need to be larger than three families.

We particularly like the wide variety of organic products available in bulk. In addition, there's also a wide array of health/beauty aids and household supplies. Most products are available either prepackaged or in bulk. You can get a small package of wheat berries or you can get 50 pounds. We buy mostly bulk quantities and caselots, often splitting them with other club members. You can usually purchase in small quantities also, even though the minimum amount may be three items.

By purchasing in large quantities several times during the year, we always have a lot of food on hand. We don't like to run to the store. For one thing it's too far, and for another, the variety is limited. In addition, every time you go to the store, you spend money. We figure the fewer trips we make, the more money (and time) we can save.

After several years of bulk ordering, we have a pretty good idea of how many supplies we need to get us through six months or a year. Grains store well in a 55-gallon drum topped with a heavy plywood cover. Tossing in a handful of bay leaves (purchased cheaply by the pound) controls insect infestations. Cornstarch, wheat gluten and cocoa last for years. Beans and dry pasta also keep well if kept dry. We even buy our shampoo by the gallon, saving on wasteful packaging and getting a good price to boot.

The structure of the club can be as formal or as informal as the people involved. Someone needs to coordinate the orders and several people will need to be available for the delivery. These jobs can be rotated, or members can serve "terms" and pass the jobs around that way. Some clubs order every four weeks or so, while others order sporadically. Set up specific rules about payments to the club for the products—is cash acceptable or should the club require checks? Who will be the contact person with the co-op? That person needs to give some financial info to the co-op. Decide where you can accept delivery—you'll need truck access and perhaps electricity for the frozen/cold stuff. Decide who will coordinate the splits of bulk items and caselots. If you can get 12 items cheaper than 10, what to do with any leftovers from the case? What happens if a member fails to pick up the food on time? Should there be a small markup to pay for any postage, phone calls, etc. the buying club incurs? Will the club actively recruit members, or should it stay at a smaller level?

Although I'm familiar only with the North Farm Cooperative, there is possibly a sponsor in your area. Good places to check are organic markets and natural food stores. Perhaps the folks at the local farmers' market would know. Look in any alternative newspapers in your area for ads.

***Update:* North Farm Cooperative, in business since 1971, filed for Chapter 7 Bankruptcy in 2002. To some extent, North Farm was victimized by the success of the movement that they had a hand in establishing. As the demand for natural and organic products increased, many North Farm members were able to find alternative sources for their natural products and sales declined steadily over the last few years.**

Economics for homesteaders:

The "antique" value of prudence
and the psychology of economics

Things prudent people should know about their money—and their future

Art Horn, Ph.D.
North Carolina

I have been enjoying the recent discussions about the core values of homesteading and Current Reality As Seen Here. Although I am a psychologist, not an economist, I have been following recent economic and social events. Here is my take on the subject:

Americans generally seem to have very little sense of history, and worse, seem to get much of their working knowledge of the world from the media, particularly television. Some of us believe that the overall picture presented by the media—that everything is wonderful and continually improving—is terribly wrong. Homesteaders seem to be one of the only groups taking preparatory or corrective action for a declining civil situation.

Throughout history people have developed a share of common wisdom, much of which is stored in popular proverbs and virtues, about the right way to live. One of the old virtues is "prudence," in the sense of having a careful or cautious stance toward the future.[1]

The virtue of prudence is woven into the homesteading movement. One way of thinking prudently about the events of our time is contained in the term "sustainability." Other ways are included in the terms "organic," "recycling" and "permaculture." The core ideas of prudence—caution, planning for adverse events in the future, etc.—are partially shared in these terms. It may be that things have gotten so imbalanced that we need to go through a generation of re-education (voluntary or involuntary) regarding the classical virtues.

Voluntary re-education in diverse things including prudence involves the modern American homesteading movement and is, I believe, epitomized by this magazine and its audience. Here we have people engaged in and sharing the learning necessary to move toward self-sustainable lives. This is not a money thing.

An example: I appreciated COUNTRYSIDE'S printing the article I wrote on the basics of sharpening and tool maintenance several years ago (79/4:67-80). I was surprised to be severely criticized about this by two authorities, one a relative who had worked in newspapers and the other a well-known "country"-type author. Both of them complained that I had given the article to a magazine that did not pay me anything and thus had been "working for free." They totally missed the point. The payment for me was in writing the article (formalizing my thinking, doing a little research, etc.) and in being able to share something practical. It is vastly more important to me that necessary information be distributed efficiently than my making sub-minimal wage writing for a highly specialized magazine.

Notably, neither of these critical "authorities" had a glimmer of understanding of the contents of the article. This is despite the fact that the "well known author" had operated a nationally advertised homesteading school for some time in the past. I guess they just purchased new knives when theirs went dull. Or maybe they didn't get dull knives because they didn't use them? If COUNTRYSIDE had to pay for content then it would be much thinner on the content, limited in what was said so as to not offend advertisers, and much fuller on the slick advertisements. This would be a much less efficient way of distributing the content. The magazine's content is what we are interested in, after all.

Forced re-education usually happens to people who have planned poorly and who end up on the wrong side of a big event such as an economic depression or a war.[2] Under these circumstances they can either learn to adapt, or perish. High-risk gamblers frequently end up having these remedial education experiences. I know

1. Prudent: 1. Wise in handling practical matters; exercising good judgment or common sense. 2. Careful in regard to one's own interests; provident. 3. Careful about one's conduct; circumspect. From: *The American Heritage Dictionary of the English Language*, Third Edition 1992.

2. I do not believe a normal person could prepare for extreme but low-frequency events such as natural cataclysms: comet strikes, etc. Common wars, active volcanoes, economic depressions and famines are much more predictable because they are more frequent and have signal or precursor events leading up to them.

3. Amazing perhaps because at this

individuals in their 50s and 60s who have all of their retirement funds tied up in highly speculative stock market ventures. They talk about their upcoming retirements. Many of these folks are going to learn that they will not be able to retire on that money they gambled away on risky ventures. Hopefully their discomfort over their losses and their newly found need to work into their nineties will be tempered by their heightened appreciation of the classical virtues.

One of the amazing aspects of our time is the almost total lack of perspective which the opinion leaders in the media and responsible positions have for our long-term situation.(3) A good book on recent (the last 80 years or so) economic history is *A Journey Through Economic Time* by John Kenneth Galbraith.(4) In this book Galbraith describes the economic history of this century with a little twist. Most of the lightweight stuff we see in the popular media describes capitalism as a sort of godlike force moving humanity toward ever greater "standards of living" (by which they mean doing less work and at the same time increasing consumption). In fact Galbraith points out that, to the contrary, capitalism has two general states or "equilibrium states," conditions which, when they are reached, tend to hold on for long periods.

The economic condition everyone seems to worship, and in fact equate with capitalism, Galbraith terms "high equilibrium." This has been the general economic situation of the USA since 1945.(5) When we have high equilibrium we have low unemployment, inflation problems, high resource utilization, high levels of waste and increasing demand for most things. Everyone else in the world would like to have this general economic state. These periods are called "economic booms."

The root cause of such long booms is a mass psychological attitude that things are going to get better and more secure (but also more expensive). Jobs will be more plentiful, credit will be more available, etc. The psychology is "Buy now, pay later." This is an adaptive attitude as the "later" involves cheaper (inflated) money.

In actuality what we have seen in the end phases of this "long boom" is that the value of money decreases faster than the typical person's ability to make it and we have real declining incomes and declining wealth (as people use credit to make up for income shortages), more bankruptcies, and frantic attempts by government and the financial institutions to keep things going.

The "low equilibrium" phase of capitalism is characterized by slow activity. This is a phase in which people do not expect tomorrow to be better than today and thus they hoard their money and act very prudently, perhaps too prudently.(6) This causes a long period of economic contraction characterized by high unemployment, scarce credit, low resource demand, low consumer demand and great bitterness and pain. Obviously these "low" conditions also reinforce each other.

The transition between "high" and "low" equilibrium states seems to me to be a "Great Depression" or a war or cataclysm of some type.

The USA has not had a Great Depression since 1929. To see one of these low phases come to life please observe the economic history of Russia since 1989. That country may have had more than a 50% drop in average living standards in five or six years.(7) The Russian economy seems to have clearly gone through a Great Depression since 1989 and now seems to be stuck in a low equilibrium phase.

Depressions are frightful to the general public. The media and political types react hysterically to the very words involved. In fact the term "depression" was so scary after 1940 that the term "recession" (meaning a less serious pause in business activity with two quarters net negative eco-

time almost everyone has college educations, advanced degrees, etc. It all goes to demonstrate that you can be well-educated and still have no common sense.

4. Galbraith, John K., *A Journey Through Economic Time: A Firsthand View.* 1994, Houghton Mifflin, NY. Galbraith worked in the Office of Price Control and Rationing during 1941 and was one of the most important economists at the heart of the war effort. This is a good, if advanced, book for home schooling. Galbraith knew most of the important economists of the century and describes their theories and impacts quite well. His discussion of low equilibrium states begins on page 74.

5. The "postwar boom" was caused by a confluence of several large trends and situations including the destruction of most of the world's physical plant capacity outside the USA, pent-up domestic consumer demand from the rationing system in place during WW II, increased GI postwar benefits and bonded debt. During the U.S. Civil War the government frequently printed money when it needed it and this resulted in postwar economic problems in the form of massive inflation. (This is the origin of the "Greenback.") They learned from this, and in WW I and WW II much of the debt was bonded, thus creating an IOU that could be traded or banked on. These aggregate conditions created a huge economic demand in the postwar period. See Galbraith p. 26.

6. Technically, this reduces stimulus in the economy by slowing the "velocity" of money circulation, the number of times during a year that a particular dollar changes hands. Also the total money supply contracts because of bankruptcies and defaults (see below). When the contraction is greater than the ability of the government to counter it through expansionary policies, then you have a real depression setting in.

7. Who can accurately estimate anything in a huge country with no reliable data collection? They have had a horrible contraction no matter what the detailed statistics will eventually state.

8. The term "demand" in economics is an estimate or actual measurement of the aggregate amount of

nomic or GNP growth) was coined to replace it. Then during the Carter administration the term "recession" was banned as also being too scary, leaving one administration economist testifying before Congress saying that since he could no longer use the word "recession" he would use the word "banana" to refer to two consecutive quarters of net GNP contraction.

The real driving engine behind a Great Depression is a period of extended deflation of the currency. People become frightened and this tends to make the depression worse. The mass psychology switches to negative expectations: "Tomorrow will be worse."

During inflation a manufacturer can make a product, place it on a shelf, and then raise prices as inflation progresses. The investment is secure if the price can be raised at least as quickly as inflation cheapens the value of money.

During deflation a manufacturer is punished for making a product if it is not sold immediately. This is because the price it can be sold for declines with time while the costs for manufacturing have already been paid. Under deflation it is frequently wiser for manufacturers to keep their money in financial instruments which will beat deflation, such as government bonds, than to lose money running a plant. People quickly realize that it is best to hold their now difficult-to-acquire money, because it will tend to buy more tomorrow. This cycles through the economy and things slow down.

At some point in these contractions the economy reaches a low equilibrium phase where people are very cautious and business activity is minimal. This reflects a systematic contraction of "aggregate demand."(8) There is no reason for this to change unless the mass psychology switches and the actual necessary economic demand can be generated.

While inflation can be fought with increases in interest rates, as those of us who lived through the "Volker era" in the mid-1980's can remember, the reverse may not work with deflation. While we can raise interest rates as high as we need to strangle demand, we cannot lower them below zero to stimulate demand. If people's expectations are negative enough, even interest rates below 1% may not be attractive.(9)

It's not just consumers who develop negative expectations. Galbraith recounts that when he was involved in mobilization of production during WW II, the government ran into resistance from the steel companies. The companies were certain that once the war was over the economy would go right back into the depression and they didn't want to be stuck with new steel mills or "excess capacity" at that point. (10)

It seems clear to me that we are headed into a deflation/depression phase. There is much anxious talk now about deflationary pressures resulting from the Asian financial catastrophe. (11) Interestingly enough, the media I see always seem to mention this and then try to make light of it. We used to call this "whistling past the graveyard." They know that if a real bad one hit, all these "Live Stock Markets Today"-type shows will be replaced with Soup Kitchen and riot footage.

People in this country are less and less able to pay for necessities. After the late 1970s American living standards were partially maintained only by all of the available women entering the workforce. Now they are all out working, and in fact are being downsized and squeezed from many directions, and still our "living standards" are falling.

In the 1980s and '90s people took out second mortgages which were not spent on their houses. The percentage of home ownership equity has fallen. Ditto for credit cards. The bankruptcy rate is rising rapidly. This by itself will probably cause a financial panic in a few more years.

Under these likely near-future conditions, what is a prudent person to do? Do you head for Las Vegas and take the long shot or to the homestead and take the sure shot?

If we study the last Great Depression we see that American social organization was very different then.

money chasing goods in the whole system or the part that one is considering. Where does money come from and where does it go? These are reasonable questions which are rarely discussed. There are several types of money. However, the most important type is the sort that we write checks for and exchange with stores etc. This type of money is created essentially out of thin air by the process of making loans. I did not believe this until I took a course in Money and Banking and worked through the details of these transactions. Lending activity is a dominant way in which the money supply "grows." Money is destroyed by defaults and bankruptcies. In a default, owed money is never paid back and is "written off." Thus, when there are lots of defaults the overall money supply shrinks. Money is truly lost at those times. If enough default activity occurs then the aggregate money supply shrinks, and thus the aggregate possible demand is lowered. Even if people had a positive attitude about the future the lack of money would have a serious slowing effect on the economy involved and would keep it in low equilibrium until the money supply was re-grown.

9. These interest rates have actually been seen in Japan in the "Post Bubble" period. Japan may be another large economy which has tipped into a low equilibrium phase.

10. Galbraith pp. 120-123.

11. I have an interest in tools and get many catalogs in the mail. Recently I received a catalog which had very nice, high quality, name brand knives from Japan and Taiwan at around 80% of retail. This was described as a "liquidation" event. It is illegal for products to be dumped here at below manufacturing costs so these price levels may give us a hint of how things are shaping up for the near future. The currently distressed Asian economies need to expand exports and are going to attempt to do this by severe price cutting. This places price pressure on US and European firms, leading to wage cuts, downsizing and other deflationary activities.

12. Lester Thurow, Asia: *The Collapse and the Cure*. New York Review of Books, February 5, 1998, pp. 22-26. Lester Thurow is a prominent economist.

Also see: Robert Novak, "Asian Crisis Far From Over" (Syndicated column) *Asheville Citizen-Times*, Saturday February 7, 1998. "Treasury and Federal Reserve officials are increasingly worried that the Asian financial crisis so threatens international banks, particularly German, that it could trigger a global recession."

13. We could argue about the fine points of this. Many of the things we can purchase today such as electronic gizmos or some health care components could not be purchased at any price in 1931. But is the experiential quality of life we can buy now even at inflated prices comparable to what could be obtained in the depression? I doubt it. It is likely many of the readers of this magazine also doubt it.

14. For instance, the price of a $50,000 mortgage would run up to the current equivalent of $400,000-$600,000 (It will still be 50 thou: it's just that your income gets cut by 7/8ths to 11/12ths) while the value of the collateral will adjust to $6,250-$4,166. Since the S & L catastrophe, banks are required to periodically revalue properties on which they hold mortgages. When the paper value has dropped below the amount owed, even though you have never even been late on a payment, you are considered to be in a type of default. The bank is then required to reduce the difference either by a lump sum payment by you, a foreclosure, or some other action. If these rules are enforced by the Feds during a general deflationary cycle the results would be a cataclysmic crash in housing values and bankruptcy of most of the banks holding mortgages, followed by a general financial lock-up. For this reason it is likely that some other "emergency" solution such as "indexing" will be put into place. Strange policies such as "indexing" are a feature of highly unstable third world economies. The U.S. Treasury has already released an "indexed" bond. These are to protect the government against the expense of repaying bonds in deflated dollars and are useless as a

Some of these differences probably lessened the impact of the Depression and the resulting "low" period substantially. These saving features are no longer present in the USA.

During the 1930s a much higher percentage of people lived on farms or had close relatives living on farms. A much higher percentage of all jobs involved agricultural activities including things like railroad freight and other shipping jobs. These activities never fall below a certain level.

There was a migration to farms, farm labor migrations, and labor camps and concentration-type camps for the homeless poor. (Read John Steinbeck's books on this era. He wrote about what he saw going on around him.) People learned to make do with anything and to recycle everything.

People who lived in the cities, it seems to me, had much greater anxiety than people living in the country. This is because city life requires economic activity, particularly constant purchases, for basic survival. This is less true on a homestead which affords shelter and produces some food and fuel. Political and social instability are features of Great Depressions and these seem to have mostly been a city phenomenon during the last Great Depression. There are a few exceptions such as Bulgaria's "Green Socialists" under Boris III and Stambolinsky, but largely the rioting and political activity occurred in cities among people who felt they had little to lose.

While a Great Depression seems to be in our immediate future, what of the "beyond the beyond"? What happens after a Great Depression? Do we drop painfully back into a low equilibrium or bounce happily back to a high equilibrium economy? This depends upon the mass psychology and the ability of the leadership to stimulate demand.

A recent article by Lester Thurow regarding the Asian crisis points to Japan as an example of an economy with unparalleled financial resources, social cohesion and great industrial and commercial capacity, but inept leadership. This has resulted in the Japanese economy not turning around following the bursting of the "bubble" mania. Despite their advantages they could slip into a prolonged low equilibrium condition.

What happens if a substantial part of the world (the USA, Japan, Europe etc.) goes into low equilibrium at the same time? How long would it take to get back to the "good old days"? I think it could take generations.[12]

Life is a series of risks under the best of conditions. We must do our best with imperfect knowledge and limited insight. How deep a hole could we fall into? I doubt that anyone expected the severity of the drop in Russian living standards following the disintegration of the Soviet Union. Do we have liabilities that could take us to this depth? Possibly so.

To take an easy one we can look at our money. Our current dollar is probably worth between eight and twelve cents compared to the 1931 dollar.[13] If a full deflationary cycle were to run its course, all the inflation has to be squeezed out of the dollar. Thus, the purchasing power of a dollar should expand eight to 12 times. Of course our incomes will also drop to 1/8 to 1/12 of current levels to reflect this.

Unfortunately the contracts we have made to pay off house notes, credit cards, etc, will not drop because they are denominated in dollar amounts.[14] These will become unpayable.

This process of general contraction takes something like a year to achieve. In the recent Russian example it took two or so years to achieve a 30%+ decline in living standards.

A personal example: My mother began working in Chicago in 1931. That year the deflationary wave associated with the Great Depression hit the local business sector. As the newest salesperson in a retail department store, she took six pay cuts in nine months. She would have been cut further but the government passed a law guaranteeing a minimum wage and stopped nationwide pay cuts once they reached that level.

Unfortunately, there is another

problem. The 1931 dollar was backed by gold. This provided a sort of floor for devaluation because there is a market for gold which is somewhat independent of the dollar. The dollar of today is backed not by gold but by the promises of politicians. Should a prudent person bet their survival chances on the promises of politicians?

What is a prudent person to do?

It seems likely that there will be a huge wave of deflation leading to foreclosures and bankruptcies. Credit card debt is essentially not collateralized so there is nothing to seize when the banks panic. The usual strong-arm collection tactics they are masters of will force people into bankruptcy when they cannot pay. Very much of this activity and the entire banking system goes into decline.

History will describe this as a "Great Depression" although the government will probably try to put some "spin" on it. Maybe the government will call it a "Great Banana" until their denial collapses. The Feds will eventually save the banking system but this will take time. All of the resulting hysteria and theatrics will aggravate a crash and it sure looks like we are headed for a long period

of "low equilibrium capitalism" following the crash.

So what is a prudent person to do?

Bear with me while I attempt to sketch the larger picture. Fernand Braudel[15] describes economies as having up to three layers, sort of like a layer cake.

The simplest (lowest), and most universal layer is at the level of the topsoil. This is the extraction layer. The layer of the farmstead, fishery, mine and forest. Relationships are face to face and face to dirt, timber and water. This level is not something that can be seen as actually distinct from the topsoil. This is where most humans have always lived. Throughout virtually all of human history over 90 percent of all humans have lived as hunters, herdspeople and peasants.

The middle layer is built on the first and is the level of commerce. Buying and selling and organization of markets occurs here. Relationships are more remote and abstract. This second layer is less extensive than the first, and not all societies have it.

The third (top) layer, built directly upon the others, is the layer of finance. Few societies have this layer. This layer is largely remote from the reality of the topsoil or face to face relationships.[16]

Financial panics and crashes primarily start in the financial layer. Recessions and depressions occur in all layers with the deeper events (Great Depressions) beginning in the financial layer and driving progressively down into the primary layer. A very good description of this process (and the reasons to be on a homestead during one) is described in J. D. Belanger's *A Place Called Attar.*

If my analysis is remotely correct, the situation seems like a no-brainer from the point of view of a Prudent Person. Get thee beyond the sidewalks and to the country if thou wouldst minimize thy discomfort! Life contains suffering. If events unfold as "My Current Reality Sees & Hears It" then we will all experience some discomfort. We may be able, by prudent action and planning, to avoid some of the avoidable discomfort.

deflation hedge for consumers.

15. Fernand Braudel: *The Structures of Everyday Life*
Vol. I: Civilization and Capitalism 15th-18th Century
Vol. II: The Wheels of Commerce
Vol. III: The Perspective of the World

Published and re-issued from 1955 until the 1980s. English language editions from Harper and Row, NY 1982 and later. Available in paperback.

Braudel was one of the greatest modern historians, and this trilogy is considered his greatest work. His description of the development of layers of economic activity is largely in Vol. II. If one would like to see what it was like to live in precapitalist Europe during "low equilibrium" times, which is from the dawn of history until the 1400s, this is in Vol. I. His description of the continuing crises of capitalism is in Vol. III.

Anyone who is involved in home schooling should read this and share it with their young ones. This is the sort of real history which talks about the daily life of common people through the past few centuries. Many of us grew up thinking that all history amounted to was dates of famous battles and political events. This is an antidote for much of that.

16. Of course the financial layer is the one that takes over and drives many decisions at the lower layers. This produces the strange conditions of "corporate farming". Once the financiers start driving these industries, decisions at the low level reflect "corporate policies," not the real topsoil, local market, good husbandry or common sense.

The collective term Hobart Rowen uses for the financier crowd is "swindler." I was reminded of this by his last book. For a deeper discussion of the role of these types in recent American history read Hobart Rowen, *Self Inflicted Wounds: From LBJ's "Guns and Butter" to Reagan's "Voodoo Economics,"* 1994, Random House, NY. This is another good, if advanced, book for home schooling. Rowen was a *Washington Post* columnist who covered the White House and political economics issues for many years.

The idea of the swindle is to get something for nothing, or at least very little. In the financial layer of the economy we have a collection of highly intelligent individuals organized as predators. They make their livings by separating common people and governments and businesses from their money.

Also see Tom Lowry "Mob Linked to Stock Fraud," *USA Today,* Friday February 6, 1998 p. B-1. The Mafia is buying up brokerages. "Stock manipulation is seen by the mob as an easy way to make money without much effort or risk," says Assistant US Attorney Cynthia Monaco.

Where the money went

Why the savings you think you have in the bank aren't really there

THE INTENTIONAL PEASANT
MARYLAND

Strictly speaking, there is not much money in this or any other country today. Almost none of it circulates. What we call money, the Federal Reserve "notes," are sometimes called fiat scrip. This means that it is money only by fiat or decree of the sovereign. It is money because the State says it is.

Further, the green "dollar bills" we think of as money represent only a small fraction of the currency that circulates. Most money exists only as bookkeeping entries in computers. One can get dollars if one wants them, but if many of us wanted them at one time we would create a "bank run," where they had too few physical dollars in stock to cover the public's demand. In such a case we'd have to wait until the Federal Reserve sent more dollar bills to the bank to cover the problem.

Strictly speaking, money has no value in and of itself. Gold and silver money does exist, but it doesn't circulate at face value because it is much more valuable as metal. Also, as Gresham pointed out, bad money drives out good. Paper notes have driven money, properly so called, out of the marketplace. This makes modern economics largely a psychological game and explains why the State is so anxious to keep a happy face on the economy.

Before getting to where the money went, we need to cover where the money came from.

All legal tender money is created by banks. No exceptions. It is created by bank loans. When John and Mary or International Cat Food get loans, they are put on the bank's record as both a debit and a credit—both an in and an out, so to speak. The bank gives the borrower a check book or a check for the amount borrowed. When John or Mary write checks from this amount they are really behaving like a sort of mini-mint, creating money as they go, money which never existed before.

When the borrower repays the principle of the loan, the money disappears again. It is "extinguished" from the bank's records. In this country, there is money in circulation only because it has been borrowed into existence. In bankspeak this is "monetizing the debt." (You thought David Copperfield was a magician?)

If the public fails to borrow enough, there is less money being created and the government has to give a war or something to make more debt.

An important thing to remember about this is that the bank can lend out from six to 11 times the amount of its deposits. This is possible because we all keep our money in the bank. It matters not whether bank A or bank B, because they balance their accounts out between themselves every evening, called bank clearing. The bank can then legally lend out this "float" many times over.

Not only is the legally required bank reserve very low: it doesn't actually exist. This is because banks can and do borrow from European banks—the so called Eurodollar market.

Because cancellation of a loan cancels six to 11 times the amount of money that was created by that loan, banks like to make increasing numbers and amounts of loans. This brings us down to where the money went.

When the public is maxed out and can't possibly support any additional monthly loan payments, we have a situation where the money supply cannot expand unless the government sends a truckload to Israel, Brazil, Uganda, or someplace. I am indebted to my daughter Merrilee for pointing out that if Mexico and Brazil suddenly repaid their bank loans in full, we would have a severe problem because six to 11 times the amount would suddenly be extinguished from the money supply.

In a similar way, if we had a depression where enterprises were going belly-up at a great rate, loans would be extinguished and vast amounts of money would disappear from the system. This is because a loan default is like a loan repayment. They are both cancellations of the loan and thereby six to eleven times the loan amount in created money. After all, loans are always repaid—by either the borrower or the lender.

The State gets its messing-around money (what it spends over and above its tax revenues) in the same way John and Mary did. But instead of going to Nevvafale National on the corner, it goes directly to the Federal Reserve. The Fed lends the State what it needs and the State gives the Fed its IOUs called bonds.

But what about the U.S. mint? Don't they print the money?

Yes they do, but the State doesn't get to keep it. They give it to the Fed for a small printing fee.

Why, you ask, do we do such a thing?

Was there some doubt in your mind about who owns the country?

Managing your money:

Cheap is good; free is best

THE INTENTIONAL PEASANT

Around any homestead, even a city-bound wannabe like this one, there is a never-ending crush of work to do. Our backs might be equal to all that strain, but our wallets and pocketbooks often shudder in anguish. The cost of a fir 2x4, for example, is breath-stopping. For people with imagination, dedication, and perhaps a little chutzpah there are ways to lower the level of fiscal pain and have a lot of fun in the process.

For those who don't feel that living cheap can be fun, come along anyway. Some day everybody may need the skills involved in getting along with less. But it really can hook us and become our favorite sport.

Here's the case: this codger is a certified book junky. The local library sells good used books for eighty-five cents. More often than not, the book one didn't buy year before last, for thirty bucks, eventually will turn up in the sales shelves. And for those with a preference for non-fiction, there isn't apt to be much competition. This very morning, beautiful big, fat books were on special sale, two for $1.50. All this is not carefully-thought-out strategy, but who has $30 for a book? Even better, pricewise, but with a rather meager selection, is the mission store, where books—any books—go for 10¢.

Out of sheer desperation years ago, when the brood was young, we stumbled on to a great truth: in America, lots of stuff goes begging. The treasure that appeared in our local dumps was amazing. It even included a working lottery wheel—which became a chandelier after we shooshed the badger off it, cleaned it up, and added chains. The wasteland out in back of a prefab-house factory yielded the material for a 12 x 20-foot yard house, needing only roof shingles for finish.

Many years ago, a large sign appeared on a sturdy old four-square house not far away on Main Street: "Let us build your business on this site." Since we all know what "site clearing" means, the thought of all that beautiful old lumber being mangled under Caterpillar treads was just too much. To condense a long tale, we approached the builder, got permission to dismantle the house, and carted the pieces off—and managed to half-again the size of our own home. Unlike the COUNTRYSIDER in North Carolina with the salvaged-but-legally-usable church timbers, the building inspectors are still waiting to hear from us.

On a smaller scale, those slightly-leaning, often-abandoned outbuildings are available to those of us who don't mind asking for permission to haul them away and who will be responsible for leaving the premises in neat order. Shipping pallets have often been mentioned in COUNTRYSIDE as another source of free-for-the-hauling material for home projects.

While probably scarce in rural areas, those official or unofficial dumps in profligate-American metropolitan settings, mentioned above, can be a literal mine of good stuff. A long-ago friend, an artist with a fevered imagination, did all of her "shopping" at the Annapolis (Maryland) dump. It loses something in the telling, but the swordfish on her wall, put together of perforated aluminum and oddments like a tin funnel and the cadaverous insides of a toaster oven, was actually stunning. So was the orphaned, legless chair hung from the ceiling beam by found parachute straps.

Most of us don't have a Bobbi's genius for seeing esoteric possibilities like this in rubbish, but to the extent we can find the time to improvise, we can save lots of cash and have a great time. The homesteader who looks first at the cost of hog panels and then—ah-ha!—at all those pallets free for the hauling, is well on the way.

People whose idea of dressing for dinner is putting on a clean sweatshirt won't be much impressed, but this peasant has the reputation of being the best-dressed man in our creaking crowd of codgers. (Codgers come from an era when wearing clothes was more or less mandatory.) Most of our people now know that the bulk of our wardrobe comes from thrift shops and the mission stores. We draw the line at underwear, even President Clinton's. As an example, within weeks just prior to writing this, the Mission produced three brand-new herringbone tweed sports jackets—that fit like the proverbial glove—for a total of $5. (Buy one, get two free.) Thank heaven for moderns and their sweatsuits! It isn't often we hit a bargain like this, but we rarely pass a thrift without stopping.

Incidentally, for those who wear woolen things, sweaters and the like, there is no better or cheaper sweater bag than the two-gallon Zip-Loc.

Having gone on like this, please accept a confession: most of the time the peasant lives in jeans or sweat-suits—which are cheap, comfortable, and easily maintained.

Yes, thrift and mission stores are great. For us, on the other hand, flea markets have been iffy; around here people seem to have an exalted opinion of the value of their castoffs and appear offended at our more realistic offers. Still, for youngsters just starting out and who need a houseful of furniture, that's where the action is. Here is the gospel according to many talented and successful interior designers: never buy new furniture. (That is, unless one is buying for a well-heeled client and is getting a commission.) Furniture is the biggest exception to our flea-market caveat. One can have a great time, lots of fun, and save important money in furnishing that first house or apartment via the flea market and, on top of this, end up with furnishings of character. Searching the classified ads can pay well, too. The rest of the designer's gospel: never buy a big white sofa and never buy anything—anything—else without thinking about it for two weeks. The obvious exception to this rule is when we've already thought about it, are looking for it, and encounter one at significant savings.

This antique computer was a real find in the classifieds; it's been serving well for years. But this was more good luck than good management because technology changes so fast and some—even with a prestigious name—aren't really built for the long haul. For techies who really know what they're doing, used electronics, especially from compulsory-upgrade cranks, can be the way to go.

Besides probing yard sales, mission stores, and flea markets, the most valuable free resource we have may well be our own labor. Goes without saying? Okay, so come dinner time, a lot of sweat equity might not seem so cheap when everybody is looking for a third helping of the mashed potatoes. Still, when labor is all we have...

As an instance, when this peasant's barber went to Italy for his third three-month sabbatical, in desperation he began cutting his own hair. It's a lot easier than people might think, after watching the barber do it for 20 years or so. A little checking around the back of the medulla oblongata from a cooperative wife might be a big help. On the distaff side of the subject, many women never see the inside of a hair salon.

After a while, we begin to look for ways to indulge our hobby and turn lemons into lemonade in the process. Some of the recipes for shaving soap which have appeared in these pages (80/2:10) may very well be the answer to the problem of those little slips of bar soap that just won't stick to the next bar. After running off a batch this very morning, old peasant is in business for another year. Of course, with his beard, there are only a few square inches left for the razor.

Possibly the greatest (cheap or free) resource homesteaders have available to them is their own ingenuity. Without doubt all this is like preaching to the choir, as many Countrysiders never miss an opportunity to substitute ingenuity for money. But those of us who are new to the concepts can use all the vicarious experience we can get. As an example, take the do-it-yourself peat moss: the leaves that drop with happy dependability every fall. Nothing cheap, in this peasant's experience, improves awful dirt like turned-under leaves. As with most other organic matter turned under, the soil will want some nitrogen: dried blood, cottonseed meal, poultry manure, and such. One of the most wasted sources of free nitrogen is what gets flushed down the urinals of the nation.

Following several years of letting earthworms do all the work, it occurred to us that our lifetimes might not really suffice to make dirt out of this unbaked pottery we find here underfoot. Maybe, we thought, we should give the little pioneers a hand. Or a fork. (Mea culpa, Ruth Stout!) This fork business is terribly painful to many of our worms who have been doing yeoman labor in our service for years. Nothing to do but grit our teeth and turn them under.

Our garden on borrowed land is divided into beds now, one forkful deep, using Peter Chan's methods he describes in *Better Vegetable Gardens the Chinese Way*. Since Tiller The Hon went to his greater reward, there is only the turning fork and low back pain. But the fork doesn't want gas, just potatoes and eggs, and it starts every time. Mostly. Then there's the blessed silence. Of course, if we were turning six acres... But how many snorting, belching Caterpillars did it take to build the pyramids, the kongs of Thailand, or light at Alexandria? Snorting, belching peasants? Quite a few.

There's a lot of talk these days about remineralizing the Earth. There was a piece not long ago in the Daily Bleah about how they're saving the Black Forest in Germany with minerals. But one of the richest sources of minerals is tree leaves, the end product of the tree's own mining of the deep earth. Why a forest would need minerals seems almost spooky. Could it be that the tree leaves in the Black Forest are being raked up? In a forest? The article didn't say. Articles rarely say much we care about and need to know.

Here in Big Town, a hundred thousand unpaid volunteers fill big black plastic bags with leaves for us peasants every fall, setting them handily at curbside where Henrietta, our Cavalier, can scarf them up. It takes possibly 20 trips with the little station wagon to get a sufficient amount to cover the small garden and to bury the fig trees for winter. Because these leaves come from widely different places with varying soil profiles, they represent a real buffet meal of minerals for the garden. The downside of an over-winter heavy-mulch is slugs, but pulling most of the mulch back and turning the soil in the spring helps control the little devils.

Probably the most overlooked resource is American paper. The bulk of course, is the printed fish-wrapper called, with a straight face, the daily news. But everything we buy comes wrapped in something and, if it isn't plastic, chances are it's paper. Since putting in the garden beds, we pile all this effluent on the walkways between them, cover this with some leaves, then sprinkle pine bark mulch on top. (Coal cinders would be better, if we had access to them, because slugs hate cinders.)

Paper is a perfectly good way to turn sod into garden-ready soil, too. One simply piles it on in the fall. It must be thick and needs weighting down against the weather. Come spring, the ground is ready to cultivate. Mostly.

One of America's favorite pastimes seems to be a kind of financial "can you top this." Many people who hover around the poverty level—intentionally or not—feel a squish of guilt in not being able to give their children the golden dump on birthdays and Christmas. In truth, when all their friends are being buried under a landslide of merchandise, it's difficult to teach our children more civilized values. After attending a $30,000 wedding reception, we found out that $50,000 is not at all uncommon. The only word that seems to fit the situation is obscene. But there it is: the only solution to the mess is raw guts on the part of more thoughtful people. And it does take courage to buck the tide.

In this peasant's experience, voluntary poverty is a trip; involuntary poverty is an abomination. Perhaps that's why we who live in the industrialized west can look at poverty without flinching. We know that, in the worst case, we can always go back to that aerospace job, or get written back into ER, or any of those other options that currently can only be pursued in an urban anthill. At least, we may think we still can.

As an aside, the medical fraternity of Greater America has a diagnosis for our, uh, *condition*. It is called autonomy-withdrawal syndrome. So as a long as we've got it, why not enjoy it? Let our tee shirts proclaim: Cheap Is Neat! (Hand lettered by ourselves, of course.)

Do you really need credit life or mortgage insurance?

Ken Scharabok
Tennessee

Credit life insurance, which pays off a loan if the borrower dies, is generally sold to people who take out installment loans or buy goods, such as vehicles, on the installment plan. On a home, it is generally called mortgage insurance rather than credit life.

As you are taking out the loan one item on the statement might be automatic credit life insurance, or you might be asked if you want to include it. However, before allowing it automatically on the loan or saying yes, you should give it some thought.

Credit life insurance is expensive and varies widely from state to state. For example, on a $10,000, 12 percent per annum loan payable over 48 months, in Tennessee credit life insurance would cost $433 over the life of the loan, versus just $156 in New York State.

In most states you have the option to either refuse credit life insurance on installment loans if you can document you have other assets which would be available to pay off the loan in the event of your death, or to obtain the insurance from a source other than the seller. Credit unions generally offer the lowest rates.

Many buyers simply don't need credit life insurance; however, it can be a good deal for people who are old or ill or who do not have enough other life insurance or other assets to cover their debts if they die.

Almost all mortgage lenders will require you to include mortgage insurance. However, here again, shop around and investigate other alternatives. For example, you may be able to have the lending institution named as the primary beneficiary on an existing or new life insurance policy. In this situation, if you die the institution receives the full insurance payout, subtracts out that needed to settle the mortgage payoff, and the rest reverts to the estate or secondary beneficiary. You will not be able to cancel the insurance without the institution's permission and the institution will be notified in the event payments are stopped.

Lending institutions may also permit you to cancel mortgage insurance in some situations. For example, say the original mortgage of $50,000 has been paid down to $25,000 and the property is now appraised at $100,000. The institution may feel confident enough on the loan to no longer require further mortgage insurance.

Like any other credit or insurance, use credit life and mortgage insurance wisely.

Managing your money:

The $700 solution

It's good to have big goals... but thinking small might help you reach them faster

MARK A. HOWLAND
CHIEF BIOLOGIST
ENVIRONMENTAL RESEARCH CORPS
(AND A COUSIN OF OL' BEN)

Many people think that the most difficult part in starting out on a mission toward homesteading is saving a thousand dollars or more. This number seems to most to be an insurmountable mountain that places their goals out of reach.

I would like to introduce Ben Franklin's "Rules of Seven" to COUNTRYSIDE'S readers. Terms in today's lingo like roll lucky sevens, or snake eyes, are actually related to old Ben's philosophy. Ben Franklin even started the country's first lottery to help raise money for his church.

Ben felt, as many of his generation did, that our counting system of 10s was not in keeping with the human spirit. In fact, akin to those who advocated the metric system with those esoteric centigrades and meters, Franklin and his peers advocated a system based on sevens. He felt that the week, divided into seven days, created a mood, an atmosphere, that creates attainable goals for those in link with that division of time.

I have modified this rule of sevens to what I call the Seven Hundred Dollar Solution. This solution has brought me wealth, material possessions, and happiness.

So many of the articles of this and other magazines are written by aspiring homesteaders waiting and dreaming until they can get to that special piece of land. Yet others are written about the failure to figure in the costs of the items needed for a homestead to succeed, and how their dreams came to a crashing halt.

The Seven Hundred Dollar Solution can put those dreaming years to productive use before that move to a homestead, or prevent a potential failure to realize the dream once there.

Let me show you how $100 a month, $700 every seven months, can provide many of the basic needs and items that assist and help realize a successful homestead.

Saving and making $700

Ever wonder why convenience stores spring up on almost every corner of America? The average markup on a convenience store item over its counterpart in the larger supermarket averages from a minimum of seven percent to a high of 49 percent (See that Rule of Sevens? I'm not making this up, the source is *Today's Grocer*). The average person in America lives three to five minutes from a convenience store (one to two miles away), and lives 20 to 30 minutes from a large grocery store (eight to 10 miles away).

For the convenience of saving 15 minutes and at the cost of saving about 31¢ in gas, the average person spends $3.43 cents every time he or she enters a convenience store. In fact, research has shown that the average person intends to go into the store to pick up a pack of cigarettes, or a carton of milk, unconsciously intending to spend less than a dollar. But in reality, the trip often includes a couple of candy bars, a newspaper or auto magazine, extra sundries, and that gourmet ice cream that just happens to be one of your favorite flavors. In states with lottery tickets, the average cost of a convenience store trip is over $7. After all, you might hit that big one!

Want to save a hundred dollars a month fast? Don't go to the convenience store.

Not only will you get savings of 7-49% by obtaining the prices a large market offers: with some discipline, these extra items will be eliminated as well. With the average person making 19 trips a month to the convenience store, savings of $25 to $50 are easy. Cut out those cigarettes, and not only do you save more, but also when you do get out to the country on your homestead, there is far less chance of burning the forest down. You'll live longer to enjoy your property as well.

Look at other costly non-necessities in your life, and $100 a month becomes possible. Subscribe to the newspaper rather than picking one up. Buy your milk at the store rather than the delivery guy who shows you that special on spray can whipped cream. Feed that wood stove a little more rather than fill the oil man's pockets.

You don't like living frugal? It's a modern society and you want to enjoy the pleasures? Well, then just try living sensibly for a month and see if it returns to you that first $100 deposit to the $700 solution. If you don't like it, go back to your other lifestyle.

If you are going to be a homesteader, the current mode of modern living (living check to check) will need to be changed anyway. I bet you won't go back. But at least at the end of seven months you'll have that first $700 to start building your dreams with.

Need $700? There are seven weeks between Halloween and Christmas. Try the advanced method, getting $700 in just seven weeks. Go into the woods and find creeping jenny or princess pine and some spaghnum moss.

Make a wreath ring out of old chicken wire and stuff it with the moss. Weave the princess pine or jenny in between the wire openings until a solid wreath effect is reached. Floral supply locations or Christmas decoration outlets will buy these ready-to-be-decorated wreaths for at least $7.

In seven weeks, you can make a hundred wreaths on weekends and nights, even in front of that mind-numbing boob tube. The moss, if moistened regularly, will keep the wreaths fresh looking, like new if stored in a cool place. It's extra money. Make your Christmas present to yourself one of your homesteading items.

Education

Do you know that a high school grad averages about $20,000 in salary a year in the U.S.? A college degree brings that up to about $35,000, a master's to $44,000, and a doctorate to $66,000.

But do you know that a professional degreed person in the U.S. averages $111,000 dollars a year!

What is a professional degree? These are the specialized degrees awarded by professional associations, trade groups, or the government.

A solid waste and wastewater technician's license takes about two months of study, about $500 in entry fees, and gives one access to a job paying, on the average, over $50,000 a year.

A course in surveying or CAD drafting takes about a year with average course costs of under $700. A surveyor's license may require apprenticeship for up to seven years. Surveyors in America average over $80,000 a year.

Beauty technician, nail care license, health care provider, child care license, animal science technician, water quality specialist, even that high school GED can be obtained for less than $700 in annual education costs.

A home welding course takes less than seven weeks to complete and a welding equipment setup is under $700, yet welders are in demand throughout the U.S.

We spend more each year on pet food and pet care than we do on humans, yet technicians to assist vets are scarce and hard to find.

Nurses with specialized training earn about 40% more than those without. The list goes on and on.

Not all of us need to spend $70,000 a year at Harvard to get ahead in the world. Find out about the professional degrees in your field of interest. Find out what minimal course work can be had at lower costs to get a leg up in that field through some type of accreditation.

Computer

The Seven Hundred Dollar Solution can provide some fun as well.

Seven hundred dollars will buy a pretty decent used or refurbished computer these days. Not top of the line, not the fastest. But it will get you one that gets you on the Internet. Check out the main mail order companies like Gateway or Dell—they have refurbished unit outlets. Get last year's technology in a refurbished unit. It will work just as well.

For less than $7 a week, you can find unlimited Internet access in most locations.

Don't be a technophobiac, thinking that going country means that you can't live with high tech.

As a research tool alone, the information on the Net will aid you in developing homesteading plans. Need solar information? Need a source for that mushroom spawn? Want to find that book on some esoteric homesteading subject? Check out the Net's online bookstore—far cheaper prices than that mega bookstore down the street. Check out companies' web sites.

Pay for that computer in seven months with a Saturday or Sunday job. It is possible to find a weekend job in some seasonal retail stores hiring for the Christmas season, greenhouse and nurseries in the springtime, landscapers in the summer. You can make $100 a month even if the jobs pay $5 an hour. You may have to put in an extra 20 hours on top of the 40 or 45 hours a week your regular job requires.

Our ancestors worked up to 18 hours a day a hundred years ago. You want to live like a king on a homestead? The best equity is sweat equity. You can bet it's hard on the family life; you can bet you will be tired. But seven months of hard work will get that computer, and you can always go back to your normal schedule afterward. Seven bucks a week for access will buy you into a few research titles on how that computer can make you money as well. Besides, there are no 40-hour work weeks on a homestead. It usually is more like 80 to 100.

Worried about powering that computer in the country? Work that second job another seven months and buy a solar panel array. Even in the poorest sun locations in the country, the 35 watts demand of a computer can be powered from any modest

A real sign of the times

The fairy tale weavers in the establishment media and Washington D.C. never tire of telling the masses about America's supposedly booming economy and widespread prosperity. COUNTRYSIDERS and others who use common sense know otherwise, but that doesn't stop the spin doctors from repeating their falsehoods.

Could the success of one especially profitable stock actually be a sign of economic deterioration?

Nashville-based Dollar General has nearly 3,700 discount stores in medium-sized towns and big cities throughout America. Dollar General's stock has risen 34 percent in the past year. Over the past decade, Dollar General has been the ninth-best performing public stock in America, according to *The Wall Street Journal.*

Many people would assume that a retailer such as Dollar General is doing great business because consumers are flush with cash. The situation is just the opposite.

Dollar General's target market is families and single people earning $25,000 a year or less. As the middle class has seen its wages erode while jobs are sent overseas, Dollar General's focus on low-priced and affordable items has made them one of the few options available to ordinary working folks with limited funds.

The Economic Policy Institute reports that households earning $25,000 or less a year are the fastest-growing income group in America. That's a completely different trend than what the "news" casters are proclaiming.—*Al Doyle*

panel system and batteries costing under $700.

Clothing

The Seven Hundred Dollar Solution can apply to clothing as well. The average man spends over $1,000 on clothing a year, a woman over $2,300 (in the industrial Northeast). Shirts, underwear, pants, and shoes as well as children's clothing make up the bulk of the costs.

Seven hundred dollars will gain you entry into a new world. How does $2.75 for a golf shirt sound? How about $4 for a brand new child's frock? Where? Same place the stores get them from of course!

Go to any yellow pages and find the listing for textile or silkscreen suppliers.

We use Carolina Made to obtain shirts bought by the dozen, hats by the half dozen, socks by the gross, dresses, etc.

The company only requires a minimum order of $200. We can mix and match sizes and colors by the half dozen.

A color inkjet printer capable of making iron-on transfers can be attached to that computer to make work logos on the shirts and other colorful designs. A set of fabric pens or paints, and artistic talent can create a new secondary income at church bazaars, flea markets, or even walking into that company down the street and asking if you can produce their work uniforms for them with personalized logos.

Besides, a case of shirts is more than you will ever need for yourself, wear the best and more colorful designs for advertising and knock that clothing bill down to under $700 by spending $700.

Shelter and food

Of course, you need some shelter to be on that land. I hate to tell you this, but most raw land you can find affordable to buy to start a homestead just does not have those rolling pastures, that cleared woodlot, that perfect sweeping driveway up to the house location.

Most land today still on the market at reasonable costs has its pitfalls. Green and catbrier, poison ivy stands, honeysuckle, and kudzu are just a few of the pleasures that await you that need to be cleared away in order to use your land. Many find that it takes more than a few weekends or summer vacations to get that land into usable condition. And that dream log cabin just doesn't go up that fast, nor does the money to build it come that easily.

Well, how about a $700 solution? For $700 you can buy Stromberg's Chicks and Game Birds Unlimited geodesic dome fasteners, a pile of mill lumber, and 8 mil vinyl greenhouse plastic to make a usable 2,500 sq. ft. shelter. The connectors are made from galvanized steel and are pre-shaped to make it possible to bolt together 2x4s into a geodesic framework.

Connector sets are about $50 apiece, seven for $350, each dome unit takes 12-2x4s at $2 each—under $200—and enough plastic costs under $200. Eight mil vinyl plastic lasts up to 20 years unlike the more common 6 mil polyethylene plastic, and can be painted for privacy shading.

Alter the dome connections to allow several units together (we use seven), and a larger roof can be placed over one's head.

Finished with clearing the land, or got that cabin up? You now have left on your property a ready-to-go greenhouse if you coated the walls with whitewash made from a $1 bag of lime, like Tom Sawyer. Or a shelter for those pygmy goats or range chickens you plan to have for a food supply.

Don't think the Seven Hundred Dollar Solution can be applied to solving this need? Well, research it. Seven hundred dollars can go a long way to creating a food supply.

Seven hundred dollars will buy enough seeds to plant over 20 acres of land—and you can grow all the food you will ever consume in a year on less than two acres.That $700 will buy a pair of breeding goats; it will buy a cow; it will buy chicks and breeding pens.

Seven hundred dollars will buy all the lumber and materials you need to build mushroom holding trays that you can set up in one of the geodesic dome units. Filled with straw and compost, or prepackaged growth mixtures such as BioMatrix from BioMass Farms that we sell, and sprinkled with mushroom spawn; button mushrooms, oyster mushrooms, Japanese shittake and enoki mushrooms and others are easily cultivated, being about a seven week crop. Some mushrooms, especially freshly grown and not dried imports, fetch prices up to $7 per pound at restaurants in any medium sized city. Plus, they are pretty tasty for your own use as well!

Water

Water is a necessity of life. Water needs for the homestead are critical to provide for animals, humans, crops, landscaping, erosion control, and other aspects.

I own a 49 acre wetlands and wildlife research station in Lakeville, Massachusetts called BioMass Farms. I did not pay a dime for the land, obtaining it through barter, but that is a story for another time. At this facility, besides doing erosion control design testing for products my firms release, we grow about 400 species of wetland plants that we use in replication planting work that is used to replace wetlands in areas of construction.

Needless to say, we need water for this—water to rush waters down a slope to test out a new erosion control product's effectiveness in stopping silt; water to satisfy the demands of wetlands' species cultivated both in greenhouses and in outside growing beds; and water to keep the fields of wildflowers we have seeded and which have matured, providing us with aesthetics and addressing the science of slope stabilization.

BioMass Farms is not unlike homesteads that have little to no access to public utilities, expensive or difficult routing to bring power to the aquatic resources, and no large ponds or rushing waterfalls that could be tapped for water easily. What we do have is a small river that borders our north and east edges of the property. What we need is a way of getting that water to our locations on the farm where we need the water with no power.

Hydraulic rams are nice, but you need a good fall of water to get effective pumping ratios. Our land changes only about eight feet in elevation over 3000', and the river lies at the lowest elevation with no appreciable fall.

Solar pumps are great, but on a wooded New England site with limited west vistas, solar well pumping, a power drainer of solar panels if there ever was one, just wasn't practical.

My local utility company has the distinction of being the numero uno company of the U.S.A. for highest utility rates. And it adds insult to injury by only giving one free pole to bring that power to you. Anything beyond 200' is on your tab.

The Amish region of Pennsylvania provided us with this seven hundred dollar solution. The RIFE Hydraulic Ram Co., founded in the late 1800s, manufactures a rather neat product called the Sling Pump.

The sling pump looks like a miniature Goodyear Blimp. At the base of the unit is a small propeller and inside the core of the blimp-like unit is a helical tube that is coiled and stacked within the unit. The propeller spins the unit in the water forcing water into one end of the helical tube. The reducing diameter of the tube causes the water to become more restricted in its coiling toward the rear of the unit, forcing the water to "spurt" ahead. The resulting action is about 1 gallon a minute, 60 gallons an hour, over 700 gallons a day. Cost of the product, just under $700.

We now sell the unit as an approved distributor in New England.

The Sling Pump: Water pumping water, with no energy requirements.

The Sling Pump has one moving part, and that's lubricated by water! We pump the water to holding tanks set at the highest part of the farm where we can gravity feed water down to our needs. We plan to add a pump every seven months or so, of course, until we have seven units giving us over 5,000 gallons a day that will not cost us a dime to pump.

The environment

You had better believe the Seven Hundred Dollar Solution applies to the environment as well. We are all responsible to provide care for the Earth that supports us, and seven hundred dollars a year spent on the environment is one investment that has immeasurable rewards.

You want to be a homesteader? Well, be a homesteader who cares about the place you live in, one who cares about the land. Take a lesson from our Native American friends: the land provides for you, warms you, feeds you; take care of it and nurture it.

- $700 can buy a good used low emission wood stove and lower the dependence on oil or gas resources.
- $700 can buy a solar panel array, not to use for the power demands of water pumping, but for the lighter demands of lighting. Reduce the need for nuclear power or air polluting coal power plants to generate electricity. Get off-grid, as they say.
- $700 will buy a power water turbine for those who have the right site.
- $700 will buy a small electricity-producing windmill.
- $700 will buy enough erosion control materials to stop that mud from the driveway from sliding into the nearby brook and clogging the gills of the fish that live in it.
- $700 will buy a Pasture Pump created by those same people at Rife Ram, a unit that has cattle or horses pumping their own water and prevents the animals from tramping in the streams and ponds to get their water and thus polluting the aquatic resources with feces, nutrients, and silt.
- $700 will buy a new AIR wind turbine, giving you free wattage from the wind, again reducing energy needs.
- $700 will buy enough filter equipment to make water potable.
- $700 will buy those unique and innovative items that helps the environment in so many ways—solar

ovens, wood water heaters, a grain mill, a beekeeper's setup.

- $700 will buy a composting toilet protecting our groundwater from its number one enemy—septic waste.
- $700 twice over will buy the top of the line energy efficient refrigerator, the top power waster in your household.

The Seven Hundred Dollar Solution provides many solutions for the environment, and the returns are both financial and spiritual.

Give it a try

For those who think the Seven Hundred Dollar Solution, as derived from my cousin Ben Franklin's Rule of Sevens might work, go ahead and give it a try.

Seven hundred dollars in seven months is an achievable goal, much more so than a thousand dollars. For some reason in our psyche, $700 is not as intimidating as $1,000, and appears to most to be reachable.

As you make more money by getting those specialized degrees, step up to the next stage—$700 saved every seven weeks. That's what I do and I am looking to be able to jump to the next level, $7,000 every seven months!

Keep making $700 extra dollars every seven months, apply those moneys in the manner I have suggested while you are planning and dreaming about that homestead. In four short years, you will have some items that can provide the basis for a good start in country living, and isn't that what we claim is all we need—a running start? Make the Seven Hundred Dollar Solution work for you.

Mark A. Howland is a wetlands biologist based out of the Northeast and considered an expert in erosion control, wetlands and wildlife issues, and storm water management. He is a distant cousin of Ben Franklin and owns BioMass. For more information on some of the products he has suggested here he may be contacted at BioMass, 15 Mohawk Ave., E. Freetown, MA 02717; 508-763-5253; www.biofence. com; www.wetlandsandwildlife.com.

Tool care for dollars and sense

Properly maintained tools will last longer, serve you better, save you time and money, and increase your pride of workmanship. Even homesteaders who are aware of this sometimes neglect garden hand tools.

Rule #1 is to never, ever leave a shovel, hoe, rake or any other tool in the garden overnight, and certainly not in the rain.

If you disregard this rule, it might be necessary to clean the blade with a wire brush, or steel wool, or a pumice stone.

Brush or hose off any dirt before storing the tool. Some people keep a five-gallon bucket of coarse sand, laced with vegetable oil, near the tool rack. That makes it quick and easy to thrust the blade of a tool into the oily sand before hanging it up, so cleaning and oiling becomes a routine.

Any tool with a cutting edge can benefit from sharpening, including hoes, shovels and spades. Stones and pebbles can nick blades, but even ordinary soil abrasion will dull them. Touch them up with a bastard mill file, using short, quick strokes, following or restoring the original bevel.

When the original varnish on wooden handles starts to wear, if not before, sand it all off with fine sandpaper. Rub the wood with boiled linseed oil, and then with steel wool.

Hang tools so they are out of the way and yet accessible, and so they will be protected from bumps and scrapes (and you will be too).

At season's end, repeat the cleaning with special care, and wipe down all metal parts with a rag and mineral oil.

The unthinkable, and Grandma Rogers

Would we want to live like she did?

The Intentional Peasant

Unless the homestead is within downwind sniffing distance of a large city, generating enough cash income to pay the taxes (and those other expenses which refuse to go away) can be a genuine problem. Cities are where the money is—extracted in every case from the countryside, the perennial milk cow of the non-producer. In the past, one was able to scare up enough casual income to rub along on, content that food and shelter were all but guaranteed by the home place. The existence of a bank loan, however, laid a frightening dimension on top of all one's "normal" needs—those expenses, so to speak, handed us by the angels. But where a banker was staring down the barrel of his mortgage, a stream of income was essential. Still, we could perhaps pull it off, given health, love, and time enough. The ends were worth the price.

But things got a bit hairy when countryside was emptied to staff the counters at McPimpleburger and Sam's Club. Earl Butz was telling small farmers to "get big or get out," for reasons not to be discussed in polite company. And the small farmer did just that; he got out, more often than not.

All the small businesses which served the farmer began to wink out like stars at dawn. Small towns and rural hamlets today look a lot like post-neutron-bomb horror movies. Making the requisite few bucks has become a genuine dilemma in many places, a situation not any more promising now, when we find ourselves eyeball to eyeball with NAFTA and GATT. No matter how much better off we may be, long term, with free trade (and the jury, as they say, is still out), a term measured in decades is not what the average person is prepared to deal with.

The upshot of this whole thing is that many homesteaders outside the reach of megalopolis may already feel themselves to be in real trouble.

It isn't pleasant to contemplate all the human misery, but failing to face reality is the first step toward total failure. One doubts that Chicken Little was a very happy bird. Even those of us who are close to or who are in major metropolitan areas are perhaps not exempt from worries about the future, given the propensity of our politicians to rattle sabers worldwide on a regular basis, given the overburdened stock market exhaling its hot breath on our mutual funds, and given the insane credit bubble inflated by American consumers.

So enough of the problem; where will we find solutions?

Well, those of us who do find answers will perhaps find them in many different places. I was thinking lately about Grandma Rogers, the last full-time farmer in her clan, as a sort of extreme solution. Grandma and her ilk were really homesteaders, but they called themselves farmers in those days because commercial farming hardly existed in Ambemarle County.

I hesitate to offer Grandma as an answer, because she would be a truly radical one. In fact, it will sound very much like a neoluddite's solution—which is about what it amounts to.

You see, Grandma's people survived on the same ground for many generations without much money at all, but her life looked a lot like a background for Gunsmoke without the gunsmoke. Although the original thousand acres was split until Grandma's parcel was just 90, it provided to be plenty, at least until the tax man cameth. But when she widowed at an early point, she lived comfortably, just as generations before her had lived, without a bank loan, running water, electricity, central heat, hot water, refrigeration, a bath tub, television, a car, a grocer, life insurance, health insurance, vacations, a computer, voice mail, a typewriter, a pager, a ball gown, Ovaltine, Barbie™, Club

Med, a cellular phone or a "regular" phone, or a second book.

Even today, there are people living without these things. She hand-pumped her water, used kerosene lamps, split up windfall to fire eight pot-bellied stoves, heated bath water for the galvanized tub on the kitchen wood-burning cook stove, used the spring house for cooling milk and butter, canned all the winter's food in Ball Perfect Masons sealed with paraffin wax, wrote the indecipherable equivalent of the book of Job on one-penny postal cards, and read The Book, which she did not understand, even with the help of the Reverend Mr. Stiff. Some said he didn't, either. Indeed, not having a radio, she relied for both society and entertainment on Sunday church. She was reputed to have seen a physician once, but generally took care of everything with a springtime purge of senna tea and a large bottle of Rub-My-Tism. The word vacation was not in her vocabulary.

Grandma had a horse and a big old rectangle farm wagon, but got a lift to church in a surrey I understand was owned by the Wheelers, her sister up on the hill. Other places, she just walked, but the people in her circle rarely were found more than 10 miles from home.

She almost always kept pigs whom (that's whom, not which) I had the privilege of feeding summertimes. (Slopping, it was called. I like pigs; I never eat them.)

Often there were as many as three dozen chickens, actual home-hatched barnies called Plymouth Rocks. (I ate those with gusto.)

There were always at least two cows, often four; one belonged to the tenants, people who often disappeared, cow and all, at midnight.

Grandma knew the railroad schedule like most today know the *TV Guide*, but never traveled by train. Her late husband had, though, and their three children were named for railway stations: Linwood, Vernon, and Velma. If the George Washington was even a minute late with its 9:05 p.m. wail, she never failed to remark it.

It probably wasn't until Uncle Linwood went to college that things began to change. His two siblings weren't really college inclined, stayed at home and worked to finance Linwood. The place became a commercial farm, of sorts, temporarily. After Linwood and a friend came up with an invention for scratching the last bit of fiber off cottonseed, sufficient to make a rayon-like thread, he got a nice job at Buckeye in lieu of cash. Then he was able to finance the electric lines, the refrigerator, the hydraulic ram and cistern for running water, and the Model T. No central heat; Grandma wouldn't have it.

This is how bad it can get; or good, if you're of hair-shirt leanings. As you probably can tell, I loved it, but only to be a summertime soldier, in June, July, and August, and only after there was running water, a refrigerator, and twice-monthly movies in Charlottesville, 15 miles in Aunt Velma's Model A. Things didn't begin to get terribly civilized until they built the movie house in Creosote. A movie every week!

But would we want to live like that, in such a primitive way? Nope. Not on your life. Nobody but the occasional idiot, such as a rare intentional peasant, and even this one has a Carmela who hates bugs and who'd rather die than fight a cook stove like Grandma's. Can't say I blame her.

Sometimes, though, it's good to step back in memory—or in some codger's memory—to square one, to basic-basic living. Nobody is apt to want to put on the hair shirt. Do without my computer? Bite your tongue! But if one had to…

Suppose for a moment we're discussing survival here. The whole point is not what we're willing to jettison today, but what we're prepared to dump on that foggy tomorrow which—let's face it—may never arrive. The people who wouldn't survive such a tomorrow are those who never thought about it: those who didn't put by some candles and kerosene lamps and lamp oil, who didn't call up about that old, cheap wood stove advertised in the classifieds, who didn't can up just a little rainy day extra for the cellar, who didn't save some of that excess warm clothing, who didn't think, from time to time, the unthinkable.

• Cut off the borders of soiled and stained flannel-backed tablecloths, as these portions are usually in good shape. Use them to make book covers for cookbooks and children's schoolbooks. They are washable and inexpensive.

• To save time and water doing dishes, wash dishes once a day. Fill a dishpan with hot, soapy water, and keep it beside the sink during the day. Place dirty dishes in it for soaking. After the last meal, dishes will wash up in a jiffy.

• Use the end-of-the-bar soap bits to make liquid soap by breaking the scraps into small pieces and putting them into an empty squeeze detergent bottle. Fill the bottle with warm water and let it sit for at least a day. Squeeze out the soft soap as needed for washing.

• Make new bars of soap by saving all soap scraps in a can. When the can is almost full, put it on the stove in a pan of water. Melt the scraps, stirring the whole time. Pour it into Styrofoam cups, old milk carton bottoms, or other throw away containers. When it hardens, peel or cut away the containers, and use the newly molded soap.

When starting a business ask "What do people need that I can provide?"

"I'd like some advice on starting a home business. What can I do to make a little money for necessary expenses without leaving my homestead?"

Homesteaders have always asked this question, but most approach it from the wrong angle. The basic idea shouldn't be "What can I do to make money," but rather, "What do people need that I can provide?"

Think about it: There's a world of difference!

Example: Many people think that because they have goat milk or rabbit meat or extra tomatoes—or because they like to make soap or candles—people will beat a path to their door, and they'll be "in business."

It seldom works that way. Goat milk and rabbit meat aren't found in most supermarkets because there is very little demand for them. When you have extra tomatoes—or zucchini—so does everyone else. In many cases you're competing with people who are giving the stuff away.

But if you ask "What do people need that I can provide?" you might come up with some very different ideas.

A reader asked, "What do you think will happen if we can't get gas? How will we get to work?"

This is the wrong question, and the wrong concern. If you can't get gas, chances are no one else can either. And if there isn't any transportation, there won't be any jobs, in the current conventional sense.

But that doesn't mean people won't need goods and services, or that other people won't be providing them.

This article offers some ideas and suggestions on how you might fill the gap.

What do you need, yourself?

One of the best and most common ways for this to happen is by discovering something you need that no one is providing. "Necessity is the mother of invention." Many new ideas come about because of one individual's need, not because that individual wanted to start a business. But if other people have the same need, there is potential for a money-making enterprise.

After tiring of the problems associated with using conventional sawhorses for cutting firewood, someone came up with an improved design. A neighbor saw it and wanted one… and a home business was born.

One man made, for his personal use, an ice-fishing rig that sounds an alarm when a fish is on the line. Other fishermen saw it and wanted one like it. Making them became a profitable part-time job.

It might not be necessary to "invent" anything. Mothers searching for a day-care provider encounter others who are also looking for such a service—and start one themselves. We have read in Countryside about a man who sells ice cream—homemade, on the spot—wherever people gather during the summer. This didn't start out to be a business. It was a charitable service for nursing home residents that grew into a business when the demand was seen.

Problems:

- Your needs might be unique, or not as much in demand as you might think. (Many businesses fail because of inadequate market research and because entrepreneurs think everyone else is just like them.)
- You might not be able to provide your product or service at a price potential customers feel is reasonable.
- Manufacturing and/or marketing might be more than you can handle: outside your area of expertise or interest, or beyond your budget.

Most "guides" are idea starters; you still have to think for yourself

There are several sources that list ideas for potential businesses. (One is *How to Earn Extra Income in the Country*, by Ken Scharabok; available for $25 at Scharabo@aol.com)

In some cases these might result in the "Eureka!" factor. You find your perfect business opportunity all laid out and ready to go. More often though, these are meant to get you thinking on your own.

And that's a big problem when talking about small home businesses. Most people don't think. They don't consider what people actually want or need; they don't adequately examine their costs and pricing structure or what customers are willing to pay; and they don't think about all of the many details involved in most businesses, from accounting and advertising to cash flow and inventories and working hours.

A lady who baked and sold cakes in her home advertised her home phone number. The telephone company required a business listing, which she couldn't afford. She quit. Details.

Few people have a clear concept of how a business operates. They think if they just provide a good or service, the money will roll in. And they generally fail.

Some people go to the other extreme. One couple was so concerned with business permits and regulations, including IRS, UPS and USPS requirements, that they neglected the core of their business. They didn't last long either.

Many people, not just homesteaders, are interested in running a small business at home, for many good reasons. Such operations are proliferating, and many are quite successful.

The keys include doing something you know about and enjoy, that a reasonable number of other people want or need, at a price that is low enough to attract and keep customers but high enough to make a profit. Cash reserves and cash flow, marketing, and customer satisfaction are only a few of the things that can make or break even a small, part-time operation.

Tens of thousands of people are becoming entrepreneurs today. Many will find success and happiness. You can be one of them if you give your project enough effort... and thought.

Successful marketers have always said "Find out what people want, and give it to them." As wants change, there will be many new possibilities for those who keep their eyes open.

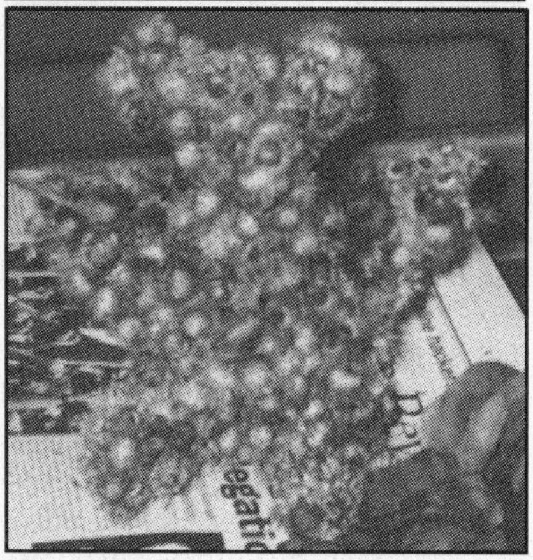

This cuddly-looking creature isn't what it seems to be. It's made of cockleburrs! B. Quintana got the idea while picking burrs off her clothes after walking around her Mooney Range Crest Farm in Pennsylvania.

Sam and Theresa Zagorski use their portable sawmill to cut lumber for neighbors. Here they're making timbers for COUNTRYSIDE's raised beds.

Learn to enjoy doing what you have to do!

DAVID HUGHES
TENNESSEE

Change is a constant, but rapid change is what has brought us to the brink of great danger. Man's world has significantly changed since the 1920s. This alteration has been pushed by "convenience" and "modernization." Both concepts are fundamentally insupportable.

Economic security is tenuous at best and improbable in today's fast-paced society. The pre-1950 small farm economy was based on diversification. Two cows, two sows, chickens and maybe sheep had to be fed by the farm's production. This was a no-debt or low-debt economy. Money changed hands infrequently, and saving was the rule.

That system involved hard work. It seems that our greatest fear as a society today is actually having to break a sweat by working at something. Sweating at play doesn't seem to bother anyone, which seems to be a curious misplacement of values.

Most people are amazed by their own ability to work hard when necessary, and they are even more astonished at what they accomplish while working. I recently mowed my orchard with a European scythe and raked and stacked the hay. I accomplished this "superhuman" feat by mowing an hour or two before work and raking and stacking after supper. This hay made in "off hours" is nearly enough to feed our beef cow this winter.

The same philosophy applies for hoeing the garden, canning and livestock care. All of these things are well within the abilities of an ordinary healthy person.

If you are making the move to a full load of farm/homestead work by building muscles and skills together, try not to overdo it. Learn to plan and manage your work and allow time for rest and play. Learn to like the things you have to do, and change will be kind to you. Remember that work is more "fun" than fun!

The beehive:

When it's springtime in the apiary

FRANK FEDORCHUK
CALIFORNIA

In northern areas where winters are cold and long, Spring is very important in the life of the honeybee. Close attention should be given to the hive at this time, because starvation is a serious potential problem.

An early Spring feeding is essential in helping to start the brood, which needs to be strong as temperatures increase. The feeding should be a syrup consisting of one part sugar dissolved in two parts water. As the temperature rises into the 60 to 70 degree range, the bees become active and appreciate the extra food source.

This is the time when Fumidil-B in syrup form should be given along with the sugar feeding. This medication can be purchased from Mann Lake, Ltd.; 1-800-233-6663; www.mannlakeltd.com.. A small bottle lasts a long time. Be sure to follow the directions closely.

Special care should be given from early Spring through May, because inclement weather can cause high mortality. Supplying patties as an additional constant food source is helpful at this time. Place them over the frame in your hives. Patties are two parts powdered sugar to one part Crisco or store brand solid vegetable shortening. Be sure to replace them every three months. Placing about a teaspoon of heavy syrup on the patties will attract the bees to them more quickly.

In early Spring the bees will work willows and maples as the weather permits. If possible, plant willows around creeks or wastelands for their Spring feeding.

As the weather warms up in your locality, hive splits can be made. If the hive is quite full of bees, remove the first and tenth frames. Then remove the second and ninth frames. Put these four frames with bees in another hive. Look through the hive for the queen. Capture her using a glass or small tumbler. Place it over the queen while slipping a post card between her and the comb. Do this very gently and then place the queen (only) in the number two hive. Then, move the number one hive a couple of feet away and place the number two hive where the original hive was. The bees will be in the number two hive. Since there is no queen in the number one hive, the existing bees there will begin the process of hatching a new queen.

By creating another nucleus of bees, swarming will be prevented. However, the first time splitting is done, try to have an experienced person help you. A smoker needs to be used carefully. Two puffs at the entrance, two puffs when the cover of the hive is removed, and then additional smoke only as needed. Keep the use minimal.

Splitting the hives isn't difficult and should be done every year or two, depending on hive strength.

Fire extinguishing powder

Combine 6 pounds fine silica mason's sand and 2 pounds sodium bicarbonate. Mix thoroughly and keep in 1 pound glass or metal containers. Locate in strategic places. When putting out flames, scatter mix on base of fire.

Mason's sand is found at building supply stores and cement plants.—*Mary Gibson, Montana*

Aaron Grady, 8, hives a swarm.

Bees swarm; boy becomes a young man

SHELLY GRADY
ILLINOIS

When my eight-year-old son burst in the house with Betsy running breathlessly behind him, I knew he had news of some importance. He had that look of grave excitement, so it was hard to tell if he brought good news or bad.

"Mom, we found a swarm of bees out on the Christmas trees." My heart leaped, then fell.

Our circumstances were somewhat peculiar. I have been the primary beekeeper in the family for our first year of beekeeping because my husband's job in the military takes him away on business a lot. Over the winter, I made my son and husband bee suits, hoping to enlist some aid for the upcoming Spring and Summer season. I needed the help because my bee suit won't fit again until after the end of May, when child number six is due to be born!

As usual, Rod, my husband, was

gone on business. He's always gone when anything exciting happens! But he had asked me what I would do if the bees swarmed this week while he was away. I'm glad he did, or I might have panicked when Aaron brought his news.

We homeschool and had studied bees the previous year so Aaron was somewhat familiar with honeybees. I always assumed he would be hesitant around them though, due to a run-in with some yellow jackets he had a couple of years ago. But, when I told him he would have to hive the swarm, he was excited and enthusiastic!

We took the whole crew out to the Christmas trees to check out the swarm and its location. I prayed it would be an easy one, but never having worked with a swarm before, I didn't really know what I was asking!

When we arrived, there they were... a great pile of bees hanging onto three branches at the bottom of a young Christmas tree. It looked like a simple matter of cutting the limbs off and putting them into a hive body where they'd hopefully take up residence.

All the troops marched up to the house to get our equipment. I had enough hive parts for two more hives, so we quickly assembled all the needed boxes, stands and tools, parceling them out from the greatest to the least. Even Rachel, our two-year-old, insisted on being included, and carried two frames of drawn comb.

Swarming bees don't sting...

Aaron put on his bee suit and leather work gloves amid words of encouragement from his sisters and I. In all my previous reading, I recalled that swarming bees weren't supposed to sting. Boy, did I hope I remembered correctly! I assured Aaron they wouldn't sting him, but made all the girls stay a good 20 feet away.

I didn't think Aaron could handle cutting and holding a branch full of bees at the same time, so I told him to hold the branch while I came in from behind to cut it. With fear and trepidation, I gingerly cut about halfway through the branch. The weight of the bees pulled the branch down, jarring the swarm, and 1,000 bees took off into the air. I dropped the clippers and beat a hasty retreat. My worst nightmare is getting bees stuck in my hair!

The swarm calmed down and taking a deep breath, I reached for the clippers that I dropped directly under that mass of bees! The next clip was successful, and Aaron ever so gently and slowly placed the branch full of bees into the empty hive body. Two more branches brought about 80% of the swarm into the hive body with the rest flying or crawling on the ground.

I marveled to see my young son so calm and fearless in a place where many an adult would tremble. He carefully assembled the rest of the hive, and fed them some syrup in an entrance feeder. He also put sugar and shortening on the inner cover to help get rid of varroa mites.

What an incredible experience for an eight-year-old. His confidence level rose about 10 times that day.

The next morning, Aaron informed me he dreamed we had another swarm. But his dream was off a little.

In the next two days, he hived three more swarms. Looks like I'm out of a job as family beekeeper.

The beehive:

Autumn care for honeybees

Anita Page

FRANK FEDORCHUCK
CALIFORNIA

September and October are harvest time for honey. Mistakes here can be costly to the bee population. The longer northern winter requires more feed and more care of the hive. After harvest, 60 pounds or more honey should be left in the hive. If there is a shortage of honey for the bees, fall feeding is essential. The following feed should be given:

Syrup: Mix sugar and water half and half in very warm water and place in a one-quart container which is the feeder jar. Punch six holes in the jar lid with a 6-penny nail. Then invert the jar over the hive or in front of the hive in a saucer. Feed one to two gallons of this mixture during the warmer days, or after heavy frost.

Placing patties over frames in hives: Patties are two parts powdered sugar to one part of Crisco or store brand solid vegetable shortening.

Most bee losses occur in the spring, February and March, at brood-rearing time when honey is used up. To prevent starvation, feeding is critical at this time, as is feeding during a long period of poor weather, cold or wet in the spring. Patties should be placed over the brood continually. Use five patties or more per hive, replacing them every three months.

In spring and fall (before cold weather sets in), Fumidil medicine in syrup form should also be given. Be sure to follow the directions carefully. Fumidil can be purchased at Mann Lake, phone 1-800-233-6663.

Giving the bees winter protection is very important. Place the hive inside a building if possible, with access to the outside. This protects the bees from wet, cold and wind, and greatly increases their survival over winter.

Apish strips work very well in winter and are a good idea for the beginner to use on his bees, although the strips are a little expensive. I don't use them extensively now, as good management seems to take their place.

Bees require little care, but if the need arises, knowing what to do is very important. The magazine, *Bee Culture,* is one of the best sources for beginners. It is very informative, helpful in answering questions, and a real necessity for all types of beekeeping for either the hobbyist or commercial beekeeper. Call 1-800-289-7668, extension 3220 for subscription or information on *Bee Culture* magazine.

I have had experience in beekeeping for many years in the northeast, along Lake Erie and the Appalachian Mountain areas, and I will be glad to assist anyone who wishes to start the hobby of beekeeping, especially seniors.

Watching bees is a very rewarding study in nature for anyone. If you should get stung by a honeybee, it is usually your own fault, although they do become somewhat testy if sickness or stressful conditions exist. Remember that the majority of bee stings come from yellow jackets and most people cannot tell the difference—so honeybees take the blame.

Honey temperatures

Q. We sometimes have trouble with our honey crystallizing. To prevent this granulation, we heat it. What should the temperature be?

We also store some comb honey in jars. What temperature should the honey be when it's poured over these combs?

A. As a general rule, honey can be heated to 160°F without harming the flavor, but it shouldn't be held at this temperature for any longer than necessary.

Extracted honey poured over comb honey should be no hotter than 140°F or there is danger of melting the comb.

Uniting weak colonies

Q. I have several weak colonies. Would combining some of them be a good idea? Is fall too late to do this?

A. Late fall is the best time to unite colonies, because they have practically no brood, and they're starting to go into the winter inactive period.

In spring and summer, colonies should be united using the newspaper method. (Set one hive, preferably the weaker one, or one that is queenless, on top of the other, with a sheet of newspaper with a few pinholes between the two. The bees will chew through the paper and unite without fighting.) In late fall two colonies will combine without the newspaper.

How to kick the smoking habit

Julie Hunter
Arkansas

Getting the smoker started was always a problem for me, and it would sometimes go out when I was part way through working with my few hives. Then I would have to contend with disgruntled bees while I finished my job!

I have given up using the smoker to calm bees down when I have to open the hive. Now I use a water/sugar syrup spray, just like I use on packaged bees when they arrive. Using a fine spray of water and sugar syrup mixed in a 1:1 ratio is just as effective as a smoker for my beekeeping chores. I purchased a two-gallon sprayer especially for this purpose. This sprayer is never filled with any other ingredients.

This method works two ways. The bees get busy engorging themselves with the sprayer syrup, and their wings get sticky with the spray, which makes flying difficult. I also soak my hands with this mixture. Bare hands and the syrup are much less prone to getting stung than gloved hands.

When removing honey frames, I place them in my garden cart and cover with a wet sheet. I can then take the frames to the kitchen without having bees follow me.

The beehive:

Adversity doesn't stop this beekeeper

Joe Leonard
Oregon

I just spent the last couple of hours elbow deep in furious honeybees. It's not a good day to work them, since it's too cool and wet, but sometimes you have to do the best you can with whatever chance you get.

We've had a really mild winter here in western Oregon. The fruits are in bloom, and the bees are hard at work. I was shocked today to see a swollen hive ready and waiting for the next honey super. I had taken my apistan strips out earlier when I had begun to see activity. Mites are terribly damaging. I lost my other three hives to them, so I'm becoming very cautious. I feared that I'd find a dwindling hive, but instead found one bursting at the seams.

I lost two Yugoslavian hybrid hives and a swarm hive last summer. The strong and sole survivor is a Buckfast hive. They were busy despite the cool weather, and very cross.

We installed two vegetable shortening patties (one part Crisco, one part sugar), set the new honey super under the previous one, and came in to lick our wounds. Actually, I only got stung twice, because I forgot to tie the legs of my overalls. The kids got no stings at all.

The Buckfast is an aggressive bee. Some call them just plain mean. Despite that, I've ordered a second package, which should arrive soon. I'll definitely remember to tie my pants legs shut when I work with them again.

About the Yugoslavian hybrids: Mites are probably why I lost both hives. They produced an excellent honey crop this summer, and they are a very nice bee. If a person was just being introduced to beekeeping, the Yugoslavian hybrids are the guys to start with. I was stung one time by a Yugo, and I'm sure it was accidental. I even worked the Yugos without veil or gloves on occasion.

The kids all became interested in beekeeping by watching me work with the Yugos, and none are afraid of bees because of those good experiences. I have ordered two more three-pound packages of Yugos, so we'll see how they do this year.

I'd like to encourage anyone who is thinking about having a go at beekeeping to do it now. The post office plans a substantial price increase for shipments of packaged bees. I ordered my Buckfast bees from Bee Weaver Apiaries, 16481 CR 319 Lynn Grove Rd., Navasota, TX 77868; 936-825-7312; www.beeweaver.com.

The Yugoslavian hybrids came from Taber's Honeybee Genetics, P.O. Box 1672, Vacaville, CA 95696; 707-449-0440; www.honeybeegenetics.com.

If you want to start keeping bees but have no experience, make the public library your first stop. Study the subject before you order bees. Your local extension agent can also help you.

Beekeeping is a fascinating and beneficial hobby that provides food. Wild bees are disappearing because of the mite problem, so it's only as more people become interested in and participate in beekeeping that we'll have the benefits provided by our little friends.

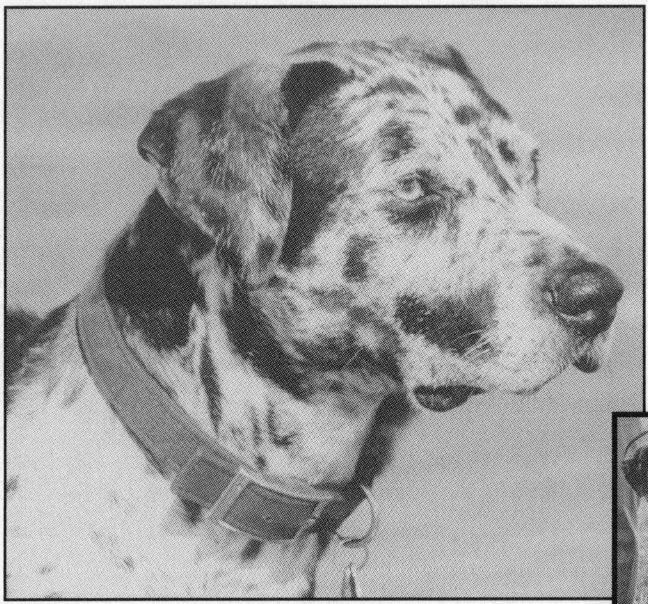

The Catahoula Leopard

Ron Stoute
West Virginia

My family has been involved with the Catahoula Leopard Dog for generations. They were always there. I never paid much attention to them until I went to college and got out into the world and saw what they had to offer in the way of dogs.

How disappointed I was with what I found! I owned various breeds of working and herding dogs from other parts of the world, the names of which I will not mention here for fear of unnecessarily upsetting any current breeders or fanciers of these dogs. The degree of congenital defects, not to mention temperament problems, simply forced me away from them. I wanted a real dog.

So I went back to my roots of some 20 years ago, back to the breed I had so foolishly underestimated in my youth!

The Catahoula is one of the very few dogs that evolved in North America. There are several theories regarding their origin, some of which are suspiciously slanted to reflect romantic notions of certain areas. Some are actually feasible. However, their origin is of little consequence to me. What's important is that they are here now and are considered by many to be one of the premier working/herding rough stockdogs in the world.

The Catahoula is a tractable dog yet a formidable protector. They are medium-large in size and quite capable of stopping any threat to their owner or property. They are great family dogs and usually require no confinement once they learn their boundaries.

Some Catahoulas are being used in search and rescue work and other areas requiring intelligence and good common sense. But the majority by far are working farm and ranch dogs, employed in the control of cattle and guarding other livestock. Around the farm, children and livestock are well protected when a sturdy Catahoula is at hand!

Many are also used to hunt wild hogs under the worst conditions imaginable. And they are just plain good ol' varmint dogs. This dog can work cattle from sunup 'til dark, and still happily hunt coon or hogs all night!

I suppose the most obvious characteristic, yet least important (at least to me), is their color. They derive their name from the leopard-like coloration which in fact is blue or red merle on a background of white and tan. Many are solid colored. Most have at least one clear blue eye—many have two of that color.

These powerful short haired working dogs have few inherited weaknesses, most being bred for function, yet they have enough "eye-appeal" to win top honors at the most prestigious rare-breed dog shows in the country.

Louisiana has chosen the Catahoula as their state dog, giving some the impression that the breed sprang from that area. More likely they evolved from the sports of lost Spanish war dogs in the mid-Atlantic area and gravitated westward over time.

The breed has been used for generations on homesteads and ranches in rural America, where they have proven and recommended themselves by deed. And they will be here long after many of these exotic dogs transplanted from other nations have failed and are forgotten.

The homestead dog:

The Fila Brasileiro

"Faithful as a Fila" is a Brazilian proverb

Lisa Ford
Washington

What breed of dog is absolutely bred to be a farm dog and a devoted family companion? In my eyes, no other breed can even stand in the shadow of the Fila Brasileiro. This breed was developed in Brazil, where crime rates are high, and the people needed a large, strong, intelligent dog to protect the estates (fazendas).

The breed resembles a Bloodhound and Mastiff cross giving it a rather massive cuddly look. Don't be fooled though. This is not a breed that will let a stranger touch its long soft ears or its semi-wrinkled face

and neck. It is no pushover and cannot be bribed into being your friend. It has what Brazilians call ojeriza or a natural distrust of strangers. This fine animal takes its job of home-guardian extremely seriously.

Surely you can tell this is not the breed for everyone. Although the breed is not taken to wandering, it should live where there is a sturdy fence or (more preferred by the Fila) in the home. This way strangers are protected from walking onto the dog's territory.

After hearing all this most people are leery of purchasing such an intimidating protector. Good! If you don't think you can handle a breed that has this much natural talent for its work then get a breed with a more mellow temperament. But, if you're still interested, this dog has much, much more to offer.

In Brazil filar means to hold or to secure. I believe this is describing the dog's heart. The devotion of this breed is legendary in its native country. "Faithful as a Fila" is a Brazilian proverb. When alone in the company of their owners, these dogs turn into comical clumps of adoration. Their place is on your feet (or your lap if you can breath beneath the 130-170 lbs. of dog flesh!) They are always alert to strange sounds but are not indifferent or aloof as are many other guardian breeds. Their list of credits doesn't stop here!

This is one of the few working rare breeds that are, in general, not animal aggressive. Mine love to have baby lambs and goats fight for "king of the hill" on their backs. They are not usually used as a flock guardian, however. Their love is for their family first. They have intensity, but nothing as keen as a Border Collie. They have been used for hunting as well. Wildcats, boar, and other such adversaries have been successfully hunted with Filas. But the job they consider their number one priority is guarding their family and their territory.

The breed standard includes fawns, reds, brindles, black-brindles, and the occasional black. Minimum height for females is 24 inches, weight 90 lbs., with males 27 inches and 110 lbs. Many Filas are in the 140-180 lbs. range. The breed is extremely agile for its size, surprising onlookers by its swiftness. The coat is short, dense, and easily maintained. The tail and ears are left natural. The Fila is athletic when you want to be, yet content to lay by the fire for days on end.

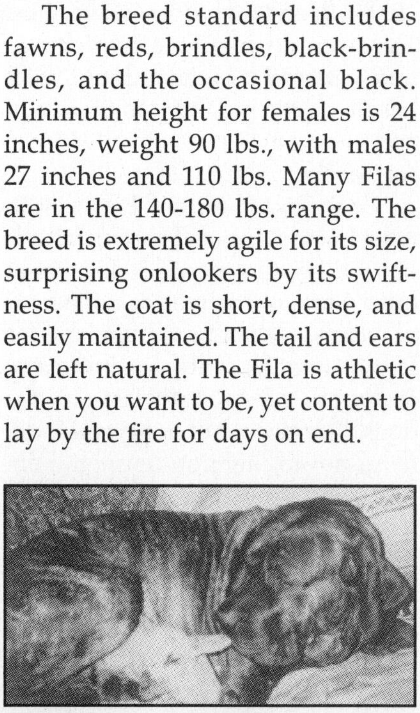

The poultry yard:

Raising meat chickens—my way

LINDA M. EVERHART
MISSOURI

I have a large library of old and new poultry books and have also been a subscriber to Countryside for many years. When reading any of these on the subject of killing chickens, I can't help but cringe. It's no wonder so many people consider this common homestead activity complicated and distasteful.

Personally, I cannot stand to see an animal suffer during the butchering process. And I have no desire to spend a lot of time doing it. The "modern" method of hanging a chicken upside down in shackles or inside a cone and cutting the jugular vein so that it bled to death in a couple of minutes and/or sticking a knife through their mouth to scramble their brains was invented for three reasons: 1) It made dry picking easier. 2) It bled the chickens well. 3) It was less messy and could be done indoors, as in a processing plant.

Before processing plants, nearly every farm wife raised and butchered her own chickens for the table. This was done outside with an ax and a chopping block or by an easier method I learned from my great-grandmother (which is apparently regional, since I have never seen anything similar to this in print). The chicken's head was removed, the body was placed on the ground and its natural reflexes caused it to jump and flop around for a while. It was then scalded and picked.

At some point in time, probably when bleached flour was being promoted as a superior product, a flopping, headless chicken in the backyard was labeled unacceptable. Excuses for dropping this practice ranged from the chance of bruising the meat to breaking bones (unattractive if the chickens were dressed for market) to simply being gross and crude. As a kid, I thought it was rather humorous. As an adult, I consider it quick, humane and practical. It also happens to be the best way to bleed a chicken completely without keeping it alive during the process, and I will prove it. Also, bruising the meat or breaking bones rarely happens if you choose a soft, grassy area of the yard to do the work.

Before I get into the instructions, I'd like to share a few pointers on chickens in general.

If you want to raise chickens for meat, and would like to end up with a product similar to (but better) than the factory kind, you need to purchase genuine Cornish-cross chicks. Make sure the "Cornish" is in the name. I prefer Super Cornish-cross, which now cost about 85¢ each.

A Super Cornish-cross chick on a good high-protein feed will dress out at three pounds or better in 6-8 weeks. These are not normal chickens, so if you have raised other types of poultry in the past you will not be prepared for these unless you do your homework.

Super Cornish-cross chickens are lazy, ugly, eat like pigs, have extremely nasty habits and wouldn't even rate in an IQ test. That is why they are perfect chickens for the beginner butcher. Not even squeamish homesteaders would mind killing these.

This kind of chicken needs lots of floor space, deep fluffy litter and big feeders. To determine how many you can handle, figure out how many basketballs you could put on the floor and still have space for feeders, waterers and walking paths.

In my opinion, an outside yard is essential. The entrances to the house must be at ground level or at least very close to it. (These birds don't climb ramps well). I simply let mine run loose during the day, although that isn't a very good description of what they do, which is waddle around a bit then lay in the shade and eat. This is the only kind of chicken I know of that will eat and drink lying down.

I don't feed medicated feed to anything we raise to eat, and the stores around here do not stock unmedicated chick starter. To get around that problem, I buy gamebird mash which costs about the same and has the proper amount of protein without the drugs. They also get plenty of table scraps.

This year I attempted to breed, hatch and raise my own chicks using purebred Barred Rock hens and Dark Cornish roosters. They were wonderful chicks, but did not gain weight very fast and became rather leggy.

Butchering

Anyway, on the butchering part. I skin my chickens, but if you would rather scald and pick, the killing part is still the best method. It takes me about five minutes to catch, kill, skin and gut one bird by myself, and I do them one at a time because skinning a chicken is much easier when the bird is still warm.

Place a large clean table in a shady spot and run a garden hose to it with a spray head that you can operate with one hand. Tilt the table away from you so the water runs off the other side. You'll need a sharp knife (fish fillet knives work best), a good pair of game shears (optional), a gut bucket, a large pot of cold or ice water for the finished chicken, a towel to wipe your hands on, a chicken catching hook and a broom handle or something similar.

Put the broom handle on a piece of flat ground near your table. This is your killing area.

Catch the chicken with as little fuss as possible. Hold it upside-down with both feet together and swing it gently back and forth as you walk to the killing area. By the time you get there the chicken should be dazed and calm.

Put the chicken's head on the ground and lay the broom handle across its neck. Step down on both ends of the broom handle and pull up firmly and quickly. (You'll be surprised how fast and easy this is, but be prepared to use a lot more muscle when killing old roosters of the laying breeds.)

Gently lay the headless bird on the ground and let it flop. Keep your eye on it so you don't lose it if it flops across your driveway into the brush. As soon as it stops jumping around, immediately take it over to your table. The bird should still be kicking.

With the game shears or knife, cut a slit in the skin below the neck (near the V of the wishbone),and pull the skin to the back as you pull the neck forward through the slit. Cut the neck off at the shoulders. With your fingers, go around the neck cavity, pulling and breaking every blood vein and anything else that is still attached. If you do all of this quickly, the blood will actually be pumped out of the neck cavity, and will squirt on you if you're not careful. The bird is now bled out better than by any other method, and you will have the proof in your hands very soon.

Now cut off the feet and the wings at the elbow. (Sorry, but you lose that part of the wing when skinning.) Pull the skin over each shoulder, off the ends of the wing stubs, off the back and breast then over and off each leg.

You should now have the whole skin, inside out, at the base of the tail. Go ahead and pull it the rest of the way off, leaving you with a skinless chicken with tail feathers.

Cut through the tail bone above the preening gland (being careful not to cut into any internal organs), and then around each side to the front to open the body cavity. Wash one of your hands and put it inside the cavity, using your fingers to break loose any tendons that hold the guts. Grab up around the heart area and pull everything out all at once.

Rinse off the bird as you admire your work, save the gizzard, liver... and of course the heart, which will be flat as a pancake, proving that this method really works when you desire a fine dressed and well-bled chicken.

Place the bird and giblets in the pot of cold water to cool them down fast. Now go get another one!

Finish rinsing, cleaning and soaking the chickens in the kitchen sink using several changes of cold water until water runs clear. Cut into smaller pieces or leave whole. Dry pack into bowls or pans, cover tightly and age in refrigerator for 24-48 hours. Fry up a big skillet-full for supper and freeze the rest.

Plastic zip freezer bags are handy, but can be very expensive. When used alone, they will not protect food from freezer burn and are hard to stack. I recommend double wrapping any food to be frozen, first in plastic wrap or bags, and then in plastic coated freezer paper secured with common masking tape. Reynolds freezer paper has good instructions for wrapping on the side of the box.

That's all there is to it. No complicated diagram or special equipment is needed. After all, didn't we all move to the country to simplify our lives?

A reader first told us about this method of killing chickens back in 1973. That reader was Pat Katz, who later became our regular Country Kitchen columnist, and a successful cook book author. (We consider her *Craft of the Country Cook* an essential homestead tool.)

As for the "regionality" of this method, Pat, who lived in New York at the time, said she learned it from a friend who learned it when he lived in Italy, where it was the normal technique.

Tips on raising chickens

Kelly F. Schaefer
Missouri

I have been raising chickens for a few years, and have some tips for fellow homesteaders who may be having some of the problems I had.

When we first built our chicken coop, we did not cover the fronts of the nest boxes. They were left open. This didn't cause any problems for the first year.

However, then I noticed I was getting fewer and fewer eggs until finally, I wasn't getting any. Obviously, one or more of the hens was eating the eggs. You would think there would be some other kind of evidence that this was happening, like a few pieces of egg shell or yolk left over. No way! Chickens are messy about everything except eating their own eggs. They devour every little piece possible with nothing left.

I remembered reading that to prevent chickens from doing this all you had to do was cover the opening of the nest boxes with some type of material, kind of like a curtain, so it would be dark and they couldn't see well once inside the nest box.

It amazed me that this actually works. They know they go in there to lay an egg, but if they don't see it they won't eat it. Well, chickens aren't known for their intelligence.

I covered the nest boxes with burlap which they thought was great fun! As they sat in there, they would pull on the strands of the burlap and add this to their nest. No amount of sewing a hem or even using duct tape on the edge would help. They just saw this as a new challenge.

Finally, my husband suggested covering the opening with sheets of rubber material he could get from where he works. This worked great. The rubber is about 1/8" thick and is nice and pliable. We cut pieces that are slightly smaller than the nest box. The chickens can easily get in and out. To attach the rubber pieces we stapled the top edge to the nest box frame.

This has worked great for a year and a half. They have made no attempt to tear these coverings apart (not that they could.) If you can't get a hold of sheets of rubber material, you could easily substitute old floor

The poultry yard:

The pecking order

MARCY & IVAN CALES
WEST VIRGINIA

If social workers are right and today's victim truly is tomorrow's predator, be well advised of this when dealing with poultry.

I don't mind poultry. I love them. I think they're great to have around, and some breeds are downright huggable. Chickens can start conversations, give you the stamp (or stigma, depending on the neighborhood) of someone struggling for independence.

They can feed you too—directly, with eggs and meat, or indirectly, with manure for the soil and their charming, heart-warming desire to peck bloody fights over the privilege of chowing down on that inch-thick tomato hornworm that decimated your prize Brandywine.

But roosters can be something else entirely, and you can see the sense some cities have in barring them while leaving you free to raise the ladies. I'm not talking about the noise, either. Noisy roosters I can live with—at least until fall. I'm talking about the pecking order, which always showed up worse in males than in females. Maybe the hens had better things to do, such as break loose, dig up my mint, burrow prairie dog holes in my rose garden, and stampede en masse all over my clovered yard, keeping me from that time-honored right to flop down in a shady spot to celebrate a rare moment of rest.

Our first rooster was a freebie. At the time, we didn't know that much about the different breeds. He and two hens in a crate had fallen off a truck on the Interstate, and Ivan's grandfather had collected them and given them to us. That raised our flock to 27, but the rooster ruled, since everyone else had been born that spring. We named him Captain Kirk, after the swaggering, puff-chested character William Shatner played to over-effect on Star Trek.

He was a game rooster, and his owner had reasons for not wanting to go to the trouble of getting him back. As spurs went, Pecos Bill would have admired them. They were half the length of his legs, monstrous horned moons that guaranteed no one could enter his yard without the Rooster Stick to fend him off. He had an ability to defy gravity, and could somehow poke his spurs into you while facing you, leaving perfect needle-like wounds in the center of grape-colored bruises. Just as you wouldn't turn your back on a rabid dog, you wouldn't turn your back on Kirk.

Needless to say, we ate him. After all his show, he couldn't even keep a 4-1/2-foot blacksnake from raiding the nests, and he was clearly unable to service our now-mature hens, so what good was he. Anyway, our other roosters, two Black Giants and a Dark Cornish, would appreciate a life without terror.

We don't know if this goose is a very ambitious nest builder, or taking advantage of the environment. Jack Schaffter, Illinois, sent the photo without any comments.

I hate to think of that dinner. Kirk's revenge extended beyond the grave, and Ivan rehashed his vocabulary of eight years in the military as we discovered the (expletive) had two layers of skin to remove. Ivan's mom Jean cooked him all day long under slow heat to no effect. "The heck with it," Ivan paraphrased as he dug in with vicious enthusiasm. "I'm still eating him."

After that, the gift of seven hens and one rooster came to us. They were huge sexlinks, looking like a bizarre marriage of Rhodes and Leghorns. The rooster was three times bigger than any other rooster I'd ever seen, and for reasons that became plain, we named him Brewster the Rooster. (If you don't know the story about Brewster, have someone tell you.) All the hens in the world wouldn't have been enough for him. As Kirk did, he terrorized the young males, but he turned out to be even more of a blacksnake coward than Kirk. At least he was a lot more tender.

The turkeys

Came another gift... Tom and Tess Turkey. Tess heard the melodic call of the Mountain Man Turkey and ran off, leaving Tom forlornly behind. Despite his size, Tom would have starved to death if we hadn't hand-fed him, since Brewster (while he lived) would keep him from the grain.

After Brewster, the Black Giants had their turn to rule, then the Dark Cornish, who by then was as fancy as a green peacock. They all kept Tom at bay, although as time passed, Tom grew ridiculously larger.

Unfortunately, we had to move, and butchered our whole flock except for Tom, whom Jean kept as a pet. He grew to be a truly stupendous bird. And now he had somebody to pick on: Max, the new Dobie-Lab puppy.

Now that Tom was big and bad, he didn't want poor Max to forget it. And Max didn't.

How could he? It didn't look like Tom would ever stop growing.

When we came to visit, there would be Tom, slowly and splendidly pacing his way... Up and down the yard.

His favorite trick, now that his head had turned blue, his tail fluffed out and beard grown to trophy length, was to trap the puppy in his doghouse. Max was a brave dog and would have protected his master from any human, but this thing was different. He would huddle in the farthest corner, barking for help until Jean chased Tom off.

It didn't take long for Jean to have enough of that. And any turkey should watch his step when Thanksgiving draws near. We visited the day before the holiday to find large feathers painting the yard like fall leaves after a high wind. Jean was standing on the porch eating a sandwich. "Care for some turkey-neck sandwiches?" She smirked.

This is what happened: Yesterday was the last time Jean cared to rescue Max. It was time to have turkey on the table, and anyway, it was Thanksgiving. Her favorite executioner's tool was a good, stout stick. With it she could crack a chicken before it knew what happened. And normally, this worked fine. While Max yelped, Jean discovered turkeys are a bit different from chickens. Tom didn't even appear to be aware that his head was being waylaid with a locust pole. He was too busy bullying Max to pay attention.

Luckily, Cousin Randy and his dog were staying over. The dog was a Samoyed with the unlikely name of Pepper. Pepper was watching the scene with interest, but politely, and did not get involved. He was a pretty good dog and didn't normally act without permission.

Jean's arm was tired of whacking. "Get him Pepper! Kill him!"

Pepper lunged. It was really too bad for him that he was a city dog. Turkeys where he came from were bald and plastic wrapped. One can understand why he chose to attack the wrong end of the tom.

Tom might have been immune to head wounds, but it dawned on him that his rear end was getting draft and turned around. Pepper was faster, and got him in the neck, and down they went. Tom was very quickly dead but Pepper by now had doubts on this thing, and every time he stepped off the bird, a reflex action would draw the leg up, causing Pepper to think it was coming back to life again.

While Pepper killed Tom for the sixth or seventh time, Jean got a hatchet, relieved Tom of his head, and said, "Go on, Max it's yours." Max peeped out cautiously, stared hard for a long moment, said "Rah!" and grabbed the head and pulled it inside his doghouse for revenge.

Cousin Randy, whose muscles were designed for lifting nothing heavier than a new Coors, was put to work hauling Tom to the picnic table; hence the feather-storm. Jean never regretted stuffing Tom the way she did, but it posed an interesting problem when he proved too big to fit in the "full sized" oven. He had to be cut up. She held up the drumsticks as proof. Wrapped in paper, they looked like bowling pins.

We all made sandwiches of a very large bowl of neck meat. It was the tenderest, most delicious meat I'd ever had.

"You know," Jean said thoughtfully, "I think I'll get another turkey this spring."

Ask Countryside:

Chicken flavor depends on breeding and management

Are there any significant differences in the flavor of chicken meat caused by genetics? What are considered the most delicious types of chicken? Is anyone breeding chickens for superior eating qualities?

It's not polite to answer a question with a question, but in this case it's necessary.

1. Do you prefer white meat, or dark? The Cornish has a considerably greater proportion of white meat to dark than does a Barred Rock, for example. So in this regard we could say yes, there are genetic differences.

2. A lot of work has and is being done on breeding for some "eating qualities." Such traits as yield of edible meat on the carcass, efficiency of gain, rapidity of gain, ratio of muscle to fat, thinness of skin, tenderness, color of skin, color of flesh, etc., are being considered in many research programs. However, most of these are influenced by the management of the birds and the manner of processing as well as the birds' genetic makeup.

I know of no specific work on breeding for flavor at present. However, in many old books we find references to the fact that chickens raised in a certain area had better flavor than others. I suspect this had quite a bit to do with how they were raised, but to some extent breeding could have been a part of it too.

Age, exercise, contact with certain kinds of soil, all have a bearing on the flavor of the meat. So does the processing, storage conditions and cooking method. At one time capons were popular because their meat was softer and juicier than roosters' of comparable age and weight. Now breeding has given us a male that has almost caught up with the capon in that he grows to a considerable weight while still young enough and inactive enough to be soft, tender, juicy and very meaty.

Note: Caponizing roosters is a surgical process that is no longer recommended.

Bloody eggs might mean a vitamin deficiency

I have a problem that is costing me money. We have a flock of Rhode Island Reds and a few White Rocks (one year old). The problem is that the eggs are bloody. It is not the meat spot: sometimes the eggs are full of blood. We do not have a rooster and have never had one with these hens. This is the first time I've had so much blood in eggs. Can you give me a suggestion on how to solve the problem?

Blood appearing in the egg is the result of hemorrhages occurring during the formation of the yolk. It is influenced slightly by many things including changes in the weather (thought to be the result of changes in barometric pressure). When more than 3-4% of the eggs show blood, I look closely at the ration of the hens. It might be low in vitamins A or K or both.

Poultry raiser wants that old-time flavor

We have been raising our own fryers for several years and they are so much better than store-bought chickens. But I have a problem. They do not have that wonderful flavor I remember from 20-25 years ago.

Can you shed any light on this? Maybe it's the feed. (We feed a pellet ration.) If you think it's the feed could you give us a formula for mixing our own grains? I tried feeding corn in addition to the pellets last year, but it didn't make much difference.

What you remember from years gone by was a chicken that grew rather slowly by today's standards. Therefore it was older than many of today's chickens when slaughtered, and the flavor does tend to be stronger in the older animal.

Also in some cases cooking methods and even the grease in the frying pan has been changed.

In general, chickens that are on the ground and pick up a few bugs and bacteria tend to have a somewhat stronger flavor than those raised in total confinement. If this is what you want, perhaps putting a shovelful of soil and sod in the brooder house each day will bring back some of the "old-time" flavor. Or if you want to go a step further, put a shovelful of fresh cow manure in the pen every day. It would have an effect.

Chickens and hot weather

We have temperatures here (in California) in the 100s for days on end, and some as high as 115°. We have Rhode Island Reds that do well but we are looking for better meat and/or egg production. What breeds are most heat tolerant?

In general, heat bothers chickens with dark colored feathers more than those with white or light colored plumage. This is especially true if shade is lacking or minimal.

We tend to recommend egg-type crosses or strains based on White Leghorns for the best egg production in hot climates. However, these birds won't be much for meat. For meat production in a warm climate we would again look to something with white or light colored feathers and try to schedule them so they would finish out at other than your warmest season.

Finding one bird good for both meat and eggs in a very hot climate would present a problem, although in theory White Rocks or White Wyandottes should work.

Several things to bear in mind when keeping chickens in hot climates are:

1. Provide plenty of shade.
2. Keep shade high enough above the birds to allow plenty of air circulation.
3. Provide easy access to drinking water.
4. Locate drinking water in the shade.
5. Provide well-ventilated nests.
6. Provide ample roosting space.
7. If birds are confined, consider fans, evaporative coolers, and sprinklers mounted on the roof to help reduce in-house temperatures.

The 10 most common poultry diseases*

1. Colibacillosis
2. Airsacculitis
3. Mismanagement[1]
4. Staphylococosis
5. Marek's disease
6. Omphalitis
7. Staphylococcal arthritis
8. Infectious bursal disease
9. Coccidiosis
10. Mycoplasma gallisepticum

*Based on reports from diagnostic laboratories in the 11 top ranking egg producing states. The data represents reports on total chickens without specificity to type: egg, meat, breeder or backyard.

[1] Mismanagement is defined as any management-related cause other than infectious or nutritional: ventilation, feed and water system failures, overcrowding and rough handling are examples.

The henhouse:

Build a neat but simple henhouse

Have fresh eggs, and dress up your yard, too!

Steve Belanger
Countryside Staff

Chickens are an essential part of most homesteads. Too often, though, they are thrust into dark, damp, gloomy, unattractive, inconvenient-to-care-for, ancient and falling down henhouses, or makeshift shelters that are just as bad.

Pity the homesteaders who have to work with such a henhouse! Pity the neighbors who have to look at it! Pity the chickens!

There is a better way, as this article demonstrates.

This henhouse is moved daily so the chickens are always on clean ground.

I needed a coop for six hens to keep the family in eggs with a little surplus for relatives. I saw a picture of a henhouse I liked in an ad in *Country Garden & Smallholding,* the British equivalent of Countryside. If anybody sells coops like this in the U.S. I'm not aware of it, and besides, it didn't look difficult to build.

Since I didn't have any dimensions to work with I just made the total floor area 6' x 6' high. I made the uprights out of 2 x 2s to keep the weight down since I planned to put wheels on it to move it around so the chickens could get fresh grass every day.

The hen house itself is two feet by six feet long and three feet off the ground. I didn't want to have to bend over to clean the house or to get eggs.

I wanted it to look good, so I used boxcar siding. Plywood would work and it would be cheaper. If you want to save even more, use what you have on hand or can scrounge. Use your imagination and see how cool a design you can make.

I put 1 x 8 treated wood on the bottom to seal it from critters. If I were only going to move it once a week or less I would have used 2 x 8s to make it stronger.

If you don't park it on a level spot the door binds on one side and when you move it, it again binds on the other side. This is nothing serious. Just lift the handle for moving it and the door works fine. Everything in life needs a little fine tuning.

I built the floor and back wall and put a door on the back to get the eggs and clean the coop. I put a big door on the front to get feeders and waterers in.

I built four nest boxes inside but the chickens take turns and only use the bottom two. There are two roosts inside the house.

We did have one problem in addition to the binding door. One evening when we came out of the basement after a tornado warning the chicken coop was laying on its side. The chickens were okay...and the coop was undamaged.

Materials for 6' x 6' movable henhouse

2–treated 1x8 12'
20–2x2 8'
4–2x4 8'
18-1x8x8 boxcar siding (or you could usefour sheets of plywood, or recycled material)
3–8' fiberglass roofing
4#–deck screws
7#–roof screws
4–hinges
2–pulls
2–swivel hasps
15' of 5' chicken wire
10' of 3' chicken wire
Total cost of materials, all new, was $255.10.

We recently moved and didn't bring our behind-the-barn treasure pile, but with recycled and scrounged materials the cost would be much less.

A door was put on the back to make the job of getting the eggs and cleaning the coop easier.

How to cull laying hens

Laying hens should be culled monthly, but eliminating the boarders is even more important in the fall.

Here is what to look for to distinguish a laying hen from a non-layer.

Present laying characteristics:

Character	Laying hen	Non-laying hen
Vent	Large, dilated, oblong, moist	Small, conrtacted, dry
Pubic bones	Flexible, wide apart	Rigid, close together
Comb	Large, full, red, glossy	Small, pale, scaly
Wattles-lobes	Prominent, soft, smooth	Rough, dry, inconspicuous

Long laying characteristics:

Character	Laying hen	Non-laying hen
Vent	Bluish white	Flesh colored
Eye	Prominent, edges white	Thick, yellow tinted
Beak	Pearly white	Yellow tinted
Face	Clean cut, sunken	Full, well fleshed
Shanks	White, flat, thin	Yellow, round, smooth
Plumage	Worn, soiled, lifeless	Loose, moulting signs

Cull after dark to disturb the birds as little as possible. Handle each bird, feel the vent, and look at the comb. Discard any showing non-laying characteristics.

If as many as 50 percent of the flock shows non-laying characteristics at one time, it may be the fault of the management. Every effort, by proper feeding and care, should be made to bring them into lay again. Allow three to six weeks, then cull.

Every litter bit helps

COUNTRYSIDE: I read that the Ohio Experiment Station has raised 30 consecutive broods of chicks on the same litter over a period of seven years. They found extra nutritional benefits in the deep litter and a great savings in labor and cost of litter materials.

How interesting that Louis Bromfield wrote in Out of the Earth that the Ohio State Experimental Farm raised 20 generations of chickens on old poultry litter with a notable reduction in the incidence of disease, a total absence of cannibalism and marked vigor and fertility. That was published in 1948!

I know farmers are not notoriously slow to change, but this is ridiculous. In case any readers are cleaning out the coop or disinfecting it for new chicks, please believe the experimental farm this time.

One word of caution: The litter must not have wet spots. It should be dry, fluffy, and odorless to create the molds and fungi which make the antibiotics and vitamin B_{12}. – *B.C., Pennsylvania*

There is nothing new under the sun. Recycling nutrients was recommended by the writers of ancient Rome when they suggested that hens be al lowed to peck at the dungheaps of the ox. Two thousand years later we found that they were obtaining vitamin B_{12} that way.

Built-up litter was advocated in the late 1940s by researchers at Ohio State and elsewhere. Much of the work was done with adult birds and about the time that caught on, industry began putting laying hens in wire cages, so it was no longer much of a consideration. The result: somebody "discovered" it all over again. Now it's the broiler industry where raising two and three hatches of birds on the same litter is commonplace.

There are, as you point out, some notes of caution to bear in mind. You can get along pretty well by putting clean litter in a clean house and stocking it with clean baby chicks. Adding more clean litter on top of the old and more clean chicks seems to work out okay. However, if a batch of chicks brings with them certain kinds of conditions and/or certain diseases break within a particular brood, the house must be cleaned completely and a fresh start made.

Did the right thing

COUNTRYSIDE: Help! I'm having problems hatching duck eggs. After a poor start last year, I ended up with a healthy pair of ducks. Last summer she laid 15 eggs and hatched 15 ducklings. With an excess of duck eggs this spring I gave some to a local school for incubation. Out of the 24 eggs, only four hatched. Of the remaining 20, five were not fertile, and 15 had developed completely but had not reabsorbed the yolk sac and died just before or during hatching. Why?

I had the same problem with my Araucana eggs that have been hatched in several different incubators. There seems to be no pattern to the hatching results. There was an average hatch of about 50 percent in three other schools that reported back. All unhatched eggs contained full term dead chicks with yolks. In some cases the chicks started to hatch then the yolk came gushing out of the hole.

What's wrong? I've been unable to get any answers from our local extension service poultry expert or from the hatchery where I bought the Araucanas. Do Araucanas have special incubation requirements? What went wrong with the duck eggs?

I'd had no other problems until about three weeks ago when I lost one of my best layers.

My rooster appears healthy and vigorous but he sounds asthmatic. When he gets excited he wheezes. He has been this way for months without any loss of vigor. Could he have something caught in his throat?

Today another problem has developed: coccidiosis. I put Sulmet in the drinking water when I first noticed bloody droppings this morning. Is there any way to prevent coccidiosis? I understand sulfur drugs are not good for ducks or geese. How do I treat them if they show signs of coccidiosis? – *D. E., New York*

An average hatch of 50 percent is not bad for small incubators run by people who are not familiar with incubation. I would suspect that there may have been too much variation in the temperature between night and day where the incubators were located.

I also suggest you check the incubators for mechanical problems such as loose wafer on the stem or switches that are not working properly. The variation in temperature should only be about one-half degree. Several other problems you could have: humidity within the incubator, accuracy of the thermometer, turning of eggs.

Araucanas require no special incubation conditions, but in the case of ducks, humidity at hatching time is critical.

The rooster that sounds asthmatic may have been the victim of heat stress. Sometimes over-heated birds are left with a labored breathing condition. It also could be the result of scar tissue resulting from a respiratory infection. It could also be a particle of material lodged in the windpipe near the vocal chords.

You did the right thing about the outbreak of coccidiosis. Using one of the sulfur drugs will usually stop it and the chickens rapidly return to normal. That is, of course, providing you spot the outbreak in time. Coccidiosis is the result of an organism so prevalent in the environment that it is impossible to escape it if chickens are raised on the floor or in contact with the soil. One way to prevent it is to raise chickens on wire because the organism must cycle itself through the soil or damp litter. However, chickens started on wire often contract coccidiosis when placed on the floor or turned out. That's why medicated mash is recommended to provide a degree of protection while the chicken builds some natural immunity. If a medication strong enough to eliminate coccidiosis entirely is used, the immunity the chicken must eventually have is not built up. So, it becomes a balancing act and the manager, by close observation, can control the outbreak until such time as the chicken builds its own immunity. A medicated feed usually allows the immune process to take place without your observing the symptoms of coccidiosis. But in the event you have mud puddles, damp litter or an excessive buildup of coccidia, the disease might break out in spite of the degree of protection incorporated in the feed.

Ducks and geese are seldom affected by coccidiosis, although certain species of coccidia are known to inhabit the digestive tract of both ducks and geese.

> Readers frequently ask us to reprint material from out-of-print issues. These items, by poultry editor John Skinner, first appeared here in 1977.

Fertility and A.I.

COUNTRYSIDE: I have heard that there are several breeds of chickens that cannot lay fertile eggs. Is this so? – *L. J. C., Arizona*

There are several breeds of chickens, as well as numerous crosses, that run into reproductive problems. The best exhibition-type Cornish, and both large fowl and bantams have problems with fertility because of their physical dimensions. Very short, heavy legs, extreme muscle development and wide bodies make them awkward. They're also subject to more stiffening of the joints with the increase in age than some other breeds of chickens. Therefore, the most successful breeders usually resort

to artificial insemination.

In some of those profusely feathered chickens, Cochins being a good example, the feathers interfere with the mating process and unless clipped prior to the breeding season, usually cause a high percentage of infertile eggs. Again, artificial insemination is the simplest answer. By using AI techniques, it's possible to extend the reproductive life of many males and also to secure offspring from injured or crippled individuals who might never have made it naturally.

This, of course, raises the question of whether or not these individuals should be mated and one can answer that only by saying that if there is a purpose in making the mating, then it is good to have the know-how. If there isn't a definite purpose for making the mating, perhaps it should not be made.

Weed seed"casserole;" music to lay by

COUNTRYSIDE: We had an incredible weed problem this year and when we harvested the soybeans we had a wagonful of weed seeds and small bits of soybeans that the combine had separated out. Our original plan was to burn it all, but it suddenly struck me that here was 30 bushels or so of perfect chicken feed supplement. We promptly built a bin in the basement and dumped it through a window.

Every morning I cook up a bucketful of the stuff (using twice as much water as seeds) and feed it to the flock. If you try this be sure to cook it well as raw soybeans can be harmful, plus you don't want those weed seeds to germinate next spring when you put the chicken manure on the garden. I still feed laying ration but the hens eat only about half as much now and they love the hot, wet "casserole" they get on these cold winter mornings. With the decrease in store-bought feed we're actually making money!

I have another idea I'd like to pass on: When we started shutting the chickens in this fall because of the cold weather they seemed to get very bored. So I took an old radio out to the hen house and tuned it to a rock and roll station. Now, anytime I go out, at least half of the flock is gathered around the radio in a rousing sing along. No more boredom for them and a good deal of laughter for us. – *D. V., Illinois*

The soybean-weed seed casserole, as you call it, is quite akin to a good breakfast of porridge for you and me. My only suggestion would be that you could reduce the cooking time by grinding the soybeans and weed seed. But I can't argue a bit with what you are doing, and obviously, your chickens are responding well to it also.

Twenty-five years ago and more, when I was running a commercial poultry farm for a large breeding organization, I put radios in the chicken house and connected them to an intercom system in my home. I had the radio hooked into the circuit with the lights so that when the lights came on in the morning, there was entertainment for the hens. This continued until I closed up for the evening.

This does two things. First of all, it accustoms the chickens to human voices and other noises so the presence of visitors or unexpected sounds does not scare them. I also think it's pretty well demonstrated by dairymen and others that music does have a beneficial effect on the performance of the animals, including humans.

Compatible peacocks?

COUNTRYSIDE: A friend recently gave me some peacocks that had blackhead disease and I'm wondering if it's safe to keep them around my goats. – *B. J. M., North Carolina*

Under normal conditions peafowl don't present a health hazard to to goats or vice versa. There's always an outside chance though, that one species could have something that would prove detrimental to the other. Generally I don't recommend keeping widely diverse species together, since the difference in habits and temperament usually creates a degree of nervousness and irritability in one species because of the presence of the other.

In farm situations where one species may be allowed to come and go from its association with the other, this is not really a problem; but in a confined situation, social compatibility does sometimes present difficulties.

Cochin will make good "Mother Goose"

COUNTRYSIDE: What breed of chicken would you recommend for hatching goose eggs? I've had much better luck hatching goose eggs under hens than I have in the incubator. – *R. M. C., Ohio*

For hatching goose eggs, I would suggest using either Cochins or Bantams. The long, loose feathers of the Cochins together with their instinct to be persistently broody, make them a pretty good choice for hatching waterfowl eggs.

With their own kind

COUNTRYSIDE: Pigs and poultry do not belong together and should not be mixed for several reasons other than transmitting tuberculosis. Poultry and fowl have a number of protozoa and bacteria in their intestines which, when ingested by other animals, can cause pathogenic responses.

A good example is salmonella. This bacteria is normally found in the digestive tract of birds. However, when a human or pig becomes contaminated the result is acute diarrhea. I speak of this example as a 4-H leader who has seen prime project hogs become acutely (and upon occasion fatally) ill from just such contamination.

Hogs can also suffer intestinal damage from eating feathers. The barbs of the feathers are quite sharp and their abrasive action on the gut wall can reduce the efficiency of weight gain and with the high cost of feed, no one can afford to keep an inefficient hog. – *P. L. P., Arizona*

I have previously recommended that it isn't the best practice to run two species of animals together. Diseases can be a problem. The difference in size and temperaments of various animal

species presents a mechanical and social problem, and you have made reference to certain disease problems.

Regarding salmonella: I can't discuss it adequately in this column, as there are 1,200 stereotypes of the organism. Some man transmits to the animals; some animals pass to man; and some of these animals transmit to each other. Many are so numerous in the environment that it is impossible to avoid them.

If it is necessary to mix colors and breeds, then equal numbers of each should be kept together all the time, starting out as early in life as possible. But when it comes to different species of animals and those of differing ages and sizes, they just simply do better when they're among their own kind.

Aquarium incubator

COUNTRYSIDE: I would like to share with you how I hatch my chicks and goslings.

Last summer two of my White Leghorn hens went broody on me, so I decided to set eggs under them. Halfway through the incubation period, the first hen quit setting and I lost those eggs.

When I noticed the second hen was going to do the same I was determined not to lose these eggs also. I remembered a friend had told me that the local grade school used 10-gallon fish aquariums as incubators to hatch chicks in the classroom.

I got my book *Raising Poultry the Modern Way* and read all about the incubation process. I needed to maintain a steady temperature for the eggs, so I used an old lamp and a treble light laid across the top to achieve the right temperature. Out of 14 eggs, eight chicks hatched.

This spring I gathered 10 goose eggs from my Chinese geese. The entire incubation time was in the aquarium.

After faithfully turning them three times a day for 30 days they began to hatch. Eight out of the 10 goslings hatched.

For those who desire to experience their own hatching and not pay for an expensive incubator, a 10-gallon fish aquarium works nicely. It may be a little more work than an automated incubator but the results are just as rewarding. – *Aaron and Abigail Brown, Indiana*

Laying problems

COUNTRYSIDE: I recently bought eight Araucana eggs from a friend and gave them, along with ten other eggs, to a hen that wanted to set. I made her a nice nest out of a styrofoam fruit box and placed it on a bench in the chicken house. Four days later I went into the chicken house and the hen had eaten the whole side of the box causing 14 of the eggs to roll onto the floor. These eggs were eaten. Now I'm worried that the chickens are going to eat the eggs out of the nest.

I have another problem with a hen that won't lay eggs in the nest. She always lays in the same corner of the chicken house. I have tried putting her up in the nest but she just jumps down and goes back to the corner.

How old should hens be when you kill them and replace them with young hens? I have read that egg production decreases after the first year. I would also like to know how many eggs I should get from a flock of 35 hens.

A hen will establish a habit of laying her eggs in the same location each time. Generally, the place they lay their first one or two eggs fixes this location. Having the nest available to the hen for the deposit of her first egg is important. Frequently, hens are reluctant to adjust to your wishes later on.

The first year of production is the most efficient. That is, hens produce more eggs and on less feed per dozen than during any subsequent year of life. As a rule of thumb, the hens that survive the first year of production will lay somewhere around 10 to 15 percent fewer eggs their second year. The eggs laid the second year will be slightly larger and the shells will usually be a little weaker than that of first year layers. However, individual hens can be found that will prove to be the exception to the rule.

Given good care you should get a yearly average of about 20 eggs per day from 35 hens—more in the spring and less in the fall. This assumes you have a healthy flock of egg-type chickens and provide them with at least 14 hours of light per day and an adequate diet.

Whey is good feed

COUNTRYSIDE: For years we've fed the whey from our summertime cheesemaking to the chickens. They prefer it greatly over water and I've read it's a good source of B vitamins which they need for egg production. They get the whey in addition to a free-range diet of garden and forest insects, table scraps, cracked corn, whole oats and stolen dairy ration. In winter they have had to do without whey as we don't make cheese then.

Now I've learned that a local cheese plant sells dried whey for $3 per hundred pounds. Is this a good price considering the nutrients it would add to our admittedly haphazard chicken diet? What does it contain anyway? Should it be fed dry or reconstituted with water? I think warm whey would comfort them on cold days. – *Peter Yronwode, Missouri*

Whey is a good product to use in poultry rations. It contains lactose and several of the B vitamins as well as riboflavin (vitamin G). The latter is especially desirable when the eggs are being saved for hatching.

Excess quantities of whey will have a laxative effect on your birds and contribute to wet litter problems when the birds are confined. Dry whey at $3 per hundred is a very good buy. You should always provide some clean, fresh water in addition to any whey given the flock.

The henhouse:

Raising chicks in a "cardboard condo"

Creativity makes up for a lack of space.

Lisa Richards
North Carolina

I am currently living in a small rented trailer on about one acre of land.

Last February I had the opportunity to obtain a large number of day-old chicks (for free). I had nowhere to put them and I wasn't sure if my landlord would appreciate chickens running everywhere. On the plus side, I also had access to approximately five to 10 pounds of free feed every week. Sooo…

I got creative. It was too cold to keep them outside and I didn't have enough lights to keep them warm, so I came up with what I thought was a novel way of coping with the problems.

Chick condos!

I took boxes and cut "windows" for the chicks to stick their heads through. This allowed light into the boxes and access to food and water which I kept in containers outside of the box. I lined the box with material and changed the lining daily. These boxes could be stacked to save space. It worked very well. The closed space helped the chicks stay warm and I had no deaths or illness with these chicks. As the chicks grew larger, I simply put fewer chicks in each box.

After three or four weeks, I bought a child's wading pool and cut a lot of small holes in the bottom. During the day when it was warm, I put the chicks in the yard and turned the wading pool over the top of them. Instant playpen for the chicks. The landlord simply thought the pool was there for the children to play in.

Next I built a small coop for the chickens I intended to keep. It was 3' x 4' with a hinged door in the roof to gather the eggs. I did a fairly neat job and have been happy with it. The front of the coop has a large open "window" area that I covered with chicken wire for the summer and heavy plastic for the winter. Then there is a small opening with a sliding door for the chickens to get in and out. I chose to make the large opening because I could use this as a dog house if the landlord refused to let me keep the chickens.

When I finally talked to my landlord, I had six-week-old chicks that were only several weeks from butchering weight, an attractive, neat appearing chicken coop to keep them in, and a free roll of chicken wire to put up a fence if he gave me the go-ahead.

This went a long way toward convincing him it would be okay. I also promised him I only intended to keep about half a dozen pullets and one or two roosters. The remainder had an appointment with my freezer.

As I promised I now have six hens and one rooster. They are very large meat birds. (They butchered out at four to six pounds at only eight or

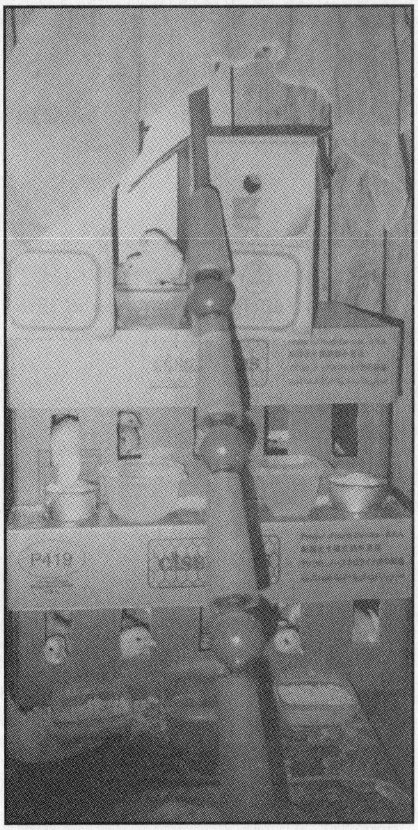

nine weeks.) I have also been very impressed with their laying ability. They lay large, brown eggs. I even have one hen that lays double yolks, regularly. I know this is a defect, but it sure makes rich cakes.

I have one hen that has been broody. I find this a plus as well. (I don't have to decide if I should or shouldn't turn the eggs.)

This letter only goes to show—if you really want to do something, you can usually find a way to do it.

The homestead chicken

Our reader surveys consistently show that the most common form of livestock on homesteads is the chicken. There are some very good reasons for this popularity.

First, while many people who are unfamiliar with farm livestock are intimidated by larger creatures, even young children are captivated by tiny, fluffy chicks.

Starting out with day-old chicks is far less expensive and requires much simpler facilities and equipment than starting out with other animals.

If a chick dies you can dig a grave with a spoon and write off the small expense. If a cow dies...well, you get the picture.

People who think they couldn't butcher an animal can raise chickens for eggs. Those who want to learn to process the meat they eat will find that learning is much easier with a chicken than with other stock.

The payback is rapid, compared with most other farm animals. You can put meat on the table in 8-12 weeks (depending on breed and other factors), and eggs in about six months (again depending on breed).

It takes much less time to gather eggs than to milk a cow or goat, and the schedule isn't nearly as rigid. And not many things offer as much homestead pride and satisfaction as comparing runny store-bought eggs with "homegrown" eggs, with golden yolks that stand up proudly in the frying pan!

And even this only touches the surface. There is the country charm of a flock of vari-colored chickens scratching in the dooryard...and so much more.

But if you have no experience with anything other than a cat or dog, how do you get started?

As with all homestead projects, the first step is getting the information you'll need to make the right decisions and take the right actions.

Where to begin

Chicks and fertile eggs are available from a number of sources. Feed stores typically sell chicks during the spring months, and some farmers also handle them as a sideline.

There is one drawback when buying close to home: If you are looking for an unusual or specialized breed, the local seller might not have the right chickens for you. But if you have your heart set on a particular breed, day-old chicks can be shipped by mail.

Catalogs from breeders who advertise in magazines like COUNTRYSIDE (check the display and classified ads as well as the Breeders' Directory of each issue) offer dozens of different breeds of chickens and other fowl. If you're like most people, the biggest problem will be narrowing the choices down to a manageable level.

With more than 350 varieties to choose from, how do you sort through various birds? For homesteaders who want meat and eggs, the first step is not to select the "prettiest" birds, but to learn about their characteristics. Then decide which breed or breeds might best suit your needs.

Chickens are divided into classes based on geographic origin, while breeds are determined by shared physical characteristics such as body shape, skin color, carriage or station, number of toes and feathered or non-feathered shanks.

A variety is a subdivision of a breed that differs in color, pattern, combs or other cosmetic details.

Let's use the Cochin breed to show how chickens are classified. Since they originated in China, Cochins are part of the Asiatic class. Varieties include white, black, buff and partridge. Cochins are known for being heavily feathered, which can be quite important to northerners who plan to keep chickens year-round.

Rhode Island Reds, Plymouth Rocks and Wyandottes (all from the American class) are among today's more popular breeds. Why are they found in so many homestead flocks? These birds along with the Sussex and Australorp are considered to be dual purpose breeds.

That means they are decent egg layers and will provide good meat. While there are better egg layers and better meat breeds, the dual purpose chicken gives the small producer a steady supply of both products from a modest-sized flock. This isn't how commercial egg and chicken companies think, as they raise birds exclusively for one purpose. For the COUNTRYSIDER, the "jack of all trades" approach usually works much better than imitating the agribusiness model.

The dual purpose birds can also tolerate less than perfect conditions. Wisconsin extension poultry specialist John Skinner recommends Rhode Island Reds for their overall hardiness and consistent egg production. He also noted that Rhode Island Reds tolerate marginal diets and poor housing conditions better than most breeds.

Skinner described Plymouth Rocks as "a good general farm chicken. They are docile; normally will show broodiness; possess a long, broad back; a moderately deep, full breast; and a single comb of moderate size."

The Wyandotte is another dual purpose bird that Skinner recommends. He described them as "good, medium-weight fowl for small family flocks kept under rugged conditions." They have rose combs that won't

freeze as easily as larger combs. Wyandotte hens are good mothers.

Despite its dual purpose designation, an Australorp holds the world record for egg production with an amazing 364 eggs laid in 365 days. This English class chicken is a meaty, medium-sized fowl.

The Sussex is another English bird, and it gets Skinner's seal of approval. He considers them to be "one of the best of the dual-purpose chickens, a good all-around farm fowl." They are also good foragers and mothers.

It is important to determine what you want from a flock of chickens before you place an order. For instance, Cornish chickens have a reputation as good meat birds, while Leghorns are often raised for eggs. Orpington chicks are not very aggressive and fare poorly when competing with other breeds.

Perhaps the best solution for the small homestead or first-time chicken flock would be a majority of dual purpose breeds along with a few "fun" specimens such as the colored-egglaying Araucana. Some roasting-sized birds such as the 12-pound Brahma can also be added to the mix.

If your main priority is eggs rather than meat, make sure your flock has at least some Leghorns. Bantam-sized birds for many breeds can also be obtained. Despite their small size, bantams do well as brood hens and foster mothers for chicks from other birds.

If you live in a hot climate or are raising chickens for meat, purchase white-plumaged birds whenever possible. For a steady egg supply, look to commercial egg layers. However, these chickens require good housing and an all-mash diet. If you have less-than-ideal housing for chickens and want to supplement the feed with table scraps, sex-link or crossbreeds can be a good choice. There are regional differences in the names of these chickens, and they are sold by local hatcheries.

Although they will never grow to the size of a plump roasting chicken, bantams can be reliable egg and meat producers. For those with limited space and feed budgets, bantams are one alternative to consider. Bantams also make good brood hens for setting other eggs.

Incubation & chick rearing

Before brood hens can go to work, there must be eggs to hatch. If you want fertile eggs, you'll need at least one rooster—a male bird who will aggressively defend his turf and crow every morning—in the flock.

Some people would rather not have a rooster, and that is your choice. If you decide to take that route, you'll have to buy hatching eggs, chicks or replacements every year. For many homesteaders, a chicken flock isn't complete without at least one strutting rooster.

There should be one rooster for every 20 hens in the light breeds and one rooster for every 10 to 12 hens in the heavier breeds. Roosters vary in fertility. Many aging males stiffen, and while still capable of producing semen, they won't pursue mating with the same effectiveness as younger roosters. Increase the male/female ratio if you have two- to four-year-old roosters.

Regardless of age, healthy males need sufficient light to fertilize the flock. Texas poultry extension specialist William Cawley explained, "The hormone level of male birds' blood must reach a particular point before the sperm in the testes will grow and mature. Light stimulates the production of these hormones. In his mind, the male can be ready to mate and may give visible signs of doing so, but until his sperm matures, he is 'shooting blanks.'"

According to Cawley, it takes two weeks longer for a male's sperm to mature than it does for a female's yolk. If you want to fertilize the first eggs of the season, place your roosters on 14 to 16-hour light days about three weeks before the hens start laying.

There is no penetration when a rooster and hen mate. The rooster's copulatory organ makes contact with the hen's distended orifice of the oviduct located on the left side of the cloaca. The hen exposes it at the moment of mating.

Some breeds have more difficulty breeding because of their feathering or dimensions. Cornish chickens, very large birds and some bantams have short, heavy legs, extreme muscle development or wide bodies that can interfere with breeding. With their heavy feathering, Cochins sometimes need a vent feather trimming before the breeding season.

Sperm stays viable in hens for some time, as it congregates in folded recesses of the oviduct. Some hens remain fertile for as long as four weeks after contact with a rooster, but fertility declines substantially after a week. Older hens stay fertile longer than younger ones.

As a sperm leaves the "nest", it moves up the funnel to the infundibulum, where fertilization occurs if a yolk is released from the ovary. Once a fertilized egg is laid, it must have proper care to hatch. Gather the eggs at least twice daily and store at a temperature of 50° to 65° F with a relative humidity of 75 percent.

Basements offer ideal conditions for egg storage. For dry conditions, one hatchery owner recommended placing eggs in covered boxes lined with three to six inches of clean and slightly dampened bedding.

Hatching eggs shouldn't be stored more than 14 days. One week is an ideal storage time. If you plan to store the eggs for more than seven days, turn them daily to prevent the yolk from floating to the surface of the white and adhering to the shell's inner surface.

Eggs from older hens hatch just as well as those from pullets. Since eggs from older hens are larger than pullet eggs, chicks hatched from older hen eggs will also be bigger.

There are two ways to incubate hatching eggs—the broody hen or the mechanical incubator. Although the incubator is popular with people who are concerned about hens transmitting disease organisms to chicks, one university study came to the conclusion that the machine-incubated chicks are "socially deprived", since the baby birds missed communicating with the setting hen in the last two days before the hatch.

Scientists who conducted the study identified 11 different calls used by the hen and chick in communication. The calls encouraged chicks to vocalize and gave them an idea that the outside world would respond to them.

Broody hens are easy to spot, since they insist on sitting on the nest when they should be out scratching for feed. Brooders will also cluck and peck at anyone who tries to remove them from the nest.

The brooding instinct is normal once hens have laid a certain number of eggs. The tendency has been eliminated in a number of breeds, but it is quite strong in bantams, Wyandottes, Plymouth Rocks, Dorkings, New Hampshires, Rhode Island Reds and Orpingtons.

Caring for the broody hen

When a hen goes broody and you decide to use her as a setter, add cracked corn to her feed for several days before placing her on the eggs. This will help her develop a warm brood pouch on her chest. Then move her to a secluded nest and give her dummy eggs to set for two days. Also powder her with an insecticide.

If the hen stays on the dummy eggs, she is a good candidate to stick with hatching eggs for the required 21 days. Warm the eggs to room temperature and set them in the nest. Large breed chickens can handle about 13 eggs.

Let the hen off the nest once a day for water, feed and exercise. Discard any egg that she pushes out of the nest; she knows the good ones. The eggs are ready for candling on the seventh day.

If the egg has a reddish, spiderlike body in it, it is fertile and the embryo is developing. If there is a black ring, that means the embryo started to develop, but has died. If there is no sign of development, then the egg is unfertilized.

Chicks should begin to emerge after 21 days. How is the hen able to sit continually on the nest for three weeks? She goes into a partial state of hibernation, as her temperature drops and her metabolic processes slow down. The hen also absorbs any immature yolks in her body.

Just because a hen shows signs of going broody doesn't mean she has to set on a clutch of eggs. If you don't want to take her out of production, you can "break" her by putting her in a broody coop. The coop should be wire-floored and about 2 x 4 feet by 14 inches high. Place it in the least likely nesting place—somewhere there is plenty of light—and mount it so it is unstable. The constant activity of maintaining her balance "breaks" the hen of her desire to set on the nest. This will take about four days.

Mechanical incubation

If you decide not to let the broody hens incubate the hatching eggs, you'll need a mechanical incubator. There are two basic types of incubators: still-air and forced-air. Either will work, provided it meets the four requirements of incubation.

Successful hatching requires a temperature of 102° to 103° F in still-air incubators and 99.5° F in forced-air; 60 percent relative humidity, increased to 70 percent during the last three days of the hatch; turning the eggs an odd number of times daily from the second to the 18th day; and ventilation to supply fresh oxygen to the embryos.

Improper humidity is the leading cause for losing chicks during artificial incubation. The membrane sticks to the chick when humidity is too low, and that prevents it from turning inside the egg. That will prevent the chick from orienting itself and pipping out of its shell. On the 18th day of the hatch, place an additional source of water such as a damp sponge inside the incubator.

Other reasons for poor hatches are infertile or old eggs; weak stock; improper egg care; shell contamination; improper temperature, humidity or ventilation; and infrequent turnings.

(Note: There has been some speculation—and experimentation—about the need to turn eggs. After reading about this in COUNTRYSIDE, several people have reported

hatches as good without turning as with turning... and with a lot less time and work.)

If you do your job, poor hatches will be the exception rather than the rule.

Caring for the chicks

Then you'll need proper facilities for the chicks. This can be as simple as a cardboard box with a heat lamp suspended over it or as sophisticated as an electric battery brooder. (This doesn't refer to a storage battery, but to an array or battery of brooders, usually stacked vertically; heated with electric.) What is important is that the chicks are kept warm and dry and have a constant supply of food and water.

For the first week, chicks need a constant temperature of 95°F. After that, the temperature can be reduced five degrees each week. If the chicks are huddled beneath the heat source, they are too cold; little birds grouped in the corners of the brooder are too warm, and chicks grouped on one side of a brooder are avoiding a draft.

Chicks in a box are well protected from drafts, but if they are in a building (such as a brooder house), a chick guard should be placed around the brooder area to protect them from drafts. Chick guards are 18-inch high circular fences, often made of cardboard, that also prevent chicks from piling in corners and smothering to death. Remove the guard after eight to 10 days.

The brooder should allow enough floor space for the chicks. Guidelines are as follows:

Age of bird	Floor space per chick
0-4 weeks	$\frac{1}{2}$ sq. ft.
4-8 weeks	1 sq. ft.
8-12 weeks	2 sq. ft.
12-plus weeks	$2\frac{1}{2}$-3 sq. ft (light breeds)
	3-$3\frac{1}{2}$ sq. ft. (heavy breeds)

Anyone who has brooded chicks can attest to the large amount of dust they produce. But not many are aware of the reason.

As feathers grow on the young birds, they are lubricated by a very fine, talc-like powder. This is why people who brood those cute, fluffy little chicks in a box in the kitchen or spare bedroom usually come to regret it!

Just-hatched chicks, whether they come from a hatchery or a home flock, have enough unabsorbed egg yolk in their bodies to live on for about 72 hours. Even with that built-in food supply, have feed and water available at all times. Chicks will readily learn to eat a crumblized starter ration if a little is sprinkled on top of a newspaper placed on top of the litter.

Chicks need the following feeder and waterer space:

Age of Bird	Feeder Space/100 chicks
0-4 weeks	12 linear ft. (2 3-ft. feeders)
4-8 weeks	20 linear ft. (2 5-ft. feeders)
8-12 weeks	30 linear ft. (3 5-ft. feeders)
12-plus weeks	40 linear ft. (4 5-ft. feeders)

Age of Bird	Waterer space/100 chicks
0-4 weeks	6 1-quart waterers
1-4 weeks	2 2-gallon waterers
4-12 weeks	2 5-gallon waterers

With your chicks fed, watered and warmed, you're on your way to having a productive flock. However, if you want only hens for eggs or want to separate the males to raise as fryers, it will be important to learn how to sex chicks. There are several ways to do this, but be forewarned: it's not easy.

Birds can be vent sexed by everting a chick's anus and examining the genital organ. This method takes a lot of practice to master. Another not-so-easy method involves inserting an instrument into the chick's cloaca to examine the gonads. The instrument is expensive, and seldom worthwhile for a home breeder with a small flock. Sexlinked birds may be sexed by their down feathers, and certain purebreds can be sexed by different feather patterns.

What's the simplest way? Just wait until the birds are eight weeks old and sex them by feathers and appearance. The hackle and saddle feathers of male chickens are shiny, pointed and glossy. Feathers on females are rounder and duller. The only exception to this guideline is the Sebright bantam, which has female plumage in both sexes.

Housing

There's no need to get too elaborate or to spend gobs of money for a chicken coop. Many fine shelters have been built with scrap lumber and odd pieces of building material.

The portable pen is a practical choice for small-scale chicken raisers. Just wheel the structure to different spots and allow your birds to browse in and fertilize different plots of land. Gardeners can use a mobile pen to reduce bug populations, and feed costs are cut significantly when chickens are allowed to eat insects and vegetation. For instructions on building one, check out the article in 82/5; "Build a neat but simple henhouse."

Karen Hayes and her husband Jack had no plans to raise "smelly" chickens on their $2\frac{1}{2}$-acre homestead. That changed when Karen rescued two escapees from a nearby chicken packing plant.

Here the Hayes' portable chicken corral is laid out, ready to be assembled.

Karen says her fences are very sturdy and easily moved to provide fresh foraging for the chickens.

This corner detail shows how the 12-ft. fences, made from scrap lumber, are fastened together.

Jack built the two hens "a pen similar to a rabbit hutch in size and shape," Karen told COUNTRYSIDE. The chickens soon began laying large eggs, and "fresh eggs started to appeal to me." So she bought two Leghorns from a friend. That led to designing a simple and economical portable chicken pen. Most of the materials used in the project came from scrap lumber.

"It's very easy to keep the chickens contained – most of the time – in the area I want them," Karen said. "During the winter months, we set the pen up in our garden area, and the chickens eat the bugs and vegetable scraps and leave their fertilizer. About every two weeks, we move the pen to a new area so it never gets too smelly and muddy.

"I have since added two Barred Plymouth Rock hens, and they are doing very well. Having the chickens out foraging has cut the feed cost considerably."

The chickens reside in two coops located inside the fencing. The roofs are hinged for easy cleaning and egg removal, and doors are cut in the side to allow the chickens to come and go as they please.

Each section of fencing surrounding the coops was

made by using three four-foot 2 x 4s. Karen stapled chicken wire between the sections, then nailed five 12-foot rails onto them. The door section was made by placing a scrap piece of plywood in the middle and cutting a door in the plywood.

Three eye-bolts that mesh together are on the end of each section of fencing. Karen slipped a metal rod through the eyes, and that holds the fence rigid. If the flock becomes larger, this style of building lends itself to modular additions.

"Any number of these sections can be joined to make a suitable-sized pen," Karen said. "They are very sturdy. When I get more chickens, I plan to add one or two more sections and make a larger pen. I also plan to make at least six more sections and use them to put the goats in an area where we have blackberry vines to clear.

"They would be very useful for someone who is currently renting a place," Karen said. "When you move, you can pick up your fences and take them with you."

While chickens often like to roam a bit, they must be protected from the elements, ever-present predators and theft. That means your flock must have some kind of housing. Again, fanciness isn't important, but the building should keep the flock at a comfortable 55° to 85°. If sufficient water is available, chickens can adapt to temperatures ranging from 0° to 100°.

Give the chickens sufficient room. Egg-type birds need two to three feet of floor space, while larger breeds do better with three to $3\frac{1}{2}$ feet. Two square feet will do for bantams.

Allow your birds to range if possible, since sunlight helps chickens to synthesize vitamin D. They will also obtain some minerals from the ground while ranging. Fenced-in runs allow chickens to get outdoors while providing protection from predators.

Chicken manure is high in ammonia and will give off unpleasant odors if it is not removed periodically. A sufficient supply of litter is needed to absorb bird droppings. Any dry, absorbent, fibrous materials can be used, such as sawdust, chopped hay, wood shavings, peat moss, finely shredded paper or sand. If there is an ammonia smell in the building, the litter is too damp. Correct this by increasing ventilation or by stirring lime into the litter to help the moisture escape.

Roosts

The house should have perches and nests. Perches should be thick enough for chickens to get a good hold while curling their toes around them. A two-inch-thick bar is good for large birds. Broom handles make good perches for bantams. Allow 10 inches of perch space for full-sized birds and five inches per bantam.

Make sure that the perches are far enough from the wall to allow the birds to sit in comfort. Eighteen inches is a good distance for large breeds, while a foot is sufficient for bantams.

It's not necessary, and sometimes not even desirable, to provide roosts for heavy-type meat birds, as the perches can lead to breast blisters.

Install a dropping pit along with a good supply of litter beneath the perch. To keep chickens from scratching in their droppings, install a removable wire frame over the pit.

Nests

It's important to provide comfortable nests for the hens in a secluded, dark corner of the coop if you don't want them laying eggs in the middle of the floor. One nest for five hens should do.

In most cases, hens will continue laying where they laid their first few eggs. If that happens, it will be difficult to get hens to switch to laying in the nests. One way to remedy this problem is by placing a nest in the usual laying spot, then gradually moving it to a better location.

Leave enough room for feeders and waterers. They can be purchased at small-town feed and hardware stores or through mail-order catalogs. With a little creativity, you can make your own from bleach bottles, coffee cans or other household odds and ends.

You'll have to completely clean and disinfect the coop twice a year. Remove old litter and droppings, then scrape away any dried manure. Scrub the coop with disinfectant, then apply a mite control. Allow the coop to air dry, and the flock can go back home again.

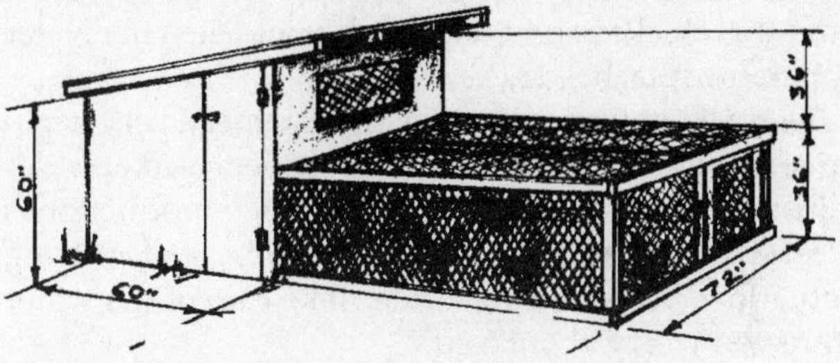

4 rafters placed 24" O.C. Cover with 1"X6"X RL, then with tar paper.

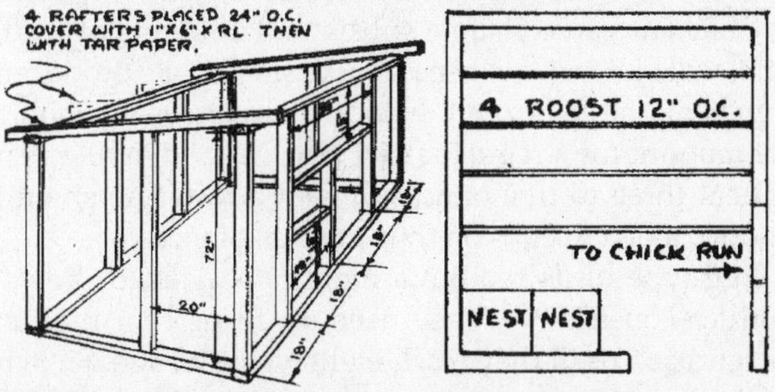

The dimensions of this house may be altered to suit your materials or the space available. Feed and water is easily placed through the door of the run, and eggs are gathered through the small door in the house. The run may be covered to provide shelter from rain and sun. The run and windows are covered with one-inch chicken wire.

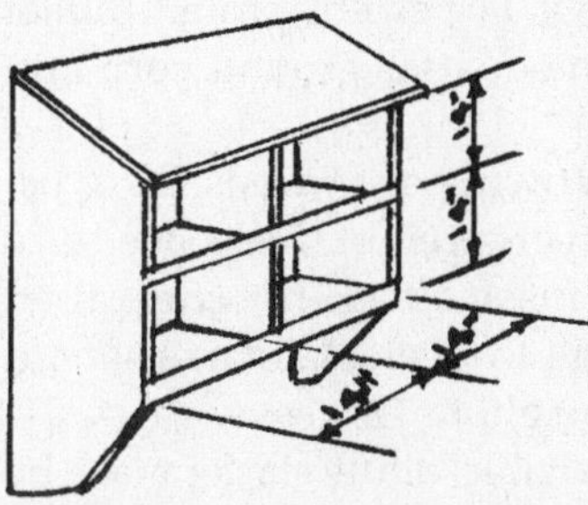

Feeding

What's the most important element in feeding chickens? Water. To quote M.L. Pierson and G.H. Arscott of Oregon State University's Department of Poultry Science, "Water, an essential nutrient for poultry, is too often neglected or completely taken for granted."

They continued, "Although no exact requirement has been established, water is necessary for a bird's growth, reproduction and regulation of body temperature. It is necessary for digestive processes and transport of nutrients and waste products and is the major constituent of all animal cells and tissues."

In studying the importance of adequate water supplies for chickens, Pierson and Arscott noted that 57 percent of a chicken's live weight is water, while eggs are 73 percent water by weight. A commercial egg layer that produces 250 eggs a year will consume 80 to 90 pounds of feed a year and at least 180 pounds of water. Hens drink more than roosters.

A number of factors will affect water consumption. Among them are the amount of feed consumed, the kind of feed (chickens drink more water when fed pelleted, salty, fibrous or high-protein types), temperature and humidity, and the water itself.

The ideal water temperature for chickens is 50° to 55°F. Intake decreases by as much as 25 percent if the water approaches the freezing point. Pierson and Arnscott found that chickens refuse to drink at all when the water temperature reaches 112°F.

Even a short time without water can mean very negative consequences for the flock. Layers deprived of water for just one day go into a partial molt. Egg production is decreased. Water-deprived broilers eat less feed, causing fluctuations in their growth rate. Take care of the water before you worry about feed.

Feed is a major expense

Chickens can consume substantial amounts of feed, and it will be a major expense for the small-scale producer. Even bantams go through 40 to 50 pounds a year. Double that amount for a regular-sized bird. A good laying hen will eat three to five ounces of feed a day. She should produce a dozen eggs on four pounds of feed.

Egg-type birds require a highly specialized diet to produce consistently. They need an 18 percent protein starter mash until they reach eight weeks of age. Switch to a 16 percent grower ration or a starter blend with 60 percent protein starter from eight to 12 weeks. From 12 to 20 weeks, layers require a 14 percent protein pullet developer or half mash, one-quarter ground corn and one-quarter ground oats.

Meat chickens have their own special needs. Birds being raised for slaughter as fryers at eight weeks need a 20 to 22 percent protein starter mash. Chickens being raised for slaughter as roasters at 14 to 16 weeks of age should be fed a grower mash from eight to 12 weeks.

If grower mash is not available, dilute starter mash by a third with ground corn or a corn/wheat mix to come up with a 15 to 17 percent protein feed. From 12 weeks until slaughter, the best formula is finishing mash or a 50-50 mix of starter and ground corn.

General purpose flocks need 18 to 20 percent starter until they reach eight weeks. After that, go with a 15 to 17 percent formula or similar blend until the 14-week mark. A 14 to 16 percent grower ration can be used after that.

There are several options for meeting a chicken's nutritional needs. A base mix, vitamin packages or concentrates for blending with homegrown grains are available. Some Countrysiders who don't grow their own grain or have limited time for mixing items just stick with a standard chicken feed.

Be sure to provide a well-balanced diet for confined birds, as they are unable to forage for bugs, seeds, greens and other nutritious chicken delicacies. Ranging can supply much of the food for 10 to 20-week pullets, but it isn't adequate to meet all the needs of meat birds or layers. That means you'll need to provide mash at all times.

Chickens need grit to digest their food. Grit remains in the gizzard—an enlargement of the alimentary canal that follows the crop—to help a bird grind up its food. Gravel, sand or other roughage that can withstand the substantial pressures (several hundred pounds per square inch) of the gizzard can be used.

Birds that range usually find enough grit, but always keep some available. Chicks should be fed grit once a week. Provide them with a constant supply for four days before they begin ranging.

Chicks that haven't had enough grit before they begin ranging sometimes become "crop bound." This also happens to older birds that have stretched crop muscles or an obstruction in the crop's outlet.

To cure the problem, put the affected bird in a coop. Place some mineral oil down its throat. Remove the soured accumulation of feed and liquid in the crop by holding the chicken upside down and massaging the crop. Give the bird a chance to drink some water, then keep it off feed and water until the crop empties.

Laying hens also need a free-choice supply of calcium for producing firm-shelled eggs. One obvious source is eggshells, but they need to be cooked to destroy any organisms. The shells also need to be completely pulverized. That will prevent the hens from recognizing the eggshells and possibly becoming egg eaters. Other good sources of calcium include limestone and crushed oyster shells. Hens also need sunlight or vitamin D to utilize calcium.

While greens or garden leftovers can be used to supplement chicken feed and grain, they shouldn't be the mainstay of the diet. Greens contain too much water to be used exclusively for chicken food.

Some homesteaders plant oats as a quick green chicken feed. If you are worried about the birds eating the plants roots and all, build a small lumber frame and cover it with a screen. Plant the framed area thickly. The chickens will graze on the oats as they grow through the

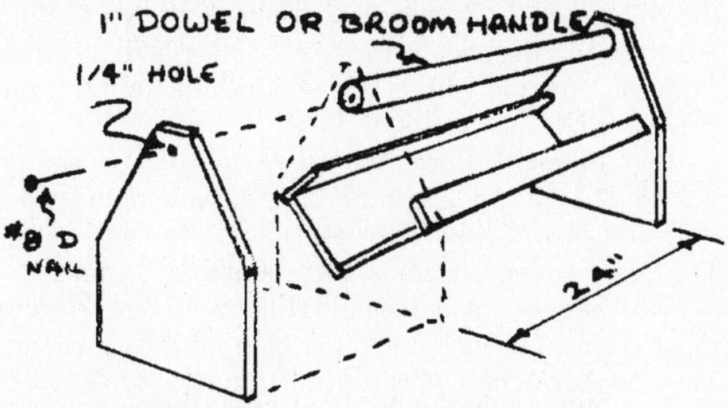

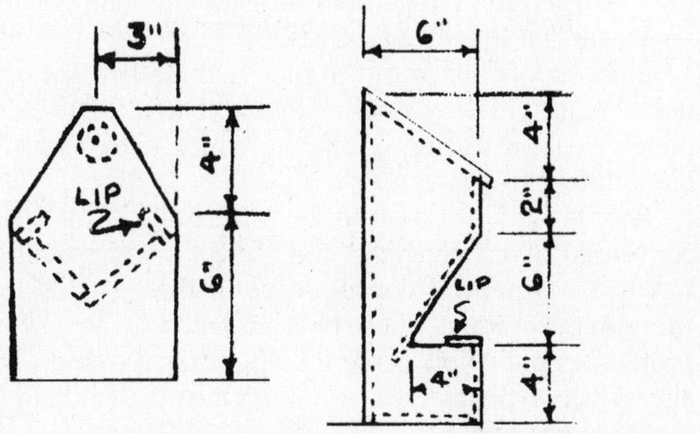

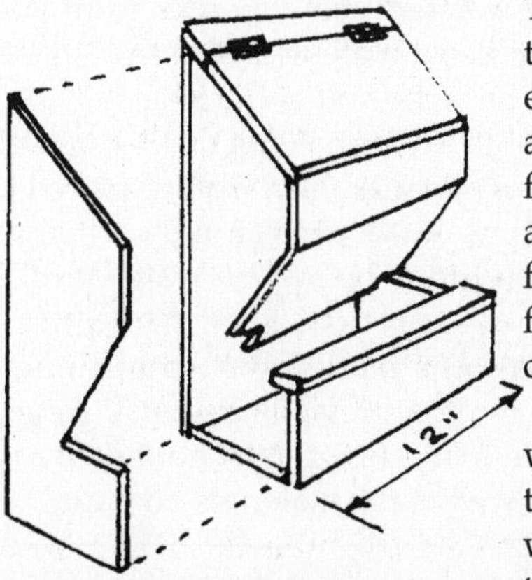

screen, but they won't be able to pull up the roots.

Don't feed spoiled greens to your chickens, and don't leave edible greens around long enough to spoil. If they aren't eaten in 20 minutes, remove the greens from the feeding area.

In the fall and winter, cut-up pumpkins, beets, mangels and winter squash all make good chicken fodder. Peelings, trimmings and leftovers can also go to the chicken coop. Such scraps may be given only to chickens that are at least eight weeks old.

Potato sprouts should never be fed to chickens.

Many readers are sure to ask, "Why does feeding chickens have to be so complicated...and expensive? Certainly, feeding chickens was simpler in the old days!"

There are two ways to answer that.

First, until early in this century, very little was known about nutrition—vitamins, minerals and such—either in terms of a body's requirements or in terms of what various feedstuffs offered. This applied to humans as well as chickens and other farm animals.

It followed that such feed supplements as fish meal, soybean meal, and other products weren't available.

One result of these scientific advances was that production and efficiency increased. Meat chickens grow faster and plumper, laying hens lay more eggs per year and per pound of feed, and both meat and eggs are much less expensive than they used to be. ("Chicken every Sunday" used to mean a certain amount of luxury; today it means nothing. Even just 50 years ago eggs were plentiful in spring and very expensive in winter.)

This leads to a problem that perplexes many homesteaders, namely, why are their homegrown poultry products so much more expensive than the store-bought ones?

The main reason is the much-heralded efficiency of modern agriculture. In the few minutes it takes a homesteader to care for a few chickens, the factory farmer can care for thousands.

But then, what would happen if those factory farms went out of production...Chicks, broilers and layers die by the thousands even now when the electricity is off for any length of time. In an economic crash, many of the farms producing for the huge agribusiness companies that control the markets might fold. In a Y2K situation, bottlenecks in transportation, finance, and other sectors could make it even worse.

Store-bought chickens and eggs would again be expensive, or not available at any price.

In that case, the "scientific feeding of chickens" would be unavailable to most homesteaders as well...and the old-fashioned methods would again come into play. Meat and egg production would fall, but some is better than none.

Chickens can live, and produce, without all the fancy scientific nutrition. They can glean a good portion of their needs by free-ranging, supplemented by table scraps, garden waste, excess milk or whey left over from cheesemaking, scraps from butchering, homegrown grain (even grain spilled or wasted by other animals), and from such items as vegetables grown specifically for animal feed and labor-intensive things like sprouted grains or boiled potatoes.

Even today, many avid homesteaders would like to raise chickens, and other animals, this way. They "can't," because they have to "compete" with mass-produced product. They know they can buy it cheaper than they can produce it, and/or they're simply too busy trying to make a living and keeping up with modern demands on their time to be able to afford to produce anything so inefficiently.

But if or when they don't have to commute to a town job, watch tv, wash the car, chauffeur the kids to school events, balance the checkbook, and all the other tasks that occupy modern Americans...and if or when chicken and eggs aren't available in stores...we might discover what true efficiency really is.

Equipment

You can buy ready-made feeding and watering equipment, but it's much more economical (and fun) to build it yourself. An automatic waterer and feeder designed by Billie R. Tylor for COUNTRYSIDE is simple to build.

The waterer requires nothing more than a five-gallon can, a pan, a piece of hose, some scrap lumber and miscellaneous hardware. Adapt the waterer's holding rack to fit your can and pan. The completed waterer is also shown. The only opening should be at the end of the hose.

To save floor space, attach the holding rack to the wall. Whether the waterer is mounted on a wall or placed on the floor, the water runs out of the can only when the water level in the pan drops below the water level in the spout.

The feeders can also be made from scrap lumber. Use the illustrations (on the previous page) as general construction guidelines. This design can be adapted to fit your flock's needs as well as the materials on hand.

Egg production

Egg-type hens will lay 220 to 280 eggs a year with proper diet and lighting. It's easy to recognize those that are laying and those that are shirking their duties.

A productive hen has a wide, deep breast and an enlarged, pliable abdomen. She shouldn't be fat. Her skin will be warm and moist, and her vent will be enlarged and moist. The good egg layer will have bright bold eyes and a warm red, waxy-looking comb and wattles.

The yellow pigment in egg layers bleaches from the body parts in a definite order: vent, edge of eyelids, 1/4 earlobes, beak and shanks. The bleaching from the vent and eyes is noticeable about 10 days after production begins. It can take as long as seven months for the shanks to bleach.

While the onset of egg production varies with diet, breeding and the season when the hens matured, most egg strains begin laying at around five months. Heavier meat-type breeds usually begin laying at six to eight months. Chickens will lay for 10 to 12 months, peaking at 34 weeks before declining a half percent a week until they molt.

Hens can lay well for another year after molting, but egg quality and quantity are usually best during the first year of production. Expect 10 to 15 percent fewer eggs the second year.

Egg size is an inherited characteristic, but eggs will get larger the longer the hen is laying. Size has little to do with quality, however, as smaller eggs tend to score higher in that department.

Adequate light is needed for steady egg production. As light strikes a hen's eye, the optic nerve sends a stimulus to the brain, then to the pituitary gland, which controls egg production. This stimulus causes the pituitary gland to release a hormone that aids in the growth and maturity of the yolk. When the yolk matures after 10 to 14 days, additional light causes the release of another hormone that frees the yolk from its follicle.

The yolk is dropped into and engulfed by the infundibulum, which is the first section of the oviduct. Peristaltic motion moves the yolk through the other sections of the oviduct. It passes through the albumen-secreting section of the oviduct, the magnum, then into the isthmus where the shell membranes are added. Next, the yolk moves to the uterus, or shell gland, where fluid is added and the shell is formed. It takes 24 to 26 hours from the time the yolk is released into the follicle until the egg is laid.

As with any process, the egg-laying process can go wrong. Decreasing length of days, disease, aging, poor nutrition, lack of water or stress can all affect egg laying. The quality of eggs from an older hen may decline.

Meat spots—small deep red chips in the eggs—occur most often in brown-shelled eggs from heavy breeds. They happen when worn-out cells from a hen's reproductive tract clump together inside the egg. Remove the spots, and eat the rest of the egg.

Blood spots are found in one to three percent of a flock's eggs. This occurs when the capillaries fail to completely seal off during ovulation, which releases some blood into the egg.

People who are new to farm-fresh eggs are often concerned about chalazae, the "cords" in egg whites. Cords are a natural consequence of the egg passing through the oviduct. These twisted strands of egg white protein keep the yolk centered. The cords unwind with age, which explains why you don't always see them in store-bought eggs.

Double-yolk eggs occur when two yolks mature at the same time. This happens most often with pullet eggs.

An egg within an egg is a rare problem that happens when a formed egg is forced back through the oviduct by reverse peristaltic action.

Egg-eating hens are the worst plague that can strike your family's egg supply. It is a difficult habit to break. One way to stop this is by building nests with inclined

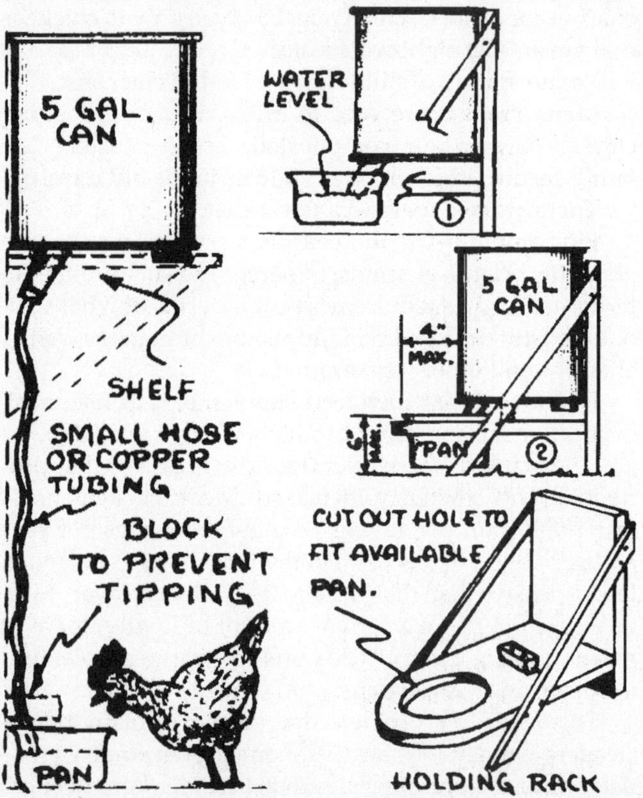

bottoms so the eggs roll out of the hen's reach. Other methods include placing unbreakable dummy eggs in the nest, frequent egg gathering, darkening the nests, and placing the nest out of the hen's normal range of vision.

Clean eggs don't need to be washed, but dirty eggs can be washed in water about 20° F warmer than the eggs. Rinse and dry the eggs quickly.

It is preferable to have nests that keep eggs clean so they won't have to be washed. Aside from the extra work, washing eggs can lower their quality...and it removes a protective coating that keeps the eggs fresher longer.

Using home-produced eggs

Unlike store-bought eggs, hard-boiled fresh eggs are often difficult to remove from the shell. You could let the fresh eggs stand at room temperature for a few days before boiling them, but that defeats the purpose of having fresh eggs. It's better to make a small hole in the air cell end of the shell before cooking.

If you prefer, you can make a small fracture in the shell of a half-cooked egg. Both methods allow a little water to come between the shell and albumen, which makes it easier to remove the shell.

One "problem" with home-produced eggs (or anything else, for that matter) is that when production is highest, the homesteader is drowning in eggs, but when production slows or stops eggs are at a premium. But eggs can be preserved by pickling, drying, freezing or storing.

Eggs do well when they are pickled in sweet, sour or spicy brine solutions. They can keep for several months if stored in the brine and refrigerated.

Cover the eggs with cold water. Bring the water to a quick boil, then simmer for 15 minutes. Cool the eggs in cold water, then peel them.

Place the boiled eggs in a jar that can be tightly closed, then pour a hot pickling solution over them. Store the sealed jar in the refrigerator. Allow a week to cure small eggs and two to four weeks for medium and large eggs.

These pickling recipes are designed for a dozen eggs. Heat the mixture to near boiling and simmer for five to 10 minutes.

Beet red eggs:
1 cup red beet juice
1-1/2 cups cider vinegar
1 teaspoon brown sugar
A few canned beet slices (optional)

Dilled eggs:
1-1/2 cups white vinegar
1 cup water
3/4 teaspoon dill seed
1/4 teaspoon white pepper
3 teaspoons salt
1 teaspoon mustard seed
1/2 teaspoon onion juice
1/2 teaspoon minced garlic

Spicy eggs:
1-1/2 cups apple cider
1 cup white vinegar
2 teaspoons salt
1 teaspoon mixed pickling spice
1 clove garlic, peeled
1/2 onion, sliced
1/2 teaspoon mustard seed

Fresh eggs can be dried in a food dryer. Don't use chipped or cracked eggs. Separate the white from the yolk, making certain the yolk doesn't get into the whites. If they aren't separated, the eggs will turn green when dried.

Add one teaspoon of cream of tartar to a dozen egg whites. Beat to a stiff meringue. Place the meringue on a sheet of plastic wrap on a dryer tray. When crisp, roll to powder with a rolling pin. Store in moisture-proof bags.

Dry yolks by spreading them on a jelly roll pan, then placing the pan on the dryer tray. After the yolks are set, finish drying on a low temperature setting. Store them just like egg whites.

Reconstitute the dried eggs by adding three tablespoons of warm water or milk to one tablespoon each of dried yolk and egg white. Gradually add and stir the liquid until a paste is formed, then add the remaining water or milk.

Eggs can also be frozen. To prevent yolks from coagulating, mix one cup of yolks with one tablespoon of salt, sugar or corn syrup. Egg whites need no special handling prior to freezing.

When freezing yolks and whites together, stir a dozen eggs with a tablespoon of salt or sugar. Individual muffin tins each hold two eggs. Completely thaw eggs before using. Plastic freezer bags may also be used.

For short-term storage, place eggs, clean but preferably unwashed, small end down in packed containers of sawdust or oatmeal. Eggs will keep several months this way if stored in a cool, dry place.

Eggs preserved in waterglass (sodium silicate) have been known to keep for as long as a year. Use fresh, infertile eggs with uncracked, clean shells. Don't wash them, since the film that helps seal the egg pores will be removed.

Scald a stone crock. Add a mixture of one part waterglass to nine parts water. The solution should be about two inches above the tops of the eggs. Cover the crock tightly and store in a cool place. Don't let the eggs freeze.

Meat production

Home-raised chicken has the same superior taste found in fresh eggs. Once you've had some of your own meat, the flaccid, chemically fed store-bought chickens will be much less appealing.(We won't even mention the horror stories from commercial slaughtering plants!)

Homestead chicken meat will be darker than the commercial variety, since the birds will have greater activity and a more varied diet than factory fowl. Commercial fryers each butchering weight—four pounds live weight, 2-1/4 pounds ready-to-cook—at about eight weeks. It takes 2.2 pounds of feed for them to gain one pound live weight. Commercial roasters are butchered at 3-1/2 to 4-1/2 months.

Chickens in Your Backyard authors Rick and Gail Luttmann butcher fryers up to six months of age and roasters at six months to a year. Older birds are used for stew meat.

There are numerous ways to butcher chickens. Regardless of which method you choose, take the birds off feed for 12 hours prior to slaughtering. That will prevent sour grain from the chickens' crops from being dispersed throughout the carcass.

Some people use a stump with two nails in it for holding the chicken's head. Chop the head off with an axe, then hang the bird upside down to bleed. Others break the bird's neck by holding the head with two fingers, thumb under the bird's chin. By swinging the arm sharply, the chicken's neck is snapped. Repeat, then hold the bird under the other arm until quiet.

Another technique involves piercing the chicken's brain with a thin knife blade. As one experienced chicken raiser described it, "The muscular contraction that follows causes the feathers to loosen, and they can easily be dry plucked." If you use other butchering methods, the chickens should be scalded in 130°F to 180°F water to loosen the feathers.

To remove the tiny feathers and hairs that remain after plucking, twist pieces of newspaper and hold the bird over the sink or stove, or outdoors. Light one end of the paper and move it around so the flames touch all parts of the bird.

There are 11 easy steps to butchering once the chicken has been plucked, pinned and vented by pressing on the abdomen to force any fecal material out of the cloaca. Follow the photos. Butchering should be done while the chicken is still warm.

Step 1 - Cut off the head, if you didn't use an axe. Save as much neck as possible.

Step 2 - Bend the legs backwards and cut through the joints to remove the shanks.

Step 3 - Remove the oil sac (dotted line) at the base of the tail by cutting under the sac to the backbone and up towards the tail.

Step 4 (Not pictured) - Remove the esophagus, crop and windpipe by pulling them away from the neck skin. Be careful not to tear the crop, as it adheres to the neck skin. Leave the esophagus and windpipe attached or cut them off at a point nearest the body cavity.

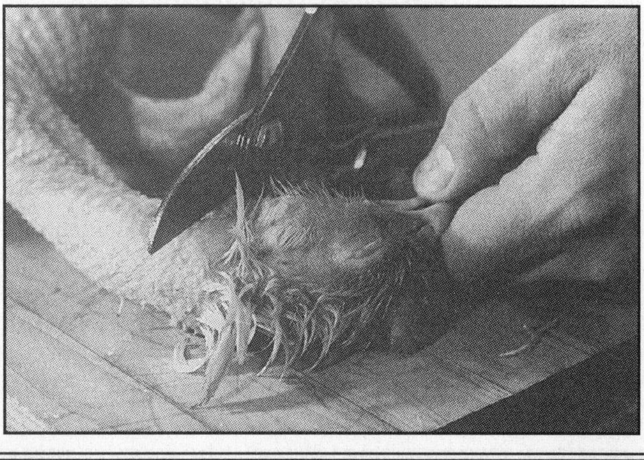

Step 5 - Cut the neck from the body where it joins the back.

Step 6 - Make a horizontal or vertical cut to remove the entrails. Insert your hand to loosen the organs. Be careful not to rupture or cut the intestines, as that would contaminate the meat. Grasp the gizzard and pull it out. The rest of the internal organs except for the heart, reproductive organs, kidney and lungs will follow. They must be removed separately.

Step 7 - Make a vertical opening in the body cavity from the posterior end of the breastbone down to and around the vent if you want to truss the bird with string and skewers.

Step 8 - Separate the heart, liver and gizzard from the intestines. With the neck, these are the giblets. Split the gizzard lengthwise through the thick muscle.

Step 9 - Carefully peel away the lining without cutting it, since it contains old food and grit. Remove it intact to prevent contaminating the gizzard.

Step 10 - Cut the green gallbladder away from the liver. It's better to give up a small piece of the liver rather than cutting too close to the gallbladder. Hold the gallbladder lower than the liver when cutting to prevent the gall from dropping on the liver and making it inedible.

Step 11 - Remove the heart and trim the top part to expose the chambers. Squeeze the heart gently to remove any blood and wash it thoroughly. Wash and chill the giblets.

Wash the chicken immediately after it is gutted. If you plan to truss the bird, do so before chilling. If the bird will be halved or quartered, cut it up after chilling.

The giblets and chicken head may be used to make a soup stock. Trim the gizzard and cut halfway around to open it. Remove the contents and lining and wash it. Remove the green gallbladder and wash the liver. Trim off the top of the heart and the rest. Pluck and wash the head.

Heat a pot of salted water and add the chicken parts. Simmer for several hours and strain off the soup stock. Vegetables, noodles, barley and seasonings may be added if you wish. The gizzard, heart and neck can be used in the soup, for stuffing or for gravy. Feed the other parts to the animals.

Stewing hens can be simmered just like soup. It will take two or three hours before the meat is tender. Remove the meat from the bones, use it in another recipe or refrigerate it. The meat works well in salads, sandwiches, soups and stews.

Homesteaders use everything they can get from a chicken!

Health care

Properly managed homestead chicken flocks are a productive source of meat and eggs. Negligence and poor management will mean health problems. Any combination of overcrowding, inadequate ventilation, insufficient water supply, lack of feeder space and long exposure to

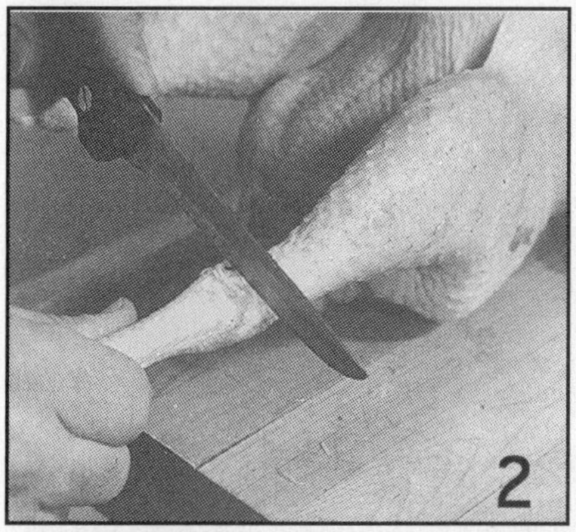

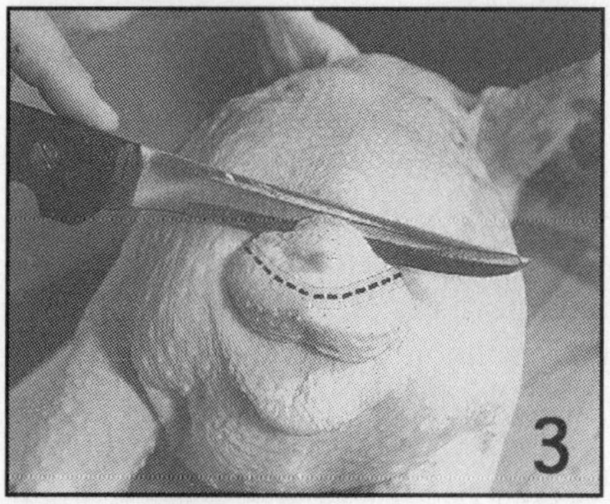

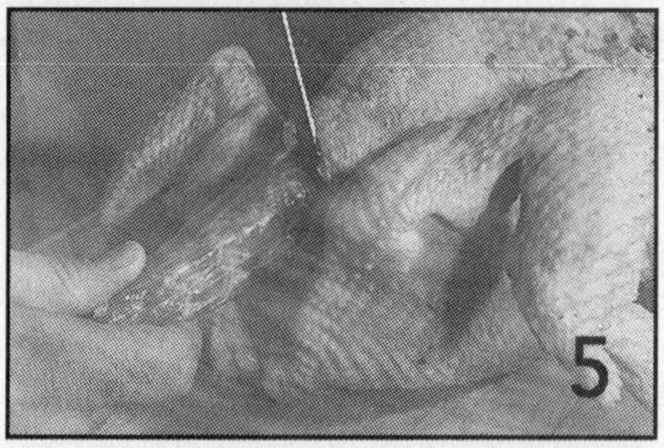

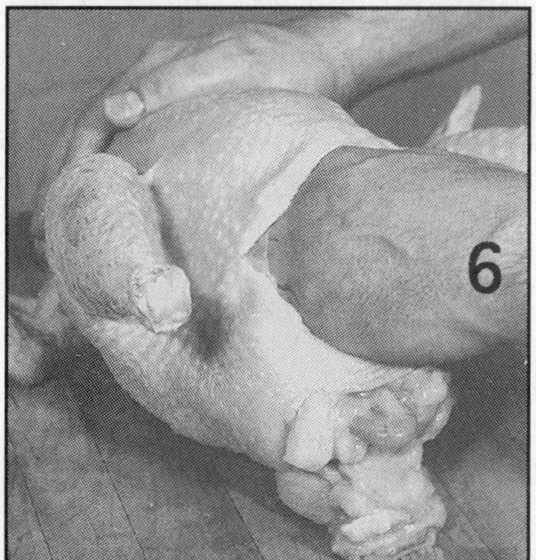

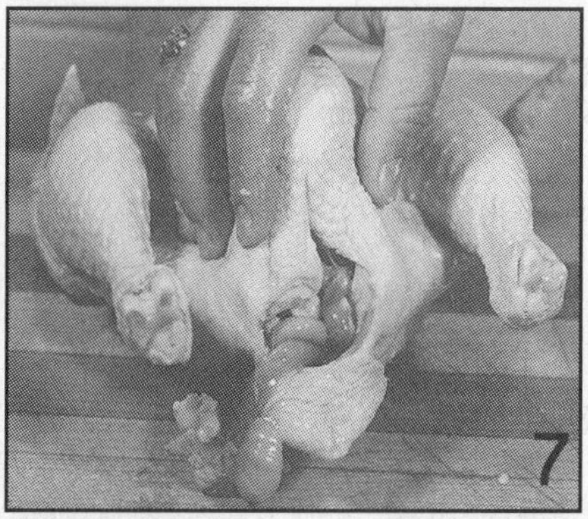

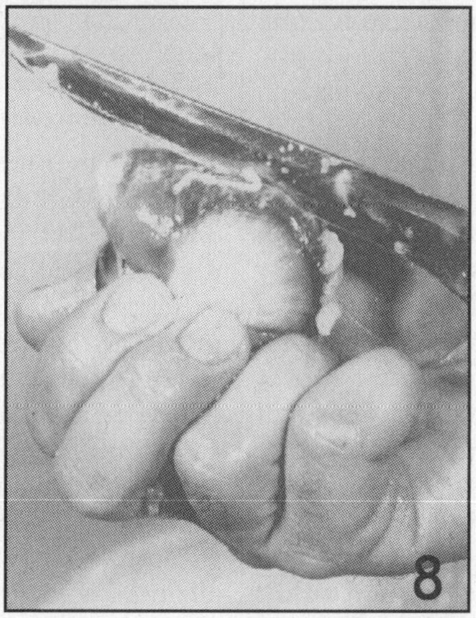

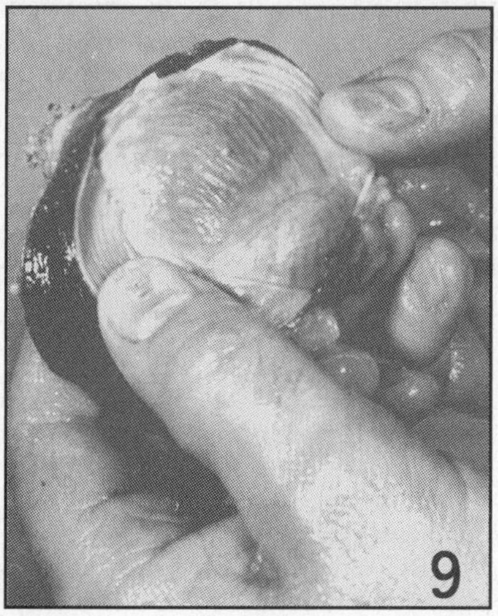

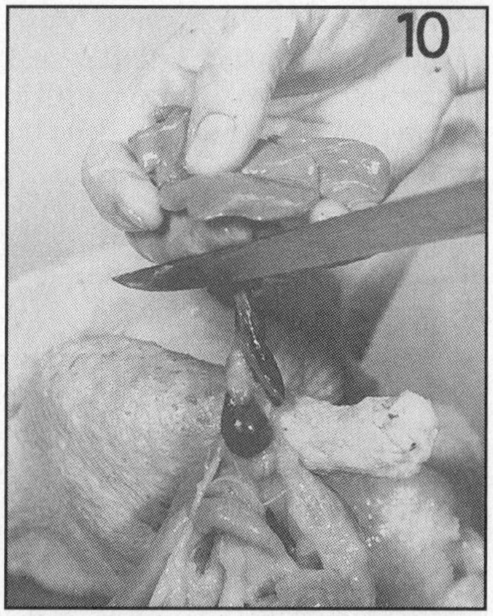

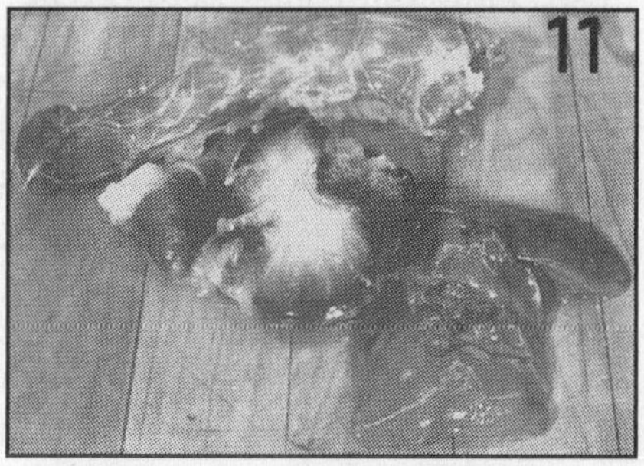

intense lighting can make a flock susceptible to health problems.

Since disease profiles vary from state to state, no single vaccination program is suitable for all flocks. Talk to an extension poultry specialist or another knowledgeable person to find out about the prevalent diseases in your area and follow a proven vaccination program.

There are some basic guidelines for disease prevention. Texas extension poultry specialist William Cawley came up with a 12-step plan for a healthy flock. He advises homesteaders to:

1. Purchase poultry from a seller with a reputation for healthy, reliable stock. Cawley recommends dealing with hatcheries that participate in the National Poultry Improvement Plan, as they offer birds that are pullorum-typhoid clean.

2. Purchase day-old poultry or hatching eggs only. If you do buy adult birds, know your source.

3. Group birds according to age and source.

4. Change litter and thoroughly clean and disinfect the chicken house and equipment at least once a year or between each group of birds. The house can be cleaned with soap and water and sprayed with a cresylic disinfectant. Diluted bleach is a good disinfectant for metal surfaces.

5. Choose a proven commercial feed designed to prevent nutritional deficiencies, especially in young birds.

6. Provide an adequate supply of fresh, clean water.

7. Have a vaccination schedule geared to your flock and geographic location. "It may be a complete program, just pox, or perhaps none at all," Cawley said.

8. Discourage anyone but you or other family mem-

bers from visiting the poultry yard. "I know this is just whistling in the wind," Cawley said, "because we backyard poultry raisers are so proud of our birds we just want to show them to everyone. But if the visitor tells you he has sick birds at home, for gosh sakes make him stand outside the fence to look at your flock."

9. Isolate all sick birds as soon as you can identify them.

10. If a disease problem develops, get an early and reliable diagnosis. Apply the best treatment, control and eradication measure for that specific disease. Cawley recommended contacting someone in the agriculture department or veterinary school at a nearby state university for a diagnosis.

11. Dispose of all dead birds immediately by burning, deep burial or disposal pit.

12. Maintain good records on flock health.

Problems will come up occasionally in any flock. Lice and mites, cannibalism and feather loss seem to be the most frequent concerns for COUNTRYSIDERS.

The body louse is 1/16 inch long and straw colored. It moves around the skin surface near the vent, thighs and underside of the belly. To control lice, place a mixture of half wood ashes and half dust in a box. Chickens will "dust" themselves and control this parasite.

Scaly leg mites cause great discomfort when they burrow beneath the scales of chicken legs. To eliminate mites, immerse chickens' legs up to the feather line in human grade mineral oil. Let it soak into the skin thoroughly. Repeat the process three times, 10 days apart. Cleaning the coop will help keep mite populations in check.

The northern fowl mite's calling card is blood-streaked eggshells. It irritates hens' vents and causes a scab to form. When the vent is stretched during egg laying, the scab opens and spreads blood on the eggs. An approved insecticide should be applied.

Red mites are blood-sucking parasites that live in the crevices of buildings and roosts during the day and feed on chickens at night. Thoroughly clean the building and dust insecticide powder directly on affected birds.

Photo by Mary & Jim Nicholson, North Carolina.

Cannibalism is a controllable problem. It is caused by overcrowding, poor ventilation, excessive heat, absence of feed and water, unbalanced diet, bright lights and other stress-inducing factors. Proper flock management can eliminate these problems. The only sure cure for cannibalism is debeaking, a practice which many small flock owners find repugnant.

Many bird owners worry about feather loss, but it is a natural occurrence for chickens. By the time it reaches maturity, the average chicken is on its fourth set of feathers. Normal activity such as wear and tear and mating are the main reasons for lost feathers. Lost feathers are replaced after a normal fall molt. Hens will lay eggs during molting, which can take as long as 10 days.

The cost/reward ratio favors chicken owners. Besides eggs and meat, there is the knowledge of poultry that one learns along with increased self-sufficiency.

The henhouse:

First year with chickens

H.G. Carlson
Montana

In the fall of 1994, we finally realized our dream of moving from the city. We wanted to start living the homestead life before we could afford to buy land, so we moved to a rented acreage just outside of town. Then, unprepared and underfunded, we launched into the two areas of food production that seemed reasonable for neophytes. We planted a big garden, and we began our love affair with chickens.

We bought mature layers for eggs and broiler chicks to raise for meat. We began the spring of '95 armed with an arsenal of books and magazine articles explaining more about raising chickens than we could ever hope to learn. However, we quickly learned that book "chickening" isn't the same as real life "chickening." We couldn't have raised chickens without help from friends who are more experienced homesteaders and farmers.

The first thing we learned was that chickens are living beings and that you can't just decide what you will do with them and what they will do for you. Despite our adherence to all the rules of chickens that we knew of, despite our doting attention, despite our care for temperature and hygiene, despite our prayers, some of our chicks died. We also found that the birds hadn't read the same books we had read.

As they grew older, they began to make decisions for themselves. They didn't follow our books. They became unpredictable. They didn't like the feed they were supposed to like. They drank more water than they were supposed to drink. They refused to be herded and they didn't go to bed early in the evening.

Chickens, we discovered, have quite an organized social structure and each one seems to know his or her place in the community. Certain ones seemed to be dominant. The roosters had their favorites. One pair (Ed and June) roosted together, apart from the others. Don't know what he saw in that chick—they all look about the same to us! If other roosters approached June, they quickly faced a formidable display of Ed's dark side—adequate to deter all potential suitors.

Are these chickens admiring the red rose because of its beauty, or because it looks delicious? Photo by P. Adkins, Michigan.

Most people don't think of chickens as pretty. They're smelly and they have a reputation for being not too bright. Perhaps this reputation is deserved. But they were the right thing for us and we just love them.

Within a few days of getting our layers we were eating fresh eggs. We found that they taste stronger, the yolks are darker from range feeding, and the whites are firmer and don't spread out so much when you drop them in a pan. What a luxury to enjoy a generous supply of fresh eggs daily! One dozen layers provided more eggs than our family of five adults could eat and it was really nice to be able to share our surplus with friends.

Someone told us that we could feed our chickens the vegetable scraps from the kitchen. We never would have thought of it ourselves. Eventually we were serving them everything that was scraped off our plates in addition to the usual vegetable peels and apple cores.

How we all enjoyed watching them run to us when we brought them a pail of kitchen scraps! It was so gratifying to feel that someone really is absolutely thrilled to see you approaching. It just plain felt good to be able to so easily satisfy them. They ran towards the scrap pail at a tilt which gave them quite a comical appearance—somewhat reminiscent of old cowboy movies where the women run across the screen with their long skirts gathered up high and clutched in their hands.

Our chickens didn't have a sweet tooth, but they seemed to like some foods better than others. For example, they stood in line for cooked beans and lentils, oatmeal, moldy cottage cheese, carrot peels, spaghetti sauce, bread and stale potato chips. They weren't excited about tomatoes, cucumbers, dried-out cake and icing, celery, broccoli, or string beans.

We joked about what the chickens must have thought of our scraps. When they saw or heard us coming with the pail, the black hen was usually the first one to get to the pan. She would quickly assess the menu and cluck out her critique to the others who rushed out of the coop like shoppers headed for a K-Mart blue light special. We think the conversation must've run something like this:

"Rose, get out here! They brought oatmeal. Oh, this is good. And look! Tomato stems and carrot peels. I just love a salad with a meal."

"Hyacinth, Daisy, Violet, Ivy, come quickly! Lily is going to clean up the whole meal before you even get here. Oh, this is tasty, what is it—spaghetti sauce? M-m-m. A little heavy on the oregano, but still very nice."

"Fern, this oatmeal is lumpy... and the toast is burned. Isn't there something else?"

"Did you try the spaghetti?"

"Fern, you know I don't like Italian. It gives me heartburn. Oh look, here's a little bit of fatty roast beef and gravy. That looks good."

"This is a good sign, girls. It's so reassuring to know that our people are eating beef."

Well, I know they don't really talk like that, but it's fun to imagine.

Anyway, I just want to encourage any citified transplants like us to try to do some of these homestead-types of things and to not be afraid of failure. If chickens aren't your thing, then try goats or turkeys or whatever.

We did so many things wrong and so many unnecessary things that we blush now to think of them. We must've been good entertainment for our neighbors.

I remember when we applied pine tar with paint brushes to the tails of the chickens in an attempt to stop pecking and cannibalism. Pine tar was on everything. Chickens were fleeing in every direction. Wearing our sloppy denim work jumpers and with bandannas on our heads, our daughter and I must've looked like we belonged to some strange chicken-painting cult. Passing cars slowed to a stop along the road so the occupants could watch the spectacle. This was not a great day in the history of chicken husbandry!

But that first roast chicken in the fall convinced us that raising chickens was worth all the inconvenience and effort.

That was three chicken seasons ago. This year's chicken catalogs have arrived and we're making plans for another round of broilers. I'm lobbying for geese again, but facing formidable opposition. (That's another story.)

Last year was the first year that we didn't have to carry a chicken book around with us at all times for a quick reference. It all becomes easier with time and practice.

I think chickens are a great way to begin as a country dweller because the initial cost isn't high compared to larger stock and they are pretty hardy. Next to gardening, raising chickens probably offers the greatest potential with the least risk of any homesteading production activity.

We've had some less than enviable experiences with geese and a skunk, and inhospitable weather, but nothing we couldn't find humorous later. Our success with poultry has encouraged us to continue with the chickens.

We're not real farmers or homesteaders. We are just regular people who are attracted to the homestead idea but have only enough courage to try it in small increments. We hope to be able to buy land eventually, perhaps before all of the children are out of the house and on their own. My husband works in town and we are looking to our "sunset" years. We are studying about raising sheep and cattle, milking goats, gardening, alternate energy sources, and self-sufficiency.

The other day I asked my husband if he would ever want to move back to town, even if it would mean renting for the rest of our lives. He said, "I never want to live in town again."

Amen.

Some practical advice on guineas

Sherry Pendleton
Mississippi

Guineas hate snakes and eat ticks. And that's enough reason to keep the noisy, bossy birds around.

One way to keep them from leaving is to let a good old broody hen hatch them. I set my first guineas under a standard Araucana hen. They were raised by her in the chicken house in pens. They learned to come back in by dark to be locked up. They also lay their eggs in the chicken house, not in the raised wooden nests but on the ground underneath. A few golf balls replacing the eggs kept them laying.

Guineas can be real mean to the chickens but somehow they seem to work things out.

Now when I incubator hatch guinea eggs, I always put some Araucana eggs in with them. Upon hatching, they're brooded and caged together. When I sell the keets, I encourage the buyer to get a couple of the chicks to raise with them. The guineas will stay with the chickens and will roost with them. They will not bond with strange chickens however—only the ones they're raised with.

One thing to remember is that guineas take 28 days to hatch and chickens, 21. So the chicken eggs should be added a week after the guinea eggs are started.

Guineas are always welcome in my garden. They can see and gobble up a grasshopper or Japanese beetle quicker than my husband surfs channels with his tv remote.

Chickens and fences

Bev Carney
Wisconsin

Fences. I've always hated them. In my youth, they were some thing to go under, around, or over—just so they didn't get in my way permanently! When I got older, I learned a partial value for fence as a trellis for peas and other climbing things. But never a big fence—nothing to restrict movement.

So when I read articles about fencing in the chickens, I thought, "Oh no, not my chickens. My chickens will have free range over our entire 1.5 acres and the acres of fields surrounding us."

Things began to change when I brought home our 10 little chicks. At first things were cool. We raised them in the bathtub. At about six weeks we put them in their coop, but first we fenced in a yard to acclimate them to the coop and to keep them safe. But a little yard—a little fence. Not to worry, the fence would come down once they were older.

And so it did. At about eight weeks we figured they were old enough to branch out on their own and we took the fence down. Interestingly enough, on their first trip out of the coop with the fence down, every single chicken stopped right at the fence line. Eventually they let loose and ventured forth, but they initially froze right at the line!

All this was in mid-July. Was I worried about my garden? Heavens no. We all know chickens are great in the garden. They eat cutworms, weed seeds, and scratch up some good dust mulch.

And so it was. The summer of '93 passed in bucolic splendor—no fences—and chickens roaming all over. As I dug the potatoes, the hens helped scratch them up. When we rototilled in the manure, they were right there, eating up the weed seeds. What fun!

Fall and winter passed and spring came once again. The girls were older and, I soon found, wiser.

Gardening began with planting the peas. Things went great until the peas had been in the soil for a few days and swelled up enough to be palatable. Whenever I looked out the window, chickens were out there scratching up the seeds and eating them!! Well, this called for emergency measures.

I couldn't fence in the garden—a fence —around my garden!! Instead, I devised a "fool-proof" system. I bought two-foot chicken wire (poultry netting, these days) and cut it in half to make 1 foot wide strips. (Don't ask me why I didn't buy one-foot wire: I have no idea.) I propped these strips up against the pea trellis and this would (of course) keep the chickens away from the pea seeds.

And it worked—until the pea vines grew above the strips. But the damage seemed minimal so we ignored it and went on to other crops.

The broccoli plants were ready to go into the ground. My husband kept insisting that the chickens would eat them, so for his sake, I made little cages for each plant out of that two-foot chicken wire. For the kohlrabi, I made a little tent of wire. This was gonna work!

Funny thing though, we seemed to have an explosion of bug problems. Something was eating the plants despite the cages. I knew it couldn't be the chickens... until I saw them munching away, sticking their beaks right through the wire.

At this point a reasonable person would have thought "fence," but no, I decided to make the cages for the plants a little wider, so they couldn't reach in.

Over the onion plants I extended hog paneling. It was curved from use and seemed to be just the thing for protecting the onions. I wasn't worried about them actually eating the onions, just scratching them out of the ground, so it didn't matter to me that the onion plants peeked out of their guard.

And it worked—kind of. The chickens didn't scratch up the onions. But they ate them! This had to stop. I had to give in. So I fenced—but just a little fence and just around the onions!

The peppers ended up with individual little cages, the carrots with fence. But the tomatoes! Goodness, they were in cages already; they didn't need fence too.

I'm embarrassed to say that it took me almost all season to realize that my girls—my sweet little chickens—were eating a hole—just one hole—out of every tomato they could reach just before it ripened enough to eat. I spent a lot of time looking for slugs and dusting the plants with diatomaceous earth to combat this alarming slug problem. Oops!

After four years of gardening with the girls, we've made some compromises. We fence everything—but gradually. When the peas go in, they get fenced. When the tomatoes start to color, they get fenced. But gradually. A bit at a time. This takes a fair amount of fence. You can fence a 60 x 150 area with a lot less fence if you do it at once and all the way around. But given the way we started, we've accumulated a lot of fence!

By the way, unless you have banties, two-foot chicken wire will work fine and is easy to erect. And it's so low you can step right over it —thus pretending it doesn't exist at all!

The new, improved chicken door

Note to all the youngsters we've been hearing from about the difficulties of getting started: Pay special attention to the first paragraph of this article, and think about it. You aren't going to accomplish all your goals overnight, and you have much to look forward to!

Arnold Gorneau
Pennsylvania

Well, the children have all grown and gone; we're down to one goat and fancy chickens, and it is time for those projects I promised I would get to "some day."

Back in the July/Aug 1996, issue of Countryside (80/4:45) I presented an automatic door to close the chickens in at night for predator protection, but it had to be opened every morning.

Rear view: This opening attaches to the coop. Photo sensor is at upper left.

Front view: Note two limit switches and clear plastic door.

The new unit presented here is completely self-contained. It opens with the sun (letting the birds out) and closes them in at dusk. Well, that's what it's designed to do.

The door, which slides up and down, is operated by a motor which gets its command from a 120 volt photo cell of the type used to operate night security lights and available at most hardware stores. There is a sensitivity adjustment.

The door is raised and lowered by a geared down, reversible motor available from American Science & Surplus (3605 Howard St., Skokie, IL 60076, Vol. 100, Jan 1996, page 74, Stock #4341, $6.50), and requires a capacitor available from the same source (Vol. 102, March 1997, page 36, Stock #26089, $1.75).

The motor, to which I attached a 2" pulley, runs at 8 RPM.

One end of the string is attached to the pulley with adhesive and passes up over a high bar and then to the top of the door, where it is attached by a paper clip. If something goes wrong, the paper clip will presumably give way.

At sunup, the door is raised to its open position and a peg near the bottom contacts a microswitch (the upper limit switch), which cuts off current to the motor. The string holds the door up all day and the chickens may go in and out.

At dusk, the photocell switches off, closing a relay (Radio Shack Model #275-217c, $6.99) which energizes the motor to go in the reverse mode. This unwinds the string and the weight of the door causes it to go down until it activates the lower limit switch which cuts off current to the motor. The door remains down until the next morning.

I used microswitches for the upper and lower limit switches, but reed switches, etc., would work.

The entire apparatus should be protected from rain and snow. I gave the wood a few coats of spar varnish.

I am indebted to my friend, Mike Halbert, who drew the schematic and paid for the relay.

All current is 120 volts; therefore, be aware of the shock hazard.

Notes: A) If the motor specified here is unavailable, try to buy the slowest (most geared down) reversible motor you can.

B) The photo cell need not be mounted on the unit; it may be mounted on the roof or wherever it might get the earliest rays of the sun.

C) Good luck.

Controlling blackhead in free range turkeys can be difficult

COUNTRYSIDE: Re: Blackhead in turkeys 81/5:83: Controlling blackhead disease will be very difficult in a free range system. Penning the birds would limit exposure to the parasite.

Once signs of illness are present success in treating is very limited. Emtryl was an effective cure, but was being used by hog farmers and was found to be carcinogenic. Metronidayol given once a month can help prevent the growth of the parasite *Histomonas meleagridis* which causes blackhead. The dosage is 10 mg per pound once a day. I have also heard of a product call Fish-zole which is a water soluble Flagyl (metronidayol). Also, regular worming can help control the cecal worm whose eggs are host to the blackhead parasite.

I began raising peacocks in 1995 and was concerned about wild turkeys spreading blackhead on the property. I wrote to the Arkansas Diagnostic Laboratory of the Livestock and Poultry Commission (PO Box 5497, Little Rock, AR 72215) regarding the discontinuation of Emtryl and Flagyl, and received this reply:

"I talked with Dr. Marilyn Baeyens who is the zoo veterinarian in Little Rock. She recommended several things. First, she advised that the birds be penned. This would limit their exposure to blackhead. The second point she made was that once the birds begin showing signs of the disease treatment success is very limited. She recommended that you place young birds on the product for two weeks when they first arrive and once a month as a preventative. The dosage she uses is 10 mg per pound once a day but she cautioned that you read and follow package instructions because the dose may vary with each product." —Paul E. Norris, DVM, Director. —*Marla Berry, Arkansas*

Family album:

These turkeys roam Laurie Miller's homestead (apparently with no problems) in New Hampshire.

How many chickens equal a pig?

We can't tell you how to compare apples and oranges, but we can show you how to compare cows and goats... at least when it comes to feed consumption!

The tool is an "animal unit," which is a common denominator for farm animals. One mature cow equals one animal unit. A mature ewe or goat is one-fifth of an animal unit: five sheep or goats eat as much as one cow.

Animal Units

Cow or heifer 2 years or older	1
Mature bull	1.3
Young cattle, under 2 years	0.8
Weaned calves to yearlings	0.6
Horse, mature	1.3
Horse, yearling	1
Horse, weanling	0.75
5 mature ewes or doe goats	1
5 mature rams or bucks	1.3
5 yearling sheep or goats	0.8
5 weaned lambs or kids	0.6
Sow	0.4
Boar	0.5
Pigs to 200 lbs.	0.2
75 laying hens	1
325 replacement pullets to 6 months	1
650 8-week-old broilers	1
35 breeder turkeys	1
40 turkeys raised to maturity	1
75 turkeys to 6 months of age	1

The Golden Rules of feeding poultry

David Bland
England

Up to 75% of the cost of poultry keeping is feed, and yet this is still an area of confusion and misunderstanding for many small producers. To try to simplify what can be a complicated and somewhat boring subject, I have set out below some golden rules which if adhered to will reduce costs and at the same time give a wider understanding of basic nutritional requirements.

Chick feeding

Chicks need to start with a chick starter crumb or mash. This contains an anti-coccidiostat and should be given until the chicks reach eight weeks of age. A certain amount of wastage is allowed for the first five days to ensure that all chicks have an equal opportunity, but from then on feed should be placed in a feeder. Hanging feeders can be used provided they are always hung with the base level to the top of the birds' backs. One can also use a trough with a spindle fitted, so that they are unable to get into the trough for dust bathing. Place the trough off the ground on bricks.

Growing birds

At eight weeks change their diet to growers' mash, but if this is not available, growers' pellets will do. Using mash will keep birds more contented and docile, thereby keeping stress and mortality to a minimum. From this stage onwards, use adult feeders and allow sufficient trough space per bird, as you would for mature birds. If you are using circular hanging feeders, then each bird will require 1" of space of the diameter of the bowl. When using trough feeders allow each bird four inches of trough space. The measurement is taken on both sides, e.g. a 12" trough times two = 24" which is sufficient for six birds.

Do not forget to use grit during the growing period, placing a fresh pile down in the run at the rate of one ounce per bird per month. It is perfectly in order to use hen size grit, but don't forget to put it down.

Laying birds

At 18 weeks of age birds will need to be changed to a laying diet. Again this should consist of a coarse ground mash, avoiding if possible layers' pellets because birds fed on pellets are more likely to become bored, encouraging other vices to set in, including one of their favorite sports, pellet flicking. Continue feeding grit as before for the rest of their life.

Grit explained

There always seems to be some confusion concerning oyster shell grit and flint grit. Oyster shell is a soluble grit, which means it is of little help in grinding feed. It would be like your dentist fitting you with chalk teeth. The only use oyster shell has is to supply calcium. Provided you are feeding your birds on a standard proprietary ration then there is no necessity to feed oyster shell. If you do, apart from wasting money, you will upset the calcium-phosphorous ratio, and your birds are likely to end up producing soft shelled eggs as well as having brittle bones and feathering — all the things, including rickets, that you wish to avoid. Do not feed oyster shell unless indicated by an expert nutritionist or a qualified poultry vet.

Flint/granite grit is used as we use our teeth to grind up food. It is insoluble, gradually passing through the system as the grinding action reduces its size. It's a very cheap but important part of the ration. It has been known to improve egg shell strength.

Feeding whole grains

Whole wheat can be fed as a scratch feed midday or

late afternoon, depending on the time of year. As with mixed grain, it should be given at a rate of no more than one ounce per bird per day. To exceed this will reduce the intake of the higher protein ration and so reduce egg production.

Under no circumstances should it be included in the morning, mixed in with the mash/pellets. Hens will pick out the wheat first and being full, will not consume sufficient protein to sustain good egg production. It takes approximately 12 hours for a bird to digest whole cereals as against mash/pellets which take a minimum of two hours to pass through the system. Feed whole wheat as a scratch feed during the hot summer months.

Mixed grain is made up from 75% whole wheat and 25% cut corn. This is an ideal feed during the long winter months, the corn giving the birds that extra heat and energy they require.

Do not use a mix containing oats or barley. Whole oats for the bird are of little nutritive value and are basically a bulk feed in this form. Hens find whole barley unpalatable and as a result it is normally left to grow in the run the following year. Feeding the correct grain will save money and keep birds healthy and active.

Winter feeding

During the cold winter months, feed if possible a higher protein ration or place a small container in the house kept topped up with either fish meal or soybean meal. Both these high protein ingredients will help offset harsh weather conditions and birds will feed from them as and when they require. In the most extreme weather conditions, a hot mash can be given near the end of the day but it must be cleared up within 15 minutes to keep the residue from fermenting. Another way is to mix a small amount of cod liver oil in with the mixed grain, just enough to make it shiny.

Kitchen scraps

I'm often asked about feeding scraps. All kitchen scraps containing salt, throw out or give to the dog. If not salted they may be mixed in with layers' mash, the latter being used for the purpose of drying off the scraps. Depending on the quantity given it may be necessary to add protein, i.e. one teaspoon of soy or fish meal per six birds.

This article was previously published in the British magazine *Smallholder*: used with permission.

David Bland has 40 years' experience raising poultry and is the author of *Poultry for the Garden*, a best-seller in Britain now in its third printing, and *Practical Poultry Keeping*, as well as a video about poultry. A resident of Sussex, England he also writes regularly for *Smallholder* magazine.

Forget potato peelings. They are more expensive to cook than to feed at all. Hens do however enjoy fresh vegetables such as carrots, cabbages, cauliflower and the like. Do not throw any of these directly on the floor of the run but hang up in net bags (those which have previously contained vegetables from the store). Cabbage stalks will give your birds hours of fun if hung up in the run. If the run does not have a covered top to suspend them from, then it is relatively easy to construct a tripod to hang the stalks on.

Heatwave alert

I know that the summer has now passed and it may be a long time before we experience one the same but did your birds and their production suffer in the heat? Like mine, they probably were inactive during the day, keeping well out of the sun, resulting in a loss of consumption and production.

There are three ways to help your birds consume the necessary protein and nutrients in a very much shorter period of time:

a) By giving multi-vitamins in the water.

b) Treating them as you would in the winter, by placing in the house a small tin of protein in the form of soy or fish meal.

c) After the heat of the day has dispersed and hens have come out of the shade, give them a moist layers' meal to encourage and increase appetite.

Water

All of the above is of little use without life's major sustaining nutrient—water. Each and every day all water containers should be washed out and refilled. During the summer months, birds need a fresh supply of cool clean water at midday as well and even a shallow paddling pool will help them to cool down. In the winter, especially during periods of severe frosts, use troughs instead of water founts and float glycerin on top to prevent the water from freezing over.

Lighting

A special word about lighting in winter: For those who keep less than 25 hens in a house, there is no need to worry about extra lighting. It is costly and totally unnecessary. Yes, their production may slow down in the winter, but towards the end of February production will pick up along with increased egg size. Over a 12 month period there will be no difference in total production. By keeping your hens happy and contented they will pay you back by producing an abundant supply of nice fresh tasty eggs.

In a nutshell

With the right size feeders positioned at the correct height and with ample space between them there will be no wastage. Feed a good quality ration and by providing plenty of clean water, you are well on the way towards producing eggs economically from healthy happy birds.

Having chickens is like a three-ring circus!

JOHN MCCLURE
TENNESSEE

When I first purchased my five acre tract some four years ago it was 100% wooded. Then came in succession a culvert, driveway, fence, clearing for a house, shop and a pond.

I decided to get bantam chickens due to their efficiency in controlling ticks. In this they performed admirably while adding to the attractiveness of the place. There was a pen available for roosting, but the chickens chose to use the cedars and other trees for this purpose. Hawks, owls and other predators took their toll and eventually eliminated all the bantam population, which at one time totaled 30 chickens.

I then decided to get some game chickens, expecting them to better withstand the predators. The rooster was a beautiful, golden-mantled specimen and the hen was a black game. Both they and their offspring have survived better than the bantams, but losses still persist.

Various antics make for interesting observation. For instance, when the young rooster saw his first brood of chicks he appeared to be in a mild state of shock, but he was tender and helpful. He found a bug to feed one of the chicks, but decided it needed breaking up. When he picked it up again, the chick had a firm hold on the other end of the bug and thus was lifted about a foot in the air while thrashing about with legs and wings. At this point the rooster, noting the determination on the part of the chick, just left the bug in his possession.

When a hen is raising her clutch the roosters have a strong tendency to encourage them to begin laying again. They often succeed and then the hen abandons her half-grown (or less) chicks. When this happens the chicks will chirp for their mother and a rooster will take over to feed and care for them, often clucking to them!

The last three hens which started laying before their offspring matured had lost their chicks to hawks, down to one, two and three respectively. The hen which had left the one chick turned up with eight new ones, but then strangely accepted her nearly half-grown chick back as part of the family.

This seems to strengthen the family unit to the extent she has only lost one chick to the hawks after three weeks! "Big Sister" helps feed the little ones by scratching for them and on one occasion I heard her cluck to them, in a higher-pitched voice than her mother!

Recently two of the chicks got into a fight and the mother paid them both no mind, but big sister stepped in and broke it up in a stern manner, swishing her tail in a demonstration of authority.

It's almost like a three-ring circus to observe these interactions.

Our male cat, Junior, lays on our goose's nest when she gets off to eat or drink. Junior sets on the eggs and keeps them warm until she gets back.—*Linda L. Kovach, Pennsylvania*

This is "Red Chicken," one of my neighbor's banty hens, loaned to me to hatch some of my meat bird eggs. My mom, Peggy Pierce, took the photo.—*Melonie Martin, Tennessee*

Photos: Mark & Joanna Lanning, Washington

Guinea fowl for tick control

Jack Sabean
Maryland

Of all the valuable things we've learned, both from Countryside and from experience, this defense against ticks is the one we really feel needs to be shared with others.

My wife and I own five acres on Maryland's Eastern Shore. In our area there is a large population of whitetail deer with their accompanying parasite, the ubiquitous tick. When we first moved here three years ago our daughter and dog would quite often return to the house with ticks on their bodies. There are several stories in our area concerning severe harm coming to local residents as a result of these tick bites, including Lyme Disease, Rocky Mountain Spotted Fever and Erlichiosis.

The second year we were here, we purchased a few guinea fowl. Ticks have been very rare in our life since then.

Our guineas are range free and sleep where they wish (usually up in the rafters of the goat barn). They get most of their own food in the summer and reproduce on their own. They require practically no care at all. Their only drawback is their alarm call, which they issue quite frequently during the daylight hours. They only screech at night if disturbed and in fact, you may find them more alert than your best watch dog.

Do not purchase adult birds and just let them loose. You will not see them again. We find it best to buy very young ones and keep them confined for a few weeks before allowing them to roam.

Once the birds are a year old they will nest on the ground, laying their eggs communally, and the adults will share the responsibility of raising the young. We once had a mother killed by a fox and the three-week-old young were successfully raised by their father.

Unfortunately, the keets spend the night on the ground for the first few weeks and we have lost many youngsters and adults to fox predation. What we do as insurance is to steal freshly laid eggs (while the adults are off feeding—they are very protective) and set them under a Bantam hen to hatch. This works well as long as the guinea babies are removed when they hatch. We keep the babies isolated until the young surviving free range birds are mostly perching up high with their parents at night. At that point we let the confined keets loose near the free range brood and they are eagerly adopted into the group.

Country words:

Most children learn at an early age that baby chickens are called chicks, baby ducks are ducklings, and baby geese are goslings. But the young of some other domestic fowl have less familiar names.

Baby guineas are keets.

Turkeys are poults.

Swans are cygnets.

And among four-footed animals:

Goat—kid
Sheep—lamb
Cow—calf
Horse—foal or colt
Pig—piglet

If overpopulation is a problem, both the eggs and the birds are edible. It is best to catch them at night when they are roosting and relatively helpless. Or you can sell the birds. There always seems to be a market for them; we get about $6.50 per adult bird at the local auction.

Spread the news and check behind the kids' and dogs' ears.

The rabbit barn:

Young rabbit raiser shares what he has learned

STEPHEN JONES
11-YEAR-OLD HOMESCHOOLER

Rabbitsmakefunpets.Ihavebeen raising 4-H show rabbits for four years. If you are considering raising a rabbit, I would like to share what I have learned.

Rabbits come in many sizes and colors. Your first decision is whether you want an indoor (house pet) or outdoor rabbit. The smaller rabbits work better in the house than larger rabbits. If you decide to keep your rabbit in the house, put cat litter and borax in the tray, it cuts down on the odor and mess.

If you decide to keep your rabbit outside, there are several things to think about in choosing a good location. Do not let the sunshine hit the rabbit. Rabbits will not move out of the sun. They will die of a heat stroke. You need to choose a location that is safe from varmints. Even small dogs could nip their toes off and the rabbits might bleed to death, while a larger dog can get the cage open. Do not let cold winds hit the rabbit. They will chill and die. As long as the rabbit is sheltered, he will do fine outside.

Cage size is another decision to make. Larger rabbits need larger cages, a 2'x2' cage is large enough for medium and small rabbits.

Another decision to make is whether you want a buck or a doe. The does are sometimes more territorial, but many make good pets. Bucks, on the other hand, are docile.

Before you buy a rabbit there are a few things to check for. You need to check the rabbit's teeth for missing, broken, deformed, or crooked teeth. Not only can they not be shown, they could die a slow death of starvation. If you plan to show the rabbit, check the rabbit's toenails for missing, broken, or discolored toenails.

Rabbits can get colds like people, some serious and some not so serious. You can tell when a rabbit has a cold by looking to see if its eyes or nose is runny. If its front legs are matted, it shows they have been wiping their nose with their front feet. They probably have a cold. Some rabbits are susceptible to sore hocks. Sore hock is sores on the feet. It is very hard to get rid of sore hocks. I suggest not buying a rabbit that has symptoms of a cold or sore hock.

After you have bought your rabbit, you need to know how much to feed and what brand of feed the original owner fed. It is better to gradually switch the feed. If you plan to feed a different brand ask for a little bag of feed.

Like kids, rabbits like treats, but too much is not good for them. One-half spoon of Calf Manna or a few black hull sunflower seeds make a nice treat. They also like half a slice of wheat bread.

If you want a good healthy rabbit you need to keep salt and mineral licks available for the rabbit at all times. Another consideration is water. Rabbits have to have clean water all the time. If a rabbit does not have fresh water, it may die.

Keeping under the rabbit cage clean is important. If you do not, your rabbit is susceptible to many diseases. The droppings you clean out are good fertilizer, or excellent in worm beds. By keeping the rabbit's area clean you cut down on the risk of a cold or diseases. If your rabbit gets ear mites, put some type of oil in their ear. If your rabbit is losing hair on the face, apply cat flea powder and reapply in two weeks.

I hope you enjoy your rabbits as much as I enjoy mine.

20 Do's and don'ts for practical rabbit raising

SHEILA HOAG

Do keep records—even if it's in a looseleaf notebook instead of a computer. In two or three weeks of hectic spring or summer activities, you might not remember exactly what day you bred that doe. And what buck was it that missed three does last fall? Records may seem to be important only for commercial breeders, but us little guys need certain information to keep our production at its peak.

• Don't leave your rabbits out in the weather. They should not be in the wind or rain and they should be able to get out of the direct sun. The heat is worse for rabbits than cold. Prostration, sterility and even death can result from temperatures above 85°F.

• Do have plenty of water available for your rabbits at all times. It should be cool, not cold, water in the summer and mildly warm water in the winter. Most rabbit won't eat unless they have water.

• Don't leave pelleted feed in bags or uncovered. Rodents will steal you blind, and contaminated feed is bad for your rabbit's health. I put my feed in aluminum trash cans with lids. Mice can't get to it and the feed stays dry and bug-free.

• Do pick replacement does early. It is six or more months before a rabbit matures. At about three years, litter sizes decrease and signal it's time for a new doe. If a doe is a good mother, save one of her daughters. Mothering instincts seem to be inherited.

• Don't feed your rabbits cabbage or anything related to it. Other vegetables, such as carrots, turnip greens and lettuce, are all right. Fruits, except citrus, are acceptable also. Other foods rabbits like include shelled sunflower seeds, rolled or crushed oats, and dried pieces of bread. If you don't feed pellets, rabbits need a salt lick.

• Do be careful if you inbreed in your herd. Inbreeding can lock in good traits—and bad ones just the same. Never keep a rabbit for breeding stock that has been sick, is mean, or that has defects (moon eye, blindness, overgrown teeth, etc.).

• Don't destroy a doe just because she loses one litter, especially if it's her first. A change of weather, intruders in the rabbitry (dogs or cats I mean), a recent move, or any number of circumstances can make a doe neglect her litter. If she cannabalizes them, put a piece of raw bacon in her cage a day before she is due. At any rate, give her one more chance. If a doe loses two litters without very good excuses, it's time for her to go in the stew pot because chances are she'll never keep a litter.

• Do pick good bucks—and keep two instead of one. Your buck is the father of every litter. The better he is, the better his offspring are likely to be. I keep two bucks because accidents do happen. Can you afford to be without a buck for even a short time?

• Don't keep a litter together more than three months. After that, they can begin to mature, and present you with unexpected litters. They will fight among themselves, also. Despite how many people think of cute, cuddly bunnies, rabbits can be vicious.

• Do let your kids join 4-H, or you yourself join the A.R.B.A. No, you won't agree with any group 100%, but both are invaluable sources of information. The local library can be, too.

• Don't keep chickens near your rabbits if you can avoid it. Rabbits can't give any diseases to chickens, but the chickens can give several things to rabbits. I'm not a vet, so I can't get technical. Ask your vet for specifics.

• Do provide expectant does with a straw-filled nestbox two days before they are due. This way, they have time to arrange the nest and get comfortable before they kindle. They will eat some straw. If they eat a lot of it, put more in unless they have pulled fur. Many times in hot weather, does will eat—or throw out—all but a small amount of straw. In that case, let them.

• Don't put new rabbits right in with your herd. Isolate them for ten days or more, to be sure they are healthy and parasite-free.

• Do get pedigrees for purebred rabbits. A lot of backyard or small farm rabbit breeders don't bother with pedigrees. These papers insure your rabbits are purebreds, and it gives you background information on them. You can also pedigree your own litters from their parents' papers.

• Don't give them damp or moldy hay. Ever.

• Do have something for your rabbits to chew on. Their teeth grow all the time. Unsprayed fruit tree twigs are good, and then they won't chew on their cages so much.

• Don't hesitate to use rabbit droppings on your garden. It is nitrogen-rich and doesn't burn or have a strong smell. It also breaks down rapidly. And what it does for your garden—wow!

• Do attend the county or state fair. You can see a wide variety of very nice rabbits there, and many are for sale at reasonable prices. Take the time to look them over.

• Don't rely on learning about rabbits from just one person. Get all the information you can, and make your own conclusions. Most of what you will come to know about rabbits will be from first-hand experience. Good luck!

Raising earthworms with rabbits in Alaska

Sue Nilsson
Alaska

Here in interior Alaska, our weather isn't a whole lot colder than Montana, but earthworms aren't native to the area and generally don't survive our winters. However, I've managed to keep redworms in my raised garden beds, winter some over, and save myself some labor.

Let me address the issue of worm beds under rabbit cages.

I've found this arrangement to be less than satisfactory, because each rabbit has a "pee corner" that creates a wet spot in the worm bed. Worms seem to avoid those areas. The only way I found to deal with the odors, bugs and excessive humidity levels caused by wet spots was to rake the beds every day.

Raking required the same amount of time and labor as daily scoop cleaning. I compost other animal wastes as well, so at first glance it seemed that separate beds were the way to go. But there is an even better way with rabbit manure.

The basic idea is this: Rabbit manure is virtually free of weed seeds and can be applied directly to garden soil without harming the plants. Rough fertilizer values are 3.7 percent nitrogen and potassium, 1.3 percent phosphorus. It's a great garden medium.

Rabbit manure doesn't have a very high moisture content. If you let it sit a day or two, it is even lighter and easier to handle. Water weighs 8.34 pounds per gallon. Composting with or without worms requires water, which means a heavier finished product and more labor.

My method is to put a small pile of sawdust under each rabbit's pee spot to capture the urine. Urine-soaked sawdust doesn't suck as much nitrogen out of the soil when it decomposes, but I choose not to use it straight in my garden. It's wet, smelly and unpleasant to work with. Every day I scoop the wet stuff and deposit it in the worm bins. I scoop the manure weekly and store it in paper feed bags which I keep in an unheated lean-to until spring. Then I run a tiller through my raised beds, pour out the manure, rake smooth, plant, mulch and let nature do the rest.

My soil is glacial deposited silt in a boreal forest area with a very low organic content. Birch leaves naturally deposited each fall may take as long as three years to decompose here. I first got worms for improving my soil and not for composting.

I learned a little late that redworms require huge amounts of raw organic materials to survive—more than most gardens can provide for them. This is the basis for the belief that redworms can't be raised in garden plots. My first batch of worms effectively starved to death.

When I first used straight rabbit manure in raised beds, I seeded them with excess worms. I reasoned that even if the worms didn't get enough to eat or survive the winter, they would at least be adding the nutrient value of their bodies to my soil. Meanwhile, I used birch leaf mulch and hoped the worms would help at least a little. Come fall, I was happy to find the worms thriving and my soil looser.

I packed the beds with straw hoping that some might winter over, but none survived that first year. However, a few more made it to spring each successive year.

The key to their survival is straight rabbit manure and high levels of organic material interspersed throughout the soil. Since I don't have many rabbits, there isn't enough manure for every raised bed I have. If I run out of manure, no amount of organic mulch is going to keep my worms going.

One last thing to keep in mind: If you free range your ducks, chickens or pigs, or let them in your garden after harvest, be prepared for a low redworm survival level. Redworms are easy pickings, as they tend to lay on top of the soil just under the mulch. They sometimes have a smell that seems to be attractive to wild birds.

The goat barn:

A frugal homesteader makes a case for registered goats

Rebecca feeds a Nubian kid.

Barbara Winters-Laport
Missouri

I'm writing this from the viewpoint of a person who has learned to be frugal. This wasn't usually by choice, but by the need to make ends meet.

I raise goats, with a preference for Nubians. Why? They are a large goat and are capable of making a gallon a day of the best-tasting, richest milk you could ask for. Due to their size, the young wethers will put more meat on the table than other breeds. They come in a variety of colors, have gorgeous long ears, and each goat seems to have its own personality. Most homesteaders are looking for a good value. If you have a couple of does that are giving a gallon a day each, you are probably happy regardless of their breed.

When looking for a sire for your spring kids, seek a registered buck who is siring daughters that are milking well. Look for a buck that is the same breed as your doe. You can contact the American Dairy Goat Association (ADGA), P.O. Box 865, Spindale, NC 28160; Phone: 828-286-3801 to get forms and register your spring kids as grade Alpine or grade Nubian or grade of whatever the breed was the sire. You will be able to get more money for your kids.

Keep a doeling and breed her to another registered buck of the same breed and you have a 75 percenter. Females that are 75 percent can be registered as American of whichever breed you are working towards. By breeding up, you increase the value of your animals.

Join a local goat club and meet other breeders. One of them will often have more good does than they need and will sell a registered purebred at an affordable price. Breeders are a source of tons of information that will help you do things more economically. Goat people are usually a thrifty lot.

Another way to increase the value of your stock is by writing to ADGA and getting the "on test" form. By working with other breeders, you can authenticate the milk-producing records of your goats. Buyers will pay more for goats that come from good milkers. If you decide not to go on test, at least keep a daily record of what each doe gives so you can use that information yourself in culling poor producers or for future reference.

Some unregistered does will milk just as much or more than some of the registered animals. But the bottom line is total income minus total expense. In the long run, you will have more profit from good quality registered goats.

Ed. note: In some regions, at some times, registered and purebred animals don't command prices any higher than grades. The time and money spent on upgrading might not be "wasted" in terms of herd or breed improvement, but it doesn't always pay off at sale time. You have to know your market.

For further reading: Dairy Goat Journal, *145 Industrial Dr., Medford, WI 54451; www.dairygoatjournal. com. $21/yr.*

Animal breeding tables

	Age of puberty months)	Interval of heat (days)	Avg. heat duration (hours)	Avg. gestation period (days)
Rabbits	6-8	—not applicable—		31
Swine	4-7	18-24	2-3 days	114
Sheep	5-7	14-20	30	148
Goats	4-8	12-25	36-48	151
Cattle	8-12	21	16-20	283
Horses	12-15	21	4-6 days	336

The goat barn:

How we built a low-cost, heavy-duty goat milking stand

Rosanne Atzet
California

We were in need of a functioning goat-proof milking stand. We have milked goats that would kick, twist and move around while we were milking. One goat would even lay down, hoping to divert our efforts.

Our pallet milking stand has helped with all these problems and more. The goats could no longer move from side to side, forward or backward to avoid milking. Even our clever "lay down so you can't get my udder" goat was controlled. We could tie a rope under her belly and to the top of the milking stand. Now she would be suspended in air if she tried to lay down. Man triumphs over animal once again.

With only four pallets you can build a strong stand by placing two upright, one flat down and use the fourth for pieces of wood.

First we connected, with nails, the bottom pallet to the outside upright pallet. Then we measured 13 inches, to be the inside distance between the two upright pallets. We nailed the second upright pallet 13 inches over, to the bottom pallet. Meanwhile, we used our chain saw to cut several pieces of wood planks off the fourth pallet. We cut these as long as possible, for they need to be at least 15 inches long. We nailed the 15 inch pieces perpendicular to the top of the uprights, thus stabilizing the milking stand. These boards were nailed along the top at the front, middle and back.

Similar pieces of wood were nailed down the front of the milking stand to prevent the goat from escaping out the front. The two boards were nailed at an angle to the upper part of the entrance for stability. On the floor inside the uprights or walls we nailed boards for a type of flooring to prevent the goat's feet from falling through.

This milking stand controls even persnickety goats, and has paid off in many ways. The girls can do the milking by themselves.

The lower section of boards from the right side was cut out to allow room for our hands while milking.

You may want to secure a feed bucket to the front. We nailed a strap with a hook to the front. We also use a rope or chain on the back to keep the goat from backing out.

We elevated the stand to make it easier on our back while milking. You may wish to put the stand on another pallet or make legs. We mounted ours on some concrete stands.

This sturdy milking stand has paid off in many ways. Now our girls (10, 8, 6 and 4 years old) can do the goat milking by themselves. The goats eagerly jump up into the stand to be milked and get their goodies.

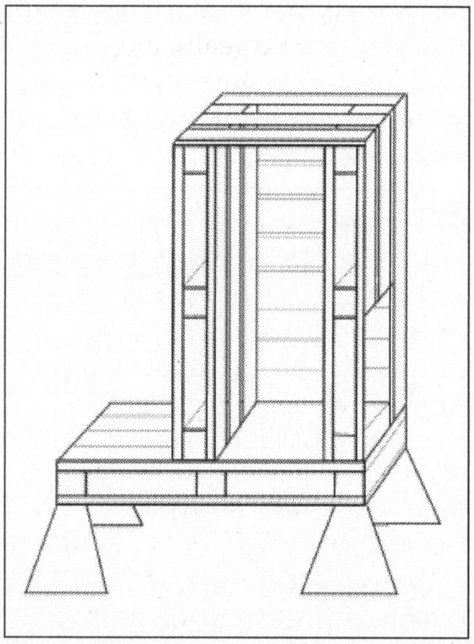

The stand was built from four used shipping pallets. It's elevated on concrete piers to make milking easier on the back.

The goat barn:

Why Oberhasli Swiss dairy goats?

ANDREW & TERRY JORGENSEN
OREGON

I've been reading Countryside magazine from cover to cover for about two years now and, like many of the people who write articles for this magazine, I have always thought it would be fun to share a few lines about what makes me love being out of the city, in the country and working harder than I ever worked when I was a "professional person."

When we moved to the country in October of 1994, my husband, Andy, thought I would want a horse. I grew up around horses and had had horses most of my life. I said "Oh, maybe someday but I'd really like a goat." Andy was very surprised. "A goat! What do you want with a goat?" I said, "I want babies in the spring."

One day Andy stopped by the feed store and there was the cutest little goat he'd ever seen (not that he had seen all that many goats, but...) He thought she looked more like a deer than a goat. He came to get me to show me this cute little goat.

We went, we looked, we bought. She was so cute and so friendly and tame. We were in love. That was Daisy Mae.

We bought her on June 1, 1995. We didn't know much about goats so we went to the library and checked out every goat book they had and read them from cover to cover. By that time we knew a little more, but we wanted to meet people who knew a lot about goats so we went to the Clackamas County Fair. There we met several people who raised and showed Oberhasli, including Dale and Loita Coleback.

When we attended the Oregon State Fair I volunteered to help Loita show her animals. I had shown fat steers as a teenager in Wheatland, Wyoming, so a show ring wasn't completely foreign to me, but I needed coaching on what to do with a goat.

We joined the Northwest Oregon Dairy Goat Association, the Northwest Oberhasli Breeders Association, and the American Dairy Goat Association. We have educated ourselves so we can raise quality dairy goats and care for them properly.

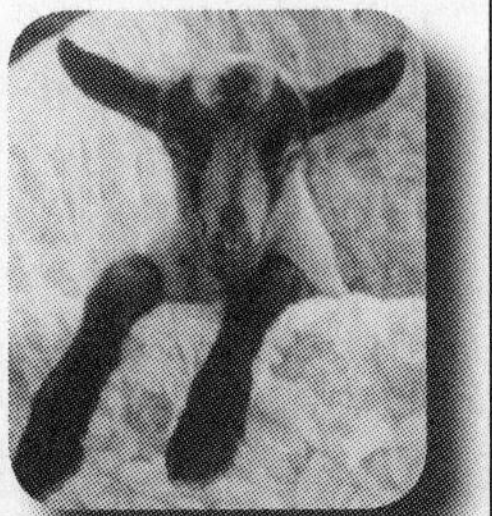

We have grown a bit since June of 1995. We now have 10 Oberhasli. We had eight kids in the spring of 1996 and 11 in '97. It makes it worth the work just to see those babies hopping!

Why Oberhasli Swiss dairy goats?

We have found them to be very hardy in this climate. They don't mind the cold temperatures and have sturdy black hooves. They are quiet (one of our requirements), they are good pack animals as well as milk producers, and they don't freak out when a stranger comes into the barn. They are a medium size and have wonderful, inquisitive personalities.

We are now very involved with this beautiful breed. We are trying to improve it by selective breeding programs and DHIA (Dairy Herd Improvement Association), a program for testing milk production, butterfat and protein percentages and improving your management. We participated in Linear Appraisal, a program that evaluates your animals compared to a standard rather than judging one animal against another. We also show in ADGA (American Dairy Goat Association) sanctioned shows. Here your animal is judged against the other animals that are in the show ring with you.

All of these things work together to aid you in making wise choices in which animals to breed to what sire, what animals are not going to produce for you, (after all, these are dairy goats) what weak points to work on in next year's kids and just who is going to be just a pet or, if you are able, just who to get rid of.

One of the goat owners who has become a good friend is Nettie Stein. She and her husband, Terry, have several of the beautiful Oberhasli breed. She tells how her father—a cow dairyman—might have reacted to the question, "Why Oberhasli?"

Ninette Stein

The larger question in my father's mind would have been, "Why goats? Why not cows?" If he were alive, I would patiently explain that goats are smaller, easier to handle, less expensive to feed, and more suited to brushy terrain. When he shook his head in disbelief, I'd deliver the "gotcha:" pound for pound, goats produce more milk. It's not unusual for our Oberhasli to milk 10% of their body weight every single day. That would have convinced my father, the dairy cow farmer.

The question remains: Why Oberhasli? For us, it started as a "color thing." After I'd whined for the umpteenth time that I wanted some milk goats, my husband smirkingly replied, "No goats… unless they look like deer." That sent us to a fair, where we saw a very few beautiful brown goats. Reluctantly, my husband let me drag him to see the beauties. Yes, he had to agree those Oberhasli goats looked a lot like deer. Bingo! I had him.

I began my research in earnest. Here's what I found about the Oberhasli breed:

Rarity: According to the registration records of ADGA, Obers are the least common goats in the US. That appealed to me. It meant there would be a better market for offspring, plus the personal satisfaction of owning something just a little "different."

Genetics: Anytime a breed is perpetuated from a small number of animals, there are bound to be imperfections. I was intrigued by the challenges of improving the breed.

Production: The first year official DHIA records were kept for Obers was 1992. They were dead last for total pounds of production. I felt there was a lot of potential for improvement; my father's training in feeding techniques were well-remembered. (I've been pleased to see much improvement, nationally. In just three years, Obers have risen from fifth to fourth in total milk production; butterfat percentage is second; protein is third.) Based on this research, I, myself, was convinced Oberhasli was the breed for us.

I was able to find an Oberhasli breeder who was willing to sell us a pair of doelings at a price within our budget. Goat books began to mysteriously appear on our coffee table, often marked at the section explaining housing requirements for goats. A quick survey of our 20 acres found a little shed that could be upgraded to the minimum requirements; after a few fenceposts and a few sections of cattle panels were added, we had a home for our new babies.

The day "Daffy" and "Dolly" arrived found my husband finishing the last gate for their new home. He was committed to providing adequate facilities, but was still uncertain about the whole project. By the time he and the girls had finished the gate, he was beginning to appreciate the winsome personalities possessed by all goats, but particularly Oberhasli.

After five years, our love affair with Obers continues. We appreciate their stylish beauty even more now that a small herd roams our woodlands. We're excited to see both total registration and production begin to climb, nationally. And we're excited to be part of a very viable Ober revo-

She raises Pygmy goats for fun... and profit

MARCIE WISE
OHIO

I've noticed many articles in Countryside about doing something you enjoy and making a little money from it. Well, that's what I'm doing. I raise Pygmy goats.

I started five years ago, after falling in love with them when seeing them at the zoo.

They make great pets because of their small size, they're inexpensive to buy and feed, and they're easy to handle and to transport.

Pygmy goats were first imported into the United States in 1959, and were sold mainly to zoos for large amounts of money. They are now raised mainly as pets and are much cheaper.

I bought my first doe kid in 1992. Of course my two daughters went with me to pick her out. The girls and I fell in love with a nice silver agouti. We took her to our mini farm, where she became our pride and joy.

The girls named her Crickett and she went everywhere with us. She even went to school. My oldest daughter had to do a report on an animal, so what better subject than the Pygmy goat? All the kids and the teachers adored her and Crickett enjoyed the attention.

When Crickett was a year old I talked with others who owned Pygmies and they encouraged me to have her bred. So Crickett visited a buck in a neighboring town.

The gestation period is approximately five months. I took all the precautions during her pregnancy. She was overdue by two days and I was a nervous wreck. I didn't leave my home for 10 days because I thought it was going to happen at any minute. (Many goats and births later, I know what signs to look for).

Sleeping benches are also good for playing on... or sleeping under!

I had even been sleeping in the barn at nights, so I was a walking zombie during the day.

My husband (who was very patient with me) kept telling me that I was babying her too much. He suggested that I go to get groceries, since there was no food in the house. Crickett was in the pasture running around so I figured it was safe to leave.

Wrong! The minute I pulled out of the driveway, my husband said later, she came in the barn and stood in the corner acting very funny. I had called my friend (who was a dairy farmer, and has helped many calves be born) to be on call. I thought I had all angles covered.

A wheelbarrow provides plenty of room for a Pygmy kid to play.

Wrong! I had no vet (since I gave all my own shots, I never used a vet). Seems Crickett had a single buck, and her pelvis was not big enough to pass it.

What a shock to us all when we ended up in a strange vet's office for a C-section. Costly too. And we lost the kid. Very disappointing and I swore no more breeding.

Wrong! During Crickett's pregnancy I had purchased more Pygmy does. They were just as sweet as our first goat but we could now make comparisons between animals. We found that not all Pygmies have the same dispositions. Some are a little friendlier than others, some like to be with people, some are very stubborn, some are very bossy to the other goats, some are hay hogs, some are very quiet (even during kidding) and some are very talkative (especially when they are in heat).

So now its time to breed again,

what do I do? I load the does in the truck and off we go.

This kidding season went well. Thank God, because otherwise I probably would have thrown in the towel. Nothing is more rewarding than seeing those little critters stand up and nurse.

I've learned that when raising farm animals you have to take the good with the bad. Not all does are good mothers. Sometimes I have to take their place and bottle-feed the kids. When you come to my house don't be surprised to see newborn kids in a box in my kitchen, if need be.

I've been blessed with many twins, a few triplets and one set of quads. I've learned a lot from other Pygmy people and we all try to keep each other informed if we hear of a new product or of a new feed, etc., or if we just want to cry on someone's shoulder because we just lost a newborn kid. The people with goats I have met are some of the nicest people I know, and I have made some very good friends.

My daughters have been in 4-H for the past four years with their Pygmies. They've taken three grand champions, and reserve champions, and both have been champion of champions in showmanship. I'm very proud of them both.

We are also members of N.P.G.A. (National Pygmy Goat Assn.) and enjoy showing our goats in Ohio and neighboring states.

I enjoy my goats very much, but they do have to pay their way. I do sell many of my kids, and once in a while there will be one that is just so irresistible that it stays! I remember the first doe kid I sold: we all cried for a day. Now it's not quite as hard to say good-bye. Once in a while when the girls hand over the kid to its new owner I notice a tear in their eye. I usually try to fluff it off with a joke or we'd all be crying. It's very easy to get attached to them.

When I say that to people they look at me like I'm crazy, unless I'm talking to a goat person. Then they'll just smile and have a little sparkle in their eye.

My girls are teenagers now and will soon be grown and on their own, but whenever they come home there will be Pygmy goats here to greet them. I can imagine myself in my later years walking out to the barn to give them warm water in the winter or to see who had new babies or just to say hi. They're a great miniature animal that old or young can enjoy.

The goat barn:

Record-keeping made easy

Nola Jones
Texas

I would like to share my record keeping idea that I use for my milk goats. I do not have registered goats, but do like to keep track of when and what I do for each of the goats.

This simple system would work for any animal. I use a spiral notebook, marking each page with an index tab. This tab has the goat's name, and/or number on it. The top line has when I bought her, the animal's age if I know, what I paid for her, and any other information I know about her.

Instead of keeping it in the house I keep it at the barn. For me this is the key to making it work. I date each entry, and note what was done. Since it stays handy, I do it as I trim feet, worm, or doctor the goat. It is also there to write in when they are bred and kidded. It seldom takes more than one line. With 25 lines front and back it will take a long time to use a page.

When one is full I will mark full over the goat's name and start a new sheet. It is fast and inexpensive. I can also see at a glance which goats I'm spending the most time on, and consider replacing them.

I don't have to worry about remembering to write it down when I get back in the house. Then if it is something I want to transfer to a more permanent record, I bring the book in and update my records.

When I go to sell the animal I tear the page out and give it to a buyer, then they have an accurate record of what I know about the goat.

Continued on next page

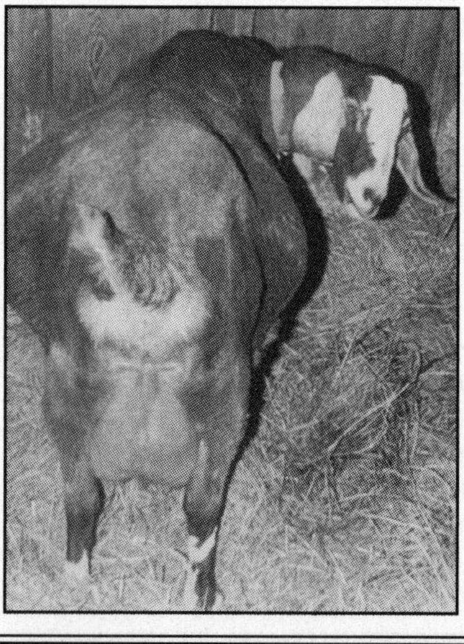

Before & after: **Robin and Crystal Kovach, Pennsylvania, hold Buttermilk's quadruplets. (See article on canned milk on the next page.)**

Canned goat milk

It is easier to store jars than trying to keep excess milk in the freezer. Canned goat milk looks and uses just like the bought canned milk; be sure to shake before using.

First, I strain my milk and freeze it in gallon ziplock plastic bags until I have enough to fill my cooker, and also have the time to can it. When I am ready to can, I thaw it in a stainless steel mixing bowl sitting in another larger stainless steel mixing bowl filled with water on the stove. This serves as a large double boiler, allowing the milk to thaw quickly.

Once it is hot, I scald my jars and can it. I can quarts at 10 lbs. pressure for 10 minutes. I have had good results with this method.

Canned goat milk II

Linda L. Kovach
Pennsylvania

I can goat milk to feed kids. It comes in very handy when a doe doesn't produce enough milk for her babies.

Strain and cool the fresh milk to 50 degrees or less. Pour it into clean glass canning jars to within an inch of the tops. Put the lids and bands on and screw them down tightly. Place the jars in a large kettle that is partly filled with water. Cover and bring the water to a boil. Let it boil for one hour, being careful that it doesn't boil down too far. Cool and store in a dark place.

We also have a Jersey-Holstein calf we bottle fed on goat milk. She is growing like a bad weed!

When we're not feeding all the milk to goat kids, I make cheese. We have two pigs and we feed them the whey from cheesemaking, mixing it with their grain. By butchering time they look like weight lifters.

The goat barn:

Exercise yard size

We have a site selected for a goat exercise yard. It's about 100 feet by 100 feet. Is this big enough to keep her happy?

For exercise alone, a yard about 10 feet by 20 feet is sufficient if it has some shade and well-drained or sandy ground so it doesn't get muddy.

Legume pastures promote production

Is it necessary to have legumes (alfalfa and clover) in a pasture? Our pasture is rocky and would be difficult to reseed, even if we had the equipment, which we don't.

If the pasture provides the only roughage the goats get, legumes could mean better milk production. But if you're going to feed purchased hay as well as pasture, spending a little extra for alfalfa could be a good investment.

The highest milk production comes from goats that aren't on pasture at all. They get top quality hay and lots of grain, and never leave the barn and exercise yard. For many goat raisers with outside jobs—and certainly for beginners—this makes a lot of sense.

You have to balance the time and expense of pasture—buying the land and paying taxes on it, establishing a stand of suitable forage plants, and building and maintaining fences and gates—against the cost of purchased feeds. In many cases, buying feed is cheaper.

People who insist on being independent of outside sources and who want their animals to live as "naturally" as possible will prefer pastures, even if the initial cost is higher and if it means having more animals to meet their dairy product needs. In this case it should be noted that some strains of goats—meaning families, not specific breeds—are said to be better adapted to such conditions. The ideal purchase would be a goat already living and producing well under such a system, rather than one living the life of Riley in a confinement system.

But here, as usual, only experience with your own animals living under your own conditions will provide any real answers.

How many goats to feed a family?

Will one goat provide enough milk and cheese for a family of three? We usually only drink milk at dinner, but we plan to make all our own cheese, and we eat a lot of it—three to four pounds a week. We would also like to use the milk for yogurt and we hope to have some extra for raising a hog. Am I expecting too much from one doe?

A milk goat will produce anywhere from two to eight quarts a day. A newly freshened doe might milk a gallon a day in April, less than half a gallon by September, and be dry by November... or she might give three or four quarts a day almost year around.

You probably won't start out with one of those gallon-a-day milkers, but if you buy a good animal and feed her right you could reasonably expect to get four to five quarts a day when she first freshens. (Remember that a mature doe will generally produce more than a first-freshener.)

It takes roughly 10 pounds of milk to make one pound of cheese. A gallon weighs about eight pounds. So if you have an "average good" goat producing about half a gallon of milk a day, you'll get about half a pound of cheese a day.

You need a very good producing doe, or else you need two does.

The goat barn:

What some people know about goats isn't the truth

Jill Abraham

All goats stink, have horns, beards, and eat tin cans.

False! While it is true that male goats (bucks) emit an aroma during breeding season, females (does) never have an objectionable odor.

Beards grow on many goats, with mature bucks displaying the longer beard and more facial "whiskers." Castrated males (wethers) and does sometimes sport a smaller goatee which is removed with an entire body clip in the spring. Beards are inherited, and some goats don't have them.

Dairy goats are fed a dairy grain ration and alfalfa hay. Available pasture and browse round out the diet. Unlimited water and minerals make a happy goat. They are very particular in their eating habits and will avoid dirty, contaminated, thrown-on-the-floor feeds.

Because their feeding and eating habits are so clean, dairy goats produce a delicious and nutritious sweet milk.

Goats do like to "taste" everything due to their curiosity. They will nibble at your buttons, shoelaces, and clothing, but if you watch them, "taste" is all they do.

Horns on a dairy goat are justly discouraged. A horned doe is a problem to her herdmates, keeper, and herself. An unintentional fling of her head or a well-aimed shove can result in injured herdmates. Horns certainly pose a problem with becoming entangled in fencing and tethers. A sanctioned show will not allow horned goats to be shown. To eliminate the growth of horns, kids of both sexes are disbudded.

This does not mean all goats grow horns. Some are naturally hornless (polled). Care should be taken to avoid the breeding of two polled animals as your chance of producing a hermaphrodite (an animal with characteristics of both sexes) is greatly enhanced.

Fact: More people in the world use goat milk than cow milk.

Goat milk does not have a "goaty" flavor when it's properly produced and cared for. It's delicious!

The sheep shed:

Sheep can utilize many grains

Sheep can live well on grains other than corn, according to South Dakota State University Extension sheep specialist James Thompson. The other grains are generally used as an energy source, and protein and mineral supplementation may be needed.

Since the protein content of some feed grains is higher than others, homesteaders will need to keep that fact in mind. As a general rule, cereal grains tend to be high in phosphorus and low in calcium. Higher-fiber grains are less suited for lamb finishing rations but are a good choice for other sheep. Some grains to consider are:

Oats: Sheep like them, and they are especially well suited as a major feed component for breeding sheep and lambs. Oats are high in fiber. Although higher in protein than corn, oats are considered to have 80 percent of the relative energy value of corn.

Oats can and should be fed whole to sheep, because there doesn't appear to be any advantage to grinding or processing.

Grain sorghum or milo: This is a popular feed in the southwestern U.S. It has a relative energy value of 85 to 100 percent of corn and is considered to have a 100 percent replacement value for corn.

Some feeding trials indicate lowered rate of weight gain in lambs that were fed sorghum grain as the only energy source when compared to corn. Mixing sorghum with other grains would be one way to obtain better overall lamb performance.

While there are no apparent advantages to grinding milo, it should be coarsely ground when used in lamb creep feeds until the lambs are six weeks of age.

Barley: It contains more total protein than corn, but has 90 percent of the relative energy value of corn because of its high fiber content. Barley can replace up to 100 percent of corn in rations for all classes of sheep. Gains are nearly equal to corn in finishing rations, but feed efficiency is somewhat less.

Sheep find barley to be highly palatable. Few digestive disturbances are reported. It can be fed whole.

Wheat: Even though it has a relative energy value equal to corn, it is recommended that wheat be fed as only 50 percent of the grain mixture for sheep. Sheep that eat high levels of wheat are susceptible to digestive disturbances and founder. Ewe rations for late gestation and lactation may utilize higher levels of wheat without any apparent problems.

Best results are obtained when wheat is fed whole, as processing makes it less palatable and produces slower gains in lambs.

Rye: This grain is more palatable to sheep than any other class of farm livestock. It has a relative energy value of 85 percent to corn and may replace 50 to 100 percent of corn in sheep rations. Rye may be fed whole without decreasing animal performance.

Millet: Its value as a feed grain is not well documented. Millet should be cracked or coarsely ground when used for sheep feed. It has a relative energy value of 75 to 90 percent and higher protein content than corn. Millet would probably work best in ewe and lamb rations.

Observations on hybrid vigor, commercial production, and homesteading

Michael Foley
Minnesota

While I generally agreed in substance with the perspective of Val Dambacher regarding raising sheep naturally in the January/February magazine, I feel I have to take issue with some unsubstantiated inferences contained in the essay.

Yes, a big ingredient to a natural way of life, as well as success in any agricultural endeavor, is to pick a variety or breed that will thrive in your area/environment! "Hybrid vigor" however, is not the mechanism that results in a large volume of milk for commercial dairymen. Rather, it is testing, recording and selecting for productivity, along with feeding and management factors. Dairy cattle are, for the most part, straight bred, and very similar in genetics; hardly hybrid.

Secondly, hybridization doesn't result in "a large, obese lamb at six months old." If properly practiced, crossbreeding creates offspring excelling either parent breed for various characteristics, one of which is growthiness; obesity results from improper feeding, not improper breeding!

I agree, "miniature is very cute," but also not very practical for anyone hoping to turn a profit in an industry where it is tough enough to do so today without handicapping oneself in any manner. Small sheep breeds, while cute and okay for home consumption if cost is no concern, are also slow growing and seldom reach weight approaching desirable for commercial slaughter. It takes processors just as much time and effort to convert a small animal to a lesser quantity of retail cuts as a larger, higher valued one.

In defense of commercial producers

Probably the most bothersome insinuation was that "commercial" producers routinely, without regard for the consumer, medicate their animals via sprays, fungicides, hormones, etc. My observations have been that this is more likely true where total confinement is employed, such as with poultry or hogs, and to some extent dairy, than with sheep and cattle which are raised less intensively and allowed room to roam and graze the better portion of their lives.

The standard breeds of these species (in my case Columbia sheep) can also be raised relatively "pesticide free!" When a rotational grazing system that allows adequate time for pasture recovery is practiced, my experience has been that only a spring pre-pasture and fall pre-breeding worming are necessary, at least in the northern climates.

Intolerance

One last observation; it's one thing to tout the virtues as you see them of your way of life, economic outlook, breed of livestock and so on. It's quite another to infer that others who see and do things differently are somehow uninformed, insensitive, greedy, lack integrity, etc. If respect for the homesteader viewpoint is to be expected we must afford others the validity of theirs.

As a semi-homesteader and agri-educator, I've observed there's not necessarily a right and wrong, all or nothing perspective to lifestyle values any more than there is for religion or politics. Intolerance for differing viewpoints doesn't foster acceptance of yours. Oftentimes I detect a veiled, and sometimes very obvious, disdain from COUNTRYSIDE contributors for those who don't endorse the Spartan existence many homesteaders see as the ultimate of virtues.

While not condoning consumerism, as an early post-depression product of an upbringing in Minnesota's northwoods where no electricity, running water, fossil fuel, heat, etc. were available, I see a big difference between such an existence being a lifestyle choice versus a dead end, no-way-out way of life. Those that have "been there, done that" as a non-choice way of life aspire to something better, just as the involuntarily unemployed desire a job with an adequate living wage. Of course they "don't get it" when it comes to the "beyond the sidewalks" aspirations of "more from less."

Almost everyone who writes about their favorite breed of livestock considers it the ideal, of course. In addition, if you're trying to sell somebody on something—be it a breed or a lifestyle—it's often tough to restrain your enthusiasm. Most people, being familiar with advertising, allow for that.

Along the same lines, most of us assume that since this is a homestead magazine, it's read by homesteaders, or at least by people with similar interests and ideals. We're part of a club where we don't have to be overly concerned about "meeting the other side," because here we're all supposed to be together.

But then, magazines don't reflect life; they portray just one slice of it, like a caricature. A magazine is a vehicle for dreams. One that strays too far from its niche has no reason for existing. For a golf magazine, all that matters is golf. For COUNTRYSIDE, it's homesteading.

Ever notice though, that when citified magazines ridicule country bumpkins, everyone laughs?

Maybe we should all lighten up.

The sheep shed:

Hair sheep provide some advantages, but might be hard to market

KEN SCHARABOK
TENNESSEE

For a homesteader interested in keeping a small flock of sheep, hair sheep offer several advantages over wool sheep.

They are more adaptive to an area with a hot Summer and cool Winter since they lose their winter coat each Spring. They do not require shearing. They have a diet similar to wool sheep, but are more resistant to internal parasites. Twin lambs and twice-a-year lambing are not unusual. Their smaller size makes them easier to work. Some lamb gourmets consider hair sheep to be far superior to wool sheep.

On the downside, there is an extremely limited consumer market and when sold, they suffer a severe price discount to wool sheep.

Last summer I raised four hair sheep lambs, two rams and two ewes, more to keep the grass clipped down around my residence than anything else. They came from a friend's flock with the understanding that I would raise them for the summer, then we would split whatever they brought when sold.

In early October I took them to a consignment auction in a Mennonite community as eight-month-old lambs. One ewe brought $20 and the other three $17 each. After commission we each netted $32—so I figure I broke even on supplemental feed.

My friend's wife died during the summer. Since she was the herd master, and he works six and a half days a week, we rounded up what we could of his flock and took them to a dedicated sheep auction in mid-October. It was a combination of older rams, bred ewes, ewes with lambs and young rams. They averaged less than $12 each after commission.

While the flock was primarily for their own freezer, they had been trying to sell freezer or Easter lambs and breeding stock with very little success.

If you enjoy your own freezer lamb, hair sheep may be a good choice due to their advantages over wool sheep. However, there does not seem to be a viable commercial market for them now or anytime in the near future.

For further information: Katahdin Hair Sheep Int'l., RR 1 Box 115, Fairview, KS 66425.

Sheep shed feedback:

Some Katahdin breeders get a good price

Al Silverio
Illinois

This is a response to Mr. Scharabok's article — I believe he's incorrect about the supposed problems of marketing hair sheep, at least Katahdin sheep.

First, let me describe my position. I've had Katahdin sheep for 11 years. I maintain a purebred flock, but I've not kept up the paper work to certify the sheep as such. I think sheep are dim-witted, smelly, bothersome things that tend to die if you simply look at them in a mean way. And I like having them around the place, keeping things chewed down, utilizing marginal land, giving me swearing practice in abundance, and teaching me humility and patience (learning to keep sheep alive and thriving requires the aforementioned personality characteristics). I'm not a big fan of sheep, whatever the breed, but I find them useful and I like seeing them on the pastures.

I agree with the positive factors seen in hair sheep mentioned by Mr. Scharabok, and while the negative aspects he noted may apply to some breeds of hair sheep, it has not been my experience that Katahdins so suffer. Much the opposite.

Selling for slaughter I take my lambs to the Springfield, Illinois collection point of Interstate Producers (309-691-5360), and I am immediately paid that day's price as determined at auction in Peoria. No quibble, no dock, and the first time I showed up with a load of lambs, the stockmen at the collection point recognized the breed and commented on the high quality. This business has many collection points.

Selling certified breeding stock is more profitable than selling slaughter lambs. And the demand is considerable, if sporadic. Foreign buyers hit our market regularly wanting hundreds of yearling ewes at a time. And the U.S. is scoured to find enough sheep to fill a given demand. Last year it was a couple hundred wanted by a Mexican buyer, and the price was in the $220-$240 range…didn't matter what it looked like: if it was Katahdin, had hair and was about a year old and female, breathing and without disease, it sold. Costs related to certification and transport to collection points got the take-home price down to around $180 per yearling, light or heavy, which beat the slaughter price of $75 to $95 depending on lamb size. To work this out you have to be tapped into the network of breeders which you can do by joining the Katahdin organization noted at the end of Mr. Scharabok's article.

Katahdin sheep are a bit easier to care for than some breeds of sheep. The ewes drop lambs like pebbles falling out of a bucket (unless you get the ewes too fat). No lost sleep for the shepherd staying up nights in the lambing barn. And the new lambs have coats like puppy fur… now that is a cute lamb.

Icelandic sheep breeders organize

The Icelandic Sheep Breeders of North America has just been formed, to provide information about the breed to the public and to exchange information among members. They will also promote the special attributes and products of these unique sheep.

Founders say the breed is famous worldwide for its soft, versatile, colorful dual coated fleece; light flavored fine textured gourmet meat; and pelts that look like long lustrous furs. These sheep have been valued for meat, fiber, and milk production in Iceland for 900 years.

Registration of these sheep in North America will continue to be handled by the Canadian Livestock Records Corporation. ISBONA has adopted the breed standards and guidelines developed in Iceland.

For more information, details on the quarterly newsletter and fleece samples send an SASE to the Icelandic Sheep Breeders of North America (ISBONA), 115772 Hwy. 395, Topaz, CA 96133. 530-495-9595; website: www.isbona.com

The sheep shed:

Sheep cotes

Ancient, but still useful

Left: Sheep wintered in a sheep cote. *Right:* Sheep wintered without shelter. (These drawings are from a book published in 1864, thus proving that exaggeration is nothing new!)

NATHAN GRIFFITH
WEST VIRGINIA

A sheep cote is a special shelter designed to protect sheep from the elements, predators and parasites. Its use comes to us from the ancient sheep-keeping regions known as the Levant (the lands bordering the eastern extremity of the Mediterranean Sea) and the land of Colchis (modern "Soviet" Georgia). The county of Gloucestershire, England has a range of hills called Cotswolds; they were named for the sheep cotes dotting the hills in ancient times. Cotswold sheep take their name from the same practice; both they, and middle East methods were brought to the Cotswold region of Britain by Phoenicians when they broke the Milesian grip on Colchis, circa 500 B.C.

Cotes consist of a small penned area, with housing for the sheep. The housing can be tall enough for a grown man to walk in, and wind-tight on the sides, Or it can be low (about three to four feet) with more open, airy sides and just a wall to the prevailing winter winds.

Originally, sheep cotes had walls of stone at least five feet high. Their area depended on the size of the flock, but rarely did they house as many as 200 to 300 adult sheep. A cote of that size would be shared by up to 10 shepherds. They weren't used in areas of low rainfall unless there was a rainy season. The Levatine rainy season begins early in December and continues until late February or March. Except at that time, Israeli shepherds and sheep left the cotes to "abide in the fields."

During the time in the sheep cotes, animals were fed stored fodder. What little grass grew inside its fences soon disappeared, and the sheep had to eat the fodder or starve. This broke the cycle of internal parasites.

Stomach worms, the worst parasite of sheep, survive winter by going dormant. Keeping sheep off pastures during early spring allowed the grass to grow taller, allowing the grass-climbing stage of the worm to starve. Even today, sheep kept in dry lots harbor no stomach worms.

Moreover, sheep kept in cotes always look better than those wintered in dark or stuffy barns, or out in grazing paddocks. Constantly inhaling fumes from accumulating wastes and the exhalations of ill animals; lack of sunshine for warmth, vitamins and germ-killing; and lack of daily exercise all hinder barn-kept animals. The constant temptation of short, sweet, winter grass induces paddock-kept sheep to neglect the hay in their feeders except when they are famished: They exercise entirely too much for the meager sustenance they wind up getting. Ewes kept for even just three weeks in a cote show amazing improvement in condition over both conventional winter keeping and during times of summer dearth.

Modern cotes consist of cheap housing coupled with sturdy, dog-proof fences which don't permit the sheep access to green grass. The system differs from the fold in that the area contained is much smaller, so grazing within the enclosure is discouraged. The best modern cotes are portable, with the shelter portion on skids, wheels, or just knockdown construction. The fence portions can be either portable electric-mesh fencing, woven-wire covered wooden or pipe panels, or commercially available galvanized stock panels. Even gates may be used, though they'd be rather expensive. A portable manger is almost essential. I show plans for the best manger design I've used in my book *Husbandry, The Surest, Cheapest Way to Leisure, Plenty, Prosperity and Contentment.*

My sheep cotes

My first cotes utilized packing pallets I got free locally, stood on end to form walls. I attached them, using baling twine, to metal fence posts (T-posts) or to six-foot lengths of 3/4 inch rebar (concrete reinforcement rod) driven about two feet into the ground. Across the top I laid cheap reject-grade wood slats, and laid galvanized roofing on that. I used old locust wood fence posts and rocks to anchor the roof from wind.

My cotes utilized an existing fence for the north boundary, and for the north "wall" of the hut portion. To block the wind, we attached a three-foot wide cheap plastic firewood tarpaulin to this wall. For sheepcote boundary fences we used the really narrow spaced "yard & garden" type woven wire attached to metal T-posts. It comes in 47 and 59 inch heights in rolls of 165 feet length, and has one-inch line wire spacing at the bottom.

We have since used—with very good results—common galvanized stock panels (four feet high) attached to T-posts with hay string. Another hut frame is one I made of one-inch galvanized iron pipe. It has runners, and a galvanized metal roof. It is anchored to the cote's north fence, which allows the attachment of a windbreak there. This also allows runoff water from the roof to go outside the cote. Pick the highest ground in the cote for the house placement.

Outdoor area ought to be between 60 and 90 square feet per head on well-drained ground, somewhat more on wetter land. Smaller areas can be employed if the cotes will be moved when the ground begins getting muddy.

The roofed area needs about eight to 10 square feet per head for ewes and tegs (unbred yearling ewes) until lambing time, when they'll need about 25 to 30 square feet per ewe with her lambs. That way you can set up individual pens for each ewe so she can bond with her lambs. Our Cotswolds are such good mothers they will allow other lambs to nurse if they don't get a week or so segregated to form this bond.

Rams are kept in their own sheepcotes away from the ewes. Rams don't eat as voraciously as ewes, and will get thin over time if they have to compete with them for food. Also, they may fight and fret over the ewes. We keep them in their own cotes, about 30 to 40 feet square for up to a half-dozen rams (we have their permanent sheepcotes on a very well-drained rocky area). They get better feed than our ewes (but less of it) because they are almost never pastured. A ram is half the flock, so never stint them, and keep them parasite-free. Of course, during tupping (breeding season) the rams graze with the ewes.

The results

Keeping our sheep in cotes has resulted in 15% to 20% less hay consumption. At the same time, we found parasite control much easier and cheaper, not only by breaking the cycle, but by making treatment far easier because of the confinement. With portable cotes, the sheep can be kept on arable land to hugely improve next year's crops. This used to be called "the golden hoof" effect. The sheep look far better at winter's end, and lamb birth weights also went up by 10 to 15%.

I don't know if the system would work for all breeds. We keep Cotswolds, and their historic fence-respecting attitudes make sheepcote management a very easy method.

Best for small flocks

Then too, sheep cote management is mostly suitable for small flock owners. True, a loss of a sheep to dogs or parasites here and there hurts those producing hundreds or even thousands of lambs. But it's far worse to self-supporters and those making hundreds of dollars/ewe annual returns on wool and specialty mutton, like many small-flock Cotswold keepers.

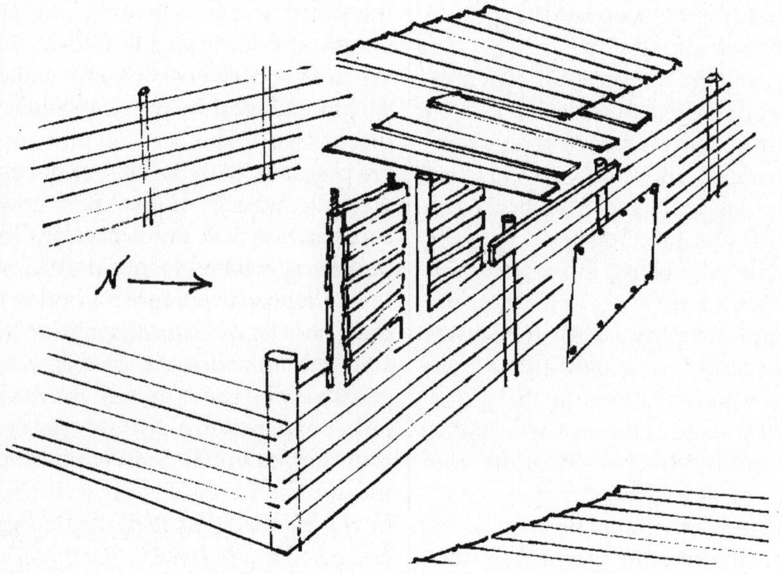

A modern sheep cote

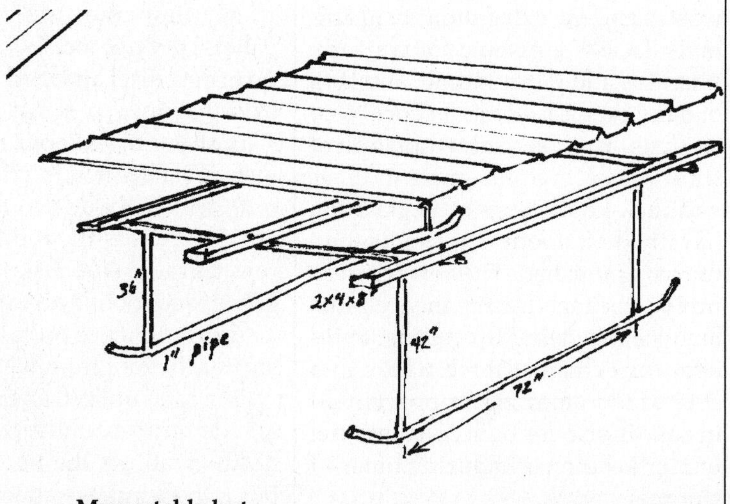

My portable hut

Raising sheep—naturally

This homesteader had some specific goals in mind, then found the breeds that could meet them

VAL DAMBACHER
OREGON

I especially enjoy reading my issues of COUNTRYSIDE because they feature organic homesteading and an emphasis on our natural way of life, the way farming used to be. I have always felt that plants and animals should be raised as naturally as possible, especially without the use of chemical pesticides that leave residues of poison on food and soil.

One key ingredient to the natural way of life is to pick the right variety of plant or breed of animal that will thrive in your area. Having organically gardened for years in the city, I knew this to be true. I also knew saving the gene pools of some of the old-time plants and animals gives us more alternatives from which to later breed hybrids. Sometimes that "hybrid vigor" they speak of breeds for one main characteristic, like a large bloom on a rose, a large volume of milk for commercial dairymen, or a large obese lamb at six months old.

My goal in homesteading, now that we finally made it to our farm in Oregon, is to be as self-sufficient as possible and still have time to enjoy life. Here's what I've discovered about sheep raising that has simplified my life and brought me one step closer to a natural way of raising food and fiber.

I picked sheep as my animal to raise because they are little and fairly problem-free if not overcrowded. They work well on a smaller homestead. I picked small sheep (under 24") because I knew I might be maintaining them myself most of the time. Besides, small feeds a family of four well without everyone getting tired

Little Richard shows his gentle nature, typical of Soays.

of it before it is used up.

"Small" or "miniature" is also very cute, and in sheep this is a niche market the commercial sheep raiser is never going to fill. I also knew I needed two or three very hardy breeds so I wouldn't be buying someone else's problems. I wanted no lambing problems, no foot rot, no sickly critters that had to be coddled for survival.

After sifting through everything I could find about sheep and a bit of trial and error, I have chosen two breeds that fit the bill for me—the Soay sheep and the smaller Southdown, called the "Babydoll".

Both breeds are generally raised in very small flocks, giving the buyer a better chance at healthy stock. It's fairly easy to watch three dozen sheep for the slightest limp or a sticker in the eye, but 300 or 3,000? That's when disease spreads. (When introducing new stock to your farm it is wise to always quarantine the newcomers at least 30 days.) Because of the hardiness of these two old-time breeds, I have been able to raise them pesticide free. They are totally organic pasture fed, without the addition of expensive poison-sprayed grain. I do supplement with a non-sprayed alfalfa/grass or clover/grass hay in winter.

The Soay sheep in particular have been found to be a gourmet treat when marinated and barbecued like kabobs, or roasted whole in a pit for a holiday feast, as many ethnic groups do. This breed is tender, very low fat and delicious. The sheep does have a very nice spinning wool, but the lanolin taste found in most lamb is missing from this primitive breed

Jack, an older Soay ram, is very gentle and tame.

that sheds each year on its own.

Managing parasites, particularly worms, is always a challenge with sheep, and no one wants to medicate if it's not necessary. I have found that the primitive breeds have a great amount of parasite resistance, and when moved from one pasture to another at regular short intervals, can be raised up to slaughter time without needing worming. Of course, this should be checked regularly with stool samples taken to the vet for evaluation. I know if I do have to worm, my lamb is still so close to naturally raised that it can't compare to store-bought. Organic wormers are used by some folks but so far tests are too inconclusive to be certain they work. I'll be testing some of these for my next project.

I live in an area of commercial pear orchards, and I know people have no idea how often and how close to harvest those pears are sprayed with pesticides, and how seldom anyone actually checks up on the orchardists. I can only imagine how often commercial meat producers must medicate their animals, spray for external parasites, use fungicides on hooves, overgrain and add hormones to the meat you're about to buy and eat.

So the answer? If you're vegetarian, get hardy sheep so the manure for your plants will not be filled with worming residue. And if you want delicious meat for dinner, get hardy sheep so you know exactly what's in that meat that tastes so exquisite.

Here is a recipe for unbelievably good lamb kabobs:

Lamb kabobs

1/4 cup olive oil

1/4 cup soy sauce, teriyaki and Worcestershire sauces combined

1/4 cup red wine, or 2 tablespoons vinegar

1 teaspoon lemon pepper

1 teaspoon dried minced onion, or 2 teaspoons fresh

1/2 teaspoon rosemary

1/2 teaspoon sage

(vary with fresh ginger, mustard or bay leaf)

Cut one roast or 3-4 chops into 1" cubes, removing any extra fat. Marinate in above mixture at least three hours, turning meat chunks as needed to thoroughly coat.

Then skewer and barbecue over medium coals, turning once, for about 6 minutes total time. Don't pack the meat tightly onto skewers as it will cook too unevenly. Meat should be tender and moist when cooked the right length of time.

Even the most doubtful will become a lamb lover if you've used a breed with mild-flavored meat.

Two Babydoll lambs lunching together.

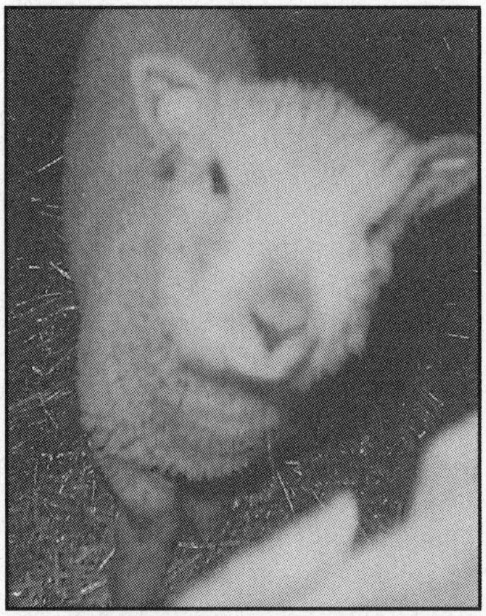

This Baby Doll Miniature Southdown belongs to Alma Whaley, Ohio.

<u>*New Q of M:*</u>

If you had five acres and wanted to be independent, how would you do it?

COUNTRYSIDE: I have a question I would like you to consider for a Question of the Month.

My husband and I are in the process of trying to acquire a five-acre piece of property. There are approximately 1-1/2 acres in yard with two houses, 1-1/2 acres in woods, and two acres in tillable land.

My question: If you have five acres and want to be independent, how would you do it in the 1990s?

I realize most people would say, "It can't be done nowadays." But that's okay. I am just interested (and perhaps some other readers are too) in learning how to make a little piece of land produce an income for a hardworking family. – *A Wisconsin Mom*

This is a mighty big question – but one of the kind we intend to pay a lot more attention to in the unsettled days ahead.

Let's face it: Most of us – no matter how long we've been homesteading or how far we've come – are dreamers. As noted in The New Pioneers (see page 67 and following) we all say we want to have a greenhouse, a root cellar, and solar power, but very few of us actually do anything to make those things realities. Yes, we have plenty of excuses, and usually even a few good reasons (like time and money!)... but this is going to have to change, and soon.

We'll be getting into that later.

But the first step is to dream without inhibitions; to decide what we need to do the job we have set for ourselves, without regard for cost, lack of skills and knowledge, time, or any other circumstances. We'll work out the how after we decide on the what.

So – let your imagination soar! Describe your dream homestead, then share your vision with your fellow homesteaders. Send your letter to COUNTRYSIDE Q OF M, 145 Industrial Dr., Medford, WI 54451.

The sheep shed:

Which breeding schedule is right for you?

With a normal, seasonal schedule, most sheep are bred between August and December. But early – or late – lambing might make more sense on your homestead.

For early lambing, ewes are bred between late July and early October so they will lamb between December and early March. For late lambing, ewes are bred from October through December and lambs are born between March and May.

A number of factors can come into play in this decision, including your personal workload during various months of the year and when other family members may be available to help with lambing. Following are the advantages for both early and late lambing that may help guide you:

Advantages of early lambing

1. If you plan to sell some of your lambs, it's possible to creep feed them and have them ready in time for the Easter lamb market where you can generally get top prices.
2. You will have fewer parasite problems with lambs on early spring pastures.
3. You are more likely to breed early-born ewes as lambs six or seven months down the road, than you are lambs born later in the spring, if that's a goal you are working toward.
4. You will have fewer fly problems at docking and castration.
5. Lambs will gain weight faster.

Advantages of late lambing

1. Building and equipment requirements are less demanding, since the weather in most parts of the country is warmer when lambing occurs. It's even possible for ewes to lamb out on pasture.
2. Mild weather means fewer chilled lambs.
3. It's easier to shear ewes before lambing.
4. Less grain is required for lambs if you have plenty of pasture.
5. Feed cost per ewe is lower.

Temperature in your part of the country is another factor to consider. In Texas, for example, where constant temperatures of 90° to 100°F. might be expected in August and September, breeding sheep later in the season would be advisable. Excessive heat not only reduces sperm production in rams, but has a definite effect on embryo survival and fetal development.

Experiments have shown that in ewes exposed to continuous 90° F temperatures on the day of breeding, none of the embryos survived. Seventy percent of the embryos were lost if the ewes were exposed to the same temperature one day after breeding. Losses continued to decrease as the pregnancy advanced.

If you are planning to breed ewe lambs from your last lamb crop, you need to make sure they are mature enough to withstand the stresses of pregnancy. Ewes can reach puberty anywhere from five to 12 months of age, depending upon the breed and various nutritional and management factors.

One university recommends that ewe lambs be healthy, strong and weigh at least 120 pounds if they are to be bred. If you want to have your lambing occur all at one time you may want to delay breeding all your ewes until your ewe lambs are ready to be bred. Or perhaps you'd rather breed older ewes early and ewe lambs late.

Once mature, ewes will naturally begin to cycle in the late summer, coming into heat every 14 to 19 days. One heat period will last 20 to 42 hours, with an average of 30 to 35 hours, and ovulation will occur toward the end of the heat period.

Regardless of which breeding procedure best fits into your homestead routine, there are some general preparations than can aid your efficiency and productivity.

For example, have you considered the "ram effect" as a method of promoting earlier cycling in your ewes? While it may be too late to take advantage of this year, you may want to file the idea away for future reference.

The ram effect comes about merely by putting a ram near your ewes near the beginning of breeding season. The presence of a ram in an adjoining pasture (where he cannot have access to the ewes, but where they are aware of his presence) causes ewes to start cycling and ovulating within 14 to 16 days.

The ram's presence also has a synchronizing effect – ewes all come into heat at approximately the same time – which simplifies the shepherd's lambing chores five months down the road.

Other management "tricks" will help enhance the productivity of your ewes as well.

If they have been kept in good, but not overly fat condition throughout the summer, they will settle better and are more likely to have multiple births.

Flushing is another method you may want to use to help increase birth numbers. Flushing refers to the practice of feeding ewes better during the two to three weeks before breeding. The increased nutrients increase the ewe's rate of ovulation, giving them —and you—more lambs.

Pasture and/or grains can be used for flushing. Paula Simmons, in her book *Raising Sheep the Modern Way* (Garden Way Publishing, Charlotte, VT), suggests you begin flushing ewes with 1/4 pound of grain per ewe per day and work up to 1/2 to 3/4 pound each in the first week, continuing to feed at that rate for the remainder of the flushing period. Best results will be obtained, Simmons adds, if the ewes are not actually mated until their second heat period, at which time they drop a greater number of eggs.

If pasture is used for flushing, beware of clovers, trefoil and alfalfa: under certain conditions the estrogen content of these forages will decrease ovulation in ewes. Check with your local extension agent for more information.

Other basic management procedures are also in order before breeding begins:

For ewes

• Be sure to trim wool around the tail and vaginal area.

• Trim feet. The extra weight ewes carry during pregnancy makes it especially important for feet to be in good condition.

• Deworm the ewe flock.

• Check for ticks. If they can be eliminated before lambing, you won't have to look for them on the lambs.

• If you are breeding during hot months, shear ewes and keep them in a cool, shady place as much as possible to prevent lamb losses.

• If vibrosis abortions are a problem in your area ewes should be vaccinated before breeding. A second injection is required three to four weeks later.

For rams

• Shear rams six to eight weeks before breeding.

• During hot weather breeding turn rams into the flock only at night and remove them the following morning. Make sure they have plenty of shade during the day.

• Worm the ram and check him for ticks.

• Allow one well-matured ram lamb for every 15 to 30 ewes. If using a yearling to five year-old ram, allow 25 to 50 ewes per ram, depending upon area temperatures, sex drive of the individual animal, and hilliness of terrain.

• Provide supplemental feed during breeding season if your pastures are poor.

• Make sure your rams are in good condition and free from parasites and disease problems.

Beef cattle:

Dehorning cattle

Ken Scharabok
Tennessee

My neighbor's aunt and uncle have a small herd of cattle strictly to produce freezer beef. Their bull had horns about 8" long. One day they found one of his calves dead in the pasture. For whatever reason, the bull had gored his bull calf. That bull then went to work for Oscar Mayer's bologna division.

Horns are relatively easy to remove. The younger the calf the better.

Electric dehorners are available at just about any farm supply outlet. They are essentially heat coils, like an electric oven, with a circular end. To use them the calf is restrained, the heated end placed at the base of the horn and rotated until the heat causes the horn button to come away from the head.

Does it hurt the calf? Yes, but for a very brief period of time. Once the skin cells around the horn base are killed, the calf feels no further pain.

When using an electric dehorner, it is critical the dehorner be rotated until the horn button comes away from its base. Otherwise, you are likely to end up with horns anyway. The wound heals quickly and, when properly done, the calf will look like it was polled to begin with.

The dehorner can also serve another purpose. Young cattle have a tendency to develop warts. If left, the warts can be transferred to other cattle by the affected cow rubbing on them or on something like a tree other cattle use to scratch. If the warts need to be removed—pulled, cut off or crushed—during fly season the wound needs to be sealed. An electric dehorner serves nicely for this purpose.

I dehorn because I am a commercial cattle producer and the feedlots pay just a little more for dehorned cattle. For a producer with only a couple of head, it is likely they will become semi-pets. Even being playful the horns can cause severe damage.

Electric dehorning is simple once you get the hang of it. Dehorners are inexpensive, about $40, last forever, and are well worth the cost to avoid potential horn injuries.

Words for homesteaders:

Everyone is familiar with the word "poll" in the sense of taking a survey of public opinion (and "polls" as places where votes are cast). But in Countryside, poll more commonly refers to the head, and more specifically, horns.

A naturally polled goat, sheep or bovine is naturally hornless. To poll an animal is to dehorn it.

Dehorning is cutting off horns that have already grown. But horns can also be avoided by disbudding, which kills the horn buds (usually with a hot iron, but caustics are also used) before they protrude.

The family cow:

Lessons of a backyard dairy

Eric Wilson
Maryland

In March of 1994 I bought a Jersey heifer calf from a nearby neighbor. She was eight days old when the farmer delivered her in the front seat of his pickup truck. He carried the calf across our yard to the makeshift enclosure I had built to keep her in until something better could be built. It was four walls of upright pallets and half of it was covered with an old, used sheet of plywood. I paid $75 for her.

Rosie, as she came to be known, was taught how to drink her milk replacer out of a bucket.

As she grew, we purchased a halter and a dog tether so she could be put out on a picket line to graze. The challenge became to keep her from pulling the picket post out of the ground or breaking the line altogether and getting loose.

As fall approached, Rosie was going to need a barn of some sort to stay out of bad weather, and a barn would be necessary to store hay for her. From the scrap lumber dumpster at my workplace I was able to find pallets, 2 x 4s and plywood. The three-sided structure looked more like a hillbilly barn than anything. But with some white paint it was prettied up. A pallet fence was built to keep the heifer in the barn area when she wasn't able to go out on the picket line.

For years I had wanted to raise a calf to be a milk cow and to hand milk her, make cheese, yogurt, butter, etc. I wanted to do it all from nothing. Raising a week-old calf to be a milk cow is a two-year commitment. Nothing is gained until the cow freshens and milk is extracted from her as a result of having a calf. Rosie became a pet.

The calf grew and so did her horns. They needed to be burnt off. She ate $100 of alfalfa hay her first winter.

When she was 15 months old we learned about how to tell when she was in heat. That's the 24-hour period when breeding is possible. We had her bred to a Jersey bull via artificial insemination.

We used an AI company called "Sire Power." The technician was friendly, personable, knowledgeable, and experienced. We had to tie Rosie in the barn and hold her against the wall to keep her still for the insemination.

It didn't "take" the first time, so three weeks later we called Sire Power again. They charged $17 the first time and $16 the second time.

Since she didn't go into heat again in three weeks, I assumed that she was pregnant. The waiting was a test of patience. I wondered every day if she was really pregnant or not. I wanted so much to be successful at this new endeavor. By winter she was starting to show some bigness around her belly, so I felt excited in anticipation of her future delivery of a calf.

The second winter Rosie ate $150 worth of hay. I figured she ate more because she was a full grown heifer and she needed to feed the calf growing inside her.

We still had a few incidents of her escaping from the barnyard. When we had a lot of snow and drifting, there was a drift on one side of the pallet fence and her manure bed had built up on the inside of the fence. Rosie took the leap and enjoyed grazing on dead grass exposed from windswept areas of the yard. Once I put her back in the fence, I nailed some 2 x 4s up to prevent her from jumping the fence again. I also made some effort to remove the build up of manure near the fence. The rest of the winter was uneventful.

As spring approached more and more people were asking me, "When is the cow due to have the calf?" I hadn't calculated the exact due date, but I figured it would be the end of April or early May. Once April came, I anxiously checked her every day. Was she having a discharge (water sack), was her breathing rapid, was she acting uneasy? I didn't even know if a cow has a calf standing up or lying down. (Lying down is common.) She was out on the picket line all the time now that the grass was green and growing. I was concerned about the picket line (a steel link chain by now) getting caught around the calf being born or hurting the weak, new-born calf. I didn't do anything about it; I just hoped for good luck.

One day when our kindergarten-aged son arrived home from school, my wife asked him to go check Rosie. He came back in the house in a few minutes all excited. "Mom, Rosie had her calf! It's so little! It's cute!" I was called at work with the exciting news. I asked some questions to make sure everything would be okay until I got home in a few hours. My wife took lots of really good pictures with the camera and on video. She oversaw the care of the cow and calf until I arrived.

Rosie didn't let the calf nurse. We assumed that she was tender with such full teats, and of course, this was all new to her. But with a neighbor's help we restrained the cow and helped the calf get its first meal. That was a very stressful day or two.

I worried about milk fever, so I made sure to give the cow enough mineral salt during the months prior to delivery. Rosie was fine—just stressed out from the experience. The calf was weak, but with a few meals of colostrum in her she was walking and stronger.

Since Rosie didn't let the calf nurse, I hand milked her the next morning. I got enough to feed the calf from a bottle. By that afternoon, Rosie was letting the calf nurse. That was a relief, but I had already planned on putting the calf in a separate stall and milking the cow, so that's what we did.

Everyone in my family wanted to have a turn feeding the calf. Of course, the calf needed a name too. "Bessie" was decided upon. She was a cute thing. I loved to pet her head and feel her smooth brown hair. She jumped around in her stall so much while I milked out Rosie that I would say she was practicing to be one of Santa's reindeer and was trying to jump into the air for a takeoff.

Hand milking a cow was a whole new experience for me. She was jumpy at first, and tried to kick me off her teats repeatedly the first couple of days. But she became used to the experience. We were like clock-work every morning and every evening. I would lead her from her picket line into the barn, tie her to the wall, wipe her bag off, pull up my little stool and start milking her into the 10 quart galvanized bucket that I purchased at Southern States Cooperative for $2.99.

Rosie gave four gallons of milk each day. Wow! She would have given more if I fed her grain, but I cut back on that because one day she gave three gallons just at the evening milking. The calf drank one and a half gallons a day. The remainder was for our use.

When I skimmed it, there was about one quart of cream in each gallon of milk. And it was the thickest, richest cream I have ever seen. It had a taste that I could never handle, though. Maybe because I milked it and smelled it all the time, I developed a familiarity with the smell that was distasteful to me.

My grandmother raved about the joy of using the cream in her coffee. My mother, who has a butter churn from 30 years ago, churned almost all of the butter that we have in our freezer and refrigerator. My brother made whipped cream to top homemade bread pudding: that was delicious! There was skimmed milk

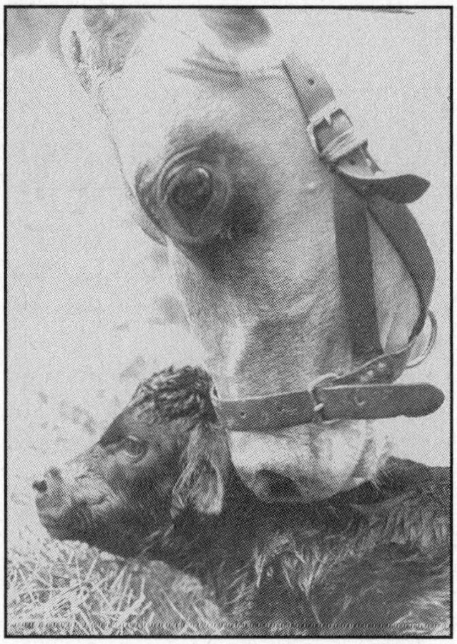

coming out of our ears. The chickens drank it, the cats and dog lapped it up, we used it in cooking, and of course we drank it when it suited our taste buds.

One evening my wife made sausage gravy using buttermilk and skim milk. The sausage was from pigs that we raised last year. That was the most delicious sausage gravy I have ever eaten.

I made cheese, too. I discovered how simple cheesemaking can be. We now have four cheeses aging on the kitchen counter. I turn them every day waiting for the rind to form. In a month or two we will sample our cheddar cheese.

There was so much milk, though. Some days it was stressful, as I wondered what I was going to do with it all. I didn't pasteurize it. I felt that it was safe enough. Nevertheless, I didn't feel comfortable selling it to neighbors. There are laws regulating such a thing!

The major problem I experienced was that it took 40 minutes to milk the cow. That was too long! Was my technique wrong? I don't think so. I believe it was because her teats were so small. I could just get two fingers on the hind teats and three fingers on the front ones. It was more like stripping the milk than milking normally. My hands would cramp up and become fatigued. After about 10 days of this I started to dread having to milk.

Nevertheless, I like the experience of rising before the sun in the quiet of the morning and being with the animals. The smells of the barn, the sounds of them eating, the beauty of the waning crescent moon rising prior to the sunrise, the warmth and softness of Rosie's side against my head, the feeling of achieving my goal of two years were all daily rewards that made it memorable.

After two weeks of milking I had to do something drastic. When I told people I was going to sell Rosie and Bessie, there were mixed replies. Some said that they understood. One told me that I had to do what made me happy. My brother said that he would buy the cow and milk her himself. I was encouraged to call the farmer from whom I bought Rosie two years ago. He said that he would buy her, but not the calf. He recommended a buyer for the calf.

Fifteen days after Rosie freshened, the cattle truck pulled up in our lane. I led Rosie for the last time across the yard to the truck. She was lured on by a can of rolled barley in my hand.

Later that evening the other fellow came for the calf. We walked down to the barn and looked at Bessie. I patted her on the head. He asked if a check was okay. I said "Yes" even though no money could replace the feelings in my heart for this dear little animal. I carried her across the yard to his truck. I thought about the day two years ago when the farmer had carried her mother across my yard from his truck. We put Bessie in the front of his pickup. She wanted to lick his ear and face. He laughed.

I didn't have any regrets. I did what I wanted to do. I enjoyed the experience. I have learned immensely more than I could learn by reading about it.

Will I do it again someday? Maybe. Right now I am just enjoying my freedom from milking morning and evening.

Last evening when I came in from doing my evening chores with the chickens I told my wife that the chickens were glad to see me. I guess what I meant was that I miss Rosie and Bessie.

What to do with a milking buck

COUNTRYSIDERS have experience, and offer advice

KARIN MACAULAY
TEXAS

I should have known that the Countryside readership would not let me down! After my call for help to gather information about "milking bucks" was published in the July/August 1997 issue, I received some very encouraging and useful responses.

The first came from Roger Ives from Connecticut. He recalls having collected semen from two milking bucks, both Alpines. He reports that "in each case the buck had excellent libido and good quality semen."

One of those bucks belonged to Marie Armstrong of New York. I contacted her, and she told me about her buck, Jeopardy. "He had so much milk in his teats that many people thought his enlarged teats were his testicles." She also provided quite impressive milk production results of his dam and offspring.

As to my worries about decreasing fertility and mastitis, she said, "He was very fertile, lots of libido... he was sold after many daughters... he was extremely healthy" and "I would not be afraid of a buck with milk in teats after my experience with this one."

Elise Presley of Arkansas steered me toward Debbie Taylor, also of Arkansas. Debbie has a milking LaMancha buck, Jupiter, who also has teats filled with milk. She describes the teats reaching a length of 3-1/2" with a diameter of about 1" but very small orifices. She has heard of another milking buck developing mastitis and nearly dying.

One interesting factor is that two-year-old Jupiter had milk only his first summer but not this year. Now I am thinking that there is a remote chance that my buck might not continue to have this problem either.

Because a problem it has become. His left teat has grown quite large and has hardened, there are some scabs on the outside. The orifices in his teats are also extremely small. Acting upon advice from Kat Thompson of Missouri, I tried to dry him off by treating him with the product "Tomorrow." This did not work. First, due to the udder being so hard, I could not milk him out. And he, much more so than any first fresheners I encountered, absolutely resents my touching his teats, making it quite an ordeal.

In addition, the tip of the "Tomorrow" tube, although quite narrow, did by no means fit into the orifice. I am now aware that I may lose him to mastitis. At this time, he is still going strong; no sign of laminitis yet.

Kat Thompson also told me that she had personally seen three French Alpine milking bucks with absolutely no fertility problems but one friend lost her buck to mastitis. Her statement, "luckily, she has some sons" made me wonder if I should not only keep his daughters but also try to keep back one of his sons, knowing that he could develop the same problem. I am still pondering this.

In the meantime, however, the doe he bred last February delivered two promising daughters. The decision has been made: this breeding season I am going to use him on as many of my does as possible. If the information I received from all these good people is sufficient to judge upon, then I am confident that his daughters should be above average milkers.

Jane Bechtel of Pennsylvania supplied an interesting article from the February 1995 issue of *Discover* magazine. Among a number of generally interesting facts (e.g., besides goats, this phenomenon applies to only one other specie, the Dayak fruit bat of Malaysia) this article by Jared Diamond states, "We've also known that many otherwise perfectly normal male domesticated goats, with normal testes and the proven ability to inseminate females, surprise their owners (and probably themselves) by spontaneously growing udders and secreting milk... Both sexes of all mammals have mammary glands. While the glands are generally less well developed and nonfunctional in males, the degree of underdevelopment varies among species." And, "It should be emphasized that male and female differences in hormones aren't absolute but a matter of degree... In particular, becoming pregnant is not the only way to acquire the hormone necessary for breast growth and milk production. Direct injection of estrogen or progesterone (hormones normally released during pregnancy) has triggered breast growth and milk production in virgin cows—and also in male goats, male guinea pigs and a steer."

And then there was the response from Karol Lowery of Texas. She owns an eight-year-old Nubian buck out of a top bloodline who, as a two-year-old, "had the beginnings of an udder." She reports that he sired normal, beautiful, show-quality babies and that his bucks went on to become herd sires. She did not change his feed, she did not milk him or treat him, she just left it alone. And this although "his udder, if anything, has gotten bigger over the years." Karol believes that trying to dry him up by the method used for does and reducing protein would "certainly not decrease the size of his udder. All it will do is weaken him." She contacted several breeders in her area, all of whom advised to ignore it.

After considering everything I have learned, I decided to do just that. If he and I are lucky, he will sire a number of offspring that may turn out to be terrific milkers. What else can one ask for?

I am very grateful to everyone who responded to my problem.

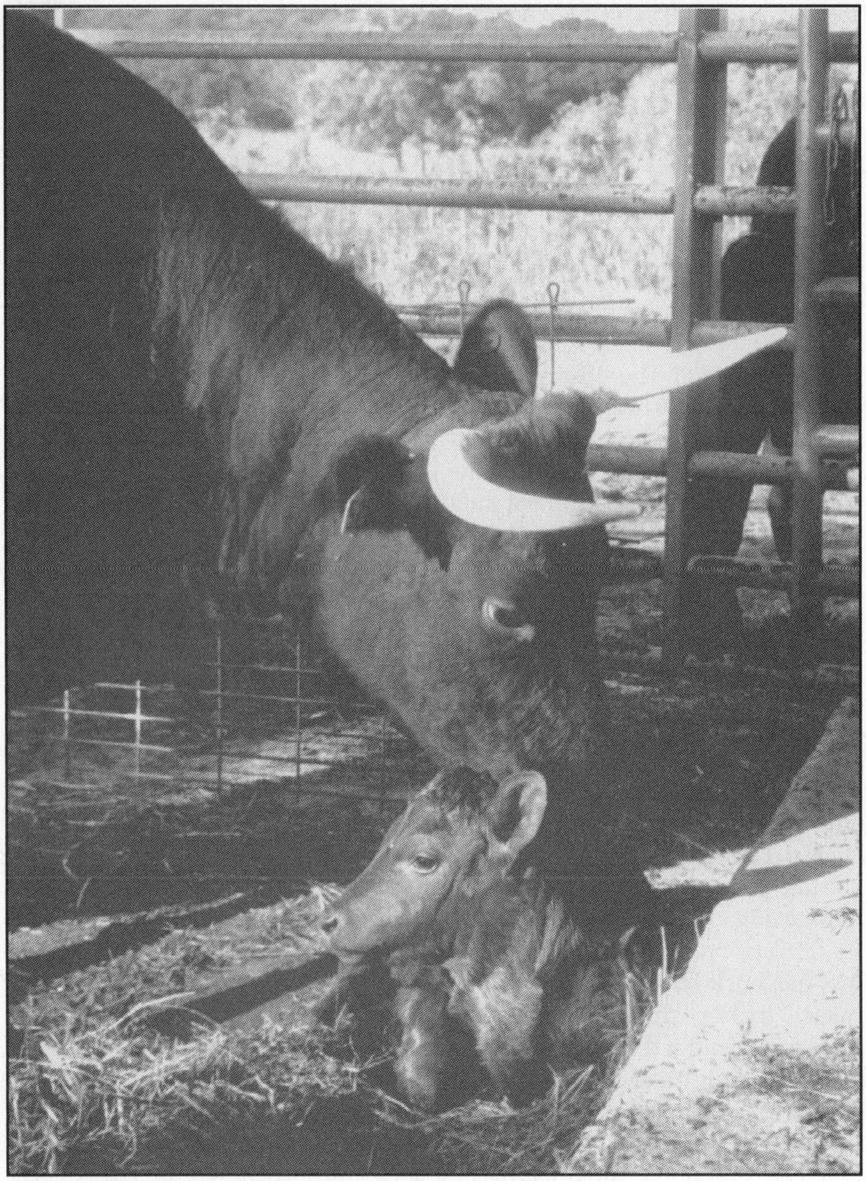

American Milking Devon: A valuable minor breed

Cindy Wilson
Wisconsin

During the bicentennial year of 1976, an effort began to locate authentic Milking Devon cattle for Old Sturbridge Village in Massachusetts. There were virtually none to be found.

A group of these Village workers teamed up with local farmers to form an organization, which has been growing annually, to find out about breeds that had once been an important part of American farm life.

In 1997, The American Livestock Breeders Conservancy (ALBC) celebrated its 20th anniversary. Membership has grown from that handful of volunteers to 4,000. The ALBC is a non-profit organization dedicated to the conservation of 100 American livestock and poultry breeds threatened with extinction.

No single organization could save 100 breeds alone, but with interaction of the ALBC members, general public, breeders and breed associations, many can participate in the ALBC's mission of conserving and promoting endangered breeds and breed-types of livestock and poultry in America. This non-profit, membership organization may engage in research, education, communication and all other acts necessary to promote its purposes.

"Rare" and "minor" breeds are minor only in that they exist in small numbers. Minor breeds of today—including asses, cattle, goats, horses, pigs, sheep and chickens—were predominant breeds of the last century and played a major role in developing North American agriculture. Characteristics of these breeds include the ability to thrive under less than ideal conditions and to convert forage and rough grazing into meat, milk and fiber. Genetic diversity, in addition to individual qualities of each breed, offers an irreplaceable resource we must maintain to be capable of responding to the changing needs of current and future agricultural practices. Once a breed is lost or destroyed, like the Lincolnshire Curly Coat pig or the Suffolk Dan cattle, there is no way to recreate them. Therefore, these resources are lost forever.

Western Europe has already lost 70 breeds of cattle and 46 breeds of pigs.

As of the 1996 census, the Milking Devon breed has 450 living females and 114 living males and has registered 831 animals since the American Milking Devon Association was formed in 1978. Wisconsin has eight farms raising purebred Milking Devons. Milking Devons can also be found in 30 other states and in Canada.

Cattle from Devonshire, England were exported to the United States as early as the 1600s. They were the first British cattle imported, although Spain had already introduced cattle in the South. Pilgrims are known to have brought the breed over from North Devon and they soon became the colonial farm's all purpose animals. They were used for meat, milk and draft, as the bulls provided a reliable source of oxen in the small New England fields of that time.

The Milking Devon is a hardy animal, adapted to survive on a low quality, high forage diet in severe climatic conditions. They are healthy, long-lived animals, marked by friendly temperaments, making them ideal family cows. They produce a gallon of milk a day with a butterfat content of at least five percent. Their small daily output is balanced by their long-term productivity. They are light-boned, so when slaughtered they yield 60% usable beef.

Historically, Devons have been held in the highest regard as draft animals. In *American Cattle: Their History, Breeding and Management,* Lewis F. Allen described the value of the Devon as oxen. "For active handy labor on the farm or highway, under the careful hand of one who likes and properly tends him, the Devon is everything that is required in an ox, in docility, intelligence, and readiness for any task demanded of him. Their activity in movement, particularly on rough hilly grounds, give them for farm labor almost equal value to the horse, with easier keep, cheaper food, and less care. For his lack of size the Devon is not so strong as other breeds, but 'for his inches', no horned beast can outwork him."

The breed has a striking appearance. Devons are a solid red, ranging from ruby or cherry red, sometimes having white markings on the tail switch, udder or scrotum. Their muzzle is flesh colored and hair around the eyes, ears, and muzzle is orange.

To be shown, Devons must carry their horns. The cow's horns are medium in length and elegantly shaped. The bull's horns are generally thicker and shorter.

Devons are of medium size. The mature cow averages 1000 to 1200 pounds; the mature bull weighs from 1200 to 1500 pounds; and a well grown ox, in good working condition, ranges from 1400 to 1600 pounds.

Even today, the Milking Devon is regarded as a valuable breed. They are ideal for the small farmer who wants to keep a small herd. ALBC Director Dr. Donald Bixby, quoted in *Country Journal,* said Milking Devons "are ideal for the small farmer. You couldn't keep a Holstein on a small farm. You couldn't afford to feed it, and you would drown in milk."

Milking Devons produce about as much milk as a goat—a gallon a day—but they are also beef and draft animals. The 1996 census found only 564 animals of the breed in the U.S.

As with all minor breeds, one does not know when their genetic contribution might be needed. The future of agriculture is not known. A new disease might crop up, a popular breed may need some help genetically with environmental survival, or agricultural systems might change. Although most present day breeders aren't anxious to crossbreed Milking Devons, documentation does exist of Holstein heifers bred to Milking Devon bulls yielding a solid black Holstein-sized animal. The activity and stamina of oxen are increased and the butterfat content of milk is also increased.

ALBC has reported Texas Longhorn cattle being bred with Devon (beef type) producing Texons.

The survival of distinct minor pure breeds is required so traits of both lines can contribute to crossbreeding.

Enthusiasm in awareness of minor breeds has mounted as artisans Aaron F. St. John, Patricia Powell Kessler and Bonnie Mohr have created paintings depicting rare breeds. These works of art have been used as promotional and public awareness campaigns for the minor breeds. The State Historical Society of Wisconsin used a photo of an oxen team in its 1997 brochure. Even musician Brian White used Milking Devons in his country music video Rebecca Lynn.

As ALBC states on the cover of its 20th Anniversary Breeders Directory, "Rare breeds are part of our national heritage and represent a unique piece of Earth's biodiversity. The loss of these breeds would impoverish agriculture and diminish the human spirit."

For further information:

American Livestock Breeders Conservancy, PO Box 477, Pittsboro, NC 27312; 919-542-5704; www.albc-usa.org;

American Milking Devon Association, Susan Randall, Sec., 135 Old Bay Rd., New Durham, NH 03855, www.milkingdevons.org.

Dick Gradwohl with a 38" miniature Hereford, while two 78" oxen look on with what appears to be curious disbelief!

Big opportunities in small cattle

Professor Richard Gradwohl
Washington

As 100-500 acre family farms continue to disappear, the small acreage family homestead farm is becoming more common. The smaller cattle breeds are particularly well-suited to these smaller farms, and their popularity is increasing. At last count there were 15 breed categories of miniature cattle in the Miniature Cattle Breeds Registry.

Arlene Gradwohl with a mini Kentshire calf and its mother.

Miniature cattle are either selected reproductions of the older breeds, or a result of several crossbreed programs. Crossbreed programs have the advantage of creating heterosis (higher performance levels) in their progeny. Whenever you cross one distinct breed with another the results can be an animal with outstanding performance characteristics.

Small cattle are easier on the land, equipment, and facilities. Those of us who once had large cattle remember the constant work on fencing, barn repairs, and hours mending broken equipment. The small animals just don't have the bulk to do much harm. Pastures seem to stay greener longer because these miniature cattle weigh less and their hooves are smaller. You don't need heavy duty equipment, and maintenance is rare.

These two Kentshire heifers are almost five months old, and only 32" tall.

Some folks with small acreage farms purchase one large animal to raise their own beef. Cattle are herd animals. You need more than one. It's much easier to maintain a small herd than a solitary animal. A solitary animal just does not do as well as two or three together. With the small breeds it is possible to put two or three animals in the same area that you might put just one large animal. This is much better for the animals.

More animals per acre is the key here. Because you can raise more animals in the same amount of space, beef production is twice to three times as much. It takes about five acres to raise two large animals, depending on location (soil and climate) and the pasture available. You could raise one or two animals per acre with one of the small cattle breeds. It doesn't take a computer scientist to figure out total beef production per acre is much greater with the smaller cattle.

These smaller cattle are 25% more efficient than their larger counterparts in terms of feed conversion, and therefore eat much less. About

1/3 the feed is typical.

Miniature cattle come closer to a family's needs than large commercial beef. One beef per locker is a lot more desirable than raising more beef than you need.

Miniature cattle can also be a great investment and at the same time be helpmates with the grass and brush. They are also much less intimidating and easier to handle.

However, the truth of the matter is that they make great pets. Most owners of these great little animals would probably never consider them for beef purposes. Because they are easy to work with, it's very easy to give them names and develop bonding relationships. On our miniature cattle farm we have Little Red, Blue Girl, Green Girl, Misty, Snuggles, Little Lady, Violet, Happy, Danny Boy, Nutmeg and quite a few others. All the girls are expecting, so we will have quite a few more.

Have we eaten some of our miniatures? Yes, we have. You can't keep all the bulls. They do produce excellent quality meat. One piece of advice: if you are going to use one or two for beef, don't give them names.

If you have questions or comments about the breeds of miniature cattle call or write the Miniature Cattle Breeds Registry. You can order a breeders' information packet on the 15 miniature cattle breeds or you can subscribe to the Miniature Cattle Breeds Newsletter by contacting 25204 156th Ave. SE, Covington, WA 98042; 253-631-1911; www.minicattle.com; info@minicattle.com.

Words for homesteaders

The above story uses two words that often confuse city people.

A heifer is a young female bovine that has not yet freshened (given birth to a calf).

A Hereford is a cattle breed developed in England, having a reddish coat and white markings.

Raising fallow deer

CLAUSE & JOANNE MILLER
ILLINOIS

When we moved to the country in the summer of '93, we began looking for some type of animal that would lend itself to our hilly pastures. We considered buffalo or emus, but heard some scary tales about them. Besides, they were expensive.

We checked into fallow deer, a European breed that is smaller than our native whitetail. They cost less than cattle, but do require eight-foot fences. That was our biggest expense. The amount of pasture needed for one cow will take care of seven deer. Their meat has no wild taste and is very lean—great for those concerned about cholesterol and heart conditions. They come in three colors: tan with white spots, chocolate brown, and white.

The following spring we purchased nine bred does, seven chocolate and two spotted. Later, we bought a chocolate and a spotted buck, each four years old. Even though they have been raised in captivity, they are naturally skittish and panic easily, although one spotted doe will eat corn out of our hand. We named her Granny, since she is older than the others and seems to have been treated like a pet.

Buckwheat is seven years old.

She is the only doe named. It is our policy to never name anything we are going to eat! The bucks will be kept for breeding only, so they became Buckwheat and Barley.

The next year, we bought 10 spotted and three chocolate does, followed by another chocolate and spotted buck. These bucks became Sorghum and Milo. Since then, we've added Oats, Rye and Wheat. Some day we might get really exotic and add Triticale and Amaranth!

We purchased a used portable hammermill to grind their winter feed which consists of alfalfa, protein supplements, corn and dry molasses. During pasturing season, we give only small amounts of this.

Our second year, 100% of the does produced babies. The third year, we had 25 fawns out of 26 does. We are really excited about these percentages.

This year we butchered eight young culls. We are not set up for home butchering, so we used the local slaughter plant. They, in turn, helped find buyers for the carcasses that we didn't need for ourselves.

We gave one carcass to a restaurant in Vermont, Illinois. They plan to do a venison night. This may open up another market for our meat. Other markets are breeding stock, trophy bucks for hunting preserves, and antlers. Our extra bucks aren't old enough yet for hunting preserves. We have shipped some antlers to a business in Wisconsin, and we have enough to send to another outlet in Texas. They are used for knife handles, furniture decorations, hat racks and other craft items.

The bucks lose their antlers in April and start the new growth within two weeks. During the growth period, the antlers are covered with a soft fuzzy layer called velvet. By the end of August, when the racks are full size, this layer comes off and they are a hard bony texture.

We now have 70 deer, ranging from one to seven years old. Rut (mating) season begins in October and lasts through December. The bucks can be dangerous during this time. Their necks swell up and they make noises that sound like an angry old sow. Naturally, we take extra precautions if we need to be in the pens. This year fawning began the first week of June.

Our deer are becoming quite a local attraction. We frequently have people come to see them. Of course, our grandchildren love to stand at the fence and give Granny her snack. We welcome visitors.

In the future, we would like to turn our north acreage (wooded, with gullies and a pond) into a preserve for bow hunters. But for now, we are happy to step outside in the early morning and marvel at their frisky antics over the hillside.

Livestock health:

Nitrate poisons livestock, silently and swiftly

Ken Scharabok
Tennessee

The following information was released by the University of Tennessee Agricultural Extension Service:

A cattle producer in Central Georgia woke up one morning to find dead cows littered across his pasture. Of 72 cows, 62 had died in one night.

An autopsy revealed that the cause of death was nitrate poisoning. The source of the nitrate was the hay provided to the cattle the previous day.

Nitrate is a naturally occurring chemical found in plants. It contains nitrogen used in protein formation under good growing conditions. During a drought, however, when plant growth slows or stops, nitrates accumulate. That's because plant roots continue to take up nitrogen, but water isn't available for plant growth.

If you cut hay when nitrate levels are high, there's the potential for poisoning later when you feed the hay. Nitrates are stable and don't degrade with time.

When cattle (and presumably other livestock} consume hay high in nitrate, the nitrate is converted to a compound called nitrite. The nitrite moves into the bloodstream, combines with hemoglobin in the red blood cells and prevents them from carrying oxygen. The result is suffocation.

To avoid a tragedy on your farm, recognize factors which will increase the likelihood of high nitrate levels in hay. Many grasses will accumulate nitrates, but pearl millet, sorghum-sudan hybrids and johnsongrass will build up high levels.

Grasses such as Bermuda grass and tall fescue which have been heavily fertilized with nitrogen and harvested under drought stress may have toxic levels of nitrates.

Pay special attention to hay fields which have had large amounts of animal manures applied to them. The rates of nitrogen applied to these fields are often several times higher than those in which artificial fertilizer has been used.

If you think you have some hay which could possibly have high levels of nitrates, contact your local Extension office. You can have the hay tested and get a feeding strategy developed.

(Be particularly cautious with hay from fields which have been heavily fertilized with either hog manure or poultry litter. Both can contain significantly more nitrogen than cattle manure. Before allowing hog manure or poultry litter to be spread on your land, even if it's free, consult your local Extension office for a recommendation on the maximum amount which can be safely spread per acre.)

Livestock health:

This scene came from "Little Farm" in Pennsylvania...with no further identification or explanation. But then, with a picture like this, what can you say? Winter on the homestead!

Watering livestock in winter

Frozen buckets of water can be a headache, especially if you have to haul water any distance. Livestock care is never as easy in cold weather as it is during the summer, but here are some ideas to make it easier.

Water piped to the barn is a blessing in any season. A hose from the house will work in summer, but when it freezes, you'll need a pipe buried below frost depth and a frost-proof spigot. With such plumbing, if you have enough animals in one class to justify a stock tank and electric heater (electricity in the barn is also a blessing), winter chores will be less time-consuming and your stock will have plenty of water.

If you provide water in buckets, teach your animals a drinking routine. Bring them warm water twice a day, making sure every animal has a chance to drink all it wants. Then take the buckets away. No more denting and smashing buckets by banging giant ice cubes out of them, and your chores will be finished sooner too. (Rubber buckets are marginally easier to deal with in freezing weather, and they stand up better, but they're still a pain. Plastic ones, of course, are impossible in this situation.)

Heaters are available for poultry waterers. Even a light bulb under a waterer can prevent freezing, if you take extreme care to ensure that the bulb and electrical components won't get wet.

An alternative might be to bring a bucket of hot water to the henhouse at chore time to thaw out the waterer and provide a new supply. This doesn't work well in extreme cold because of the shape and constrictions of chicken waterers. It's somewhat more satisfactory with some rabbit waterers that are wider at the top than at the bottom.

Another alternative is to have spare watering utensils. Bring one with fresh water and take the frozen one to a warm place to thaw out. This is especially handy with rabbits, even using ball-point waterers.

Although not solutions in really cold weather, there are a few tricks you can use that will help on days when the mercury hovers around the freezing point. One is to be sure the water container is in the warmest possible location, and in the sun. Don't give the animals way more than they will drink: it's easier to deal with a little ice, than a lot. Make sure they have plenty to drink in the morning and evening, but remove or empty the containers at night.

Don't worry about providing heated water, thinking it will take longer to freeze. It won't.

Chores in winter are seldom as pleasant as they are in summer, but with a little thought and perhaps creativity, you can see to it that your animals have enough to drink without spending all of your time on the bucket brigade.

Winter livestock care

Ken Scharabok
Tennessee

Unless you live in a severe winter climate, most livestock does not need to be housed during winter months. They will grow a heavier winter coat and build up a fat layer under the skin to help insulate them. However, this is not to say some winter protection should not be provided.

For the most part, winter protection should be offered in the form of a windbreak which allows the livestock to soak up whatever sunlight is present, while at the same time keeping them out of the wind chill influence.

One effective windbreak for an open pasture is in the form of a 90° right angle shape. Draw one on paper and note that it offers 360° wind protection. Put the point of the wedge into the prevailing wind.

Such windbreaks can be of natural or scrounged material. One possible plant for a natural barrier is the American Arborvitae, which is an evergreen. When purchased in quantity, they cost about $1.50 each. A wedge with 75' legs would run about $75.00.

For scrounged material, check with local companies which replace single and double-wide garage doors. Quite likely they will allow you to haul these off to avoid having to dispose of them themselves.

If your pasture area is all in one field, a single windbreak should be sufficient. If you are practicing rotational grazing, one possibility is to build more than one windbreak and leave pasture gates open as necessary to allow livestock access to the windbreak when they need it.

While comfort of the livestock is one consideration, the economic aspect is that the less energy they have to expend keeping warm translates into less feed you have to provide to maintain them at a certain level.

How to weigh livestock without a scale

We often want to weigh animals...for medicating, marketing, or record-keeping.

Small pigs are commonly weighed on hanging scales. You can weigh a chicken or a rabbit on a kitchen scale, or a bathroom scale. Many animals can be weighed by weighing yourself on a bathroom scale, then weigh yourself holding the animal.

But what do you do when the critter is too large to lift or hold? Here are some suggestions:

Pig: To estimate the weight of a pig, measure the heart girth, and the length from between the ears to the base of the tail. Then, heart girth X heart girth X length divided by 400 = the weight.

Sheep: To estimate the weight of a sheep or goat, measure the heart girth from a point slightly behind the shoulder blade and behind the elbow. Measure the length of the body from the point of the shoulder to the point of the rump. Then:

Heart girth X heart girth X body length divided by 300 = weight in pounds.

Example: A ram has a heart girth of 39 inches and a body length of 33 inches. How much does it weigh?

39 X 39 = 1,521. 1,521 X 33 = 50,193. 50,193 divided by 300 = 167 lbs.

Steer: To estimate the weight of a steer, use this formula devised by Prof. James A. Bennett, of Utah State Agricultural College:

[(Heart girth in inches X 27.5758) - 1049.67] X 1.04 = Live wt in lbs.

Example: A steer has a heart girth of 63 inches.

Multiply 63 by 27.5758: 1737.2754.

Subtract 1049.67: 1737.27 - 1049.67 = 687.6.

Multiply the remainder by 1.04: 687.6 X 1.04 = 715 lbs.

The heart girth is measured around the body just in back of the shoulders. Pull the tape snug.

For the most accurate results, keep the animal off feed and water for at least 12 hours. Be sure the animal is standing squarely on all four legs, with the head up in a normal position.

How to make rennet

Rennet is used to coagulate milk to make cheese. Today it's generally purchased from cheesemaking supply houses, but here's how it was made at home in the old days.

Clean the stomach of a calf as soon as it is killed, scouring it inside and out with salt. When perfectly clean, tack it on a frame to dry in the sun for a day.

Cut it in squares and pack it down in salt, or keep it in wine or brandy.

When you want to use the rennet, soak a square half an hour in cold water, wash it well, and put it in the milk tied to a string so it can be drawn out without breaking the curd.

How long does it take to do chores?

Enterprise	Feed	Water	Clean or groom	Bedding	Care of animal/ products
1 cow	2-3 times daily, 12 min. each	With automatic waterer, none. By hand, 5-10 min.	8 min. daily	Daily, 15 min.	Milking, twice daily, 20 min. each
2 goats	Twice daily, 12 min.	Daily, 5-10 min.	Daily, 4 min.	Daily, 4 min., 4 times annually, 2 hours	Milking twice daily, 10 min.
2 sheep	Twice daily, 10 min	Daily, 5 min. trimming, crutching, docking, etc.	Periodic hoof 4 X yr., 2 hrs.	Daily 2 min,	Variable
1 steer	Twice daily, 15 min.	Daily, 5 min.	-0-	weekly, 2 hours	-0-
1 veal calf	Twice daily, 20 min.	Daily, 5 min.	Daily, 2 min.	Daily, 10 min.	-0-
25 hens	Daily, 2 min.	Daily, 3 min.	-0-	Weekly, 25 min.	Daily, 5 min.
12 ducks	Daily, 2 min.	-0-	-0-	Weekly, 15 min.	-0-
3 rabbits	Daily, 7 min.	Daily, 8 min.	-0-	Daily, 6 min; Weekly, 15 min.	-0-
4 bee hives	-0-	-0-	32 hours per year	0	Variable
1 horse	2-3 times daily, 15 min.	With automatic watering, none. By hand, 10 min.	Daily, 15 min.	Daily, 15 min.	-0-

The pig pen:

Little pigs don't get fevers... and that's bad

When little pigs get sick, they don't get a fever. And that can kill them. Studies at the University of Missouri-Columbia have shown that a newborn pig's immune system does not respond to a disease challenge by producing a fever. Instead, the newborn's body temperature can drop to sub-normal levels—and that could help explain death rates in baby pigs.

Currently, 12 to 15 percent of piglets die before they are weaned.

"Loss in body temperature contributes to the pig's poor growth and even death," said Bob Matteri. He and John Klir, both USDA Agriculture Research Service scientists, are the first to identify the previously unknown mechanism in baby pigs that contributes to lower body temperature.

"We found an immaturity in the pig's immune response, such that the newborn does not develop a fever," said Matteri. Now he's trying to figure out why that happens. Once we know that, we might be able to supplement feed so the little pig won't run out of energy stores."

"We have created an experimental model to help show why some animals get a fever and some don't," Klir said. "The model will be used while working with pigs in controlled environment chambers to improve the newborn pig's chance of survival when challenged by diseases."

Saving little pigs is a worthwhile effort. U.S. Department of Agriculture scientists estimate that saving one piglet per litter born in the United States is worth $350 million dollars annually.

How to repair shoes

MARY GIBSON
MONTANA

Ralph Eich of Shelton, Washington asked about shoe repair so here is what I have on the subject.

Ripped seams

You need a packet of hand sewing needles. The packet contains different shaped needles, each about 4 inches in length and designed for a specific purpose. You will need extra long thread, either carpet thread or polyester-cotton-wrapped thread.

1. Pull apart the seam until you meet resistance. Stop at this point. Remove all old stitching.

2. Choose the proper needle from the kit. If your hand will fit behind the seam, a straight needle will work. If the seam is located close to the shoe toe, select the curved needle.

3. To sew a fine seam, use single thread. Use double or even triple strands of thread when the original holes are large enough. For a more water resistant seam, first coat the thread with wax.

4. Close the seam by sewing through the original holes. Take care not to enlarge them. Make stitches taut.

5. Secure the finished seam by repeating the final stitch several times; a knot is unnecessary. To achieve a smooth finish pound or rub the stitching into the leather.

Attaching leather half-soles

Sewing on new half-soles will require a last, an item not easily come by. Search second hand stores, antique stores, etc. Made of metal, it resembles an inverted leg with a foot (for holding the shoe) and is attached to a wooden base. (See illustration.)

In addition to a last, you will need clinching nails and an awl for making new holes in leather. You can make

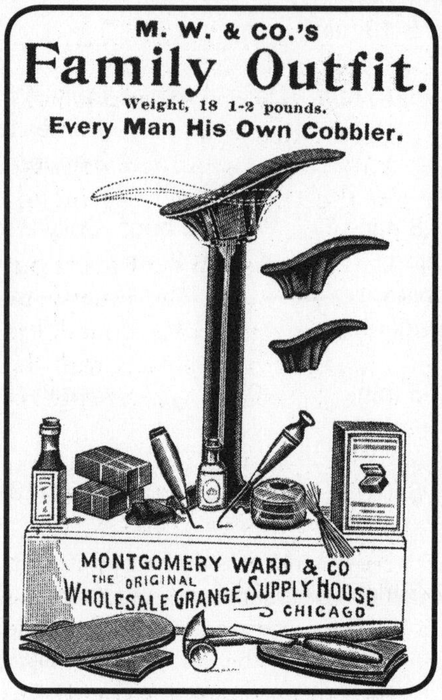

one from a hardwood dowel of a size that fits your grip comfortably. Drive a long, heavy nail perpendicularly through the center of the dowel, allowing a portion of the point to extend beyond the wood. Hammer the extension flat against the wood to secure the spike in the dowel. Flatten the nail head with a hammer and grind it to a smooth point with a coarse file.

1. Buy precut half-soles, or purchase leather and cut your own.

2. Soak the half-sole or leather piece for 10 minutes in tepid water. This makes cutting and sewing easier. Then wrap newspaper around the leather to absorb excess water.

3. If you are making a sole, place the sole of the shoe on the leather and trace around it. Carefully cut along the outline with a sharp knife.

4. Place shoe on the last. With a pen knife or razor blade, cut the old threads on the original half sole. Lift the sole and separate it from the shoe with a somewhat diagonal cut at the arch.

5. Bevel the new half-sole so that it slightly extends over what remains of the old sole.

6. Clinching-shoe nails range from 3/8 to 7/8 inch in length. Choose one a half size larger than the total thickness of both new sole and shoe. Hammer in about 9 nails along the juncture of the new and old half-soles. Next nail down the tip and sides of the half-sole.

7. Using a sharp knife, trim the edge of the sole for neatness.

8. Cut a shallow depression or trough on the sole's bottom where the stitching will be. Having the stitches recessed protects them from wear.

9. With the old holes of the shoe welt (a strip of leather sewn in the seam between the upper of a shoe and the sole to reinforce their joining) to guide you, use the awl to make holes from the topside in the half-sole. Every other hole will be enough.

10. Take a waxed strand of thread 3 feet long and thread two needles, one at each end of the thread. Begin at the first hole closest to the arch. Run the needles consecutively through the same opening, one needle in one direction and the second needle in the other direction. Sew such opposing stitches all around the sole. To secure the final stitch, either sew the last stitch several times or make a knot. Cut excess thread.

11. Complete your work by pounding down the depression made for the stitches in the sole. Rub all the needle holes, stitches and cracks with wax or shoe polish.

Sewing needle for leather

Take the "key" used to open sardine and ham cans. Straighten the handle end, and hammer and file, or grind it to a point. Thread sewing material through the slot at the opposite end.

Making tire tread shoes

Becca Haughn
Ohio

This is in response to the request for possible shoes in the future when we'll need to make and repair our own.

To make tire tread shoes you'll need:

An old tire and inner tube
Carpet tacks
Chalk or soap
Mat knife
Scissors
Hammer

Trace each foot with chalk or soap on the tire. Mark your left foot as right and right foot as left as the pieces will be turned tread side down.

Cut out pieces with a mat knife. It will be tough to cut.

With your scissors cut two strips from the inner tube, 3-4 inches wide.

Put your foot on the tire cut out (tread side down). Lay inner tube strip across your foot and mark the point for attachment even with the bottom of the sole. Cut the strip on lines.

Fasten strip to sole with hammer and tacks. Repeat for other foot.

They should be ready to wear.

As you become comfortable with these perhaps you could come up with your own creations. Enclose it for winter-type wear, thong it for flip flops, or perhaps you could raise them to be boots.

I've heard that these treads can be applied to worn shoes, etc. to extend their life.

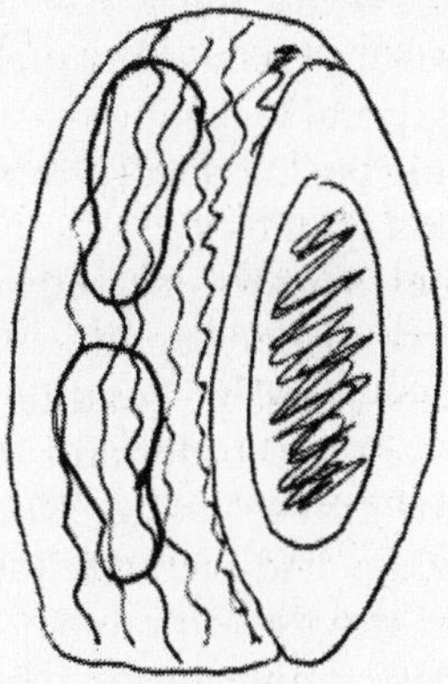

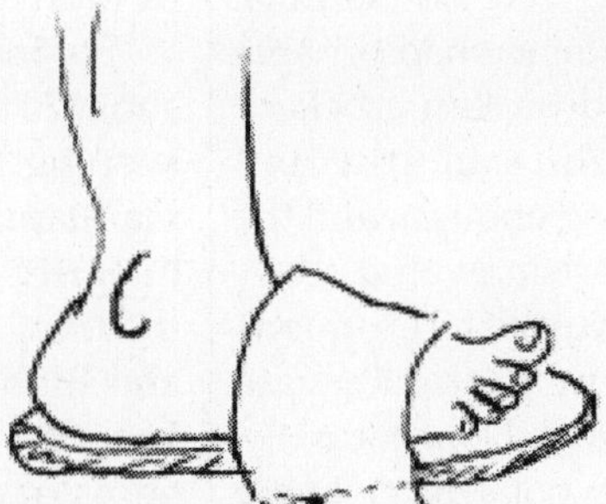

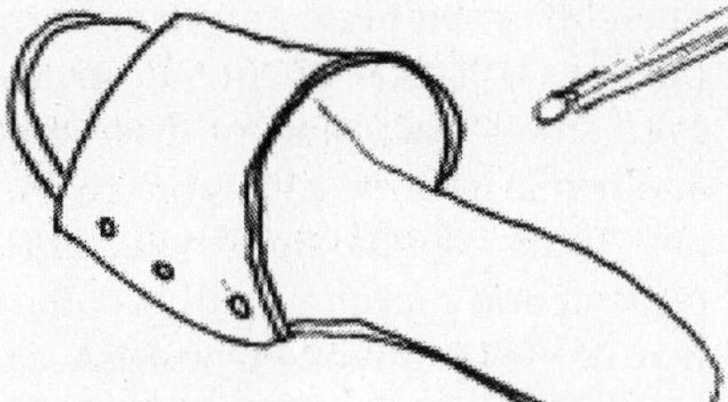

Becca Haughn

How to repair a sock

One old sock will repair two socks. Remove the portion for sock to be repaired.

Cut toe and sole pieces from another sock and stitch as shown. Sew new toe and sole to bottom of old sock.

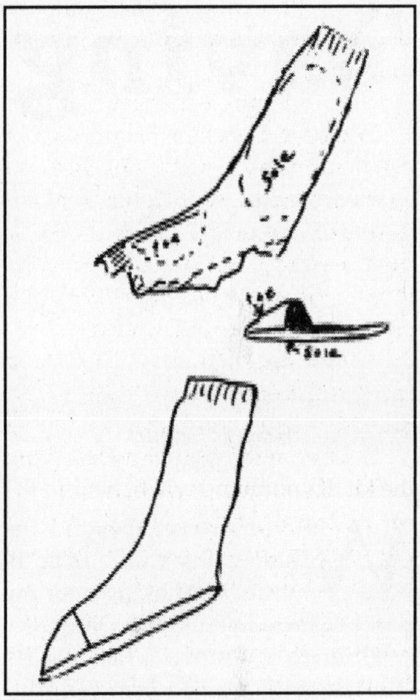

Combat country mud with this homemade boot remover

You can construct your own boot remover with three pieces of scrap plywood or other wood, two nails and two wood screws. (See the diagram for instructions.)

To use, just hold the baseboard flat on the floor with one foot and pull the other foot into the concave cut. Pull up and one boot is off. Repeat for the other foot.

This works well for boots of any kind and is great in the winter or in the mud of spring and fall. – *Jim & Julie Hunter*

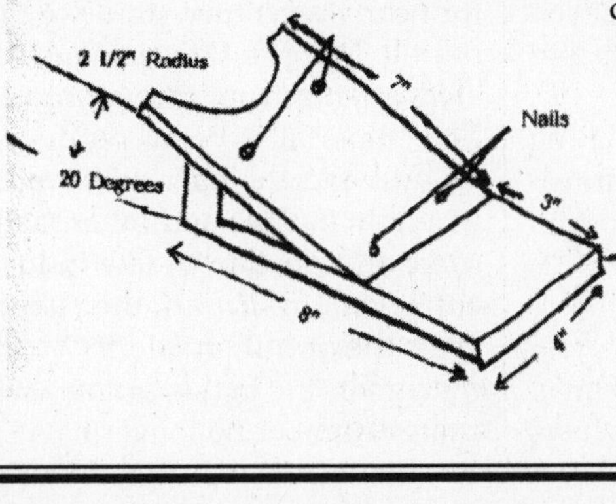

It's not just recycling: it's saving the good stuff

JAMES F. GILFILEN
OHIO

We progressed beyond the sidewalks a little over 10 years ago, taking over my parents' farm in southern Ohio.

Prior to the move, I had used a short moving van to bring in four maximum weight loads of collected junk from our former home in Denver, Colorado. With the old barn so full that a person could not walk through safely, I had to solve the space problem soon.

I took evenings after work to dismantle an old house in the local village for wood to begin an additional storage building. This building is two stories high, on a 20' x 32' concrete pad. After more than six years, this building is so full that you have to "kick a path" through to find anything.

At present I am contemplating ways to add some more room for junk, using the wood and tin from an old barn I moved for a neighbor.

The rationale behind it

Collecting good old stuff may seem irrational to folk who have been reared to pitch out anything not immediately usable. Please let me reason with you who maintain this idea.

Before the age of efficient manufacturing, all things were used until they were no longer economically repairable. Then they served one last purpose: heating the house for a short while. There were no landfills. Instead, each residence had an area where bottles and broken crockery were dumped. You can still find these if you dig long enough, and the bottles are of surprising value.

During the Industrial Age, goods were produced at a greater rate than they were used. Consequently, the sellers had to convince people to throw away stuff and buy new things. This worked reasonably well for nearly a century, until we threw out the Monroe Doctrine and tolerated buying from foreign markets. This material is being produced at an ever-increasing rate by people who pay income and other taxes in some other nation. A few industrial entrepreneurs in another country keep the profit, while 99% of the consumers are in this country where a large number no longer have high paying jobs.

In the light of this reasoning, why do we still maintain the old mentality of "junk it and buy new"? I hope some readers wake up before we become slaves to the state because of ever-increasing taxes. If the grass roots begin general recycling in earnest, maybe big business will rethink its motives and methods.

For instance, a nearby local city of about 20,000 population has difficulty keeping streets in usable condition, maintaining law and order and the integrity of the infrastructure. When the local workers had plenty of jobs and high pay it was no problem to keep the taxes coming in for these necessary benefits. Presently, taxes must be raised to do any rebuilding. Incomes will consequently drop, and even smaller amounts of discretionary funds will be available to buy new things. Dumpster diving, trash picking and recycling will become a way of life for anyone who wishes to survive and stay warm.

My wife of 40 years is very patient with me, making little effort to guide me into more "sensible" modes of thinking.

Where I work, an effort is made

to collect and recycle paper from the offices. The recycler does not take slick paper, nor newsprint, nor boxes. That stuff is hauled to the landfill. For every pound of paper that is recycled, probably 99 pounds is rejected and trashed.

The whole scene of trash and landfills is frustrating to the sensible person who rejects the false idea behind them. America needs to find some good use for unwanted items and stop using landfills. Government will certainly not support poking through trash piles. In our nearby city, there is a law against dumpster diving.

The businesses that have arisen from the need to reuse good stuff are few. Goodwill stores, the Salvation Army stores, and an assortment of "near-new" shops are making their effort to keep good stuff alive. Of course, the producers of new stuff will balk noisily and mightily at this effort, but we need to impact the whole system to bring about preservation of our resources and our scarce, heavily taxed money.

It's like having a hardware store in your backyard

Some examples offered: I like to poke around the barn and my storage buildings to find a "new" shovel or hoe. If I need a board I need only to go out back and fish one out of the treasury there.

I take all offerings graciously. My co-workers give me their old engine oil which I spread (without EPA approval) upon my gravel road to keep down the dust. (See note.) There is a use for anything. If not for me, maybe a friend needs something I have.

Hardly a week goes by that I do not find some articles of furniture thrown out where I work. I have given many nice broken office chairs to a friend who is unemployed and repairs them to sell. Re-use just makes good sense. Throwing away repairable items does not make sense.

A short time ago, a fellow of the same persuasion as I brought me two pickup loads of new clothing patterns from a defunct local sew shop. So far, my wife has sold or disposed of about 200 of them, which hardly scratches the surface. I hope to sell them this summer at a local flea market. Those patterns carry a price of $5 to $10 each!

Last summer a contractor gave me about 1,500 square feet of used rubber roofing material as he was removing it from one of the campus buildings. It kills weeds en masse, and will eventually be a watertight liner for a good size pond.

A local enterprising person hauls wrong colored and outdated house paint from a certain class A paint company's stores, and sells it nearby for $3 to $5 per gallon. Where do you imagine I got all the nice matching color of paint for all our building roofs? About 20 gallons at $3 per is pure gold. I got 25 gallons of 20-year outside house paint for the same price, and it is living up to its guarantee. That is first class recycling!

About a year ago, the university pitched out about 50 bags of 12-12-12 commercial fertilizer that water damaged. I worked hard to collect 14 of them out of the dumpster. I don't use it here, but somebody surely does.

The school changed the pool filtration system and pitched 25 big bags of diatomaceous earth; guess how I dispose of them.

Common old freight skids can be used for fences and pens, and pallets to keep firewood dry. Years ago I figured how to saw them up without hitting a single nail, and they make very good dry firewood.

The local library fills up a large dumpster each week with outdated magazines and unusable donated books. Needless to say, I have a good magazine collection.

The possibilities are endless.

Granted that all folks are not as "lucky" as I am, but persistence pays off.

One thing that helps me is the pride that these tradition bound, "mountain" people have. They would pass up a penny on the sidewalk, because it would somehow demean them to bend over and pick it up. No one—I mean it—will scavenge in a dumpster around our town. Even the street people avoid them. This nation will have to learn someday to get serious about recycling.

I hope some more of you folk have been sparked to get interested in saving the good stuff.

***Probably all homesteaders are in favor of recycling. However, many will be alarmed at some of the suggestions in this article.**

For example, most homesteaders (we hope) will frown on spreading used motor oil on a road to keep down dust. The contaminated soil and/or water resulting from this form of "recycling" makes it a very poor solution indeed. The only proper way to recycle used oil is to take it to a recycling center.

It should be noted that the diatomaceous earth used in swimming pool filters is not the same as the diatomaceous earth used by gardeners and livestock raisers.

Family album:

Virginia Minden-Mills, Rio Linda California, is developing a breed of rabbit she calls the Velveteen Lop. These unidentified young ladies obviously approve.

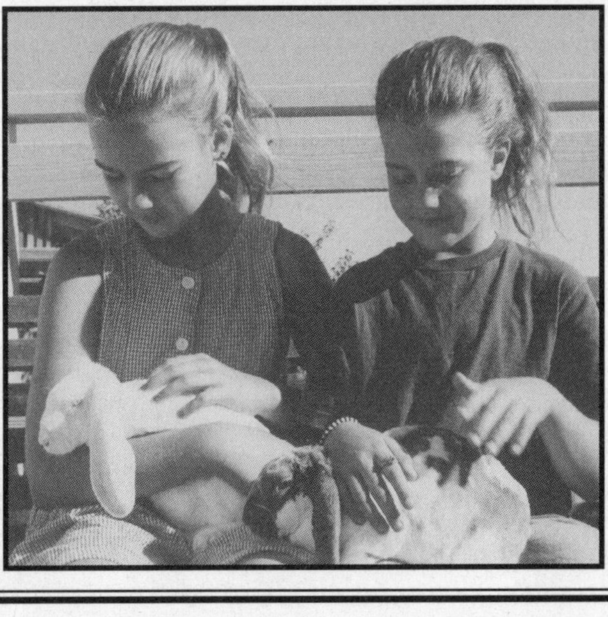

Activities for indoor fun

MARY HEALY
MONTANA

Playdough

This recipe for playdough makes a nice soft dough that will last for up to a year in the refrigerator, or several months in a covered container on the counter. It tastes terrible and could make a child feel ill if eaten, but is not dangerous to eat. I suggest this for children over age two who will understand not to eat it.

2 cups flour
1/2 cup salt
1 tablespoon alum
2 packages Kool Aid drink mix (unsweetened)

Mix the above ingredients in a saucepan, then add the following:
2 cups water
3 tablespoons oil

Mix and cook over medium heat for 5-10 minutes, stirring continuously. When the mixture has thickened and forms a ball it is ready. Before it is ready it will look awful and be slimy and lumpy, and your arm will be about to fall off. Keep stirring, you are almost done. When it has formed a ball, take it out of the pot, and place on the counter to cool. Knead with a little extra flour to get rid of the lumps.

Provide rolling pins or short dowels, cookie cutters, and small containers for the pretend cook in your family, or get out the toy cars and make roads and landscapes. Children aged 3-5 particularly like this activity, but anyone aged 1 to 90 will enjoy the feel of this dough.

Purchase alum in the pickling or spice section of the grocery store, or better yet (and usually cheaper) at the drug store or a tanning supply outlet. The alum is a pickling and preserving agent used for pickles and tanning hides. Kool Aid provides the color and a wonderful fragrance, but can be substituted with food coloring.

Fish pond

Children love to fish in a pretend fish pond, and will fish over and over, even for the same things.

The easiest fish pond is made of paper fish with paper clip noses, and a fishing pole made of a short sturdy twig with a string fishing line, and a strong magnet for a hook.

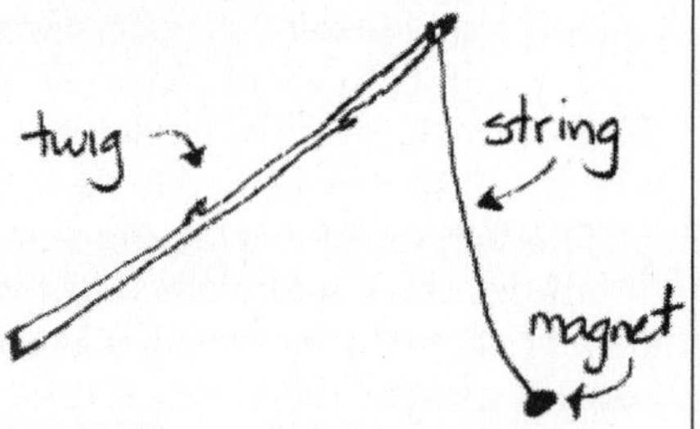

Cut out several fish from different colors of scrap paper or light cardboard (the heavy paper and cardboard will require a stronger magnet). You and the children could color the fish with markers or crayons. Attach a paper dip to each fish and throw them on the floor behind the sofa, or into a large cardboard box "lake." Have the children take turns "fishing." For older children, put simple math questions or reading words on the fish, and have them answer the question when they catch a fish.

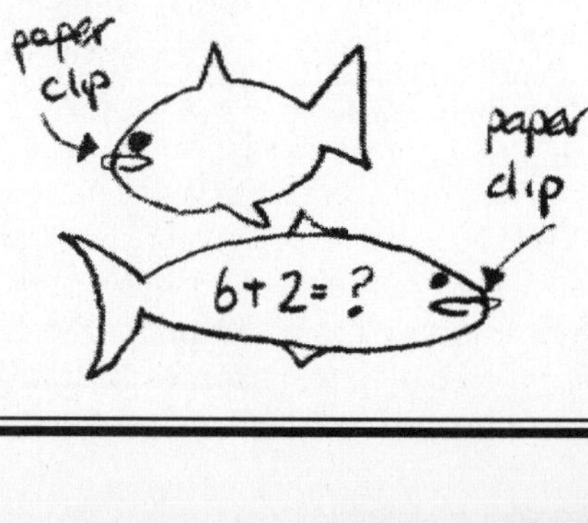

If you have the time to be the fishy helper, you can look around the house for small objects such as pencils, socks, toy cars, cookies etc. and attach them to the fishing line by removing the magnet and tying a spring clothes pin for quick "fish" changes. If you have older children, they could be the fishy helper for you. The fishy helper hides behind the sofa or a large box with his supply of "fish" and attaches an object when the child throws his line "into the water."

Dress up hats

Children have wonderful imaginations and can turn themselves into someone else with the simplest of props. Shannon's favorite has always been queens and princesses, but your children will adapt these simple hats to whatever their current favorite is.

Cereal or cracker boxes make wonderful crowns. Open out the box, trim off the top and bottom flaps and measure out a piece about 4-6" wide and a little longer than the size of your child's head. Cut points or other fancy designs on one long side. Have your child decorate the crown with markers or crayons, fabric scraps (glued on), or aluminum foil (this is a great use for used foil that has small tears in it, as the tears don't matter here.) Tape, glue or staple the hat together to fit the child's head. This hat can be painted red to be a fireman, have buttons glued on to be a jeweled crown, or be whatever your child wants.

For an old fashioned princess hat, take a large piece of paper such as used gift wrap, paper grocery bags, newspaper etc., and roll it into a cone. Adjust the bottom of the cone to fit your child's head, and tape, glue or staple shut. Trim the bottom edge to make it round. Attach a string or elastic to keep the hat on. If desired, attach some strips of newspaper, scrap fabric or leftover gift wrap ribbon to the point of the hat for streamers. The streamers should be very light or the hat won't stay on. Get out your old shoes, that dress you never wear, some beads or gloves and watch that princess emerge.

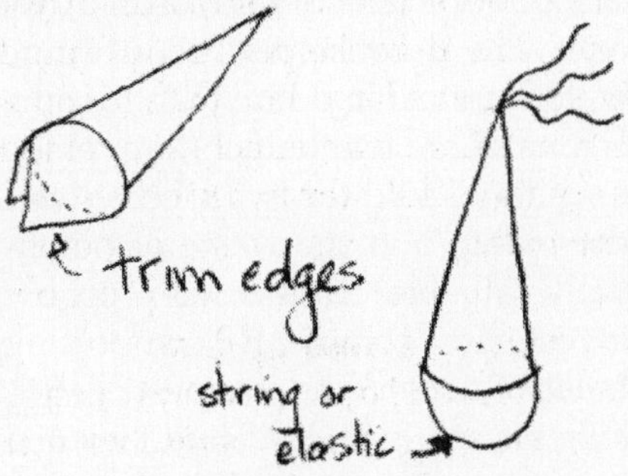

Christmas projects for children:

Cornstarch clay for ornaments
1 cup cornstarch
2 cups baking soda
1-1/2 cups cold water

Mix cornstarch and baking soda together in a pot. Add the water and cook over medium heat until the mixture looks like mashed potatoes. Pour the clay out onto the counter and cool. Knead until smooth.

Use cookie cutters to cut out Christmas shapes, or use your own imagination to make Christmas tree decorations, gift tags, window ornaments, etc. After shaping, allow to dry overnight. Paint and if desired, cover with shellac, clear nail polish or liquid plastic to make it shiny.

Glittering stars

This simple project requires white craft glue (in a bottle with a nozzle) and glitter. Protect the table with newspapers or a plastic table cloth. Use a piece of freezer paper or waxed paper as your work surface. Using the white craft glue, "draw" a star or other holiday shape on the waxed paper. Sprinkle heavily with glitter.

Allow to dry for at least a day. Shake the excess glitter onto a clean piece of paper and return it to the glitter container for your next project. Carefully peel the paper from your ornament. Hang your glittering stars from the Christmas tree or the windows with ribbons or string.

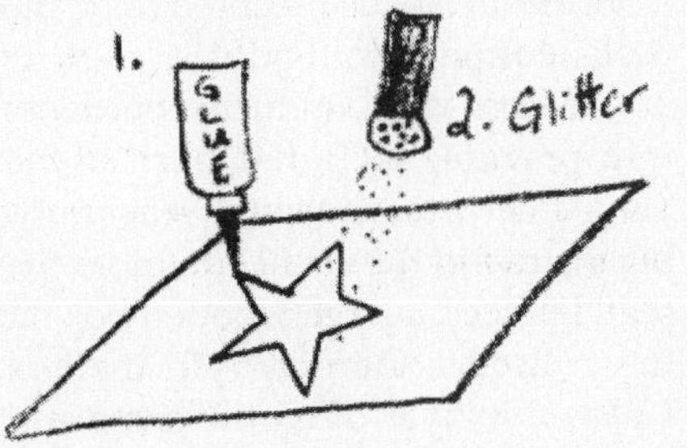

"Stained glass" snowflakes

Paper snowflakes are fun to make and are wonderful decorations for your windows during the winter. Smaller children will need help to fold the paper into sixths or eighths to get the repeating snowflake pattern.

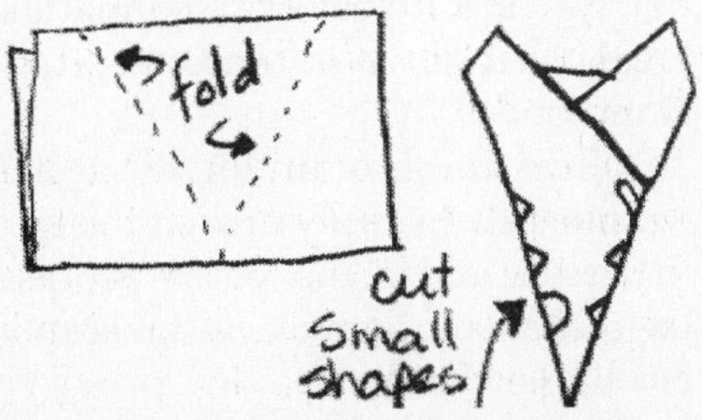

For the older child who wants to try something new, collect some old crayons, and some waxed paper. You will need an iron for this project, so be sure to have supervision for those not experienced with an iron. Cut two sheets of waxed paper the same size. Lay some old newspapers on the ironing board and lay the first piece of waxed paper on top of it. Using an old knife, scrape some wax from the crayons onto the waxed paper. Experiment with different colors and amounts. Lay the second piece of waxed paper on top, cover with more newspapers (2 or 3 sheets is enough), and iron for 5-10 seconds or until the wax shavings are melted. Now, use your new "stained glass" to cut out a snow flake. They look best hanging in the window for the sun to shine through, but you can use them anywhere to make it look wintery.

Shortbread is simple!

Here is a recipe for the child who likes to bake. It is simple enough to manage alone, but ask for help setting and using the oven.

2 cups flour
1/2 cup packed brown sugar
1/2 teaspoon salt
3/4 cup butter, chilled

Mix dry ingredients. Cut in butter with a pastry blender, and then mix with your hands until it forms a soft dough. Press into an 8" x 8" square pan. With a fork, poke holes in the surface of the dough. Bake at 350 degrees for 20 minutes or until just starting to turn brown at the edges. Cut into squares while warm, but allow to cool in the pan. A small plate of these cookies makes a nice gift for a neighbor or friend.

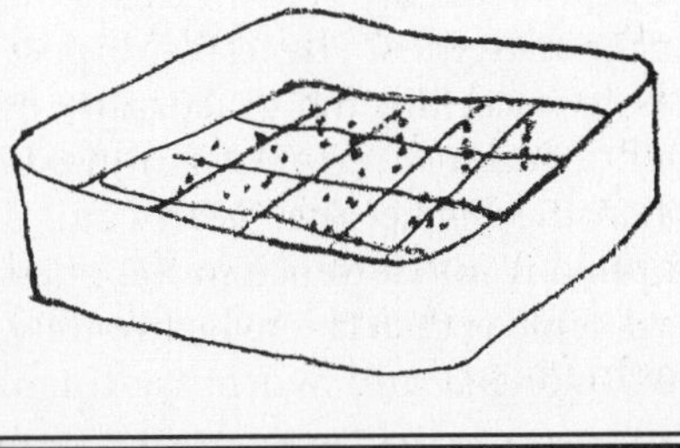

When the earthquake isn't the only "emergency"

In search of the perfect composting toilet

Christopher Nyerges
California

I had to chuckle when I heard of a family who decided to shorten the length of their "survival test" because their porta-potti broke.

The family wanted to see how well they'd fare in their urban home if an earthquake severed all utility lines and truck routes into the city. So they turned off their water, gas and electricity, and only used the food, water, candles, and what-not that they had stored in their home. They called off the test when their emergency toilet ceased working properly. But why did they stop their test when it was just becoming real? After all, when a crisis is suddenly upon us, we have no time for buying an alternative toilet—you just use what is available.

The area of human excrement is possibly the most overlooked area of personal disaster planning. Why? Because in our sophisticated modern society, you use the toilet, flush, and forget. Yet, properly composted, human excrement can be a valuable source of fertilizer and even burnable gas, as the Chinese have proven. (There are over 7.2 million methane digesters in rural China which use human and animal wastes to produce fuel and fertilizer for about 35 million rural people.)

I once exclusively used a simple bucket toilet in my Los Angeles home for three months. The test's purpose was to ascertain the practicality of such a toilet after an earthquake. When the bucket was nearly full, I emptied it into a trench in the outer yard, which I then layered with straw, earthworms, and worm castings. Eventually, I planted tomatoes in the trench.

The simple bucket was not difficult to use. In fact, the real challenge was to test various methods of combating the "outhouse odor" which many would find offensive. Putting lemon juice and baking soda into the toilet after each use seemed to be the best solution to foul odor.

Another test I conducted outdoors in a private, secluded part of the yard. I set up a hospital seat potty, but instead of the usual pot under the seat, I placed a large wooden box on the ground underneath. In the box I placed a layer of earthworms and worm castings and some partially decomposed straw. I covered over each use of the toilet with another layer of earthworms and worm castings. The system was amazingly simple, odor-free, and fly-free.

The real key to the success was the addition of the earthworms. The worms (I used redworms) are rapid reproducers, and they continually burrow and digest organic matter, breaking it down into nitrogen-rich plant food.

When the box under the toilet became full, I simply moved the box to the side and let the worms process the contents. I then placed an empty box under the chair.

The idea for this toilet came to me when I was observing the worm farm I had established under my rabbit coop. With the regular rabbit droppings and urine which dropped through the screen bottom of their cage into the worm farm below, the earthworms rapidly proliferated. With the presence of worms processing the rabbit droppings, there was a conspicuous absence of flies around the rabbits.

I was also motivated to pursue this project for another reason. Anyone who is concerned about huge water waste in modern toilets (some estimates are that half of the average household's water is flushed down the toilet), and the waste of potentially valuable fertilizer, has probably investigated commercial composting toilets. But even the cheapest of such toilets is nearly $1,000. Thus, I wanted to find an easier, cheaper method that would still conform to all standards of health and cleanliness and ease of operation.

My worm toilet is an ongoing project, and I have more tests to try. Yet, the potential seems most obvious. Not only could such a toilet save vast amounts of water: it would be economically viable if set up properly. In wilderness areas, such as at National Parks and at remote cabins, such a toilet makes far more sense than the current outhouse method where the contents are only considered waste matter at best and a health hazard at worst.

If readers have any suggestions, comments, or questions, I'd very much like to hear from you.

Nyerges is the author of several outdoor and environmental books. The schedule of his classes is available from School of Self-Reliance, Box 41834, Eagle Rock, CA 90041 or on-line at http://www.self-reliance.net

Our suggestion would be to read *Humanure Handbook*, by Joe Jenkins. $19.00 plus $2.50 S&H from Countryside Bookstore, 145 Industrial Dr., Medford, WI 54451; 800-551-5691; www.countrysidemag.com.

First a flood. Then a fire. Now he's waiting for El Niño

DARYL KEECH
CALIFORNIA

In our last episode of "The Perils of Daryl," Northern California was flowing toward the sea. (COUNTRYSIDE 81/3:40) Fortunately, the rains quit, and the land-shift stopped. Community, state and federal agencies worked fairly well at recovery. But above all else was tremendous individual effort.

The signs of the flooding are more subtle now. It appears as debris layers high in old oak trees or in fence lines.

Not so subtle is the obvious fear at the news of the largest El Niño this century forming in the Pacific. Southern California usually bears the brunt of this weather phenomenon, but spin-off can send heavy rains north too. Oh, that tricky jet stream.

The rains, as usual, spurred a great spring growth. The orchard and garden at JayHawk Ranch were especially productive this year. The grasses grew so tall, new additions—two Herefords—were placed on the pasture. Some people will go to any length to avoid mowing. Alice and Rosie are contentedly munching their way around.

Their personal effort, however, didn't impact the thousands of acres surrounding the ranch.

Late September, in the early afternoon, the phone rang. The neighbor's suggestion to look north revealed a startling sight. A pillar of smoke looking like an atomic blast or Moses on the move stained the clear blue sky. More ominous yet was the hot, dry north wind. The lazy afternoon received an adrenaline wake up call.

After a short period of running in place ("where are my pants?") the sprinklers were activated. The simple "bayonet style" sprinklers affixed to each roof edge soaked the asphalt shingles and within minutes was soaking the ground in overlapping arcs.

This fire destroyed more than 100 homes. On the brighter side, 300 were saved, some because the owners were prepared.

The previous work of disking the property line and the general "greening" of the area added a sense of confidence. A little last minute mowing (how did that grow so fast?) and the ranch was ready.

As the hours passed, the trail of smoke grew larger...and closer. At dusk, it was as wide as an outstretched hand. In the night, the glow was like city lights just beyond the ridge line.

The wind, usually calm through the night, continued whistling. By morning, the fire had grown to 5,000 acres. A thousand fire fighters had gathered to combat the monster. Two- and four-engine bombers dropped their magenta dusts. Helicopters released bucket-loads of man-made downpour. Throughout the day the fight was waged against a slippery foe.

The second night the smell of smoke was in the air and ash fell on the ranch. Not much sleep was to be had that night. "Check the sprinklers, eye each roof, scan the horizon for the 10,000th time."

By morning the fire was 50% contained and the wind died down. At the end of the day the threat was generally over.

In the days following the fire, officials announced that over 100 homes were destroyed. A more optimistic statistic was that 300 homes were saved from the flames. In no small part this was due to fire resistant roofing materials, brush clearance, fire resistant trees and shrubs, and good old green grass.

One photo in the local newspaper showed an undamaged home 100 feet from another that was ashes and twisted metal. A forlorn chimney rose from the ashes. The owner of the preserved home gave the most credit to the hours of watering and sprinkling before the fire reached him. You won't find an argument here. Is that the tooting of my own horn I hear, or the Horn of Buckland?

The skies are gray today. Is this the first touch of El Niño?

We seem to be living in interesting times.

GRIDLOCK

beyond the sidewalks

Dudley Moor
Massachusetts

Another reason to live beyond the sidewalks had its first anniversary last Labor Day weekend on Cape Cod, Massachusetts.

Potential for disaster was in the air as hurricane Edouard loomed large on the radar screen. The dangerous and fast moving storm was gaining speed and forecasters predicted landfall would take place in a matter of hours at Chatham, Massachusetts. Thousands upon thousands of vacationers began to flee for the two bridges to the West, the only way off this once rural peninsula.

What followed was a traffic jam one expert called the worst in Cape Cod history. New England's playground became a monumental exodus as cars of every size and description, trucks, motor homes and campers all left at once. The entire Cape was in gridlock and Governor William Weld declared a state of emergency, with the National Guard ordered to stand by and the state police ordered to remain on duty until further notice.

An Army Corps of Engineers' analysis says it would take 13 hours to clear the Cape and "most observers agree even that estimate is highly optimistic." On a good summer weekend the population here swells from 200,000 to 500,000 if you include the day-trippers and the people on longer vacations.

***

The eye of the storm was to strike 70 degrees west longitude, which was exactly my position as I worked hurriedly to secure some aquacultural tanks and pump systems near Stage Harbor. All around me fishermen of all types secured boats and gear to ride out the closing storm.

As the wind and surf began to pick up, I headed for home past a group intently listening to a weather radio on the pier. I was not prepared for what I encountered next.

Needing to cover only a few miles,

Shelves were cleaned of water and canned goods. Batteries were solid gold, and buying gas was out of the question. *Artwork by Dudley Moor*

I entered the main road and quickly found myself in the middle of the worst traffic chaos I have ever driven in, through, or around. The traffic was gridlocked over 30 miles from the bridges and most drivers were looking feverishly for short cuts and back roads to escape the area.

I attempted to make a stop at the grocery store for some last minute hurricane provisions and encountered more confusion and uproar as shelves were cleaned of water and canned goods. Batteries were solid gold and a gasoline fill was out of the question.

I arrived home after driving more than an hour to cover those few miles through what to me was total anarchy. Some people were not stopping at stop signs, cutting others off, making U-turns, and losing patience. It was a scary, ugly scene that opened my eyes as to what might develop when there are too many people in too small an area with an impending crisis spinning like a buzz saw and approaching fast.

Driving laws, rules and regulations, and common courtesy were nonexistent (not that they exist all that much in an urban commute anyway) and Cape Cod public safety officials do not really know how to prevent this chaotic evacuation from happening again. One can only wonder, along with public officials like Representative Thomas Cahair, what would happen if there were some kind of accident at the Pilgrim Nuclear Power Plant in near-by Plymouth. It is a frightening thought.

We are an "at risk population." One should add this category to the ever-growing list of public safety considerations such as air pollution, contaminated water, crime, and the quality of life, when looking closely at relocation.

The experience during the approaching hurricane was a valuable lesson for me and my family. This beautiful place which was once quaint fishing villages, small farms, and listed on all the maps as rural, is now a traffic jam every summer and officially a metropolitan area. We also know that things can quickly go from bad to worse during a crisis with this sort of people density.

Our only storm damage was to the vegetable garden as the eye of the storm took a right turn out to sea at the last minute. However, a storm still rages in me to live in less crowded conditions, and we will soon be heading for the country to live beyond the sidewalks.

A sociologist studies homesteading

Homesteaders—the New Pioneers

***New Pioneers,* by Jeffrey Jacob; 278 pages, $26.50; Penn State University Press, University Support Bldg. 1 Ste C, University Park PA 16802 (ph 800-326-9180); (reviewed by Jd Belanger, COUNTRYSIDE Editor)**

This book is about homesteaders who are just like you... about homesteaders who are nothing like you... the webs that connect all homesteaders... and homesteading as a bridge to a sustainable future.

Based largely on a survey of COUNTRYSIDE readers, New Pioneers is sprinkled with personal interviews and in-depth case studies, all held together with some astute observations and postulates.

COUNTRYSIDE itself is an eclectic melange—some would say a hodgepodge—of colorful people, apparently disparate lifestyles, and conflicting ideas. New Pioneers sorts out this confusion by separating the parts into neat little piles, then putting them into pigeon holes that connect them in ways that make sense.

A prime example of this is the sorting of homesteaders into seven different classifications. For anyone with a restrictive view of homesteading, this categorizing alone will be a real eye-opener. What's more, Jacob is able to use his COUNTRYSIDE survey results to tell us exactly what proportion of homesteaders can be assigned to each category. (See box.)

None of this is particularly surprising, nor in conflict with the readership studies COUNTRYSIDE has conducted over the years. But it's obvious from letters in the magazine that many people have a very distorted view of who and what "homesteaders" are. No matter how many times the editor points out that the vast majority of homesteaders have "normal" jobs and lives (Weekenders, Pensioners and Entrepreneurs comprise 77% of the total), the idea persists that all homesteaders must live entirely on the bounty of their homesteads, with minimal cash income also provided by the homestead. In reality, a mere 3% are in this class.

This example alone might give many homesteaders a new perspective, and possibly new hope and inspiration. At least they can stop berating themselves for being failures, or some kind of "halfway" homesteader.

Imagine how much less confusing some matters would be, how much less conflict we might see in these pages, if every correspondent would be identified by their homestead category. Just as Purists and Weekenders obviously have much in common, they also obviously and necessarily do things differently. It would certainly help in many cases if readers would at least be aware of these differences.

Another question of "perspective" is more problematical, but of vastly greater potential importance. This involves the main theme of the book—back-to-the-landers as "new pioneers."

Jacob isolates one issue as both

What flavor homesteader are you?

Here is a breakdown of homesteader "types," as defined by Jeff Jacob, based on his survey of COUNTRYSIDE readers:

44% are Weekenders: Have full-time employment away from their farmsteads, but spend their free time (weekends, early mornings, and evenings) working on their property.

18% are Pensioners: Retired and supported by pensions (social security, investments, and retirement plans).

17% are Country Romantics: Take part-time or seasonal work, then spend the rest of their time at work and at leisure on their property.

15% are Country Entrepreneurs: Major source of income comes from small business on property (cabinetmaking, welding) that does not directly involve farming.

3% are Purists: Invest only part of their time growing a cash crop on their property, for just enough cash income to survive in a monetized economy; otherwise subsist from the resources of their own property and barter relationships with the neighbors.

2% are Microfarmers: Devote most of their working time to the intensive cultivation of cash crops on their property—usually fruits or vegetables with high market value.

1% are Apprentices: Learn the back-to-the-land craft while working on someone else's farm.

(From *New Pioneers;* Table 5. Back-to-the-landers: a typology)

This list is not only a key to Jeffrey Jacob's book: it's essential for understanding COUNTRYSIDE, and homesteading itself.

critical and central to the movement: sustainability. As he points out, "...the good life was to be found in a more democratic 'small-is-beautiful' society, whose everyday life would be closely connected to the sustaining power of the land."

The problematic part is how many—or even whether—back-to-the-landers would agree with the premise, or to what degree.

As an example, in 81/1 we printed a number of responses to someone who could see no value in homesteading.

After reading this book it would seem that the ideal reply to that person would have at least mentioned the concept of sustainability. Yet, the dozen or so replies printed made no reference to what Jacob considers the keystone of homesteading.

Our question then becomes, is Jacob endowing homesteaders with a nobility we don't deserve? Or is this noble purpose so taken for granted no one has openly mentioned it in almost 30 years' worth of COUNTRYSIDES? Or is he telling us something we have been only dimly aware of and unable to put into words—in effect, handing us a rationale we can readily and perhaps even gratefully accept, and work on developing?

In spite of the thousands of letters from homesteaders I have read in almost three decades, I honestly don't know. Even considering the seven classes of homesteaders, the answer isn't clear. It's possible that many of us are working on a goal without being consciously aware of it, unflattering as that might be.

A more likely explanation, however, is that we are working on a number of goals and ideals simultaneously, and thus find it difficult to separate them or sort them out. If this is the case, Jeff Jacob has indeed given us a valuable tool, not only as a movement but as individuals. He might not be telling us anything we didn't already know, but he is helping us to focus more clearly.

Jacob brings up another crucial factor that, on the surface at least, is troubling. He says that as a group, we don't put our money where our mouth is. "The back-to-the-landers of course are not paragons of sustainability virtues. They practice anything but lives of pastoral asceticism, as they accumulate a collection of consumer-society accessories from microwave ovens to chain saws. In addition, to the extent that their behavior actually reflects sustainability norms, they lead decidedly unbalanced lives. At its most general level sustainability entails a shift in the direction of one's personal energy not only away from preoccupation with material consumption but also toward the development of a wide range of relationships, from personal, family, neighborhood and community relationships to relationships with nature, and the supernatural, and with ideas (the life of the mind). While smallholders do possess an extraordinary sense of pragmatism as they balance the multiple demands on a finite amount of time against their commitment to self-reliance and voluntary simplicity, their primary source of gratification remains the private pleasure of enjoying nature on their individual homesteads. But in their relative neglect of community relationships they ignore potential sources of solidarity for the defense and promotion of their chosen way of life." (Emphasis added.)

"I want to ask difficult questions about the back-to-the-landers in the context of a worldwide consumer culture that is threatening the integrity of the earth's support systems."—*Jeffrey Jacob, in "New Pioneers"*

The "primary source of gratification" was clearly evident in the replies to "the lady who doesn't get it," cited above—and indeed, in most of COUNTRYSIDE.

On the other hand, discussions of "community" indicate that many homesteaders would find something to argue with in Jacob's assessment of "relative neglect of community relationships," and perhaps even more in regards to "the defense and promotion of their chosen way of life." Many will deny that homesteaders neglect community relationships, even on a relative basis. And many others will protest that they have no need or inclination to defend or promote their chosen way of life.

Jacob does touch one raw nerve. He points out that very few of us have actually made much progress toward even our basic and materialistic goals. A perfect example—and an almost humorous one, because we see it so often in the pages of COUNTRYSIDE—is that while almost all of us want and plan to have a greenhouse and a root cellar, very few of us have acquired these ascribed essentials.

Nevertheless, "in spite of its reclusive character, latter-day homesteading does constitute a break, however partial and imperfect, from the mainstream consumer culture. If a prerequisite for a sustainable future is a fundamental, society-wide change in consciousness, regardless of how narrow, the back-to-the-landers have traveled at least partway down that road."

Again, this could be a backhanded compliment... or it could be accusing homesteaders of failing to do something they had no intention of doing in the first place. But this brings me to why I consider New Pioneers such an important landmark in the evolution of modern homesteading.

Many of the concepts Jacob discusses have seldom or never been examined in COUNTRYSIDE, much less in the other back-to-the-land journals, past and present, that eschew philosophical considerations.

Is this because people simply aren't interested... (and therefore it doesn't sell magazines)? Maybe it's not important... although many topics of considerably less importance are routinely discussed by COUNTRYSIDE'S correspondents!

Or is it that no one has ever before spent 13 years examining the responses to hundreds of copies of a 12-page questionnaire, and sorting and codifying what even its participants consider to be a loose and highly individualistic coalition into a sociological phenomenon and force?

My bias is obvious, but I would definitely prefer to think that Jeff Jacob has uncovered something of tremendous importance to homesteading as a movement. Even though much of his book will incite controversy among those of us who see homesteading as the wave of the future in one guise or another, I believe some of his basic tenets could serve as a starting point for developing an entirely new homestead outlook. If enough people were to follow through on his ideas, we could easily show that homesteading, far from being a quirky lifestyle, is in reality a hands-on philosophy that is building the foundation for a sustainable future for all of society.

This is, admittedly, an academic sort of book. As a summary of a survey, the statistics are unavoidable. Even then, it's difficult to imagine anyone but a COUNTRYSIDE reader being able to understand, much less enjoy, most of it!

On the other hand, if we give serious consideration to Jacob's view of homesteading as it relates to the "sustainability" of our world and civilization, that kernel alone could make this an extremely important book.

Naturally, I wish everybody would read *New Pioneers*. Homesteading would gain instant credibility, and even respectability. It's easy to write off or even scoff at misfits who want to "go back" to old-fashioned ways of doing things. Seeing homesteaders as visionaries who hold a key to the future is quite another matter. (Show this book to your friends and relatives who think your homesteading is just "hobby farming," or better yet, to those who think you belong in the looney bin.)

Since that's probably impossible, I'd settle for seeing every COUNTRYSIDE reader reading this book. Even that would go a long way toward polishing the image of homesteading... and it would make editing this magazine a great deal easier!

Another guy who "just doesn't get it"...

New pioneers... or country bumpkins?

COUNTRYSIDE: I have been meaning to write and tell you about the losers we have in the Neillsville, Wisconsin area. But I think this clipping from *The Clark County Press* pretty much covers anything I could say! —*Willy Frederiksen*

Karnitz starts his column by saying "I'm beginning to think some people are taking this 'back to nature' thing a little bit too far." He tells how he notices a magazine advertising 40 (actually it was 42) "true-life stories on how real people, just like you and me, left their busy, unsatisfying lives to live in the country."

He forked over $3, and "later found, to my dismay, that most of the testimonies weren't from starry-eyed dreamers who reverted back to 'the old ways' but a collection of societal misfits who thought it was 'cool' to live without the pleasures of a flush toilet. Most of the magazine dealt with how to get started in the country (i.e. buying property, building a house) with no money."

Then he says the average letter reads something like this:

***

Dear Country Bumpkin magazine,

Me an' my husband done decided to take an' move to the country last year. We'z tired of runnin' water, crime, and jes' barely gettin' by.

We done sold our house, pulled up stakes and set out for the woods. We were shore lucky. We done found a two acre parcel on a dead-end road with no electricity nor no runnin' water. Here's the best part—it 'uz only $20,000.

Well, winter wuz comin' so's we decided we needed a house for in which to live. We commenced to diggin' a basement by hand but it started snowin' and we had to move into our camper.

There we wuz. No jobs, no water, electricity or amenities. No nuthin'. But happy, shoot yes, we wuz happy. No feudin' over whether to watch All-Star Wrastlin or TNN on the television. We jes' set and talked.

It shore wuz a long winter.

Come spring, we planted a garden and dug an outhouse. It 'uz shore nice.

We don't got no health insurance. We don't believe in no doctors. We buy all our clothes to rummage sales. We don't buy nothin' new. Why it's almost be a sin to spend money on anything. To heck with progress, we got each other.

The neighbors think we're a mite weird, but that ain't nothin' new. Let 'em keep them fancy trappins' We don't want 'em.

We luv our life on this here dead-end road.

Love to you-all.
Ornery in Ogalla

***

Dear Country Bumpkin magazine,

Isn't progress wonderful? I just can't wait for the next century to arrive.

He-he-he!

Laughingly yours,
Chad Karnitz

***

Editor's note: It's hard to believe that this fellow and the folks who

praised that issue were reading the same magazine.

He obviously "doesn't get it." But then, he isn't the only one.

Certainly, it would be easy for someone to read one issue of a homestead magazine and get the wrong impression—especially when that issue is largely devoted to people who are just starting out with few resources. Maybe someday we'll have a Question of the Month devoted to wealthy people (like newspaper reporters?)... which will lead others to say "Homesteading is just for rich people, not common folks like us." Of course, neither view is accurate.

The fact is, homesteaders are indeed "new pioneers" working toward a sustainable future. We are ahead of the times; those who don't get it are the ones living in the past. This alone is enough to make us different, and therefore sometimes misunderstood.

We can suffer the snickering cynics in silence, knowing they'll see the light soon enough. When the next century arrives, we'll be waiting for them.

Sue Robishaw's book entertains and informs

Sue Robishaw and Steve Schmeck are what might be called "pure" homesteaders. They live in an owner-built underground solar-powered home in the northwoods of Michigan's Upper Peninsula. They are about as self-sufficient, or at least self-contained, as anyone could hope to be. At one time their main livelihood came from carving and selling wooden spoons.

This book is an account of their over 20 years of "homestead adventures:" finding land, designing the house, building the house, and living in it the homestead way. It describes their water-pumping windmill, solar food dryer, photovoltaic system... and what they eat (including recipes and a "shopping list" for an entire year, including two bushels of potatoes, 25 pounds of peanut butter, and 123 pounds of oatmeal). Seed-saving, the outhouse, making maple syrup and the greenhouse, it's all here, making this one of the most comprehensive manuals on homesteading we have seen.

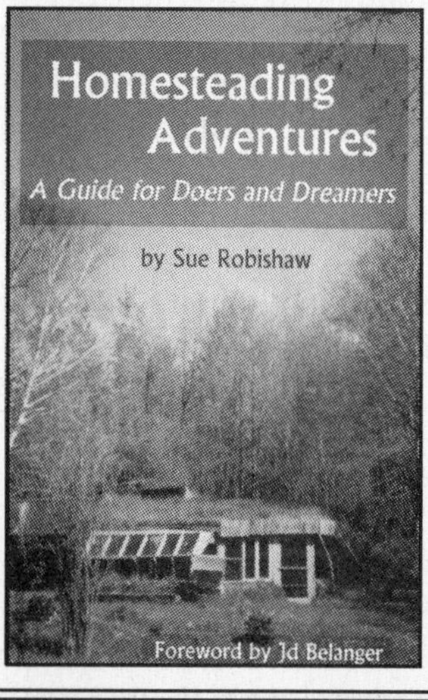

And yet, *Homesteading Adventures* isn't exactly a manual. While it will certainly serve as a guide for many people, it's much more readable and interesting than a "manual."

One reason is the unusual presentation. Most of the book is based on two fictional characters (JJ and Cindy Lou) who follow the homesteader around, pestering her with questions. At times they seem to be caricatures of wannabe homesteaders: they're a bit outrageous (as when they talk about growing oranges in the U.P., and dressing in white to help harvest "fluffy white potatoes") and the odd dialog takes some getting used to.

However, these odd and outrageous characters serve to contrast with and highlight Sue Robishaw's wise and gentle advice. Instead of a lecture in the form of a manual, this book is a conversation between a highly experienced homesteader and couple who know less than nothing about it. Even the greenest novices will be able to feel good: They at least know more than JJ and Cindy Lou!

Another reason this book will hold your interest, regardless of your level of experience, is the overall tone, the spirit of homesteading the author displays throughout. She describes a life that most people can only dream of—and which many today might not even be able to imagine. And yet, the peace, the simplicity, the satisfaction of that life are bound to appeal to many people in today's bustling and confusing world.

The sometimes outlandish JJ and Cindy Lou could make this book unreal if not for the steadying presence of the very real and down-to-earth Sue Robishaw. In addition, however, the many excellent photographs clearly demonstrate that this is no work of fiction, or theories of a dreamer.

Anyone interested in homesteading is sure to enjoy, and benefit from, this very readable book.

***Homesteading Adventures, A Guide for Doers and Dreamers,* by Sue Robishaw; 303 pages with index; illustrated; paperback; $16.98 + $2.50 S&H; Countryside Bookstore, 145 Industrial Dr., Medford, WI 54451. Ph: 800-551-5691.**

Alaskan, welder, single female homesteader

Jenny Bell-Jones
Alaska

"How did those who've done it, do it?" (or words to that effect) was a recent Question of the Month and since a heavy snow fall is preventing me from "doing it" outside today I decided to get busy with pen and paper.

What I am "doing" is homesteading in interior Alaska on 73 acres which I was lucky enough to be able to purchase for a very reasonable price earlier this year. OK, OK, I can already hear those voices whispering "trust fund baby" and "lottery winner," and a few folks are probably thinking that I married some corporate executive and took off with the money... But no—no one was that generous in my youth, I rarely remember to buy a lottery ticket, and at 50 years of age I don't consider myself grown up enough yet for marriage!

Let's get serious: How did I do this?

For starters, you should know that I've participated in some form of "homestead style" living for most of my life. I grew up in Scotland in a family that gardened organically, used many types of natural resources, and recycled before it was called recycling. I learned to hunt and fish, and lived a lot in remote areas, both alone and in community situations, on both sides of the Atlantic. I was taught self-sufficiency at a very early age: Mom used to send me out in the backyard to cook my own dinner when I was about eight; I had my first manual laboring job when I was 11. I've continued the lifestyle whether I was living in the country or the city, and I've lived in several of the biggest.

In other words, I practiced. Now, that does seem to be a theme running through a lot of the Countryside correspondence so I won't elaborate on it. However, I do consider it to be of great importance for the beginning homesteader.

By now I'm probably sounding like a '60s flower child. Wrong again. I'm pretty much a redneck, a high school dropout who has worked in a blue collar job about all of my life. I immigrated to the states with no personal resources and worked my way into the position I'm in now.

Becoming a better welder

And I do mean worked: This is a very important ingredient in achieving homestead ownership and success. I worked my rear end off—12-hour shifts at the plant. If overtime wasn't available I took a second job—usually low paid and rarely something I enjoyed. I make good money now but I worked up to it. I started in the shipyards as an apprentice on the equivalent of minimum wage and before that I shoveled horse manure for an even lower wage. I worked and studied and became a better welder. But it came slowly and not without going without a lot of things that others consider essential. There were months when I slept in my truck while on out of town jobs, and my health has suffered from long hours inside dirty boilers. Without the help of good friends I don't know if I could have done it: friends are important too!

But it brought results and now there is a 73 acre parcel down the road from here with my name on it, and a little cabin (12' x 17') that I managed to set up by converting an existing shed before the snow flew, ready to move into in the spring—my first construction project!

So I've covered practice and hard work (and friends, don't forget friends!) but there's a third ingredient in the recipe without which the place I have now would not have been possible: I established credit.

"Oops, she started talking a foreign language," I can hear some of you saying. Even worse, I'm about to mention the dirty "M" word—money! Sorry, folks, but it's important, and it seems to be the thing that some of us have the most trouble with.

Well, I certainly did at first, for two reasons. First, I understood nothing about finance beyond the fact that my paycheck always seemed to be too small; and second, because the idea of having any amount of money and being in any way involved with "investments" or "credit" seemed to me to be like sleeping with the enemy. Fortunately, a friend convinced me that establishing credit was not going to make me a social outcast, and my ex-husband (a really great guy with whom I parted on good terms) helped me fill out the paperwork and get started.

Establishing credit

I started small; a $150 loan from the credit union got the paper trail going. I obtained a couple more small loans, never borrowing more than I was sure I could afford to repay, and paid them off in a timely manner. Then I bought a small rural property with an "owner will carry" mortgage. I rented it out, worked like crazy, and paid the note off early.

By now I had an "A-1" credit rating without ever having had to make a monthly payment over $200. I got a couple of gas cards, and a Visa card, and continued to pay on time, being careful never to charge frivolous items.

After a few more years and a couple more real estate deals I finally started to shake the "money is an evil thing" idea that I had carried around for so long, and to evaluate investing.

I found out that "investing" covers a wide range of financial avenues and does not necessarily mean that you sink all your money into some employee abusing, earth polluting corporate conglomerate.

Once again I kept it simple; a basic IRA, some items on which I knew the long-term resale value would be excellent, and another piece of property which I purchased as part of a rural housing cooperative (another good possibility for folks who can't afford the place they want on their own). And again, I paid off early.

By now I was being offered credit every time I opened my post office box. Me, the scruffy construction worker with the "unstable work history" who averaged a change of residence at least every three years, was being begged to accept the American Express Platinum card!

The final result of all this endeavor (for me, the paperwork involved was much harder than a 12-hour shift in a hot boiler) was the place I have now. You see; the reason I got that good price I mentioned earlier was because it was a cash price. The owners would not carry a note—no ifs, ands or buts. I had part of the money but I needed to borrow $20,000 and borrow it fast, because at the price being asked, the place would not be on the market long. And I wanted it badly—I had finally found a place to settle down. Thanks to that good credit rating that I had worked so hard to maintain, I was able to walk into a bank I had never set foot in before, unemployed, dressed like a backwoods trapper...and walk out with the loan I needed.

Money is a tool, and like any tool, if you use it safely it won't hurt you. But like any tool, we need to learn how it works in order to use it to our best advantage.

These days it is almost impossible for a young family to save a large amount of cash, but it is possible for them to save something, no matter how little, and it is possible for them to establish credit. Just remember to start small and never, ever accept more credit than you know you can afford to pay off.

A good rule

My own personal rule (because I'm subject to frequent layoffs in the construction industry) is "will I be able to make the payment if I'm unemployed?" If I can't, then I don't take on the payment. I absolutely won't touch an adjustable rate mortgage (I don't visit casinos much either), and I won't take on a loan that penalizes early repayment. (Some do—be sure to check!) I have to budget very carefully because of my on again/off again employment. For someone with a steady job it's a bit easier, but I recommend always staying a payment or two ahead in case of an emergency.

A homestead and a house in town: same principle

What this all boils down to is that someone who wants to buy a homestead needs to go about it the same way as the family that wants a house in town: establish credit, save whatever you can, and then look for a place you can afford.

Of course, there are problems associated with financing rural properties that are different from a place in town. One is the fact that very few lending agencies will give a real estate loan or mortgage on vacant land. The place I bought here has no house on it so I had to get a personal loan; this meant a higher interest rate and a shorter loan period: therefore, larger payments.

One place, two views

If the place you want does have a home it may not qualify for a loan if it does not meet "conventional" housing standards. When I was living in Arizona I found a place I really liked and needed to borrow from the bank. To me the place was perfect—it was zoned agricultural and had a "habitable" house with a great view in a nice neighborhood. The bank appraiser saw it a little differently: an overpriced, pieced-together miner's shack with no foundation on a dirt road with the other residences in the vicinity in similar condition...and told me not to waste my time or hers by filling out an application.

So folks looking at rural properties are more likely to need an "owner will carry" situation. There are more available than some people realize. Some have minimal down payments, especially if you show the owner that good credit rating you've built up.

Something else which people moving to the country for the first time tend to neglect is resale value. (Yes, I neglected to consider this with my first place and took a severe loss when I sold.)

Let's say you've found the 40 acres of your dreams: it's cheap, beautiful, the seasons are mild, there's lots of wild game, and you just can't wait to move. Two years later you've drilled three wells (how cheap is it now?) and still haven't hit water. You hate the rednecks and the range cattle that visit your unfenced "ranch liquidation" on a very regular basis. You've been unsuccessful in all your applications for the big game tags, you can't find employment and the "for sale" sign goes up.

Bad financial move. Not just bad, terrible! Even supposing you can find a buyer, you won't recoup your investment because you haven't owned it long enough, and if you can't find a buyer you're stuck!

Before buying, check into other properties in the area. How long has the place you want been on the market? How about other similar places? Beware when you are told that property prices "have remained stable for several years." This does not mean that property has been selling regularly, and could also mean that the "stable" prices are very low prices—maybe lower than what you paid for your place!

I know I've probably created some controversy with all the "money talk," but I do believe it's a tool that very few of us can avoid contact with today, and we will all be better off if we learn to use it correctly!

To those who don't have a place yet, I wish the best of luck. Keep searching, and in the meantime learn how to get the best use out of all your tools and resources!

Is your glass half empty, or half full?

JUDITH A. UTTENREITHER
DELAWARE

I've put a lot of thought into the question about getting started without a grubstake. My first thought was that a 31- and 47-year-old should know how to manage money and be able to save. But then I thought that everyone has their own strengths and weaknesses. Everyone does not get to the same point at the same age. I can see that with my own children.

Another thought that crossed my mind was we've been "over programmed" with consumerism. At every turn we are being bombarded with retailer greed. This has been going on for over 50 years. Some more than others fall for their traps.

Instant everything. You no longer have to save for anything—just whip out the plastic and it's yours. Worry about paying later. Our courts are now backlogged with record high bankruptcy cases.

Years ago you had to be 21 and have a stable job to get your first credit card. Now banks set up booths on college campuses during registration. Please tell me how an 18-year-old with no job can pay their credit card bills? Then Bank B will give that same 18-year-old a card simply because Bank A did. They charge to the limit and what does the bank do—raise the limit. So that 18-year-old student is able to get even further in debt.

And too many do. Trust me, I know too many parental horror stories. My best friend's daughter declared Chapter 13 at the ripe old age of 20! She is far from being alone.

Our government has certainly helped. You don't have to stand on your own two feet and make it on your own. Of course, after about 60 years the light bulb finally went on in the dimly lit minds in Washington. So now we have welfare reform.

With all these factors we have become a nation that acts like a bunch of two-year-olds. Just gimme, gimme, I want ______ and now! Too many people are not satisfied with what they have or are willing to make do with what they do have.

Jd was right when he said COUNTRYSIDE is loaded with ideas and helpful tips. Many of us practice them. But on the other hand, too many don't want to do anything to help themselves get from point A to point B, slowly, thoughtfully and carefully. Just give it to me now. Then they whine because the Smith's budgeted, saved, did without, recycled, etc. to get from A to B. They just want to snap their fingers and they're at point B—a homestead, or whatever.

What is a homestead? Like COUNTRYSIDE says—it's what you make of what you have. It could be an apartment in the country or the city. It could be a home in the 'burbs or rural America. It's where you are or are going in your mind. If you always say the glass is half empty that's where you'll stay. But if the glass is half full, you're halfway there. It's just like the difference between Haves and the Have-nots. It's your outlook.

Let me give you a few examples.

We have lived in Delaware for about a year and a half. We were transferred from Pennsylvania with all of two weeks notice! We live in a resort area where land and housing prices are through the roof. In order to use the relocation package (which we couldn't have afforded not to use) we were limited to five acres or less. But we couldn't afford five acres with a house.

A litany of Haves and Have-nots

So, I "Have Not" the five acres I would love to have, but I "Have" 1½ acres and a nice house. I "Have Not" the chance of ever realizing my dream of having a large pasture with my own Clydesdales. But I "Have" fun watching and feeding sea gulls on my one-and-a-half. I "Have Not" the big garden I had in Pennsylvania through hard work. I "Have" been able to slowly reclaim the very neglected mess my one-and-a-half was in. I "Have Not" anything put up from last year's disaster of a garden—weed and ant filled overly high raised beds built by the former owner, that dried out too quickly no matter how much I watered. I "Have" six new raised beds in a new location that, knock wood, are doing nicely.

I have not been able to reclaim enough for a bigger garden so I can put up food for this winter. I have enough for this summer, some for my folks and the freezer. I have not the nice two bin compost area I designed. I have one-half the pallets I need for the job. I have not the henhouse and greenhouse I can envision on each side of the unfinished side shed. I have the hope and dream of it being finished. I have not the fruit orchard I can envision out back with all kinds of semi-dwarf trees and a big multi-type berry patch. I have two apples and one walnut tree that the previous owner planted and then forgot about.

Again, through hard work and lots of TLC, I have what appears to be a bumper crop. I could go on and on, but I think you get the picture.

By the way, our "start" was a small row house in Baltimore City that no one wanted. Talk about sweat equity. From there, we again bought an older home in the 'burbs that no one wanted. Sweat equity again.

We have worked hard, put in thousands of sweat equity hours, saved, recycled, did without, etc. to be able to be where we are today. Still not my dream of a big farm—but in my mind I'm fulfilled and happy.

If you'll excuse me— I have some baking, weeding, digging, watering, bug picking, etc. to do on my little homestead. Then I'll see if there are any gulls to be fed, and there are the new kittens to be cuddled.

Come to think of it, my glass gets fuller every day.

Shelter:

Enjoy country living sooner, with temporary housing

Develop raw land, or recycle a house?

Apparently, many people assume that homesteading means starting out with land that has no buildings: the first task is to build a house.

Like many assumptions, this one is both unfortunate and wrong. Many homesteaders (if not most of them) come out way ahead, both financially and in terms of time, by buying a piece of land that at least includes a livable house. Just having a well, road, septic system and electricity in place can be worth a small fortune in some areas.

For every homesteader who believes that building one's own shelter with one's own muscles and brains is an integral part of the lifestyle, there are several who are equally convinced that bringing a neglected house back to vibrant life is a high form of recycling... as well as a few others who simply want to unpack, and then get on with the gardening and livestock husbandry. And this doesn't even consider concerns over the "suburbanization" of the countryside, with houses (and wells and septic systems) sprouting on five- or 10-acre parcels. Rehabilitating an old farmstead might be more Earth-friendly.

A beginning homesteader will have more than enough to do without building a house. In addition, in many parts of the country, existing livable houses cost a lot less than building from scratch. Best of all, those on a budget can often profit by buying a fixer-upper: they at least have a roof over their heads while doing the remodeling as and when time and finances permit.

In other words, like many of the articles in COUNTRYSIDE, this one offers some good ideas... but not all the details apply to everyone. You don't have to live in a temporary shelter, or even build a house from scratch, to be a successful homesteader. But if you do, here's how.

WARD ENGELKE
WISCONSIN

More than one-third of the average American's after-tax income is devoted to shelter, usually in the form of rent or mortgage payments.

For those wanting to start homesteading, this is not very good news. After acquiring the land, a house has to be built. This, added to current shelter costs, may make homesteading impossible. (See editor's note in box.)

What is really important when homesteading? The number one goal is to get onto the land. Once on the land, all other dreams can start to be fulfilled. With that being the goal, let's look at ways to get on the land sooner.

Today, if a person works from ages 20 to 65, it can be fairly argued that 15 to 20 years of their life was spent just to keep a roof overhead. Where did we go wrong? Before we escape to our homestead dream the housing problem needs to be defined so we aren't destined to repeat it.

Why are Americans willing to spend one-third of their working lives in economic servitude? The question can be answered in two ways.

Two problems

First, most people were never told about any other way to get a house. From childhood on, most of us are taught that the only way to get a house is to go to the bank, get a loan, and spend the best years of our life paying twice the house's worth to the bank. Americans then jump for joy when a bank "condescends" to loan them mortgage money for 30 years. They count it good fortune, but the radiance is short-lived and routine sets in. The bank's "benevolence" becomes a burden and life becomes centered on how to make the monthly payments. This is all in the name of "security."

Second, and perhaps more important, most Americans are not willing to lower their comfort level for a short period of time in order to gain fiscal freedom. We accept and live by a prepackaged, standardized housing philosophy. This forces people, moved by fear, to tolerate housing that is overpriced, inadequate for their needs, and in most cases crippled by planning restrictions. Feeling that this is the best it gets, people begin to rationalize the compromising housing choices by saying, "We can turn the basement into a family room" or "The living room is too small, but we do have two and a half baths." Because of our addiction to comfort, people are moved to accept housing which is less than it could be.

Housing trends in history

Our addiction to comfort began with the turn of the 20th century. A quick trace of average houses from the 1900s will show how comfort standards or "needs" increased while family size decreased.

During the economic boom of the 1920s many people built houses that were called "expandables." These were built with a basic finished first floor that included two bedrooms, living room, dining room, kitchen and small bathroom. To accommodate future family growth, the unfinished attic was fashioned in such a way to allow the upper level to be finished when the need arose. This type of house was popular in various forms for about 20 years.

In the 1950s housing underwent a big change. Suburbs became the place to live. Housing suffered because most houses were built in tracts. With tract housing the potential owners got to pick the colors of the walls, carpet and type of exterior siding. There was no room for expansion and people began to "outgrow" houses. More than any other feature, the picture window became the selling point for these plain houses. A bath-and-a-half became the standard.

With prepackaged housing well established in the 1970s, floor plans became limited and individual options became almost non-existent. Most builders went to a feature selling aspect, selling something that is visually or emotionally appealing without interfering with the structural part of the building. This is when whirlpool tubs, "deluxe lighting," wood trim choices, fireplaces, and other options became as important as the floor plan. Homeowners began to see features as the reason to move into other houses.

Now, near the close of the century, the options have almost taken over what people look at when purchasing a home. With that attitude among so many buyers, it's no wonder housing has increased in price while the desire to start small is almost non-existent.

As an example, my in-laws bought a house in the country for a good price. In order for them to move, their house in a major metropolitan area must sell first. Their problem is the house built in the early 1960s is "too small" for families today. This house is about 1,200 square feet with a finished basement, natural fireplace and a third of an acre lot (rare in the city). Moreover, their garage is not attached to the house, therefore people would have to walk outside to get to the car.

When this house was built some 30 years ago this was state of the art. Now people can't see how anyone lived, to say nothing of raising a family, in such "primitive" housing.

Changing attitudes

The consequence of the current housing philosophy is that we accomplish exactly the opposite of what we set out to do. Rather than attaining greater security, we are less secure because our responsibility is delegated to others.

The money for our house is given over to the bank. The house design and construction is shifted to either a builder or Realtor, who do not have our needs in mind. The result is our self reliance is false because of these outside factors. Rather than working the land and planting a large garden or purchasing some small animals, we have to work outside the homestead to pay for the house. If a person wants to successfully homestead and save years of work, this current attitude needs to be changed.

We need to plan for basic survival—shelter, food, fuel. That doesn't mean giving up every type of comfort, but it does require a new look at our lifestyle and an honest look at our options. Although this article focuses on shelter, the principles can be applied to other areas of our lives.

Temporary shelter

The temporary shelter plan in-

Homesteaders have many housing choices

Tim and Patty Gamble, New York, elected to rehab an 1800s farmhouse. Patty said there were "no windows, no furnace, no bathroom, no electricity—you get the idea."

Recently she sent this picture, calling our attention to the all new ("Yea!") windows. "And how nice it is to use an indoor toilet. Hopefully a tub will follow soon." (See page 69 of this issue for their current arrangement.)

"Hopefully winter will skip us this year as we haven't done any insulating yet and only hooked up one stove. Well, I can dream, can't I?"

"We've rebraced the basement and jacked the floor almost even. The new tin roof should be here any day."

Clearly, this is as much of an adventure—as much work—and as satisfying—as carving a brand-new homestead out of the wilderness.

***Right:* Charles and LuVerne Davids spend winters in Arkansas, and summers in their owner-built cabin in northern Minnesota.**

***Below:* The Gamble house.**

volves building a small, livable, low-cost structure on the land, and living in it while building your permanent house. There can be many variations, but the potential advantages in all are the elimination of interim shelter costs, the gain of building experience, the gain of knowledge about the land and the gain of a useful outbuilding after the permanent house is built.

Usually the temporary shelter can be put up in several weeks. After the shelter is up, the move to the land can be made and the portion of the budget formerly devoted to rent can now go toward materials for the new house.

To begin, an average shelter will cost somewhere between $10,000 and $15,000. This might sound like a lot of money, but consider that a down payment on a house would be about the same. In addition to the elimination of a mortgage payment, there will be further savings because there will be no travel costs to the building site.

For those who think renting is the best option, consider that if a small apartment is rented for two years at $700 per month, which is the average in a large city, the cost would total $16,800. That money wouldn't be invested into anything except the landlord's pocket.

The shelter cost will be the best hedge against rising real estate prices and building costs. By living on the land without rent or mortgage payments the savings towards the house accelerates more rapidly.

Types of temporary housing

There are many different types of temporary shelters. Your needs will dictate what type you require.

The simplest is an older mobile home. You can find them in many different price ranges and styles. A mobile home is the quickest way to get onto the land, although it is the least cost-efficient option. If choosing the mobile home option, consider all the costs involved in setting up the trailer. There is the moving cost, setup charge, septic and water, skirting, and other smaller costs.

The other consideration is what is going to be done with the trailer after the permanent house is built. If the trailer is going to be removed afterward, factor in that cost from the beginning.

A garage provides experience

Another option is constructing a garage and turning it into a small house. If you're not confident about building the exterior shell, act as your own general contractor for the project. I would suggest that the interior work be done yourself. This type of project will give you valuable experience when it comes to your permanent house. A standard 2-1/2 car garage (26' x 28') will provide 728 square feet of living space. This may not seem like a great amount, but consider most two bedroom apartments are only 750 to 800 square feet.

After moving to your permanent house, this could be used for a home business, shop or guest house.

Many other types of cottage buildings could be used, such as A-frame buildings or insulated pole buildings. If you want an error-free home, buy a set of building plans for simple framed buildings at any lumber yard. There are hundreds of them. The result from any of these will be a well-constructed functional home. Sometimes plans can be adapted fairly easily to use rough-cut or recycled lumber, which will lower the cost and bring more individuality to the structure.

Consider the final house

You should give some thought to the final house, even during the construction of the temporary structure, as this would be a good time to practice the building techniques which will be used on the main structure. It's better to make beginning mistakes on a smaller temporary structure rather than the bigger dream house.

For example, people often decide on a site without considering whether the concrete truck can get to it. Why build a stone shelter if the desired permanent house is going to be a traditional log home? This will give experience in building and will be architecturally complementary to the permanent house.

The temporary shelter will also give you the advantage of having built on the land when making practical decisions for the main house. By living in the shelter you'll get a feel for a certain view, how the house will react to cold winter winds, and ease of construction. This will also enable you to customize the house to catch the cool breezes in the summer or have the morning sun at your breakfast table. You'll be able to talk with the neighbors about the elements peculiar to the area and find sources of cheap material.

The buildings discussed here are temporary, with the exception of the mobile home, insofar as human habitation is concerned. These shelters may be incorporated into the final house plans or can be turned into another type of building. Some thought should be given to the final state of your temporary shelter. If woodworking is going to be important in your homesteading, plan that into your shelter design.

A couple I'm acquainted with turned a temporary shelter they lived in for several years into the main building for their maple syrup business. In doing that, they figured the savings over constructing a new building was enough that they were able to plan for future growth and gather equipment needed for future expansion.

Most new homesteaders start with a common background of inexperience in construction. This lack of experience often evolves into a lack of confidence.

The temporary shelter concept has been around since the 19th century. Many people who settled in the United States and Canada started with small buildings that became a storehouse or some other building on the homestead.

If getting onto the land to start your dream is most important, consider building or getting a temporary shelter. It's better to be cramped for a short time in order to plan for the debt-free house, rather than be comfortable and never gain the freedom to realize your homesteading dream.

Despite problems with excessive heat retention, quonset houses are the most affordable and practical for the Krafka's needs.

We wanted out!

A thriving nursery business satisfies their craving for economic freedom and a rural environment

Barbara Krafka
Florida

Rick lived in an apartment complex called the Haystack. I rented a one bedroom efficiency at Orange Tree North. Agricultural names appealed to our homesteading souls, but the fact was, we were crammed into sardine box housing in the suburbs of Orlando, Florida. To rescue ourselves and each other, we married in 1979 and made our break from the concrete.

Our homesteading was born of a passionate desire for economic freedom and a craving for a rural environment. We were both employed in the Apopka, Florida foliage plant industry, so our dream was to operate a little backyard nursery on our own country land. What made us successful? What made our homesteading dream come true?

1. We prepared. Our career experiences, our volunteer work, our education, even our recreation was always focused towards the homesteading goal. Since our teen years, both of us had worked in nurseries. Then we studied ornamental horticulture in college. Our hobbies in college gave us knowledge and practice toward a rural lifestyle while we were still city dwellers. Rick baked bread. I made jellies and canned vegetables. Yes, even in teeny-tiny apartment kitchens. We grew vegetables in containers on balconies.

Volunteering for nursery-owning friends to load trucks or work trade show booths taught us the glamorous and the unglamorous aspects of nursery lifestyle; there were few surprises when we got out on our own. We knew what sitting up all night during a freeze to tend heaters meant. We knew hurricane preparations.

We chose to focus on flowering tropical vines, (mandevilla, alamanda, stephanotis, jasmines); crops difficult to grow but high in demand. We never sold second quality material; threw it out instead. As a result we had a waiting list of customers and stayed sold out for years in advance. We never had to advertise.

2. We started small and grew slowly but debt-free. We bought our country land... 2-1/2 acres of burnt-out orange grove with a tiny house and a decent barn. Although we immediately built a fiberglass mist house and began offering liners to other nurseries, we kept our full time jobs. (It would be four years 'til the nursery could support us full time). Every dime went back into the business and we only bought fertilizer, pots, soil, additional greenhouses, etc. when we could pay cash for them. Likewise, we offered no credit to customers. This was contrary to industry standards, but not to our lifestyle principles.

3. We stayed focused. Selling plants was enough. We turned down chances to sell vitamins, soap, roof coatings, etc. We ventured into animal husbandry once. I paid a man for some geese which I thought would keep the nursery weeded and insect free. Three months later, I paid the man to come round up and remove those territorial, customer attacking beasts. We stick with what we know.

The freezes of 1983 and 1989 which devastated Florida were a blessing to us in two ways. First, we were able to purchase 15 adjoining acres after the citrus died. Second, we had plant material to sell that had survived the cold due to our hard work protecting it with plastic blankets and irrigation all night. Several boom years followed as people and businesses replaced their damaged landscapes.

Altogether we were able to become debt free on 17 acres in 17 years. We are rooted in and here to stay.

There's a seemingly small point here that's worth noting: "The freezes... which devastated Florida were a blessing to us..."

This isn't like getting a lemon and making lemonade, nor is it the same as falling into a pile of manure and coming out smelling like a rose. It has to do with planning and preparation.

Many homesteaders, to some degree or another, plan and prepare for "survival," thinking of things such as losing a job, blizzards, earthquakes, extended power outages, or even an economic crash. Planning and preparation no doubt would have helped this nursery business survive the frosts... but it did even more!

No matter what form "devastation" takes, somebody is going to profit from it. That "profit" might be in the form of money (the Krafkas sold replacement stock), the opportunity to acquire more tools of production (in this case, land), or even the ability to help family or friends who are less prepared or less fortunate.

This example demonstrates that you don't have to hope for, or even expect, a disaster, to prepare for one. It can be an ordinary everyday way of "doing business."

Since the goose fiasco, Kay earns her allowance as the weeder.

But if disaster strikes, your chances of survival are increased...

And you might even come out ahead.

Holiday in Holland makes them appreciate Texas

Becky Vandenberg
Texas

My husband John, six-year-old daughter Victoria and I just returned from a trip to visit my Dutch in-laws in Holland. The last time we were there was seven years ago, before we moved beyond the sidewalks to our little six acre piece of Heaven.

Having the space, quiet and freedom here on our farm now really accented to us the misery of "close living" people sometimes must contend with. It made us more than glad to get back to the East Texas forests and our simple lifestyle.

Did we get criticized when we moved? Not by many. Most just questioned why my husband would want to commute an hour to work each day. But we had a vision of preparing a place of refuge for the days of hardship that will come. We were blessed to find not only the farm of our dreams but also the big roomy home of my dreams. Therefore we have opened up our place to friends, family and sometimes strangers who need to "get away" from the city rat race for a breather. This has resulted in probably less than six weekends in 3-1/2 years that we have not had extra people here with us. On several occasions we have had as many as 10 for long weekends.

Don't get me wrong: we are not running a hotel or resort. Our guests help out with the chores, having great fun at it, while not realizing they are actually working on a farm.

I homeschool our daughter and have had her city counterparts here for a week at a time for "visits" that were both fun and educational for them. Why, this place is a science fair all by itself.

As for socialization, here in our area there is a little country society all its own, including the Lions club, homemakers clubs, a homeschool support group, softball leagues, numerous churches and even a dieting club. Neighbors can be counted on when needed and the favor is returned in their times of need. It's amazing how many people actually live hidden away in these piney woods.

I'll share an experience my Dutch mother-in-law had during WW II. As a young woman, she lived with her family near Rotterdam and food was almost nonexistent. However, she was engaged at the time to a man who lived way out in the country. He was able to continue a bit of farming without the Nazi's confiscating his vegetables. He would smuggle potatoes to my mother-in-law in the city, which was the only way her family survived that winter. One day a neighbor knocked on their door and begged to buy their potato peels to eat. If it wasn't for that country boy more than one family in the city would have starved! Think about it.

King Cotton or Killer Cotton?

Conventionally grown cotton is one of the most heavily multicided plants around, using 10% of all pesticides produced worldwide. Growing the cotton for a new conventional cotton T-shirt represents one third of a pound of insecticides, fungicides, et cetera-cides and chemical fertilizers.

Also to be considered is the dioxin produced during bleaching, the chemical defoliants used to remove leaves prior to harvest of the cotton bolls, and other chemicals used in processing.

Maybe we don't need new T-shirts, unless they are organic.

Cocktail party conversation:

Amaze your friends with these little-known facts

Interesting items that surfaced when the editor cleaned up his computer...

An ostrich oddity

The British *Country Garden & Smallholding* now includes an 8-page insert called Ostrich Review. From this we learned that the ostrich is the only bird that urinates. (Monthly, £23.95 per year outside UK; Buriton House, Station Road, Newport, Saffron Walden, Essex CB11 3PL)

Ostriches in New Zealand

Meanwhile, the head of a New Zealand farm organization, speaking about farming in that part of the world 10 years from now, predicts that "There will be more trees as sheep, beef and dairy give way to forestry. *But* the hillsides won't be dotted with ostriches. These are more likely to be given away as pets."

Homesteading by another name

Also via the New Zealand publication *Rural Garden* we note that their term for homestead is "lifestyle farm." (Rural News Co., PO Box 3855, Auckland 1 New Zealand; bi-monthly, $22 [New Zealand] per year.)

When is a fir not a fir?

We will never again refer to Douglas fir trees. According to Arbor Day, the proper spelling is Douglasfir—one word. Or hyphenated.

The reason: it's not a fir.

After being discovered by botanists around 1800 it was variously classified as a fir, spruce, hemlock and pine. In 1825 explorer-botanist David Douglas showed that it should be classified in a separate genus of its own. Its Latin name is *Psuedotsuga*, or false hemlock. –*Arbor Day*, An Official Publication of the National Arbor Day Foundation, PO Box 81415, Lincoln, NE 68501

Define "small farm," please

A few readers think it's silly to discuss the definition of "homesteading." So what would they think about a high-level meeting to discuss the development of a uniform USDA definition of "small farm?"

It happened! Representatives of the Agricultural Marketing Service, CSREES, the Economic Research Service, the Farm Service Agency, the Food and Consumer Service, the Foreign Agricultural Service, the National Agricultural Statistics Service and the Rural Development mission area all got together to define a "small farm."

And what did they decide? Considering that we're talking about a committee, and a government one besides, the outcome shouldn't surprise you.

"As a first step, participants decided to share their working definitions of 'small farm' with one another in order to obtain an overview of various definitions. They expressed their intention to arrive at a more uniform 'small farm' definition pending further discussion."

And pray tell, what are some of the terms these folks now use for "small farms"? They include "small farm," "medium farm"—and "large farm."

Sex change operation

Researchers at England's Manchester University and Scottish Agricultural College claim they can increase the number of female chicks hatched in incubators by changing the sex of some male embryos.

They reduce the incubator temperature for short periods during the first three days of incubation. (Temperatures and times were not given.)

Bet you didn't know this!

A ram sheep or buck goat responds to olfactory stimuli from an estrous ewe or doe by exhibiting the Flehman response. (Head back, mouth open, lips curled back.)

Vegetarian water

Here's a bizzare story that helps illustrate just how complex—some might say wacky—our little planet has become.

Some vegetarians in England are refusing to use tap water. They recently found out it's filtered through charcoal.

Charcoal made from burning bones.

Bones of sacred cows, from India.

Sacred cows' bones are preferred because they're allowed to live out their natural lives. Their old bones are brittle, and make perfect material for charcoal filters. Using cattle from Western societies that slaughter them young for beef wouldn't work as well because their bones are relatively soft.

Some people were glad to hear that the bones were imported. At least they're not using mad cows.

The machine shed:

Tool, toy or trap?

Important principles for equipping your small farm

Selecting farm tools: Part I

Jeff Rast, Farmer/Director
The Center for
Small Acreage Farming
Idaho

I can't recall a day in my life when I didn't like tractors. Their big gripping tires, shiny paint jobs and beefy power have attracted me since the day I could play in a sandbox without adult supervision. Even today, I find it difficult to walk onto the premises of an equipment dealer and admire some heavy metal without eventually thinking "Yep! Gotta have that one." For years now I've been in the grips of some Pavlovian reaction of salivating over every Kubota I see. Perhaps it's incurable.

But it isn't just the sit-and-drive tools that tempt me. I get the same twitching reaction every time I drive past the BCS dealership or see a Troy-Bilt ad in a magazine. Mind you, I'm not getting paid to drop these names in front of you. It's just that these power units and more have been a source of "tool temptation" for me for quite some time.

But are they really tools? They could be. Then again, they could be little more than pricey toys or, worse yet, expensive traps. It all depends on one's own unique situation. What constitutes proper equipment for one farm might not work quite as well on another farm. In fact, spending money on inappropriate equipment could seriously eat into your profits, if not devour them altogether.

I have run through the whole spectrum on how to properly equip my 10 acre farm. (We intend to never have more than 3.5 acres in intensive vegetable, fruit and herb production, including a small greenhouse. The rest of our farm is devoted to pasture and hay as well as a small homesite.) I've considered all the options from a 4WD Kubota with front-end loader, tiller, transplanter and snowblower, all the way to the other end of the continuum where we do everything with hand tools and hire out the snow removal.

This decision process is difficult for those of us who want to earn a respectable income, using little to no debt, but do not have a net worth high enough to make the banker smile. It's even tougher for us easily tempted tractor fans. But there are some helpful principles and guidelines to consider in order to equip your farm with appropriate tools and technology.

This article is the first in a series on equipping your small farm. Future articles will explore the principles that help one navigate through all the options, temptations and conventions which are too easily taken for granted. Then the series will provide a look at different types of tools and equipment, listing their intended uses as well as their advantages and disadvantages. For now, though, let's consider the question, "Is it a tool, a toy, or a trap?"

It's a tool

Look up the word "tool" in a dictionary and you'll find a wide variety of definitions. Perhaps the most encompassing is "Anything regarded as necessary to the carrying out of one's occupation or profession." But the phrase "regarded as necessary" is so often abused in farming, regardless of the scale of the farm. So much of what we regard as necessary comes to us via marketing, peer pressure and some pictorial conception of what a farm ought to look like.

But what do you really need? For something to qualify as being necessary to your profession as a farmer, it must help you profitably produce food, feed, fiber, etc. while regenerating the land. If it doesn't help you produce the product, it's not a tool. If it doesn't help you care for and regenerate your land, it's not a tool, at least not in the long run. And if it doesn't allow you to accomplish those two tasks at a profit (assuming you're marketing well), it's simply not a tool. Or rather, it's the wrong tool for your situation.

Both large-scale industrialized farmers and small-scale farmers are equally prone to buy inappropriate equipment which undermines the sustainability of the farm. It can take plenty of disciplined thought and paper work to finally decide on what you need for your farm. We'll take a look at some of the guidelines to consider later on.

It's a toy

While we've got the dictionary open to the Ts, let's see how it defines "toy." Yep. Thought so. It means something to play with. And that's just how so much of the equipment purchased for many farms ends up being used.

I once had the opportunity to participate in a tour of some large-scale grain and potato farms. One immense farm we visited was truly impressive. The shop was massive, with three ceiling-mounted engine hoists and enough gadgets to give a mechanic the impression that he just passed through the pearly (or rather the oily) gates. In another shop(!) on the farm, the son pointed out some of the machinery they used to produce all their potatoes and grain. One large, relatively new combine was parked regally in a corner. "We don't really use it as much as we thought we would when we bought it. I hate to admit it, but I guess it's just a big toy—a really expensive one." I appreciated his honesty.

On the smaller end of the farming spectrum, I see plenty of small farms with more tractor parked around than could probably be justified in terms of profitable production. But many of these farmers know that. They wanted a tractor and could afford one. These people are hobby farmers or gentlemen farmers. They are in a position where they can farm for recreation. The tractor doesn't need to pay its way. The farmer knows it's not paying its way and that's just fine with him or her. This is legitimate. In these situations, the tractor is a toy. Admittedly, it's a refined, sophisticated and expensive toy with many useful functions, but it's still what I would classify as a toy.

It's a trap!

However, a tractor or any other piece of equipment becomes a trap when it (1) was purchased to pay its way in profitable farming and (2) is perceived by the farmer to be paying its way, but, (3) it is not paying its way. This is where people can really get themselves into a bind. Over time, equipment which falls into this category eats away at the farm's income without the farmer ever knowing it. The culprit is hidden costs which cannot be found except through careful accounting.

It's not enough to purchase a used piece of equipment in reasonably good condition at an excellent price. That is important as far as it goes. The problem is, it doesn't go far enough. The hidden costs will rob you even more effectively than a street-polished pickpocket. At least in the case of pickpocket thievery, you discover fairly soon that you've been robbed. But the hidden costs can go undetected for so long that you'll blame your lack of profitability on other factors. That can make matters even worse.

Those most prone to get bit by the trap are the ones who "fly by the seat of the pants." These are the ones who overestimate the quality of their own instincts. Some of these people are a bit lazy, but most are hard-working, zealous farmers.

An accountant friend of mine has ways of spotting these people at tax time. The most obvious are those who bring their receipts in a shoe box or some dynamic equivalent. The one common trait these people share is their lack of current, detailed, orderly records. But even detailed records aren't enough if you don't account for depreciation (cost recovery). Let's begin looking at some very basic cost considerations in avoiding the trap while purchasing tools.

"Careful! It might be a trap!"

Crunching the numbers

Any piece of equipment you buy has numerous costs associated with it. These fall into two broad categories: ownership costs and operating costs. Understanding the difference between the two is crucial to your profit potential.

Ownership costs are fixed costs in that you spend the money every year whether you use the equipment or not. The real kicker, though, is that most of these costs are non-cash in nature and thus constitute those hidden costs which will gobble up profits if you don't account for them.

Usually the biggest hidden cost is depreciation or cost recovery. I find it helpful to think of this as replacement cost. The point here is that no equipment lasts forever and likely will need to be replaced eventually. I think the most responsible way of dealing with this is to set aside a certain amount each year to be used to replace the equipment.

Other hidden ownership costs include interest on the investment (if you've taken out a loan for the equipment)*, insurance and shelter.

Operating expenses include the obvious items such as fuel, lubricants, repairs and maintenance. The older the equipment, the higher will be the operating expenses, and the lower will be the hidden ownership costs.

***Even people who don't borrow should consider the opportunity cost. If you hadn't spent the money, it might be earning interest, or it might have been put to some other productive use.**

Jeff and his wife, Carol, juggle equipment decisions on their small farm in Idaho. Jeff also directs The Center for Small Acreage Farming which publishes a monthly newsletter and workbooks for small acreage farmers.

The workshop:

Eliminate stale fuel problems

SwampFox
Florida

If you have ever forgotten and left gasoline in a power tool over the winter, you know how it can foul up the fuel system. When I swapped some know-how for a tiller that had not run for over five years, I was faced with a classic case of crudded up fuel tank and carburetor. I decided to eliminate any future problems.

On small gas powered tools like my chainsaw or weed trimmer, I simply turn the unit upside down, drain the gas tank and start the motor. When the engine runs out of gas it is ready to be stored until the next time it's needed.

For something the size of a 5 hp tiller a different approach was indicated, so I explored the possibilities. For this type of tank a petcock of the type used as a drain in automobile

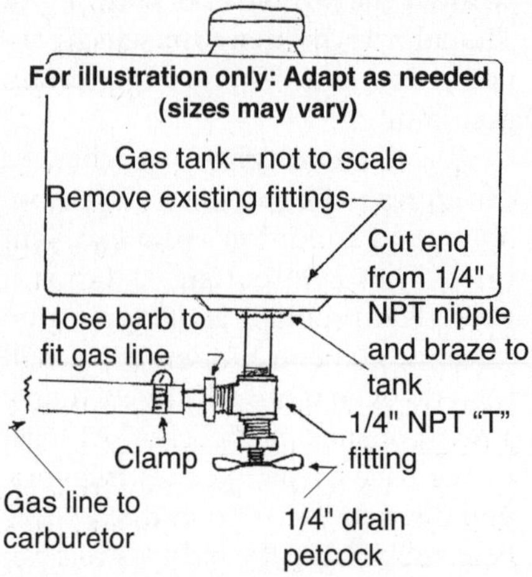

radiators seemed the best suited. These can be purchased at most car parts or hardware stores.

After determining the lowest point in the gas tank and marking it, the tank was removed and a hole was drilled for the petcock to fit into. It needs to be a tight fit, so I drilled the hole slightly undersized and reamed it to allow the petcock to thread into the sheet metal.

The next step was to remove all paint and dirt from around the area. After that, the petcock was threaded in about 3/4 of the thread and adjusted to lay flat against the inside tank bottom. I used a low temperature silver solder, also from the hardware store, to attach the fitting to the tank. Regular soft solder can be used, as no great strength is required at this attachment, but I prefer the silver solder.

Look at the photo and you can see how the finished installation works. When you are ready to store the tool for a length of time, simply drain the gas, start the motor and let it run until it quits. The few drops of gas left will evaporate and cause no problems.

An added bonus of this petcock is that you can easily drain any water that might get in the tank.

This method applies to a metal tank. If you have a plastic fuel tank the fitting will have to be epoxied into place. Do not drill any holes until you are sure the epoxy will work on your tank! You will have to experiment with the type of plastic on your particular fuel system to find the right one. J&B Weld, available at most auto parts stores, would be a good one to try on a number of plastics. Some, hardly anything will stick to.

If you look at the drawing you can see how to add the petcock to a tank with a bottom outlet. These will be found mostly on larger mowers, lawn tractors, etc. Simply remove the original fitting and add the parts as indicated. Use only silver solder or silver braze to fasten these fittings, because strength is required at this attachment point.

A word of caution: Be positive that all gas fumes are gone from the tank before attempting to solder or braze the fittings in place.

Preserving gasoline

Jim Rogers
Oregon

My question asking how to preserve gasoline was answered by about a dozen helpful Countryside readers from all over the U.S.

It seems there are two products on the market that can be added to gasoline to prevent it from deteriorating. Most readers recommended Sta-bil which can be purchased at Wal-Mart and some other stores selling auto supplies. A small container of Sta-bil costing $3.97 will preserve 20 gallons while the larger container costing $8.97 treats 80 gallons.

I phoned the company that makes it (Gold Eagle Co. in Chicago) and asked how long the fuel would remain fresh. They knew it would last for at least five years and thought it would probably last indefinitely if kept in sealed gerry cans in a cool place.

Another product called Gas Saver Plus is available by mail order from several businesses selling preparedness supplies. This treats 160 gallons for $15.65 (plus $5.95 shipping) or 320 gallons for $27.95 (plus $7.95). Phone numbers for a couple of these dealers are 1-800-866-4876 and 1-303-277-0305.

It's a good idea to have fuel containing this stuff in any engine that isn't run for long intervals (such as an emergency generator).

Homesteaders and the law:

Dog does its job, gets owner in trouble

Last week my dog bit someone. The dog was doing his job protecting our property. Now we face a huge fine, and might have to kill the dog. Let me tell you our story.

As I came in the door from picking up my husband from the hospital, the telephone was ringing. It was someone from a doctor's office, asking if our dogs have had rabies shots. (They have.)

It seems that someone had ordered flowers to be delivered with a "speedy recovery" wish for my husband. The floral delivery person came to our farm, ignored the closed chainlink gate and came up to our porch. To open the gate, he had to reach across a large sign reading "Warning: Security Dog On Duty." He later was quoted as saying he did not see a dog, so thought it was all right to come in.

Well, the dog didn't agree with him! For his trouble, the guy evidently had his pants torn, and was bitten on the leg. According to the doctor's office caller, it was not a puncture wound; just an abrasion.

So far the delivery person has not reported the bite to the humane society. One of our good neighbors did! No neighbor called us, but one of them called the humane society, telling them we were harboring a "vicious dog" that attacked a person, and tore up his leg very badly. (Not true.)

The humane society called yesterday as a follow-up to the "incident report." I was informed that should the "bitee" file a complaint, we would be ticketed. I explained about the closed gate, sign, etc. She informed me that signs such as ours made us even more likely for a lawsuit, as that was admitting we knew we had a "bad dog."

Now, this dog is a working Australian Shepherd. He was bred to help on the farm, including herding and protecting. Should we have to leave our property unprotected, and our animals subject to harassment and/or attack? Evidently, the law thinks we should.

In this area we have lots of problems with coyotes, raccoons, and dogs running at large. Also, the crime rate has gone up dramatically, with bold, daytime robberies. What are we to do? Is there no more common sense? Without our Aussies, we would be losing animals, equipment, etc.

We purchased 15 acres here in 1959, with much scrimping and saving. In 1961 the adjacent 10 acres with a small house and dilapidated barn became available. We were sweating blood, but went into debt and bought it. It wasn't easy; we went without many things, but wanted to raise our kids in the country. Now, the city is closing in on us. We are at the mercy of the Growth Management Act, run by three non-elected appointees of the governor. These three people live in a metropolitan area three counties away from us. They have never seen our property, yet they now have the right to decide what we can, or mostly cannot, do with it.

We have always expected to divide the property into smaller parcels someday, and sell it to provide a retirement income. When we purchased it, there were no firm zoning laws. Then it was zoned to one house per every 2-1/2 acres. Okay, we could live with that. But now, in their great wisdom, the powers that be have down zoned us to one house per 10 acres. They are saying smaller is urban sprawl. The good citizens who have moved into the many, many apartment complexes now located within a couple of miles of us want to be able to "enjoy the rural atmosphere." None of them have offered to help pay our taxes, clean the barn, tend animals, etc. Yet their wishes outweigh ours, even though we have been here, improving and nurturing this place for over 35 years.

Many years ago we made the mistake of putting in a small pond. Our ducks and geese enjoyed it, and we sometimes used it for irrigating. Now we get huge flocks of wigeon and Canada geese coming in. They devastate the pastures, pulling grass out by the roots. Another "good neighbor" likes to see them, so has requested that the county designate our property as a wetland. It's not, but we may lose our rights for using it. (Not our privilege for paying taxes on it, though.) We have a small stream on the acreage. Now the Department of Fisheries wants us to fence off 50 feet from both sides for the full length of the property to keep livestock out of it. We have maintained this for over 35 years! Now some apartment dwelling "expert" is going to have jurisdiction over our property.

Maybe I should just face the facts... it's not our property anymore. – *Frustrated Farmer, Western Washington State*

This suburb is not a good place for geese

It happened in Will County, Illinois:

A resident of a "semi-rural suburb" where lots average three acres got fed up with a neighbor's pet goose who used his pond as a bathtub... and his lawn as a toilet. He brained the goose with a shovel.

He was fined $250 and was sentenced to four months supervision by a judge. (The goose owners wanted him jailed, "so he could think about what he did.")

Someone who heard about it gave the family two replacement geese. They didn't last long, but the neighbor wasn't a suspect. They were killed by coyotes.

Time off:

Let's go to the Fair!

Jan Hoadley
California

Start planning now to enter your county fair as well as, if possible, the state fair.

Sandra Kayser told us about her success with garden produce (81/5:33), but there's a huge assortment of other projects you can enter at the fair. A mainstay of many homesteads, in addition to the garden, is canning. Jars of vegetables, jams, jellies, relishes, sauces and other items are put up for practical use... take the best jar of each to the fair! This isn't a waste either, as you get the jar back.

Baked goods—breads, pies, cakes, cookies—all have categories at the fair. Candies from fudge to peanut brittle have classes in many fairs. Most allow you to pick up the items after the fair is over—so again, no waste of food. Pick the most evenly matched cookies or candies, done but not showing traces of being burned. Pies and breads cover a wide variety. Some fairs have special classes for items made with honey. Some fairs have classes for honey in jars and pieces of comb in a jar. The premium book gives you all the information you need: how many cookies, what size jars to use, what kinds of pies are available.

Photography offers a special appeal for many. You not only preserve images of your special place in the world and can win prizes for it (more importantly, sharing it with others who come to the fair to watch!) but afterwards you have special, personal gifts for Christmas or to hang on your own wall. Look for the unusual way to project yours.

One photo I took has been to three fairs and has won two firsts and a second, and it wasn't taken with fancy equipment. A good 35 mm camera, a roll of black and white film and knowing a little bit about goats created a photo that has gotten many comments not only from fairgoers and judges but from customers at work, where it normally hangs in my office.

Anyone who's had goats can appreciate the lengths they'll go to for goodies. I walked to a shady tree with my girls, pulled a branch down to tempt them, and stood back a few feet. Sure enough, two stood up on their hind legs, reached with their fronts and pulled the branch down for a treat...but the branch can't be seen clearly in the photo so it appears they are reaching for the tree above.

Another winning photo is my Border Collie and ram. Both were hot and found a shady tree. They lay down just a few feet away from each other and again, a photo opportunity.

I've seen many creative, clever photos from other people, such as the toddler with the "Got Milk?" shirt and a Holstein calf reaching up to nose the child. Scenic photos, children with animals, flowers, animal babies and unusual poses all get looks.

Crafts are another area that many talented homesteaders can enter, from quilting to sewing to wreaths and hundreds of others. When you're spinning the wool and taking it from there into a sweater or afghan think of entering the item in the fair—homestead produced from start to finish. Many crafts can be made for competition then later given as Christmas gifts—with the ribbon still attached!

Still more ideas lie in animals. Look at the premium book. Perhaps you have some especially nice Barred Rock hens this year, or a very good lamb.

Be sure they meet the requirements before entering! At one fair last year I saw many birds disqualified—six pound "bantams," New Hampshire hens entered as Rhode Island Reds, Buff Orpingtons that were barely five pounds. If you have doubts, look in poultry catalogs and books for qualifications. If it says your breed should be five to six pounds and your hens are, consider taking them. Look for good feather plumage, straight tail carriage, bright eyes and good temperament. The latter is not judged but many little fingers—and big ones—get stuck into the cages!

If you have a lamb you're thinking of putting in the freezer and he's the right weight, see if your fair has a market class. Some have an entry fee that covers the cost of the butchering—you show the animal live, they haul him to the butcher then he's judged as a carcass meat animal. You get him back for the freezer and the butcher will cut to order (an additional charge). These classes also may be offered for market pigs (should be a "terminal show" — don't bring diseases back to your other pigs, if any!) and beef animals. The latter should be well broke to lead. Look in the premium book for weights required and other specifications.

Horses and dairy animals also have classes at most fairs. Sometimes these are one day events: you truck in, show, and then go home.

However, a word of warning if you take animals: Have someone available to watch over them. Animal rights people have been known to turn animals loose and/or put antifreeze in the water, which will poison and kill the animal. Aside from that, many fairgoers are totally unaware of farm animals and will try to feed them (goats, sheep, and poultry especially) any number of fair-bought goodies which may not be the best thing for the animal!

Some fairs offer special competitions — a salsa event or educational emphasis. Some fairs will mail you the entry book. You can enter by mail then go to drop off your exhibits (nonliving of course) at a certain time. Some fairs have a horticulture division where you can enter houseplants, bonsai and container grown plants. Flowers are another possibility—cut fresh for display not only for the fair but throughout the season for your home!

It doesn't take lots of money to be competitive at fairs. It takes knowing what you're doing and a little bit of luck. Many of the items can be used later at home or—as previously mentioned—given as gifts. Either one offers two uses for each item. Look on it as a learning experience. Perhaps you'll learn something that will not only make a winning entry but increase safety or efficiency at home. One jar I entered drew a comment of "not full enough" and I learned what to look for.

On the other hand, my first attempts at canning brought ribbons from the county fair as well as one winning second place at the state fair! One cookie entry was judged as being slightly burned. I disagreed at first but pulled the next batch out a little sooner… light brown, not medium brown… and not only do they do better but taste more flavorful too.

As Sandra said, do what you're doing anyway. It's not necessary to put extra work into the entries.

In some cases it can lead to income

aside from the fair. Perhaps your first place fudge results in people asking to buy it, or your champion "other breed" sheep results in someone wanting to purchase stock or meat, or your chickens bring in egg customers who were looking for fresh eggs but were unable to find them. Make up cards to put on the cages after judging, especially if you did well. Secure them so the animals can't reach them!

As I said, it doesn't take expensive efforts to win. I just entered things I was doing anyway. I've had Top Individual Hen, Top Trio under one year, Champion Dorset, Reserve Champion Hampshire sheep, Champion and Reserve "other breed" sheep, Junior Champion (over all breeds) dairy goat, as well as many first place wins with chickens, ducks, sheep, goats, cattle, canning, baking, photography and several other enjoyable activities.

Those that didn't win...no big deal! The non-placing jars of vegetables, fruits and jellies still feed your family; the third place sheep still produces lambs for the freezer every year; the sixth place goat still provides plenty of milk for the household. And those crafts that don't win still can be much appreciated gifts. I don't appreciate my animals any less if they win or don't place at all as long as they're doing what I want them to do—the ribbons and pocket money are just extra. Many of my birds were purchased from the same places many of you get birds from—McMurray and Cackle hatcheries. One sheep was a retired 4-H ewe—she and her offspring still did well at the shows and in the breeding classes she got many comments about holding together well as a four-year-old, then five year-old, then six-year-old. A few goats were former 4-H projects. Individual care given on a small farm can put a sheen to the feathers or shine to the coat that the "big guys" don't take time for. Few believed that the day before the show my "Top Individual Hen" was scratching for bugs in the garden and pestering the horse to get bits of grain he dropped. Or that the "Top Trio" roosted in an outside pen with a small A frame shed for shelter. Yet time after time spectators and judges marveled. What did I feed these birds? Their feathers are beautiful and they're so big and healthy looking! One judge—unfamiliar with my Barbados sheep—asked which one I thought should be first. When I didn't hesitate in pointing to Holly he asked why. I said she had twins that year and raised them on grass whereas the other had a single, but he couldn't tell that by looking at them. The Barbados cross lambs got considerable attention. (What breed is that?!")

Think it over… think about what you can do and plant in the coming months to take an active part in your county fair. Then just do it!

I've heard many fairgoers say they have nicer (sheep, goats, birds, etc.) at home. Fine. Bring them! Have some competition! After all, in the end that's what fairs were designed to do… find out who has the best animals, crafts, food products, etc. You can learn a lot, even if you aren't there for the judging. If you didn't win, look closely at those that did. Ask the superintendent if she/he isn't too busy for comments. And bless the judges who take the time during hectic judging to leave comments so we can all learn a little more!

Arts & crafts:

Make your own greeting cards with
Creative rubber stamping

Ariel Mars
Oregon

If you want to make your fortune, buy shares in greeting card companies.

Have you shopped for greeting cards lately? The day I pay $3.50 for a greeting card that someone looks at once and tosses, other great cataclysmic events will occur. The lowest price I found for a card at our local store was $1.25 and let us not mention the highest.

Consider the alternatives: 1. Don't send cards. (Defeats the purpose.) 2. Recycle cards. (Okay, but certainly not very personal.) 3. Make one on your personal computer. (Possible, if you have a personal computer.) 4. Discover rubber stamp art.

A year ago, after my shocking experience at the greeting card store, I met Candy, the "stamp lady" who has been rubber stamping for a number of years. Previous to that my experience with rubber stamps had been "return to sender" and "copy." You can imagine that I was not overly enthusiastic when she said, "I make my own." (Read in visions of cut and paste.)

Revelation! She doesn't just make cards with a stampedy machine: she has created some beautiful one-of-a-kind works of art.

Second revelation: stamps can say anything, generic or personal, and there are thousands to choose from.

Expensive? You can buy a stamp and an ink pad for the price of one of those "nice" cards at the greeting card store. Like anything else, you can spend whatever you choose, but being basically frugal I want to spend as little as possible, using materials I have on hand, and I want it to be reusable.

My first stamp cost $3, the ink pad was on sale for $3, and I used one really pretty paper that I cut off the bottom of a magazine advertisement. I folded the paper to envelope size, stamped the front, wrote Happy Birthday inside in nice lettering, and was very satisfied with the results. Good first start.

Check out the paper you normally throw away. We get so many catalogs, letters, annual reports, etc. that the supply seems endless. Not all of it will be useable, but some of the companies use very nice paper and they certainly aren't afraid to use a lot of it. A local engineering company will occasionally let one of our members sort through their throwaways and it is a gold mine of colored and textured papers. Printers often have scraps left over and one local printing company sells their leftovers for 50 cents a pound. A pound of paper makes a lot of cards!

Then there are the "How to Rubber Stamp" videos, self explanatory, very inspiring, springboards for greater and more creative efforts. There are magazines devoted to nothing but rubber stamping. One magazine is The Rubber Stamper, P.O. Box 420, Englishtown, NJ 07726 (bi-monthly, $25 per year), another is Rubber Stamp Madness, P.O. Box 610, Corvallis, OR (bi-monthly-$24 per year). Most rubber stamp companies put out their own catalogs for $2 to $8. To save on expenses four of us subscribe to a stamping magazine and then pass it around. There are websites devoted to rubber stamping on the Internet.

Rubber stamp clubs are another way of sharing without a lot of expense. Our stamp club, Stampers-R-Us, has meetings devoted to sharing catalogs from stamping companies, learning special techniques from other members who have taken a professional class, even philanthropic projects. Our philanthropic project each month is to donate a card or two each for the use of the local convalescent center to send to their patients who have no family or friends locally, or to give to patients to send to others. This year we stamped and donated two dozen calendars to give to the local senior center to distribute, sell, or give as bingo prizes. Cost? Minimal: each member donated $1.26 and their expertise and time.

My most recent purchase was a small hippopotamus stamp, a small bird and a small sheep, all of which were on the bargain table at $1 each. Combined with another dollar stamp of a music note, I stamped on the front of the card at the top, a hippo, halfway down, I stamped the bird, and at the bottom two sheep. The message was explained inside under duplicate images, surrounded by music notes. (Hippo—Birdie—Two Ewe.) Absolutely a hit at the birthday party and I can use it over and over.

Once a year there is a Rubber Stamp Convention in our neighboring city that has over a hundred vendors from throughout the United States offering stamps, magazines, accessories, catalogs and nearly everything else a stamper could want. These are held in major cities throughout the United States. Demonstrations are given by experts and the stamp stores in the area usually invite some of the celebrity names in stamping to put on a free demonstration of the latest techniques.

Cute sayings abound. One of my favorites is the goofy goat stamp, around which I usually make a few marker point flies and toss in a tree or some grass as a surround and then inside I use something like, "Stressed, anxious, weary, fed up? Yes, and you?" Or the new one I am having made, (Yes you can have your own made) "My husband said it's him or the goats... The goats are still here."

For many of us who raise goats or other animals, losing one of them is traumatic. When one of my friends loses a goat or other pet, I usually stamp a picture of that type of animal on the outside of the card, pen

in a blue tear in the corner of its eye and stamp the inside with "I think of heaven as a garden, where I shall find again those dear ones who have made my world."

Why stop with cards? You can stamp fabrics, ceramics, lampshades,

stationary (makes a great, inexpensive gift at Christmas or birthdays), name tags, envelopes and just about anything you want to personalize. You can make your own stamps with an eraser-like material or even a potato. You can simply stamp or you can emboss, (stamping with a raised image), stamp on metal, make collages with stamps and found objects, use water color techniques, anything you want to use to individualize your creation.

Rubber stamping is terrifically creative. If you doubt this, give three stampers the same stamp and blank cards. It is a fun shared experience. And it is nice when people oohhh and ahhh and think you are just "so clever" and the card looks "so expensive" and the recipient spends more time admiring the card than the gift.

The simplest stamps are the best. When I first started stamping I bought some really ornate angels. They are beautiful, but how many cards of beautiful ornate angels do you need?

The stamps I use most are the ones of an empty canning jar, an empty tote bag, a few single flowers and grass. Think of all the things you can use to fill those empty spaces.

Stamps can be purchased already mounted on wood, or unmounted which means just the rubber image (you also need a cushion to mount it on). It is a simple technique to mount your own stamps on wood, or with the new acrylic or Velcro methods. I really like the acrylic for stamps you don't use a lot. Unmounted stamps can be purchased for about half the price of already mounted ones.

Basic technique:

Paper, matte (dull finish) paper is easier for the beginner. Graduate to the glossy, glitzy later.

Stamp: Better to buy one or two small simple stamps than one expensive ornate one.

Stamp pad: Several kinds. I like the pigment pads, but you can use any pad made for rubber stamps.

Accessories: Limitless, but look in your kitchen and bathroom for unused woolly metal scrubbers, sponges, makeup wedges. The key is to find something that will pick up color and stamp with a good texture.

Colored markers: Water soluble, wide tip if you only have one kind, but both wide and fine are useful to accessorize your stamp. They can also be used to color in portions of a stamp you want in a different color. Just use the colors you want on the stamp itself (remember water soluble), blow on the stamp with moist, hot breath and stamp.

Lay down several sheets of absorbent paper, (preferably not newspaper) one on top of the other, as your base to work on. Have your supplies at hand. Place your chosen paper on top of the absorbent sheets, take your stamp in hand, tap onto the ink pad half a dozen times to ink it and place the stamp firmly down on one spot of the paper and exert pressure for a few seconds. Success!

But the stamped image may look a little bare. Using another color ink pad, tap your make-up or other sponge on the pad and sponge in background color, or stroke your colored marker directly onto the sponge and then stamp. You can create beautiful skies with just one color of blue depending on how heavily or lightly you apply it. Grass can be made with a grass stamp, of which there are multiple kinds, or you can use the same background technique and fill in the stems with your ink marker. (Remember, all grass does not grow straight up.) Curl up the corners of your sponge when you are tapping to avoid sharp corners in your background. Tap your woolly scrubber onto the ink pad and use it to make some great background bushes.

You can buy bare tree stamps or you can combine the woolly scrubber bushes onto some branches and trunks you make with your ink markers.

Clean your stamps with a mixture of a window cleaner and water (half and half). You can either spray it on and blot it off, or use a fuzzy paint pad in a container, saturate it with the mixture and pat the stamp clean and then blot off with a towel. Recently we have been using baby wipes as cleaners and conditioners for our stamps. One or two set in a plastic container are quick, easy, and last a really long time. Always clean your stamp after using it. Your images will stay crisp and clean and your stamps will last longer.

I have used one goat stamp for years to personalize the letters I send to people inquiring about my animals. When they see the Nubian head and the sticker red heart I put with it they immediately identify with my herd name.

Did I say this was cheap? Hmm, it can be. But you must exercise great restraint because all the attention you will get will remind you of the great stamp you saw at the store last week which would be just perfect for...

Could Abe Lincoln afford one today?

The cost of log homes is rising. The price of eastern pine, one of the main types of wood used in log homes, increased about $30 per thousand board feet last year, to about $480. Previous annual increases were more on the order of $5.

In addition, at least one nationwide insurance company no longer insures log homes because the cost to repair a fire-damaged log building was far higher than expected. In one case it cost $110,000 to make repairs that would have been about $40,000 in a stick-built home, the company said. – *Wall Street Journal*

Sources of work clothes

If you are in an occupation which wears out work clothes fast, request catalogues from The Working Man, PO Box 140204, Nashville, TN 37214 (615-883-1530) and Walt's Wholesale, PO Box 208, Darlington, SC 29532 (803-393-8081). An example of pricing is four pairs of work pants and shirts for $21.95.

An outhouse I'll never forget...

DOLLY HANCHETT
MICHIGAN

Some years ago, in Colorado, I stopped at a trading post to buy some junk I didn't need. I asked the man if there was a bathroom and he said sure, out back. So out I went.

I don't know why, but I always have to look down the hole before I sit down. What a shock! There was nothing there but space. This guy built an outhouse overhanging a canyon! He'll never have to dig another hole, but I couldn't sit down for fear I would topple it over.

Old technology:

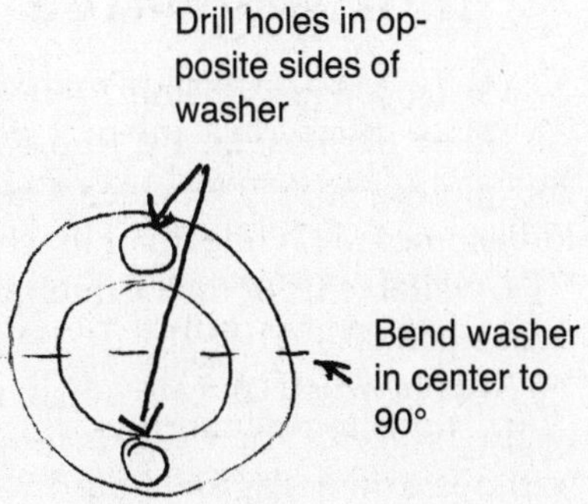

Diagram 1

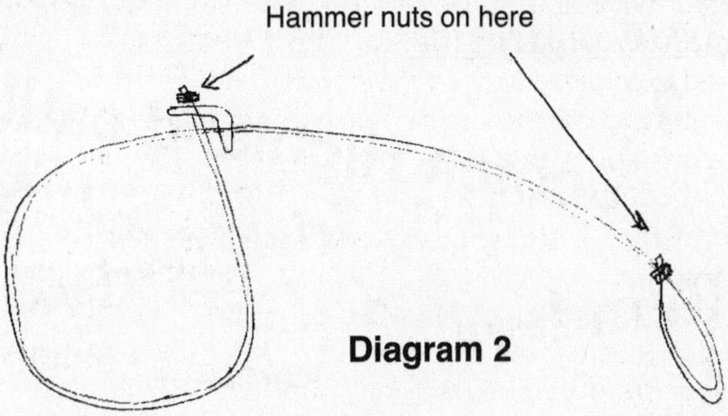

Diagram 2

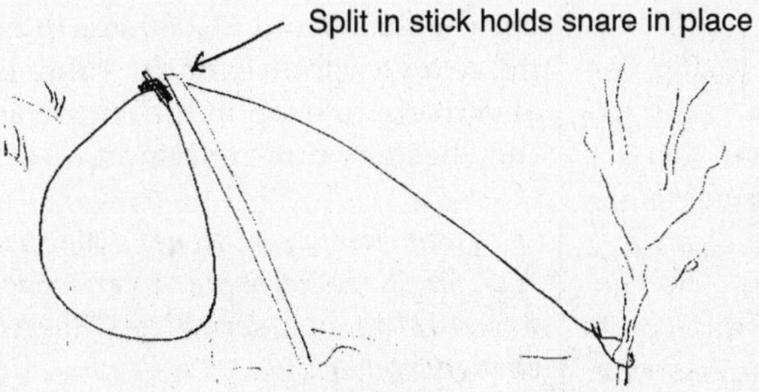

Diagram 3

The ancient skill of snaring

Jim E. Johnson
Louisiana

Our forefathers scraped an existence out of the wilderness and had to survive on what was available. They planted crops and harvested game from the woods and fields. But contrary to popular belief and what we have read and seen on television not all game was harvested by hunting.

Native Americans used traps of all sorts and ingenious methods to procure game. The white settlers brought steel traps, which were hand forged and very expensive. Some adopted the Indian methods of game procurement and started using deadfalls and snares. Today the same methods can be employed to produce food for the table or to rid the homestead of a nuisance predator.

Snares have evolved from a simple noose made of vines or leather into today's modern snare constructed of aircraft cable. This cable can be purchased at most hardware stores and comes in sizes varying from 1/16" in diameter to as large as 1/8". Around the farmstead 1/16" or 3/32" will handle any size animal you want to catch.

A lock is designed from a bent washer and stops are made on the cable from tempered steel nuts. A hole is drilled on opposite sides of the washer (see diagram #1) and bent at a 90 degree angle. The cable is placed through the hole and a nut is smashed on the end of the wire. Nuts must be heated in a fire and allowed to cool. This takes the temper out of the metal and allows it to be smashed on the wire without breaking. The threads in the nut grip the wire and will not slip off.

The wire is placed through the washer as in diagram #2. This can make the snare either a locking or a non-locking device. The difference is a locking snare when closed does not open but only becomes tighter and a non-locking does not. Some states have laws against locking snares so be sure to check local regulations before setting and using snares.

On the opposite end a loop is formed so the snare can be tied off or staked.

New snares should not be dyed or colored. All you should do is boil them in a mixture of baking soda and water for a few minutes. In a few days they will take on a light gray color which blends in naturally with the surroundings.

Setting is quite simple. A noose is made about the size of the target animal's head. It is placed in the trail where it is traveling. A split is placed in a stick to hang the snare from and stuck in the ground next to the trail (diagram #3). Secure the snare to a bush or stake and open the loop to the size you need and place it in the split end of the stick. The stick keeps the snare from falling down or being knocked over.

The beauty of snares is that they are simple in nature and very easy to use. Also they can be selective, whereas steel traps generally are not. They can successfully take beaver, otter, coyotes, rabbits, mink and raccoons. They also would be a very good item to carry in a survival pack, not only because of their effectiveness, but also their light weight. Rain or freezing weather does not affect their operation so they are always ready to use.

Ask Countryside:

? Scotch Highland cattle ? Irish Terriers ? Alpacas ? Reindeer ? Kerosene heater wick ?

RESPONSES PROVIDED BY
KEN SCHARABOK, TENNESSEE

Q *I would like to know more about Scotch Highland cattle.*

A Contact the American Scotch Highland Breeders Association, Box 81, Remer, MN 56672.

Q *I am seeking information on raising reindeer in Wisconsin: availability of stock and feeding requirements.*

A Contact the Reindeer Owners and Breeders Association, 2921 N. 6th St., Kalamazoo, MI 49009; 269-375-2448; roba_association@hotmail.com; www.reindeer.ws

Q *I am seeking information on Irish Terriers and Alpacas.*

A For information on Irish Terriers contact the Irish Terrier Club of America, 416 Arlington Ave., Naperville, IL 60565; 630-420-2271. For other dog breeds contact the American Kennel Club, 5580 Centerview Dr., Raleigh, NC 27606; 919-233-9767; www.akc.org. The address of *Alpacas* magazine and the Alpaca Owners & Breeders Association is PO Box 1992, Estes Park, CO 80517-1992 (800-213-9522). Alpacas seem to be destined to be the next "hot" rare breed. If past experience holds true, a breeding pair bought today for $30,000 will be worth only a fraction of that value several years from now. Alpacas currently provide between $500 and $1,000 worth of fleece a year; however, its value is also likely to drop in the future as they become more common.

Q *I am seeking an owner's manual for a Sears kerosene heater, model #564402130, in order to learn how to change the wick.*

A For a couple of bucks extra the place where you bought the replacement wick will also likely install it for you or you can likely do it yourself by just taking the heater apart until you get to the point where it becomes obvious how the wick is replaced. Chances are you might not even have to replace the wick. Try trimming the top and moving the wick up a little. I have been using the same wick in my Kerosun heater for over ten years. The owner's manual for my Kerosun recommends letting the unit use up all of the available kerosene periodically as this helps to keep the wick cleaner.

Q *I am interested in raising Nigerian Dwarf goats but the information available on them is rather limited. Can anyone provide additional information?*

A You might start by contacting the Nigerian Dwarf Goat Association, 3636 Cty. Rd. 613, Alvarado, TX 76009; 817-790-8559; info@ndga.org; www.ndga.org or try looking in the Encyclopedia of Associations at your local library. You may have to call the research department at a larger city main library to find a copy.

Book reviews:

How to live mortgage-free

Mortgage Free: Radical Strategies for Home Ownership, by Rob Roy; 280 pages, paper; Chelsea Green Publishing Co., White River Junction VT (Available from the Countryside Bookstore, 800-551-5691.)

Anyone who is not already living in the house of their dreams—and without a mortgage—should read this book next weekend, if not sooner. But then, almost anyone will enjoy and profit from Rob Roy's facts, anecdotes and musings.

Mortgage Free is part philosophy, part building manual, and part autobiography. It not only says a great deal about shelter—how to think about it, plan it, and acquire it—but it also covers a great deal of what some of us call homesteading.

Rob notes that there are three types of people who live without mortgages: the rich, the poor, and the smart. With this book, you can be among the smart.

He points out that historically, human shelter cost nothing—like the nests and dens of other animals. Then in the Middle Ages, it was common for a serf to work three months for the lord of an estate, in return for a house, land on which to grow food, and a communal defense system.

Today we work the first 140 days or so of the year just to pay taxes. And since the average American family spends 32 percent of its after-tax income on shelter, we work another 90 days just to have a roof over our heads.

This means most people don't earn any money they can actually spend on food, clothing, or anything else, until well into August. If we think of serfs as just a notch above slaves, he wonders, then what's the word for us?

Rob Roy claims that being enslaved by a mortgage is ridiculous, and totally unnecessary. And he lays out personal experiences, observations, and strategies that will enable almost anyone to be mortgage-free.

Although well known for his expertise on cordwood construction, in this book Rob considers virtually all the options, with emphasis on the use of indigenous materials.

The real value of this book, however, is not to learn how to build a house, but to learn how to think about a house.

But because thinking about building a house, yourself, with indigenous materials and no mortgage, obviously requires a positive attitude toward independence, simplicity and frugality, these are woven into the fabric of the book.

Most of the "radical strategies" won't seem radical at all to COUNTRYSIDE readers. What's more, these strategies are so clearly explained and logically stated that it's difficult to think that anyone could consider them radical. This book makes the "conventional wisdom" about housing seem pretty ridiculous—but it does it with common sense, humor and grace.

Topics covered include the grubstake, finding land, temporary shelters, and many interesting and valuable anecdotal references to home design and construction. But you'll also find useful information on alternative energy, and even intensive gardening.

Rob Roy freely draws on Thoreau's *Walden,* which this book is quite similar to in several respects. It's humorous, insightful, and at the same time practical in many areas, some far removed from providing a mortgage-free shelter.

Independent thinkers will find it stimulating and entertaining, even if they have no intentions of building a mortgage-free house.

How to live without television

"The White Dot Newsletter," quarterly; $8 for four issues; The White Dot, PO Box 577257, Chicago IL 60657.

"The White Dot" is subtitled Survival Guide for the TV-Free and fits in nicely with the homestead philosophy. A statement on the contents page says "Welcome to the White Dot, a newsletter for television-free households. (Or) maybe you own a television but find it unsatisfying to watch." Who, us?

An interesting autobiographical article by Brian Kologe, who dumped his tube 27 years ago, is a highlight of the issue. He gives concrete examples of all the things he was able to do without tv sucking away his energy. He also prepares those about to become tv-free by explaining what boredom is and how it can be an impetus to action.

While some of the articles seem unnecessary (a scathing review of something called the Recovery Network, which features televised AA meetings is given) but this criticism of the network seems like preaching to the choir. Presumably, anyone reading this newsletter already feels tv is junk, so what's the point of reviewing shows or, in this case, entire networks? (Besides, to me it sounded like one of the few things on tv that would be interesting and worthwhile to watch!)

A cute feature in Issue No. 7 is the "Life of Waste-O-Meter" which clearly gives the number of years you'll spend watching tv if you live to 40, 50, 60, etc., (according to the figures about the average hours of tv watched). And "Unattached and Unplugged" is a column by a single male who is tv-less and deals with that all-important question: how does a single male handle life without sports on tv?

It's rare to find a magazine with an individualist flair that dovetails with COUNTRYSIDE. But this newsletter does, since it's for people who "do" rather than "watch" life. I think that the "Letters" column, which runs to two pages (because without tv, one has more time to write letters and more brain cells available, apparently, to make them thoughtful!) makes for interesting reading, including as it does testimonials from people who have discovered or rediscovered what it feels like to live life instead of watching a little or big black box.

One woman describes a probably commonplace occurrence: "I grew up hearing 'Shhhhh!!!' whenever I spoke while tv was on!" (Nowadays, with tvs on 24-7—that's 24 hours a day, 7 days a week—in many homes the kids would never get a chance to talk at all!)

And other readers who desire a tv-free life describe what it's like to live with a spouse who'd sooner give up the spouse than Channel 2 or HBO. (Sounds pretty similar to those COUNTRYSIDERS who are married to city folks who just don't understand.)

The name The White Dot comes from… the white dot that older folks will remember when a tv's knob was turned off. (For the youngsters in the crowd, "turn the knob" was what people did before remote controls were invented. Yes, we actually had to walk up to the set itself to change the channel!) —*Reviewed by Linda Westley, California*

How to spin without a spinning wheel

Spindle Spinning: From Novice to Expert, by Connie Delaney; ISBN 0-9660952-0; 80 pp; paper; $12 + $2 S&H; Kokovoko Press, Route 3 Box 134, Corinth, KY 41010.

Spindle Spinning explains the simple process of spinning wool and other fibers into yarn using inexpensive handspindles. To make learning easy for beginners, the complete, illustrated guide gives step-by-step instructions that begin with selecting and preparing wool for spinning. By the end of the book, the reader will be able to spin fine silk thread.

The lessons begin on a top-whorl spindle and continue to show the best methods for all types of spindles, including bottom-whorl, Turkish, Navajo, and various supported spindles. Simple instructions for making several types of spindles are included.

Detailed and illustrated instructions explain basic skills and more advanced techniques for plying, winding on, wrist distaffs, skein-making, and improving speed. The book also includes sections on types of wool, other spinning fibers, and troubleshooting.

Emergency in the countryside? **Do-it-yourselfers to the rescue!**

Ariel Mars
Oregon

EMERGENCY!
POLICE! FIRE! AMBULANCE!
DIAL 911!

Doesn't take a rocket scientist to figure out that one does it? So what happens if there is no 911? You're on your own. Not a strange concept for most homesteaders, in most situations, but a pretty frightening ordeal for people who are not prepared for any emergency, minor or major.

In our county the law enforcement system deals with life-threatening situations on an immediate basis. The exponential population growth, the large geographic area of our county, and the static if not lesser amount of officers has brought us to an expectation that any other "emergency" will be handled on as-an-officer-is-available basis. We've learned to live with that.

But do we expect the fire engine, the ambulance and life flight to be there when we need them? How about a minor disaster? Or a major disaster? What about a 7.0 earthquake, a volcanic eruption (not unheard of here on the Pacific Rim), or the 100 year flood we keep having on the average of every 30 years? Who are you going to call and will they be there if you need them, if you can get through?

Beyond our own personal preparedness, even homesteaders don't usually give this too much thought. The time has come for us to start thinking about it. Your government already is and, as in most things, they are not usually the first to the table.

We recently attended a community involvement meeting sponsored by our county. The first words out of their mouths were "in the event of a major emergency, you people in the outlying areas need to be able to sustain yourselves for a minimum of three days." Sustain, as in no police, no fire, no medical, no help.

FEMA (Federal Emergency Management Agency) is sponsoring a program that could mean not only your survival but those of your neighbors as well. Homesteaders do help each other: it's a way of life. Don't expect everyone to live that life or have the skills necessary to help and when an emergency happens it will be too late for most people to start learning.

Before we get too critical of others we need to ask ourselves how much we know about emergency preparation. Sure, I know about the flashlights, portable radios, water, emergency food, etc. What do I know about fire suppression, triage, disaster medical operations, light search and rescue or disaster psychology? How can I help myself and my neighbors become an effective emergency management unit with little or no outside help? It brings home a very important homestead principle—we need each other to survive, despite our predilection for rugged individualism.

In our local area FEMA training is available through CERT, Community Emergency Response Teams. We have been involved in a seven-week training exercise which provides us an opportunity to learn and practice and be prepared in any major emergency situation. One of the most important lessons to learn is that your greatest skill will lie in organization. Know what to do when the situation arises, have your equipment on hand and know how to use your equipment in an orderly and beneficial fashion.

Fire suppression: We learned what extinguishers to use (when is the last time you saw yours, if you have one?) and how to use them. What are the three major classes of fire that we could expect to deal with? Class A, ordinary combustibles, paper, cloth, etc.— a water extinguisher or a dry chemical type is appropriate. Class B, flammable liquids, oils, gasoline, grease, etc.—a foam or dry chemical type is appropriate. Class C, electrical equipment—use a foam or dry chemical extinguisher.

Using them is simple: PASS. Pull the pin, Aim the nozzle, Squeeze the handle and Sweep the fire. Check to make sure you have fire extinguishers in place, that they are fully charged and that all members of your family know how to use them. Hints like aim at the base of the fire, not the flames, is just one of the informative points this class teaches.

Disaster medical operations: How can you do the greatest good for the greatest number of victims? The number of victims will likely exceed local capacity for treatment and the survivors will have to help others. Is triage a word you associate with MASH or ER? Triage is a French word meaning "to sort." Victims are evaluated, sorted by immediacy of treatment needed and set up for immediate or delayed treatment. To do the greatest good you must begin at a single point and work out quickly through your victims, assessing the injuries and assigning a designation for the rescue workers to follow. The goal in triage is to identify victims, overall, not fixate on one individual's injuries.

The rescue workers follow with actual treatment. The classifications are I for immediate, D for delayed or DE for dead. The immediate (I) victim has immediate life threatening injuries: treat these first; Delayed (D), injuries do not jeopardize the victim's life; Dead (DE) no respiration after two attempts to open the airway. CPR is not performed in a disaster environment. Remember, the greatest good for the greatest number.

The three life threatening conditions to be given priority are airway obstruction—use the head tilt, chin lift method (the most common airway obstruction is the tongue); severe bleeding—direct pressure, and/or elevation; and recognizing and treating shock—rapid, shallow breathing, cold pale skin, failure to respond to simple commands—keep warm, elevate feet, lay victim on back.

There is also training in splinting broken bones (magazines, cardboard or newspapers make a good temporary splint), the three types of bleeding, arterial, spurting blood; venous, excessive blood flow; capillary, oozing blood, and the methods of treating each.

Burns are addressed: the types of burns, 1st degree, reddened dry skin, pain, possible swelling; 2nd degree, blistered skin, wet appearance, also possibly pain and swelling; 3rd degree, whitened, leathery or charred skin, painful or relatively painless. Remove the victim from the burn source, cool with water (do not use ice, it can cause hypothermia), elevate extremity above heart if possible; do not apply antiseptics, use only a sterile dressing. A dressing is applied directly to the wound, a bandage is used to hold it in place.

Search & rescue:

The objectives of search and rescue are to realize that you should not put yourself in jeopardy. You should try to rescue the greatest number of people in the shortest amount of time, and lightly trapped victims should be rescued first. They may be able to help you with others.

The procedure for search and rescue is an outline for the course contents. Gather the facts, assess the damage, identify your resources, establish the rescue priorities, conduct the rescue, and evaluate your progress.

Most survivors are in the void spaces of collapsed buildings, such as where the middle collapses and the ends lean against the wall, also under tables and desks and other furniture. Call out, "If anyone is in here, come to my voice." Listen. Use a systematic search pattern, bottom-up, top-down, right wall-left wall, etc. If you come in the door or other opening, start by going either right or left along the wall and keep that pattern throughout your search. It may also be a way of rescuing yourself.

Learn about leverage and cribbing. Even a small person can move heavy objects with the proper blocks and levers. Learn rescue techniques. We're all pretty familiar with the fireman's carry that we see on tv and in disaster movies. How effective that will be when you are 125 pounds and you are carrying a 250 pound victim remains to be seen. It is an option. Placing the victim on a rug, board, or even dragging them by standing behind them and pulling them out with their clothes are also options. While the best method, if time and circumstances allow, is to determine injuries and stabilize the victim, there might be times when this is not a possibility.

Disaster psychology & team organization:

It helps to recognize the emotional phases that survivors go through during and after a disaster. The impact phase where the survivors do not panic and may show no emotion; the inventory phase when the survivors assess damage and try to locate other survivors; the rescue phase where emergency services personnel, including CERT's, are responding and survivors are willing to take their direction from these groups without protest. Remember that stress can lead to unusual behaviors. Don't take anything personally. People's reactions are often due to their inability to cope with the disaster itself. Maintain a professional demeanor, listen, establish rapport and respect confidentiality.

Each member of a CERT team is given instruction and training in all of the above areas and in much greater depth than has been discussed here. Our CERT team, being the first in our county, was given without cost a Community Emergency Response Team Participant Handbook (a super resource and review manual), a hard hat, a reflective vest, an all-purpose tool for turning off gas and other utilities as well as other functions, plus latex gloves, bandages, dressings for training, etc. Even if there is a cost, it's dollars you will never regret spending.

What to do when a power outage puts a chill on most activities... but takes it out of your freezer

If a power failure puts the refrigerator and freezer on the blink, what can you do to salvage foods?

- **Keep the refrigerator and freezer doors shut when the power goes out. Open the freezer or refrigerator doors only to add dry ice or other frozen foods. Both these items will help keep temperatures low.**
- **Never open the door just to check on how the foods are doing. It only lets precious cold air out.**
- **When electric power is restored be sure to check foods to determine the extent of thawing.**
- **Get rid of any food that is off-color or anything with a suspicious odor. Never taste meat, poultry or other foods that are suspect to see if they have spoiled. This is an easy way to be exposed to botulism poisoning.**
- **Meat that still has ice crystals present or that has maintained a temperature of 40° F for less than two days can be safely refrozen. Some quality may be lost in refreezing, but the meat will still be wholesome and safe to eat. Eat refrozen foods as soon as possible.**

In addition to training each of us to assume a disaster preparedness/ response role in a major emergency we have also learned a great deal about our own strengths and weaknesses and our ability to cope not only with monumental disasters but more effectively cope with our own personal responses. We are going to continue meeting with our team members and working within our community to assess potential problems and prepare emergency plans before they are needed.

We have a much better understanding of the functions of emergency personnel, especially those of the Clackamas County Fire District #1, who conducted this training. It gives us the ability to assist in even minor disasters when trained personnel have other areas where their professional training is needed more urgently. It has also very importantly established a rapport within our very diverse group and with the trained fire personnel. We are working on an ongoing program of area assessments, procedures for control, identifying skilled residents, and increasing community awareness. Several of us are updating our CPR certifications and one member is a ham radio operator who will be offering training to help us get our ham (amateur radio) license. In our county there is a core of ham operators assigned to fire stations and other strategic locations to help emergency personnel (fire, police, etc.) communicate with each other in the event of an emergency communications system failure.

We may not have 911 or police, or fire, or life flight, or ambulances, but we won't be completely helpless. We will have a trained core of people who care about each other and their neighbors and who are trained and prepared to do something when 911 doesn't answer.

It is impossible to cover all the valuable information we received in this class. How does it apply to me and what can I do about it anyway? The major cause of injury in the Loma Priada, California earthquake, was cut feet from broken glass. You can always keep a pair of shoes beside your bed. It's a first step.

For further information about CERT programs contact the Emergency Management Institute, FEMA 162825 S. Seton Ave., Emmitsberg, MD 21727 or visit the website at http://training.fema.gov/emiweb/cert/.

Thoughts from CERT member Ariel Mars:

CERT training brings a new attitude toward Big Brother

Having just completed the disaster preparedness training offered by FEMA, the Community Emergency Response Team classes, and having written about my experience to share with other COUNTRYSIDE readers, I should have a feeling of accomplishment and satisfaction.

No.

Rugged individualism, self-help, do-it-myself, beholden to no one but willing to help when and if I am needed or asked, describes the average homesteader, in my opinion. In re-reading my article, I found myself quite shocked to have written in essence that I expected the government to provide emergency services such as fire, police, etc. I expected to be taken care of no-matter-what and the shocking part was that it might not happen.

We give lip service to maximum independence and self sufficiency. That should mean that I shouldn't have great expectations of being "cared for" by Big Brother. I try to live that kind of life. I highly value privacy and being able to take care of my own problems. So, why on earth would I expect to be taken care of! I sense a fundamental flaw in my thought process.

The final exam for the CERT classes was a three part hands-on exercise. Understand that at all times there were trained emergency personnel there, ready to step in and keep us on task. Government, in the large sense of an organized sponsored body, was being represented. It would be unrealistic to say that we weren't very apprehensive about actually doing, in a simulated emergency, all the procedures we had been taught, but the trained personnel were there.

The actual final exam consisted of suppressing a large fire contained in an open steel tank. Standing there with the fire extinguisher in your hand you were mentally rehearsing PASS, (Pull the pin, Aim, Squeeze, Sweep). We were all okay with that. We'd practiced, an actual fireman was at our side, and one of our classmates was there with another extinguisher acting as a safeguard. We were backed up by trained personnel.

The second part of the exam consisted of going into a smoke filled "burning" building, complete with timber and steel hazards, simulated arcing electrical wires, upturned furniture, and finding our "victim." Most of us hated the thought of doing this but we had received instruction. Once again the instructor was there, we more or less remembered what we had been taught, and we were working as a team and we found our victim. We were backed up by trained personnel.

The third part of the exam, which we thought would be a breeze, was going into an actual classroom, no smoke, no fire, just overturned tables and chairs, to triage a group of carefully made up victims. Remember, the trained personnel are at your elbow. This is an exercise; no way can you blow it.

It surprises me that any of us made it through. The victims were so well made up that the bone sticking through the bloody leg looked real. Oozing wounds and screaming victims were everywhere. I fervently prayed that I would never see the real thing. And I was so thankful that my sponsored organized body (the fire department-government) was there!

Being grateful is good for the soul. Perhaps for the mind also. The more I thought about how dependent we were on the professionals (government) in this situation, the more I thought about how dependent we are on our established government in all areas of our lives. Instead of seeing them as a roadblock or an adversary or an expected service, I was put in a situation where I was truly grateful to have a backup. I was truly glad to have Big Brother there with me and for the training that I had received.

There are a lot of things I don't like about government—inefficiency, lethargy, bureaucracy, minding my business are just a few. I appreciate what I learned in the way of techniques and procedures in this class, but what I truly have learned to appreciate is that we have a lot to be grateful for in our own everyday lives that is provided by the "government".

Maybe we are too quick to condemn that cop who gave us the ticket, the bureaucrat who makes you fill out the same form you filled out last week in triplicate, the road crew that blocks your way to work to fill the potholes, the planning department that makes

Disasters take many forms, and can strike anywhere. The two inches of solid ice shown in these photos knocked out power over a wide area for five days in 1994. ***(Nancy Johnson, Tennessee)***

you get yet another permit. It's easy to become angry, resentful, and just plain tired.

I wonder, though, how many of us take time to be grateful for the cop who died while trying to stop an armed robber, or the bureaucrat who enforced the rule on wiring your house and saved you from a house fire or the road crew that clears the way for the emergency crews to get to your home and help you.

The next time I have to deal with one more rule or ordinance or resolution, I am going to think back on my CERT training and remember how grateful I was to have someone from the "government" there to help me. This was just a training session, we all knew it was a training session, and I can't begin to express the relief and gratitude that we had for those professionals (from our government) who helped us in that particular situation and prepared us for ones to come.

Do I still have expectations? Yes. But my expectations don't include the government solving my problems (even when I wasn't aware of that expectation): just helping me to solve my own with the proper training and a better attitude.

Perhaps this wasn't a moment of deep psychological truth but it was, on reflection, a "change my life" experience. We do need each other, we do need government, we do need to remember to be part of the solution and not the problem. Mostly we need to take a good hard look at our own expectations and biases.

My ideal homestead:

"I'm amazed at how much I have accomplished on my to-do lists!"

WENDY MARTIN
VERMONT

I have been planning my ideal homestead ever since I was a kid. I grew up reading a few books about the wilderness and homesteading, over and over. My favorites were books by Bradford Angier like *Skills for Taming the Wilds, How to Build Your Home in the Woods* and *On Your Own in the Wilderness.* Then there was *The New Way of the Wilderness* by Calvin Rutstrum and *Wildwood Wisdom* by Ellsworth Jaeger. Then I found *Five Acres and Independence* by M.G. Kains and *The Have-More Plan* by Ed and Carolyn Robinson, and all the books by the Nearings. From there I read anything and everything I could get my hands on about building, organic gardening, homestead animals, etc.

I have always kept journals. This has been very helpful. I tried to write down all my dreams, schemes and big ideas. I sketched out details, made lists and kept a bibliography.

To this day, I am amazed at how much I have accomplished on my to-do dream lists!

Once I knew what I wanted, I could take advantage of things I gleaned or salvaged or got cheap at a garage sale. Projects came together as time, money and scrounging permitted. I have lived in all sorts of situations from middle-class kid to college student to corporate America technician to homeless to a rented cabin to owning my own underground home and organic farm.

Wow! Was I ever happy when I got here and could put down roots! I've been here 10 years now. I started with a 14 x 28 ft. one-room underground house with no running water, bathroom, kitchen, electricity, etc. There was a big overgrown field by the road that was full of brambles, bushes, poplars and small evergreens. I had been living in a tent all summer before moving here. I had virtually no money.

I located a spring, developed it and ran a pipe to the house for gravity-fed water.

The only cooking amenities were the wood stove and a "barbecue window." I opened a window, started a fire with sticks and newspapers, and cooked most things in a wok over a makeshift grill. First I got a "free for the taking" gas stove that was outside, hooked to a small propane tank. Eventually I got room to put it inside. There was a closet into the earth that we used for a root cellar. Our "kitchen" was a piece of plywood with holes that two buckets hung in. Gray water had to be taken outside. The toilet was a five gallon bucket under the loft.

A great deal of progress has been made in 10 years.

Over time the house and out buildings expanded. We added a bedroom for my daughter, a bathroom, a root cellar, a solar greenhouse, an outhouse in the field/garden, a chicken coop, tool shed, apprentice trailer and a sweat lodge.

I cleared the field and started making raised beds. I planted an orchard of apples, plums, pears, cherries and blueberries, elderberries and raspberries. A row of lilacs and rugosa roses were put on the bank near the driveway, backed by highbush cranberries and forsythia.

There are patches of Jerusalem artichokes, asparagus, strawberries, horseradish and comfrey.

After years of doing without, we got on the grid. I tried to hold out for solar and/or water power, but didn't have the money. That's definitely a dream for the future, but not a high priority right now. I enjoy the computer for getting on-line and the satellite tv system. We still have all our pre-electricity systems in case of power outage.

The house is heated by two wood stoves. If I had my druthers I'd have a masonry fireplace—the kind with lots of mass that utilizes quick, hot burns. They aren't cheap, though. My second choice would be to have an outside wood furnace. Dragging lots of wood around, both outside and inside gets old.

The spring is covered by a simple wood cap. My dream is to build a stone spring house where I could store things. I'd also like to have a water storage tank and bury the water lines deeper.

The solar greenhouse has 55 gallon drums of water and a rock wall to help soak up heat and give it off slowly. It's 12 x 48 ft.

In my dreams the greenhouse is glassed with low-E or some other energy efficient glass, instead of the durable, serviceable but ugly woven greenhouse plastic.

At this point hot water comes from the wood stove in winter and 100 feet of black plastic hose in the greenhouse in the summer. I would like a hot water tank and maybe a glazed box for better solar gain.

The gas stove is okay... but my real dream is to have a restaurant model with a broiler. It would be great for preserving and day-to-day cooking. When I dream big, I imagine myself with an AGA... a stove that has a lot of mass and is always "on." Oh yeah, I'd like a masonry bread oven in the house and am planning a Quebec-style (or Bread and Puppet style) outside brick oven.

For the house, I'd like a workshop/sewing/crafts room with lots of storage space and big counters. Around the outside, it would be fantastic to have a huge covered porch—maybe with a summer kitchen. And wouldn't it be great to have a round, stackwood sauna!

I've gotten good at scrounging used and new lumber, but if money weren't an issue, I'd have a portable sawmill... or even a chainsaw lumber maker sounds good.

The geese and chickens have their own homes and the tools have their shed... but imagine a barn!

I could have everything better consolidated and maybe even have an apprentice apartment. The rototillers would all be in one shed and the cider press could have a permanent home. Gee, maybe I could even park my truck out of the way of freezing rain and blowing snow!

Ohhh... if I were more organized, maybe there could be a real sugar house instead of an outside pot and finishing the syrup in the house. And it would sure be great to have some beehives.

Hmmm... for power outages I have a 12 volt power supply, camping equipment, a dynamo radio—but a big generator could keep the freezers going and I could still watch my favorite home and garden tv shows.

The grapes are doing okay, but if I were good, I'd put up a fancy trellis. The raised beds are easy to reform each spring, but it would be nice to have permanent sides of logs or boards.

There's a packing shed for keeping freshly picked veggies out of the sun. The water comes to it via hydraulic ram pump into sinks. One improvement I've often dreamed of is to have a deep stone/gravel floor for better drainage.

I have a three bay compost bin made from pallets. Ideally, these need replacing as the pallets are truly becoming part of the compost. As long as I'm dreaming, it would be nice to have the compost enclosed in screening to keep out the skunks, raccoons and deer. We have a compost tumbler made from 55 gallon drum on a stand. I love it for mixing potting soil each spring. In my dreams it is kept well painted.

The greenhouse, though large, is never large enough! I always end up making hay bale cold frames and putting the hardier stuff outside ASAP in the Spring. Of course, in my dream there are well-insulated permanent cold frames.

When it comes to work—this is the 8th year of Peace & Carrots Farm CSA (Community Supported Agriculture). In my dreams, it all runs smoothly. Apprentices always work out and help is available when I most need it. Picking days are celebrations and everyone is eager to do their best! The beds are weeded and mulched, the successions are timely, the paths are mulched and everything is labeled.

The most outrageous dream...

I think my most outrageous homestead dream is fencing. Instead of the four foot welded wire fencing that encloses an acre, I'd have high-tensile fencing eight feet high around all two acres of the gardens."

Deer are the biggest impediment to a successful garden here. Heck, as long as I'm dreaming, I'd like outriggers of electric fencing to go with that.

When we do custom rototilling or cider pressing, I put down the tailgate of my pickup and strap the equipment to the truck. I keep a beat-up camper on the truck all the time. My homestead dreams include a new pickup or at least a trailer to tow equipment or my 4WD ATV. I use the ATV to go from the house to the field, to transport groceries, to haul wood, to pick and haul veggies. A dream homestead would have a small tractor with a bucket loader and several garden carts for the ATV.

My daughter is homeschooled and our house is full of thousands of books. My ideal homestead would have a library that is well organized. We could walk to the shelves and find exactly what we were looking for! There would be neat stockpiles of supplies like paper, notebooks, craft supplies, etc. The encyclopedias would always be arranged from A to Z and there would be two phone lines—one dedicated to the computer.

What I have learned

Okay—enough! What I have learned from writing this is that homesteading is an ever-evolving process. A real homesteader can find happiness in making-do, recycling and scrounging.

If everything were perfect, the challenge and some of the charm of country living would be missing. Our dreams keep us focused and learning. Our needs and wants keep us building and growing. There will never be enough time or money to "do it all," but dreaming about the possibilities can be very satisfying.

It's great to see what we have already accomplished and are energizing to make plans for the future.

The machine shed:

Selecting farming tools: Part II

How much mechanization do you need to accomplish your goals?

JEFF RAST, FARMER/DIRECTOR
THE CENTER FOR SMALL ACREAGE FARMING
IDAHO

In Part I of this series (82/3), I bared my soul. Truly, I suffer from an incurable affection for tractors and almost any kind of machinery. Let me confess further that I have no longing to be cured from this affliction. But this passion of mine complicates the process of buying only the equipment I need, and no more.

Deciding whether the equipment you want to buy is a tool rather than a toy or a trap can be very difficult. Ultimately, this decision must be based on sound economic principles. Last time we just started into some basic economic considerations. Now I'll share some other principles a little more in depth.

If you're like most people, you probably don't enjoy the study of economics. In fact, you'd probably enjoy a swig or two of cod liver oil more than enduring the following financial considerations. However, these principles will affect your farm business whether you want them to or not. So I'll try to make this as painless and enjoyable as possible.

As this series develops, we'll analyze the functions for which various tools and technology must be adapted. Interpreting those functions in light of the size and unique characteristics of your farm will help you decide on the types of tools and/or machines to use. You may even find the use of draft animals to be appropriate for much of your farm.

Rhea Moore, Texas, uses his John Deere to build a "tank." (That's what they call ponds in Texas.)

His wife, Patsy, with a bit of teasing familiar to many equipment owners, calls this rig "his big boy's toy."

Regardless of the specific directions you take, these principles will apply to one degree or another. Let's start with the most basic.

What's its purpose?

The primary purpose of machinery is to replace labor.

Please don't feel insulted by the simplicity of this statement. Any tool, regardless of its level of mechanization, is purchased to replace labor. Even a shovel replaces labor, reducing the amount of time required to dig a hole if one were to use a sharp stick.

On a much larger scale, this principle lies at the heart of declining employment in farm communities. As the level of mechanization increases on farms, the demand for laborers on those farms declines.

But how does this principle apply to your situation? It all depends. What size is your farm? How much income do you want to derive from it? How much time can you (and your family, if applicable) give to your farm? How much money can you afford to invest in tools and machinery? How strong and healthy are you and anyone else who will work on the farm? How much hired labor do you want to use? All these factors work together to determine the level of mechanization appropriate to your situation.

If your farm is extremely small (less than an acre) you'll probably be operating a mini-farm which is (or should be) very labor-intensive using mostly hand tools such as a spade, spading fork, U-bar and the like. An economical roto-tiller might be your highest level of mechanization. For larger farms, the level of mechanization involved will increase, and could allow for using draft animals.

Health considerations are also very important. The doctor says I am in pretty good health. However, having injured my back in an auto accident years ago, I suffer recurring back problems. Consequently, I need a higher level of mechanization than I would if my back were sturdy.

How much mechanization do you need to accomplish your goals given the nature of your farm and your financial and labor constraints? Be honest!

Timing is everything (sometimes)

Depending on your enterprise mix, timing of operations can make a big difference to your productivity and profitability. This is especially true if your mix includes highly perishable fruits and vegetables. A very small operation may have an average work load which would not require the use of a tractor. However, work loads during peak times may be such that access to a tractor could be necessary to get everything done on time.

Keep in mind, though, that I said access to a tractor, not ownership of the tractor. If there are plenty of custom equipment operators around, you may not need to own the tractor. However, timing can be critical. Even an abundance of custom equipment operators in the area does not guarantee that they can meet your timing requirements. When it's time to make hay, everybody is making hay.

One way to avoid the timing crunch without incurring a need for extra equipment is to customize your enterprise mix to spread your operational demands more evenly throughout the year. There will still be those unavoidable peak times, though.

New or used?
That is the question.

In the previous article in this series, I touched briefly on the subject of ownership or fixed costs versus operating or variable costs. The relationship between these two sets of costs lies at the heart of deciding whether to buy new or used machinery. Fixed costs such as depreciation, taxes, interest, insurance and shelter remain much the same each year whether you use the equipment or not. Variable or operating costs such as fuel and repairs vary depending on the hours of use.

Purchasing used machinery lowers the overall fixed costs, but the variable costs will increase as maintenance and repair costs increase on used equipment. At least initially, one could say that smaller operations are better off purchasing used equipment in order to keep the fixed costs lower. However, there are too many qualifiers involved to make such a statement with much authority.

Balancing out the lower fixed costs of used equipment are factors which can be remembered with the acronym: CROSS. The Condition of used equipment and its Reliability can be woefully deficient compared to new machinery. Then again, a used tractor which has been lovingly restored or well-maintained may be just the ticket. The Options of used equipment are usually just a fraction of what new equipment has. Although, while the used equipment may not have all the options you want, it may have all you need. Finally, will the used equipment give dependable Service and be of sufficient Size to accomplish the work?

If you have good mechanical skills and can properly and promptly maintain and repair machinery, then you are more likely to benefit by purchasing used equipment. If you have a green thumb, but find that you're all thumbs when it comes to mechanical maintenance and repair, then you probably ought to select a newer piece of equipment in good operating condition.

Keep your cost per unit competitive

For you to operate a profitable farm business, you need to ensure that your equipment cost per unit of product is at a competitive level. The higher your fixed costs, the more units of product (pounds of tomatoes, pints of strawberries, tons of hay) you must produce in order to pay for your equipment and still make a profit. Variable costs are not such a significant factor on this point as they vary according to the amount of product produced or number of acres farmed.

It is all too common for farmers to become overinvested in machinery. Having too much money invested in machinery will gobble up your profits and undermine the health of your business. To compensate, you'll have to scale down your equipment or scale up your farm. The former almost always solves the problem more sustainably than the latter.

To calculate your costs per unit attributed to a given machine, first determine your annual fixed costs (depreciation [purchase price divided by number of years of use], interest, insurance, and shelter). Estimate your annual units of production for a given enterprise: pounds of carrots, for example. Then estimate what portion of a machine's time will be devoted to the enterprise in question(i.e. 10%) and multiply that portion by total fixed costs. Finally, divide the portion of fixed costs by the total units of production for the enterprise. That will give you your fixed cost per unit.

For example, let's say you expect to produce 7,000 pounds of carrots. Then let's assume your fixed costs on a tractor will be $2,500 per year. Only 10% of the tractor usage will be for the carrots, so $250 of fixed costs will be apportioned to the carrot enterprise. $250 divided by 7,000 pounds equals 3.57 cents per pound of carrots attributed to fixed costs for the tractor. If you're selling your carrots for 45 cents per pound, then 8% of your carrot income goes to pay just for those fixed costs. That may or may not be competitive depending on your total production scenario and market for your carrots. But you need to know these costs in order to determine whether or not your equipment is contributing to or detracting from profitability.to accomplish those functions.

Tillage tools

Selecting farm tools: Part III

Jeff Rast, Farmer/Director
The Center for Small Acreage Farming
Idaho

One of the most enduring symbols of modern agriculture is that of the moldboard plow. After all, this was the tool that turned under the perennial, native grass prairies of the Midwest and Great Plains so the ground could produce annual crops like corn and wheat instead. But even though it is such a time-honored symbol, the moldboard plow is a relative newcomer on the farming scene, having been impossible prior to the development of steel in the early 19th century. (Ed. note: The forked plow, however, dates back to Mesopotamia, before 3000 BC.)

Today the array of tillage implements is as diverse as the average fisherman's tackle box. There seems to be a tool for nearly every purpose, if not more. But let's sidestep the status quo for a moment and ask what it's all for.

Why tillage? I'm not asking this rhetorically. When answers to such questions seem glaringly obvious, it's wise to reflect on the words of Wendell Berry: "Seldom do we know what we're doing, because seldom do we know what we're undoing." Because tillage disrupts natural processes more than most agricultural practices, we need to carefully think about the purposes of tillage.

Very briefly, the main purposes of tillage are: 1) to prepare a suitable seedbed, 2) to eliminate competition from weed growth, and 3) to improve the physical condition of the soil. Within this third purpose, I would include the incorporation into the soil of compost, animal manures and/or crop residue. The best tillage system or systems to use must accomplish one or more of these purposes effectively and efficiently while improving the condition of the land.

Control of both wind and water erosion becomes a key consideration in deciding which system to apply. And in arid regions, you want to select tillage practices which conserve soil moisture to the greatest degree possible.

As a general rule, a desirable seedbed is one that is mellow, yet compact enough that the soil particles are in close contact with the seed. The seedbed should be free enough from crop residue that interference with the emerging seedlings is kept below a tolerable level. Furthermore, you want the soil to retain enough moisture to germinate the new seed and sustain plant growth. This last point obviously isn't so critical in areas which receive plenty of rain during the growing season or even where adequate irrigation water is always available.

It's all too common in many farming areas for people to practice "recreational tillage." In other words, more tillage is used than is necessary to accomplish the needed results. In fact, recreational tillage has done more to harm our soil base than anything short of regular soil fumigation. To avoid the short-term financial waste and long-term environmental waste of recreational tillage, always bear in mind the purposes of tillage, along with Wendell Berry's words.

Throughout the balance of this article we'll consider each purpose of tillage and the implements used to accomplish them. Furthermore, we'll look at the benefits and detriments of each practice. Keep in mind, though, that this is not a discussion of the principles and practices of tillage. The focus here is only on the equipment options.

Seedbed preparation – primary tillage

Moldboard plow: Since I've already mentioned it, let's start with the moldboard plow. As this implement is drawn through the soil, it shears off a "furrow slice" of soil and inverts it to one degree or another by means of a three-directional wedging action caused by the curved blade. The soil is broken into lumps and may even be pulverized to some degree, depending on the moisture content of the soil.

Not all moldboard plows are created equal, though. Large, breaker types with a long moldboard are designed to take out virgin or tough sods and completely invert them without breaking up the soil. On the other end of the spectrum is the stubble plow, which partially turns under grain stubble while pulverizing the soil.

The power requirements on moldboard plows can be high, though. For average depth stubble plowing (relatively light duty), about five drawbar horsepower are required of a tractor for each 14 inch bottom or blade of the plow. For deeper plowing, turning sod or using larger bottoms or blades, more horsepower per plow bottom is required. Heavier tractors in the 20 to 40 horsepower range can effectively pull up to a three-bottom plow for most purposes. Smaller tractors, like Kubotas, for example, may have sufficient horsepower, but lack the weight and wheel diameter to effectively pull moldboard plows of anything but the smallest size.

In light of Wendell Berry's words, bear in mind that moldboard plowing "undoes" much. As a very disruptive form of tillage, it can be easily abused through overuse. Such a warning hearkens back to the early 1940s when Edward H. Faulkner wrote *Plowman's Folly*.

In light of Wendell Berry's words, bear in mind that moldboard plowing "undoes" much. As a very disruptive form of tillage, it can be easily abused through overuse.

I am of the conviction that there are only two contexts in which the use of a moldboard plow can be justified. The first is when a stand of native or perennial vegetation is to be "taken out" in order to put in another crop. If you are considering taking out a native meadow, give careful thought to the matter! Native meadows tend to have a high level of biological stability which will be dramatically reduced by turning it under with a plow. You may be much better off in the long-run to save that meadow for grazing livestock.

The other context in which the use of a moldboard plow can be justified is to mix (not invert!) crop residue, compost or livestock manure into the soil. (Inversion of the soil undoes the natural stratification or layering of beneficial microorganisms in the soil and actually hastens the disintegration of the soil. As one Native American said long ago as he observed the moldboard plow in action, "Wrong side up!")

Chisel plow: In response to the erosion problems of the moldboard plow, the chisel plow was created in the 1930s. It tills as deep as 16 inches by lifting and loosening the soil without inverting soil layers. Consequently, it also leaves much more crop residue on the surface, providing additional protection against erosion. Perhaps its greatest benefit is that it provides the deep soil preparation without inverting the various layers of microbial populations. This leaves the soil in a more vigorous and vital condition.

The chisel plow amounts to a series of stout C-shaped shanks measuring about two inches wide and up to 24 inches from top to bottom. Different types of tips can be mounted on the ends of the shanks to modify the chiseling action.

Broadfork: For very small farms which are highly labor-intensive, the broadfork provides excellent deep soil preparation. Also called the U-bar, the broadfork resembles a large spading fork with two vertical handles. The fork is about two feet wide with stout teeth spaced every four inches or so. The teeth can be anywhere from 12 to 18 inches long. Some garden supply and tool businesses offer the broadfork for sale. Mine is a large, sturdy version custom-built by a friend and board member of The Center for Small Acreage Farming, Ken Backstrom.

To operate, the fork is held with the teeth vertical on the soil surface. This leaves the handles tilted slightly forward. As the operator steps on the cross bar, the teeth are pressed into the soil, sometimes with a slight lateral rocking motion for heavier soils. Then the operator leans the handles backward which brings the teeth up thus loosening the soil without inverting it. The fork is then placed six to eight inches back and the procedure repeated.

I've used my broadfork a couple of years now and consider it a marvelous invention. Not only is it an effective way to prepare soil deeply, it also provides great exercise for the upper body. For operations less than an acre, the broadfork represents a good choice for deep tillage if you're in reasonably sound physical condition. Even with my recurring back problems, I consider the broadfork to be a valuable asset.

In the next issue, we'll explore tillage equipment further by looking at secondary tillage implements.

Vanishing old-time skills:

The science of making moonshine

This article is unusual in several respects.

First, we don't normally print material from anonymous contributors, but this is an exception, for reasons that should be obvious.

We also don't normally print information on illegal activities, and we're not recommending this one.

Why tell you how to do something, then tell you not to do it?

Because making moonshine is one of those disappearing arts & sciences that ought to be kept alive, at least on paper. And being curious folk, many homesteaders have doubtlessly wondered about this arcane topic but didn't know who to ask.

But there's another reason, of special importance to those who have the guts, imagination and desire to prepare for any kind of prolonged crash.

Whether or not you enjoy a nip now and then yourself, good whiskey is among the most valuable barter goods around. Unlike most hard goods, it's "renewable" – but only if you know how to make it yourself. And although lots of people know how to make many useful things, very few people know how to make whiskey, especially good stuff.

Here are some tips from one of those people.

Few old homesteader skills are as shrouded in tradition, folklore and gross misinformation as that of making moonshine. Attempt to discuss the process with a person who has interest in the subject, and you will most often find that they are very reticent to allow "science" to conflict with "tradition." Old-time methods can represent a tried and true process, but they can also represent years of repeating a myth. The production of homemade wines and spirits combines the sciences of microbiology and chemistry, both of which are controlled by very rigid physical laws.

Such was the case when a friend decided to give it a try, with me acting as a "consultant." I immediately found myself contradicting my friend's uncle who had "always done it that way." He never sprouted his grain, never cooked it, etc., etc. (He also admitted that it had a kick, but it tasted like – –!)

The mash

The first step is the preparation of the mash. Corn and wheat both produce an excellent product, the latter having a slightly more delicate taste. Milo produces an almost tasteless product that can be used to make gin, vodka, and especially schnapps.

Whole grains are primarily starch, and starch is not fermentable. Therefore, the starch in the grain must be converted to a fermentable sugar. Even the seed itself cannot use its store of starch until it converts it to a biologically usable sugar.

When a seed begins to sprout, it releases alpha and beta amylases (enzymes) which convert the starch to sugars. Thus the first step is to sprout the grain, to convert the starch to maltose. This is called malting.

Soak the grain in a burlap bag or container for approximately 24 hours. Place the bag (or spread the grain out in a large sink or stock tank with a screen over the drain) so that it can drain. Keep the grain moist by regular sprinklings with water until the seeds have produced sprouts an inch or more long.

The tough part is grinding the sprouted grain. A food chopper or electric meat grinder will work, but it is a slow and a very laborious process. Adding small amounts of water while grinding will help ease the process to a degree.

Once ground, most people will start the fermenting process. Wrong! Not all of the starch is converted to sugars at this stage, and you will be wasting most of your grain, not to mention imparting some very undesirable flavors to the end product.

The process of converting the residual starch is called mashing. The enzymes are activated in the temperature range of 140° to 155° F.

Place the mash in a large container with about an equal volume or slightly more of water. With constant stirring so that it doesn't scorch, raise the temperature to 150° F. Allow it to cool back down to 140°. Place a small amount of the liquid in a cup or saucer and add 1-2 drops of tincture of iodine. If the iodine produces an intense purple color, starch is still present. Repeat the cycle (it may take 1-2 hours) until the iodine retains most of its reddish-brown color. This indicates that you have converted most of the starch.

Place the hot mash in a large plastic container and allow it to cool. This will allow even more time for the enzymes to work.

Fermentation

At this point you will need a beer hydrometer. The mash will normally test between a 5% and 10% potential yield of alcohol, depending on how much water you added to the mash and how well you converted the starch. Add sugar until the hydrometer indicates a potential alcohol reading between 13% and 15%. A bushel of wheat or corn will require about 50 lbs. of sugar. (For information on making sugar, see COUNTRYSIDE 59/1:10-11 and 71/3:9.)

Use a good beer or wine yeast to inoculate the mash. Bakers' yeast does not tolerate the higher levels of alcohol toward the end of the process as well as the brewing yeasts. Add the yeast as soon as the mash reaches a temperature of about 90°. Wheat, especially, has a natural thermophilic (heat loving) yeast that is not killed in the cooking process. Also, if you still have a high content of unconverted starch in the mash, it will foam like crazy, not to mention tasting like "Uncle's"!

Anaerobic fermentation produces a greater yield of alcohol than will be produced in an "open" container. When yeast has contact with oxygen it tends to produce more yeast and less alcohol. When it is forced to metabolize the sugar in an oxygen deprived environment, it produces more alcohol and fewer new yeast cells. Tightly tie or tape a large plastic bag over the container, which will act as an air lock. Don't forget to punch a tiny hole in the bag to allow the carbon dioxide to escape or the bag will blow off (one of those things that tend to go bump in the night).

The cooker

The distillation vessel and condenser must be made of copper or stainless steel, fitted with a removable top that will hold pressure without leaking, and must be equipped with a pressure gauge. Vaporized alcohol is highly flammable and explosive. A plugged tube can produce a terrible explosion! If you think a steam boiler explosion is awesome, try one that is filled with a volatile vapor!

Furthermore, do not use any soldered joints unless you use silver solder or the non-lead variety.

The construction and design I will leave up to the individual. If you don't already know the engineering requirements, and don't have the means to properly construct your cooker, then leave it alone!

You must also have a good heat source. A wood fire may be "traditional," but it is dangerous and inefficient. Even a small distillation unit requires an intense amount of heat, because you will be boiling a large volume of liquid over a very long period of time. A large propane or natural gas burner works much better and you can control the heat.

Hint: A cooker mounted in a steel drum wrapped with insulation will be well worth the effort.

In addition to a cooker, you will also need a condenser to cool the steam. This can be as simple as 25-50 feet of copper tubing coiled in a small steel drum filled with water. The tubing should be at least 3/8" to 1/2" I.D. Again, if you don't have the resources to braze the inlet and outlet of the tubing to the drum and the tubing supports inside, leave it alone.

Last but not least, you will need a proofing hydrometer and a graduated cylinder large enough to float it. Although moonshining is illegal per se, these are readily available from most beer/wine supply stores. Get one that reads from 0 to 200 proof.

Moonshining

Distillation is the fun part, but is quite time consuming. A medium sized cooker will produce about a gallon an hour, so plan to blow the entire day (or night). Turn the burner up to "full ahead frantic" until you begin to see fluid coming from the condenser, and then turn it down until the gauge reads no more than 2-4 lbs. pressure. Alcohol vaporizes at a lower temperature than water, so the first product to come off is almost pure ethanol at about 190 proof. It is tasteless and will burn with a colorless flame, so don't get your outlet too close to the cooker! As the quantity of alcohol in the mash begins to deplete, the amount of water in the fluid increases.

You will need a large container in which to empty your "drip jug". If you do it right, 30-35 gallons of mash will produce about 6-7 gallons of final product.

The natural grain flavors begin to come off with the water. As the percentage of water increases, so does the intensity of the "flavor." By experience, the best balance of flavor/alcohol is about 100-105 proof. If you try to get it much lower, it will begin to taste like Uncle's stuff. By the time the bulk product is diluted down to the proper "octane" the liquid coming out of the cooker will test 40-50 proof or lower. Taste that, and you will get an idea of how strong the grain flavor is becoming.

Rather than discard this residual alcohol, keep saving the over-run in a separate container until the liquid coming out of the condenser tests about 20 proof. Add this to your next run.

Headaches, hangovers, methanol and fusel oils

Many people are concerned with the accidental production of methanol (wood alcohol) which can cause blindness. In the old days, moonshiners often used wood barrels for "thumper barrels," a process where the steam was allowed to partially condense and run back into the still in order to raise the "octane" of their product. Under these conditions of heat and moisture, some distillation of the wood might have occurred. Primarily, the problem was caused by unscrupulous prohibition-era bootleggers who added the cheap methanol to their product to increase the volume. Methanol cannot be produced by the distillation of grain "wines" in stainless steel or copper vessels.

Fusel oils can be totally removed very simply with charcoal. But you cannot use the barbecue kind! You must make your own from white oak. Old oak pallet boards work great.

Cut the boards into roughly 1-inch squares about a foot long. Rick these up on a clean surface such as a piece of metal or a brick floor as if you were building a square tower. Leave about a half-inch space between the sticks so you get a good draft. The trick is to burn the entire tower down to coals as evenly and quickly as possible. By the time the tower has collapsed, the coals are ready to quench with water. Allow the charcoal to dry, then add enough of the charcoal to your bulk vessel to the point that it covers the entire surface. Most will sink to the bottom after a few days.

You will notice after a day or two that the product is completely clear, but will have a slightly "harsh" taste. This is where aging comes into play.

Aging: Fact versus myth

Aging is a biological process, but is has absolutely nothing to do with time per se. Everyone will tell you that the "good stuff" must be aged in a charred oak barrel for years. Bull puckey! You can accomplish the same thing in two weeks.

The characteristic golden color and smoothness that most often contrasts the commercial stuff from the crystal clear "shiney" is obtained from wood tannin. After the charcoal has had about a week to absorb all the fusel oils, add about a quart of cherry wood chips and about an equal volume of white oak chips. Red oak produces some undesirable off-flavors. You want them to be fairly fine to maximize their surface area. Running the wood through a planer or over a jointer produces the best chips.

The color will begin to form in 24 hours. Keep a close watch on it at this stage, as the "whiskey" flavor will develop quite rapidly. Start tasting it daily beginning about a week after you have added the wood chips. It will be done somewhere between 10-14 days. Much longer than that and it will begin to develop a very undesirable strong "oaky" taste.

Carefully siphon it off into bottles, preferably through about three coffee filters. As you get to the bottom of the container you will begin to pick up a lot of "fines" (charcoal dust). Drain the bottom slugs off into another container and let them settle. Once the jug has cleared, you can siphon it off as if you were racking wine.

The "proof" is in the pudding!

Like cooking, there is an element of art in whiskey-making that cannot be imparted by the recipe. This is gained by experience and careful observation. Contrary to what many will believe, the stuff made with this process will be of better quality and taste than any of the commercial products.

Thinking that we were making some pretty good product and fearing that our judgment may have been prejudiced by our pride of authorship, we conducted a blind taste test with about two dozen friends. We asked each person to taste a small quantity of a very expensive commercial product and our own, and to tell us which was the "shiney." Without a single exception, everyone thought the shiney was the expensive commercial product, and vice-versa. We then told them which was which. After they recovered from the surprise, they often said that the commercial product (which they thought was the shiney) tasted like cough syrup compared to the homemade product!

Although testing for residual fusel oils was beyond our technological abilities, my friend accidentally did it the hard way. He confessed that he was having such a good time "sipping" the product one weekend that he didn't pay any attention to the declining level in the jug. In his own words, "I got all four feet in the trough Saturday night, and I just knew I was going to wake up the next morning with one heck of a hangover! And would you believe, I didn't even have a headache!"

Making brandy

Brandy is nothing more than distilled wine, but don't try to salvage a "bad" wine by making it into brandy. You will end up with bad brandy!

The very expensive imported products are usually made from champagne, but an excellent product can be made from fermented apple cider.

The malting step is not required. Use the pure juice without any added water. Add enough sugar to bring it up to a potential alcohol reading of 13% to 15% and use a good wine yeast.

In contrast to distillation of whiskey, in which the flavor intensifies in the over-run, the "brandy" flavor is strongest right from the onset and becomes milder as the water content increases! Apparently the esters responsible for whiskey flavors are water soluble, whereas the apple flavors are alcohol soluble. Thus, when making brandy, the trick is to stop the process before you lose all the good flavors, as opposed to preventing them from building up too strong. With apple brandy, this will be at about 90 proof.

Use the same charcoal and wood chip process as in making shiney. Due to the lower alcohol content, you will probably need to leave it on the wood a little longer in order for the alcohol extraction of the tannins to be accomplished.

Again the "proof" was when a friend tasted it and he thought he was sipping at least a "30-dollar brandy."

Schnapps

Excellent homemade schnapps can be made from a bottle of commercial vodka or your own "milo base." To an empty 1-liter bottle, add 1/2 cup sugar, 2 ounces (60 ml) glycerin, and 7 ml of peppermint extract. Fill the bottle with the vodka/shiney and shake until the sugar is dissolved. No one will ever know it's not a commercial product.

Glycerin or "glycerin oil" is a heavy weight alcohol and is used in a number of food products to thicken and/or make them smooth. It is often available in drugstores, and is sold by wine/beer making distributors as "smoothy" or some name to that effect.

Bootleg vodka and pork, too

In Russia, making bootleg vodka is a cottage industry. (The product is called samogon, meaning "self-distillation.") All it takes is a sack of potatoes or grain, half a sack of sugar, a pinch of yeast and a radiator from an old truck or tractor to serve as a condenser, and you're in business, according to Cyril Muromcew in *The Wall Street Journal.* He adds that "Russians, being masters of evasion and camouflage, often keep pigs in the vicinity of the still to mask the fine aroma of samogon in case the militia should come sniffing around."

News from Spaceship Earth:

The sorry state of public education

"However mediocre the educational attainments of the average U.S. child, our best students are still the best in the world."

That, according to Chester E. Finn, writing in *The Wall Street Journal*, is how many in the school establishment "have explained away a ton of evidence of meltdown in American primary and secondary schooling. But they've just lost their excuse.

"It turns out that U.S. high school seniors – including the best and brightest among them – are the worst in the industrialized world in math and science. It also turns out that the U.S. is the only country where kids do worse the longer they stay in school."

Among the 21 countries participating in the math portion of the Third International Math and Science Study, U.S. students scored ahead of only Cyprus and South Africa, and were 100 points behind the leader, the Netherlands. Science scores were slightly higher, but still trailed 15 countries, including Iceland and Slovenia.

Among the top-performing 10% to 20% of each country's students, the U.S. scored second from the bottom in math, and dead last in science.

Mr. Finn concludes that the public school system is "an ossified government monopoly that... needs a radical overhaul. For starters, control over education must be shifted into the hands of parents and true reformers – people who will insist on something altogether different rather than murmuring excuses for the catastrophe that surrounds us."

Aren't you glad you raise your own?

The bacterium *campylobacter* kills an estimated 1,000 people a year and causes indigestion and diarrhea in millions of others. It was found on two out of every three chickens at stores across the country.

Campylobacter was found four times as often as salmonella in the chickens purchased for a study by *Consumer Reports.* Although it's the most widespread cause of food poisoning in the United States, the government does not require that chickens be tested for it.

Industry spokesmen said it would be impossible or too expensive to eliminate all contaminated chickens.

Thorough cooking kills the bacteria.

How to get rid of fleas

Fleas multiply rapidly in warm weather, and can become a real nuisance. They can also be difficult to control. The first step is not to reach for some kind of poison to eradicate the pests, but to learn about their life cycle.

Fleas lay their eggs – up to 50 a day – on animals. However, the eggs soon fall off, most of them usually dropping where the animal spends most of its time, resting or sleeping. If this is in your home, and the eggs are in the carpeting or on furniture cushions, this is where you should focus your flea control efforts.

The eggs develop into tiny, worm-like larvae which remain hidden where the eggs dropped. They feed mainly on adult flea droppings, which accumulate where the animal rests.

The larvae become pupae within a small, silken cocoon, where they stay for two to four weeks or more. This cocoon protects the pre-adult fleas from insecticides, which means that even if you treat an area with insecticides, those in the pupae stage will still hatch and you'll have fleas again.

Here's how to get rid of fleas, according to Mike Potter, extension entomologist with the University of Kentucky.

First remove all toys, clothing, and stored items from floors, under beds, and in closets. Remove pet food and water dishes, cover fish tanks and disconnect their aerators. Wash, dry-clean or destroy all pet bedding.

Vacuum the entire house thoroughly. This will remove many of the eggs, larvae and pupae, and help make those remaining more accessible to the insecticide. Make sure you discard the vacuum bag as soon as you're finished.

The most effective treatment formulations, Potter says, contain permethrin, which kills the newly emerged adults, and methoprene or pyriproxfen to aid in long-term suppression of eggs, larvae and pupae. "Remember to follow label directions carefully and to keep pets off treated areas until the insecticide has dried completely," he says.

Expect to see some fleas for two weeks or longer after the initial treatment. Continue to vacuum to help further control the problem

"You should also treat your pet. A variety of on-animal products are available, including some very effective formulations dispensed through veterinarians."

According to Potter, the best way to use these pet-applied products is preventively, before fleas have gained a foothold in your home.

While most flea problems can be eliminated by treating the pet and the home, sometimes it may also be necessary to treat the yard, especially if the pet spends a lot of time outside. Special formulations are available that can be applied with a hose-end or pump sprayer.

Another case of mistaken identity

We add this to our collection of mistaken identity stories that show most Americans have come so far from their agricultural roots they don't know one animal from another: police in tiny Hinsdale, Illinois were dispatched in search of what a caller said was a wandering mule.

It was a cow.

Pigs in America

European pigs were introduced to North America by the Spanish. In his exploration of the Southeast which started in 1539, Hernando De Soto included 13 sows obtained from the Caribbean stock introduced by Columbus in 1493 during his second voyage. De Soto's herd grew to 700 by the time of his death three years later. As he explored the Southeast, some pigs were traded to Native Americans and others escaped confinement, spreading their range and population. The second introduction is believed to have occurred in what is now New Mexico by Spanish explorers and settlers in the early 1600s. For a fascinating book on pigs, see if your local library has, or can borrow, PIGS from Cave to Corn Belt by Towne and Wentworth. —K.S.

Stealing pigs is more profitable than raising them

On a cold night in January, British pig farmer Stanley Wiles heard his pigs squealing. When he went to check on the cause of the commotion, he surprised three thieves.

Two of the men fled, but the third climbed up on a slate roof, then tried to jump down. He broke his leg.

The 65-year-old farmer grabbed the much larger 37-year-old thief by the shirt, and punched him, then ran after the other two. They escaped.

When he returned, the first fellow was crawling on the ground, but he grabbed the farmer's leg. The farmer, who thought he was outnumbered 3 to 1, in the middle of the night, kicked him, breaking his jaw.

The farmer was fined $166,800.

Small farmers pay for the privilege

Farm numbers in the U.S. peaked in 1935, at 6.8 million.

Today there are fewer than 1.9 million.

Sixty percent of them—1.1 million—are "small" farms, meaning they have annual sales of less than $20,000. They own 29% of the farmland held by farmers and hold 39% of the farm sector's net worth, but they only make up 4% of all U.S. agricultural sales.

However, small farms account for about 20% of the hay and tobacco produced, and 11% of the cattle, sheep and wool sold.

The Census of Agriculture reports that 75% of small farm families say non-farm occupations contribute significantly to their household income. In fact, most lose money on farming.

Oil and the food supply

It has been estimated that a 10 percent reduction in oil supply would increase the prices of fruits and vegetables by 55 percent. Oil is used not only for fuel for tractors and trucks, but for drying grain, producing pesticides and fertilizers, and more.

Population dwindling in Great Plains

A decade ago, two East Coast professors caused a stir in the Great Plains when they suggested that the entire region be turned back to the buffalo. When they said it's too hot, too cold, and has too short a growing season to be of much use to humans, they got death threats from some of the natives.

Today, it might be happening.

"Our countryside is just emptying out of people," said Roger Johnson, North Dakota's agriculture commissioner. "It's just scary."

In many small towns the only thing growing is the cemetery. Younger people are leaving and old people are dying. Farmers are giving up. Schools, churches and stores are struggling. Small is getting smaller, and fears are growing that some places now are just a generation away from extinction.

The last person most people see before they die is their doctor...

Drug reactions kill more than 100,000 Americans a year, according to the Journal of the American Medical Association. This is not the result of mistakes by doctors prescribing drugs or of patients taking them, but the nature of the medications themselves.

Virtually all medications can have bad side effects in some people. "We want to increase awareness that drugs have a toxic component," said Dr. Bruce Pomeranz, a study author and a professor of neuroscience at the University of Toronto. "It's not rare."

Deaths from drug reactions often go unrecognized, Pomeranz said. A death certificate might list a stomach hemorrhage as the cause of death, without mentioning the drug that caused it.

In 1994 there were 106,000 hospital deaths from medications and about 2.2 million non-fatal drug reactions.

Experts, of course, say that medications do far more good than harm and people shouldn't stop taking them for fear of reactions.

The same experts sing a different tune when the medicinal doesn't come from a pharmaceutical laboratory.

***

In 1996 alone, physicians wrote 2.8 billion prescriptions... about eight for every American. —*Pills That Work, Pills That Don't*, by Gideon Bosker, M.D.

Hot foraged food

Ukrainians have been warned not to buy chanterelle mushrooms and blueberries from outdoor markets.

Several samples have been found to be radioactive. Authorities say the mushrooms and berries are often gathered in areas contaminated by the Chernobyl nuclear disaster.

First cloned calves are Japanese

Two calves, cloned from cells from an adult cow, were born in Japan in July. This was exactly two years after the birth of Dolly, the British sheep that made history by becoming the first clone of an adult animal.

Workers in skilled trades are becoming scarce

About 65% of high school graduates go on to college, causing labor shortages in some of the basic trades such as carpentry, plumbing and welding. This might change. Comparing the two, one employer said "At the end of four years, one will be $40,000 in debt and looking for a $10-an-hour job and the other will have no debt and already have a $20-an-hour job."

Unhappy high-tech workers

Half of technology workers wish they had studied something else in college, according to George Mason University. The reason given by 75% is that they want more "enjoyment."

Do we need this?

"I think we are in a phase of 'Build it because we can" rather than because people want to buy it. Just because something is technologically possible does not mean we should make it." (Market researcher Nick Donatiello, in an article describing a new Japanese computer with internet capabilities, a radio, and tv, all built into the door of a refrigerator.)

Tax money flushed away

The National Park Service has accepted drastic reforms in its construction policies, mostly aimed at its Denver design center. About 250 jobs were eliminated, along with other measures. The action was spurred by the news that at Delaware Water Gap National Recreation Area near Milford, Pennsylvania, a two-hole outhouse cost $785,000.

Another factor in Park Service costs was untouched. Half of the NPS construction budget consists of projects the service doesn't want, but which House members insist on in their districts.

Climate change benefits Alaskan farmers

Some people still argue about whether global warming is real. Not farmers around Delta Junction, Alaska. They can see it in their bank accounts.

Dennis Green, who farms 7,000 acres that until the 1970s was permafrost, got an oat crop last fall...plus an unheard-of additional crop of oat hay.

Winter nights used to see temperatures of 50-60 below (growing zone 2). The last couple of years it's been 20-30 below (zone 4). Scott Hollembaek now burns only 10 cords of firewood instead of 20, at $50 a cord. And his herd of Black Angus and bison are eating much less just to survive the winter.

The leap to zone 4 also opens the possibility of growing many crops that wouldn't survive in zone 2.

The warming has brought both costs and benefits to nature. Three million acres of spruce forest are beginning to show damage from spruce beetles, which are moving north. But while the spruce forest sheltered relatively few animals, the area is now home to ducks, bear, moose, and songbirds, including robins.

Roads and houses are beginning to sink into the ground as the permafrost melts.

The area was opened to agriculture in 1978, when a state program cleared more than 156,000 acres. Most of the new farmers only lasted a few years before throwing in the towel. That's when Hollembaek bought a 937-acre plot for $1. Not $1 per acre: $1, period.

Land in the area is now selling for $375 an acre.

University of Alaska weather charts show a gradual warming trend over the past 30 years. The growing season has lengthened by about 20%. However, not all farmers subscribe to the global warming theory. "Thirty years ain't enough to tell you anything," one told a *Wall Street Journal* reporter. "This is all Al Gore smoke-and-mirrors B.S."

Although he doesn't believe in global warming, he's getting an alfalfa crop three years out of four, in an area where, a few years ago, alfalfa could be grown at all.

Another warning on antibiotic overuse

Not long ago, science predicted that infectious diseases would be wiped out by antibiotics. Recently, however, they issued yet another call for their judicious use. Overprescribing is causing germs to mutate so rapidly that the medicines no longer work when they're really needed.

Every pediatrician in the U.S. has been provided with brochure to hand out to parents, urging that they not demand the drugs for every sniffle. Antibiotic use in children under 15 is three times higher than for any other age group. Up to 40 percent of antibiotics prescribed for respiratory and ear ailments are inappropriate, according to a microbiologist at drug maker Eli Lily & Co.

More than 90 percent of staph aureus strains are resistant to penicillin and related antibiotics.

Despite several years of warnings, overuse of antibiotics continues, making them less effective as the bugs adapt.

Just-in-time groceries

The average U.S. city has a two-to-three day supply of food. The Northeastern states import more than 70 percent of their food. (Shouldn't you be growing more of your own?)

Despite medical progress, TB is still a killer

The leading cause of death for women age 15 to 44, worldwide, is tuberculosis. More than 900 million women of reproductive age suffer from the infectious lung disease. TB now accounts for 9% of deaths of females in this age group, more than double the 4% rate for war.

Young entrepreneurs

Of the 5.6 million Americans going into business for themselves in 1996, almost 30% were 30 or younger.

Wiretaps set a record

Wiretapping by government agents set a record in 1997, according to a report by the Administrative Office of the U.S. Courts. The 1,186 wiretap requests approved by state and federal judges was a three percent increase over 1996. Each one listened in on an average of 2,081 conversations...a total of 2.27 million.

Athletes on steroids are starting young

Some boys and girls as young as 10 are taking illegal steroids to do better in sports, according to a study in Massachusetts. Of 965 youngsters questioned, 2.7% use anabolic steroids which build muscles but also damage the liver, stunt growth and cause long-term ailments.

Because a cycle of steroids costs several hundred dollars and "I don't know a lot of 10-year-olds who have a couple of hundred dollars," University of Massachusetts researcher Avery Faigenbaum said, "I think we have to look at parents. I think we have to look at youth coaches."

Lightning rods help protect buildings

Do you need lightning rods?

The risk of lightning striking a building involves five criteria, according to the Lightning Protection Institute (LPI):

- The type of structure;
- its location;
- its construction;
- surrounding topography;
- local lightning frequency.

LPI notes that nearby trees do not offer protection. In fact, they can create a "side flash" of lightening to your house or other buildings.

For information on home lightening protection, send a SASE to LPI, 3335 North Arlington Heights Rd., Ste E, Arlington Heights IL 60004.

Why we should keep vehicles longer

80% of the energy consumed by a vehicle during its life is in its production.

Why using discarded pallets is a good idea

There are 1.5 billion pallets in the United States...six for every American. About 40% of domestic hardwood lumber goes into pallets. (Hardwoods make up about 27% of U.S. lumber production.)

Homesteaders have told of numerous uses for discarded pallets, but one comes with a cautionary note. Somebody sold pallet wood as firewood...and was sued when a customer had a stove overheat.

Easy-to-get mortgages increase delinquencies

Mortgage delinquencies—late or missed payments—reached 4.25% by the end of 1997, according to the nation's largest private mortgage insurer, Mortgage Guaranty Insurance Corp.

One reason has been that mortgages have been easier to get. According to a housing industry spokesman, "We lowered down payments from 5% to 3%. We said we won't require reserves anymore; two months' was traditional. We raised the debt ratios (portion of income that can be used for mortgage payment) from 26%-28% to 33%-38% and we went to alternative credit, from a minimum 24 months (of good credit history) to 12 months. And while we'd always considered that the absence of credit experience was a bad thing, now we said 'No credit is good credit.'"

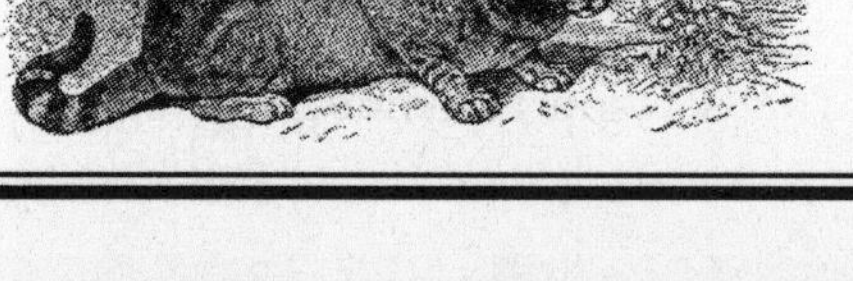

Home ownership increased (to 66%), but so did mortgage delinquencies.

However, credit, or lack of it, isn't the only reason, or even necessarily the main one. Company research showed that even people with good credit can get into trouble... and those with no credit can avoid it. The difference is a strong sense of commitment.

Modest means isn't one's downfall so much as the inability to plan and sacrifice, the company notes.

A strong sense of commitment... an ability to plan...and sacrifice... attributes that are part of the homestead mindset.

Why we prefer organic gardening

The EPA has set standards for heavy metals in sewage sludge fertilizers as follows (in parts per million):

Arsenic	41
Cadmium	39
Copper	1,500
Lead	300
Mercury	17
Nickel	420
Selenium	100
Zinc	2,800

But fertilizers made from sewage sludge might not be the most serious problem for gardeners who use stuff from bags. Other forms of fertilizers have no EPA standards for heavy metals.

And if you're still not concerned, maybe you'll be interested in knowing that it was recently revealed that some fertilizers even contain toxic wastes... and it's perfectly legal.

A sack of 20-20-20 contains 20 percent each of nitrogen, phosphorus and potassium. The other 40 percent is "filler," and fertilizer manufacturers don't have to say what that consists of.

The machine shed:

How to determine how fast a farm or garden tool will cover a given area

Ever wonder how much faster you could do a given field or garden job if you had a machine that was a little bigger, or went a little faster? Ever want to estimate how long a job will take with a given piece of machinery?

The following chart will be very useful for these, and other applications.

The "width" column refers to the width of the implement: mower, tiller, plow, cultivator, whatever. The "miles" column shows how far you'll travel performing the operation on one acre.

Example: You're buying a new mower for your half-acre lawn. How much longer will it take to mow with a 20-inch wide machine versus a 30-inch machine?

The chart shows that with a 20-inch swath you'll travel 4-9/10 miles to cover an acre. With a 30-inch swath, it would be 3-1/3 miles. Divide by two for your half-acre and you'll see that your 20-inch mower will travel a bit less than 2-1/2 miles and the 30-inch mower will travel a bit over 1-1/2 miles.

If you want to take this further, say you estimate an average speed of 3 MPH with both mowers. At this rate the smaller one will cover your half-acre in a little less than an hour; the larger one will require just over half an hour.

As for overlapping, breakdowns and pit stops for lemonade, use your own judgment and experience.

You can, of course, use the chart to evaluate machines of other sizes. If you trade in your six foot hay mower on one that's 10 foot wide, you know that the six-footer (72 inches) travels 1-2/5 miles to cover an acre. The 10-footer is the same as two fives (60 inches), or half of 1-3/5 miles per acre, or about 4/5 of a mile per acre.

Width of a tool (in inches), and the distance traveled per acre (miles)

7	14-1/3	26	3-4/5
8	12-1/4	27	3-3/5
9	11	28	3-1/2
10	9-9/10	29	3-1/2
11	9	30	3-1/3
12	8-1/4	31	3-1/5
13	7-1/2	32	3-1/10
14	7	33	3
15	6-1/2	34	2-9/10
16	6-1/6	35	2-4/5
17	5-3/4	36	2-3/4
18	5-1/2	37	2-2/3
19	5-1/4	38	2-3/5
20	4-9/10	39	2-1/2
21	4-7/10	40	2-1/2
22	4-1/2	48	2-1/12
23	4-1/4	60	1-3/5
24	4	72	1-2/5
25	4	84	1-1/6

How much does it cost?

On the average, the annual fixed cost for a tractor is $455 per $1000 of new cost for the first year; $95 the second; and $89 per $1000 for a tractor three years old. This continues declining to $38.80 per $1000 for a tractor 15 years old.

How much time will it take?

Spading an acre of land by hand, according to one source, takes 20 days. Working it with a rotary tiller takes only a few days. But plowing it with a three bottom 14" plow takes 0.83 hours and with an eight bottom 16" plow, 0.22 hours.

Seeding with an eight foot grain drill requires 0.37 hours per acre; planting with a two row 40" corn planter requires 0.45 hours per acre; mowing with a seven foot mower takes the same; and combining with a six foot grain head will take 0.71 hours per acre.

Note to beginners: these averages do not take into consideration rocks, clogging with weeds and trash, break-downs and inexperience!

How long will it last?

According to the American Society of Agricultural Engineers, you can expect a tractor to be good for 12,000 hours (compared with 2,250 for a pickup truck). Tillage tools—plows, harrows, discs, etc.—last an average of 2,250, as do mowers, manure spreaders, balers and side delivery rakes. Seeding equipment should be serviceable for an average of 1,200 hours, according to this group.

The average tractor in the U.S. is used about 600 hours a year, which makes that 12,000 hour useful life 20 years.

Should you farm it out?

Consider the benefits of owning your own machinery as opposed to hiring the work done. Being able to time field operations properly can make a big difference in yield and quality. Bad weather can really put you in a bind if you're relying on someone else to get your hay in the barn—or even if you're doing the job yourself with inadequate equipment. You take your chances with weather in any case, of course, but you can help tip the scales in your favor.

Can you justify the expense?

Machine ownership—of tractors or rotary tillers or anything else—generally is more profitable in proportion to the extent of its use. This formula is used by farmers to determine at what point it is more profitable to own equipment than to lease it or hire a custom operator.

The break-even acres (or hours) BEA equals the total annual fixed costs TAFC divided by the custom rate per acre (or hour) CR minus the variable cost per acre (or hour) VC.

$$BEA = \frac{TAFC}{CR - VC}$$

Old technology:

Leaching lye from wood ashes

This method, patterned after one used by the early settlers of North America, produces soft soap by combining fat and potash (lye obtained by leaching wood or plant ashes).

This recipe has been tried successfully with waste cooking grease, olive oil, peanut oil and cocoa butter.

Equipment needed:

- Several medium sized rocks.
- A flat stone with a groove and a runoff lip chipped into it.
- 5-gallon wooden bucket with several small holes in the bottom. A hollowed log with the same capacity can be used.
- Collection vessels for the lye. These should be made of iron, steel, enamel, or clay. An aluminum vessel should not be used, since lye would corrode it.
- Small twigs.
- Straw.

Materials

Five gallons of ashes. The ashes may be made from any type of wood, but hardwoods yield the best lye. Ashes from the burning of plants and leaves of trees may be used. Ashes of burnt seaweed are particularly useful as these produce a sodium-based lye from which hard soap can be made. Lye leached from the ashes of plant life (excepting seaweed) is potash or potassium carbonate (K_2CO_3), an alkali. This alkali reacts with fat to form soft soap. Ashes from other materials such as paper, cloth, and garbage cannot be used.

Two gallons of soft or medium-hard water.

Pile the rocks so that the flat, grooved stone rests evenly on the top *(see Figure 1)*. Set the wooden bucket on this stone.

Method

In the bottom of the bucket, make a filter to trap the ashes by criss-crossing two layers of small twigs and placing a layer of straw on top *(see Figure 2)*.

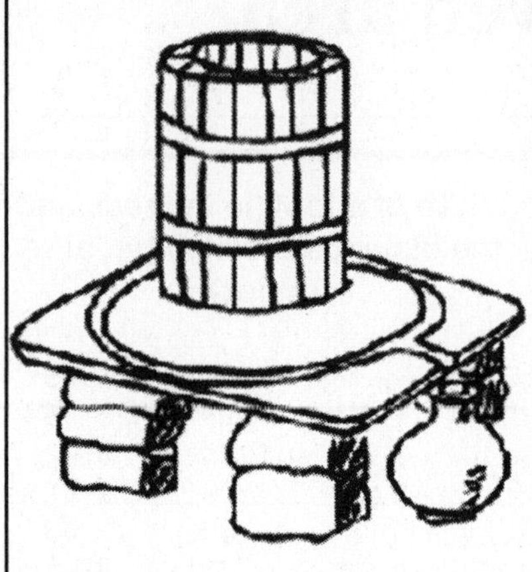

Figure 1

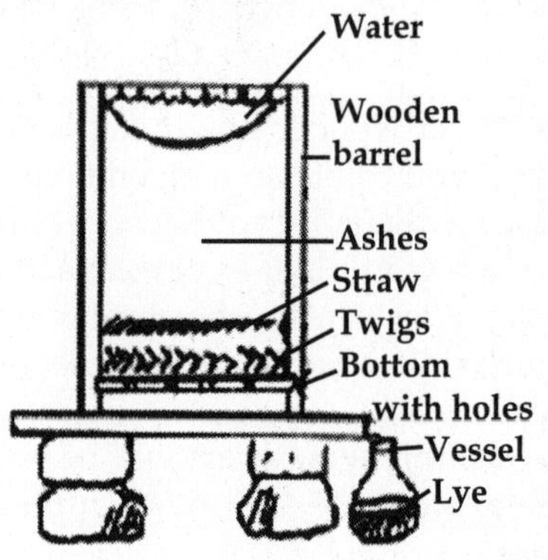

Fill the bucket with dry ashes. To keep the lye from being leached accidentally, the ashes must be kept dry before they are used.

Pour warm water into the bucket, making the ashes moist and sticky. To make sure that the water passes through the ashes at the correct rate for leaching the lye, move the ashes up at the sides of the bucket to form a depression in the center.

Add all the remaining water in small amounts in the following manner: Fill the center depression with water; let the water be absorbed; fill the depression again.

When about two-thirds of the water has been added, the lye or potash, a brown liquid, will start to flow from the bottom of the bucket. Use more water, if necessary, to start this flow. The lye flows over the flat stone into the groove and then into the collection vessel below the run-off lip. It takes about an hour to start the flow of lye.

The yield from the amounts given here is about 7-3/4 cups. The results vary according to the amount of water loss from evaporation and the kind of ashes used.

If the lye is of the correct strength, an egg or potato should float in it. A chicken feather dipped in the solution should be coated, but not eaten away. If the solution is weak, pour it through the barrel again, or through a new barrel of ashes, or concentrate it by boiling. A bushel of ashes is about the right amount for four pounds of fat. This proportion is cited in soapmaking recipes of the colonial period in the United States, but many of the recipes of that era differ on the proportion of ashes to fat.

(This article first appeared in COUNTRYSIDE *in July, 1971.)*

Soapmaking today, even among crafters who make their own, has become more of a science than an art. But even though early soapmaking required a good deal of experience (acquired by watching Grandma and Mother) and was still touch-and-go, the basic process was simple.

In a 10-gallon cast iron pot suspended over a brisk fire, melt down 12 pounds of clean, rendered beef tallow. Slowly pour in lye water "of sufficient strength" (one old recipe tells us), about 20 gallons in all. Stir with a wooden paddle until the soap is done (another call for art and experience). Remove from the heat, cool, and pour into a wooden barrel.

A planning guide for the future

What to do now

How far have you progressed with the Y2K preparation plans suggested in the last issue?

If you're average, probably not very far at all. There isn't any significantly new information to alarm you, no real reason to panic, and you don't want your friends and neighbors to think you're a nut. You have decided to "wait and see."

***

This is one of the most vexing aspects of Y2K: We just don't know. Nobody does! The experts who blithely assure us that nothing bad is going to happen have no more proof than the experts who say it will be the end of the world as we know it.

We can't even give up and just go along with the crowd, because we don't even know what the crowd is thinking. One survey (taken in June by the Information Technology Society of America) reports that 80% of those polled fear their financial records will be distorted, and 50% are worried that they'll lose their jobs. (The same poll said about 25% of Americans believe the Y2K problems will force them to change their lifestyle. How so many will lose their jobs and savings and not change their lifestyle isn't explained.)

However, another survey, taken at about the same time, claims that almost half of all Americans know nothing about the problem, and a large percentage of those who do thought it was already taken care of!

***

No matter which survey we go by, it's clear that those who are both aware of the problem and concerned about it are in a small minority... which brings us to our lesson for this phase of the countdown.

That small minority has already snapped up all available steam and diesel generators. Purveyors of dehydrated foods are backlogged. Sellers of many non-electric appliances are reportedly out of stock.

The explanation is simple. A few years, even a few months ago, most tools and supplies for self-sufficiency merely trickled off the shelves, with sporadic sales to the few "weirdos" with a survivalist bent. There was no point in stocking, or even manufacturing, more.

Therefore, when the trickle became a flood, the shelves were emptied, the pipelines were depleted, and manufacuring capacity can't keep up.

And that's with only a small percentage of the people even looking for such goods, and with more than a year yet to go—maybe.

What's going to happen when more people become aware and educated?

We might liken this situation to a pool fed by a small trickling stream. One deer and her fawn drink from the pool daily, but that's doesn't effect the water level.

Then one day a herd of thirsty buffalo thunders up to the pool. They drain it, trample the mud, and there is no water for the deer.

Walton Feed sells food reserves, mostly to Mormons. Although they are encouraged to stockpile food, not all do it. If they did, Walton Feed couldn't meet the demand.

Enter non-Mormons. Walton Feed is sold out.

***

The point of all this is that if you haven't already made certain preparations, it might already be too late.

What's more, if you're "waiting to see what happens," you're in a very large group. When you get the signal — whatever it might be — so will a few million others watching or reading the same news. Then it will really be too late.

***

Let's get back to our main theme, our over-riding concern, our consuming interest in the Y2K problem... or opportunity. That is, if you have longed to be a homesteader, maybe for many years, but never got around to it, this is your perfect chance. And it could be your last chance.

But you're already being trampled at the exit, in large part not by homesteaders, but by people who are concerned about surviving Y2K.

It's true, maybe nothing will happen. And to brighten that possibility even more, maybe after 2001 or so when the Y2K survivalists go back to the rat race (if they do) you might be able to pick up their homestead tools, or even their homesteads, for pennies on the dollar.

But if something does happen... if you're cowering, hungry and cold, perhaps in a riot-torn city, when you really wanted to be on a homestead even in the best of times... you're going to be very, very unhappy.

If you still haven't done anything to prepare because you felt you didn't have enough factual information, plug these ideas into your decision-making and see if it helps.

***

If you have started the actions suggested here last issue, stick with it. Continue to learn, practice, and perfect your skills. Continue to accumulate tools and supplies as your circumstances permit. And here are some additional ideas:

√ Classes are starting in September... Many vocational schools, community colleges and others offer courses that could be very helpful to homesteaders. It might be breadmaking or sewing, gardening or welding or small engine repair. Dozens of these could be very useful... no matter what happens. (Some might even consider computer courses.)

√ Practice more frugal living. Select one day a week (or a week) when you don't use electricity, or the car, or when you only eat the simple foods you might expect to have to live on as a homesteader... or Y2K survivor.

√ Strive to establish and maintain a positive outlook! Even if your primary concern is surviving disaster, think of the preparations as homesteading. Dispel fear. Replace it with the pleasure and joy of learning and doing. Erase any feelings of hardship or deprivation. Instead, think of the satisfactions of simple living.

Be happy, have fun... but keep your powder dry.

A new urgency

Much of our correspondence recently has shifted from "How do I get started in homesteading?" to "How do I prepare for (Y2K or whatever)? The following letter is just one of several like it that arrived before our first Countdown to Year 2000 issue was mailed, and the pace has increased considerably since then.

The shift in emphasis might seem subtle, but it's significant. The question now is much more urgent. We can no longer advise newcomers to start slowly, not to go into homesteading but to grow into it. Anyone not already well on the way simply doesn't have the luxury of time. Setting priorities and cutting corners wisely is now more important than ever.

COUNTRYSIDE is placing renewed emphasis on the basics of homesteading to help newcomers get up to speed as quickly as possible and as a refresher course for the rest of us. (The 10 "Countdown" issues will also be an excellent reference source.)

But basic how-to information doesn't address what might be even more important needs: How do we set priorities, and how do we cut corners wisely?

This letter is fairly typical in its indication of these problems.

COUNTRYSIDE: What if something happened? "Something" as in a natural disaster or a man-made one – it makes no difference in the large scheme of things. Something that brings life as we know it to a standstill. No electricity – no refrigerator, no freezer, no instant hot water, no furnace, no microwave, no lights, etc. No electricity and the stores would close. What would I need to keep my family safe, warm, well-fed and healthy through all of whatever happens?

The major priority right now, as I see it, is to get in a woodstove. Without heat, not a whole lot else is going to matter in the winter months. And of course a supply of wood, because obviously a woodstove is pretty useless without that.

I have no real idea why I feel so strongly about this whole thing, but I do. I have plenty of theories, and a couple of real good thoughts, but that isn't really the point.

After the woodstove and wood supply, I'd say medicine. Mostly like Tylenol for us and the kids. Having fever reducers could be a major factor if anyone was to get sick.

Sometimes I think I'm wasting my time and energy on all of this, but what can it hurt to be prepared? I figure if I'm prepared and nothing happens, so what – we have extras. On the other hand, if I'm not prepared and something happens, I dread to think of the possibilities. To me, being prepared is the most obvious plan of action. If nothing else, at least I feel a bit more secure.

After the woodstove and medicine, food will be a big issue. The garden is planted with all kinds of things and I want to learn to can it this fall. My potato patches are all tilled up. I just haven't had the time when it's not raining to get them in the ground.

I want to have plenty of potatoes and vegetables on hand. I could stockpile cans of vegetables, but what about the next year when the stores are still closed and I haven't a clue how to grow or store anything? I'd rather learn by trial and error now while there is still room for mistakes than trying for the first time when it is absolutely necessary that we keep everything.

I realize there is a lot of projection in all of these thoughts, but again, I just feel so strongly about it for reasons I can't even explain.

Then, of course, sugar and flour. I wonder if maybe I've read too many historical romance novels, but they always buy their sugar and flour from somewhere and up here in the North country, it is not as if I can grow it all. I wouldn't have the first clue what to do with it if I did. There's a bit of honesty.

Another is, I have no idea how to bake bread from scratch. How does it rise? I mean, back in the old days before you went to the store and bought packaged yeast (which I have a huge problem with), how did they do it? I can't get the rapid rise yeast to rise at all. That is a big joke at my house, but I would like to learn.

I'd like to get chickens, too. My husband keeps talking about building a chicken coop, but so far that's as far as it's gotten. One more thing I feel we need...chickens for eggs and for meat.

Stockpiles of coffee, peanut butter, pastas and that sort of thing. Cocoa and snack-like things for the kids...and myself at certain times of each month.

Matches, a big pile of them. Spices of course. I wanted to start my own herb garden this year, but it didn't happen. Maybe next year. Certainly not a major priority.

I feel very blessed to have what we do, which by some standards I'm sure is not much, yet by others a whole lot. It just depends on the view. I have a 30-year mortgage (28 left) on a run-down house in the country on almost an acre of land, 1/4 of which was covered with bamboo. (I'm still fighting that battle.) I have my children, 1-1/2 and 8 years old. We have junky furnishings and the house is most always cluttered, but we have each other, and through it all, I guess that is what matters most.

Someday I hope to be completely prepared. I hope it's soon enough. We're working on it. Some days my husband rolls his eyes when I mention the subject, but most always he's very understanding and supportive.

– Kathy, New Hampshire

Two things strike me about this letter.

First, the priorities seem to be a little out of kilter. Granted, we're all different and have different needs, and this isn't as bad as the lady who put cosmetics and hair spray at the top of her list! But a woodstove — and Tylenol — aren't likely to be urgent items unless more basic needs are met first.

In an effort to be helpful (or at least thought-provoking) I would suggest that food and water head the list. You can probably stand a lot more cold than you think you can, and at least in a temporary emergency, warm clothes and blankets will suffice. Also, in a system of priorities and triage, heat is essential only part of the year, even in New Hampshire: food and water are requirements at any time.

Breaking this down further, short-term supplies are essential, and in most "reasonable" scenarios, this would be adequate. But we'll also continue to hammer at the idea that homesteaders have enough food to last from one season to the next... rather than relying on industrial agriculture and its distribution system to produce, process and store it... simply because that's a big part of what homesteading is.

The catch is that most people not only don't have such stores: they don't know how to provide them. Gardening, canning, raising chickens, and even baking bread, are learned skills. They require knowledge, tools, and practice. People who think they'll pick up these skills (to say nothing of the tools and supplies)when it becomes necessary are deluding themselves.

There are some short-cuts to be sure, and even the most experienced and well-prepared homesteaders tell themselves they'll do more "when the time comes." But generally speaking, the most important skills aren't acquired overnight.

Where does this leave people who are still in the starting gate?

I hate to admit it, but their top priority at this time is not to become as self-sufficient as possible as quickly as possible. Becoming a self-sufficient homesteader in less than two years simply isn't a realistic goal.

Anyone sincerely concerned about survival in the next few years who doesn't have a normal homestead supply of homegrown food on hand and little or no experience in producing it has no choice but to stock up on purchased food.

This needn't be, and in most cases shouldn't be, the expensive "gourmet" meals. Obviously, neither should it be frozen, or supermarket junk food.

Certain canned foods would serve the purpose if they can be protected from freezing. But dry or dehydrated products should get the most attention.

The "survival" types of dehydrated foods are already in short supply. But peas, beans, rice and other grains, powdered milk and pasta are available in bulk from food co-ops, and even some supermarkets.

If you find this disappointing because you want to be a homesteader, be consoled by knowing that most homesteaders still buy things like peanut butter, flour and sugar.

And if you have or can provide proper storage conditions (see the root cellaring article in this issue), you might also consider buying potatoes, carrots, onions and similar commodities in bulk, from growers.

Some people will protest that the grocery budget for next week is already strained: How are they going to pay for next winter's food in advance?

In the case of store-bought items, it's not necessary (yet) to purchase it all at once. Pick up a few extra cans of tomatoes or jars of peanut butter every time you shop. It won't seem like a major expenditure, even if you have to squeeze it from elsewhere in the budget.

But then too, you'll want to use these foods, rotating and adding to your supply as you do.

That might mean learning new or more ways to use potatoes, beans, or rice. Using flour instead of buying baked goods. Making your own pasta.

The bright side is that you are learning to be a homesteader... you are actually doing something of a homestead nature... even though you didn't producethe raw products yourself! And that's a wonderful start.

Insuring your family's food supply is the top priority, but that doesn't mean you can't work on others at the same time.

Unless you live in a warm climate, you can't garden for the next several months, but you can continue to gather information, perhaps collect needed tools, and make plans.

Find that woodstove, or an acceptable substitute. Be sure you have the right kinds of tools and appliances. (Microwavable dishes won't work on a woodstove.) In brief, once you have that basic food supply, short-term as it might be, you can go on to develop a more self-sufficient homestead with increased security and confidence.

The "triage" or priority-setting discussed here should be applied to everything else on your list. For example, several readers have asked about livestock: How essential are they?

At this point you might have enough time to get involved with animals...but only if the more important things are taken care of first, with the money and labor available. Meat, milk and eggs can add considerably to your comfort level (and manure to your garden productivity) but they aren't essential to survival. If you're in a position to have livestock, fine. If not, start collecting vegetarian recipes.

Comfort level! That's what this is really all about. A person with a good supply of firewood and Tylenol or cosmetics—but no food—obviously isn't going to be comfortable.

Secure the basics first.

Then, as circumstances allow, increase your comfort level.

And eventually, if all goes well, you'll find yourself with a full larder, a productive garden and animals, a warm house, interesting things to do and think about, a happy heart and a satisfying life.

You'll be a homesteader.

The comments about not knowing why there are such strong feelings about matters of preparedness and survival are interesting in that they too are not at all unusual. They have been around far longer than any talk about Y2K or other millennium events.

We can speculate on several possible reasons. However, we merely make note of that now to distinguish it from the mass hysteria that will most likely occur in the future. After a few highly visible events make it to the evening news, and greater numbers of people decide that even a meltdown is a very real possibility, preparation will be a different story.

If or when that happens there will be even less time to get ready, and our advice will be a lot grimmer.

Handy hints

• Hang bars of deodorant soap in apple trees to keep deer away because they don't like the smell.

• Before going to work in the garden, scrape your fingernails over soap. When you wash your hands after the work is finished, the soap under the nails will wash away, leaving clean fingernails.

• To keep pets out of your flower beds, sprinkle beds liberally with black pepper. They don't like the smell and if they get too close they have sneezing fits.

• Keep two old socks in the back of your car or truck and put them over your hands when you have to change a tire, brush snow off the windshield, etc.

What to do now

A planning guide for the future

√ Take inventory: Where are you right now in terms of preparation? List all assets, including tools and skills.

√ Set goals: Where do you want to be in the future and when? Do you want to be ready to be totally self-sufficient, is it okay to merely have a stockpile of essentials, or will you just wait and see what happens?

√ Set your course to meet those goals: Subtract what you have from what you want to determine what you still need.

√ Make your plan: Decide how you're going to get what you need to reach your goal. Set priorities (triage). Concentrate on the most important or essential needs first. Set a timetable for yourself.

Suggestions:

If you are in the city and you're totally convinced that is not where you'll want to be, get out now!

If you're in the country but don't have a working homestead, start building one now. In most parts of the country it's not too late to start or expand a garden: July/August is the best time to plant crops to be harvested in fall.

Construct rabbit and poultry facilities, and stock them.

Acquire the books you'll need for advice, now and later.

Plan to save seeds from open-pollinated crops. While getting seeds next spring might not be a problem, the future could be a different matter: you'll need the experience for next year's harvest.

Preserve food, from your own garden if you have one, or from farmers' markets if you aren't that far yet. Get the equipment and information you'll need. Better to have failures now (and learn from them) than when they could be critical.

If at all possible after all the above, get out of debt. In any event do not incur more.

If you are already comfortably situated on a working homestead with everything you need in place, check closely to see if you missed anything. Now is the time to start gathering less-essential goods that will add to your security and comfort.

Be sure to rotate stores to keep everything as fresh as possible. Consider adding to your stores to help those in need.

Make any repairs, replacements or additions you might have been putting off: if you're going to need a new roof in a few years, get it now instead. If you've been meaning to get a tetanus shot, get it now. If you need dental work or new glasses, take care of it now. Don't put off what you can do today.

Fighting fires — and fear — in Florida

Kathleen A. Roberts
Florida

I'm writing from a war zone. Not literally, but it might as well be.

Helicopters are flying overhead with loads of water. Forestry men are on the scene with heavy equipment, cutting fire breaks. There is a flurry of excitement and fear among my neighbors as they douse their homes with water and set sprinklers on their roofs to ward off any stray sparks or flying ash.

It wasn't until a forestry man cut a fire break to our back field fence that reality hit me full in the face. We could very well lose all that we had worked so hard for! With teary eyes and disbelief, I mentally surveyed the land and all that we had done, including the pig pen, chicken coops, and rabbit hutches. At least I didn't have to worry about turning the animals loose, as a bobcat previously took care of them.

What's most important?

It was time to decide what we valued most. People and pets came first, obviously, but what can't be replaced? Photo albums and family videos were first. I was never so happy that I have been organized as I was at that time. All of my albums, dated and in order up to the very month, were easily packed. A neighbor agreed that these were among her valuables, but they were scattered all over her house. She was unable to locate them.

Important papers are second. I keep them in a portable file. They include car and home titles and birth certificates. Get your papers in order now. Better safe than sorry.

Although my neighbors quickly packed VCRs and videos, I figured these could be replaced. I wanted to pack things that could not be replaced or purchased.

My father-in-law died recently, and he built most of our furniture. These things are irreplaceable. We loaded as many of the smaller tables and items as we could on my husband's truck. The quilt my daughter made when she was eight years old came along. Don't be overly concerned with store-bought items. You'll want to take everything. We did.

One month later...

I'm writing this a month later. Our homestead is still intact, and we are very grateful. However, we are not out of danger yet. Wildfires still rage all around us. We live on the edge, afraid to even go to the grocery store for fear of what might happen when we are gone.

It is times like these when neighbors pull together and become more trusting and helpful. I let a neighbor know when I go anywhere now and leave a key in case my cat and dog need to be evacuated quickly. At night, the smell of smoke often wafts through the air ducts and unsettles me to the point where I can't get back to sleep.

Lessons learned

This wildfire experience has made us think differently.

We are going to buy a pump that will let us empty the swimming pool if we need to save the home. We are also planning to buy a pitcher pump that will let us draw well water during a power outage. A larger generator that can run the refrigerator is also on the list. What items can you buy or save enough money to buy? I think these firestorms are just the tip of the iceberg for nature shifts.

This is a strange Independence Day, as fireworks are banned. A nearby county has evacuated 120,000 people.

Talk about confusion! All major highways are closed. Alternate routes are closing due to the smoke. Traffic in town is stop-and-go, and a lot of people can't get to work. I ran across elderly people who seem displaced and confused as they asked for directions.

Another lesson learned: Keep some cash on hand for emergencies. A credit card will get you a hotel room, but most fast-food places won't take Visa or MasterCard.

Shelters don't allow pets. Make animal arrangements beforehand. One dog was found chained to a tree. What a sad fate for a loyal companion.

There is a dusk to dawn curfew. Anyone caught roaming the streets will be carted off to jail. It sounds unbelievable to those who are not living it.

In case you have to file for disaster aid, you'll need to have the address and zip code of the damaged home or property, the Social Security number of you and your spouse, directions to the damaged home and a daytime phone number where you can be reached. The toll-free number for disaster aid (FIMA) is (800) 462-9029.

Exhausted firefighters and foresters are relieved by the National Guard as well as firefighters from Alaska, Idaho and California. My sense of pride in humanity has been renewed. The firefighters have received such an outpouring of donations of beverages and food that the excess is going to area shelters.

Just one looting

I have heard of only one looting story. The poor woman had just come home with groceries and had to evacuate before she could even put the food away. When she returned, the groceries along with her children's video games, tv and VCR were gone. That was an isolated case, as the community has pulled together.

There have been over 1,800 wildfires since May 25, and they are still burning as I write. There is concern that the various blazes will merge into one solid wall of fire.

I hope no one has to go through the fear we have experienced. We need to prepare for any emergency.

Construction:

Make it square, plumb and level

We know the shed or barn or bookcase or cage we're building should be level, parallel and plumb. And you'll want to have it in a certain place in relation to a property line, existing building, or other feature.

If the project is larger than a bread box you'll need a 50 feet or 100 feet tape. String or 60 pound test fish line will do.

Measure two equal spaces off your starting points and you'll have the far side line if you included the size of your building, or the near side if you haven't included the building.

In order to square a building, whether it's square or rectangular, measure diagonally until the corners are established. It doesn't matter if the object is a cage measured in inches or a building measured in feet, the principle is the same. Of course the tape has to be held taut. "If you sag it you lose it."

Another way to check out an object is to take what they call a 6-8-10.

If you take three straight 1x4s or 2x4s and lay them out this way and nail all three corners, you'll have a large true right angle. If you don't slam it around too much it will remain true. Wouldn't hurt to check it from day to day to see if the measurements stay true. Wood, especially green or wet, has a tendency to shrink, twist or sag. In a built up and well nailed structure, this tendency is held to a minimum.

Multiply the 6-8-10 proportions and with three 100 foot tapes, steady hands and clear thinking, you can establish a true corner and two sides at the same time.

Take a 6 foot flex tape and play around on the kitchen table and you'll get the picture real easy.

Establishing an elevation

You can establish an elevation with a transit or a line level or a water level made with a common garden hose.

If you can't get a friend with a transit to help you, get two 50¢ line levels from your hardware store. They just hang on a tight line. According to the bubbles in the levels, you raise or lower the line until the bubble is on center. I like to use two line levels 1/3 of the way from each corner if over 20 feet. Not as good as a transit, but pretty close.

Of course after line level is established you measure down to establish the foundation top.

Don't trust your string lines overnight without restretching.

An old millwright trick to establish identical elevations from one side of a wall to the other is with a simple garden hose, especially if the wall is concrete or brick. This takes two people talking back and forth and adding water to the hose with a pitcher or can. When each person says the water is flush with the top of the hose, you are level.

The plumb bob

You can buy a $50 or more mercury plumb-bob... or you can hang a stone or filled bottle or wrench on the end of a string and accomplish the same thing.

Let's assume you have a wall. Nail an overhanging cleat or bracket so it sticks out a few inches. Hang your weighted string on it, and when it stops swinging, the distance at the bottom will be the same as the cleat overhang at the top. Pull the wall in or out to make it plumb, and anchor it.

Watching your weights

There are roughly 3,500 honey bees to a pound. There are 8,000 houseflies to a pound.

There are 600-1,000 apple seeds to an ounce. The seeds per ounce for some common vegetables: beans, 100-125; beet, 1,600; broccoli, Brussels sprouts and cabbage; 9,000; carrot, 23,000; celery, 72,000; sweet corn, 120-180; cucumber, 1,100; eggplant, 6,500; lettuce, 25,000; onion, 9,500; pea, 90-175; pumpkin, 100-300; radish, 2-4,000.

A wispy dandelion? Only 35,000—less than half as many seeds per ounce as celery.

Heat value of wood

This table by the U.S. Forest Service lists the relative heat of 33 dry woods, with hickory equaling 100, and compares densities to water. Denser woods burn longer; less dense woods ignite and burn faster.

Species	Density	Heat Value
Osage orange	.78-.83	112
Dogwood.	.70-.79	100-107
Hophornbeam	.70-.75	100-101
Hickory	.70-.74	100
Oak	.60-.73	86-99
Black locust	.69-.70	95-98
Blue beech	.65-.71	93-96
Beech	.64-.66	89-91
Hard maple	.58-.65	83-88
Birch	.55-.64	79-86
Mulberry	.59-.63	84-85
Apple	.58-.62	83-84
Ash	.57-.61	81-82
Southern pine	.51-.60	73-81
Elm	.50-.59	71-80
Walnut	.52-.55	74
Soft maple	.47-.54	67-73
Tamarack	.49-.53	70-72
Cherry	.50-.52	70-71
Sycamore	.49-.52	70
Gum	.48-.52	69-70
Douglas fir	.45-.51	64-69
Sassafras	.44-.46	62-63
Chestnut	.42-.44	59-60
Spruce	.41-.44	59
Tulip or yellow poplar	.40-.42	57
Hemlock	.40-.42	57
Cottonwood	.38-.41	54-55
Balsam fir	.36-.40	51-54
Redwood	.33-.40	47-54
Aspen	.37-.39	53
Basswood	.37-.39	53
White pine	.35-.37	50

Recommended clearances for woodburning devices

	Radiant[2]	Circulating[3]	Supple-mental[4]	Cookstove or Range	Pipe
Ceiling	36"	36"	36"	30"	18"
Front	48	48	48	—	18
Side	24-36	18	36	24	18
Rear	36	18	36	24	18

[1]Information adapted from NFPA bulletin No. 89M, 1976 edition.

[2]A radiant stove is one with a single layer of metal enclosing the fire, such as a Franklin stove.

[3]A circulating stove is one with a second metal jacket enclosing a space for heating and circulating air.

[4]A supplemental heating device is one such as the Add-A- Furnace.

Smoking stove causes concern

I have a problem with my woodburning stove. Every so often, when I open the door, smoke pours out, even though the damper is wide open. What can I do about this? – S.K., Minnesota

The problem most likely is poor draft. This can have several causes. Here are some things to check.

Chimney height: A chimney lower than the peak of the roof can result in downdrafts. Nearby taller buildings or trees can also affect the draft.

Exterior chimneys: A chimney on the outside of the house often results in poor draft, particularly when starting a fire. Such a chimney is cold, and slow to heat up. (It also promotes creosote accumulation.)

Elbows: If you have any 90° elbows in your stovepipe, try replacing them with 45° elbows. This will decrease the resistance found in the sharper angled pipe.

Chimney cap: An uncapped chimney can cause downdrafts. Also, there are special caps that claim to offer extra protection from downdrafts in difficult locations.

Fresh air: Fires need air to burn. If your house is too tightly constructed or insulated, you might have to install a fresh air kit to provide air for the fire.

Exhaust vents: If you notice the problem when you're running a kitchen exhaust fan or clothes dryer vented to the outside, it may be due to negative pressure inside your home.

Chimney liner: If your chimney is unlined, or if the liner is not properly sized for the stove, a poor draft will result.

Chimney cleaning

Before hiring a chimney sweep, check with your local volunteer fire department. They may inspect and clean chimneys free or for a voluntary donation.

Heating with kerosene requires caution

An old-fashioned method of heating homes and farm outbuildings is making a comeback, bringing hazards perhaps not familiar to a new generation of users.

In the last few years, use of kerosene heaters in homes and farm buildings has expanded significantly, with an estimated 15-16 million now in use, said Larry Piercy, Extension Safety Specialist with the University of Kentucky College of Agriculture.

"Many homeowners now use kerosene heaters to supplement their central heating system to heat a small area in the home," Piercy said. "They also are used in greenhouses, garages, basements and workshops as well as for emergency heating situations during power outages."

They are handy to have around, but old-timers who used kerosene as a primary heat source decades ago can tell the new generation a basic fact about kerosene heaters.

They can be dangerous.

Potential hazards include indoor air pollution, fire caused by a flare-up of the wick flame, burns from hot surfaces and fires from improper storage of the fuel.

"One hazard which should never occur," Piercy said, "can occur if gasoline is used in kerosene heaters. Gasoline should never be used as a fuel in these heaters."

Newer kerosene heaters do have more safety features than the ones Grandfather used to use, but care still needs to be taken, Piercy said. Buyers should look for improved guards or grills that reduce the risk of accidental contact burns. Heaters should have a manual shut-off device that allows for quick turn-off in emergency situations such as an uncontrolled flare-up from the wick fire. They should have a mechanism which prevents the wick from being retracted to a hazardously low level.

"Buyers should look for a heater that has been tested and certified by a nationally recognized testing laboratory," Piercy said. "These kerosene heaters have met specific safety standards."

Finally, the owner needs to familiarize himself with basic safety knowledge regarding use of the heaters.

- Read and follow the manufacturer's labels.
- Provide adequate ventilation. If your house is tightly sealed, open a window slightly. Inadequate ventilation could cause headaches, nausea or breathing difficulties.
- Set the wick according to manufacturer's directions. If the room becomes too hot, turn the heater off or open a window. Lowering the wick does not reduce the heat.
- If an uncontrolled flare-up occurs, use the manual shut-off switch. Do not try to move the heater or attempt to extinguish a kerosene heater fire with water or blankets.
- Make sure the chimney is seated properly on the wick assembly to avoid sooting and fire hazards.
- Place the heaters at least three feet from combustible materials.
- Do not use the heater in areas where flammable vapors are present, around gasoline, paints or solvents.
- Do not leave the heater unattended. – *Reprinted from 1992*

How big is a doghouse? As a rule of thumb, make it one-third longer and one-half taller than the dog, and the width, two-thirds of his shoulder height.

In cold climates, the house should have a vestibule, which should be twice the width of the dog and 2" taller than his shoulders.

A small amount of unslaked lime will keep green scum out of livestock water tanks.

Check stored grains for spoilage

If you're storing grain—whether you grew it yourself, bought it at harvest time prices to save money, or gleaned a neighbor's cornfield—be sure to check it occasionally to spot problems before they become serious. Otherwise you might lose a good portion of your investment.

Check for mold, insects, and heating. (The three are often related.)

Molds can develop when grain moisture exceeds 14 percent and the storage temperature is greater than 40°. Once mold activity begins, additional heat and moisture are released by the developing fungi and the problem accelerates.

Mold growth may or may not be visible. Watch for crusting, or moldy odors.

One way to fight mold is to cool the grain. Large bins commonly have fans for this purpose. If you have oats, wheat, barley, etc. stored in wooden bins you might have to remove it and aerate it before returning it to the bin. Be sure to clean the bin thoroughly before putting grain back into it. If you have small amounts in garbage cans or similar storage receptacles, removing and aerating it is a much simpler chore.

Handle shelled corn like small grains. Ear corn—stored with grain still on the cob—is somewhat easier to store, because the cob draws moisture from the kernels. However, a crib with good ventilation is still a necessity.

Saving small farms

About 300,000 American farms have disappeared over the last two decades as big agribusiness grows ever more centralized—a trend that won't stop without immediate action, according to a federal commission's report.

Agriculture Secretary Dan Glickman, who appointed the commission, said, "I want to see small farms grow and prosper and get ahead, not just survive."

A small farm grosses less than $250,000 a year and is run primarily by families. The report suggested 146 ways to bolster small farms.

Becoming self-sufficient in less than 18 months isn't a reasonable goal, but here's

How to get started

My husband and I are "farm-sitting" for a couple who gets COUNTRYSIDE and we are both very impressed by it. I stayed up until 3 A.M. this morning reading the latest issue, which came yesterday. Enclosed is our subscription.

I would like to ask your opinion about a couple of questions.

1. Is it really "doable" for us, city folk, who have little know-how, little money, and only 18 months to become self-sufficient?

2. If so, where do we start, practically speaking? If not, would it be a good idea to offer our services to a bona fide homesteader in return for food and shelter?

Perhaps a future issue could include advice on what to do if you're in a situation like ours. — *Brian & Karyn Oneel, Ohio*

People who have read this magazine regularly know that becoming self-sufficient in 18 months (now maybe 14), starting virtually from scratch, isn't a reasonable goal. And anyone who has tried it knows even better.

I have been preaching about this for 30 years from two different angles, both of which seem even more pertinent today.

First is the widespread notion that because we live in such a high-tech world filled with scientific marvels, we are somehow "smarter" than our ancestors. The implication is that even an uneducated dolt can easily learn to do the simple things they did to survive.

That we are not all that smart can easily be demonstrated.

Even a child can flip a switch and flood a dark room with light. But how many of today's adults could start a fire without matches, or make a candle? How many even highly educated people could make a light bulb, or a generator to light it, or the wires to connect the two?

Extend this across the length and breadth of what we do to survive today, and the problem should be obvious: We are all specialists, and very few people have the capacity to perform even the most basic tasks from beginning to end. It's not just a joke to say that we learn more and more about less and less until we know everything about nothing at all.

The division of labor that was both spawned by and still fuels the Industrial Revolution has put self-sufficiency almost on a par with rocket science: way beyond the reach of most mortals.

Farming provides an excellent and pertinent example, because farmers used to be self-sufficient, and self-sufficiency implies a certain level of farming. Farmers used to plow with horses and mules that replaced themselves, they sowed seed they saved from the previous harvest, and they stored and ate what they produced.

A modern farmer couldn't make a tractor from scratch, the way he could breed a mare. He couldn't produce the fuel and lubricants to run it, like he could produce hay and oats for his team.

Today's farmer doesn't save and plant open-pollinated seed. He buys hybrids, and now even genetically altered seeds from gigantic specialized corporations (filled, of course, with highly specialized workers).

He doesn't have a cow, a pig, a few hens, a variety of crops to feed them all, and a garden to provide his food. He has hundreds of cows, or thousands of pigs, or tens of thousands of chickens—and nothing else. He grows corn, or wheat, or soybeans, and nothing else.

He sends thousands of pounds of milk to market, but buys cheese, butter, ice cream and yogurt at the supermarket. He sells tons of wheat for pennies, then buys bread and cereal for dollars.

Division of labor is good, by Industrial Age standards. It's efficient. It produces more goods for more people at less cost. It increases profits. The effects on the planet, society, and individuals haven't been tallied up because they have been so hard to document in dollars and cents. They don't show up on computer spreadsheets.

But extreme division of labor has also rendered every one of us, as individuals, totally helpless. We are captives of the industrial system. "I will program your computer if you feed me," but "you" consists of an intricate impenetrable maze of specialists, none of which can exist without the others.

Because of that division of labor, we can fly across the country without knowing a thing about aerodynamics, or even baggage handling systems… unless one of those happens to be our specialty. We can undergo a complex and dangerous medical procedure without knowing a vein from an artery. We can sit down at a computer and surf the world wide web even if we don't know a bit from a byte, and we can sit down to a table laden with wonderful food even if we couldn't tell a potato from a pigweed in the garden.

Because we can do and enjoy all these, and because we know so much about our narrow specialties, we think we stand head and shoulders above those "backward" people who, if they were here today, wouldn't even know essentials even our children take for granted—like programming a vcr.

Hicks. Hayseeds. Clod hoppers. Those were some of the sneering titles the Industrial Age applied to people who didn't jump on the technological bandwagon. Those, and "jack of all trades, and master of none."

These are some of the reasons so many people don't accept—and can't understand—things like the Y2K situation. Division of labor has blinded them to the basic and stark realities of survival. Their specialization has led them to rely on other specialties they know nothing about, to the extent that they think "they" will take care of any problems. The technological advances of industrialized society have created a false pride in what they consider their accomplishments and capabilities.

How our ancestors learned

This explains, to some degree, how we arrived where we are today, and why a few of us have warned about it for decades.

But it also explains why becoming self-sufficient in a matter of months is all but impossible.

Children today learn at an early age how to turn on a light, the tv, a faucet. They can use the microwave, make a phone call, flush the toilet.

They have no idea whatsoever how any of it works—neither do most adults—but that doesn't matter. It's there, and it works, and they take it for granted.

Now go back 100 years or so.

Children learned at an early age how to gather eggs, plant seeds, weed a garden. They watched Mom and Grandma bake bread, make soap, preserve food. They saw Dad and Gramps harness horses, butcher hogs, make sausage.

As they grew older and stronger, they were expected to help. And eventually, they could do all of these things, and more, by themselves.

They didn't suddenly decide to become self-sufficient, and they didn't learn everything overnight. It took years.

Can't we speed it up?

"I understand all that," you say, "but can't this education be speeded up?"

Well, yes... and no.

You can read, take courses to learn various homestead skills involved in self-sufficiency, even become an apprentice. But even if you can absorb all that concentrated book-learning (which even hands-on classes amount to, really), you won't be ready for the ebb and flow of real world cycles.

In a setting of self-sufficiency, seeds are planted in the spring, plants tended during the summer, crops harvested and stored in fall. To get real-life, real-time hands-on experience will take a year.

But what if this year is wet, and next year is dry? What about late frosts in spring, and early frosts in fall? Every gardener can tell tales of going years without problems with potato bugs, bean beetles, onion thrips or fusarium wilt, and then... pow. We start learning all over again.

Every year is different. It's generally acknowledged that when even an experienced gardener starts over in a new location, it takes three to five years to become familiar with the new conditions.

For livestock and other projects, the learning curve is even longer.

It's not impossible, but...

That doesn't mean it's impossible, or that you shouldn't at least make a start. It just means you shouldn't have unrealistic expectations.

In the past we suggested that you not go into homesteading, but grow into it. Today, for those concerned about Y2K, that might not be an option. Those people will have to make other arrangements.

How to make a start

You aren't going to become self-sufficient, or even self-reliant, in one year. But you can make a start. So your first task is to insure that you'll survive long enough to become self-sufficient.

Offering your services to someone who is already there, or even half-way there, could be a good option. The problem is finding such a situation... and perhaps even more important, finding a situation that will work. In more than 30 years of observing such arrangements, I have seen many problems, and I'm not aware of even one that has worked out over the long term. Depending on who's telling the story, the apprentice is either treated like a slave, or is a lazy good-for-nothing. You get the picture.

Buying time to learn

Lacking that, the next logical

Family album:

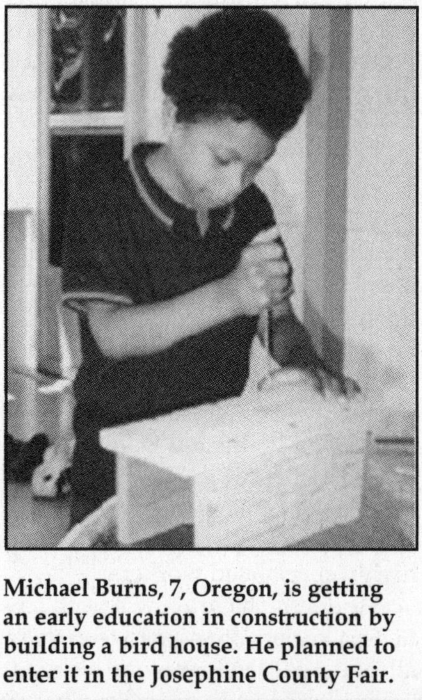

Michael Burns, 7, Oregon, is getting an early education in construction by building a bird house. He planned to enter it in the Josephine County Fair.

approach would be to give yourself enough time to learn and practice self-sufficiency skills. This amounts to priming the pump.

If you were already self-sufficient, you'd have a year's supply, or more, of necessities in your larder and storerooms. But since you didn't produce those supplies yourself, you'll have to obtain them elsewhere.

That could mean buying nitrogen-packed freeze-dried food, or grains and other raw staples, or canned and packaged goods from the supermarket, or a combination. The goal here is to buy time, to assure yourself that you will at least survive while you go through the learning process.

If you don't have enough money to buy groceries for next week, you obviously aren't going to buy groceries for the next year or two. That presents other problems.

If I were in that situation I'd do three things. First, I'd get permission to glean farmers' fields after harvest. We have done this with potatoes, onions, and corn. You might have more, or less, or even none, in your area: You'll have to do some diligent searching.

Gardeners also often have a surplus that only goes to waste. And how many times have you seen trees laden with fruit that the homeowner considers a nuisance rather than a blessing? You don't need prime apples to make sauce, or to dry them.

Such gleaning might be considered a more "civilized" form of foraging, which is the second thing I'd concentrate on. (In some situations it might be the first.) There are books on edible wild plants, and in some places you'll even find classes, where you'll get expert guidance and hands-on experience.

And third, I'd sell everything I could possibly do without to raise money to fill in the gaps in my food storage plan. (This would include essential equipment and tools for both garden and kitchen.)

Division of labor is a valuable technique. Like many other things, it can be taken to extremes (as noted in the article on this page), but even early hunter-gatherers used it. Old-time homesteaders certainly did.

This means "self-sufficiency" shouldn't imply doing everything yourself. That would be inefficient... and impossible.

It also means you don't have to know everything to survive on a homestead if you're aligned with a "community" — even a community of two — when different people have different skills.

Keep this in mind as you learn. Ask not only what you need to know, but what will make you more valuable to others.

Getting educated

The next step is to go after that self-sufficiency education in earnest. Read books and magazines. One in particular is highly recommended: *How to Grow More Vegetables* (than you ever thought possible, on less land than you can imagine), by John Jevons; Ten Speed Press, Berkeley, CA. Study the pertinent material. Make notes. Make plans.

Take classes. Join clubs, including goat, rabbit and poultry clubs, if those are included in your goals. If there is a Master Gardener program near you, or an organization where you can meet and learn from other gardeners, go for it!

Order seed catalogs. Study them. Based on what you have learned and planned, place your order.

At the same time, start gathering information and equipment for preserving food.

Then use your new knowledge to do what you can, when you can, where you can.

You won't be self-sufficient. But with a lot of attention, some work, and a little luck, you'll produce enough to live on. You're on the way.

Be businesslike: Cultivate a homestead attitude, set priorities, and get to work!

COUNTRYSIDE: I have just been reading the Sept/Oct issue and my heart is racing with fright. As part of a family of four, there is more than myself to worry about.

My husband thinks the thoughts and ideas that I get from COUNTRYSIDE are weird. Oh, he doesn't come right out and say so but, with the way he looks at me... why would he have to say anything?

We live on one acre of land and are doing nothing to be self-sufficient. I brought up the subject of chickens once and he just laughingly brought it up with a family member. Boy was I hurt. What is it, don't black families want to survive and just live better and more peacefully?

My question comes because of our lack of preparedness. Are vacuum-packed seeds a viable option for late comers? He does know how to garden *if* he has to.

This short note feels like an incredibly bold move. — *Pam Pitts, Pennsylvania*

This is another letter involving priorities. (See page 337.)

One top priority is to avoid fear. We don't talk about what might happen to frighten anyone. These are merely possibilities to consider, evaluate, discuss, and then act upon according to your convictions and capabilities. Instead of being afraid, develop a homestead attitude.

A reluctant mate makes it more difficult. But we've heard from other women in similar situations who planted gardens and raised chickens on their own... and got help when their mates learned how good fresh eggs and vegetables were!

Vacuum-packed seeds can be a "viable option" for anyone, under certain circumstances. But they hardly qualify as a top priority for those who have done nothing else.

You don't need long-term storage as much as you need to learn to plant and save your own seeds.

Ideas to help in preparing for emergencies

The message: Quit waiting to live life!

COUNTRYSIDE: First let me say that we are not running around, half crazed out of our minds with panic or paranoia. We have long prepared ourselves, mentally, physically and otherwise, to live without centralized food, medicine, and fuel. We simply think it is not sustainable, safe, or sane to think that others will always be there to provide all your basic survival needs.

For many years, we have planned and dreamed of our homestead, only to be continually trapped in town, for many reasons we are still trying to unravel. The towns we've lived in are really country towns, and we've learned many valuable skills. I have learned outdoor foraging for food and medicine, gardening, how to cut firewood, etc. John learned how to build houses. We have been gardening, sprouting, and cooking our own food and more for a long time. I have read book after book on building, alternative energy systems, root cellaring, gardening, greywater and the like.

I feel confident with my knowledge. But we are (eeek!) tenants. Renters unable to build root cellars, composting toilets, powerless water systems and the like.

Last year, when the power in our mountain town went out for three days we had no water, heat, or cooking facilities. We felt the terror of being at the mercy of the grid. We have been determined to get to our homestead/land by this fall. We plan to set up solar, bike and water power systems. We plan on heating and cooking with wood, building a root cellar, and planting a small orchard.

We are not motivated by fear. We are motivated by passion about the "good life" we want to create. We are motivated by a desire to live in harmony with the Earth and its cycles. We are motivated because homesteading is the dream we have shoved on the back burner one too many times. We are motivated by love; love of ourselves and each other, compelling us to take every step we can toward creating security, harmony, and balance, for us as well as our neighbors on this Earth.

The true message for us is: *Quit waiting to live life!*

So, here is what we have done so far.

1. We took full inventory of every tool we own including flashlights, contents of our household tool box, and garden equipment.
2. We made a list of all the activities we would like to do on our homestead, including building a simple cordwood house.
3. We made a list of every tool or supply we would need to do each activity such as planting and pruning an orchard, or pumping and heating water for our home, or fencing animals, or growing, storing and preserving food.
4. We checked each list against our inventory list. Whatever was not in our inventory, we placed on a list called "Needed Tools and Supplies."
5. We have started going to yard sales, reading classifieds, and generally looking around for the items on our list.
6. We cleaned out our entire rental home and created a pile of unnecessarys we are going to sell.
7. We bought Rob Roy's book *Mortgage-Free,* and we are calculating realistically (for the first time) what we want to pay back, as opposed to spend(the two are often unrelated).

The next part of our plan consists of these steps, which we are working on right now:

8. Rent a small storage unit to store supplies and tools we find, scavenge or buy to later use on our homestead.
9. Have a yard sale.
10. Place a classified ad for land in the paper of the rural area we want to move to, about an hour from here. The ad will read more like a personal ad, explaining a bit about who we are and what we are doing and looking for. We plan to get inexpensive land with owner financing, short term, and a fair interest rate. (So far we have found one interesting place, in the local classifieds, but the old-timer is getting sentimental about the land and now may not sell.)

More steps will be added as we go. We have long been debt free. We buy used cars and other goods for cash. We haven't shopped at a mall since we were teenagers (we don't like them!). We don't have a tv, although I use my computer for writing manuscripts and e-mail. I would give up my computer in a minute and write longhand, but editors simply won't allow it!

The benefit of this lifestyle is that our habits won't change much when we get on our land. To us, homesteading begins as a state of mind that believes simplification of life brings pleasure. If the centralized systems we are now dependent on for our very sustenance go down, creating mass suffering, the real culprit will be us, the world citizens, who forgot the most basic farmer's adage: don't put all your eggs in one basket! – *Indra Sena*

Home education:

A student writes: Home education is a good choice

MICHAEL VON ANSBACH-YOUNG

The author was home educated from third grade until the completion of high school. He currently studies computer science by correspondence. He is 16 years old.

I still remember our official first day as a "homeschooler." I was in third grade, and my brother was in first. To be honest, I couldn't see the sense in being taken from a comfortable academic environment, only to be placed at the dining room table to do my schoolwork. After all, how can you have school at home?!

It felt funny to have Mom as a teacher, but alas, my skepticism was short-lived. By lunch time I had completed far more schoolwork than I would have done at "real" school—in this case, a private Christian day school—and was excited over the notion of only a half-day of heavy academics! The afternoons were spent doing "fun" stuff like reading and pursuing individual interests. In my case this was writing. While I was yet rather young—about nine—I commenced writing a book. After forty-some pages, I recognized that my main characters weren't getting anywhere. Hence, that project never came to fruition, although my love for writing has continued to this day.

Relatives and friends—or anyone who wondered why we weren't in (traditional institutionalized) school—were more skeptical of my parents' educational choices. They feared for the mental deficiencies that we would undoubtedly develop, and they feared, above all else, for our lack of proper "socialization."

Today, you'll be hard pressed to find a homeschool skeptic among our relatives and friends.

Academically, my brothers and I have consistently scored far above government-educated peers in national tests, including SAT, ACT, and CTBS. We've all scored consistently in the ninetieth percentile, the national average for these tests being the fiftieth percentile. Homeschoolers have little trouble getting accepted into colleges and universities.

Socially, I consider myself well-rounded, although I confess that I haven't been exposed to the violence, sadism, racism, and secularism that plague too many public schools. Psychologists hold that children must have excessive interaction with peers in order to properly develop their personality, but I hold to the common-sense notion that social graces are best learned from ones' parents, and that any society that rejects or ignores the wisdom of elderly people is apt to make more mistakes than are necessary. Believe it or not, I do find that being at home has been a negative social experience, I "get along" with my family quite well! And also, it is apparent that I am very comfortable conversing with senior citizens, businessmen and tradesmen, clergymen, peers—in short, anyone and everyone, and on many different topics.

Statistics reveal that home education is a viable educational alternative, from practically any angle.

Some people, for instance, may wonder whether home education is affordable. To quote the most up-to-date source presently available: "A cost-benefit analysis revealed that an average of $546 spent per home school student per year yields an average 85th percentile ranking on test scores. Compare this to the average annual expenditure of $5,325 per public school student to achieve only an average 50th percentile ranking." (Home Education Across the United States, 1997, Home School Legal Defense Association.) This report can be read in its entirety on the HSLDA web site (www.hslda.org). Perhaps the question should be asked: "Can you afford not to homeschool?"

After meeting a college student who dogmatically stated that governmental "education funding should never be decreased," I confronted him with such statistics. He discounted them on the basis that "standardized tests are inadequate to thoroughly test knowledge of a subject area." Let it be said that while recognizing the limitations of standardized tests, I still believe that you do have to know something to do well on them, and you have to lack that something to do poorly. I suspect that this "something" may be knowledge.

There is still much that could be said, based on some of the statistics before me. But take my word for it: the story of home education is a success story, regardless of socioeconomic status, parental teacher certification, or various other factors.

My thesis is that there are two primary reasons for the success of homeschooling. First, and most importantly, no one has a more legitimate interest in the education of children than do parents. Parents educate for love, not for money. Parents (should!) really want their children to succeed, and so they will put forth the effort to help them succeed. Although there are many wonderful people teaching in the institutionalized setting, very few can effectively duplicate the love and concern that most parents have for their children.

Second, home education allows individualized instruction. There are many books and resources expounding on the simple fact that all children do not learn the same. Curriculum can be hand-picked to account for differences in students. In this way, home education encourages individuality in students, unlike government schools where children of the same age are generally expected to learn the same thing in the same way at the same time.

Because so many people have chosen to home educate—it is estimated that there were 1.23 million home educated students in the fall of '96—there is a wealth of information and resources on the subject. It would be futile to attempt to list these resources here. Your local library should have at least a few resources on home education, and these resources should point to more resources, which should point to more resources, ad infinitum.

You can take my word for it, or you can trust the statistics, but any way you look at it, the message is clear: home education really works!

Melissa and Melanie discovered a new interest in Irish step dancing... but they're back in the goat business, too.

Family life:

Teenagers find other interests—but return to homesteading!

PATRICIA LOCKWOOD
TEXAS

As our children grow older things begin to change, for us as well as them. We change from marathon runners to chauffeurs. We are no longer just physically tired, but mentally. Their questions become more complicated. Shades of gray appear in all matters.

All this has nothing to do with our children's behavior. My four are great kids and I haven't anything to complain about. However, I am noticing that things in our house are changing, as three of them are now teenagers.

We have raised animals and tried to live as self-sufficiently as possible for many, many years now. But in the last couple of years the children's interests are changing. Animals are no longer their whole world. They have even discovered you can purchase clothes from places other than second hand shops and yard sales. They even want store bought soap. For a dedicated homesteader like me, these things are close to heresy.

My husband and I decided to let them have it their way for a bit and we sold all our animals except the dog and cats. The chickens stayed: they're mine! The children were so excited that we saw life their way. We really didn't, and we felt pretty certain we knew the eventual outcome of all this.

The children slept in, and ate breakfast at lunch time. They read books, and walked around our land without having to watch where they stepped. They stored their bikes in one of the now empty barns.

And promptly began to miss the pesky critters. They wouldn't quite admit to missing all the work, but they did make little comments about this or that animal and wondered if the new owners were taking care of them right.

Pretty soon old photo albums began to appear. "Remember this?" "We won't have to break ice this year for watering the animals, but we won't have new kids to feed either." Things were starting to change.

Eight months went by without any critters and no chores to speak of. We never went to the feed store. Never even signed up for 4-H. One rather "bored" day, the girls were talking and my 14-year-old confessed. She missed her goats and sheep. The truth poured from the 17-year-old too, "Things just don't seem right."

A few phone calls later we had managed to buy back three of our goats. The children have found their way back home to homesteading. And once again the spinning wheels are spinning, the milk buckets clanging and there's homemade soap in the soap dish. The back hall is full of muddy boots and the boys are looking at seed catalogs with thoughts of planting. The compost pile is growing and it seems life is headed back in the right direction. My husband and I have a smile on our faces.

We knew all along it would be like this. It's in the blood.

The machine shed:

Instead of a trailer, consider a carry-all

MEL CRAIN
MISSOURI

When I bought my small, old T-20 Ferguson tractor, a carry-all came with it. I had seen carry-alls of all sizes at auctions and paid little attention to the one that came with my tractor. It was made of steel, five feet wide and four feet long, with a one-foot sideboard.

I didn't have a wagon or two wheel trailer. I planned on buying one or the other when one came available at an auction but, what the heck, since I had the carry-all, I would use it until something better came along.

That was two years ago. I am no longer looking for anything else.

Tractors such as mine are notorious for poor traction when pulling a wagon under slippery conditions. They're "light in the rear-end" is how the locals describe them.

A two-wheel trailer would be nice for some things. However, I have discovered that the carry-all is the handiest for me on our 40 acres.

Yes, something larger would be better, occasionally. When hauling larger items, such as fence posts, there are times when I must make more than one trip. I can haul three or four fence posts, a roll of wire and my fencing tools just fine.

I can take the carry-all into many spots that I could never get into with a wagon or trailer. Turning sharp corners is a cinch.

We heat our home with wood and I have found nothing better than the carry-all for going through the thick, heavy timber, being selective, thinning a tree here, a tree there. I cut the wood to length on the spot and haul it out. We cut our wood in the round. The small logs, four to five feet long, are ideal for our furnace. Making three trips a day, we store over a half a cord of wood in our woodshed.

Yes, when I have the carry-all loaded, I must back up the steep ridges in the timber to keep the tractor from tipping over backwards. My small tractor is too light in the front end for the added weight in the rear when I have a load of wood.

If you use a carry-all, you must be conscious of the fact that the tractor will tip over backward with too much weight. As with most things involving homesteading, it pays to exercise a little common sense occasionally.

I wouldn't be able to get a wagon into our timber with the narrow trails we have. I refuse to cut trees unnecessarily, just for a wider road.

If I used a two-wheel trailer I would have to park on the trail and skid a log back to the trail. Then I would have to cut the log to length and load it. After two or three logs I would have to hook the trailer up and drive down out of the timber to our wood shed.

We own 40 acres, most of which is hardwood timber, with a few acres of meadow. I have yet to find anything better for getting wood from the timber to the wood shed than my carry-all.

On our homestead the tractor and carry-all are in constant use. Our garden is laid out with a six-foot-wide alley down the center so that we can drive the tractor, with carry-all, right into the middle of the garden. We can haul mulch, compost, you name it, and spread it easily from the carry-all. When the lift is left up it's almost exactly at waist level, ideal for unloading.

Last fall, I was busy re-roofing our

The carry-all that came with Mel Crain's Ferguson tractor changed his mind about needing a wagon or trailer for homestead chores. He uses it to haul firewood (above), and garden produce (right). The height is convenient for loading and unloading.

home when the winter squash began coming on like gangbusters. Normally, my wife or I would have loaded the squash in our wheelbarrow and hauled them to the house. My wife's back was bothering her, so she used the Ferguson and the carry-all. With the alleyway, she never had to carry the squash more than 10 feet.

I know there are better tools for each specific job, but I can't afford to buy specialized equipment for each situation. Besides, I have better uses for my property than parking farm equipment that I might use just once or twice a year.

Last winter I discovered another benefit. We are the only house on a dead-end road, with a steep hill between us and the highway a quarter of a mile away. When the road becomes too slippery because of snow, we must park our car at the highway and haul groceries, etc. to the house in the carry-all.

Last April, we had a surprise: 26 inches of heavy, wet snow. Out of curiosity, I jumped on the tractor and drove it through the heavy snow to the highway. In an emergency, my wife or I could haul the other to the highway, where an ambulance could pick us up. With the weight over the rear wheels traction is great.

My neighbor hauls a few bales of hay to his calves each morning using his flatbed carry-all mounted on an old Cockshutt tractor.

Carry-alls are relatively inexpensive. I have seen them sell at auctions for as little as $15. They come in all sizes and shapes for any size tractor, from a small one such as I own up to very large ones for larger tractors.

I am sure a carry-all is not for everyone. However they are overlooked more than they should be. Take a look. You might be surprised.

Help for the homestead machinist

Art Horn
North Carolina

The Home Machinist's Handbook by Doug Briney, TAB BOOKS, Blue Ridge Summit, PA 17294-0850. I got my copy from Grizzly for $19.95. (Grizzly has several catalogs of woodworking and industrial tools and machinery. The catalogs are worth having. Retail is by phone and credit card. You can get them at http://www.grizzlyindustrial.com or 1-800-523-4777.)

I was going to write an article which contained some of the information in this book. Topics like tapping threads and reading blueprints are areas which typical homesteaders need to know about but which there is very little in print. Mr. Briney has saved me the trouble and provided us all with a great beginner's book with clear illustrations. I have looked at a number of more advanced books on machining but these require a deeper educational background than a nonspecialist will have.

The first few chapters of this book are of general interest to those of us who need to deal with problems such as replicating a spare part from a drawing or sketch; measuring in tolerances, occasional use of calipers or micrometers, etc.

Chapter 1 involves reading prints and why the different illustrations for a part are made the way they are: orthographic projections, sectional views, etc.

Chapter 2 involves basic measuring tools, including a very good illustrated two pages on how to read vernier calipers, three good pages on vernier micrometers, etc. Verniers are simple once you know how to read them and like Sumerian or Greek if you do not. Vernier calipers are cheap and allow good precision measurement.

Chapter 3 involves hand tools and basic layout techniques such as scribing lines on steel plates, punching places for drilling, etc. These techniques are not likely to occur to anyone "out of the blue" yet you need them when attempting to fabricate a replacement part or make something new.

Chapter 4 involves basic bench tools such as vises, grinders, saws, abrasive selections and drilling, reaming and tapping. This discussion is worth the price of the book alone. I personally find that drilling is one of the most useful technologies I use. Drilling is cheap and can be kept cheap if you maintain your equipment and know what type of drill can be used where. Tapping threads is something I learned in the machine shop. This is a totally critical technique to understand when you need threads in or on something. It is not something that is intuitively obvious. His illustrations of tapping procedures (four pages) are about the best I have seen for a beginner.

Chapters 5-8 are on lathes and milling machines and their operations. These are somewhat specialized. I only have one neighbor, a retired machinist, who has a metal lathe at his place and I have the only wood lathe among my friends.

Chapter 9 is on materials and covers things like materials properties, the differences in things like cold rolled and hot rolled materials, codes for different alloys and cutting nonferrous materials including aluminum and plastics.

Chapter 10 involves basics of heat treating. This includes small shop methods or blacksmith applications. It is not bad to know how to set up a little temporary furnace with a propane tank and some bricks and hardwood ashes that will allow you to heat treat some small part, which you had to fabricate for your old tiller, whose manufacturer went out of business in the 60s...We have all faced this sort of problem.

I really enjoyed discovering this book. Now if I could just figure out all those formulae in Pocket Ref I could almost be an engineer? Hmmm?

The Countryside calendar:

What homesteaders are doing in late June, July and August:

Now, of all times, is when we're eating fresh-from-the-garden meals. Even those who don't do much preserving should be making very, very few trips to the grocery store at this time of the year.

• Stop cutting asparagus by mid-June. Topdress with 3-4 inches of good compost.

• Remove suckers from tomatoes. The fruits will be larger.

• When runner beans reach the tops of their poles and attach themselves, pinch out the growing points. This lets them concentrate their energy in producing pods instead of new growth.

• Nip off seed heads of onions and shallots so the bulbs form properly.

• Check carefully for insect problems, and take any necessary action. Pay special attention to those that might be hiding in foliage.

• Water as necessary, paying special attention to cucumbers, tomatoes, runner beans and celery.

• To make sure you continue to eat from the garden even after others have hung up their hoes for the year, the fall garden should be well underway.

• Brussels sprouts, cabbage, and broccoli seeds should have been started in May or June for transplanting in June, or early July at the latest. Leeks should also be planted now. You'll want pencil-thick plants, at least 10 inches long, planted nine inches deep in rich soil. Leeks are good replacements for early potatoes, which can be lifted now.

• Sow turnips and rutabagas. When seedlings emerge, be on the lookout for flea beetles. Control them with frequent cultivation. Note that they dislike shade.

• Sow lettuce, in a place where it can be kept cool. This is a succession crop only: thin plants, but don't bother transplanting after mid-June.

• Plant carrots and parsley for winter use. Thin carrots as they sprout, but be careful to disturb the soil as little as possible to thwart carrot flies. The smell of crush foliage also attracts them: don't leave thinnings in the row. Their eggs hatch into grubs that bore into the carrot roots. Allow half an inch between plants. As these grow, further thinnings will provide tiny carrots for eating while an ultimate spacing of four inches will result in large roots for winter.

• When digging early potatoes, move and disturb as much soil as possible to discourage new weed seedlings, which still have plenty of time to sprout. Depending on your soil and available space, this ground can be used for late crops.

• Watch for blight on late potatoes — brown blotches on the leaves, and sometimes stems as well. A fungicide might be called for to save the crop. Tip burn might be caused by unusually warm and dry weather. If scab disfigures the tubers your soil probably isn't acid enough: did you make the mistake of adding lime or wood ashes to the potato plot? Keep Colorado potato beetles and red slugs in line by hand picking.

• Harvest beans and cucumbers while still young for best quality and to keep the plants producing.

• Canning, freezing and drying of many crops (depending on your location) goes into full swing toward the end of this period.

• In the barns: Be sure all animals have plenty of fresh, clean water at all times.

• Keep them cool and provide shade. Rabbits will appreciate milk cartons of frozen water in their hutches… and remember, excessive heat will render bucks sterile.

• If your broilers are ready to butcher, do it. Feeding them beyond their ideal weight (depending on breed) is a waste of money.

• Keep an eye on pastures: avoid overgrazing.

• Will you have enough hay for winter? If not, look around to see if you can make more from "wasteland," or if neighbors have any to sell. Check hay in the mow for heating.

• Plan early to save seeds from open pollinated crops… starting by not planting those that will cross-pollinate near one another. (This distance is at least 700 feet for corn, depending on terrain and other factors affecting wind pollination.)

How can I make fly paper?

32 oz. rosin
20 oz. rosin oil
8 oz. castor oil

Heat in an aluminum or enameled pot on a gas stove, stirring until all the rosin has melted and dissolved. While hot pour on firm paper sheets of suitable size which have been brushed with soap water just before coating. Smooth out the coating with a long knife or piece of thin flat wood and allow to cool.

If a heavier coating is desirable increase the amount of rosin used. Similarly a thinner coating is gotten by reducing the amount of rosin.

The finished paper should be laid flat and not exposed to undue heat.

The Countryside calendar:

What homesteaders are doing in September and October:

• Inventory your winter supplies. Remember the advice for beginning woodburners: Cut as much firewood as you think you'll need, and then cut another stack just like it.

Actually, your firewood should have been cut, split and stacked months ago, but now is the time to make a final check. Ours has been drying, under cover, outdoors, but now is when we move as much as we can into the house. We have a wood furnace in the basement and store several cords of wood there, but we don't move it too early because of humidity problems if the wood isn't totally dry. When we start building fires just to take the chill off, the added humidity is no longer a problem. (Some people are also concerned about insects coming into the house on the wood or under the bark. They only store small amounts inside. But it's nice to have enough for that first "unexpected" cold snap.)

• If you had a crop failure in any of your staple products—maybe potatoes, or dry beans, or tomatoes—either make up the loss by buying or bartering from a neighbor or farmers' market, or select a substitute.

• Take the same inventory of your livestock needs.

• Cull laying hens heavily now.

This is also the time to cull other livestock. Butcher or sell any animal that isn't paying its way rather than wasting expensive feed and precious time on it over winter.

• Clean wild bird feeders. Have enough feed?

• Check all house and outbuilding windows and doors for drafts. Make repairs or weather-strip now when you can still work without dressing for arctic conditions.

• Clean up the garden. Hot compost or burn weeds and crop residue that might cause weed or disease problems next spring.

• Pot a few tomato, pepper and parsley plants to bring indoors or into the greenhouse or cold frame to extend their growing season. Many herbs can be potted and grown indoors over winter.

• Green tomatoes, picked before frost and kept in a dark cool place, will ripen over time.

• Spread compost or manure, or mulch. If possible, avoid leaving soil bare over winter.

• Heavily mulch carrots and other crops to be left in the ground. This is an ideal use for leaves.

• If you're short on mulch or compost materials, pick up bags of leaves city folks set out for the trash collectors.

• Plant winter wheat and rye, even if only a few square yards in the garden. In zones 3-5 the deadline is generally September 15: you want enough fall growth to sustain the plants over winter, but too much might contribute to winterkill. If in doubt, watch your neighbors who plant wheat or rye, or ask your county agent.

• Clean, sharpen, oil and properly store all gardening equipment.

• Winterize all gas engines. Add stabilizer to filled gas tanks. (Empty tanks can lead to rust.) Drain oil and remove and inspect spark plugs. Follow manufacturer's directions for preparing for extended storage. Check antifreeze, batteries and oil in vehicles.

• Check out all hunting equipment.

• Inventory and inspect winter clothing. Do your leather boots need oiling or new laces?

• As days grow shorter, you might notice that previously unused light bulbs are burned out...in vehicles, barns, and yards. Have replacements ready.

• Spend some time with your production records while they're still fresh. Make notes to plant more, or less, of certain garden and field crops. Note which varieties from which seed companies did well, and which were duds. Be sure your saved seeds are properly stored and (if necessary) protected from freezing.

• Are you ready for the first blizzard or ice storm? Kerosene, candles, staple food supplies, water, extra gas safely stored in approved containers.

• Inspect the root cellar regularly for spoilage and proper ventilation.

• Don't dig horseradish until after the first frost or it won't have any zing. Carrots are sweeter after a frost.

• Gather hickory nuts immediately after a frost, before the squirrels get all of them.

• Is your plumbing ready for freezing weather? Drain pools, bird baths, hoses, and outdoor faucets that aren't frost-proof. If you've had frozen pipe problems, heat tape or insulation might be in order.

• How are your tires? You might need snow tires, or chains. Have winter emergency kits in all vehicles: a blanket, matches, canned heat, tow strap or chain, jumper cables, candy bars or dried fruit.

• Clean your chimney!

Seed longevity

If you save seeds from one growing season to the next, how long will they remain viable? Assuming they are properly stored and cared for, here's what to expect:

Seed	Years
Asparagus	2 to 3
Beans (all kinds)	2 to 3
Beet	3 to 4
Broccoli	5 to 6
Carrot	2 to 3
Cress	3 to 4
Corn	2 to 3
Cucumber	8 to 10
Eggplant	1 to 2
Endive	5 to 6
Leek	2 to 3
Cauliflower	5 to 6
Celery	2 to 3
Corn salad	2 to 3
Onion	2 to 3
Parsley	2 to 3
Parsnip	2 to 3
Peas	5 to 6
Pumpkin	8 to 10
Rhubarb	3 to 4
Squash	8 to 10
Lettuce	3 to 4
Melon	8 to 10
Okra	3 to 4
Spinach	3 to 4
Tomato	2 to 3
Turnip	5 to 6
Pepper	2 to 3
Radish	4 to 5
Salsify	2 to 3
Herbs	
Anise	3 to 4
Balm	2 to 3
Basil	2 to 3
Caraway	2
Coriander	1
Dill	2 to 3
Fennel	2 to 3
Hyssop	3 to 4
Lavender	2 to 3
Sweet marjoram	2 to 3
Summer savory	1 to 2
Sage	2 to 3
Thyme	2 to 3
Wormwood	2 to 3

Suggested storage times do vary greatly. Temperature and humidity are primary factors, but we can't discount the conservatism of the person making the suggestions. We would prefer to err on the side of caution.

Freezing colostrum

Freezing high quality colostrum is a good management practice for the home dairy, and for shepherds. You never know when the need for colostrum will arise.

For calves, colostrum to be frozen should be taken from an older cow that was dry for at least four weeks, did not leak prior to calving, and was properly cleaned before milking the first colostrum. Similar considerations apply to sheep and goats.

Freeze colostrum in meal-size packages. Ice cube trays are ideal for sheep and goats, and reclosable plastic bags are fine for cows. The cubes can be removed from the ice cube trays and placed in plastic bags.

Thaw frozen colostrum slowly, in a warm water bath, so the antibodies will not be destroyed by excessive heat. Do not use a microwave oven, which will also destroy the antibodies.

The first feeding of colostrum is the most important meal in an animal's life... its first vaccination. That meal can be assured by having a supply of frozen colostrum on hand.

At an auction, hay sold for $197 a ton.

How much is a 50-lb. bale worth?

The "logical" way to figure this is: 2,000 lbs. (one ton) divided by 50 lbs. = 40 bales in a ton. $197 (price of a ton) divided by 40 (the number of 50 lb. bales in a ton) = $4.925 (cost of one bale).

But there's an easier way. Multiply the number of pounds per bale by the price per ton, divide by 2, and point off three places.

50 X $197.00 = 9850. Divide by 2, point off three places, and you get $4.925 a bale.

Do you have enough grain in the bin and hay in the mow?

Here's how to measure your stores:

A bushel of grain occupies 1.25 cubic feet of space. So all you have to do to estimate the amount of grain in a bin is to multiply the length X the width X the leveled height of the pile of grain to get the cubic feet, and divide by 1.25.

If you're not much for goesintas and you don't have a calculator handy, multiply the cubic feet by 0.8.

Of course, if you have a round bin or tank, you'll have to use πr^2 X height to get the cubic feet. And π, as everyone knows, is 3.14159265. We all know that from the mnemonic, "How I need a drink, 'specially on Friday night!"

The process is similar for hay and bedding—but these products are measured in pounds and tons, not bushels. So here we have to know the weight per cubic foot, or the cubic feet per ton.

Material	Wt./cu ft	cu.ft/ton
Hay, loose, in shallow mow	3.6-4.2	475-550
Hay, loose, in deep mow	4-5	400-500
Hay, baled loosely	5.5-6.6	300-360
Hay, baled tightly	6.6-8.3	240-300
Straw, loose	3.5-4.5	450-570
Straw, baled	6-10	200-300
Straw, chopped	5.7-8.0	250-350
Savings, baled	20	100
Mixed ground feed	30-40	50-67

Livestock Weather Hazard Guide

High temperatures and high humidity combined create killer conditions for livestock, especially if they're being transported. This livestock weather guide will alert you as to when to be especially careful while handling animals. To use the guide, first know the temperature and humidity (actual or forecast). Find the temperature in the left column. Follow a straight line to the right until you reach the column below the actual or forecast relative humidity. The number you find there is the temperature-humidity index, which tells you the weather stress category (alert, danger or emergency), and how safe your confined livestock may be.

Alert (75-78): Additional precautions may be needed to avoid losses or to prepare for worse conditions.

Danger (79-83): An index in this range threatens confined livestock. Take precautions to keep animals cool.

Emergency (84+): Means trouble. Don't move animals. Provide shade and plenty of drinking water.

Dry Bulb Temp.	Relative Humidity (%)																			
	5	10	15	20	25	30	35	40	45	50	55	60	65	70	75	80	85	90	95	100
75°F.									70	70	71	71	72	72	73	73	74	74	75	75
76							70	70	70	71	72	72	72	73	74	74	74	75	76	76
77						70	70	71	71	72	72	73	73	74	74	75	75	76	76	77
78					70	70	71	71	72	72	73	74	74	75	75	76	76	77	78	78
79				70	70	71	72	72	73	73	74	74	75	75	76	77	77	78	78	79
80			70	70	71	72	72	73	73	74	74	75	75	76	77	78	79	80	80	81
81		70	70	71	71	72	73	73	74	75	75	76	77	77	78	78	79	80	80	81
82		70	71	71	72	73	73	74	75	75	76	77	77	78	79	79	80	81	81	82
83	70	71	71	72	73	73	74	75	75	76	77	78	78	79	79	80	81	82	82	83
84	70	71	72	72	73	74	75	75	76	77	78	78	79	80	80	81	82	83	83	84
85	71	72	72	73	74	75	75	76	77	78	78	79	80	81	81	82	83	84	84	85
86	71	72	73	74	74	75	76	77	78	78	79	80	81	81	82	83	84	84	85	86
87	72	73	73	74	75	76	77	77	78	79	80	81	81	82	83	84	85	85	86	87
88	72	73	74	75	76	76	77	78	79	80	81	81	82	83	84	84	85	86	87	88
89	73	74	74	75	76	77	78	79	80	80	81	82	83	84	85	86	86	87	88	89
90	73	74	75	76	77	78	79	79	80	81	82	83	84	85	86	87	87	88	89	90
91	74	75	76	76	77	78	79	80	81	82	83	84	85	86	86	87	88	89	90	91
92	74	75	76	77	78	79	80	81	82	83	84	84	85	86	87	88	89	90		
93	75	76	77	78	79	80	80	81	82	83	84	85	86	87	88	89	90			
94	75	76	77	78	79	80	81	82	83	84	85	86	87	88	90					
95	76	77	78	79	80	81	82	83	84	85	86	87	88	89	90					
96	76	77	78	79	80	81	82	84	84	86	87	88	89	90	91					
97	77	78	79	80	81	82	83	84	85	86	87	88	90	91						
98	77	78	79	80	82	83	84	85	86	87	88	89	90							
99	78	79	80	81	82	83	84	86	87	88	88	90								
100	78	79	80	82	83	84	85	86	87	88	90	91								
105	80	82	83	84	86	87	89	90	91											

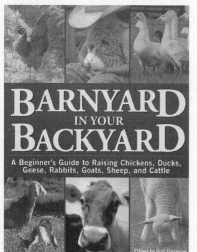

A living from the land:

Fee hunting

KEN SCHARABOK
TENNESSEE

Opening up farms or forest lands for paid hunting access may provide a profitable opportunity to some landowners. In addition, gaining control of poaching, unwanted access, vandalism, negligent damage and damage of an excess deer population to gardens or crops is a primary concern for some landowners.

Paying hunters can deter trespassers. For example, some years back one writer to this magazine complained that just about everyone in their area felt they had the right to hunt on their newly acquired property since all previous owners had allowed it. In this case, leasing the land to a responsible group of hunters may have aided this situation in that it now became the responsibility of the hunters to control who else had access to the land.

Control of the deer population can also be a major concern. For example, the population of whitetail deer in 1942 was estimated to have been 3,000 for the entire State of Tennessee. Today, the population is estimated to be 800,000 and increasing steadily.

What might a hunting lease be worth?

In my area of Tennessee (considered to be among the top deer, turkey, dove and duck hunting areas in the state), per acre hunting fees range from $1 to $10 per year. The difference is determined by opportunities and amenities and whether or not the hunting is for a limited season, such as dove only, or exclusive rights to all game available during all seasons.

Your local Extension Service agent should be able to help you determine a fair price for your particular situation. The agent may also be able to provide a sample hunting lease, liability release and hunting access permit. In addition, if you advertise, the price may be established through the equivalent of competitive bidding.

Some types of leases:

Annual leases are normally the most popular. These leases usually include the right to take all game species during their respective seasons. Annual fees can be assessed on a per-acre basis or a lump sum. Landowners often reserve hunting rights for themselves and their immediate family, and annual leases may also include camping and fishing privileges.

A cooperative landowner-hunter relationship may evolve into a multi-year or long-term lease. It is not necessary, but most annual leases include the option for lease renewal upon expiration. Once a desirable relationship is established, marketing effort and landowner involvement is minimal compared to other arrangements.

Groups or hunting clubs which lease on a multi-year or long-term basis usually perform habitat improvements, put up posted signs, help maintain roads and fences and patrol the leased property to protect against trespassers.

Under a seasonal lease, a landowner specifies the species of game to be taken. For example, by specifying only quail be taken from one group, opportunities for harvesting deer or turkeys may be marketed to another. In this manner, a higher annual income might be realized, but it involves more marketing and landowner management.

Short-term arrangements usually involve daily, weekend or weekly hunts. Short-term leases are most successful near populated areas where the demand for hunting opportunities is strong, but hunters may only be able to go hunting a couple of times a year.

Short-term arrangements are sometimes offered by someone who has leased the hunting rights on an annual basis from the landowner and then acts as a broker, subleasing the hunting rights. Under this situation landowners might receive a higher annual lease fee than otherwise.

The income from hunting rights can be enhanced by offering amenities, such as providing guides, lodging, meals, entertainment, pre-hunt game releases and intensive habitat development. Another possibility, if you offer bird shooting, is to provide an area where the hunters can practice by shooting sporting clays.

For most landowners, the most practical opportunity may be a long-term lease to a responsible hunting club.

For liability purposes, many landowners leasing to a hunting club require it be incorporated, carry liability insurance, such as $500,000, and to also release the landowner from any liability from its use of the land.

Opportunities to market the availability of hunting rights might be classified advertisements in your state's Farm Bureau publication, regional publications, state hunting magazines or the local paper. Also contact your local Extension Service, as they may be receiving calls from hunters looking for opportunities and they can then be referred to you.

Contact your attorney, insurance agent and local Extension Service agent for assistance in the development of hunting lands and leases.

Fencing a creek

Most people resign themselves to replacing flood-ravaged fences. This homesteader is more creative!

Beverly Sandlin
Minnesota

A small meandering brook runs the length of my pasture. It winds its way through a rock-strewn stream bed, between moss covered tree trunks, seldom reaching more than a foot in depth except for an occasional pool created by nature's handiwork.

This creek is one of the main reasons I settled here 13 years ago. On a bright day glints of sunlight play irresistibly across its face. In winter, snow caps the rocks and contrasts its whiteness against the chilly dark channel. The creek is restful and brings me a peace of soul I never found in urban settings. But its beauty belies its potential to wreak havoc with the land and my fences.

My little brook is listed as a dry run on area maps. Years ago, before conservation practices on the farms surrounding me became widespread, the spring that trickles life into my creek would dry up every summer, leaving the skeletal rocks of the stream bed parched and exposed. Yet, it would rage with a furious silt laden torrent when seasonal thunderstorms belched sheets of rain onto the three square mile watershed it drains. The raging flood tore trees from the banks, catapulting them into the waters; rolled enormous boulders from their resting places to spew them like a giant's marbles across the land; and of course, ripped any fencing in its path into a caricature of tangled wire, wood and posts.

Even with good conservation practices, my creek still floods. And when it floods, the fencing I have erected across the creek to keep my horses secure in their pasture is defenseless to its brown, foam tipped, tearing fingers. When the waters subside there is the inevitable chore of checking fences to secure the livestock. I have found pieces of my fence as far as a quarter of a mile down the stream bed.

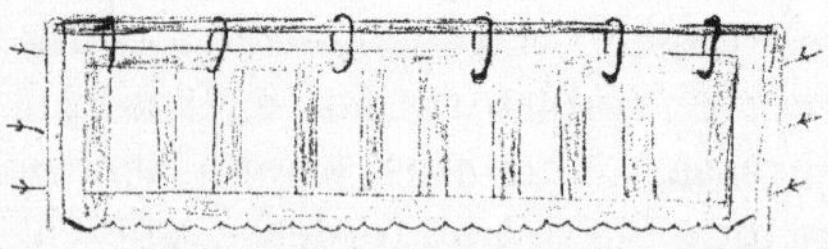

I no longer attempt to span the stream bed with high priced, long fence boards. Barbed wire invariably tangles and breaks from its posts to lie in either heavy sodden strands of braided weeds and branches or a murderous entwined coil waiting to ensnare man or beast. Cable held secure to the posts but, when caught by the plummeting roots of a flood impelled tree, yanked half my fenceline down. If I raised the fence to allow the water to pass under it, invariably a pony or donkey would slip under it. It was a frustrating six-year-long war.

Creek fencing became an obsession. I talked about it with whoever would listen. The old timers would invariably nod their heads in appreciation of the dire situation and give a candid comment like, "Yup, cricks are nice, but ya gotta pay the toll," or "Pears like a Jeckle and Hyde sit-e-ation, what ya plan on doin' 'bout it?" I'd just shake my head. If I knew, why would I be asking? I talked with store clerks who sold fencing, but most had never put any up, and weren't of much help. I talked to the extension agent. He wasn't any help at all. I checked out books from the library on fencing, but not one covered flooding creeks. I drove around the countryside assessing other farmer's creek fencing. It appeared that everyone who had a creek simply resigned themselves to fixing fence after a flood.

Later that year the kids and I went on the Minnesota Donkey and Mule Association's annual trail ride. It was held at Jim and Carolyn Burnap's 1200 acre ranch/farm. On the trail ride I spied what appeared to be a long narrow wooden gate suspended across the river that bisected their cattle pasture. Ah ha! A flap-type flood fence that floated when the river came up and hung imposingly when the river was at its normal level. They apparently didn't have trouble with trees sweeping down the river at flood stage or the flood gate would have been torn from its supports long ago. But it did give me an idea.

I was close enough to current to utilize electric fence. One horizontal line was run fairly high to be out of the reach of passing tree roots and branches. Vertical strands were attached at one foot intervals to the single horizontal line and hung to nearly water level. Flood water would simply lift and short out the electric wires tripping the circuit breaker. Trees, branches, etc., could flow right through the vertical strands without catching or breaking the wire. After the flood, just trip the circuit breaker to kick in the electric again. And when the creek was down, any beastie that decided this veil of wire strands looked like an easy way out need only step into the water, brush against the innocent hanging wires and receive a nasty jolt to discourage wandering.

I don't believe I have won the war. But for the past seven years, I have won every battle the creek has yet mounted against my fence.

Lyme disease: Is there a cure?

Not according to conventional medicine, but...

Anonymous, R.N.
Virginia

Several years ago a Countryside reader wrote about her four-year, unsuccessful battle with Lyme disease. She exhausted her finances and was left to battle the crushing effects of this devastating disease.

For several decades, as a registered nurse, I have studied and researched nontoxic therapies that heal without causing further damage to an already damaged body. Having cancer myself, I was forced to find alternative answers to a death-dealing problem. I had seen too much of the other side of the coin.

Lyme disease is relatively new, being isolated in the 1970s. It is now known to exist in at least 19 countries and 24 states in America. In 1984, 1,498 cases were reported. Since doctors are not required to report this disease, and very often it's not diagnosed correctly, this figure is undoubtedly low.

In 1970 Polly Murray and her family, in Lyme, Connecticut began suffering from an unexplained illness. She had been hospitalized for skin problems (rashes), fever and "arthritis" problems in her neck, jaw and various joints. For a time one of her sons became paralyzed in his facial muscles and developed joint swelling. The doctor told her he had juvenile rheumatoid arthritis.

But this did not satisfy her. She began studying technical literature. She discovered that juvenile rheumatoid arthritis was both rare and noninfectious, yet her whole family and more than 30 of her neighbors were coming down with these same symptoms. She repeatedly reported her findings to the state medical authorities, requesting an investigation. Others also began reporting similar findings. But the health experts were not interested.

Eventually, Dr. Allen Steere, a Yale medical school teacher, began interviewing affected people in Lyme. Many of them told him they first got a reddish, "bull's eye" type of skin rash before feeling ill. (Some did not.) Dr. Steere connected the disease to the deer tick. The disease, Steere found, had been described in Europe as early as 1909.

By then other researchers were working on the problem. They found that dogs as well as humans can contract this syndrome, and that migrating birds are carrying it into southern states such as Georgia and Texas. Dr. Andrew Spielman, Harvard medical entomologist, identified and named the tick species—*Borrelia Burgdorfor.*

The adult female deer tick is about half the size of the ticks commonly found on dogs. She has a rounded black spot over nearly all of her upper back. The lower back and sides are reddish or reddish brown and they have a fringe of scarlet around their hind parts. The adult male deer ticks are all black and smaller. The immature ticks and larvae are very small and are the primary transmitters of the disease.

One problem in correctly diagnosing this infection is that in perhaps 25 percent of the Lyme disease cases, the skin rash fails to appear. Thus, these victims might not then, or ever, realize why they are having these physical problems.

First-stage symptoms include the reddish skin rash, headaches, fever, chills, drowsiness, aches and a flu-like or meningitis-like condition. Second-stage effects are meningitis, paralysis or cardiac irregularities. Third-stage effects usually include arthritis, and occasionally chronic skin disease or neurological disorders. Constant fatigue and lethargy make it impossible for some people to continue their livelihood, and life itself becomes a constant struggle.

Currently, orthodox medicine uses mostly antibiotics to "treat" the disease—but says there is no cure. Antibiotics are creating serious problems today in many patients' immune systems. There is, however, a cure that is effective in about five days. This may seem incredible, but it has been proved.

In Lyme disease the patients' blood Sed-rate rises steadily—which means the cartilage (the body cement) is being dissolved and the body is battling a cartilage disease. One of the best solutions—if not the only real one—is vitamin C given intravenously.

The amount is (and please don't be shocked, because it will not harm, but heal) is 25 grams (25,000 mg) per day for five consecutive days. Then you are well.

The vitamin C kills the organisms that are causing the cartilage destruction. This is the same treatment that healed Norman Cousin of the cartilage disease that was attacking his body. (Read his account of this in his book *Anatomy Of An Illness*).

A few years back, a friend's mother contacted me about her losing battle with Lyme disease. For four years she was given antibiotics without effective results. She finally became bedridden. I suggested the above treatment and she began searching for a doctor who would give her vitamin C IV. Some doctors who give chelation therapy will also give vitamin C IV, but not all, because the FDA doesn't consider it "orthodox treatment" (although they have no cure!).

My friend's mother found a doctor who agreed to give her this treatment. In five days she had no further signs or symptoms of Lyme disease. Today she remains well and says she is enjoying life again and feels great!

Alternative medicine:

There are many home remedies for warts

Liquid nitrogen worked for them

In response to the request in COUNTRYSIDE for a home remedy for warts, I am sending one that worked for us.

It is rather interesting to note, however, that it is also used professionally by doctors.

There is a short story attached to it. Before my retirement, I used to deliver semen and liquid nitrogen to farmers so that they could breed their own cows through artificial insemination. Since we already had liquid nitrogen, a doctor who wanted to use it in his practice requested that we sell him a liquid nitrogen storage tank and refill it regularly.

He used the liquid nitrogen to remove warts, charging $15 per wart. He used something like a long Q-tip to reach the liquid nitrogen in the tank which would then be transferred to the wart, freezing it.

To treat our own warts, we simply taped a Q-tip to a measuring stick with masking tape and held it in the liquid nitrogen 'til the liquid stopped fast boiling. Then we took it out and applied it to the wart until the wart and a small area around it turned white. In a few days the frostbitten area would peel away, and no more wart.

Did it sting? Yes, but not too much. If a large wart were treated, one might take aspirin to ease it, but it really wasn't necessary.

The doctor was quite pleased with his results and once told me of using liquid nitrogen to treat cancer. He showed me a before and after picture of a woman who had cancer in her nose. He said that surgeons had recommended cutting off the nose, but he had treated with liquid nitrogen and destroyed the cancer, leaving the nose in a normal condition. He said the freezing only destroyed the abnormal tissue.

If anyone needs reassurance about using this, let me tell you what he told me. Another doctor asked him about using the same treatment, so I got to sell the other doctor a tank and fill that one too. Shortly thereafter, the first doctor told me that the other one called him up and said, "What should I do? The wart didn't come off." He told him to do it again.

In fact, that is what we did. If we didn't freeze enough area to get rid of the entire wart, we simply did it over.

So, if you know a farmer who has a liquid nitrogen tank, ask him if you can use it to treat the warts. (It only takes a little to do the job.) If the farmer knows about this use, he may even give some gratuitous advice. If he doesn't, he might be very interested. – *John Bender, New York*

Or – try Bactine

In regard to the boy with warts. Try Bactine. It's a mild antiseptic which worked for me and my boys. Doctors laughed when I told them about it. I dabbed it on with a cotton ball whenever I thought about it. I hope it works for you too – it couldn't hurt anyway. – *Virginia M. Dahlke, Minnesota*

Some old-time remedies for wart removal

***The People's Home Medical Book*, written in 1910, lists these home remedies for warts:**

- **Milkweed: Bruise milkweeds and apply the milk that runs from them to the warts several times a day and they will soon come off.**
- **Arbor Vitae: Rub the warts frequently with the gum from the arbor vitae tree.**
- **Ashes and vinegar: Burn some common willow bark, mix the ashes with strong vinegar, and apply frequently.**
- **Baking soda: Dissolve enough common baking soda in water to make it thick, rub it on the wart as often as you please and it will soon disappear.**
- **Iodine: The application of iodine will remove warts.**

Use masking tape

When I saw the request from John Fraley for a wart cure I was going to respond to him, personally. But then I decided everyone ought to know this cure, because I know it works!

Use masking tape! My grandfather passed this one along many years ago when I was young. I double or triple the tape now because today's tape is much thinner than it was years ago.

Cut a piece a bit larger than the wart, stick it on and leave it there a couple weeks. Don't worry, the good brands will stay stuck. I use a bandaid to camouflage the looks when I "go out."

Check the wart in a couple of weeks. If it's not gone, use new masking tape for a couple weeks more – try not to leave it uncovered too long. I think the lack of air is part of the cure.

I've never had a wart that stayed longer except a plantar wart on the ball of my foot – ouch! After using the tape two months, I gave up. Then a month later I noticed the wart was gone! Who knows, maybe it's coincidence, or maybe my body's learned to fight the warts off, but I've kept my hands and feet wart free for many years now with this method.

By the way, this same grandfather, who was born in Belfast pre-1900, worked as a carpenter all his life. He also played soccer. When he got a cut, he used the lining from the inside of a fresh egg-shell to cover it up. Has anyone else heard of this? – *Wartless, but still too embarrassed to talk about it!*

Just before going to press we received a fax from John Fraley, who reported that his request for help resulted in 57 responses... and the warts were gone in six days.

Home health:

To ward off colds and flu

Daniel E David
California

Many a coughing and sneezing folk seem to have a "good" home brew remedy for cold and flu. Well, I don't claim to have a cure, but I do indeed have an amazing elixir that wards off a cold if it's taken at the cold's onset… in other words, when symptoms of sore throat are first felt prior to a cold/flu. This is an old family recipe that originated in Spain. My dad called it vino ron (wine/rum) and he never missed a day of work in his life for sickness. I call it poppy-seed rum wine. It ought to be patented! Try it and you'll see why.

Here's how it's made.

Take a bottle about the size of a standard soda bottle. Fill it three quarters of the way with standard poppy seeds that can usually be bought in bulk. Fill near to the top with the strongest rum attainable, leaving room for the juice from two or three lemons. Shake the contents once or twice daily for about two weeks.

After two weeks, strain out the seeds in a coffee filter and discard them. Then add a dark pinot noir or burgundy wine. Use equal proportions of treated rum to wine.

The mix is kept in a dark, cool place, and is supposed to age a few months before using. But I have used it fresh and found that it had almost the same remarkable effects to ward off flu and cold. I don't know why this super elixir isn't sold. I'm certain that it would probably put quite a few folks out of business.

I must caution, however, that it tastes like the dickens. I use some treated with honey for children. And all that's required when one first begins to feel a sore throat coming on after being around folks with full-blown colds or flu, is about three measured tablespoons.

Here's to your health!

How to make cough drops

Evelyn R. DeWitt
Texas

While commercial cough drops are readily available, it is much more fun and probably just as effective for some people to make their own. The cost is less, and I believe the quality is higher.

Honey/Horehound/Mint Drops

1 quart water
1/2 cup fresh or dried mint
1/4 cup fresh or dried horehound
1/4 cup chamomile (optional)
1/4 cup rose hips (optional—or powdered vitamin C can be used)

Add any other herbs you want. Steep above ingredients at least 20 minutes. Strain. To strained liquid add:

2 cups granulated sugar
1/2 cup honey
1 teaspoon cream of tartar
1/4 cup lemon juice (optional)

Stir all ingredients together and bring to a boil. Cook over medium high heat to hard crack stage (300°F). Do not stir while cooking.

Take extra caution not to burn or scorch the mixture during the last few minutes of cooking. Watch carefully when it approaches crack stage.

Pour into shallow buttered pan. When the mixture begins to "set up," score it with a knife into small squares. After it is set, break into squares.

This mixture can also be poured and pulled like taffy and cut into pieces.

This is a basic herbal drop recipe. Herbal ingredients may be added or substituted according to individual preferences.

A note on horehound: This exceptionally bitter herb is truly incredible at relieving sore throats. When mixed with a sweetener it is indeed more palatable, but it still has a unique flavor which some people find objectionable. If you find the flavor too strong for your liking, cut down on the amount of horehound. Indeed, it does not have to be used at all, but its pain-killing and decongestant properties to me far outweigh any negatives the herb may have. Anyway, I like the flavor!

Finding horehound can be an adventure unto itself. It is usually found in spring, early summer and fall around horse stables, wells, and the base of trees. It is easily distinguishable as it looks like thick-leaved mint but it has a powdery-looking coating which gives it a distinctive "dusty" look. Underneath each "set" of leaves is a cluster of small flowers in a ball shape. When the leaves are crushed there is a medicinal odor.

Bees love horehound flowers, so be cautious.

Usually when you find horehound you will find a lot of it, as it seems to like to grow in clusters. You may want to take a little extra to dry for later use, or dig some to transplant to a more convenient location.

Horehound also makes a lovely dried wreath, and someone told me it is a natural mosquito repellant.

Reprinted from Volume 79/3.

Cough medicine

1 cup boiled honey
4 tablespoons peppermint oil
1/2 teaspoon eucalyptus oil
1/3 teaspoon clove oil
1 tablespoon licorice powder
Add or not a bit of cayenne.

For colds
2 parts thyme
2 parts sage
2 parts fenugreek
1 part cayenne
Mix and put in capsules. Take one with each meal. – *Madonna Wilson*

Old-fashioned cough syrup does the job

When I was a child my mother made a cough syrup that seemed to do the job every time. It was made by thinly slicing a peeled onion, then layering each slice with sugar. Tightly cover. After a few hours in a warm place the sugar will be dissolved into a thick syrup. One teaspoon of this worked as well as the store-bought medicine.

Reprinted from Volume 71/6.

Ear infections and pacifiers

Researchers at the University of Oulu in Finland have concluded up to 25 percent of ear infections in children under three years of age are the results of use of a pacifier. When children suck on a pacifier they produce increased amounts of saliva, which can be a cozy home for viruses which cause middle-ear infections.

How to relieve a headache without medication

Jim Hunter
Arkansas

During a recent conference on preventative medicine for laymen we were given a list of things to try to help relieve a headache without resorting to pain medicine. Homesteaders might find them of value, as our family did.

1. Soak in a warm bath with shoulders and neck submerged.

2. Stand under a warm shower and direct the water over the shoulders and neck.

3. Think warm. Sit in a comfortable position and close your eyes. Imagine yourself someplace warm. Let your hands and arms grow warmer and warmer until they are too hot to touch. This will redirect the blood flow from the head to your hands.

4. Along the same lines, place your hands in hot water (safe to the touch, not boiling) for the count of 30 to redirect the blood flow from the head to your hands.

5. For sinus headaches try accupressure. The effective point is in the center of the eyebrows. Run your finger along your eyebrow. When you notice the tip in the surface feels like two bones joining under the skin you have found the point. Your supraorbital nerve is closest to the surface in your head here.

Use the knuckles of your thumb to press on this point, as well as the point in the middle of your eyebrow, right over the pupil. Press until you feel pain. If you don't feel pain, you probably are pressing in the wrong place. Press both sides at the same time for best results and hold for 15-30 seconds.

6. Relax all of your muscles group by group. Take a comfortable position with your hands in your lap or lie down with your feet against somethig heavy. Close your eyes.

Begin with your fingers and tense each set of muscles for a count of 10. Then let them go limp. Move to your hands, wrists, forearms, upper arms, shoulders, and neck.

Lastly make a frown with your forehead. Tighten these muscles. Hold for a count of 10. Then relax those muscles. You might also want to tense and relax your facial muscles, your eyes, your cheeks, and your lips.

Make beauty products at home

You can make many of your own salon-quality beauty products at home. For example, to treat dandruff crush up 30 aspirins, put them in your regular shampoo and shake the mixture well. Apply, wait a couple of minutes and then rinse. As a color enhancer for blond or light-brown hair brew a cup of chamomile tea, let it cool, comb into your hair and leave it for 20-30 minutes before rinsing. For dark-colored hair, use cold strong coffee instead. Spray on stale beer as a setting gel. For additional information, see if your local library has or can borrow a copy of *The World's Best Kept Beauty Secrets* by Diane Irons.

Home health:

Aromatherapy: A home remedy whose time has come… again

NANCY EISCHEN
MINNESOTA

"I'm not going to the doctor unless I'm dying!" Haven't we heard that before? This has to be how many home remedies came about. But how about the natural cure that's been around for centuries? Essential Oils.

Remember in the Bible where Moses used hyssop oil for protection? How about the thieves who robbed from the dead? What did they use so as not to get sick themselves? How about the plagues? How did they fight off the disease? Essential oils.

Today this is called aromatherapy, and it's not just breathing in essential oils to overcome mood swings. When applied to the body, essential oils enter the bloodstream quicker than if taken by mouth. If applied to the feet, essential oils affect every cell of the body within 20 minutes.

But how can this help my backache after being in the garden? By knowing which oils to rub on the aches. The health benefits of essential oils have filled volumes. Research has proved that essential oils reach the body's cells when synthetic drugs cannot. This may be the reason that so many antibiotics don't work for people. Folks have developed a resistance to the synthetic drug. But essential oils pass through the body's cells, bringing the much-needed oxygen to them. This is how disease starts, lack of oxygen in the body and breakdown of the body's cells.

It is beyond my scope to say just how essential oils do their thing. I just know they help relieve my headaches and backaches, heal cuts and bruises, and just overall help me cope. There is even a blend I mix up in the summer to keep our state bird, the mosquito, at bay. I find it much more pleasant than the store-bought sprays.

Essential oils can also be used around the house to disinfect, deter unwanted pests, purify water and air, chase mold and fungus, and freshen musty odors. Moths, mosquitoes and mice don't like lavender. So a few drops of lavender oil on your skin before going to the garden can prevent you from being eaten alive. If you should cut your finger while in the garden, keep that lavender handy. A drop or two will keep the cut from being infected and promote quick healing. Don't forget to wash the cut, too. It may heal too fast and leave dirt behind!

Not sure about the water on your new homestead? Take lemon oil with you. A drop to a pitcher full will purify it. A friend of mine relayed this story to me. She was in Mexico on vacation and we're all told "Never drink the water!" She did drink the water, but added fresh squeezed lemons to every glass. She never got the nausea like her companions did! Lemon oil is also a very good air purifier. Try removing oil and grease spots with lemon oil too.

We've all experienced the effect of peppermint on an upset tummy. But did you know peppermint oil also can reduce fevers? Peppermint is an excellent way to cool the body even on hot summer days.

Don't forget the rosemary – the herb of remembrance. I keep reading more and more about the research being done with rosemary and Alzheimer's. A drop or two of rosemary put in a pan of warm water on the back of the stove can oxygenate the brain cells to overcome mental fatigue. What do you suppose it could do for just remembering the new neighbor's name?

It's hard to list all the benefits of essential oils. I find it just amazing that they've been around for centuries, yet we keep learning new things about them.

Using essential oils

Cuts & bruises: Put a drop or two of lavender or tea tree on the cut.

Headaches: Use a drop or two of lavender on the temples or the back of the neck.

Hay fever: Chamomile, eucalyptus, lavender and rose can be used alone or in a blend. Diffuse or rub a drop on the nose.

Insect bites: Apply lavender or use 3 drops of thyme in 1 teaspoon cider vinegar and apply to bite.

Constipation: Try fennel, ginger, orange, rosemary or tarragon. Mix one of these oils with a vegetable oil and massage over lower abdomen three times a day.

Corns: Chamomile, lemon or peppermint. Put a drop right on the corn.

Sunburn: Spray or rub with chamomile and lavender. To prevent blistering, apply 2-3 drops of lavender.

Toothache: Apply chamomile or clove oil on location and along the jawbone.

Foot odor: Mix 1 tablespoon baking powder with 2 drops of sage. Put in a plastic bag. Shake and eliminate lumps with a rolling pin. Put in shoes.

Insomnia: Chamomile, clary sage, lavender or geranium. Use in diffuser, or hot water bowl before bed. Even better, take a warm bath with a drop or two of oil.

Itching: Lavender or peppermint. Apply on location.

Lice: Eucalyptus, geranium, lavender, lemon or rosemary. Apply oil(s) to bottom of feet and also rub over scalp three times a day.

Muscle aches & pain: Birch, ginger, nutmeg and rosemary. Mix any oil with a vegetable oil and rub in.

Insect repellent spray: Combine 5 drops lavender, 5 drops lemongrass, 3 drops peppermint and 1 drop thyme and put on feet or add to a cup of water and spray on.

Cautionary note: Be careful when applying spice oils (cinnamon, clove, ginger) to the skin. They may irritate the skin. Dilute with olive or vegetable oil.

Living with nature:

Poison ivy:

Why it's a pain, and what to do about it

Some people are so sensitive to poison ivy that the slightest contact causes blisters and swelling, while others can pull it up barehanded with little or no adverse effect.

The different reactions arise from varying degrees of allergy to an irritating oil found in poison ivy's leaves, vines and roots.

The oil is urushiol, and you don't even have to touch the plant to come in contact with it. If you can't imagine where or how you developed a poison ivy reaction, it's possible that your dog ran through a patch, and the oil was transferred to you when you touched the animal's fur.

When poison ivy burns, there is urushiol in the smoke.

Identification

All poison ivy leaves are composed of three leaflets. Some of the plants have clusters of whitish-green drupes, a berry-like fruit that serves as a winter food source for birds. Later in the growing season the leaves turn red.

Poison ivy is a perennial. If you just cut or pull it it will grow back. If you keep cutting it with a mower or weedeater the roots will eventually starve and die.

Spraying with 2,4-D will control poison ivy in grassy areas, and selective spraying with a two percent solution of Roundup or other product containing glyphosate will usually kill the plant with two or three applications, but even some nonorganic weed experts admit that chemical control is a risky proposition, especially around the home.

The best solution is digging the roots out with a shovel, wearing gloves. Throw away the gloves when you're done: gloves that have touched poison ivy can cause reactions even a year later.

Scrub up with an alkaline soap. Lye soap or Fels Naptha are recommended. Do not use soap that contains cold cream or oil, because it will just spread the urushiol around.

Clean tools with a solvent that will break down the oil, such as Pine Sol or Simple Green. Ammonia, paint thinner or acetone will work.

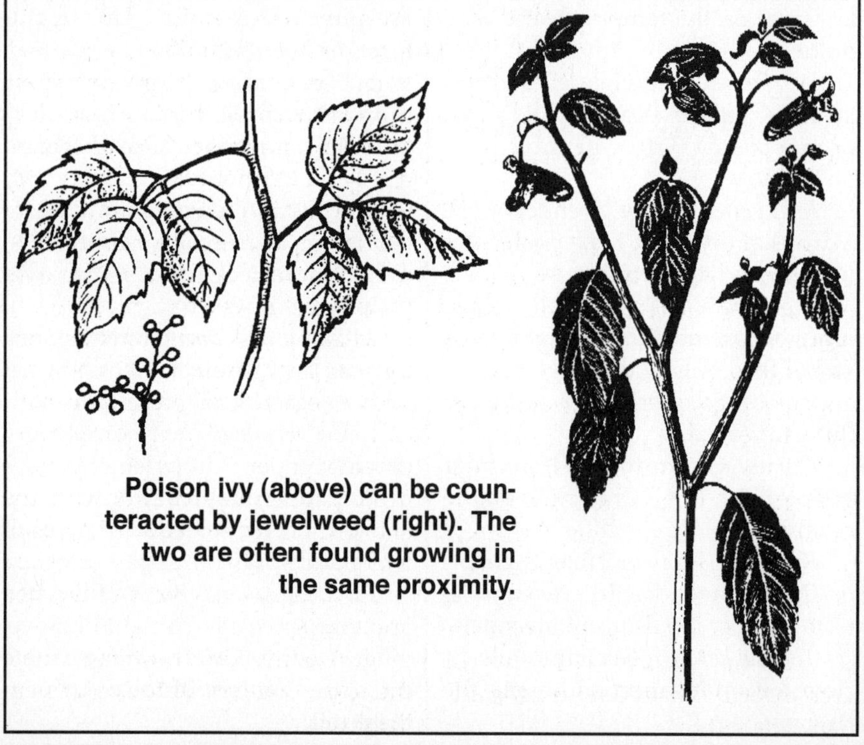

Poison ivy (above) can be counteracted by jewelweed (right). The two are often found growing in the same proximity.

A natural remedy

If you come into contact with poison ivy and have a reaction, a number of commercial products can provide relief. However, you just might find one of nature's own remedies growing in the same area as the poison ivy: jewelweed.

This member of the impatiens family is a tender, succulent annual often found in extensive patches in damp woods. It can be found from Nova Scotia to Florida and southern Alaska to Oregon. Its a tall plant, sometimes reaching four feet under favorable conditions. Leaves vary from tiny to about 3" long, egg-shaped with a point on the outer end, and widespread serrations.

Jewelweed supposedly got its name from the way rain and dew stand on the leaves in sparkling round gem-like drops. It is also known as touch-me-not (which might also be applied to poison ivy!). This is because the 3/4" seed pods that develop from the yellow flowers suddenly split when touched. The two sides curl back into tight spirals with an audible snap, scattering the seeds over a wide area. This explains the dense concentrations.

Jewelweed is a tender plant with many branches that contain a light orange juice. Rubbing freshly crushed jewelweed over skin exposed to urushiol will prevent, and perhaps even heal, poison ivy rash.

Native peoples are said to have also used jewelweed to treat itchy scalps, athlete's foot, and other kinds of dermatitis.

Irradiation and mad cow disease: What! Me worry?

Or... you might want to raise your own

Ken Scharabok
Tennessee

This article is sure to raise a few hackles, so we might point out that the author's views aren't necessarily the views of COUNTRYSIDE magazine.

But then, I get so weary of people who worry themselves to death about what they eat. Fat? Cholesterol? Salt? Gimme a break already!

There's another aspect that puts irradiation, in particular, into perspective. Just a few years ago our mail was running strongly against microwave ovens. Haven't heard a word about that, lately. (I was dead set against them too, but not because of any real or imagined health hazards: I just like to cook! And yes, we do have a microwave now too.)

Speaking of that reminds me: It took some major advertising campaigns to convince housewives that buying foods in tinned cans wouldn't poison their families, when that method was new.

There are, of course, other concerns connected with the use of hazard materials. But look at the brighter side. If any of the bigger problems discussed in this issue set us back a few years, a lot of technology-based concerns will simply disappear!—Jd

Your favorite uncle is coming over for dinner and you know he really likes his steaks rare. You take out a steak which has been in your refrigerator (not the freezer) for about a month, unwrap it, slap it on the grill until it just says ouch on both sides and then serve it "hot and bloody" as some say. Through all this you have no fears of that nasty old E.coli being an uninvited dinner guest.

Impossible? Not if the steak had been irradiated before being put into a sterile, air-tight container.

Irradiation is the process under which food stocks are passed through equipment in which they are subjected to a powerful electronic beam from a radioactive source, such as cobalt 60. The process has been under development since 1908 with much of the research being lead by the U.S. Army. However, even with proven research, its introduction as a common procedure in the U.S. has been delayed, primarily by Congress labeling irradiation as a food additive, rather than a process, such as canning.

Food stocks subjected to irradiation do not become irradiated any more than your luggage does when it goes through an airport scanner. What it does do is either render sterile or kill over 99.9999 percent of harmful organisms in the food stocks and will even protect such bulk items as grains through preventing insect damage during storage.

The extremely small change in taste and texture for most food stocks caused by the irradiation process cannot even be noticed. While there is evidence irradiation can decrease the amount of vitamins in food stocks, the decrease is not drastic and can be replaced by other sources. Irradiation also damages some food enzymes, but ordinary marinating and cooking methods do this as well.

Some of the advantages to be offered by irradiation include:

1. An estimated one-third of the food grown in the U.S. is wasted as a result of spoilage. Thus, the foods being produced will feed more people.

2. Irradiation opens markets for U.S. perishable food stocks to be sold to countries with little or no refrigeration capability.

3. The average amount of energy required for processing and preserving food stocks using irradiation is less than one-fourth that required for freezing and less than one-fifth that required for canning.

4. While such organisms as salmonella, E. coli and botulism can be killed by thorough cooking, the risk of contamination of other food stocks during the preparation remains, such as using a cutting board on which you have cut up a chicken contaminated with salmonella to also cut up vegetables for a salad. It is estimated in 1997 there were 10,000 deaths in the U.S. from tainted food and 130,000 cases of illnesses caused by contaminated ground beef alone. If you have had "stomach flu", chances are fairly good it was actually a dose of food poisoning.

5. Irradiation delays ripening of many fruits and vegetables, meaning longer bulk storage, shipping and shelf life times. Irradiated meats also have a longer shelf life.

6. Reduced exposure to toxic and carcinogenic substances such as methylenebromide, ethylenedibromide and ethyleneoxide commonly used to disinfect fruits, vegetables and spices and nitrites employed in curing meats. The latter reacts with protein when cooked, resulting in nitrosamine, a known carcinogenic. By using irradiation the need for such substances would be drastically reduced, if not completely eliminated.

7. Irradiation greatly lowers the amount of energy required to cook foods since higher temperatures are not required solely to kill harmful organisms.

8. A combination of the above can lower the cost of food stocks to the public.

There have even been some unexpected side benefits. European winemakers have discovered irradiated grapes yield more juice than untreated ones. Irradiated wheat produces a larger loaf volume. Irradiated barley gives a seven percent higher yield during malting. Some dried beans cook in less time. Prunes dry quicker and some meat becomes more tender.

On the downside, such foods as cucumbers, peaches, leaf vegetables and milk products either become soft or develop an off-flavor when subjected to irradiation. Thus, irradiation is not a magic bullet which can be used on all food stocks.

Irradiation has been approved for many spices, fruits and produce for over 10 years and was approved for some poultry and pork uses since the early 1990s. Late 1997 saw the approval extended to red meats. (Note: It's still illegal to sell irradiated beef, pending USDA guidelines on packaging and dosages, expected later this year.)

At this point the primary elements holding back more widespread application of irradiation are the investment required for the equipment and packaging changes and a perceived lack of acceptance by the general public. However, it should be noted it took almost 100 years for canning to be fully accepted, and other methods such as freezing, freeze-drying and microwave cooking also met initial consumer resistance.

Irradiation supporters include such groups as the World Health Organization, the American Medical Association, the American Meat Institute and many scientists. Those opposed to its further development and use include nutrition and consumer groups who fear trading a problem with harmful organisms today for irradiation may produce potentially greater problems in the future.

The debate over irradiation seems to follow that over such developments as the polio vaccine. Nothing is perfect and the risk certainly seems to be acceptable.

Mad Cow Disease:

While the press loved the cute name of mad cow disease, this disorder is more properly known as bovine spongiform encephalopathy (BSE).

It appears most species have their own form of spongiform encephalopathy.

Human spongiform encephalophy (HSE) occurs naturally in about one-in-one-million people world wide each year with it almost exclusively being seen in older adults. In the U.S. some 200 new cases are diagnosed each year and in England, the hotbed of BSE, some 50 new cases a year can be expected.

BSE first came to the attention of scientists in the 1980s when cattle, particularly dairy cows, started to develop tremors, aggressiveness and decreasing coordination until they died. Autopsies revealed their brains resembled sponges with air pockets. It was eventually traced to sheep carcasses which contained the sheep disease of scrapies having been processed into cattle feed. Somehow a disease which hadn't been known to be transferrable between species did so. Over 170,000 cattle in Europe, predominately in England, are believed to have contracted BSE.

In 1986 English officials were surprised when several young adults come down with what was originally thought to be HSE. However, further testing revealed the link to BSE through the consumption of beef products contaminated with either BSE infested cattle brain or spinal tissue. In all, some 20 cases of BSE in humans have been detected.

Further research on BSE has turned up some scary aspects.

- The transmission agent does not appear to be either a bacteria or virus, but rather a protein. It was previously thought only an organism which contained nucleic acid could reproduce. Current research thinking is a deformed molecule of protein attaches itself to a healthy protein molecule and deforms it. The original molecule then detaches and it and the newly deformed molecule go in search of other normal molecules.
- The transmission agent is extremely resistant to common sterilization methods, such as bleach, alcohol, boiling or exposure to other chemical agents. Researchers have reduced BSE infected tissue to ashes and the transmission agent could still be detected. Even irradiation has not proven to be an effective preventive method.
- Tests with cows revealed as little as one-quarter teaspoon of the transmission agent given as feed causes BSE.
- BSE was even transmitted to cats through processed pet food.
- The gestation period can be a number of years.

On the bright side, the decreased number of cases indicates BSE in humans has largely run its course in England and there is evidence only those with a particular susceptibility through their DNA makeup are at high risk.

Imports of beef to the U.S. from England were banned in 1989 and all known cattle which were imported since the outbreak of BSE have been tested with negative results. Almost all of these animals were purchased by the USDA and destroyed. There has yet to be a single case of BSE detected in the U.S. associated with eating beef or the use of any cattle byproduct.

There is a long list of both wild and domesticated animals which are known to develop variants of spongiform encephalophy. In Kentucky, at least 11 cases of a spongiform encephalopathy in humans have been associated with the practice of eating fried squirrel brains, a delicacy in some areas.

While the risk of anyone developing BSE in the U.S. appears to be extremely, extremely remote it still makes sense to not eat either the brain or spinal tissue of any animal. (The BSE transmitting agent has not been detected in muscle, fat, organs, milk, etc. – only in the brain and spinal tissue of infected animals.)

The health concerns associated with both irradiation and mad cow disease in the U.S. seem to be overrated. What say you?

Homestead health:

Upgrading the standard first aid kit

ABBY STOUT
CALIFORNIA

When preparing for an emergency, every aspect of one's day needs to be assessed.

You need to consider unforeseen difficulties. Supplies that are supposed to cover certain areas are often not up to par. Let's consider one small, but important piece of the puzzle: the emergency medical kit.

Since our property is very remote and we have a small child, I bought the best kit I could get at Wal-Mart before we ever began working on our homestead. I found it to be sorely lacking the first time we had an injury.

I wouldn't recommend purchasing such a kit, as they are basically for city or car use. The standard kits are filled with Band-Aids, horrible child-safe scissors, a few small packages of antibiotic ointment, a little tape and gauze and one-time use hot and cold pads. All of this stuff is good, but it's obviously missing a lot.

Here is what I would add to the kit:

Visene/eye drops for treatment of eye trauma or cleansing. Buy lots more Band-Aids, gauze, at least two tubes of antibiotic ointment, and (most importantly) sports tape. It can be used to adhere gauze or to tape sprains. They are good for preventative care and protection of old injuries. Look at a football game—everyone is held together with this stuff. Johnson & Johnson makes several sizes (two-inch is a good multi-purpose choice), and some store brands are available. Get at least three rolls.

Extra hot and cold pads and Ace bandages are a good idea. Get good stainless steel scissors and have them sharpened before putting them into the kit. The Gingher brand is outstanding.

If you panic under pressure, add a well-rounded medical book. Children's medical books are sometimes best, as they explain things.

Finally add some sealed bottled water, Pedialite and some oral antibiotics. Your doctor will usually give an extra prescription if you ask, or these items can be bought over-the-counter in Mexico and carried back legally to the U.S.

Extras: If you use herbs, add those to a first-aid kit. If you take prescription drugs, get extras and put them in the kit so you know where they are. Depending on your preparedness level, I'd also put in an extra bottle of multi-vitamins and vitamin C.

Don't get hurt if you can avoid it. More importantly, don't be foolish and unprepared!

Tough, willing, and able

Tough, Willing, and Able, *by Lois Flansburg Haaglund; 160 pp, 45 B/W photos, paper, $12; Mountain Press Publishing Co., 1301 S. Third Street W, Missoula, MT 59806; 1-800-234-5308, web: www.mountain-press.com.*

This is a story about a family. But it's neither an ordinary story, nor an ordinary family.

It begins in 1925 with Jim Flansburg's (the author's father) accident in a logging job and follows him and his kin through the Depression and beyond, as well as going back to his own father's adventures. There are some good stories here, and many modern homesteaders will identify with life in Montana during that period.

For example, when Jim married Eunice in 1928, they lived upstairs in the auto repair garage he bought when he thought his logging career had ended. Originally it had been a livery stable. There were cracks in the floor and gaps in the walls... except for the back wall, which was only a tarp. (Jim thought that was convenient because he could easily toss firewood into the house.) It was the best place he had ever lived, and it was his: he couldn't understand why his new bride wasn't as happy with it as he was.

"On October 3rd of 1929 there was the usual traffic on the highway. The next day October 4th, the stock market crashed. By the 5th no one was travelling—that is, no one but the rumrunners, for they were the only ones with any money." And then the highway was moved, so even the rumrunners didn't stop to buy gas.

That's when they moved to nine acres, built a log home, got horses and two cows, a root cellar and an icehouse. Whatever money came their way went for things like garden seeds.

This book will provide some entertaining light summer reading.

Question of the month:

What does it take to be a homesteader?

We asked what drives you toward your homestead goals, and what characteristics are most helpful. Here are some of your replies...

MEL CRAIN
MISSOURI

I became interested in homesteading over 25 years ago. I was in my early 30s, and unhappy with working at what Helen and Scott Nearing called "sweat labor."

Idealistic, perhaps. I know I was concerned with what humankind was doing to the environment and all the ramifications that had for the future.

However, I was also married and had a small daughter and son. I remember reading an article in the original TMEN about a young couple with a child, who were homesteading in New England.

The young man stated that even though they had no health insurance or extra money for health needs, their lifestyle would protect them. If this protection proved insufficient or they had an accident, society would provide for them.

While I believe there should be a "safety net" for those who for reasons beyond their control are unable to provide for themselves, I believe that first, we should depend upon ourselves to provide. For me this is reality. With a wife and children to provide for, homesteading of the type espoused in MEN at that time was out of the question, so my homesteading was confined to dreaming.

With the birth of our second child, it was time for a larger house. We purchased a large, old house in a small town, on the edge of a large city in Iowa. I immediately started a small garden.

For me it was an extension of my childhood. We had always kept a large garden when I was a child and because of our circumstances, learned to do with less.

Because of being raised to do with less and because of my quest for independence, I stayed relatively debt-free all the years my children were growing up. If you owe money to others, your life is not your own. Someone owns you, whatever the friendly banker may tell you.

The small 10 x 15-foot garden that I maintained served us well for a few years. My first experience with mulch came there. I experimented with grass clippings, carpeting, newspaper and hay.

My late aunt purchased for me, as a Christmas gift, an annual subscription to the original *Organic Gardening and Farming* magazine. When each would arrive, I would read it from cover to cover, learning and dreaming.

My wife, who had no experience with being self-sufficient, took little interest in the garden. Nonetheless, I went on alone with my dream.

A few years passed and I was able to purchase a vacant lot next to our home. Here I was able to grow a much larger garden and produce more varied foodstuffs for my family and I could grow enough to preserve some of it. My wife became involved with the canning and freezing, another step closer to my dream.

I made most of the mistakes that beginners do. I grew too much of this, not enough of that. However, over the years, with experience, things balanced out.

My first experience with fruit trees was a disaster. Yes, I put wire cages around them in the winter. However when the snow became deep enough, the rabbits stood on the snow and ate the tops out of my trees. Something more learned for the future.

My wife, who when we were married wouldn't eat a tomato, strangely enough by this time had learned to enjoy them. They are now one of her favorite foods.

I ran the gauntlet of married life, living in the suburbs, raising my children, little league, school and community activities, college for the children. While I did this, I was always the square peg in a round hole, always out of step with the rest of society. However, each year I managed to maintain my garden. My wife had other interests, so I lived my dream alone.

Obviously, with the changes brought about in them, I stopped subscribing to the above mentioned magazines. One year, friends of ours gave us a gift subscription to COUNTRYSIDE. We have renewed it ever since.

My wife began reading it regularly. For me it was nice to know that there were still people out there like myself, pursuing their dreams, each in their own way.

One day, my children were adults and my responsibilities to them had changed. At about the same time, I qualified for early retirement from the factory I had worked in for over 30 years.

I informed my wife of my dream

that I was now able to pursue and she decided to give it a try. We began trying to decide where to live. It took over two years.

It was another year before we were able to sell our home and move. All that year we looked for property in southern Iowa or northern Missouri. We rented a home in northern Missouri and kept looking, using the services of Realtors on both sides of the border, as well as personal ads that we ran in the local shoppers. We must have looked at over 500 pieces of property. When you have waited as long as I have, you tend to be choosy and learn to be patient.

After two months renting a home, one of our ads was answered and we found what we were looking for. A secluded 40 acres, 27 of which is in hardwood timber, the remainder in pasture. There are two ponds, the house was in decent shape and I have a view of my dream each morning at the breakfast table.

By the time I retired, I already had acquired most of the tools I would need—rototiller, chain saws, etc.—and much of the experience. I have since purchased a small old tractor and some equipment to go with it. I don't know how anyone gets along without a small tractor on a homestead of any size.

We have lived here over a year now and the work at times seems endless. Today I will finish reroofing the house. The only reason I was able to afford this place was because it had been allowed to run down.

It being September, my wife is putting the finishing touches on the canning, drying and freezing from our 40' x 80' garden.

The garden patches and second pond, as seen from the house.

Our propane tank was filled today for the first time in a year. Soon we (yes, my wife helps) will begin cutting our wood to heat our home. The propane is used for our hot water heater and to heat our home should we go away in the winter.

My wife is now learning to take pride in being self-sufficient. Our freezer is full of beef, lamb, pork, chicken and some vegetables. The shelves in our "cold room" in the basement are full of colorful jars of canned vegetables and meat, along with winter squash and both kinds of freshly dug potatoes. Popcorn and onions hang drying in our glassed-in deck.

I wish I knew what attributes it takes to achieve the way of life that I have now. Obviously perseverance is one of them.

Our youngest daughter, while visiting last year, asked me how I knew so much about how to do so many different things. My answer was simple. I am willing to try anything once and I am always willing to learn from others.

I hope this article helps others who might wish to live as we do. If I have any advice, it would be to never give up, keep your bills paid and never stop learning. Above all, keep on dreaming.

Luxury and convenience have nothing to do with it

Roberta Edmonson
Louisiana

What does it take to be a homesteader? Well, first and foremost, it takes someone with a love for the countryside and the country style of living. Whether a person likes conveniences or doesn't want any luxuries at all has nothing to do with it.

I choose to live away from the sidewalks simply because I love the country, and what I can do and have here. I could never survive in the city. I like space and lots of it.

It is such a joy to go out in the morning, tending to the animals; watching the ducks waddle down to the pond; and having Ethel (our pet goat) come over and give me a "kiss" on my cheek.

I like digging in the dirt, and then harvesting the fruits of my labor. There is nothing prettier or more satisfying than a pantry full of glass jars filled with canned produce from the bounties of your own land.

I suppose some folks would say they want to be self-sufficient, and not have to depend on the outside world

CHANGE

is a part of life...

We get older... and smarter!

How one homestead couple makes work easier with a few simple changes

JERRY B. NOVOSAD
TEXAS

Some of us have been reading COUNTRYSIDE for several decades, and, like it or not, we are not as young as we used to be. In some cases we are not as healthy as we once were either. There will come a time for us to think about slowing down. And this slowing down will obviously affect our homesteading activities.

At least that is the case with Dottie and myself. Our children, who used to really make the homestead hum, are now grown and have moved away. We are not that old, only in the late fifties, but Dottie has been plagued by osteo-arthritis for a decade or so and I had a serious heart attack in September of 1996, so we had no choice but to downsize the homestead.

By downsizing I do not mean that we are phasing out of homesteading. Rather we are reducing the scope of our operations to make them more manageable, especially in the areas requiring strenuous physical labor. For one thing, we have reduced our fruit orchard from about 60 to a dozen trees. Twelve trees are not a burden to take care of and we still produce enough for our use. We simply don't have a large surplus to sell or give away. The big fruit orchard has been turned into a pasture of improved grass for the cattle. It requires little maintenance other then fertilizing and shredding once or twice a year, a job I enjoy doing.

Second, we have given up the hogs. This was a difficult decision, since the hogs always ate the garden and orchard surpluses, and thus provided an important part of the recycling process we prided ourselves in. They also provided roasts, pork chops, ribs to barbecue, and were an important ingredient of the venison and pork sausage we made every year. We still make the sausage because lean pork and venison fits neatly into my controlled diet, but I'm sorry to say that we buy the pork in town now.

We gave up the hogs because they required feeding and watering every day, became hard to manage when they got bigger and were especially difficult to deal with at slaughtering time. We have not yet dismantled the hog pen. It sits there clean and empty. Maybe one day we will have hogs again. We will just have to wait and see how things go.

What do we do with the excess produce and spoiled fruit from the homestead? Our laying hens consume a surprising quantity of it, the cattle get much more than they used to, the wild birds and animals get their fill, and the rest of it goes back into the garden to be recycled. We throw the unused materials directly into the garden and disk them under after the harvest.

Since there are no hogs and only a dozen or so hens to feed, the corn patch has been reduced to six rows about two hundred feet long in the spring and six rows during the fall growing season. We have a planter and cultivator, so the work is not that difficult. We still raise enough roasting ears for ourselves and for our family and a small surplus to feed to the hens or to put out for the deer, quail, doves, raccoons, squirrels, and other creatures that live on or visit our homestead.

The size of the garden has also been greatly reduced. We feel that we can't get along without our cucumbers, green beans, squash, and tomatoes, but we now plant only enough for ourselves and for our family. If we have a poor crop and don't have enough vegetables to can in the spring, we plant a fall crop. Our pantry is not as full as it used to be, but, frankly, we still have almost everything we need. The truth is that we used to put up too much and wound up giving away jars and jars of pickles, beans, and pickled peppers each year to make room for the fresh crop. Now we do not run much of a surplus and sometimes we even run out before the next season arrives.

Our garden does not look as pretty as it once did because we weed it only about 30% as often as we used to. In spite of the grass and weeds, the garden still produces enough for our needs. The corn patch is even more neglected. Last spring we planted the corn and cultivated it three times without ever putting a hoe to it. We wound up raising some Johnson grass and wild sunflowers along with the corn, but we still had plenty of roasting ears for everyone and had enough corn left over to feed to the laying hens and wildlife. I noticed more quail and doves in the corn patch this year, perhaps because of the Johnson grass and sunflower seeds. We plan to do it the same way again next year.

We have also become quite maintenance conscious and are attempting to reduce that never-ending work as much as possible. This may go against the grain of some homesteaders who take pride in using packing crates and other scrap material in their operation, but we are gradually turning more and more to steel and concrete and vinyl and other more permanent or maintenance-free materials.

Our hog pen has evolved through the years into steel hog panels reinforced with steel posts and a concrete floor with some dirt area to allow for rooting and wallowing. The shelter is constructed of rebar and tin. The pen has not needed any maintenance for several years and needs none now. We also constructed a loading chute out of hog panels to make that job easier. (As I talk about it, I'm tempted to hitch up the trailer and go buy a couple of pigs. Better first check with my executive partner, though.)

We had vinyl installed on the eaves of our house and hope to do the walls as soon as the budget allows. Our barn is about 75 years old and has a tin roof that looks good for another 25 to 50 years. The walls, however, are made of wood and are in need of repair and painting. Rather than doing that, we plan to cover the walls with tin or corrugated vinyl if they hold up long enough for us to get the money together.

We own 62 acres, and it would be easy to lease out the cattle pastures to someone else and thereby reduce our activities to the three or four acres of yard, garden, and barnyard; but we have chosen, for the time being, to keep our cattle herd. The cows have been carefully culled and are gentle and relatively easy to manage. We have reduced the size of our herd from 20 to 13 mother cows, so that we have plenty of pasture for grazing and baling hay. Thus we enter the winter months with good supplies of hay and do not have to spend as much time hauling out extra feed. We use the big, round bales which are put out with the tractor, thus eliminating the physical labor of handling the traditional square bales. We hire the baling done. The other tractor work, such as shredding the pastures and putting out fertilizer, is therapy for me.

Working the cows during the spring is a problem, to be sure. But last spring we had a family gathering at the homestead, and everyone pitched in.If family is not available in

This DR® Trimmer was expensive, but it helps a great deal in keeping the weeds down under electric fences and other places on the homestead.

This steel gate cost nearly $70, but it should be there, maintenance-free, for a long time. The barn in the background needs attention, but continues to hang in there.

We use the tractor as much as possible in controlling weeds in the garden. This is our fall corn being cultivated, with the spring crop in the background. (Note that the Novosads live in Texas.)

The chicken tractor, constructed from steel cattle panels, tin, and other scrap materials, saves labor and is pretty much maintenance-free.

the future, we plan to hire someone to help us. We also have a dedicated and helpful veterinarian in the area who is always willing to come out to tend to an ailing or calving cow and whose prices are very reasonable.

By the way, we have given up our old practice of raising our own heifers into mother cows. From now on we plan to buy a mature mother cow with a healthy calf by her side when we need to replace one of the old ones. This eliminates the headache of dealing with heifers calving for the first time. The loss of a beautiful heifer named Jessica, who was to be a gift to our grandson Jessie, helped make that decision.

For those who are curious about the financial aspects of the cattle operation, let me explain that I am a full-time community college instructor and Dottie is a part-time real estate agent. The cattle provide enough income to pay for the fertilizer, the hay baling, the maintenance of the fences, and our property taxes, with perhaps a little left over for Christmas.

We still raise watermelons, but instead of planting five or six acres and selling them, last spring we planted only a small patch which was easily handled and still provided plenty of melons for our annual Fourth of July family picnic. I planted them in such a way that all grass control could be taken care of with the tractor cultivator except for one trip through the patch with a hoe, which took us about half an hour. The looks on the grandchildren's faces as they feasted on the delicious red, ripe melons made the effort of raising melons worth it, in our opinion.

We used to feed the surplus watermelons to the hogs, but this summer we made an interesting discovery. Someone told me that cattle will eat watermelons, so after the harvest, we broke open a few of the cull melons and then let the cows in. They loved it! Two days later the patch was clean except for a few goat weeds. They ate every melon, all the vines, and all of the grass that grew along with the melons.

Our fences still need maintaining, but we do that a little at a time and

The large fruit orchard has been converted into a pasture of improved grass. Maggie seems to approve.

We decided to repair and make use of these old discarded steel gates. They should last, relatively maintenance-free, for a long time.

Dottie's ringneck dove cage is made from an old steel frame which at one time had been a wild hog trap. It doesn't look like much, but it's pretty much maintenance-free.

The wooden frame of the outside sink rotted and fell apart. It was rebuilt with treated lumber that should hold up much better.

are gradually moving more toward durable steel fence posts. Our corral and working pens are made of steel and require little maintenance other than a paint job once every half-dozen years or so. We use expensive rust preventative paint in order to make the paint job last as long as possible. Yes, the pens would work even if they were not painted, but we have our pride and choose to have them looking good. That gives my brother-in-law and other city inspectors one less thing to criticize.

We now use only the best paint that money can buy because we found it to be less expensive in the long run. We use metal-based paint rather than outdoor latex for all outdoor jobs. Indoors we use the latex paint, but even there we are moving more toward paneling in order to reduce the maintenance. We have found that paneling now comes in many attractive designs, some of which look like expensive wallpaper. The one-eighth-inch paneling is inexpensive and can be nailed or glued directly onto the sheet rock walls.

All of the above may suggest that we are right on top of everything, but, to be truthful, we are not. The yard is no longer as neat as it used to be and some things are left undone. The cattle trailer, for example, has not been painted in years. When we bought it about 20 years ago, it was red. About ten years ago we painted it blue. Now it is a three-toned trailer, spots of red and blue set in a background of brown rust. We felt embarrassed to take cattle to the auction in the trailer until we learned that some cattlemen, homesteaders perhaps, have trailers that look worse than ours. As for the shiny thirty-thousand dollar trailers wheeled in by the gentlemen ranchers from Houston who have bought land in this area, we mostly ignore them. The other day we were taking Rosie to the vet and a lady at the grocery store asked us what we are doing with "that big cow in the trailer." I told her we were giving Rosie a tour of the town and also taking the opportunity to show off the trailer.

Yes, we thought about selling the farm after my heart attack, but we did not think about it very long. We feel so much at home here and an apartment or a house on a lot would probably drive us crazy or at least propel us into a premature senility. So we are still here enjoying the homestead and modifying its function to suit our present situation. I hope that 25 years from now we will still be here. If we are, I'll write and tell you about it.

Homestead changes can take many forms

Note: This is an update to a story titled "The community of Wal-Mart" (80/6:23) in which Jaci Pumphrey described the difficulties of living alone on a primitive fledgling homestead, and how friends and co-workers at Wal-Mart came to her aid.

Jaci Pumphrey
Washington

It has been two years since my beloved died suddenly. We were budding homesteaders and I was determined to keep the dream alive. I read all the articles about single ladies making their way alone and all that. Believe me I tried, but I found myself sorely lacking the "man" skills.

I tried using the Skil saw and found it was too heavy and bulky for me to handle safely, so I went back to a hand saw. The chain saw was replaced by a bow saw, the framing hammer with a "ladies" size. It was all I could do to keep the old truck on the road and after several "mechanics" really screwed it up, I found myself with an unroadworthy vehicle.

Drawing water from the deep well was such a chore that the garden ended up with only a small, withered harvest unfit for preserving.

I faced one failure after another. Still I hung on, until one day I went up on the roof to clean the chimney for the coming season. When the brush stuck in the chimney and I nearly lost my balance 20 feet above the ground I sat down on the ridge of my beloved dream and came to the realization that homesteading takes two. And I was only one.

When I came down from the roof that day I was looking at my dream differently. When my aging parents called for help it was almost a relief.

I closed up the cabin, parked the truck, packed three suitcases and my dog and flew to the Pacific Northwest. I never intended to stay forever (and still don't), but for now, this will do.

In fact, I'm kinda liking the idea that going potty in the night doesn't require a flashlight and shoes. And there's this nifty little thing in a recessed part of the kitchen counter that has shiny knobs...when you turn them water comes out—hot and cold!

Have I "copped out?"

Not at all. I found a cute little house close to my parents so that I am able to keep them independent. The lot has nothing but a shed and an untamed lawn on it and during this winter I am building raised beds so come spring I will be ready to landscape with garden plants and herbs.

Yes, I'm off on a new homesteading experience—one that I can handle by myself.

Meanwhile, I'm entertaining the idea of selling the Ozark 'stead. That decision has not been made though... maybe if the right buyer came along it could happen but until then I'll be growing (both literally and figuratively) in the city and making my homestead a reality.

Tips for Southern living

FROM THE OBSERVANT NOVICE
FLORIDA

1. To keep **fire ants** and **cockroaches** out of outside pet food dishes, coat a thick unbroken line of Vaseline all around the lower rim of the dish. Set the dish up off the ground (on a board) and reapply Vaseline every four weeks or so.

2.To keep **fire ants** out of the yard, having a man around to pee on the mound is sometimes helpful and so is sprinkling used coffee grounds over the mound. I've been sprinkling Epsom salts (magnesium sulfate) on the mounds this year and have had surprisingly good results. A single application of Amdro at about 9-10 in the morning does the trick for really bad mounds at the base of, and under, the stairs leading outside. If you make it a habit of stepping on and disturbing the mounds (quickly with boots on) or regularly mow over the mounds, the ants will eventually move on.

3. If you don't want **cockroaches** in the house, all pet foods, cereals, grains, snacks, fruits, sugars, honey, anything packaged in cardboard or paper (even paper over aluminum) should be kept in the fridge or in glass or plastic airtight containers. Any used food containers to be taken to the dump for recycling should be rinsed, dried, and put in a garbage can outside the house. Clean up any spilled or spattered cooking oil/grease/butter as soon as possible. Store blankets, sheets, towels, and seasonal clothing in plastic bins with tight lids. Allowing an occasional **wolf spider** and/or common **skink** lizard to take up residence will keep roaches at bay. (Field mice will too, but they can do a lot of damage and create a lot of stink in the meantime). If your wolf spider dies, then it is likely that you have no cockroaches!

If you find pieces of cockroach wings on your bathroom floor each morning you probably have a family of mice living with you. They are generally noisy from midnight 'til light.

To get rid of mice, find the hole where they are coming in and place D-Con mouse bait or a trap with peanut butter there. Duct tape a small box of D-Con on the top side of the septic pipe that runs under the house (the most favored path of invading mice) and be sure your pets can't get at it.

To keep cockroaches out of your shop area, get rid of all paper and cardboard (they eat it and live in it) and put your nails, screws, etc. in glass jars.

4. I've used, and continue to use, whole **bay leaves** in my livestock grain bins (carefully tied inside a leg of old used panty-hose) for a year now and rarely see cockroaches in the bins and never see any other kind of insect. Be careful that the leaves cannot be accidentally fed to your livestock: bay is poisonous.

Plastic garbage cans with tight lids and bungee straps to secure the tops works fine for grain storage until just one adventurous squirrel figures out the secret and lets all of his buddies in on it. Use metal cans for grain storage. Trust me.

5. If you feed **whole or cracked corn** to any of your ruminating livestock, especially in warmer months it is a good idea to stick your head in the grain bin and take a good whiff before each feeding. If it smells sweet or musty, dump it... or you could be dealing with a severe case of acid rumen in 24 hours.

6. If you have **Johnson grass** in your proposed pasture area (it grows to about four feet tall and is a fire hazard in the winter), mow it and keep it mowed short for a year before putting your animals on it. In the spring let your animals feast. It's excellent ruminant forage and my donkeys like it but horses, I hear, don't.

Broadcast seed of better grasses over it for a couple of years.

If your stock can't keep up with the growth of the Johnson grass, mow it and keep it mowed short. Eventually the "good" grasses will displace the Johnson grass.

7. I've heard that keeping a tom cat around will keep rattlesnakes away because they do not like tomcat urine. I can attest to the fact that I never saw a rattlesnake during the five years that my neutered 14-year-old boy cat was here. About two months after he died, I saw three five-footers in the yard! I inherited an old female cat from my brother (my place has been a retirement home for pets of city dwelling relatives) and never saw a rattler on the property since. So it could be that cat pee, male or female, does the trick.

8. Coral snakes, also deadly, are common here and are found under

Family album:

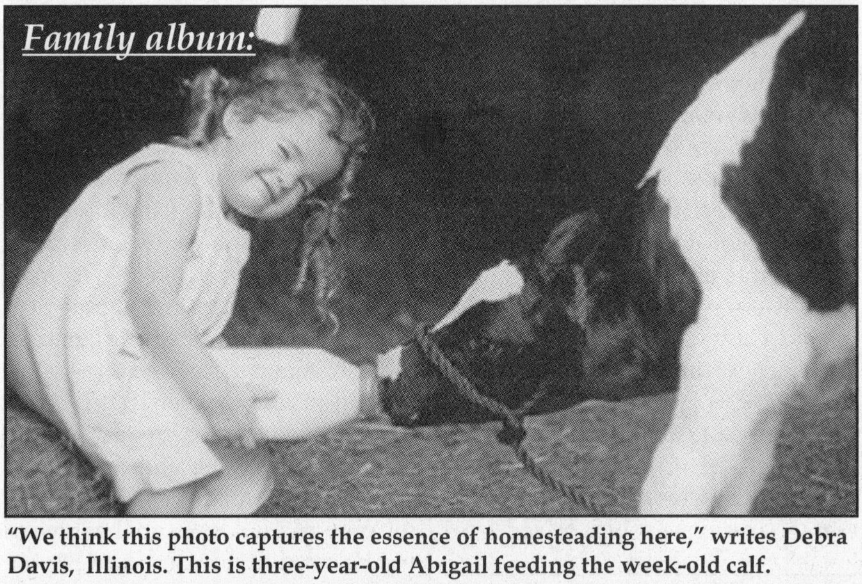

"We think this photo captures the essence of homesteading here," writes Debra Davis, Illinois. This is three-year-old Abigail feeding the week-old calf.

oak leaves and piles of brush in the fall and spring. Always wear good leather gloves when picking up leaves and brush. I don't know what will deter coral snakes but I regularly cut them in half with a shovel if they match the description "yella touches red makes a fella dead!" I have noticed that in years when there's a good supply of common black snakes around, I haven't seen any corals.

9. A good coating of **yellow mustard** will keep the dogs with chewing problems away from your garden hoses. If they still insist on chewing, they need a new home.

10. I keep **a bar of hand soap** in the toe of old nylon stockings hanging at several of the water spigots around. That comes in real handy for quick outside wash-ups and lasts a real long time.

11. If you need a good **abrasive cleaning** of your hands, use the pumice stones sold as briquettes for gas barbecue grills. Keep one at each of your spigots. They work great!

12. Cut up aluminum soda cans make good **rustproof and cheap U-brackets** to fasten (using aluminum roofing nails or screws) PVC pipe in insulation to posts or walls.

13. It's a good idea to patrol the inside perimeter of your fence on a regular basis and pick up any **trash** that might have been tossed in: glass and plastic pose real hazards to livestock. Garden refuse thrown over the fence from an indiscriminate neighbor can cause major belly aches because any sudden change to the diet of any animal is hard on their systems. If you can, talk to the offending neighbor and remind them what "no trespassing" means or, better yet, take a basket to the neighbor and ask them to deposit their garden refuse in it for you to pick up and dole out to livestock in a humane way or put it in your compost bin!

14. There are **times when things get a little tough** on the homestead. The interesting thing is, so long as I "keep the faith" (in simple living), I'm forced to learn new things so that what seemed tough before — no longer is.

A satisfying way to live!

CONNIE B. SNYDER
FLORIDA

I never heard the word "home stead" in connection with the way I live until I read this magazine. This was just the way we lived. I've been homesteading most of my life. My husband is a city boy, not used to doing without or making do. He's been raised to believe more things mean a better life, but he's learning.

The best times we've ever had were when we would build a fire in the back yard, then cook and eat our supper outside. The kids would chase fireflies, the dog, or each other. We'd watch the stars come out, listen to the owls and whippoorwills, and stare into the embers of the dying fire until Mr. Sandman came to carry each of the children off to Dreamland.

How can anything top that? What does the tv or some amusement park have to compare with the closeness and the tranquillity of an evening like this? And this is just one aspect of homestead living. There is so much more.

Homesteading is the satisfaction of our own sweat and tears making the land we have a part of us; being in tune with the seasons and cycles around us; the sweetest tomatoes this side of heaven right in our own backyard; being entertained (and exasperated) by the antics of the animals doing some of the craziest things.

I could make a list that would circle the Earth and back again, but anyone who homesteads knows all of this already. People think we're strange, but I can't understand why anyone would want to live any other kind of life. It's hard work and an endless job; but at the end of a day, when I'm bone weary and bed ready, I can see what I've done and sleep with a contentment that only a homesteader knows.

A distrust of experts serves them well

DEBORAH WOODBURY
UTAH

Homesteaders have a few characteristics in common, such as hardheadedness and a determination to make things work. Another quality that has run through our homesteading life is the distrust of experts. Whether it's baking your own bread or building your own house without a contractor, you have to ignore conventional economic theory that says to leave things to specialists.

One example is home-building. We bought an old rundown brick and adobe house that we're redoing almost completely. Conventional wisdom — our neighbors — told us to knock it down and bring in a prefab. Aside from the fact that we don't want to live in a manufactured anything, it would have been too expensive. Hiring a contractor would have been many times faster, but we'd be paying for it for the next 30 years. My husband prefers to work on our own house rather than at a "job." This year we'll earn hardly any money, but he'll save us about $80,000. Add $160,000 that we save on mortgage interest, and that's not bad wages for 1-1/2 years of hard labor.

It took us four years from the time we purchased the house until the work started. During that time we read, studied, figured, asked questions, studied more and figured more. As a result, we have been able to avoid just buying into the standard solutions. Some of our solutions are conventional, many are not. The unconventional ones are either cheaper or better in some other way. We also had the leisure of gathering materials and appliances for cheap or free.

I'm not against expertise. I value others' experience to save us trouble and time. The experts that are useful are those who share and advise, then let you make the decisions. The experts we avoid are the ones trying to sell something.

After having our first baby born in the hospital, I knew I wasn't going back. Our other two children were born at home under the watchful eye of a midwife. She used her expertise to give advice and deal with the technicalities of childbirth, but I was in control before, during and after the birth. It made all the difference.

Our oldest child is school age now, and we see no reason to turn him over to the education experts. After all, no one knows him like we do. Education is a high-stakes game, involving billions of dollars, hundreds of industries and people from the classroom teacher to the state legislators and even the president. But what do any of those people know about my child that I can't figure out? (We are both college-educated, and approve of higher education. The first 12 years of my schooling, however, was largely wasted. The university allowed me to pursue my interests and learn from people who practiced what they preached.)

There are many more examples. We learned how to raise goats from others with goats, not the feed company or even the extension service. (Some people like the extension service. I haven't found them relevant.) I sew clothes because I know what I like better than the fashion industry. My husband builds furniture that is sturdier than the stores' and fits our home.

There is more than one way to make yogurt, teach a child to read, insulate a wall, or perform most of the other tasks in life. A homesteader has to trust his instincts, not be afraid to experiment, and remember that the fun is in the journey.

A desire to live simply

GRACE BROCKWAY
NEW YORK

Simply put, a desire to live simply is the biggest reason I'm a homesteader. Given a choice between spending a day wandering through a shopping mall or staying at home and doing the laundry by hand in washtubs, with soap I made myself, canning vegetables from my own garden, baking bread, or building a new outbuilding out of recycled wood, there's no question which I would prefer.

It feels like such a waste of time to follow the pursuits that are so important to non-homesteaders. I've had people comment about how much time it takes to do laundry the way I do it, but it's my time to spend as I wish, and it gives me such a feeling of satisfaction to actually participate in the cleaning process, rather than to simply throw the clothes into a water-wasting, energy-consuming noisy machine and walk away.

That sense of accomplishment seems to be the main motivation for most of my homesteading pursuits. Combine that with how good it feels not to have to spend my hard-earned money on products that are overpackaged and full of who-knows-what, and you'll begin to understand why I'm a homesteader. I never sat down and thought about how I want to live my life; I'm a doer, rather than a ruminator. My gut feelings lead me to follow the path I've chosen.

A strong dislike of technology is certainly another driving force for me. I've often thought I was born about a century too late because the noise of modern machines is so offensive to me, and I know that a desire to get away from all the humming and whining is also a motivating factor for doing things the "old-fashioned" way.

So now, what are the personality traits that are most important for accomplishing my goals? Well, as you said, the most obvious is a willingness to work, but I think that even more than that it's that working is enjoyable for me. It's a gusto for life, a desire to fill each day to the fullest.

Now, there are folks out there who have this same drive, but they funnel it into sports, into play, and I simply can't understand that. What a waste of time! Maybe that's part of the work ethic I inherited, but I could never feel comfortable with spending vast amounts of money and time in the pursuit of something so useless, so transitory. Actually, I couldn't feel comfortable spending vast amounts of money on anything, but I could part with it a lot quicker if I were getting something permanent and useful, like land.

A second personality trait is a strong sense that frugality is a virtue. Waste not, want not. I'm also very practical, which ties in with the frugality. My house is not a showplace by any means. It's functional, practical and comfortable. Same is true of my garden and yard. Useful outbuildings, yes. Miles of lawn, no.

I'm also something of a hermit at heart, which fuels my desire to be independent. I'm happiest when I can stay home. Anything I can make for myself allows me to meet this goal by requiring fewer trips to town, which is also why I'm so enthusiastic about buying in bulk.

So, it's obviously an emotional rather than an intellectual force that motivates me to be a homesteader, and my practical, independent nature that allows me to pursue that goal.

Three generations share homestead experience

Darlene Lund
Washington

What is it that drives me toward my homestead goal? What characteristics are most helpful in that endeavor? Like so many of your readers I have been wanting to write for a long time. This question finally inspired me enough to take time out of my canning to respond.

I will start with a little background. My husband is now a retired firefighter. He is 53 and I am 52. We first made the sacrifice to move to the country away from the city of Seattle in 1973. He commuted 80 miles to work while I got all the farm experiences when he was gone. At that time, we feared we were in for a catastrophic time in our country and wanted to be as self-sufficient as possible. But that concern was just the motivation we needed to do what we had always wanted to do, get out of the city rat-race. We wanted to train our four children (ages 5, 7, 9 and 12) to be hard working, caring and charactered. We felt that would be best accomplished in a farm environment. We bought a four bedroom farmhouse with a couple of outbuildings on 20 acres for $23,000. We sold our house in Seattle for enough money to make the down payment with enough left over to remodel the farmhouse.

Our adventure began. We set ourselves up to be as self-sufficient as possible. We had our own sawmill. We raised all our fruit, berries, vegetables, eggs and beef. We had as many as four milk cows. We had all our own butter and milk. We sold the excess milk and used the rest to raise pigs. We did our own butchering. We did our own curing of bacon and ham. I even used the intestines of the cows for the casings for summer sausage. We canned hundreds of quarts of produce. My husband built a large barn using poles that he cut, cedar siding that he milled, a shake roof that he split himself!

Our children made their money from the farm. They had a truck garden, sold goat milk, had a boar service and sold berries. We raised all four of our children on that farm. Our youngest was all set to buy the farm from us after we built a new "getaway" house overlooking Puget Sound. Our middle son also lived on the acreage.

My husband retired after 28 years with the Seattle Fire Department. We were also full-time pastors. Our house was a beautiful retreat but we found we could "escape" but not "live" there. We found that we wanted the same lifestyle for our grandkids that we had wanted for our children, and so did they. At the same time we were experiencing a major "burnout" in our ministry involvement. But this time Thurston County was so permit-happy that we could not all live on the 20-acre farm. We decided to try to buy a larger property that we could all live on with plenty of privacy and "community."

We like to say we got the last good farm buy in Lewis County. We sold both our 20-acre farm and our new house and bought and paid for 100 acres with the cutest Victorian farmhouse, large garage, large barn, a year-round creek and a gorgeous view of both Mount St. Helen and Mount Rainier. Our youngest son was deeded five acres and he built a new house on it. Our middle son bought a new large double wide which is across the field from us. Now we have six grandsons living here. Our other two children visit often and also enjoy the produce from the farm! How appropriate that the children that worked the hardest and the longest on our first farm share in the experience of living on our present farm.

We retired from our pastorate two years ago, but we really just "changed jobs."

We are once again homesteading with our extended family. We have worked extremely hard the last five years. We remodeled the house, built a new shop, cleaned out debris, cut down trees, fenced the entire acreage, restored old fruit trees to production, put in a huge garden, built a greenhouse, made the yard a perennial cottage garden. My husband did a ton of cat work. We hay 50 acres, have 27 beef cows, and one milk cow that we all take turns milking. Once again the excess milk goes to the pigs. We make apple juice together as a family project. We have nut trees. We all have gardens, so if one item fails in one of the gardens we can cover it. We have grapes, raspberries, blueberries, and strawberries. We butcher together. We raise chickens and share the eggs and responsibilities. We all rely upon wood heat, and have enough trees to meet all our needs. We have the children "in common." We share the same values so the grandkids are in a wonderful environment.

We are still driven by the idea that should a major collapse take place our family can survive and thrive in it. We are driven by the idea that so few people even know how to do what was only natural one generation ago. We want the grandkids to be among those who do know! We constantly rehearse to the grandkids how blessed they are to get to live on a large farm. This year the two four-year-olds and the six-year-old were delighted to be able to help with the haying, "We get to turn bales, Grandma!" What a treasure for them to participate with their extended family getting in the harvest for the cows and to pay for the taxes on the farm. How better to teach them hard work and how to be part of something bigger than themselves?

They are also "getting" to help bring in the wood for the winter, and snapping the beans for canning. They couldn't wait for Daisy the milk cow to come fresh so they can have lots of milk again. They love to feed the calf, get the eggs, eat the fresh apples, pears, and carrots from the garden. They share in the satisfaction of making our own sausage, and trying it out to see if the taste is okay before doing the whole batch. They love the beefsticks Grandpa made and the whole process of smoking the bacon and hams. This Saturday the three oldest will go to the local farm sale with Grandpa to buy some more baby pigs to eat the excess milk and become our future ham dinners. The oldest has helped me put away some of the seeds for next year's garden. They beg for the pickles in the brine curing, and love to eat the early tomatoes with their own salt shaker. For them to experience the making of the horseradish sauce (which they won't eat) and the sauerkraut (which they like) is something few children will ever experience.

We want that for them enough to make this farm our priority rather than spend our children's inheritance traveling. This is what motivates us. If the world goes to hell in a handbasket our kids and grandkids can make their way! That security is something that will go with them for the rest of their lives. We believe that just the learning of the lesson, or the work, is not the only thing they are gaining. There is an old saying, "teach the hands to many things and the mind will flourish." We believe this is true. There are so many spiritual truths communicated through natural processes. There is so much outworking of a philosophy taking place when three families work together. There is a place of peace and protection provided for us all.

The characteristics that we share among us that make our endeavor work are having the same values and vision. We are all hard workers. We are all able to communicate well. We have good boundaries. We love truth. We know how to "in love prefer others" and when to do it. We all have a good sense of humor. We all make the Bible the final word in all things practical. The grandkids, like their parents, are being programmed according to the principles found in Proverbs. We know how to "agree to disagree" without breaking our fellowship. My husband and I feel that we are experiencing a great reward from God for our faithfulness to apply His principles in the raising of our children.

Lawman seeks peace

Harold Clouse
Texas

I've worked in law enforcement for the last eight years. Working in law enforcement you learn to watch and read people, and I have seen all kinds.

I've noticed that people seem to be growing in two different directions. The majority are caught up in the ever-growing technologies of computer advances. These people spend all of their time at computer terminals; on the Internet, searching cyberspace, and playing computer games. They can't wait to get, and master, the newest software. If you try to talk to them all you get is a discussion on the future of cyberspace.

The other group is much smaller, but consists of various groups of people all searching for the same thing. Homesteaders fall into this group. They aren't necessarily opposed to technological advancement; they just don't find peace of mind in them. They come from all walks of life, but share a desire to live in harmony with this world, the way God meant us to. In seeking this "peace and harmony" they turn to the beginnings of mankind. God created us, originally, to care for the animals and plants in the Garden of Eden. We take care of them and they take care of us. We have fallen far from this harmony with the garden. Our spirits are now uneasy because our lives are stressed and twisted. Those of us who feel this uneasiness seek a way back to that harmony and homesteading is definitely in the right direction.

My wife and I are saving up for our homestead and have already started showing our children how rewarding it is to have the skills to provide for oneself. I have worked in a hard and stressful career, but nothing compares to the satisfaction I get when I work at home, building, planting, raising animals, and teaching my children to do the same. When I spend a day working with my hands to benefit my family I am bone-tired, but there is a peace I don't find in anything else.

That peace is what I believe all homesteaders seek and once you taste it, you crave more until it's all you ever want to do.

A love of the land

Roberta Edmonson
Louisiana

What does it take to be a homesteader? Well, first and foremost, it takes someone with a love for the countryside and the country style of living. Whether a person likes conveniences or doesn't want any luxuries at all has nothing to do with it.

I choose to live away from the sidewalks simply because I love the country, and what I can do and have here. I could never survive in the city. I like space and lots of it.

It is such a joy to go out in the morning, tending to the animals; watching the ducks waddle down to the pond; and having Ethel (our pet goat) come over and give me a "kiss" on my cheek.

I like digging in the dirt, and then harvesting the fruits of my labor. There is nothing prettier or more satisfying than a pantry full of glass jars filled with canned produce from the bounties of your own land.

I suppose some folks would say they want to be self-sufficient, and not have to depend on the outside world for anything. That is well and good if you have the means to do it. Most of us don't.

I guess what I am trying to say is, homesteading has to be in your blood. It has to be the love of your life. It takes different strokes for different folks. Homesteading is not for everyone.

Now to try and answer some of the questions you put before your readers. I think technology is wonderful. Without it where would we be today. However, I think there will come a time when we will have to learn to live without it. The more technology a nation has, the more wicked the nation becomes. Whatever humanity is left on this Earth will have to learn to make do with whatever resources we have available. I feel sorry for everyone when that time comes, but feel more so for the people who are living in the cities. They won't have very much to fall back on.

But, aside from all that, that is not why I do what I do. It fulfills my inner need for peace and serenity. It gives me a sense of accomplishment when a batch of soap turns out right or the dill pickles stay crisp.

No, everything does not go smoothly all the time. But that's life. When we fail, we just try, try again. That is how it is with homesteading. When you're doing something that you love, you don't give up.

I hope that with all my rambling, trying to put my thoughts into words, I have not made you think I make no sense at all. I can't speak for everyone, I can only speak for myself. Thanks for giving me that opportunity.

Step lightly on the Earth

L. H. Scarbrough
Colorado

While pondering the question of the month "What does it take to be a homesteader?" I made a list. Included are practical skills, imagination, common sense, ingenuity, logic, and an appreciation for your surroundings, not to mention a good measure of intuition. (It's amazing what you can learn if you just "pay attention.")

But the most important skill to being a good homesteader, on my list, is to always step lightly, to make the least amount of impact on my surrounding environment, whether it be in the fuel efficient car or the lack of poisons in my garden and under the kitchen sink.

We bought our homestead about five years ago. It's 35 acres with a small pond, a creek, a mountain (8,800 feet above the sea), and a two bedroom mobile home with a septic system. There is no power here yet, but we plan on putting in a photovoltaic system.

It took the first four years to discover the various dump sites left around the place by the previous owner. One was obvious; on the edge of the woods near the driveway. One was disguised as a dam on the pond. We discovered this when a wet spring filled the pond and washed away part of the dam to expose things like an old screen door, some garden hose, carpet, plastic bottles, pieces of Formica and particle board. We spent a summer cleaning and fixing that mess.

The last dump site we found was the most frightening of all. After two years of one delay after another, we finally had a well put in. One month after the well was dug, it became artesian. Water was spilling over the top of the casing and pooling around the base of it. We needed to dig a trench to channel the overflow away from the well head. About the third shovel full of dirt yielded some broken glass. It only got worse from there. We dug out and hauled off five 30 gallon trash bags of used oil filters, old batteries, miscellaneous auto parts, broken bottles and lots of cans.

I was so furious at the previous owners who probably had that, "It's my land, I can do whatever I want," mentality. What he doesn't understand is that it is not his land. In the grand scheme of things, he is only the caretaker for just a minute, and look at what he's done with his minute. He only had the property for three years.

Can you imagine the horror of realizing that you've punched your $4,000 well right through an old hidden landfill? Fortunately, the first 50 feet of ground is a solid cap of granite above the water source, which has acted as a shield to protect it from contamination. The water is fine.

Back to the subject at hand: What does it mean to be a homesteader?

It means being responsible for your little corner of the world.

It means not taking more than you can give in return.

It means being respectful of both the past and the future. Respect the past for its simpler way of being and doing. And respect the future by using the insight that is taught by the past.

It also means being responsible for your own past and present, and the future of generations yet to come. And to learn from others' mistakes as well as your own.

Homesteading also means experiencing that wonderful, dog-tired feeling you get at the end of a long, hard day of accomplishments. And the satisfaction of taking a break from your labors to enjoy the soaring hawk above you or the occasional bobcat or deer or bear that happens to stroll by. Or just sitting back and enjoying the song of the frogs or the crickets.

Homesteading, for me, is to be just another piece of the puzzle, instead of the manipulator of the puzzle.

Remember to step lightly, and don't forget to have fun.

Country neighbor... in an apartment:

She does a lot with very little land

LYNN C. MAUST
PENNSYLVANIA

Some good things don't last forever. This little country town didn't. Our once-beautiful farmscapes have nearly all vanished under the earthmovers, replaced by developers' overpriced, oversized, tastelessly ostentatious dwellings. It is now a suburb of Philadelphia.

Growing flowers and vegetables helps ease my distress at our losses.

I'd like to encourage others living in areas similar to mine. Even a backyard (or, in my case, part of a sideyard) can be transformed into a bouquet and food-producing bit of acreage!

Six years ago I began with an idea for a small, curvilinear flower bed, hand dug with a spade, beneath a dogwood on part of the lawn at my apartment building. (My landlord has been very accommodating.) The garden gradually expanded to include four more beds and a patio beneath the shade tree. What began as a very part-time hobby grew to a daily passion.

Perennials have come to dominate my flower beds, while vegetables have become really productive due to lots of soil amending.

As an aside, I highly recommend three old books on "farming" which moved me and taught me a great deal. *Malabar Farm, The Farm,* and *Pleasant Valley* are all by Pulitzer Prize winning author Louis Bromfield. Your library may have copies, or you can purchase them from Malabar Farm State Park, 4050 Bromfield Rd., Lucas, OH 44843-9745. These writings are among those few that sometimes enter and change our lives. After being fed from the author's insight and knowledge of country life, you'll discover you have developed a finer, greater love and respect for creation and the soil.

Lynn Maust grows an amazing variety of vegetables and flowers in the sideyard of her apartment building in Pennsylvania.

As an encouragement to single women (of which I am one) I have, from the beginning, worked these gardens on my own, utilizing books, magazines, tools purchased as needed over several years, my trusty cart, and the trunk of my once-pristine Toyota Camry—and of course, COUNTRYSIDE, always.

The vegetable beds contain carrots, lettuces, radishes, onions, garlic, sweet and hot peppers, tomatoes, string beans, peas, spinach, beets, potatoes, parsnips, cabbage, and summer squash, with marigolds and petunias throughout. There are more than a dozen kinds of flowers, including a bleeding heart five feet in diameter!

Yes, you can get all this into a small area, with planning on paper and by a scaled chart/drawing and lots of thought and care. It came together 80% as planned.

You will never know such a special sense of accomplishment and security until you have planned, plotted, tilled, planted, fed, watered and prayed for God's provision from the soil.

Begin with even one packet of seeds, or one plant and a spoon for a spade. (I still use a teaspoon for transplanting garden thinnings.) A new and rewarding time of your life awaits your action. Cease dreaming and planning and do where you are, now. You will be in preparation for getting further beyond the sidewalks and will be a step closer to that goal, if and when your time comes.

Meanwhile, reap some rewards now!

Storm diary:

"We settled into new habits and a new rhythm that was somewhat slower, much quieter and very pleasant."

Jane Keon
Michigan

After a storm uprooted trees, flattened barns and shut down electrical power throughout our area, I spent one evening in the light of an oil lamp looking through Lehman's non-electric catalog to see if there was anything I wished I had during power outages. A small, stainless steel coffee pot and a pyramid toaster to set on top of the woodstove would have made breakfast nicer. Other than that, I looked at pictures of all the non-electric items we were presently using and felt grateful to have them.

We own two Aladdin oil lamps and we use them winter evenings instead of electric lights. They put out light equivalent to a 60-watt light bulb, and the quality of the light is soft and glowing. In fact, when the electric lights came back on in our house four nights after the storm, I went around and turned them off to continue writing in the lamp light!

This spring we sent for a composting toilet from Lehman's, and it is working very well so far in our upstairs bathroom. A compact unit made by Sun-Mar, it has a built-in electric fan that we plug in sometimes when the moisture level gets high in the chamber. It also has a built-in heater that we may use this winter since we don't heat the upstairs of our house. So far, though, we haven't really needed either of the electric features. After 20 years of talking about getting a composting toilet, we finally did it! (They cost less now than they did 20 years ago.) If we find that the toilet upstairs works satisfactorily, we'll go to that system downstairs, too, with a larger composting chamber in the basement.

The rugs needed vacuuming before the storm hit, so after two days into the power outage, I got out my little push sweeper. It did a fine job of getting up everything, even the cat hair.

We've used a wood heating stove for years, but I've never really cooked on it. Along with the coffee pot and pyramid toaster, I plan to order a book that tells how to use a heating stove for cooking. I especially missed my oven during the power outage, and today I've been baking like crazy—bread, cookies, granola.

We picked our first strawberries the day after the storm and wanted biscuits for shortcake. My husband had the charcoal grill going for venison steaks, and he preheated a deep cast iron frying pan and lid in the coals. I cut out the biscuit dough and plopped the rounds into the skillet. In 10 minutes they were done. They rose quite well and were wonderful!

We're very lucky to have two flowing wells on our property. One is a very narrow stream of water, fluctuating from a quarter inch to a half inch in diameter. The other fluctuates from nothing to an inch. We pipe both wells to our goldfish pond that is right outside the kitchen. I was able to water our goats, sheep, hens, broilers, rabbits, dogs and cats with ease, even if it took longer to fill the buckets, and we had good, safe drinking water for ourselves.

A concern we are facing is losing the flow of these wells. A nearby "farmer" has put in deep wells for irrigating extensive corn fields. The flowing well on the property of neighbors about a quarter mile from us has dried up, and they believe it is due to the deep irrigation wells. With that worry on our minds, we've been discussing putting in a well on property we own across the road. Lehman's has supplies for wells and pumps. We live on a river, but it is polluted with DDT and other chemicals contributed by Velsicol Chemical Company. (Just last week the press announced that our stretch of the river produced the most DDT-contaminated fish ever found in the U.S.A. How nice.) Another fresh water source is rainwater, which we intend to collect by putting eave troughs on our barns and getting some kind of tank to contain the water.

Storm-toppled trees took down stretches of our electric fence wire, so even a solar-powered fencer wouldn't help us right now. But after we get the trees cut up and the fence fixed, I'd like to invest in a solar-powered fencer. They make good sense. Too bad they cost so much.

A few years ago my husband fixed up an overhead gasoline storage tank. It was about half full when the storm hit. Gasoline stations were not able to pump gas because of no electricity, and our son and daughter-in-law were almost out. We were able to fill up the tank of their car, which gave us great satisfaction, especially my husband. But we can see the necessity for more gasoline storage for an extended outage, especially if we run a gasoline-powered generator, as we did this time, to keep the freezer and refrigerator going.

Keeping our venison, rabbits and chickens frozen was the most expensive part of this power outage. We ran our old World War II generator continuously and it did a fine job, with some babying by my husband, but it cost about $5 a day in gasoline. Also, the starter on our one-year-old freezer burned out, probably from the fluctuations in voltage. Our meat is presently in our son's freezer and we have ordered a new part for ours. Even though I use my canner to put up soups and stews made with some of our meat, I still think we rely on the freezer too much. We are talking about canning most of this year's deer, and also rabbits and chickens as they are butchered. Yes, it's more work than simply wrapping the cuts and storing them in the freezer, but I think it would be worth the peace of mind in an extended power outage. The Lehman's catalog carries some huge canners that fit on more than one burner...they would make the job go faster.

Lehman's also carries propane-powered refrigerators and freezers. The freezer is quite small and it sounds as if it struggles to maintain a zero temperature, but the refrigerator is almost as large as our electric model, and figuring shows it would cost less to run. We are going to send for literature on the refrigerator.

We don't yet have propane, and the gas company's lines don't come out as far as we live, so we use a lot of electricity! Last summer my husband bought a used, 1,000-gallon propane tank and we did a pretty good job of nestling it in so it doesn't look like a behemoth in the yard. He plans to plumb the house for propane this fall. After using a propane-powered camp stove during this storm, and seeing how little gas it took for cooking and heating water, I now know that 1,000 gallons will last a long time! Plus, with a gas stove, I'd have an oven for baking!

The other big area to think about is washing clothes. The Lehman's catalog offers several non-electric options. What we did this time was use the gasoline generator to provide electricity to run our automatic washer. We carried in 16 gallons of water from the flowing well for the wash and 16 more for the rinse. After the clothes spun, I hung them on the line. It really went very well.

Even though the 50-year-old generator does the job, I'd like to have another one on hand. I saw one running off the PTO of a tractor on a neighboring farm. That's something to save some cash for.

In addition to the woodstove, composting toilet, lamps, sweeper and other non-electric items I've mentioned, we also own a hand-cranked cream separator, grain mill, meat grinder, and noodle maker. For an extended time of no electricity, these would be even more appreciated.

It was interesting to find that after about two days and two nights into the outage, we quit flipping on electric light switches and turning on the faucets! We settled into new habits and a new rhythm that was somewhat slower, much quieter and very pleasant. Today, though, I'm using our computer to word-process this letter.

H-m-m-m. Maybe I need to track down an old manual typewriter...

Unwanted paper is put to good use

ROBERT YORK
FLORIDA

Some people weep and wail about a lovely freebie as if it were a curse. I'm talking about so-called junk mail.

There are pearls of usefulness to be found in the clutter. There are catalogs with tools, gadgets, clothes, etc. you won't find in local stores, along with coupons or discounts on many items.

But most valuable is the paper. I learned this by accident.

I had an old solid fuel furnace and saved all burnable trash for it in a barrel. All the unwanted mail, magazines, and newspapers went into this barrel.

One rainy day I discovered a leak and placed the barrel under the leak—temporarily. All the papers got soaked and mushy. I stirred it around to loosen what had stuck to the bottom and dumped it outside where it dried.

I found the ugly lump weeks later, chopped it into chunks, and found it burned beautifully in my Franklin stove!

Now I happily dump junk mail into my water barrel to soak. I churn it when I think of it, then plunk the wad on a slanted board to drain and dry.

Reprinted from COUNTRYSIDE, *March/April 1997.*

Country neighbors:

Homesteading in suburban Connecticut

Hannah holds a Rhode Island Red hen.

DONALD & LAURA MITCHELL
CONNECTICUT

We have been subscribers for a few years after finding our first issues at the library. I went to search for reading material on raising chickens, and up popped COUNTRYSIDE. The library had three years' of back issues, and we read them all pretty fast. We decided to subscribe so we could keep all future issues.

We were both raised here in South Windsor. We met in high school and were married in 1986. We first lived in an apartment before finding a house we liked and could afford.

It came with an acre of land and no next door neighbors. The house was in a rural part of town with over 1,000 undeveloped acres behind us and woods across the street.

There is an overgrown farm with an old tobacco barn and dairy barn near us. We have plans to buy this property, but still must decide if we should move to a less expensive area where we could acquire more land for less money. There is an ever-increasing amount of wildlife in our area. We frequently see wild turkeys, deer, blue herons and even a bald eagle. Howling coyotes and screaming red foxes have awakened us at night.

I restored a collapsed chicken coop. A farmer down the road gave us some chickens, and they give enough eggs for our family. I found out about a nearby livestock auction and came home with a few more chickens, two turkeys and two geese. My wife thought I was crazy!

We went back to the auction a few weeks later, and we came home with a goat. We named her Molly. She was a pregnant (unknown to us) Alpine cross with horns. We discovered her condition when we found Molly nursing a newborn kid!

Donald spraying fruit trees.

Laura likes the sheep.

Eventually, we had to find a new home for her, as her horns became too dangerous around Hannah, our pre-school daughter. Since then, we have had a few dehorned goats, but they are too hard to contain on our property. This wasn't too much of a problem until someone built a brand-new home on an acre lot right next to ours.

They were very excited when they found what they thought to be deer tracks right next to their home during construction. After they moved in, I tried raising the fence and repairing the holes, but the slope of our yard made it easy for the goats to get a running start to jump over five- and even six-foot high fencing.

Then our problems began. Our new neighbors made it very clear that they didn't like the way we made use of our land. First they contacted the town hall to find out what the rules and regulations were for raising chickens, especially roosters, since ours started crowing about 4:00 A.M. The town contacted us and said that we were okay, since there had been chickens on the property for years. Even with the town in our favor, I decided to build a coop on the other side of our property and leave the goats in the older building.

Our neighbor hired a surveyor because he was unsure of the actual property lines. It was found that the old chicken coop sat right on the property line. He hired an attorney, and we were served a letter that we had to sign. It gave us permission to keep the building there and house

our goats as long as we maintained proper insurance and upkeep and made no additions to the building or the number of goats in it. After we sold the goats, I took down the part of the building on their property. They soon erected a six-foot high stockade fence.

Raising chickens has proven to be successful for us. The extra meat and eggs we sell provides us with enough to pay for the cost of raising the whole flock. We've also had some successful chick hatches with our 42-egg Hovabator incubator system. We have raised several different breeds and really enjoy our Araucanas best.

We have even hatched some wild turkeys, pheasants and peafowl. We occasionally buy chicks from various hatcheries, and the catalogs are very helpful in learning about the different poultry breeds.

Despite the farm-like setting, the animals have upset some neighbors.

In August 1996, my wife bought a registered two-year-old Dorset sheep and her lamb. Since she is an avid knitter, my wife is very anxious to raise these sheep for their wool. The manure is great for the garden! This past May, we had them sheared, cleaned the wool and mailed it off to a spinnery in Maine. It came to about six pounds of spun wool.

The sheep are costly, because we have to buy hay at $3/bale. We buy grain in bulk from a local mill. By shoveling it into barrels and loading it ourselves, we pay half of what it would cost bagged from a feed store. This is also how we buy our chicken feed. The sheep are very easy to care for. They stay in a three-strand electric fence and are very gentle with the children.

We homeschool Hannah (7) and Jacob (4). Our days are filled with many of life's lessons as well as academics. We put together our own curriculum, which is mostly Catholic material. Our faith is very important to us, and we would like to see our children carry it on through the examples taught at home.

Hannah, 6, and Jacob, 3, with Annabelle and Emma, the Dorset sheep.

We decided to use an independent midwife for the care of our future pregnancies after the premature Cesarean birth of our daughter at a city hospital. With our second child, my wife again experienced premature labor at seven months, but she used herbs and herbal tinctures to stop the labor. She had our son at home two days before the due date.

In all that we do, our lifestyle is as simple as possible. We feel it is important to make use of what is available. We use a lot of our land raising fruits and vegetables, including several rows of berries. My wife cans jelly and jam with the grapes from our 50-year-old vines. The growing season here is from late April to October and can be extended into November for hardier vegetables. We freeze most of the vegetables.

I work outside the home as a truck driver. I start very early and come home early enough to give me time to do homestead chores.

To us, homesteading means providing for ourselves as much as possible and spending time at home. We would like to do more. This will require at least a few more acres. We are interested in raising cattle. I am very interested in old-time dual purpose breeds such as the Devon and Shorthorn. Someday we hope to raise goats again along with a pony and maybe even a donkey.

We are thankful for what we have been blessed with. We hope our children will forever hold the memories of their early years at our Humble Acre.

The barn, under construction, with family help.

Barn number two, built of logs, houses sheep and chickens.

Country neighbors:

Despite ups and downs, they're making it in Michigan

TIM KAUFMAN
MICHIGAN

My experience with homesteading is that the "ideal" of total self sufficiency usually doesn't happen. There are many aspects of this lifestyle that are fruitful and rewarding, but most people are forced to adapt homesteading to their own unique setting.

My wife has a farm background, while my father was a part-time farmer and a minister. He didn't encourage my farming interests and suggested that I pursue other vocations. There was a sense of practicality in that advice, as land and equipment prices were skyrocketing back in the early '70s. Despite that, a longing to continue in some type of farming or working the land was never extinguished.

Our Michigan homesteading efforts have been assisted at times by my wife's farming family. The soil is somewhat sandy, and topsoil is thin. Because of the lake effect, weather in eastern Michigan is very unpredictable and prone to extremes. There has been very little snow here for at least the last six years.

Many "small" farmers in this area also work in auto-related factory manufacturing jobs. The practical side is that reasonable farm expenses can be written off against the factory wages, resulting in tax savings. This is changing, as the automakers are downsizing and laying off workers. Young people must usually look elsewhere or move to find work, as there is little new hiring in the auto plants.

The first homestead effort

Our first homestead effort involved renting a farm house with a large old hip roof barn. We were beginning careers in teaching and social work and starting a family at that time. Needless to say, we were very busy, as we were also looking for land to buy and ways to build our own home.

We broke sod on a small garden patch behind our house and cleared the straw-filled barn and ran an underground electric wire to it. I built stalls and a hog feeder with old lumber. Skills learned while working construction jobs during college are often more useful than a bachelor's degree.We have enjoyed raising egg-producing chickens, sheep and feeder hogs with varying degrees of success and laughable failures. Our first garden was flooded out because of heavy rain, and our house was nearly flooded. This was caused by a clogged ditch and improperly sized drain tiles.

Three-quarters of our six-week-old chicken flock were killed, probably by a weasel. Our third batch of laying hens was a complete failure. It seems the mail-order company made a switch and sent us all roosters! We did successfully raise a pair of feeder pigs. Two ewe lambs who both had untroubled single births were raised in a fenced area of our yard. Even though it was rented, we did much work on the house, including a reroofing, remodeling and adding a woodstove insert in the fireplace.

Heavy traffic provides experiences

While we liked the home and barn and enjoyed watching the crops being tilled on the neighboring 35 acres that my in-laws farmed at that time, we were often frustrated by the lack of privacy and heavy traffic that passed by on the four-lane highway next to the house.

Large tanker trucks literally shook the house and knocked pictures off the wall. We had many unusual experiences, including being awakened at 2 A.M. by a drunken man requesting that I pull his car out of a ditch. Once that happened, he seemed to sober up quickly and gave me $50.

Other odd incidents included rude people who would stop and use the front yard for a bathroom or drive back to our barnyard to do the same. A van load from a church youth group once stopped to spend the evening while their vehicle was being repaired. They later sent my three-year-old son a stuffed animal and thanked us for being answers to a prayer, angels for providing them shelter until the van could be repaired.

On another occasion, a group of jolly, friendly carnival people stopped while I repaired a broken water hose for them. We fed them sandwiches and hot chocolate and listened to their interesting stories about carnival life. Much to our dismay, we discovered a couple of days later that they left behind a large horde of fleas.

There was the time when my wife had a harrowing experience with our typical Great Lakes clear weather windstorms. I had just laboriously chopped out a tree that had grown into the wall of an old tin storage shed. Unfortunately, I later learned that it was the only thing anchoring the building.

Hay is cut with a borrowed tractor and stacked by hand.

The next time a windstorm came up, my wife was shutting the blown-open tin shed door. The whole building left the ground. Through God's protection, she was standing upwind of the building. Half the shed landed in an apple tree while my three-year-old son and five-year-old daughter watched the whole spectacle in horror. I was able to take the tin shed apart and salvage the materials.

Less-than-adequate tools

Fortunately, I have been able to progress from chopping wood with a hatchet. It has been a long, frustrating process having to make do and improvise with less than adequate tools to do the job. Hard financial times have always necessitated choosing wisely and using old salvage items as much as possible. We enjoy going to auctions and buying nuts and bolts and old tools at reasonable prices.

My wife has also enjoyed going to garage sales and has saved much money by spending countless hours repairing and refinishing beautiful furniture. We have been able to furnish most of our house for a very reasonable cost.

After four years and an aborted effort to buy the property, the absentee landlady asked for the home and acreage, and the opportunity came to develop some property not far from my in-laws' farm. There was much work involved with building the small 24' x 32' Cape Cod-style home, which has a roofed porch extending all along the back.

We literally had to mow down a flat area of seven-foot-high field corn. We hired the foundation and heavy roof framing work out. Otherwise, I was able to do much of the building myself, which included moving the shell of the building when it was only half done. The inside finishing required many long nights. Even after nearly 15 years of living here, the work is not completely done.

However, I can't remember a more enjoyable time than when we worked together to build our home. We were later able to expand our living space by skills gained in doing electrical wiring and finishing the basement. One of our many trial and error experiences was the unwise judgment of starting our house in the fall. The cold weather and short days made it hard to shingle the 45-degree roof and putting on the rough-sawn clapboard siding in the blowing wind and snow.

Another mistake

Another mistake was putting our wood stove block chimney up through the middle of the home. It is not as safe during a chimney fire, and it is also much harder to climb the roof for chimney cleaning during the winter. (Frequent chimney cleaning is something I strongly recommend.)

If possible, choose a site on a natural rise for better drainage away from the basement. Look for a place that has some established trees. It has been a long, uphill battle getting trees to grow here, as we have endured a tree mortality rate of nearly 75 percent. After 15 years of hand watering and fertilizing, we finally have a windbreak stand of pine trees on both ends of the house site.

The jury is still out on my dubious efforts to plant a row of pine trees along the north and south perimeters of the surrounding 40 acres we now have. There is much evergreen loss because of the large deer population here. I have learned that saplings do better if an area of about two feet in diameter around the trees can be kept clear of weeds.

A slow, frustrating process

Being able to make practical use of our surrounding acreage has been a slow, frustrating process. There are 15 tillable acres, with the balance in dense brush and wet woodland. We have put pasture fencing on three of the tillable acres and added four acres of fencing in the woods, as the sheep thoroughly enjoyed mowing down the brush and eating the leaves off the numerous thorn bushes.

We have also expanded a pine tree planting on three poorly drained acres. Local soil conservation districts can be a good source of reasonably priced evergreens. We have harvested hay from a naturally gone back to grass and clover parcel.

Our attempts to store the hay in an outside haystack have met with mixed success. I would be interested to hear from other readers what the process is for building an outside hay storage stack which can be constructed to shed water and minimize spoilage.

Jacob, 6, with the first lambs born after the switch to fall lambing.

Financial considerations prevented us from purchasing a tractor for many years. One concession we made was buying a Yamaha 250 Moto 4. It has proven to be invaluable, as its towing ability is amazing. We use it to haul freshly cut firewood to our heating stove. The Yamaha maneuvers easily in our dense swampy woods. When it gets stuck, you can easily lift it out of a rut or soft spot.

The Ford 9N

After years of fruitless searching for something at a reasonable price, we purchased a Ford 9N tractor along with implements. There was much satisfaction that came with finally having the necessary equipment to plow a three-acre patch. It was hard going, as that section had already reverted to a thick sod after a couple of years without tillage. We are uncertain about how we will utilize the section, as we have no planting implements.

We hope to plant an extra-large area with sweet corn to share with family and friends. I also want to try putting in field corn. Unless another method falls in our lap, we'll have to hand pick the corn. One of our traditional fall jobs is to pick up dropped ear corn in the surrounding harvested fields to supplement winter hog feed needs.

Some of my methods such as hand-harvesting hay have caused chagrin from my "conventional" farming neighbors, but we have decided not to be overly concerned about that. We just do the best we can with what we have. Contrary to stories about rural neighborhoods, our experience of neighbors being helpful in this area is rather infrequent. We are thankful to have extended family here, as we trade farming ideas and labor.

A career setback

In my early 40s, I endured a career setback. I went from being a white-collar professional to working as a custodian with a school system. While shedding the unbelievable stress was a relief, the sizable pay cut was hard. We were able to regain health insurance benefits after a scary year of having no coverage.

The practical repair, gardening and food canning skills we had gained through homesteading helped during the financial crunch. The gardening and canning skills belong to my wife, who learned them from her parents. In this day and age of widespread downsizing and layoffs, we urge everyone to stop using high-interest credit cards. Begin an aggressive plan to pay off all debts while incomes are allegedly "up" and times are at least artificially good.

A grim word of warning: Unexpected, forced mid-life job/career changes are almost the norm rather than the exception today. We had started such a plan of debt reduction, but had not gotten as far as we would have liked before my job change. As a result, we experienced much heartache. With God's help and the support of a helpful church family, we survived with our home place intact.

To assist with the financial deficit, we converted a room in the loft of our barn into a living area for our niece. As a result, I needed to change where our usual assortment of feeder pigs (always raised in the winter to minimize odor and flies), three ewes and the egg-laying chicken flock stayed. Due to lack of funds, we had to use native resources.

My son and I spent last fall building a 13' x 22' shed-shaped log barn on a poured cement slab. We moved our animals in before the roof was completely finished. We cut the logs in our woods and ended up with a solid, usable structure which I hope to eventually expand with conventional post barn construction.

The children enjoy country life

Our three children have enjoyed living in the country, and they have learned to love the outdoors. There have been some disadvantages. We live on a gravel road 14 miles from where the kids go to school. They have a 55-minute bus ride, and we incur extra auto expenses driving to school events and music lessons. The degree of interest in farming and homesteading varies among our three children. We don't force the issue.

They have learned many skills by working as a family. Children should be given meaningful work. It is better to work with them rather than sending them off to work alone. My middle son and I have taken on several small roofing jobs during the summer. He has learned valuable skills in the process. I also had him work with me on machinery maintenance. My mechanical skills have never progressed much beyond routine maintenance. However, I have found that frequent oil changes, lubrication and replacing filters goes a long way in lengthening the life of machinery.

A winter water solution

One problem with living in Michigan is having stock water freeze during the winter. I was able to remedy that by installing a ground level one-trough hog waterer. Chickens and sheep also have access to the waterer. It has saved us much trouble, and the animals do much better with a readily available supply of water. It is easy to maintain and runs on 110-volt power. The element and thermostat have only had to be replaced once in 10 years of service. I have also found that building solid alleyways between the stalls to be much preferable to chasing pigs all over an open barn when loading them for the butcher.

No summary of our homesteading effort would be complete without mentioning our faithful collie. He loves following the tractor on woodcutting treks, and he has been a great playmate for our children. Laddie always wants to be right at your side as you step outside to start chores or any other project. He miraculously survived unscathed after being hit and knocked out by a speeding garbage truck.

Long-term goals

Long-term goals include resuming full use of our tillable acreage and finishing a small cold-frame greenhouse to realize my wife's dream of expanding an herb and heirloom plants business. I also hope to expand my sheep flock to 20 or so ewes while improving success in birthing and expanding my knowledge of sheep health practices.

Homesteading doesn't always involve taking the "easy" road, but I recommend it for an improved quality of life and the rewards found in wholesome family living. While goals may never be fully accomplished, there is always room for growth in any situation.

Family album:

This Pilgrim gander is owned by David James, Alabama.

Economical ideas

• Cut aprons in bib shapes from old shower curtains to provide protection when doing jobs that are messy or wet. Sew on ties at the neck and waist.

• Recycle a pump spray container to hold cooking oil. Use it to spray skillets before use with a little oil to keep things from sticking.

• Why spend money on expensive shampoos when you can buy the cheapest and get your hair just as clean? And if you dilute it with water, it'll last even longer.

If you're bothered by static or tangles, beat an egg at slow speed in a mixer and add it to the shampoo. Unflavored gelatin added to shampoo (about one tbsp. per cup) also takes care of unruly hair.

Adding lemon juice or stale beer to shampoo will make dull hair shiny. For fragrance, use your own scent. If you have dry hair, use an oil-base perfume; use an alcohol-base cologne for oily hair.

Country neighbors:

They didn't know they were homesteading!

D.J. Hendrickson
Oklahoma

In raising our four children, we gardened and raised our own meat whenever possible. Homeschooling provided most of the education, and the children always helped us with the care of the garden and animals. We didn't know we were homesteading. We just wanted better food and a better education for our children.

As the kids left home, we bought 20 acres on a lease purchase with $1 down and a balloon payment due later. A binding legal contract was drawn up. We were pleased to find a drilled well and an electric pole. We moved into a small town 15 miles from our land so we could be close enough to work on it.

We desperately wanted to live on our property, but couldn't afford to build. We also didn't want to finance a mobile home. What could we do?

There was a dirty old school bus at a farm auction. It had been used to house goats and a donkey. We joked about the idea of living in a bus. At the end of the auction, we were the proud owners of that bus for $185. On the trip home, towing the bus, the brakes gave out halfway down the steep hill into our valley. Despite that, we managed to get the bus home without mishap.

During this time we had been clearing trees, installing a pump and pressure tank for the well and building a well house and outhouse. The outhouse was just a seat and floor with promises from my husband to add walls "soon." As deer season approached, I demanded walls and a roof. I didn't want to be the first "whitetail" shot that year!

The wasp and mice invasions came a few days after we brought home the bus. Those battles were fought and won. We started cleaning the bus, which had been partially converted into a camper with a stove, sink, cabinet and two tables. The stove didn't work, but I found a good one for $20 at a garage sale. We added an apartment-size refrigerator ($65) and a wood-burning parlor stove. It was installed over one wheel well with plenty of fireboard. The stovepipe went far above the top of the bus.

My antique bed went across the back of the bus. Carpeting, shelves, running water, electricity, a stereo, microwave, cable tv and a phone rounded out the upgrade. I also added a rose border, wreaths, dried flowers, lace curtains, pictures and air conditioning. Some of these things weren't totally necessary, but they did make for a very homey bus.

The property also came with a chicken coop, which we promptly filled with chickens. We have horses, one of which pulls our buggy.

We've lived in the bus for 15 months and found it to be great alternate housing. We would like to build our own cabin, but our jobs keep us away a lot. We'd like to change that soon and hope to add goats, pigs, a milk cow and possibly rabbits.

There is a need to prepare for the year 2000. We hope to be debt-free with a good supply of tools and knowledge. I've had a desire to learn herbal medicine and wild food gathering and preparation. We would also like to learn soap making, hide tanning, canning and food drying.

When living in the country, one must learn to deal with all the wild animals. I've killed seven copperhead snakes. One of them bit my husband, but he did fine. They were all within 50 yards of our front door. There have been many bobcats, skunks, possums, raccoons, spiders and scorpions. Part of this is because we are the only people to live on this property in many years. It is 8-1/2 miles off a paved road at the end of a dead-end road near a river. We love it and hope to never leave.

My advice would be to make the move now if possible, learn all you can, and prepare. Housing can be almost anything that keeps you warm and dry. It's hard work, but this is a wonderful and peaceful life.

Preparing for Y2K? (Yawn.) They're homesteaders!

In Michigan's northwoods, they're always prepared

Deborah Moore
Michigan

With Y2K quickly approaching, food storage will become a dire matter of necessity. Here is how we address it in the woods of the Upper Peninsula.

Food storage is my favorite subject! It feels like I've been doing it all my life. As a young newlywed and mother, I tried my best to give my family the most for the least cost. That often involved buying in bulk and/or on sale and storing what wasn't going to be immediately consumed. Sound familiar? My purpose for food storage now is much more defined—survival.

Does that sound extreme? Not to me. Our winters here in the Upper Peninsula of Michigan are long and snowy. Our snow totals for the past three years were 263, 278 and 186 inches for an average of over 20 feet per winter. We live two miles from the nearest dirt road. That's a lot to plow, so we are snowed in. It's not that big an issue, since neither of us works outside the home. We park the Jeep on the road and snowshoe out to it when we have to go to town.

We have to make sure that we have enough supplies in November to last until May. Granted, there are a few things we bring in, like fresh greens, but we have everything we need. Most of what we keep on hand will last a lot longer than six months. Necessity is how we got started on our intensive food storage plan.

Here are a few things to consider along with suggestions based on our experience.

Inventory

How did I know what to store? I didn't. I guessed the first year, then I took an inventory on Nov. 1. Afterwards, I kept track of everything that was added to the supplies, then I took a second inventory on May 1. That gave me a pretty good idea of what we used over a six-month period. It's simple, and you have to start somewhere.

Date everything. I keep a heavy marker on the shelf closest to where I unload groceries. Just the month and year are needed. It will take a few extra minutes to date those 12 cans of evaporated milk, but you'll know which ones to use first. You can see at a glance what is and isn't being used and what to rotate.

Space

Allocate storage areas for both food and other necessities. Ours is 250 square feet in the basement. We have 12 shelf units, six feet high with five shelves each. Shelves can be removed to provide space for larger items. I also use thin wooden separators to make it easier and more stable for storage of glass canning jars. The very top shelves are used for storing seldom-used items such as canning kettles, food presses, the manual apple corer and cherry pitter, empty jars, blankets and seasonal clothes.

It makes sense to keep the vegetables in one spot, fruits and jams together, with meat and soups in their own place. This also makes taking inventory much easier. It rarely takes more than half an hour to complete either the spring or fall inventories.

Everyone knows what they like and what they want to have on hand, but there is a need for deeper thinking. Knowing we may not get out of the woods for weeks at a time has really helped us realize what is most important for our food storage. I have a penchant for Caesar salads, so I store one tube of anchovy paste per month. We both like turkey, so I buy several when it is on sale and spend the next three days cooking and canning meat and broth.

Flour is stored in a mouse-proof galvanized trash can, double-lined with heavy galvanized trash bags. Even though our basement tends to be damp, we've never had a moisture or bug problem. Sugar is stored in a five-gallon bucket with an airtight Gamma Seal on it. We use Gamma Seals for rice, salt, pasta, dry beans, brown rice and powdered milk. One basket is filled with this year's potatoes. I store garlic in oil-filled jars. The bulbs last for an entire year, and the oil is marvelous to use!

Food storage suggestions

If food storage is new to you, here are some items that you might want to buy in bulk and keep on hand: flour, sugar, salt, yeast, rice, baking soda, dry milk, dry beans, bouillon, oil, shortening, lemon juice, coffee, tea, soups, canned meats, fish and poultry, vegetables, fruits, spices and herbs. How much you store depends on your own situation.

Gardens will become a prime source for food storage and preservation. I keep literally dozens of extra boxes of canning seals (dated, of course) in an airtight box. Jelly wax can be reused, and it saves seals. Allow some space for open pollinated seeds.

We may need to adopt new ways of eating and cooking in the future. You might be able to grow your own wheat and make flour, but where are you going to get vanilla, cinnamon or nutmeg? How about pepper and salt? All of these items except salt were considered to be exotic spices not so long ago, since they came from Asia. Ask yourself what you need to make your favorite dishes or to stay happy, and stock up accordingly.

Since we live off the grid (we have solar), we can everything and don't store food in a freezer, but that's something else you can do. Meat procured in the winter can be stored outside in an animal-safe box.

Personal items

What about the "other things," those often neglected necessities? Are they really necessities? Do you need them, or just want them? It's your attitude towards them that counts.

You might run out of dish soap, bar soap, laundry detergent, tissue, deodorant, shampoo, razor blades, toothpaste, toothbrushes, Vaseline, floss, talc and hand cream, but you'll make do. If you don't want to run out, store enough to have until you learn how to make your own. Make a list of what you really need to have and things you want to have. Figure out the cost and get things on sale. I might buy a dozen deodorants or 20 tubes of toothpaste at once. I incur strange looks from the cashiers, but I don't care.

If you have lamps, how many extra wicks and how much kerosene do you need? Even if you don't use them all, wicks will last a long time, and they make good barter items. Don't forget extra glass globes. What about matches? That's another good barter item.

You'll want to have an extra gasket or two for your wood stove. If you live in a frigid climate, snowshoes and extra rawhide are a must. This is the time to acquire extra thread, fabric, needles and other sewing items. We will be putting in extra sausage and wine making supplies. How about a honing stone? Make a list.

Since our boys are grown, we stockpile for just the two of us. If your homestead includes children, everyone involved should be making a list. It could even be turned into a game for the youngsters.

Medical supplies

It takes us an hour to reach the nearest medical facility even during the summer. Will it be in business in 2002?

Our first and foremost line of medical defense is caution. A bad cut could spell disaster, so we are extra, extra cautious with our physical safety. In the three-plus years we have been homesteading, neither one of us has been sick, and we attribute that to our lack of exposure to people who are sick.

A glimpse of Deborah's food storage area. When you get 20 feet of snow a winter and live two miles from a road, you don't rely on supermarkets to store food for you.

Despite that, there are always emergencies to consider. Here's what we keep on hand for worst case scenarios: A good basic first aid book (read it now, because you won't have the time to do it during a real emergency); Band-Aids, bandages, gauze, gauze pads, tape, elastic and butterfly bandages, lots of aspirin (could be your best barter item), peroxide as a disinfectant, tongue depressors for finger splints, eye wash and cup, a magnifying glass, tweezers and needles for wood splinters, arm sling, cold and allergy pills and cough drops. Don't forget vitamins.

Entertainment

Everyone needs this. A plastic storage box could contain things like pens, pencils, paper, drawing materials, games, cards, dice, a journal (we're in for some interesting times!). Paul is a stained glass artist. He stocks up on glass and other materials before the snow flies. Ever try snowshoeing with a sheet of glass? With what he has now, he could stay busy for a long time. I have enough embroidering floss for many projects.

With solar power-charged batteries, we watch videos for entertainment even though we don't have tv reception. We watch movies from the library and trade videos with our neighbors.

Books

You can never have too many books, both for education and entertainment. How-to books will be very important in coming years. Other topics to consider are medicine, herbal medicine and animal anatomy; wild food and plant identification; and repair manuals for any machinery you have.

A delicate subject

Weapons bother some people, while others couldn't care less. We are basically peaceful people. Our philosophy is live and let live, but leave our stuff alone. We hope that whatever weapons we have will be used only for hunting food, but we know that in the coming years, there may be a need to defend ourselves and our homestead. If you have a gun, have plenty of ammunition, and store it in a dry place.

I guess our own storage system covers much more than food.

"Homesteaders are anti-tech? Nonsense!" says Larry Elliott as he demonstrates his 36-volt DC 12 hp tractor. The 32" tiller works up 400 sq. ft. of sod per charge, or 600-700 sq. ft. of loosened soil. It recharges from the solar array in 7-8 hours. It also has a 42" mower deck.
And in a few weeks, he promises, this tractor will be hydrogen fuel cell powered.

Note the greenhouse frame in the background.

His homestead has everything... almost

Larry Elliott
Oregon

I have been a subscriber for almost 25 years. I have seen some good issues, but July/August and September/October proves that it only gets better. The Y2K stuff and the book sections really got to me. I would not change a word if I had written them myself. You are right on target.

Thoughts on the grid: A couple of weeks ago, I called a cousin who works as a systems engineer for a large East Coast electric utility. I asked him, "Bill, do you think the grid will go down on Jan. 1, 2000?" Without so much as a hem or haw, he said, "Bet on it." As he sat and stewed on who he was telling this to, he backed off by saying "Be some blackouts and maybe some interruptions in service, but I don't expect it to be too bad."

He did volunteer that they felt it was cheaper to let systems go down and fix them as failures occurred rather than try to head them off at the pass. Read between the lines.

To those people who say "If all hell breaks loose, then I'll make a change. What's it take to plant a garden and raise a pig, anyway?" I say it takes a lot more than you think.

Case in point: I transplanted myself to a new area last July. Because I was remodeling the house, building a new shop and setting up the place as my "ideal" homestead, I didn't have time to garden. This year was the first time my garden area was plowed in 30 years. I have gardened for many years and even got myself certified as a Master Gardener by the Extension Service this year.

My garden? Very poor. Little organic matter, and the fertility of the soil is less than optimal. Couple that with our excessively hot weather, and you have poor yields. Enough harvest to can and put away for the winter? Barely enough for one person, let alone a family. Good things don't happen overnight.

A little off the subject. Ever hear of Ted Kaczynski, the Unabomber? I'll bet a lot of readers answer in the affirmative. How about his manifesto? Read it? Probably very few. Well, I just read it. Was it poorly written? Yes! Was it rambling? Yes! Was it boring? Not really.

A lot of what he said sounds like this magazine. He saw many of the shortcomings of our industrial/consumer/materialistic age. He saw how so much of what we take for granted is "anti-human." How our lifestyle is more in tune with the bar scene in Star Wars than it is to the final scene in It's a Wonderful Life where Clarence finally gets his wings.

Ted's problem is that he could whistle the tune, but could never remember the words. He didn't really live the lifestyle. He lived in Never-Never Land and paid the ultimate price. He not only has to live in "their" world now, but he will never live in ours. Reality never knocked on his door. What a waste.

Speaking of reality, every time I get a new Countryside I read the letters and articles from people who say, "If only I had everything necessary to live the lifestyle, I'd be a homesteader." Or "We have been homesteading for a couple of years now, and it's a struggle."

As I read these comments, I think of how truly fortunate I am and then usually end up with more than a little envy of those same writers. Why? I have just about every conceivable "homestead" item you could imagine. I own 12 acres free and clear right off the banks of a river with nothing but farm land, barns, sheep, goats and cattle as my scenic view. No neighbors crowding me now or expected to in the future thanks to Oregon's land use laws.

I don't need the grid, since I have my own large solar array and a large wind turbine. All of this goes into a state-of-the-art inverter that powers the latest in high-tech refrigeration, freezing, clothes washing and even lighting. I have a solar-powered half-ton pickup truck. Even my garden tractor/tiller is solar powered. The freezer is full of beef and chicken, and my old Karr kitchen range complete with dry wood and a well-insulated home should see me through the winter.

So what am I complaining about? The writers to whom I refer speak in terms of we, not I. This is very important and often overlooked. Usually, if not always, the writers are married with at least a couple of kids. They feel disadvantaged? Remember, the community that Jd speaks of when he describes the 2100 era is one of commitment, hard work, community involvement and men and women working together to make a better life for themselves and the next generation.

I don't think he is talking about men still sitting around in their earth bermed homes wishing that the women he meets will not only find homesteading appealing, but will seek out that lifestyle and not consider those who do to be kooks.

I find it ironic that so many women write in and express their desire to live the homestead life. I could count on one hand the number of women I have met who didn't think homesteading was crazy or "just like living in a cave." If you are not willing to lower your standards and are not yet married in the eyes of God, expect to live through the Y2K crisis alone.

I would give up all that I have to meet this elusive female only to be better off afterwards. If I can do this alone, think of what we could do together. I don't mean to get carried away, but this is true. Anyone who is setting off to survive Y2K alone without at least some committed assistance is in for a rough haul.

Several issues back, I had an article that talked about generators, inverters and solar power. I received a ton of letters. Very few had a return envelope, but I answered them all. Most letters asked how they could apply the technology to their needs. Many were excited and ready to commit to this form of power. In almost every case, I replied that this technology would work for them, but it would require them to step outside of the box (Jd's phrase; My favorite is "Imagine the impossible. Then do it.") and make changes in their lifestyle.

I never got so much as a thank-you or reply. Perhaps many dreamed the dream, but few were willing to live up to it.

Preparedness on a budget

Daryl Keech
California

In my job as an ICU nurse, we "hope for the best, but prepare for the worst." This idea is also useful in preparing for unsettled times.

There is potential for at least temporary failure of utility-delivered electrical power. Those who use freezers should consider a backup method. Canning has been in use since Napoleon's time, and it's a good method for fruits, vegetables and meats.

It is prudent to gather the equipment now even if you don't plan to use canning as a primary system. Canning jars, water bath canners and even pressure canners are available at yard sales for a fraction of what they would cost new. I would like to suggest yard sales and thrift stores to keep preparation costs down.

A word of caution: The jars must be free of cracks or chips, and the sealing ring on the pressure canner must be in good shape.

Sealing rings and a good canning book are also reasonable. Unreasonable is having a big freezer full of meats and produce spoil on the third day of the power failure.

If you depend on a public utility for gas or electricity to power your stove, consider purchasing a used gasoline camp stove.

Dehydration is another possible method of preservation. Here in California, we can use sun power for drying even in winter. Window screening in a 1 x 4 frame is positioned in a sunny spot. Some people burn a little sulfur under the tarp-covered frame to preserve color and as a bug control. Frames are brought inside at evening to protect against dew. During a warm Indian summer, the fruit takes on a leathery feel and is ready for storage in jars.

I dry vegetables crisp to be used in soups and stews. I suggest that you avoid drying meat. Smoking is a superior method for preserving meat, and you avoid the risk of spoilage and food poisoning. Jerked meat is palatable and stores well in those mayonnaise jars. Larger cuts can be smoked in a closet-sized box.

(Ed. note: Our consultant in such matters insists that smoking does not preserve meat. Jerky can be made in an oven, without smoking.)

The idea is to introduce relatively cool smoke rather than cooking the meat at higher temperatures. This usually means a separate smudge fire piped into the smoker. I use fruit woods pruned from the orchard or oak from the woodlot. Avoid resinous woods that impart an unpleasant taste.

Some of our friends use a commercial cannery owned by the Mormons. They are canning bulk items such as flour for long storage.

Try this method if you decide to collect supermarket food for storage: If you use three cans of pork and beans in two weeks, next time buy six cans for that same period. You haven't spent much extra, and extended your supply by two weeks. Do the same for other foods and products like toilet paper.

Look for those "loss leaders" to really stock up. Although paying in chunks instead of nibbles might seem difficult, it will cost less in the long run.

We store bulk items like sugar, salt, flour, grains and nuts in five-gallon buckets. We have collected lots of them, and they keep the critters out.

Water storage isn't high on my list of priorities, as I have my own well and independent power. Plastic gallon milk jugs are everywhere for water storage. The type with screw-on tops are best. After thorough cleaning, fill with clean water and eight drops of household bleach. Be sure that the bleach contains hypochlorite as its only active ingredient.

If you've used up all of your potable water, other water should be stirred, strained and treated with 16 drops of bleach per gallon for emergency use, according to a FEMA manual.

Clothing, especially children's, should be considered. They grow so rapidly that seams could be splitting tomorrow. Check thrift shops and garage sales for items that are a size or two larger than needed now. My favorite hiking boots cost only a few dollars at a yard sale.

For transportation, my best suggestion is to cruise yard sales for bicycles. It's not necessary to have a 21-speed mountain bike. Personally, I use three-speeds most often, and that or even a single-speed cruiser is enough for me. A handy person can attach a riding mower cart for transporting bulky items. If it's necessary to park those cars for awhile, think of all the "practical" aerobic exercising. Bet those gym memberships will be way down.

The tractor is considered irreplaceable on our ranch. Enough diesel fuel for a year is stored. Hoses, belts, filters and parts that sometimes break (linkage, pins) are also kept in stock. This is nothing new for most farmers who plan ahead to save on down time. Parts break at the most inconvenient times.

Some would consider their cars irreplaceable. I have to admit that a 20-mile one-way commute would be most difficult for me. One hundred gallons of gas would go a long way towards buffeting that hardship. Those pickup truck storage tanks look like just the thing for home use. They can be filled by five-gallon cans with fuel stabilizer added. By the time that store is exhausted, everyone would be out, and the highways would be safe for bicyclers.

In the event of such a disruption, I suspect that our hurry-up attitude will go by the wayside anyway. Off-the-homestead sweat labor over any significant distance will be impractical. Many jobs will be non-essential and cease to exist. Many salespersons may have nothing to sell and no customers. Some skilled trades will remain in demand. A handyman can be very popular in a time of shortages of new parts. Health care will enter a new era. The emphasis will be on local care rather than the "ship them to the specialty hospital" mentality.

I thank God we decided to move to the rural foothills. With crime as it is in times of relative affluence, I can only imagine how it will blossom in times of real shortages. America today is a long ways from the '30s and '40s in terms of family relations and the work ethic.

Our family preparations include classes in self defense and karate. We have acquired firearms. We also took the time to become proficient with them. Please don't misunderstand me. I'm no Rambo. That is, unless he's a little pudgy, graying, and zeroing in on 50.

We may be entering an era of increasing self-reliance. I would rather be in a position to offer assistance rather than requiring it. One of the guiding principles of our ranching effort is to grow no more than what our family can care for. I remember the year Gov. Pat Brown refused to allow Mexican farm laborers into California for the harvest. His idea was to open up those jobs for unemployed citizens, especially welfare recipients. That was the year the produce rotted in the fields.

There is still time to gather vital items at low cost. If the time comes when those same items are a necessity, the cost will be high, and some things will be unobtainable at any price.

Goat milk butter the simple way

Dorothy Jones
Wyoming

You can make butter out of goat milk, and you don't need a churn. This is how I did it.

Since milk pans are no longer available, I used two shallow kettles, about four inches deep and 14 inches wide. The milk sat in the refrigerator for 72 hours before the cream rose to the top.

I skimmed the cream and beat it with an egg beater for a while. It turned into whipped cream! I beat it another minute or so, and it got thicker. Then I took out the egg beater and stirred it with a spoon. It became grainy. Thin, tiny drops of moisture appeared in the bottom and sides of the bowl. It was buttermilk. I poured it off from time to time and kept pressing the butter against the sides of the bowl to squeeze out the buttermilk. Then I washed the butter with cold water. Goat butter is white and tastes a little like cream cheese.

My goats like to get out of the yard and go someplace different for a walk with me every day. Our outing is the highlight of their day. We walk along the river. The goats trot ahead, looking for willow branches, Russian olive leaves and other things to browse. They remind me of kids on an Easter egg hunt.

Country neighbors:

She just calls it "living"

Yvonne Shilling
Kentucky

I had never really thought of us as homesteaders, but... I don't think I'll ever forget the remark made to me seven and a half years ago: "It sounds like you're going to be homesteading. Good for you!"

I'm sure the look on my face was a reflection of the uncertainty of all the plans our family had at the time. But in the winter of 1989, the principal of Parkway Elementary seemed to have some sort of insight into the "way of life" we were about to journey into. You know, raising your own animals for food, growing a sustaining garden, constructing outbuildings and a cistern, etc. with not a lot of knowledge of any of it.

It wasn't really until we started reading Countryside that I came to realize that maybe we really are what he called homesteaders. I mean, I always thought of homesteaders as courageous ones who loaded up their covered wagons and traveled west to tame the wild frontier. We, after all, had a van, gravel road, and were moving to the southeast only 22 miles away! Homesteaders had to lay claim to the land they wanted, establish a water source and living space, clear land for their animals, garden and crops. They had to contend with the natives. But, as I look back, weren't we doing the very same things they were? We did have established boundaries but had to contend with the "natives" to keep them. We too had to establish a water source, clear land, etc. Hmmm.

We had just moved back to the states from Germany and I wanted desperately to have our own sense of reality and earth to begin to grow strong and healthy roots into. So I called about a tract of land advertised in the paper, made an appointment to look at it, and we found our home. It had been almost devastated by logging the year before, but in our heart's eye we saw the beauty it would hold once it had a chance to recuperate – something I could relate to very strongly at that time.

Our new homesite was without power and water, so we set out building a concrete block cistern in the dead of winter. If it was above freezing we hauled water in 30-gallon plastic trash cans to mortar those blocks. An old mobile home was hauled out and the electric run (it was too necessary to have at the time). All this took place on what was the flattest part of our land, up by the road front in full view of any passerby. And it seemed awful funny at the time that there were so many passing by... there was only one family a quarter of a mile from us on our mile of dead end road. Not many would stop. They'd just drive past real slow, faces to the windows, and sometimes wave. I am quite sure we were a sight to behold!

Anyway, we moved in and are raising chickens for eggs, meat and sometimes to sell, sheep for meat and their wool, pigs, goats and our share of dogs and cats. I dry our clothes on lines outside and inside next to the wood burner when it's raining or snowing. We cut wood for heat. We bale hay by hand using a BCS to cut, the truck to pull the hay rake and a tobacco box resemblance to make the bales (thankfully we only have five acres to bale this way). I make our soap and candles, grind wheat for our bread, spin our sheep's wool to yarn and am learning to weave it. We buy in bulk with a food buying club and we homeschool our two children.

We now have claim to 38 acres that I consider to be my garden. There are wild black raspberries, black cherries and blueberries, paw paw, persimmon, black walnut and most of our medicinals I wildcraft for. And a variety of flowers to enjoy fresh and in dried form year round. I do try to maintain an established vegetable patch, but it generally looks as wild as the rest of the "garden."

We have two really nice springs, one of which now supplies all of our water needs. That cistern has been transformed into a root cellar with our school house built over the top of it. My parents have moved from Ohio and are now our neighbors and business partners. We are starting to do crafts to sell. Our business is named Country Ridge Crafts.

Homesteading, though? I reckon so, but I just call it living.

Lynn Hesselbrock sent this picture of daughters Katie and Emily with this note: "As you can see, the adjustment from city life (as ours was) to country life indeed can be a joyous event." These Pygmy goats are the first livestock on their homestead in Kentucky.

Country neighbors:

A day in the life of a homesteader

The "routine" of homesteading is anything but!

Gilliam Y. Parrish
Oklahoma

I don't know if this Sunday was a typical day on the prairie; some are worse and some are better. But it did prompt me to make this little summary, dedicated to all those folks who, with the best of intentions and no experience, want to get out to a homestead and raise animals, possibly because of John Denver's memorable line "Life on the farm's just kinda laid back..."

Morning: Drive down and get the Sunday paper (the mail box/news box is a goodly jog from the front door). A bit foggy. However, nothing obvious is wrong, and notably our ram Toodles is not running around loose.

A few weeks before, Toodles had gotten out and, strolling up to our front door while we were away, saw the reflected male sheep in the storm door and rammed it. He shattered the glass but that apparently made the reflected ram go away. He didn't keep hitting it, which saved the glass in our main door and may have kept a ram out of our living room. Nevertheless, after spending $150 for repairs, we like to make sure Toodles stays contained.

Wife Vicki goes down to milk the cow; comes back, and reports four of our ducks (a mother and three good-sized babies) are missing. A pack of coyotes has been howling at our back fence at night. Our Great Pyrenees dogs, Candice and Chelsea, normally keep them at bay, but with all the fog, could some have slipped in and...? Vicki also mentioned she hasn't seen one of our cats in days.

I put on my sloppy clothes and head toward the barn, detouring when I arrive to check for new chicks under one of our hens. We had already extracted a dozen chicks, which were currently residing in a warm box in our kitchen and frankly, smelling the place up. Moving the chicks out to the barn is on our list of things to do today, but we never do get around to it. Anyway, after prying the hen off the nest with the handle of a broom (which she pecks quite vigorously), no new chicks appear and I drop the chicken back on the nest.

Vicki notices one of our four geese is down in the pasture. She treated one of them for some sort of infection a while back, and we assume this is the same one. I grab it, and we move it to a cage with some medicated water and grain to eat. Ultimately, it doesn't make it. (The four geese had been sent into the fenced pasture because of their tendency, when running around completely loose, to help themselves to all the chow in the dog feeder. We still have a pesky turkey that pulls the same stunt, although he hasn't come real near the house ever since Vicki caught him there and plucked out a goodly portion of his tail feathers.)

I throw hay and grain to assorted creatures. Some of the smaller fowl are promptly attended to, since they have a tendency to be underfoot and even peck your ankles until they get some grain. I head out to the pasture to check for the lost ducks.

This turns up nothing duck-wise (not even suspicious piles of feathers), but isn't a total loss since it reveals a few places where our strand of electric wire near the bottom of our fence is down. The wire is there to keep the Pyrenees from digging out; the cattle paneling which we installed at great expense around all 12 acres is not enough by itself to accomplish that task. The last time our Pyrenees got out, Candice was hit by an automobile. One large vet bill later (the vet bound her broken leg in a hot pink cast—because she was a girl, of course), we had to keep Candice in a small isolation pen for a couple of months waiting for everything to mend. She's okay now—but we have a strong incentive to keep the electric wire up and functional.

Projects for the morning include building a new pen for some peafowl we are obtaining, and installing a new gate in the cow enclosure so Vicki won't have to keep crawling over the barbed wire twice a day to milk the cow. I am delegated the peafowl enclosure; we decide to simply carve out some of the chicken house yard space for them. The original chicken house yard had been built on one of our "off" days, and had promptly collapsed in a tangle of boards and wire. But our son had just rebuilt it, and just putting in a divider to keep the chickens away from the peafowl is one of the easier (albeit time consuming) tasks of the day. With much of the project completed, we break for lunch.

Afternoon: Following lunch, Vicki calls several friends and spreads the tale of our sad loss of the ducks. I'm still a bit skeptical—lots of animals seem to turn up after a while, although we seldom have a clue where they were hiding—but I must admit I don't know where the ducks are.

Next on the agenda is picking up a couple of feeder pigs. After hooking up the stock trailer and while heading for the gate, Vicki mentions that she'd been reading a book on llamas. We had just gotten two llamas and, so far, they hadn't caused a problem of any kind. But it turns out that many, many different kinds of common plants can make llamas ill, and we needed to do some additional work to police our property to get rid of those plants.

Oh, and we needed to call somebody out to cut down all the oak trees on our 12 acres, since llamas can get sick on the acorns. I groan loudly.

We make it to the breeder's place, and get the pigs without incident. Leaving, my wife inquires if he knows a place to pick up some bales of straw. He knows a place, but at a price per bale we would be reticent to pay even for good hay. The weather hadn't cooperated this year, and hay was fetching top dollar. Straw had apparently followed hay up. We shake our heads and get in the vehicle.

Back at the ranch...

Arriving back, we prepare the pig paneling, which includes dumping over a heavy trough of dirty water.

One diversion occurs when Vicki notices Candice has somehow gotten a long string of baling wire stuck in her tail; when I go to try to remove it, Candice tries to run, and I end up holding on to the wire to stop her. She finally allows us to examine it; there's no way it's going to twist loose, and we end up cutting it out.

Back to final preparations on the pig pen. When time comes to move the baby pigs, I go into the stock trailer and grab a pig by its back legs. This works tolerably well (and doesn't hurt the animal) but as I remove the dangling pig from the trailer, all the dogs try to get into its face to sniff it or— in our other dog Spiro's case, tries to bite it. Spiro isn't a Pyrenees, is less tolerant of the other animals, and has had some bad experiences with pigs.

Much yelling and screaming later, the pigs have been successfully relocated. We head back to the house to wash our hands; we're too dirty to sit.

Evening: In preparation for getting the peafowl, I return to the peafowl enclosure to finish that task. A bit later I am joined by Vicki, who says the peafowl folks are unavailable and we will have to get those creatures another day.

Still down by the peafowl enclosure, I note one of our male goats is lying down on his side. I walk over to him and bend down; he's awake but doesn't move.

We had just lost a baby goat a few weeks before, which I found lying on its side in a puddle, breathing heavily, and which we couldn't revive. This buck doesn't seem to be breathing heavily, but being down on his side isn't a good sign.

I call for Vicki; she advises me to lift him to his feet, which I do. He doesn't seem the worse for wear, but why was he down in the first place? Vicki, quite upset, decides to worm him and forces some wormer down his throat, only to note afterwards that she'd used the wrong wormer. Oops. About all we can do is to feed the poor fellow some Pepto-Bismol (yes, it works for animals too), and hope for the best. We keep an eye on him, and he doesn't seem hurt by that either. (He does, after all, have the stomach of a goat.)

However, when Vicki calls a goat breeder later in the evening, he says that when a goat has gone down on its side like that, it will almost certainly die after a while. Not what we want to hear.

Nevertheless, the goat incident is followed by some good news: the missing ducks come waddling up, as if nothing had happened. Vicki can't make up her mind if she wants to strangle them or hug them; she settles for dropping some grain for them.

I finish the peafowl enclosure while Vicki milks the cow again and pours the raw milk to the pigs; then, we head inside.

Dinner is nachos, because they are easy to fix.

Night: I sleep pretty well, but sometimes it's an accomplishment on the prairie. I recall that Marlon Brando was once reputed to say he couldn't sleep in the country because of all the noise; folks who think the city would be noisier just don't understand the situation. The dogs keep roaring off, barking up a storm; probably the coyotes at the fence again. And the cow keeps mooing. She had been upset a week or two earlier with the "loss" of her calf (we had it butchered; delicious by the way) and had mooed all that night, but had seemed to get over it. I'm not clear what she's mooing about tonight (is she in season?), but it is irritating. At least the guineas aren't throwing a fit.

Morning: As I prepare to go off to my day job, Vicki mentions the missing cat has reappeared. An indication, I hope, of a better day.

The "Saturday night bath routine" on some homesteads is as interesting and fun-filled as the other daily happenings described in the accompanying story. Here, four-year-old Cassie Gamble enjoys an en pleine aire scrub behind the barn. Her parents are Tim and Patty, and they live in New York.

The Nichols' retirement home is a dream come true.

Country neighbors:

Dreams do come true!

Ruth M. Nichols
Florida

Our lives changed drastically four years ago when my husband's mother made it possible for him to acquire 160 acres of land that had been in the family for over 100 years. This has always been my husband's favorite piece of property. Every time we drove past it to visit his parents, he would say "That would be a good spot to build a house." Wetlands cover approximately 70 acres, providing a home and food to alligators, marsh hens, egrets, bald eagles, wood storks, etc. The remaining acreage consists of improved pasture, a two-acre stocked fish pond, and massive oak trees wherever you look. It is located just 20 miles from the place we called our home for almost 30 years.

My husband, Andy (a native Floridian), and I grew up on farms; his father owned a large ranch in Florida and my father sharecropped in Virginia. When we married in 1968, we wanted some acreage but we knew it wasn't within our budget.

I already owned a home situated on an 80' x 150' lot just two miles from the center of a small town in Central Florida. The neighbors' property line came within seven feet on each side of the house, but we decided to live there until we could afford something better.

Years passed and we reared four wonderful children. During that time we often reminisced about our farming days, days when you knew your neighbors' first and last names, days when watching the clock was less important, days when crime was practically unheard of, days when a man's word was his bond, and days when people routinely met at tent revivals and/or community festivals. We longed for the privacy, tranquillity, and spaciousness that we knew as youngsters while growing up in the country. Land prices in this area of Florida kept soaring, but we continued to dream and never lost sight of our goal.

After Andy's mother deeded us the property, the first thing we did was to buy a tent and "camp out" there every weekend. We invited our now adult children and their families and friends to camp with us and they agreed that it was a wonderful place. It offered something for everyone; fishing, canoeing, and long walks, but most importantly for us, an opportunity for our children and grandchildren to experience the tranquillity and sense of well-being that farm life can offer. The fact that we all could commune with nature was an extra blessing. I can't begin to describe how much we love this land we call Big Pond Farm.

I am fortunate in having married a wonderful and talented man. My husband has taught heavy equipment mechanics at our local vocational school for over 18 years. That in itself speaks for his dedication, but that is not what I think makes him remarkable. What makes him remarkable is that he has accomplished this after having survived a terrible motorcycle accident at a young age which resulted in the loss of his right hand and half of his right arm. Doctors had given up any hope of him surviving, yet after months in the hospital, he went on with his life. I met him in 1966 when he was 30 years old and we married two years later. I have yet to find something that he can't do nor have I ever seen him fail to finish a project. He continues to amaze me and others with his ingenuity and creativity.

As a teacher, Andy has the summer months off, so we decided to spend these months at the property mowing, trimming trees, repairing/building fences, building farm sheds, etc. Andy grew up on a ranch so he taught me the ins and outs of fence building, how to handle barbed wire safely, how to drive an old John Deere tractor, and the thousands of other things I needed to know about farming.

When the end of summer came, I announced to my husband that I wasn't going back home. Upon hearing this, he immediately went into action. We gave our large home to our youngest son and he agreed to assume the small mortgage still owed. Next Andy obtained building permits, had electricity put on the property, a well drilled and a septic system installed. Another of our sons is a carpenter and since he was between jobs, we hired him to build a retirement home for us. I worked on the house with him every day and Andy worked most evenings and weekends. It took us one year to finish it but that is another story.

Knowing that we needed something to live in while we built our retirement home, he asked the carpentry shop students at the vocational school to build him an 8' x 12' shed. The shed was completely finished on the outside and had two windows and a large door. We finished the inside of the shed just as you would a regular room, then added a window air conditioner, sleeper sofa, refrigerator, shelving, a kitchen cabinet, and a small microwave. We added an 8' x 8' deck and covered it with an aluminum roof to give us more living space.

Our small cabin had no running water inside. Andy put a water heater outside and we bathed using a shower head hung on an oak tree; the shower was enclosed by a curtain. His mother gave us a huge cast iron sink. We put this outside and connected it to the water. We cooked our meals outside our "cabin" using a propane camping stove which belonged to Andy's father. Our bathroom consisted of a rented portable toilet which, to my way of thinking, is just one step below going behind a tree. I had the same aversion to outhouses when I was a child. Only after the spiders were dispatched could I get on with my business. After living in a four bedroom home for so many years, this was indeed roughing it and it took some getting used to.

Summer nights on the porch of our little "cabin" were only bearable if our bodies were covered in mosquito repellent. Since we had so much water on our property, mosquitoes bred at a rapid pace. When the sun went down, they began to attack. As winter progressed and evening light shortened, we went inside no later than 6:00 p.m. Most of those nights

This pond, stocked with fish, gave Big Pond Farm its name. The windmill aerates the water. The fish died without it.

were spent working on our home, reading, or making plans for the farm. We didn't watch television for three months.

One winter morning my husband and I were sitting on our porch drinking coffee when we spied two bald eagles in the wetlands basin. They obviously had found a snake, rat, or something edible and were enjoying their meal. My husband and I smiled as we watched these magnificent birds eating. This was far more pleasant than our mornings in that subdivision for all those years.

Andy and I knew the property taxes on 160 acres would be enormous unless we qualified for an agricultural tax exemption. With this knowledge, we planted 2,000 pine trees, not only to act as a buffer for the Interstate 75 traffic on one side of our property, but to later produce an income and to qualify for the tax exemption.

Now, I don't want COUNTRYSIDE readers to get the wrong impression. We are not wealthy people and when I say we planted 2,000 trees, I mean Andy and I did the work. We do all the work on our farm, with only the occasional helping hand from family or friends. We are homesteaders who think there is a world of difference between hiring it done and doing it yourself. We think if you know what is involved in getting it done, you appreciate it more.

We acquired seven sows and a boar to raise hogs for market and our family. A bread store sold us day-old bread for $8 per pickup load. We also bought commercially produced feed by the ton and stored it in 50-gallon drums.

The hogs quickly multiplied. For months the hogs stayed where they belonged, but eventually found a way out of their enclosure. Andy had chased hogs in his youth and detested that job. Not being a particularly religious man, I'm sure his cursing our hogs didn't help his case any. When we could afford to put up more field fencing and hog pens, they were finally contained.

All the hogs were sold within two years because we couldn't make a profit. I now believe that corn in Florida brings a much higher price than say in Iowa.

Around the same time, we also bought a herd of goats and let them range free on the property. Their upkeep was not expensive and they helped keep the grass and weeds under control. We had to sell them too after realizing what the coyotes were doing: one for you and one for me.

I raised chickens for a time, which provided my family and customers with fresh brown eggs. It didn't take long for us to see that red-tailed hawks will take up residence, and

The farm entrance is attractively well-marked.

prosper, whenever chicken is on the menu. They, together with the foxes and bobcats, eventually put me out of the egg business.

We still wanted our land to produce some income, but what now? After we got rid of our goats, there was nothing to eat grass so we had to start mowing again. Not only was it quite expensive and time-consuming, but by the time I finished, I had to start all over again.

We found the solution! As we could afford it, we bought cattle, one or two at a time, from reliable sources. We didn't feel comfortable buying at the market just yet. We built cross fencing, installed waterers where needed, built cattle pens and feeding sheds.

At this time we own 20 head including Tux, our bull. All our cattle are named and are so gentle we have only to wave a feed bucket in front of them to pen them for working. They now mow the grass and we realize a handsome profit from the calves. This is definitely the route we will continue.

I just recently got first-hand experience in pulling a calf. I called Andy at work to ask him to come home and help me, but the calf was born just before he arrived. I felt so proud one would have thought I had given birth, not the cow. Every day brings new challenges and life is never dull for a stay-at-home granny.

We have only one other animal in addition to our cattle, but we consider her part of the family. Bessie, our two-year-old dog, is a Catahoula Leopard and German Shepherd mix. Intelligent, loyal, and a great guard dog, she protects our cattle and pretends she knows how to work them. She swims in our fish pond and since the occasional alligator leaves the wetlands to enter the fish pond, we never know if or when Bessie will become gator food. She doesn't know she's living dangerously.

This 8' x 12' shed—built by Andy's vocational school carpentry students—was "home" while the main house was being built. After living in a four-bedroom home for almost 30 years, this took some getting used to!

To oxygenate our fish pond, we installed an aerator. It was beautiful and did a great job, but it cost us $90 to run it for one month. We disconnected it.

Well, Florida heat is severe and our fish began to die. We lost a total of 140 fish, mostly large bass.

Andy's father had purchased several Aermotor windmills 50 years before, one of which was still on Andy's cousin's property across the road from us. Andy and our three sons brought the windmill to our place, repaired and replaced parts, and erected it on the upper side of our fish pond. The windmill pumps water from the pond and sprays it back in. I'm happy to report, no more fish kills. People often stop and take photos of the windmill in action. I guess the working ones are becoming a rarity these days.

Andy and I lived in that little shed for one full year while our house was being built. I even prepared traditional Thanksgiving and Christmas Eve dinners for my large family while living there.

We wouldn't recommend such cramped quarters to others unless you and your spouse have a great relationship, pioneer spirits, and can laugh easily with each other. If we could live that year over, neither of us would change one thing. It was a wonderful experience, a once-in-a-lifetime journey, despite all the hard physical labor involved, the daily emergencies, and our small budget. We gained a little more self-reliance, serenity, tenacity, and a proud yet humble feeling from that experience.

Andy and I have coffee every morning now on the porch of our retirement home. Me in my porch swing, he in his rocking chair, together we survey our kingdom. Our land and house are completely paid for and we are extremely happy and thankful.

We have only one regret and that is that we couldn't make the "move" years ago. We believe that you can overcome any obstacle and grow even stronger for having done it. Yes, dreams do come true!

An invitation to South Dakota

D. L. Flyger
South Dakota

Over the years a few Countrysiders have written to me after reading some of the articles I've contributed, wondering what South Dakota is like.

I have often wondered why more homesteaders don't choose South Dakota. Our state is not very populated and if the truth be known, we are not anxious to have riff-raff move in. But Countryside readers for the most part are fine people and we could use a few more fine people.

I don't know what people envision when they think of South Dakota. My people have lived here since the 1860s so they were the real, true homesteaders. I went to college in a southern state and found that most people have no idea where South Dakota is even located. (For those of you who are in that category, we are just south of North Dakota!)

For a good description of South Dakota, one needs only to read Laura Ingalls Wilder's books. Five of them have South Dakota as their setting. I am afraid things have not changed drastically since then.

For the most part South Dakota is prairie or farmland. There are not a lot of trees, but contrary to popular belief, trees do grow here. We just do not have natural forests as some places do, except for the Black Hills area.

Also contrary to popular belief, South Dakota is not as flat as a table. Some areas are, but the state for the most part is gently rolling and the Black Hills are really not hills but mountains.

Our state is divided into two basic regions which we refer to as West River and East River, as the Missouri River divides the state in half from north to south. The West River area is semi-arid, short grass prairie suited to ranching. The eastern part of the state contains some very good farm land and gets more precipitation. The very eastern third of the state is not that different from Minnesota and Iowa.

Some people have joked that our climate is like Siberia, but that is far from the truth. We do have hot summers. But the humidity is not terribly high, making the warm weather bearable. Winters can be something else. We like to complain about our winters, but there are places that have worse weather, such as northern Minnesota, and we probably all secretly are a little proud about what the rest of the world thinks our weather is like.

There are numerous abandoned farmsteads in the state, as the population was much bigger in the 1930s than it is today. Farms continue to grow larger as young people head for the cities and older farmers retire to town. Many of these retiring farmers would be happy to sell their farms to families who would be willing to live in the buildings. Some are even happy just to rent the buildings out.

Six years ago we purchased a 16 acre farm site for $5,000. For our money we got an old run-down barn, two nice garages, several small brooder houses, a hog house in fair shape, and a good poultry house as well as a small house, orchard, and a large grove of trees. The place adjoins a small lake and is located along a good highway.

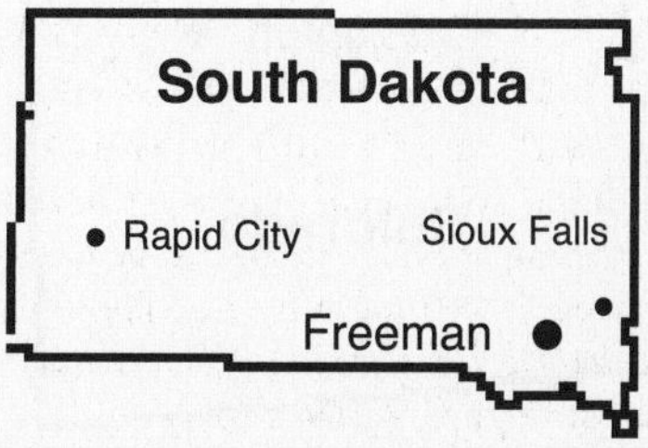

The one drawback is that the well on the property is very deep; around five hundred feet, which makes it by far the deepest well in these parts. There is another well on the place which was not in use that is only 45 feet deep. It was known to run out of water in dry years when the previous owner had a lot of cattle to water, but I think it would do for a homesteader with just a few head of stock.

The home schooling laws in South Dakota are among the finest in the nation. We also have open enrollment in our public schools. We also still have one-room schools in our state. I have taught in one for the last 14 years.

Jobs in rural areas are not terribly plentiful and anyone can tell you that our wages are about the lowest in the nation. Yet our cost of living is not as high as some places. There are currently many job openings of all kinds in Sioux Falls, our largest city, which is just a little under an hour's drive from here.

Many people are moving out of Sioux Falls to small country places. My folks live on my grandparents' farm, which is about a half hour drive from Sioux Falls, and the price for an acreage there has skyrocketed. The farm yard next to them recently sold for $60,000. It did have good water, about seven acres, a nice grove of trees and a beautiful set of buildings and a house.

There is plenty of wildlife here for those who enjoy hunting and trapping. And our many lakes and rivers provide a fisherman's paradise.

Living in South Dakota is not for everyone. Even Laura Ingalls Wilder left here to go to the Ozarks. But then our ancestors left the Ozarks to come here.

If you suffer from *The Little House on the Prairie* syndrome it might be worth a look-see. Every time I think the grass is greener on the other side of the fence I am reminded of our Old Order Amish friends from Ohio who visit South Dakota twice a year and spend a week each visit. They say South Dakota is "old fashioned" and they "like to come here for the peace and quiet!"

Country neighbors:

Successful gardening takes more effort in Colorado

R. F. Whelan
Colorado

Most of my effort at this homestead has shifted away from critter husbandry and toward energy use minimization and veggie-based food self-reliance. Critters are out until I choose to stop taking multi-week vacations, or some mutually acceptable neighbor-based back-scratching barter presents itself.

Free to travel

At present, for me, one aspect of independence and self-reliance—that part away from the homestead—means the ability to go where I want to go, when I'd like to, for as long as I can afford to. Mostly that means car/foot camping-based travel within the western U.S., sometimes alone, sometimes dragging a thought-provoking expensive engineless glider behind to indulge in a hobby of little apparent socially constructive value. (But on the other hand, I've gotten really, really good at predicting and judging weather! Maybe picnic consultation is a moneymaker...)

At the homestead, most effort goes into maintaining my investment (keeping a good roof overhead, etc.), upgrading where desired (converting a leaky screened porch of little practical use into a sunroom/greenhouse), and gardening.

In these parts, unlike most areas east of the 100th meridian, you don't just throw seeds on the ground and step back hastily to avoid getting hit by plants. So even if you're directly lazy, as am I, successful gardening takes a certain amount of effort. More than in Maryland, in my experience.

Last summer for example—if you go by averages—there was sufficient moisture since mid-May to suggest supplemental watering might not have been necessary.

Averages lie: the six weeks of dusty hot and dry between mid-June and the end of July made even native ground covers go dormant. The monsoon-based frog-stranglers afterward made national news. Both entirely typical. You don't successfully garden out here without some ongoing direct attention.

Since all my water is paid for—as opposed to from a well—cost, soil, and semiaridity (about 13" of annual moisture) serve as "figure out how to use as little water as possible" motivators. Each year I experiment with different veggies and different watering techniques (including not watering). Experimentation is part of the fun.

Sunken wide rows

My soil is mostly river sand (which I'd rather have than the more common clay hereabouts), not on a flood plain. Though quite fertile, it dries out appallingly quickly from germination and timing-critical sustenance perspectives. For row crops I currently favor combining use of sunken wide row (I can flood saturate the root zones prior to vacating the place) and black soaker hoses (for germination and labor-minimal on-site attention). The sunken rows are also helpful for capturing what natural moisture does fall. Mulch is another useful water-stretching tool. Raised beds here in my soil aren't necessary and might well be counter-productive, not to mention more work.

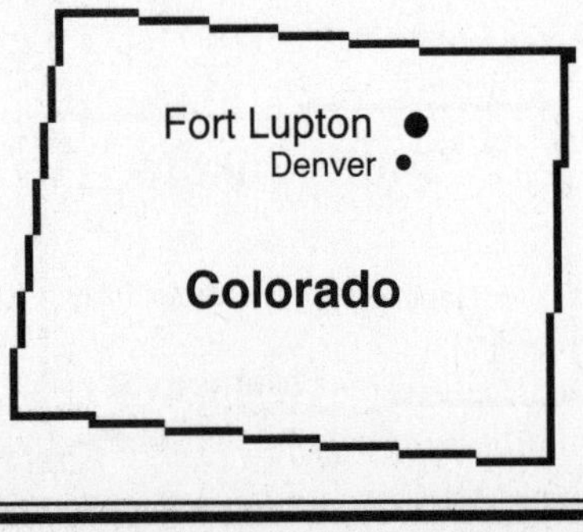

For creepie-crawlie plants (melons, etc.) mulch and inverted milk jugs work pretty well. Obviously the "bigger milk jug' concept extends itself to however long an absence one might choose to make. Because I use a tiller (a nice, red, rear-tine jobbie which works as advertised) for seed-bed prep and some ongoing weed maintenance, I don't use water-retaining devices such as sunken tires around plantings. They'd no doubt help...if I chose to make that particular labor tradeoff.

Pest control

So far, insect pests (mostly Colorado potato beetles, squash vine borers and tomato hornworms) have been acceptably controlled by a combination of planting timing, hand picking, and crop rotation. Learning the life cycles of these critters really helps minimize garden losses...not to mention personal effort! For planning purposes, I do expect to lose some of each crop to mother nature's other critters.

Incidentally, I "maintain" a nearby weed patch (dry pond) which grasshoppers (even in a "good year" the west has a veritable host of these buggers!) seem to prefer over the garden.

You also don't garden out here without a genuine appreciation for whatever bounty happens to do well each year... assuming you don't lose everything to hail.

So my canning skills, and "freezerable" and "how best to store" knowledge have grown each year to the point where store-bought veggies have gone from the "necessary" to the "why not?" category. It proved relatively easy to become "boughten-independent" in cucumbers/pickles, summer and winter squash, Jerusalem artichokes, radishes, tomatoes, potatoes, bok choi and string beans.

So far, depending mostly on how the "Mmmm...tastes good; think I'll use this regularly," and long-term storage aspects went, each year another veggie gets new seed-saving attention.

For the past two years home-grown garden veggies have been used year-round. Anymore, only mushrooms and an occasional bag of frozen broccoli remain store-bought. (Broccoli grows great out here, but I'm squeamish about those fiendishly camouflaged cabbage caterpillars which become visible only on the fork!)

As noted, all vegetarianism tendencies flow not from religious or animal rights reasons, but for reasons of laziness (oriental style veggie/pasta dishes are really quick to prepare, not to mention good tasting... learned a lot in three months on a job in Singapore), and cost irritability. Also, at present, freezer space is limited...though thanks to COUNTRYSIDE I can now easily see myself making the transition to a chest-style freezer using home-grown critter meat if/when travel habits change.

For some years now, store food-runs have been to purchase staples (rice, noodles, flour, cereals), dairy products (skim milk and eggs mostly), and the odd spice. Hating to shop, batch-buying was a habit entered into even when living within walking distance of grocery stores; presently the nearest pizza joint is 14 miles distant.

The bread machine stays

In the same vein of lazy self-sufficiency, perhaps the finest blend of old and new technologies I've come across so far is a bread machine. I wouldn't sell mine until your offer price exceeded its value and the nuisance value of having to go and

get a new one by a truly significant amount! Having made many a brick both by hand and in the machine, there's something to be said for having a machine do the work...at your convenience!

Survival of the fittest

The other day I was picking sand-cherries for my first stab at jam (came out runny, but eminently usable); this was about a week after polishing off the last of my first-ever plums (Green Sage—self-fruitful, yummy!). It dawned on me my Darwinistic tree and shrub planting efforts have had a measurable effect. Some 50 new trees remain alive (perhaps the same quantity don't!), all without supplemental watering beyond their first summer. (Eleven total were here when I moved in. My annual live-stock order has leaves and a hyphen rather than fur.) This ignores various shrubs and vines. No luck with kiwis, but two kinds of grapes are now bearing.

Mint jelly is in the works in the next week or so. With some Spring luck, next year might be a peach and apricot year, and maybe even an apple year. (The trees are still youngish. The cider mill awaits the apples' first coming...) I now usually get a few raspberries each summer to tease the palate, too.

While I'm a long way from being self-sufficient in food—don't ever plan or expect to attain it—meals are a lot more satisfying, not to mention tasty—than they would be if I got everything from the store. Also, I'd rather spend the time here dinking in the dirt than running errands in the car.

Lawns are out

In a similar theme, lawns are out. A longer term goal is to end up with a totally maintenance-free yard. Low-growing native grasses fit the bill; prairie, if you will. (That's what it was before white farmers.) Presently, expanding prairie patches exist amongst various lethal weeds (goathead and sand burrs), hanger-on annual weeds, annual grasses, and tolerated tall-growing cool-season grasses. I'm no horticulturist, but there are over a dozen different kinds of grasses pre-existing on the acre; there might even be some of the head-shaking (in the west!) eastern bluegrass.

A fearsome tire-eating patch of goatheads (looked like a healthy growth of crownvetch!) is finally yielding to napalm strikes (propane torch) after no success with blind hope, plastic sheet sterilization, and agent orange (chemicals). Sand burr control is down to time-minimal selective uprooting around the yard's perimeter. Undesired annuals are yielding to pre-seed setting mowing; similarly, desired annuals are encouraged by mow-timing. Presently, it won't win any *Better Homes & Gardens* awards, but it wouldn't catch the attention of most lawn-loving, buttinsky suburban ordinances, either.

So what's a homesteader to do with all the free time made available by not mowing every week, not having to set garden water, and not taking care of critters? For starters, I've climbed all the trees in the yard big enough to climb...

I don't know if I'm getting old, tolerant, or just lazy, but I let one of my editorial pet peeves slip through in this issue.

I hate the word "veggies." But so many people use it these days... what the heck.

(In case you're wondering, other word peeves include "baby" chicks—or calves or puppies—and "hot water heater." If it's not a baby, it's not a chick [or calf or puppy] either! And why in the world would you want to heat hot water?)

On store-bought broccoli: I can't help but wonder why the store-bought stuff does not have worms. What did they put on it to get rid of them? I can float the worms off with a good soaking in salt water, but nothing's going to get rid of the poisons on those "veggies."

Country neighbors:

Minnesota homestead odyssey—and no regrets

Cinderella Fay
Minnesota

You can get out of the city if you really want to, even if you don't have much money. Remember though—you'll have even less money when you get where you're going, so be sure you're willing to learn to live without it.

Six years ago we lived in Norfolk, Virginia: me, my husband Brian, and our eight children (ages one to 12.) We decided we wanted to be in the country. The plan was to save up enough money to buy some land.

We didn't do anything especially clever to save money. We shut off the air conditioner and learned to sweat comfortably. We ate less expensive food (rice and beans, casseroles, etc.) We stopped eating out and taking vacations. We shopped at thrift stores for clothes and household items. We canceled our health insurance. I realize that may not be a wise choice for everyone but we figured we could pay a hospital (if we ever need to) monthly payments as well as we could an insurance company, and then at least we would have actually incurred the charges.

We both had 401K plans where we worked and had the maximum taken out of our paychecks. This was probably pretty stupid, since there was a 10% early withdrawal penalty, but we didn't know that at the time. Then again, we never saw the money, so we didn't spend it either. We did open a savings account at the bank as well, and socked away anything else we could.

When we did spend money, it was on supplies for the move. We went to

flea markets, collecting tools, mason jars, big kettles, etc. We bought a 36' x 16' army tent for $50. We also bought two new chain saws on sale. (They turned out to be a waste of money. They were cheap ones and didn't last six months. If you're going to buy a chain saw, buy a good one. We have a Jonserud now.)

Every time I went grocery shopping I bought extra canned goods and packed them away in boxes in the garage. The same went for bandaids, shampoo, bug spray, toothpaste, toilet paper, etc. By the time we moved, three years later, we had quite a cache.

We began our land search in northern Minnesota. After the first year of saving we went there and looked at a few places. The property we wanted was 38 acres, all wooded. The cost was $13,000. We didn't even have half that much, but were able to put a down payment on the land and pay off the rest at 9% interest. We took some pictures and had them enlarged to 8 x 10s, which we posted at home and on our desks at work. For the next two years we made our land payments and put every other dime we could in the bank.

Once the land was paid for we had rummage sales and sold pretty much everything we owned outside of what clothes we absolutely needed and our move supplies. We did keep the mattresses off the beds so we'd have something to sleep on in the tent. We gave our notices at work and paid off outstanding bills. Between our 401Ks, what we'd saved the last three years and what we made off rummage sales, that left us with about $10,000.

We rented a big U-haul to make the 2,000 mile journey. That cost about $800. I drove our old pickup and managed to fit five of the kids in there with me. (It had a 1/2 crew cab.) The back was full of rabbits we had been raising for meat in the city. (Incidentally, we had to go to court over that about a week before we left Norfolk. We were fined for keeping more than one rabbit within city limits. You can have up to five dogs though. Go figure!) Brian drove the U-haul with the other three kids. It was crowded, hot and nerve racking.

When we got to southern Minnesota we stopped at my brother's house. He had found us a tractor ($1,200 International Super H). We arranged to have that trucked up to our land, 400-plus miles north. That was another $200.

When we finally arrived at Pitt, Minnesota and parked on our property, we had one day to unload and return the U-haul. All of our belongings were literally dumped in the middle of the woods in a little clearing. We camped that night and started cutting poles for the big tent. It ended up taking three days to secure the tent properly (actually improperly is more like it but when we got done it was solid at least.) As we got the last bit of our stuff moved in the thunderstorm started. We found out where all the leaks were right away!

The first things we did were build an outhouse, have a well drilled, and start a pole building. That pretty much did in the rest of our savings. Good thing we brought all those groceries.

We were in the tent from May 15th to October 22nd. The pole building still did not have a floor or insulation but it had real walls and a little more space (28' x 60'). It snowed October 23rd. I knew it was snowing because that is what woke me up—snowflakes blowing in through the cracks in the tin walls and landing on my face.

Three years later, we are still in our pole barn, with many improvements. The logs for our house are cut and peeled. We cleared the house site, brought in fill and collected field stone from farmers' rock piles. This past week we finished the cornerstones and are beginning to put up the foundation walls.

We have chickens, pigs, two milk goats and our rabbits. We built a barn from lumber we salvaged by tearing down an old house for someone. (That was a really big, dirty job and I wouldn't want to do it again if I didn't have to.) We have an acre garden cleared and producing nicely. Our soil is sandy so we are gradually building it up with compost and manure. Brian put in the beginnings of an orchard last spring.

I waitress in town 10 miles from here and Brian drives school bus during fall and winter, which leaves him summers free to work at home. We manage fine. It's hard work and I'd be lying if I said we haven't had some really miserable experiences. Winters here can be tough. Forty-below isn't unusual. Don't laugh, but our first winter here all we used was a Ben Franklin fireplace.

We still have a long way to go but are meeting our goals steadily. When we moved here I had a little money and no patience. Now I have no money and a little patience—and no regrets!

Country neighbors:

They quit the rat race, cold turkey

LARRY & SUSIE WRIGHT
MISSOURI

I would like to relate our experience of moving from the rat race and big city to the country. It's been almost three years since we moved, but feel that it was only yesterday.

I was an operations manager in Erie, Pennsylvania, working seven days a week—a salaried position with no extra pay for overtime, at least 10 hours a day, with almost no days off. I had just put in 93 hours for the week when I was informed that I was to make a truck delivery to Cleveland, Ohio. (This was the weekend off I had worked so long and hard for.)

I just handed in my keys and left…knowing not where, or what I would be doing.

To make a very long story short, we bought a house and property, sight unseen, in Buffalo, Missouri. (We even got a loan over the telephone.)

After six months, we finally sold our house in Pennsylvania. We were overjoyed at the transaction, since we were at the point of losing the house and starving.

This was only the beginning. The transaction was blocked because there wasn't a death certificate for the previous owner. We had paid to have this searched when we bought the house, and we finally made it clear that since this was the same lawyer that should have searched it before, the transaction was cleared to sign.

We had to vacate at closing so we were almost fully packed. We had ordered a 25-foot truck, which I called weekly to confirm. It turned out to be a 20-foot truck. We had to leave prized possessions behind.

After all the delays, we finally got on the road. Since Erie is the utmost

Guts like this aren't a requirement

The stories on these two pages are the kind that give some readers the wrong idea. To fend off the protests of those who think it's madness to buy a house, sight unseen—and in a town you have never even visited!—as well as to warn those who think this is the way all homesteaders do it, here are some notes:

We, personally, would never even consider such a move. But on the other hand, neither would we bother to investigate dozens of places with hundred-point checklists, the way some people do. We prefer a happy medium. (We have never seen the place that is ideal in every respect, or that remains so after you live there awhile. Perfection is nice, but adaptability is better.)

Likewise, COUNTRYSIDE is by no means suggesting that these correspondents' experiences are either recommended or typical.

However, homesteaders are individuals, each with their own ideas and ideals. We're always ready to report on what these real people are doing in the real world… especially when their stories have happy endings like these do.

part of Pennsylvania, we had snow... lots and lots of thick white stuff. The first day we traveled 30 miles in four hours on Interstate 90 west. On the third day we arrived in Buffalo, Missouri, a town we had never seen. A quiet place...homey...right in the Ozarks... just like Mayberry. A good night's sleep was in order.

The next day we signed the papers and had immediate possession of the property and house (which we still hadn't seen.)

Three days later we still weren't in our house. We were camping out in our van in the driveway.

The people finally moved out and left behind the "leavings" of cats and dogs in every room, "fist" holes in the ceiling, dried food everywhere and an infestation of fleas that would kill horses. We ended up "camping" in the yard some more until we could burn the carpets, clean the house, and set off "bug bombs." The first night we did spend in the house, we had every cup, saucer, bowl, pot and pan scattered about to catch the "running" (not dripping) rain.

Three years later, we are still here, with major improvements.

There has been a major "invasion" of newcomers to the area because of the great Ozark country and the so-called cheap rates. However, we were shocked to find that the tax code taxes the chickens, ducks, and animals, as well as anything else you own. We were targeted when, after being here a year, our house and property value doubled. (We protested and won.)

There are jobs an hour or so away, but industry here in Buffalo is frowned upon because it would be in competition with the farmers. I took a job paying one-half of what I was making in Erie, but with less stress, more time and freedom, and taking one day at a time and loving it.

The neighbors will do anything for you. One asked if it was okay to plow my driveway... no charge. He does it for everyone on the road. He told me that if I ever needed any tools to ask him... if he didn't have it, he would get it for me.

We are doing very well after downsizing to the country.

We still miss the things of the big city, some of the simple things people in the big city take for granted... such as private phones. Some people in the area have been promised private lines for more than 10 years and are still on party lines. We totally miss the convenience of the different stores, especially grocery stores and the competition which results in the low-priced specials. After being an operations manager and now a custodian, it is mighty hard to take it when people tell me you can't change it... it's been like that for years.

My wife and I believe that the time is near for an economic breakdown for many reasons and we have been trying to prepare ourselves for the last three years. If you don't have it to begin with and you survive on almost nothing, then when something happens we think we have a fighting chance. We have downsized, but we're living better now—and loving it.

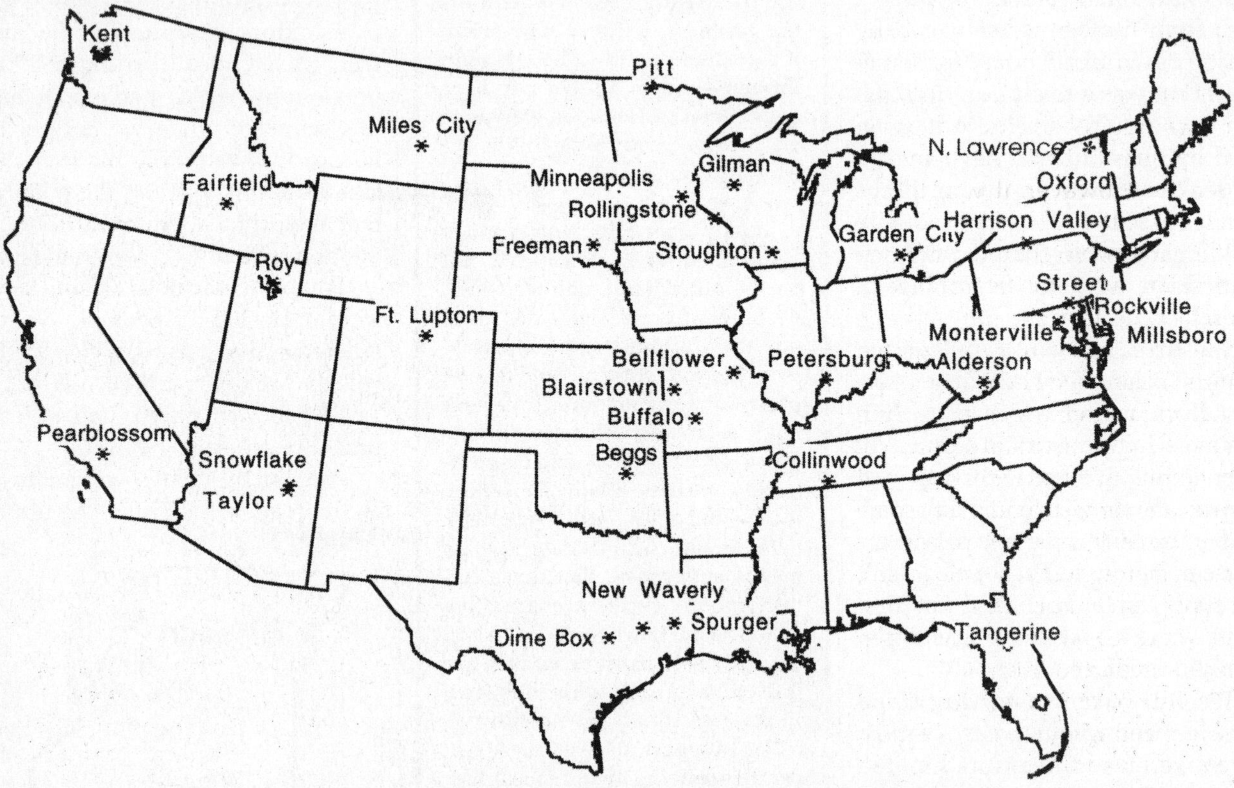

These are some of the places our correspondents are writing from.

Whatever works for you

MAGDA & PETR LISKA
MARYLAND

What a wonderful issue! As always, Countryside writers seem to discuss and reflect on exactly what I am wrestling with at any particular time in my life. The November/December Question of the Month made me realize several very important things:

Everyone seems to be finding their own way of getting started. No magic formulas, no instructions on the box, just whatever works for you! So my way must be okay after all. As impatient as I have been feeling lately, this is still the right way for us.

Let me backtrack.

We first saw our land on Earth Day, April 21, 1990, and we closed on it by June of 1990. We named it Eco Acres. However, it was not as simple as that.

We had searched for four years. At first we went to Realtors, with virtually no money and only a vague feeling that "we want to live in the country." Later, we had just enough for a down payment, plus more accurate knowledge of what we wanted. (When looking at land we had learned about many things: flood plains, covenants, taxes, surveying, perc tests, septic systems, wells, water tables, soil types, on and on…and not least of all, we discovered our own likes, dislikes, needs and dreams.)

Finally, we ran an ad, describing ourselves and what we were looking for. We received three responses, all of them on target!

We put a deposit on 25 acres. (We had originally thought we couldn't possibly get more than two. We talked the owner of an 80-acre tract into carving out 25 for us.) Six acres were fields, the balance wooded, although a five-acre corner was being logged at the time. The owner financed us with a 10-year loan and we made sure that the monthly payments were low enough to manage under almost any job situation. We scrimped and paid it off in three years!

Wouldn't you know it: just when I thought we had reached the point where I could leave my very stressful city job and our extremely rundown rental house (complete with slumlord), the adjoining 19 acres came up for sale. Hmm. Okay, stay longer at the city job, take a five-year loan.

This time we paid it off in two years, but we had to sell three acres with road frontage and a big old tobacco barn in order to get a jumpstart on our payments.

In retrospect, had I actually considered moving onto raw land, with no structure at all? What was I thinking? That would have been a recipe for failure.

By the time we were debt-free on the land we had also managed the following:

The 12' x 18' weekend cabin was built (took us 36 weekends, made out of recycled materials except for the roofing materials and nails); the orchard was planted; and we had built a garden shed, storage shed and a tractor shed. We put up two solar panels (currently used to run a fan in the cabin in the summer), and planted the decorative herb

Petr's pride in his shiny IH Farmall Cub is evident, and justified!

This is the view from the cabin window. Note the solar panels at the bottom left of the top center pane.

and flower garden which flourishes around the cabin (where originally there was only bare hard-packed earth left by the logger's equipment). There are raised beds with a wide variety of vegetables, strawberries, two 25-foot-long rows of asparagus, another "middle" garden for the tomatoes, green peppers, hot peppers, beans…and then the "farthest" garden for potatoes, corn, peanuts, tobacco, and the big vine stuff like squash, melons, gourds and even more beans.

We traded the use of our upper pasture as grazing for the neighbor's cows in exchange for some great sturdy fencing. (They even installed it and showed us how to do it in the future). Bonus: the farmer now keeps an eye on our property (and his cows) when we are not there.

The same farmer, now a wonderful friend, helped us locate and pur-chase an old tractor. It's an International Farmall Cub, manufactured by the company he used to work for in the 1940s. He helped us search one in good condition, and taught us about maintenance, even helping us to restore it. (Cosmetically—after all, it's an antique!)

We've built a pond, a joint project with the same farmer and a bordering neighbor. It is 90' x 180'. (This could be a whole story in itself.) We thought it would be such a simple project. Two years and one dam burst later, it was finally finished last fall. It looks great and should last my lifetime anyway.

We bought a Hydro Ram from Lehman's non-electric catalog and we are ready to set it up so we can get running water up to our gardens. We are currently using rain water collected in barrels and also in those "Rubbermaid" 100-gallon livestock troughs. They're made of fiberglass, and when they cracked they were thrown out by the "horsey-set" (wealthy folks back in the exclusive parts of suburbia). We used a simple fiberglass repair kit available at any auto parts store (about $10) and fixed and recycled them. One has even been sunken into the ground to make a lovely lily pond, which frogs just love and my dogs find a convenient watering hole! So far those repairs have lasted over three years.

So why haven't we made the move? Because we allowed ourselves to get sidetracked. Since we continue preparing and working hard towards the eventual move, I realize that isn't necessarily as bad as it feels.

One reason is because Eco Acres is 3-1/2 hours from where we currently live, which is near our elderly parents (one of whom has fairly serious health problems). It is our moral duty to be available to help the family in an emergency. Reality check: if we make the move now and become intentionally poor as a result, what if we don't have the money for transportation back and forth if a parent is hospitalized (currently a distinct possibility)?

Reason (excuse) number two is, we found a great buy on an older home, one block away from where we were renting in the suburbs of Washington, D.C., three miles from my job. I found it while walking the dog. The sign had just gone up. A 45-year-old house, the original owners had been retired and living on their dream homestead for three years already. It is a big mortgage compared to the very low rent we were paying, but the house was a bargain, no question. I question the wisdom of making the purchase, but it seemed like the right thing to do at the time. Getting into this house for practically no money down (as first-time home buyers), having reduced taxes because of the interest payments, and having the wood stove cranking in the sun room in winter, all make me feel like it was worth it, for a while.

That "while" leads me to another reason: my husband's career as an artist is finally starting to look promising, and being close to the city seems necessary for continuing the successful establishing of his contacts and sales. We figure that once his career is firmly launched, his actual studio could be anywhere!

Finally, even though my job is super stressful, there is some comfort in the good salary, the necessary evil of having good health insurance and the ability to save some now for retirement, while I still can.

I guess what all this boils down to is the fact that we are not ready yet and I have to face it. I'm a firm believer that things always work out for the best. I'm still relatively young (44) and my husband is 47. Looking back, I would have liked to have started when I was 18 (think of the energy level!), but I was city-raised and in a different frame of mind then.

We've cleared ground in the woods for a stackwood house. We were dreaming of a tire-house but we've been given a two-story, 22' x 26' 100-year-old chestnut hand-hewn log tobacco barn to move, so we will recycle that into a house.

Being that we are still in the city/suburb, we continue to gather the cast-offs of modern society. The following were all free: an African Gray parrot, two ringneck parakeets (mated pair), a purebred Australian shepherd from "Aussie" rescue, a Dominique rooster (we gave him to the farmer), rabbits, enough glass for home building and a large greenhouse, doors and more doors, wood paneling, lumber, windows, a rototiller (needs handles but runs), a wheelbarrow (had a flat tire so someone threw it out), gutters, rain spouts, flagstones, cinder blocks, bricks, work benches, mountains of wood chips and mulch, good hardwood pallets, tons of rugs (great to use for garden weed-free walkways), and from our suburban neighbors (especially the landscaper—bless him) oodles of plants, all varieties. As you can imagine, this list still grows!

We go to Eco Acres every week and though I long to be there permanently (I always feel like I'm home there and hate to leave), I know when "moving day" comes, we should be well prepared, more than I could ever have hoped for back in 1990.

So, back to the beginning...thank you COUNTRYSIDE writers for helping me resolve to be more frugal, more focused, and to recognize what we have accomplished so far. I had been wrestling with a "just move" versus "never going to get there" mentality. Now I clearly see that though it's taking us a little longer, it's better for us to do things our way.

The Liska's cabin isn't their full-time permanent home, but after reading about other homesteaders in recent COUNTRYSIDES, they're confident that whatever works for them is just fine.

Book review:

Guide to the next American migration

***Boom Counties: A Guide to Wealth and Serenity in a High-Risk Economy* by Jack Lessinger, Ph.D, 289 pages, paper, $89. SocioEconomics, Inc., P.O. Box 113, Bow, WA 98232.**

Author Jack Lessinger is known for his analysis of future "boom counties" where urban escapees are most likely to settle. In his latest book, Lessinger provides a historical overview of past trends and a completely new approach to country living.

Creator of the term "penturbia" that describes areas beyond urban and suburban zones, Lessinger divides 709 penturban counties into five categories ranked for potential growth. Obviously, the top-ranking counties are touted as the places to be for future population surges and real estate appreciation.

That is precisely the opposite approach that most COUNTRYSIDERS would take. Over the years, many readers have related sad experiences of finding their once-rural homestead being surrounded by encroaching suburbs. For those who don't want to be pushed out of a comfortable country home, it might be wise to avoid the trendier places.

Lessinger's proposed "penttowns" might work for former city dwellers, but they would hardly be ideal for COUNTRYSIDERS. Under the penttown plan, something like 2,000 acres would be purchased for a new town. Residents in mobile homes and condominiums and businesses would occupy 200 to 300 acres. The balance of the land would be left for open space.

Penttown residents would be allowed to live in the development for 20 years and have a share in the proceeds of the sale of the entire 2,000 acres. Lessinger expects the profit potential to be substantial. Aside from the open space, living in a condo or mobile home site is no different than any faceless city or suburb. Residents would not have their own acreage for food production or private land.

When the $89 price, complete lack of homesteading information and the sometimes academic tone of the book are considered, it's safe to say that *Boom Counties* would appeal to few COUNTRYSIDE readers. – *Al Doyle*

The homestead lifestyle:

To be a homesteader, believe in yourself, and persevere

PATRICK RAILEY
DELAWARE

What does it take to be a homesteader? Several things come to mind.

Probably the first is that we are still working toward the goal of homesteading and maybe we always will. Certainly we have made progress (i.e. starting a home business, having a garden, etc.), but there is still much to accomplish (finding our "perfect" place in the country, raising livestock, and more).

So I think perseverance is definitely a trait that homesteaders need, not only to reach their goals but also to maintain them. This may sometimes be overlooked since, theoretically, you are doing what you enjoy and want to be doing. But certainly there are bumps even in the smoothest of roads, where determination and perseverance will see you through.

An example would be having the garden all worked up in the spring, organic matter added, seedlings (that you cared for the past month or two indoors and in cold frames) set out, and just when you think you can relax... a severe thunderstorm jumps up and wipes out much of your work.

You now have two options. First, you could give up on the garden this year saying it just wasn't meant to be. Or, (the homestead way,) you can gear yourself up to do it all over again. This type of "if at first you don't succeed, try, try again" attitude, has helped get us to where we are and hopefully will continue to do so.

Another important quality is believing in yourself. We know very few people that have homesteading as their goal. Most of our families politely smile and nod their heads when we discuss our plans, but secretly think we are half off our rockers. And although our neighbors are rural folk, they still maintain outside jobs and have limited interest in being totally self-sufficient. So that leaves my wife, Rose, and I to look to each other for support and encouragement.

And that has made a tremendous difference for me, having a loving and caring partner to work with. I know that without that, we would never have been able to accomplish what we have.

Our son, Sam, is also an inspiration, as is the second child we are expecting in January. In part, our homesteading goals are driven by the fact that we want to give our children a safe and healthy lifestyle in which to grow up, sound values to live by, and practice in skills that will nurture and maintain the natural environment in which we live.

"More conventional" lifestyle lacked joy and satisfaction

JIM MAKI
OHIO

What does it take to be a homesteader? I can only speak from personal experience without starting to guess, so let's go there.

I tried a more conventional lifestyle, but there was little joy or satisfaction in it. As a matter of fact, most of my fellow workers and business associates seemed quite unhappy. And they had chased the "almighty dollar" for much longer than I.

Many people were unethical. Some excused cheating as long as they profited from it.

I asked many of these people where they saw themselves in another 10 years or so. Most expect to be in the same position making more money, or perhaps being promoted and making even more. Yet, even those in the higher positions didn't seem to enjoy their work, nor were they any more ethical.

So, one very strong factor for me in choosing the homesteading lifestyle was the desire to live according to my convictions and morality. I don't have to compromise my principles to earn my way.

There are many other factors which contribute to my pursuit of the lifestyle: A desire to be close with nature, a desire for independence, a desire for healthy food, a willingness to learn, and outlets for my creativity, which abound around the homestead.

I do so enjoy building my own home and workshop or laying out the garden beds. It's like seeing your thoughts and visions made real by your own two hands.

Too many neighbors crowding your homestead? Look on the bright side!

KEN SCHARABOK
TENNESSEE

A lament often heard in publications such as this is from people who bought their homestead or small farm well outside of a populated area only to have subdivisions built around them over the years. Instead of cursing this, you might use it to your advantage.

Suppose you are interested in a nice place while you are working, but have plans for something larger or in another area when you retire. You might take anticipated population expansion into those plans.

For example, you buy a place now for $X per acre and 30 years later it is worth several or many times that. Sell it for the best price available and then look for your dream retirement place, very likely fully paid for by the property's appreciated value.

In addition, the population around you in later years may well lead to supplemental income in the form of processed small stock or farm-fresh eggs and vegetables. Pick-your-own options might include a small orchard of dwarf apple trees or an acre or so of sweet corn.

Consider it the equivalent of another Individual Retirement Account.

On the other hand...

JD BELANGER
EDITOR

Anyone interested in pursuing this with any seriousness should get a copy of *Boom Counties,* by Jack Lessinger, Ph.D. (SocioEconomics, Inc., Box 113, Bow WA 98232; $89.)

In this book, Lessinger discusses the waves or migrations that have occurred in the United States since its founding, and the consequent effects of those migrations on real estate prices. By extrapolation, he then points to the areas—generally rural, today yet—where he expects to see the greatest growth, and therefore real estate values.

While this book was written primarily for investors (you can tell by the price, and by the review on page 409) or for those who want to avoid sinking money into depreciating real estate and to invest in land that will increase in value, it also has a curious connection with COUNTRYSIDE'S view of homesteading in the 21st century.

In a nutshell, the natural flow and cycles of social evolution are changing values and outlooks, and are leading Americans in the direction of what we call homesteading.

There is, of course, another angle to all this. Many present homesteaders will bristle at Ken's suggestion. They have worked hard and long to create their homesteads. They want to live on them and enjoy them without the hassles and changes brought in by citified neighbors. Their reward lies in the homestead itself—the soil that was built up over the years, the fruit trees that took so long to mature, the buildings and fences—not in money. In most cases, making a profit would be of little consolation because money can't replace what they're losing. And worse, they no longer have the energy to start over... and many don't have the time to start over. The years of lost or lowered production involved in a fresh start, plus the additional labor, added to the emotional distress often present in such a situation, simply aren't worth the money.

And that's without mentioning capital gain taxes.

In this situation, Lessinger's book might be used in a manner diametrically opposed to his apparent intention. Instead of looking for boom counties to move to, the homesteader seeking peaceful isolation might want to know where they are so they can be avoided.

Tips for frugal homesteaders

* Put a bit of petroleum jelly on the base of a light bulb before putting it into an outside light fixture to make it easy to remove when it burns out.

* Save the wooden roller and slat from worn window shades. Buy an inexpensive plastic tablecloth and cut it to the size of the shade. Hem the bottom to fit the wooden slat and glue or staple the top to the roller. This makes a great custom made shade for a little money.

* Use broken dishes at the bottom of flowerpots to provide drainage.

* Bend the tines of an old fork to make a small hoe for use in window boxes or flower pots.

* Cut carpet or rug scraps or good pieces of old rugs into a circular shape and back it with a disk of heavy cardboard. Put a hole in the center of the circle and use it for a quick car polishing attatchment by screwing it to the drill disk.

* When you receive a double-fold greeting card with blank panels, open the card flat and cut off the half with the writing on it. Refold the portion with the illustration, and use the blank page as a note card.

* Snip corners from old envelopes and use them to mount photos and souvenirs in scrapbooks or photo albums.

* Old shower curtains can be hung behind lightweight draperies in the winter to prevent drafts. The extra layer creates a pocket of dead air that helps to insulate the room from the cold air outside the window.

After chores:

Working at home requires a sense of humor!

Memo—
Before answering the phone, put out the rooster!

JANE KEON
MICHIGAN

I was on the phone with my editor at the *Saginaw News* when Rarie the Rooster crowed from where he stood on top of the washing machine.

As quick as I could I laid a hand over the phone, hoping the editor would think anything but that I had a chicken in the kitchen with me. I was new on the job and most of the people at the paper knew me only from conversations on the phone. I could just imagine what impression I would make if they learned I'd let a chicken in the house.

"Is that a rooster crowing?" the editor asked.

"I'm afraid so."

"Is he right outside the window or something?"

"Or something."

Rarie crowed again. "Er-er-er-er-ooo."

"It sounds like he's right by the phone."

So I explained that our eight-year-old rooster's circulation wasn't what it used to be, and when the outside temperature dropped below 20 degrees, we had to bring the old boy inside to keep his feet from freezing.

I thought to myself, if only I hadn't answered the phone in the kitchen. If only the editor had called a half hour later, when Rarie had warmed up enough to go back to the barn. I was pretty embarrassed.

It was in sophisticated clothes and a businesslike manner that I had driven the 30 miles from my farm home to the city of Saginaw to accept the position of Gratiot County Correspondent. Going from writing articles for a local newspaper with a circulation of 4,000 to a regional paper with 65,000 subscribers seemed to call for a little urbanity. Well, so much for my veneer of urbanity with a rooster crowing over the phone.

Rarie wasn't the first chicken to come into the kitchen of our 100-year-old house. When we moved here, the neighbors had told us about Mrs. Creger's chickens. She just left the back door ajar so that the chickens could wander in and out at will. Visitors would find chickens roosting on the backs of chairs in the kitchen, and even on top of the refrigerator.

When I heard that tale, I vowed that even though I was a softie around animals, I would never become eccentric enough to let chickens in the house.

But Rarie wasn't just a chicken. He was a really great rooster, who needed a little extra hospitality in his old age. He'd already lost some toes to frigid weather, and the ends of others were suspiciously dark.

The attributes that made him a great rooster were these:

1. Fiercely protective of the hens, but friendly with people.
2. Tolerant of the older dogs, but not afraid to light into the pup who tended to rile things up in the chicken coop.
3. Even in old age, a consistent father of dozens of colorful chicks, with dispositions as easygoing as his own.

What more could anyone ask of a rooster?

His only defect was that he didn't know enough to keep quiet when I was on the phone.

Another editor called from the *Saginaw News* later in the morning to check some details on an article with me.

"When am I going to hear that rooster go cock-a-doodle-doo?" he asked.

"Oh no," I groaned. "I suppose the whole newsroom knows about the rooster?"

"Hey, it's not every day we city folk get to hear a rooster crow in someone's kitchen!"

What could I do but laugh?

I told him to call the next morning between 7:30 and 8:00, when the sun was coming up, but only if it was below 20 degrees.

I figured if I could laugh about it, I wasn't eccentric. At least not yet.

Home business hazards

With the tremendous increase in working at home today, stories abound about the problems encountered when trying to make a good impression on a client. Most, of course, concern family members.

One home worker whose office is next to the laundry room tells of the time his young daughter got out of the bathtub and came to the laundry in search of clean clothes. His wife, not knowing he was on the phone, said in a very loud voice, "Are you running around naked again?"

Beyond the sidewalks, animals often play a large role.

In the days before COUNTRYSIDE magazine, our home business was The Countryside Print Shop. On the phone, I had just identified myself by the company name when a rooster outside the window let loose with a very loud, clear, and drawn-out cock-a-doodle-do.

There was a moment of silence. Then the person I was calling asked, in all seriousness, "Did you say Countryside Print Shop, or Pet Shop?" — *Jd*

After chores:

"Green Acres"—the tv show in real life

Being married to a non-homesteader requires a sense of humor

Sherry Pendleton would rather spend time with her chickens than travelling or entertaining. Her husband is cast from a different mold.

SHERRY PENDLETON
MISSISSIPPI

My husband just got through reading aloud the airline rates for a wonderful package deal to Branson, Missouri. He pores over travel sections of the newspaper with the same passion I do the seed and poultry catalogs. Our interests are about as similar as Bill Clinton's and Newt Gingrich's.

We daily replay our own version of television's "Green Acres." My husband's idea of country is any place with less population than New Orleans. My idea of a city is anywhere with more than one traffic light.

We finally got our 30 acres and country cottage, but you know who insisted we keep the city house too. As we stood looking at this lovely wildwoods, he saw himself as the English lord of the manor, entertaining guests every weekend and strolling through the dell. I saw myself as a pioneer woman, tending my garden, caring for my goats and chickens, making cheese and gathering eggs.

Our differences soon clashed into a full fledged War of the Roses. The more I fought for every spare minute in the country, the more he battled to travel and entertain. One round he wins, so I'll go on a trip with him. The next time I win, so we'll build poultry pens. He wins this weekend to entertain. I win the next to work in the gardens.

He fills our social calendar with dinners and dos; I counter with hatch dates and incubators.

He wheels and deals thousands in the business and the stock market. I nickel and dime sales for my chicks and guineas.

His idea of fun is a crowded room filled with overdressed, oversmiling, overtalking manicured stuffed shirts with cocktails in one hand and plastic plates of tidbits in the other.

My fun is growing my own organic vegetables, gathering eggs, raising poultry, learning to use wild foods like the Indians did and propagating heirloom roses and flowers.

His idea of "good food" is a restaurant dinner consisting of a big ol' hunk of red meat with gobs of carbohydrates on the side. This is following a 12-hour work day and eaten about an hour before bedtime.

I could live well on my own fresh grown tomatoes, peas and okra, and hot cornbread. A bit of my bees' honey on a good hot biscuit really gets me going.

He thinks a meal without meat is like a train without tracks: just doesn't go.

We are in an endless deadlock. Will be, I guess, until one of us dies. I've told him if he dies first, I'm putting an ad in the paper saying, "Wanted: husband with a tractor." He says if I die first, he's putting one in saying, "Wanted: wife with suitcase in hand, ready to go."

If I dare to give an inch, I'll soon find myself in an airplane on the way to some steel and concrete wonder. If he gives an inch, I may soon be driving that tractor I want (without a new husband).

After chores:

Farmers Anonymous

Pat Weerts
Wisconsin

I'm married to a farmer-turned-lawyer... so much a farmer I can see his bib overalls through that dark pin-striped suit everyone else thinks he's wearing.

We can't go for a ride without having him cluck over the farms that have thistle growing in the pasture or too large a pile of manure—sure signs of a careless farmer.

But what makes him maddest are the farms where the cows are left to lie in dirty lots. Makes him angry that those farmers don't appreciate the fact that they owe their livelihood to those cows. Seems like they deserve more respect than that. And it just makes sense to avoid mastitis and high bacteria counts.

On the other hand, I suspect that he's just plain jealous that they get to farm full-time.

When my husband and I met, we were in our final year at the University of Minnesota. He was an English major who studied literature, yet wrote pieces for an agricultural journal on the side. Later he wrote short stories about his experiences in Afghanistan as a young Peace Corps volunteer in a drought relief program. I didn't have a clue he was a farmer. Oh, don't get me wrong, I knew that he had grown up on a farm, but I did not in any way understand the depth of that influence on him, and in consequence its influence on my life.

I understood when he suggested that we move to his brother's farm in Springfield, Minnesota, just a few miles from his parents' farm, that we were farming to raise money to allow him to write. Boy, was I wrong. He didn't have a minute to spare. He worked from sunup to sundown. He milked with an old Surge milker, carrying the heavy machine to the metal milk can fitted with a filter on top to screen out impurities. He and his father and brother all worked together to get everybody's crops in the ground, harvested and stored. I, on the other hand, was trying to cope with babies, no hot running water and a very cantankerous wood stove. We fell into bed each night exhausted.

It wasn't long until the local creamery betrayed local farmers by announcing, with very short notice, their intention to quit taking our canned milk, carefully delivered every morning in silver metal cans beaded with moisture from the cooling tank. We were faced with the choice of putting a very expensive addition on the barn, with a bulk tank and pipeline system, (all to the extensive specifications of the State of Minnesota), or losing our income.

Not only could we not afford to remodel the barn, as we were milking only 13 cows, but we were concerned about putting this kind of investment in a rented farm. My husband's brother, our landlord, did not want to sell the place, as he was hoping that his two junior high school aged sons would need a place to farm when they grew up. We were forced to try to get a loan and buy our own place, or leave the farm to do something else.

When I asked my husband whether he could see himself doing anything else, he answered that the only other thing he thought he might like to do when he was a boy was to be a lawyer. He didn't seem real sure that this was the right thing to do, but we were pressed for time and had to make a decision.

We decided that we could not go into the debt required to buy our own place because a milk check just wouldn't stretch to repay the loan and feed us too, so he opted to reeducate himself in a higher paying field. He went to the University of Wyoming Law School to study Land and Water Law. This too was an outgrowth of his love for the land.

I thought after he'd become a lawyer our lives would be different. I believed that his income from the law would support him so that he could continue his writing, but I was wrong again. He quit writing, and the "farm" in him came along with us as we scoured the countryside, looking for a place that could take a few good cows. Sometimes he didn't even look at the house. He went straight to the barn, and if it had a good feeling, he'd take the place.

We raised long-horned cattle on the grasslands of Gillette, Wyoming, and registered Ayrshires, Guernseys and Jerseys in Wisconsin. Even after we lost money three years in a row raising replacement heifers, he persevered, saying that farming was unpredictable and that prices would rise again... they always did, didn't they? Three years later, he's still hoping.

What is this farming thing that holds and carries him this way; holds his heart like I can never hope to? Is there no AA for farmers?

Now when I am struggling with cancer and fear for his future alone here on this big old homestead, I ask, wouldn't it be better to move to a smaller place and sell this farm so he won't have so much to take care of when I'm gone? The answer is a startled, absolutely not! Don't I understand the value of the land?

Silly me. Thinking we were talking about money, I told him that housing prices were at the highest level I had ever seen. Why, he could sell this place and buy a smaller place. He could pay for it outright and still have money left over to pay the taxes. He looked at me like I had just stolen his firstborn child.

Well, I'm not sorry I married him, but I've learned my place in the scheme of things... somewhere just slightly ahead of a herd of red cows and a rusty old Allis Chalmers tractor.

Current reality as seen here:

Chicken Little was right!

The sky is falling, but hardly anyone seems to notice...

Al Doyle
Colorado

According to Bill Clinton and the mainstream media, the American economy is humming along at a record clip. Prosperity abounds, and baby boomers are making a killing in the stock market, according to the New York Times and Money magazine.

Where does that leave Countrysiders and the much-maligned "doom and gloomers" who expect hard times and a major economic decline? Are they way out of step with the trend? Maybe they're just not smart enough to pick the big winners on the Dow.

For decades, a number of authors and concerned citizens have been warning of a collapse in the current system. The masses have been conditioned to view such folks as lunatic fringe elements who actually want to see civilization self-destruct.

Such reasoning is utter nonsense. If I witness an 18-wheeler crashing into another vehicle, do I want the unfortunate victim to suffer? Of course not. However, I have a duty to see life realistically and not through rose-colored glasses.

According to the "happy days are here again" crowd, anyone who dares to question their hyper-optimistic clichés is a masochistic party pooper who has no right to be heard, lest their ignorant pessimism pollute public opinion.

This bias is strongly reflected in the so-called "news" programs and print media. As someone who formerly worked for a large newspaper and has written more than 100 articles for various magazines, experience has taught me it doesn't take long to learn which subjects and stories are politically correct.

These "guidelines" are never written down, but they are understood. It's somewhat similar to being asked for a "tip" by a Mexican cop. You know quite well that he's extorting cash from you, but you shut up and go along with the game. So it is with the mainstream media.

Occasionally, the truth slips out, but one must know where to find it. Look at the three-paragraph fillers on page 17, the obscure little stories in the back of the financial pages or somewhere behind the obituaries for the issues that should be prominently featured. A growing number of thinking people have given up on the controlled media and now rely on alternate sources for information.

With the non-stop media bombardment about the alleged prosperity in America, how many adults have heard that bankruptcies are at an all-time high and rising steadily? That's right. Bankruptcies in our "prosperous" nation are now running at an annual rate of 1.3 million and heading upward.

If bankruptcy is a major growth industry, what does that say for the accuracy of the prosperity message? The problem has gotten so serious that Congress recently looked at the bankruptcy laws and discussed whether they should be changed to make walking away from debts more difficult.

Prosperity hypsters like to point to "record low" unemployment as a sign of overall affluence. As the old saying goes. "Numbers don't lie, but liars use numbers." And the Beltway gang can hide the truth with the best of them.

If someone spends months looking for work and gives up in despair, he is no longer counted as unemployed by the government. The millions of older workers who wanted a job but have been forced into early retirement over the past decade have also been deleted from the unemployment numbers. Non-government economic statistician Al Sindlinger puts the real unemployment rate at around 10 percent.

Federal unemployment statistics provide a rough measure of how many jobs are out there, but they deliberately ignore the quality of the available work. Here's a common example of how the decline of the middle class is described as an "economic boom" by politicians of both major parties.

Joe Lunchbucket is a skilled blue-collar worker. Sadly, Joe's $15-an-hour job has just been exported to Mexico or Red China thanks to NAFTA and GATT.

Despite the layoff, Joe is optimistic about his employment prospects. After all, he's a capable tradesman with an excellent record at his previous positions.

Joe's unemployment benefits run out six months after the layoff, and he drops off the federal unemployment listings even though he still hasn't found work. Always a hustler, Joe puts together some handyman and house-painting jobs before finding a full-time position six weeks later.

Is life back to normal for the Lunchbuckets? Hardly. Joe now earns $8/hour, and his benefits are far skimpier than what he had at his previous job.

Although Joe and his family have taken a huge cut in income, everything is just dandy, according to the government's unemployment report. Joe had a full-time job before the layoff, and he now has another one. The family's situation is unchanged, according to the bureaucrats at the Bureau of Labor Statistics.

But wait! Could the Lunchbuckets actually be in a better economic position than they were before the layoff?

To make up for some of his huge pay cut, Joe delivers pizzas two nights a week for minimum wage plus tips. The family is still in the hole, so Brenda, Joe's wife, now works part-time at K-Mart for $6 an hour. The Lunchbuckets somehow manage to juggle their work schedules as they also care for Joe Jr. and Becky.

Now it gets truly Orwellian. According to the BLS, the Lunchbuckets are overflowing with prosperity! Joe had just one job a year ago, while Mrs. Lunchbucket was a full-time mother. Today, the family has three jobs, for a net gain of two jobs. Thank you, Slick Willie and Newt Gingrich! We appreciate the bountiful fruits of your mythical economic boom.

This hypothetical story has been lived by tens of millions of Americans. The precise details vary from person to person, but the trend towards lower wages and part-time jobs is moving faster than a Camaro in high gear.

For a large segment of the populace, the '90s have been anything but financially rewarding. This economic depression is happening quietly, as it hits a few families or one town at a time.

Skyrocketing indebtedness has disguised the drop in disposable income, but "buy now, pay later" can't last forever. Depending on who crunches the numbers, the average American family now owes $12,000 to $16,000 in non-mortgage debt. The piper must be paid eventually, and he's coming to the end of his song.

Car leasing is a classic sign of the times. Just a few years ago, most new car buyers made monthly payments from three to five years and eventually owned their vehicles outright. As bad as that borrowing was, it is downright miserly when compared to leasing.

Under a lease, the "buyer" makes a monthly payment for two to four years. At the end of the contract, the leaseholder hands the car back to the dealer. He or she owns nothing but memories.

Financially strapped consumers are attracted to leases because they can drive a new car with very little money down. Like the fox offering to guard the henhouse, car dealers are aggressively promoting leases as a way to make their products "affordable." At the present rate of economic erosion, American debt slaves will be leasing cars from the salvage yard in a decade.

There are several reasons why most people don't understand the times. Some actually believe the fables from Washington and their lackeys in the press. Many others are too tired from working long hours for lower wages to think about how things have changed for the worse in America.

Perhaps the biggest reason for the lack of public perception is what I call the "tv mentality." In the make-believe world of the lobotomy box, the "complete" history of World War II or the French Revolution is covered in two hours.

Such superficiality also reigns in public school courses. In many high school history books, no more than a page is devoted to the Great Depression. Combined with the quick-fix mentality that is absorbed by tv junkies, countless students are left with the impression that America went to bed prosperous one night and woke up bankrupt the next morning. This erroneous view of history leads people to ignore important signs of the times today.

Indications of a coming calamity were evident for several years before the stock market crash in October, 1929. Things went steadily downhill until 1933, plateaued for four years, then dropped again in 1937.

Not all segments of society suffered equally or simultaneously. Farmers were in a depression before the Crash of '29, and things got even bleaker in the '30s. Auto workers were especially hard-hit, but auto mechanics who were willing to accept reduced wages could usually find work.

Those who warned of perilous times before the Depression were scorned as pessimists and fearmongers. Even in the midst of the collapse in 1930 and 1931, various public figures parroted the line that there had been a momentary pothole in the road to riches, but good times were just around the corner.

Don't sneer at today's nonconformists who are warning of an economic crisis in the near future. The trend has already begun. It just hasn't been recognized by the masses yet. That gives you much-needed time to prepare for what lies ahead.

Disturbing signs of the times...

A recent headline (on a story buried in the back pages of newspapers across the country) read, "Demand for emergency food and shelter up, mayors say."

In the 29 large cities in the survey, requests for emergency food rose an average of 16 percent, the largest increase since 1992.

This is, as the story put it, "despite a surging economy and low unemployment."

But then what of those who aren't that desperate? Many of those are surviving by maxing out on credit cards, the "125% home mortgage" (taking out a second mortgage, so they often owe more than the home is worth – up to 125% more, instead of the "normal" 80% equity most lenders demand) – and bankruptcy.

One recent *Wall Street Journal* article told of a man in his 20s who declared bankruptcy to wipe out his $20,000 debt. The next day he bought a new car... and got a new credit card. With bankruptcies running at 1.3 million a year, he obviously isn't alone. We can assume that these people wouldn't think of committing robbery with a gun, but doing the same with a piece of plastic is okay in their eyes.

Stories like these are routine, today. Those who embrace the homestead philosophy, who actually enjoy taking responsibility for themselves and living simply, might be a minority. But they also might be the only sane people left.